REGNUM STUDIES IN MIS

Child, Church and Compassion

Towards Child Theology in Romania

Series Preface

Regnum Studies in Mission are born from the lived experience of Christians and Christian communities in mission, especially but not solely in the fast growing churches among the poor of the world. These churches have more to tell than stories of growth. They are making significant impacts on their cultures in the cause of Christ. They are producing 'cultural products' which express the reality of Christian faith, hope and love in their societies.

Regnum Studies in Mission are the fruit often of rigorous research to the highest international standards and always of authentic Christian engagement in the transformation of people and societies. And these are for the world. The formation of Christian theology, missiology and practice in the twenty-first century will depend to a great extent on the active participation of growing churches contributing biblical and culturally appropriate expressions of Christian practice to inform World Christianity.

Series Editors

A full listing of titles in this series appears at the end of this book

REGNUM STUDIES IN MISSION

Child, Church and Compassion

Towards Child Theology in Romania

William C. Prevette

James,
Thanks for sharing your personal
journey from medicine to the "pastorate"
on the mission of God. This book is
a window into part of my story working
with children + youth over the years.
Several years ago God led us to Romania
+ to OCMS. I never thought I would finish
this but I was helped by many friends
just like you.
Grace + peace to you,
Bill Prevette
Feb. 2012

First published 2012 by Regnum Books International

Regnum is an imprint of the Oxford Centre for Mission Studies
St. Philip and St. James Church
Woodstock Road
Oxford, OX2 6HR, UK
www.ocms.ac.uk/regnum

09 08 07 06 05 04 03 8 7 6 5 4 3 2 1

British Library Cataloguing in Publication Data
A catalogue record for this book is available from the British Library

ISBN: 978-1-908355-03-4

Typeset by Words by Design
Cover design by Words by Design, Image © Getty Images
Printed and bound in Great Britain
for Regnum Books International by Marston Book Services Ltd, Didcot

The publication of this title was made possible by the financial assistance of the Boys and Girls Missionary Crusade (BGMC) Fund of the (US) Assembly of God World World Mission through the Europe Office (Greg Mundis, Director).

Contents

Acknowledgements

This book began as a PhD thesis and is published with the help of Regnum Publishing and encouragement from friends at the Oxford Centre for Mission Studies. Whilst writing the final draft of the thesis, my wife and I lived in the Southern part of the U.S.A. I learned a phrase that summarizes my gratitude in finishing the manuscript. *'If you ever see a turtle sitting on the top of a fence post, the odds are pretty good he did not get there by himself.'* I find myself in a comparable place as the fortunate terrapin in this parable. The book in your hands is the outcome of input and encouragement from dozens of individuals who helped me reach the top of the proverbial fencepost.

I am deeply indebted to my academic supervisors, Dr. Haddon Willmer and Dr. Don Ratcliff who taught me to pursue excellence in research. Their constant encouragement and oversight made the completion of this work possible. My supervisors taught me through example, that God is patient with our humanity.

The Oxford Centre for Mission Studies (OCMS) provided a contextual framework for thinking and mental discipline. During my study, I commuted twice a year from Bucharest to Oxford where I found additional support from Chris Sugden, Damon So, Bernard Farr, David Adams, Ben Knighton and others who became friends, colleagues, and advocates. I learned the importance of a spiritual research community; OCMS became an essential emotional, academic, and spiritual resource in my life. I am especially thankful for Alan and Mary Reed who opened their home to me during my many residential stays in Oxford; who are now a part of my new English family. Dr. Wonsuk Ma, the current director of OCMS was most emphatic that I publish the book and assisted in the final preparation.

I owe a special thanks to Lidia Balcanu and Radu Suteu, who worked in my Bucharest office and served as research assistants. The accompanied me on almost every project visit, transcribed notes, worked with data entry and gave meaningful input to my case analysis. I was also assisted many other friends in Romania who helped with translation, electronic filing, phone calls, emails, and locating documents from FBOs and churches.

There are over 150 individuals I could thank by name for their time and input in my field research. Danut Manastireanu and Dorin Dobrincu helped me immensely in my early efforts to understand Romanian evangelicalism. Cristi Soimaru, Otinel Bunaciu, David Chronic, Carolyn Rennie, and Anna Burtea – these individuals represent many others working with FBOs and churches. This book brings together the voices of Romanian and Western FBO directors, staff, church pastors, and volunteers. I acknowledge their input into this study and their years of dedication serving children. I have been inspired by their faith, love, and service.

Finally I think of my missionary colleagues and extended ministry 'family'. Bob and Carolyn Houlihan, Doug Petersen, Byron Klaus, Alan Johnson, Craig and Dana Mathison, Greg and Sandie Mundis represent this group. Byron and Doug suggested working with OCMS. Alan offered moral encouragement and practical suggestions on how to budget time and mental resources. Greg as my regional director (Europe), Craig and Dana as my area directors (Southeastern Europe) gave me encouragement to carry on in research and writing when I thought I would never finish and should go back to 'regular missionary work'. Bob and Carolyn through their prayer and friendship were a constant source of inspiration. I thank these friends for believing in this project and me when I was unsure of the process and outcome. I acknowledge my own organization, the Assemblies of God World Missions who gave approval for this study and supported the research and BGMC who assisted with the publication. I trust this effort will be of some use to our colleagues and friends who are now serving children in crisis around the world.

Preface

As I write this preface in the summer of 2011, the world's attention is focused on a growing famine in Sudan, Ethiopia and parts of East Africa. Images of suffering children are used to 'tell the story' and solicit aid from international donors. In response, governments, NGOs, charities, churches and faith-based organizations are mobilizing relief. Not so many years ago, as the Soviet Union was breaking apart and Eastern European countries were experiencing the end of the Cold War, a similar crisis for children was made public in the nation of Romania. Following the collapse of Nicolae Ceauşescu's socialist government in 1989, more than 100,000 children were living in state institutions. These were poorly funded and inadequately maintained by the state. Western news cameras brought the tragedy of Romanian's orphans and abandoned children to the attention of the world.

This book is the outcome of more than twenty years of working with children, youth, churches, and faith-based organizations. The personal background that led to the study is provided in the first chapter. What began as work with troubled youth in urban Los Angeles, led to work in the slums of Bangkok, Thailand, continued on to Phnom Penh, Cambodia, and then to Bucharest, Romania. This book is written in the first person, something professional academics typically don't recommend. It is an academic study; however, I have tried to capture in the writing a practicality that characterises those who engage with children in crisis.

I began my work with children and youth as an activist and interventionist, not an academic or policy advocate. I believed it was important to help children and youth escape danger or exploitation - that they learn of Christ's love and have an alternative to life on the streets. I learned important lessons as a practitioner but had little formal training in psychosocial development or moral formation of troubled youth. My personal experience is reflected in the narratives of many participants who became the focus of this research. Similar to many of my colleagues, I desired to help children but invested little energy in systematic psychological or theological reflection. It seemed clear from scripture that we should care for the 'least of these'. Through trial and error, I became increasingly aware that that my interventionist approaches to children and youth in crisis were inadequate.

I had gathered from experience and reading that several methods were advocated as effective faith-based interventions for children in crisis. Some promoted church planting, others community transformation with the child as the focal point, others maintained that the physical, psychosocial, and spiritual needs of children were best addressed in the context of family, and others believed that ministries should be based and carried out in and through the local church. By the mid 1990s, the term 'children and youth at risk' was increasingly used to describe a demographic of young people 0-18 years of age[1] who are 'at risk' from poverty, abuse, war, ethnic marginalization, sexual or street exploitation, institutionalization, lack of access to basic education, social services and health care. When there is dysfunction in families, communities, or society, children are usually the first to show signs of suffering. In some ways, children are like 'canaries in a mine shaft'; they provide a focal point for discovery and encounter of perilous aspects of our world that are often ignored.

During 1998-2002, I travelled internationally as a programme development specialist evaluating childcare projects in India, Nepal, Bangladesh, and Southeast Asia. I communicated with international leaders from World Vision International, Compassion International, and Tearfund, U.K. and took the opportunity to study their organizational histories and missional methods. These colleagues reinforced my intellectual commitment to a 'holistic' framework that professed to include both evangelism and social concern based on the kingdom of God, shalom, and social justice. I maintained that Faith-based Organizational (FBO) work with children should include the local church. In each country I visited, I observed that FBOs and churches were often working with different agendas for children.

In 1999, I connected with the Viva Network, based in Oxford, U.K. and attended several international conferences. I met leaders of international FBOs that had been steadily professionalizing after years of experience working with children and the poor; they were well funded and free to respond in the present. I also recognized that the FBOs were using terms that most local pastors and churches rarely used: 'programme log frames', 'community poverty assessments', 'well-being indicators', 'domains of transformational development', 'child protection policies', and 'impact assessment'. Some FBOs talked about 'reconnecting' with local churches,[2] but I did not hear similar language from local churches, at least not the ones where I was investing most of my time. I began research with the Oxford Centre for Mission Studies in 2002; this coincided with an intentional move to Romania to conduct research and work with children in crisis.

I conducted a structured five year investigation of the relationship between selected Faith-based Organizations and Romanian evangelical churches as revealed in their action for children in crisis in the time frame 1990-2004. The analysis describes missional assumptions, activities, and patterns that

---

[1] The age of childhood has been socially constructed over many centuries (Cunningham, 2005). I will examine this further in Chapter 2.

[2] For instance see 'Strengthening our Bridges' (2002), World Vision International.

characterized FBO-church partnership. In the early 1990s, international FBO response was largely reactive and at times disempowering towards evangelical churches. This led to a 'division of labour' as FBOs responded to human, physical, and psychosocial needs of children and churches provided what they understood as 'spiritual' care for children. Whilst much positive work was done with children, I sought to understand if FBOs and churches sought to integrate their eternal and human concerns for children. Did the imposition of short-sighted agendas of the church on the FBO or of the FBO on the church undermine collaboration; did these actions neglect the concerns and voices of the children? Does FBO and church collaboration open dialogue about what God intends when he places a 'child in their midst'?

I believe this study demonstrates, in the Romanian context, that children in crisis serve to open new horizons in missiology and theology for FBOs and churches working towards partnership that honours God. '*Embracing tensions in partnership for children*' is discussed as the core category to aid in the integration of eternal and human concerns and how the 'Evangel' might be more fully discerned in FBO-church partnership. My goal was to create a contextual account of selected FBO-church partnerships that was sensitive to each side's assumptions, values, perceptions, interventions, and organizational actions. It is my hope that those working in other contexts with churches and FBOs that are concerned for children in crisis will find insights in this book to inform their future collaborations and actions. To God be the Glory if that is the case.

Dedication

To my wife Ky and my son Daniel. We have walked together through many difficult and wonderful experiences as our family's spiritual journey has taken us to Southeast Asia and Eastern Europe. I could never have begun this work, much less completed it without your support, love, and encouragement.

This book is devoted to those who make up the family of God, the churches, the organizations, men, women, and especially children.
True parenting, teaching, disciplining requires children
as signs of the logic of the Kingdom of God.

Foreword

All life is meeting. Every baby's birth makes a new meeting between strangers deeply but precariously bonded. In a mobile, interactive, interfering world, meetings are innumerable, tangling and unpredictable. Much depends on what people meeting are able to give when they come face to face. Things easily go wrong; communication becomes miscommunication and even war, so the world is in a mess. The game, Scissors, Paper, Stone, reminds us not only that meetings fail and frustrate but that there can be a perverse delight in using them to defeat and shame the other. And yet, above all that, meeting blossoms into the joy and goodness of life.

This splendid book invites us to think about what has gone on within one recent major intercontinental, intercultural meeting. Walls that had prevented or warped meetings between the Soviet empire and 'the West' came down in 1989-1990. Meeting was again possible, after many decades. Early euphoric hopes that a new beautiful world of prosperity, freedom and peace are now much chastened though not unfruitful. Why has the initial promise of the meeting been so hard to realise? What did different people bring to this meeting? How far were they equipped to make a success of it?

The meeting of different kinds of Christians as well as the meeting of Christians with non-Christians has been part of the historical substance of Christianity from it's beginning, as the New Testament shows. A meeting between Christians carries no guarantee that it will blossom into long-term fruitful relationship. We may say that we are 'all one in Jesus Christ', but how is that spiritual reality or ideological concept actualised in the manifold judgments and practical acts which our daily and local meetings are composed of? How far do Christians – individuals and organisations – know themselves? How far are they able to change, to think out of the box of their culture with its ambitions and underlying assumptions?

The encounters between Faith-based Organisations and Romanian Evangelical churches in the years after the fall of Communism show how Christians can have difficulties in meeting the Brother-Stranger and how they can learn and grow when they persevere in trying to preserve the bonds of Shalom in its fullness. This is a history, which called for detailed, sensitive, and systematic investigation – it gets it in this book. But the history further required an investigator who was more than an excellent collector and analyst of data; it needed someone to stand in the middle of the meetings and non-meetings, sharing in this history as a learner and enabler.

I value this book for the information it gives about a significant process in recent Christian and inter-cultural history. And more: I value it as testimony to the service of the engaged researcher, who meets his ‘subjects’ not as ‘cases’, but as friends striving hopefully together in response to the common calling in Christ. Meeting, as this book lets us see it, did not happen only between ‘civilizations’, or between business-style organisations and local communities, but in the hearts and minds and living of individual participants. This kind of research requires more than a computer – it requires companionship and communion. Mary who ‘kept all these things in her heart and pondered them’ was also pierced to the heart by a sword, thus modelling a participating researcher, pondering, suffering, and serving in the story of Christ in the world.

Haddon Willmer,
Emeritus Professor of Theology,
University of Leeds

List of Abbreviations

ADP	Area Development Programme (World Vision)
BMS	Baptist Missionary Society
CD	Church Dogmatics
CEF	Child Evangelism Fellowship, U.S.A.
CMS	Church Missionary Society
CRY-UK	Care and Relief for the Young U.K. – FBO
CRC	Convention on the Rights of the Child
CRN	Children's Relief Network, U.S.A. – FBO
DCP	Department of Child Protection – Romania both local and national offices
DFID	U.K. Department for International Development
DTGO	General Directorate of Technical Operations (Romanian security police)
EFMA	Evangelical Fellowship of Mission Associations
EU	European Union
FBO	Faith-Based Organization
IMC	International Missionary Council
INSR	National Institute for Statistics, Romania
KRA	Key Result Areas
MARC	Mission Advanced Research and Communication Centre
MDRI	Mental Disability Rights International
NGO	Non-Governmental Organization
NAPCR	National Authority for the Protection of Child's Rights (Romania)
OCI	One Challenge International
OCMS	Oxford Centre for Missionary Studies
SIDA	Swedish International Development Agency
UNICEF	United Nations Children's Fund
USAID	United States Agency for International Development
WCC	World Council of Churches
YWAM	Youth with a Mission

Case Abbreviations:

ACVN	Brasov Centre for New Life Association, Romania
BF	Bethesda Foundation, Romania
CoH	City of Hope Association, Romania
IDC	Heart of the Child (Inima De Copii), Romania
L&L	Light and Life Foundation, Romania
MoM	Mission of Mercy, Romania
MWB	Mission Without Borders Foundation, Romania
Ruth	Project Ruth Association, Romania

Ţoar	Ţoar Foundation, Romania
WV Ro	World Vision Romania
WVI	World Vision International
WMF	Word Made Flesh Association, Romania

Identifiers used in Interviews:

FBOL	FBO Leader or Director (sometimes both pastor and FBO director)
FBOS	FBO Staff
I	Interviewee – confidential participant
Pas	Pastor of Romanian local evangelical church

Chapter 1

Introduction

Reflection from my research journal – February 25, 2003, sent to a colleague by email:

> I have been in Romania for five months, and it seems every day I have a conversation with a missionary, a pastor, or an FBO leader who has had a conflict with the 'other side'. When I started here last August, it seemed it would be a straightforward matter to investigate Western agencies working with local evangelical churches and understand how they were working together to assist children. I am learning the 1990s was a time of concentrated (chaotic?) activity with very little coordination between the agencies or the local churches. Yesterday, a Western mission leader told me that his organization was reassessing its entire approach in Romania. Today another Romanian pastor told me felt he had been 'used' by a Western agency when they arrived here in 1992. I am not sure whether I will be able to get the sort of data I need to build a case for FBO efficacy – or if I made the right choice to do research in this country.

Looking back, these musings reflect the confusion of a novice researcher attempting to decipher a puzzle with no picture on the box to guide him. When I wrote this memo, I had recently begun a new missionary assignment in Romania and Eastern Europe. After five years of research, I can make limited claims to having solved the enigma of church and organizational partnership in reference to children in crisis in Romania. I do have more informed opinions about FBO-church partnerships, but I also have more complex questions. I have learned that research is one way of systemically describing what is complex, messy and when first examined, very confusing. The presentation of problems, methods, findings, and analysis as described in this book may give the false impression that research is a linear task; it categorically is not. Before discussing the objectives, research questions, overview of findings, and chapter layout it may help the reader to understand my personal interest in children, FBOs, and local churches.

Personal and Intellectual Background for the Study

In Chapter 4, I define my role as a 'reflective practitioner' (Schön, 1995). As one of the research instruments, it is important to acknowledge my personal rationale for the study (Mason, 1996:42). I was raised in a Methodist children's home in the U.S.A. with 300 other children. There I experienced the 'blessings and limitations' of institutional faith-based care for children. I grew up in an atmosphere of strict discipline, forced church attendance, and frequent episodes of violence. Children lived in houses with up to 20 others with one set of 'house parents' – some were kind and others abusive. I had no idea that this experience would set the trajectory for my life's work. I rejected God's claims on my life at the 'mature' age of 15. I studied chemistry and political science in University and spent the following ten years in 'off-shore' business (legitimate and not so legitimate) before an encounter with Christ in 1982 redirected me to work with troubled youth in the inner city of Los Angeles and the slums of Asia.

After completing training for ordination and earning an MA in intercultural studies[1], our family moved to Thailand in 1989. We spent the next seven years as denominational missionaries working in church-based community programmes caring for children 'at risk' from sexual trafficking and those living in overcrowded slums. Following the political changes after the collapse of the Soviet Union, I worked with other Western faith-based organizations[2] (FBOs) and local churches establishing programmes for children in Cambodia, Laos, and Vietnam.[3]

In Cambodia, our agency's work with children was ancillary; priority was given to church planting and evangelism, but by 1996 we had over 2,000 children in our 'projects'. Our response to children employed what I came to understand as a '*so that*' approach; our missionaries worked with suffering children 'so that' they could 'reach them with the gospel'. Children were seen as 'lost' and needing Christ, they also provided a 'means' to enter a community and work with adults. The nucleus of this research project began as I struggled with tensions in our organization. As country director, I mediated between personnel who were managing 'projects focused on children's physical and psychosocial needs' and others who said childcare projects were incidental to 'church planting and preaching the gospel'. I had read widely in missiology (Bosch, 1991)[4] and 'holistic mission', but my intellectual journey did not

---

[1] I did the MA at Fuller School of World Missions, Pasadena, CA. At that time, there were no courses focusing on children 'at risk'.

[2] In the last 20 years, policymakers have begun looking to churches, synagogues, mosques, and other 'faith-based organizations' to play a greater role in strengthening communities. According to Vidal, faith-based organizations are of three types: (1) local congregations (2) national networks, which include national denominations, their social service arms (for example Baptist Social Services), and networks of related organizations and (3) freestanding religious organizations that are incorporated separately from congregations and national networks such as World Vision International (2001:4). I differentiate between FBOs (as social service agencies) and local congregations or churches.

[3] Our organisation, the Assemblies of God, prioritized working with local churches. In 1990-1991, we signed protocols with the Cambodian, Vietnamese, and Laotian governments as a Christian NGO to set up schools, orphanages and programmes for children who had lost their parents during the Khmer Rouge holocaust and Vietnam War.

[4] I follow Bosch's definition of missiology: 'Missiology, as a branch of the discipline of Christian theology, is not a disinterested or neutral enterprise; rather it seeks to look at

resolve the dichotomistic approach to mission that bifurcated human need and eternal realities. This became more focused as the suffering of children drew me into their painful human situations. In the early 1990s specialists began describing these children as 'children at risk' (Kilbourn, 1995).[5] In this study, I use the term 'children in crisis' to designate those living in situations of abuse, exploitation, and institutionalization.[6]

I was asked by our sending agency to relocate to Romania in 2002. I began structured research in order to understand the factors that had enabled or hindered FBO and church collaboration to assist children between 1990 and 2004. This was not a purely theoretical inquiry, the research was informed by 20 years of field experience and a gap I identified in mission research concerning 'holistic mission' with children specific to the situation in Romania.

Rationale for the Research in Romania

Romania provided a specific context and factors important to the inquiry. I conducted a number of preliminary interviews to assess the scale of FBO intervention in the country since 1990. International social welfare journals described the arrival of hundreds of NGOs to assist 120,000 institutionalized children languishing in state run orphanages (Groza, *et al.*, 1999). Other children were abandoned or orphaned, victimized by neglect, on the streets in dangerous situations, or living in extreme poverty. FBOs had been arriving since 1990, some working with local churches, others were not. There was a relatively strong indigenous evangelical church in Romania. I found no systematic research to assess or measure the scale or impact of FBO-church partnership.[7] I define partnership as two or more autonomous bodies sharing complementary gifts and abilities to achieve a common goal (Rickett, 2000:4). Mission partnership had been studied in other contexts as an expression of the body of Christ.

---

the world from the perspective of the Christian faith. Such an approach does not suggest the absence of critical examination; as a matter of fact, precisely for the sake of the Christian mission it will be necessary to subject every manifestation of the Christian mission to rigorous analysis and appraisal' (Bosch, 1991:9).

[5] The term 'at risk' was borrowed from the social sciences and was probably first used in medical work as 'at risk of contracting a disease'. The wording implies that a child may not actually yet be in a crisis, that is, children and youth have not yet experienced suffering or some forms of deprivation. The terminology has been widely adopted by FBOs and NGOs and can be problematic.

[6] 'Crisis', as I am using the word, has at least two meanings: a) possible turning point which occurs at a crucial or decisive time (for better or worse), and b) time of danger or trouble which threatens unpleasant consequences.

[7] In Chapter 3, I cite studies of NGO activity that implicitly includes FBO work. World Vision International (WVI) had published reports of its activities in its journal '*Together*', and the Catholic Charity Caritas had also documented its work. These studies did not investigate FBO-church collaboration.

> Partnership in mission belongs to the essence of the church: partnership is not so much what the church does as what the church is: churches theologically belong to one another, for God has called each 'into the fellowship (*koinonia*) of his Son, Jesus Christ our Lord' 1Corl 1:9 (Kirk, 1999:187).[8]

The initial months of research involved background study in Romanian culture and history, specifically concerning Romanian evangelicalism and the structural factors that are presumed to have resulted in the crisis for children from the institutions. I expanded my reading in the fields of child and human development, organizational development, partnership in mission, leadership, and mission theology. Where appropriate, I interact with this literature in the analysis. In 2003 I was invited to participate with a group of scholars and practitioners who had begun work with 'child theology'.[9] This study incorporates empirical research, theological reflections, and makes suggestions for future practice.

Preconceptions, Objectives, Research Questions, and Methodology

Having recently moved to Romania, the research was designed as exploratory and as a learning vehicle; I was not able to rely on prior local knowledge or people networks. This served as an incentive to conduct additional interviews throughout the study. I also held a number of preconceived ideas and convictions. I held at least two assumptions concerning local churches: evangelical human resources are grounded in the local church and local churches usually remain in communities after FBOs have come and gone.[10] Romanian believers had endured several decades of persecution under the communist regime; I assumed they were people of strong faith and commitment to Christ. I did not know just how 'hardened' some of their faith categories had become. I had limited knowledge of local church commitments towards children. Some of the FBOs working in Romania I knew from other countries, the majority were unknown to me.

---

[8] Kirk goes on to say, '[The] failure of different churches, agencies and individual Christians to work together wherever they can has a detrimental effect on mission. It causes a credibility gap between reality and the message. Though the Gospel proclaims that faith in Christ brings reconciliation, a healing of divisions and a release of love into situations and relationships, people often see Christians adopting policies that are based on suspicion, guilt by association, and conspiracy theories (Kirk, 1999:201).

[9] The term, 'Child Theology' has been coined by Keith J. White, Haddon Willmer, and John Collier, leaders of the Child Theology Movement, see www.childtheology.org.

[10] Colson (1992) observes, 'in our search for something worthwhile, we lose sight of a simple truth: that, when it comes to spiritual maturity, God has provided no alternative to the loving discipline of the visible church' (1992:65). See Chapter 4, *The Story of the Church – Timişoara* in which Colson documents the beginning of the Romanian revolution from the church of Laszlo Tokes.

The research was intentionally based in a local context; theory or core categories emerged from the voices and actions of the study participants. There are general statements about Christian interventions with children at a world level but research at a local level provides particularity.

> What at first glance appears to be the largest world religion is in fact the ultimate local religion...The strength of world Christianity lies in its creative interweaving of the warp of world religion with the woof of its local contexts (Robert, 2000:56)

I also held preconceived ideas about 'holistic' mission that included the *vertical* dimensions of the gospel, that is, our obligations towards God in Christ and God's actions towards us and the *horizontal* dimensions of the gospel – our obligations towards neighbours and enemies. Despite the claims of some who argued for 'mission *as* transformation' (Samuel & Sugden, 1999), I recognized there were tensions between advocates of 'church growth' and advocates of 'holistic mission'. In a review of sources written prior to 1990, children in crisis had been largely overlooked in both church growth and holistic accounts. I concluded that research based in a contemporary local context had potential to advance the discussion.

An initial objective of the research was to address efficacy[11] in FBO-church partnerships. I would investigate how they had been working together and provide an assessment of their methods employed to care for children and youth at risk. A systematic study was planned to identify interventions that were producing 'change' in children's lives and factors that enabled FBO-church cooperation. An outcome of this assessment was to suggest a theory or core category (Glaser & Strauss, 1967) generated from the data that might enable closer cooperation of FBOs and churches in delivery of care for children.[12] As the research progressed, I become conscious of a number of unpredictable factors in the data that needed attention in analysis beyond assessing 'efficacy'.

The research was undertaken to answer a central question: *What factors enabled or hindered international and local FBOs and Romanian evangelical churches to collaborate in ministry with children in crisis in the time frame 1990-2004?*

I followed two directions of inquiry: 1) a critical assessment of selected FBOs and churches to examine interventions, use of structures, organizational competencies, leadership skills, outcomes, and collaboration and 2) an analysis

---

[11] Efficacy as used here means the power to produce a given effect or outcome; the production of the effect intended, as in, the efficacy of a FBO-church partnership to 'rescue' children from threatening situations; the efficacy of prayer.

[12] As a practitioner, I had worked with FBOs that paid little or no attention to churches and others that worked in close cooperation; I assumed there must be reasons for this practice, but I had never stopped to analyze the problem.

of the missiological and theological assumptions and perceptions of both FBOs and churches. Several parallel questions were addressed.

1. What were the socio-structural factors in communist Romania prior to1990 that contributed to the crisis for children and how did these factors influence Western FBOs and Romanian evangelical churches that responded to these needs?
2. What were the expectations of Western FBOs and Romanian evangelical churches of one another following the fall of communism in reference to children and youth?
3. As FBOs entered Romania in the early and mid 1990s how did they learn about the needs of the Romanian evangelical churches and children in their communities?
4. How do FBOs and their Romanian partners understand the role of the local church and what were their perceptions of the local church in meeting the needs of children?

Midway through the research I framed a pair of more salient questions to assist in analysis:

5. To what degree does theological or missiological reflection shape the process of FBO-church collaboration in their mutual response to children?
6. Have theological and missiological assumptions been modified in FBO-partnerships? These latter questions added a dimension to the study that was not anticipated at the onset and contributed to the final stage of analysis.

Questions one, two, and three shaped the first phase of the research. Through literature and interviews I was able to answer question one; the period leading to the fall of Ceauşescu and failed state policies concerning children are well documented. I also found secondary sources describing the influx of Western mission agencies in the 1990s but few were specific to church, child, and mission. There was little documentary evidence describing FBO activities outside individual promotional reports. Phase One included creating a database, visits to projects, 60 guided interviews, and analysis to develop case criteria generated from axial coding. In Chapter 4, I discuss these methods, case selection, the interview process, and case study protocol.

The research fell into three overlapping phases. Phase One revealed the complexity and diversity of FBO activity, necessitating a selection of cases representative of the types of FBO-church partnership. Phase Two was a cross-case investigation into the perceptions and assumptions selected churches and FBOs held of one another and children, generating additional data concerning programmatic outcomes. Phase Three involved a critique of 'holistic mission' in FBO-church collaboration and identification of the core category with implications for factors shaping partnership.

Overview of Findings – Changes in Perspectives During Research

I will outline some of the key findings, explaining how my perspectives and methods were altered by unexpected outcomes of the research. The study was conducted between 2002 and 2007 while living and working in Romania.

Pragmatism coloured my early approaches. I focused on systematically collecting data from interviews and empirical evidence of what was 'working' and what 'was not working' in FBO-church partnership, that is, how they were actually helping children. I established a rationale for case selection and intended to build an argument for 'holistic mission' with children. I assumed I could shape the data into a neat package and present a formula such as: 'If FBO and church do x, y, and z then they will generate holistic outcomes.' These were untested presuppositions and assumptions that were modified in the analysis.

The inquiry, as designed in Phase One, was too linear and required adjustment in a number of areas. I had assumed that FBOs and churches were willing to collaborate and social concern was 'integral' to partnership; this was not the case. Asking questions about 'FBOs from the West', 'local concern for children', and partnership dynamics required sensitivity and patience in the interview process. FBO-church collaboration in the 1990s had developed without a clear pattern or theory guiding childcare practice or partnership. The terms 'holistic' and 'transformation' were used in many imprecise ways; I could not give a coherent account how FBOs used these terms. Very few churches used them. Whatever notions I had brought about 'holistic' mission from other contexts were far from 'integral' to FBO-church partnership in Romania. The definition of 'holistic' required more testing and assessment.

The data in Phase One provided evidence of activism on behalf of children. I identified several positive outcomes in partnership but found more issues of conflict and misunderstanding including: FBO accusations that churches lacked concern for street children, pastors acting as gatekeepers, disagreements over which children should receive care, and church allegations that FBOs sought to control projects. There was a distinct 'division of labour' between FBOs and churches. Much FBO activity in the early 1990s was reactive and disempowering towards local churches. The research shifted from simply asking 'What was working for children in FBO-church collaboration?' to causality and influence. Why were the FBOs taking most of the responsibility? What sorts of churches were more likely to engage with children in crisis? What enabled FBO-church partnership to overcome suspicion and mistrust?

In Phase Two, specific cases were chosen to display variation on a number of continua. This enhanced the external validity of the findings and more importantly provided insight into theological and organizational values. Both FBOs and churches had agendas: churches were concerned with presenting the gospel and preparing believers for eternity; FBOs were concerned with helping children who were dealing with pain in the present world. Romanian churches were committed to their theological views of salvation for children and Western FBOs to their concepts of holistic child and community development.[13]

I considered FBOs and local churches as expressions of Christ's body as in Romans 12:4-5 where each member contributes according to their gift but all members belong to one another. During case study analysis, I gave greater attention to the 'theological aspects' of the study. I was not trained as a 'systematic theologian' and felt a certain inadequacy addressing the theological questions that continued to arise in the cases.[14] Discussion of sin, salvation, eternity, and God's intentions were never far from the surface in the research. I sought in the analysis to explicate how FBO-church partnerships were participating in God and His redemptive mission. I have done what I could to become more competent theologically in the process.

Phase Two became an intensive effort in 'listening' carefully to the cases, asking what churches and FBOs expected of God in their work with children, and ascertaining if they were engaged in critical reflection on the '*Evangel*' in their pragmatic interventions. Western FBOs were operating programmes, supplying financial resources and expertise. Romanian evangelicals were driven to prove to their Orthodox neighbours and themselves that they were working with 'real and serious' evangelical Christianity. Suspicion, overwork, anxiousness, and competition were indicators of little attention to the Evangel of peace or consideration of 'the child as a language of God' in missional activity. I began to suspect that some partnerships had reduced their mission to children to a fiduciary relationship[15] instead of an invitation to learn more of God in Christ. There were few forums where FBOs and churches could engage in meaningful dialogue.

---

[13] Both sides of the partnership relied on theological assumptions; churches were working primarily from a gospel of repentance and conversion while FBOs were mixing Western views of child welfare with a gospel of social concern (see Chapter 7).

[14] As mentioned above, my formal training in missiology included social science, leadership, development studies, urban studies, and some anthropology. I had limited training in theology simply because it was never required by my denomination for ordination (that may be hard for some readers to understand). I thank Dr, Haddon Willmer for encouraging me to carry on in this research as 'practical theologian' who devotes intellectual energy to listening to what one believes God is saying in a given situation.

[15] By 'fiduciary' I mean that churches and FBOs were acting as legal guardians of the kingdom for children; they were not allowing the children to inform their understanding of the kingdom. Children or elderly people typically need a fiduciary. The person who looks after the assets on the other's behalf is expected to act in the best interests of the person whose assets they are in charge of. This is known as 'fiduciary duty'. In Matt. 18:1-5, Jesus seems to turn adult logic 'upside down' when he places a child in midst (Matt. 18:2-5). He comes to the anxious and arguing disciples and reminds them that 'entering the kingdom' requires a different sort of living and learning. I will discuss the 'child in the midst' at several points in the analysis.

FBO-church partnerships in the 1990s had been characterized by activism with occasional intentionality in partnership. The 'energy' came in the form of finances and programmatic incentives, the 'push' of numerous Western agencies coming to Romania to establish a presence whether invited or not, the 'pull' of Romanians who have gone to the West looking for resources and partners. I surmised that FBOs launched a new faith-based sector for children with little 'dialogical space' for theological reflection.[16] At the programmatic level, thousands of children had been helped. The FBOs made a significant impact (positive and negative) on the evangelical churches and in turn the churches started shaping FBO agendas. By 2004, several churches that were initially reluctant to work with troubled children were becoming more socially concerned and proactive. After completing fieldwork, I identified the key factors that influenced FBO and church response to children and how the partnerships described outcomes in the lives of children; these were written up as 'initial findings' in late 2006 and labelled as four central categories.

In 2007, after stepping out of the 'white-water' of fieldwork and missionary responsibility, the third phase of research began.[17] Further analysis illuminated what I had glimpsed earlier when I labelled *Side A* and *Side B*, where:

- *Side A* (concerns from Above) represented God's actions toward humanity and our response. Church-based perceptions and interventions were focused on 'saving' souls of children for eternity, bringing children into a relationship with God, and reflected a serious concern for the transcendent nature of God.[18]
- *Side B* (concerns from Below) represented human actions in the present towards children. FBO perceptions and interventions were focused on the physical and psycho-social realities of children, 'saving them from suffering' by addressing moral formation, education, community and human development, family, and health.

---

[16] The 'dialogical open space' is my term for creating a safe space to allow listening to one another and entering into the narrative of scripture – activities that are necessary for spiritual reflection and growth – personally and institutionally.

[17] This was the result of either (a) the fruit of following the procedures of Grounded Theory after identifying four central categories and searching for a Core Category or (b) my becoming more integral to the study and the reflective process.

[18] Wells observes, 'Theology has often struggled to know what to make of the spatial image implied in transcendence' (1994: 92). Is God's transcendence to be understood as something that is 'above', 'beyond', or 'within'? Barth argued for the infinite qualitative difference in the being of God as compared with our own and spoke of this in terms of hiddenness: 'our knowledge of God begins in all seriousness with the knowledge of the hiddenness of God (Barth, CD II/I:183). Moltmann makes divine transcendence a 'this worldly matter' and links it to the coming age that would qualitatively differ from the present. See Lord (2003) for a missiological discussion of Moltmann in dialogue with other scholars on 'transcendence and immanence'. For a review of relevant literature see Wells (1994:92 footnote 4).

God's 'actions towards humanity' can be taken from texts such as 2 Cor. 5:18-19. 'All this is from God, who reconciled us to himself through Christ … that God was reconciling the world to himself in Christ, not counting men's sins against them'. I approached the findings with an awareness of the difference in FBOs and churches, which can be described *broadly* by the contrast between God acting in Christ and human beings and organizations doing good in human ways with human resources and wisdom. Sometimes, Christians see that good action in faith includes and interweaves both sides, but sometimes they are separated and contrasted. Bosch notes that the relationship between the 'evangelistic and the societal dimensions', between the eternal and the human, constitutes 'one of the thorniest areas in the theology and practice of mission' (Bosch, 1991:401).[19] With volumes having been published on holistic mission, I was unsure in the earlier phases of study what I could add. I was confronted with evidence of bifurcation and the realization something was missing in my analysis.

I found little evidence that either churches or FBOs were trying to critically *integrate Side A* and *Side B*; the partnerships had not articulated a coherent missiology for children. I refer to this as 'a side by side approach'. The term 'holistic' was used by FBOs, but the word was used as a 'catch-all phrase' and more careful theological reflection was indicated. Children were an object of intervention, but the 'child in the midst' (Matt. 18:2) was not serving as a theological pointer to what God might expect of FBO and church.[20]

I argue that FBO-church partnership in Romania must engage in more missiological reflection and suggest that 'child theology' and Christology provide clues as way forward. If '*Side A*' is not meaningfully integrated with '*Side B*', then churches may remain pietistic and concerned only with vertical dimensions of the gospel for children. FBOs tended to leave the work of *Side A* to the churches. If 'Side B' is not meaningfully integrated with *Side A*, it may result in the FBOs delivering effective social services for children but embracing a secular eschatology. Churches tended to leave *Side B* to the FBOs.

---

[19] The contrast in these terms goes back more than a hundred years in missiology. More recently, there was the argument generated around 'Renewal in Mission' prepared for the WCC Uppsala Assembly in 1968. This saw salvation as coming in many different ways and forms, which match up to the scope of human well-being, which is the will of God. It produced an evangelical reaction, seen for instance in Beyerhaus, who authored the 'Frankfurt Declaration' (1970) which said in part that mission is the church's presentation of salvation appropriated through belief and baptism and the primary visible task is to call out from among all people those who are saved and to incorporate them into the church.

[20] Willmer and White, in working with the Child Theology Movement, have put forward the thesis: a 'child in the midst' acts as a theological clue about the nature of the kingdom of God. Willmer suggests that Jesus *placed* a child in the midst of a theological discussion (Matt. 18:1-3) as a 'pointer to the kingdom of God' and 'a point of entry into the kingdom'. 'Jesus the Word makes the child one of God's languages, a theological language' (Willmer, 2004:2).

Part of the challenge is a 're-visioning' of holistic mission for children in the Romanian context.

I re-examined the case study data asking; 'What is the evidence that God is working in both the human and divine dimensions in partnership?' This led to the creation of two axial categories that embraced the data and factors shaping partnership. They are represented here by two inclusive disjunctions.

1) **Structural responses to children**– what are the possible organizational means to help children in crisis? In Romania this has been polarized between 'FBO' and 'local church'.

FBOs as mobile organizations	**Local churches as embedded organizations**
An organizational systems approach	Local churches rely on faith and scripture
Mission that relies on FBO as structure	Mission that relies on local church
Outcomes measurable 'in this world'	Outcomes are eternal and beyond this world

2) **Who is ultimately responsible for the action and intervention?** This question asks who is responsible for providing the solution. This too was polarized in the findings.

Human solution – key actor: Man	**Divine solution – key actor God**
Reliance on social science	Reliance on Bible and God's grace
Human health and physical care	Sin, redemption, conversion of soul
Child well-being and psycho-social indicators	Love, mercy and life in Jesus as indicators
Horizontal dimensions of the gospel	Vertical dimensions of the Gospel

Cases were plotted in a 'four quadrant' model, which led to a heuristic lens to include both axial categories and synthesize the central categories.[21] The core category was identified as 'embracing tensions in partnership for children'. Embracing requires not ignoring or attempting to abolish tension but living with uncertainty and ambiguity while following God and honouring His intentions for children. The use of terms such as 'holism and integration' in mission with children logically includes the idea of relationality and encompasses both tension and discontinuity. Theological learning and struggle is integral to embracing tension in partnership. Categories of certainty and entitlement can be exchanged for fidelity to Christ, mutual embrace of the cross, and deeper *koinonia.* In this manner, partnership can move forward, not stagnant but full of life and freedom, something like the child – she is moving,

[21] This heuristic is the result of several schematics and data displays (see methods). This is the sort of reflexive and progressive thinking that arises from ongoing interaction with data in qualitative methodology it informs both method and analysis and as I see now very important to pushing through on research.

she is fragile, she has every potential for both good and bad. I suggest that children in crisis act as theological pointers.

Acknowledgment of Limitations

The research is limited to a single country context. Romania provided a reasonable 'field of study' as there was a high concentration of FBOs and churches in a relatively small geographical space. The access to local FBOs, pastors, and churches aided in local data collection and understanding the complex phenomena of partnership but there are inherent limitations upon generalizabiltiy (Johnson, 2006:13). The study investigates phenomena that are not static, every FBO and church interviewed is still actively working with children. This study is something of a 'history of the present' (Garton Ash, 2001). The investigation is limited to *Evangelical* FBOs and churches. I do not investigate Orthodox and Catholic FBOs as I determined this would be problematic.[22] I partially based this decision on feedback from other Romanian scholars engaged in evangelical-Orthodox dialogue.

The study draws insight from evangelical missiology and theology as applicable to children in crisis; obviously these disciplines are broader than my application. I do not claim that every FBO and church in Romania conceptualizes partnership as described in this study. Based on the scope of the survey in Phase One, I suggest that the cases selected were representative of the types of FBO-church partnerships existent in the period 1995-2004. The analysis is drawn from specific cases and churches at a specific time and situation. Application that moves beyond those limitations, as in comparing this research with other work concerning church, child, and mission in other contexts must be done with critical assessment.

My explication of FBO and church perceptions and assumptions of children, FBO-church collaboration, and outcomes should be understood as a limited report. The models and descriptions I offer were generated following specific methods of data collection, interviewing, and participant-observation. These methods are not infallible; also I acknowledge the inadequacies of my powers of explanation, human finiteness, and fallenness. I do not take it as self-evident that only one interpretation can be made of this data; someone with a different set of questions would have interpreted FBO-church partnership in another way. My particular background, interests, and experience have influenced this

---

[22] Problematic in the sense that gaining access and building trust with research participants was integral to the methods chosen for this research. In several communities, the act of interviewing leaders of Orthodox and Evangelicals could produce suspicion on both sides. I suggest that further research to the depth and degree of this study is needed concerning Romanian Orthodox activities directed towards children. Such research would provide meaningful questions and comparisons. Currently two Orthodox priests are considering the topic.

account. There is additional and possibly more significant subject matter waiting to be discovered in Romanian evangelical work with children.

As a 'cultural insider' to the Western FBO side of partnership, I have tried to remain critically aware of my own blind spots and invest additional effort in learning to 'listen' to the narratives of FBOs, Romania pastors, and other participants. Suspicion and lack of trust are dominant cultural traits in Romania. I have maintained general confidentiality with the participants and sensitivity to the implications of their involvement.[23] There are bound to be some 'correct' responses that influenced the research findings, these are hopefully balanced by the willingness of others to 'tell their story'. I have learned to take a more 'critical' stance towards information I collected and my interpretation of it. Where possible, I validated oral and written sources with cross-references. On those occasions where I may have misrepresented the motives or thoughts of the research participants, I acknowledge the failure as my own.

Significance and Contribution of the Research

The significance and contribution is in three areas: 1) to studies with children in crisis in general and faith-based responses in particular, 2) to the study of evangelical missiology[24] and theology with children in the Romanian context, and 3) to the study of FBO-church partnership with application to other counties in Eastern Europe with an Orthodox majority. Bunge states, 'issues related to children have tended to be marginal in almost every area of contemporary theology' (2001:3). Concerning evangelicals in Eastern Europe, Volf says they must 'develop a theology that is sensitive to the needs, struggles, and aspirations of the churches and peoples in these countries' (1996:28).

Mission to children in crisis is an emerging field of scholarship in evangelical missiology.[25] FBOs continue to increase their efforts to assist

---

[23] In some cases I was asked to keep the conversation confidential; these 'hidden' transcripts have impacted my analysis and thinking. In cases where names are used in the text, this has been done with permission.

[24] Missiology has been further defined by Tippett in reference to local churches as: 'the academic discipline which researches, records and applies data relating to the biblical origin, the history, the anthropological principles and techniques and the theological base of the Christian mission. The theory, methodology and data bank are particularly directed towards … the growth and relevance of congregational structures and fellowship, internally to maturity, externally in outreach as the Body of Christ in local situations and beyond, in a variety of culture patterns' (1987:xiii).

[25] Oxford Centre for Mission Studies now has several scholars studying youth and children. There are graduate courses offered in North American mission training institutions concerning mission to children, including Wheaton College Graduate School, Fuller School of Intercultural Studies, and Biola University School of

marginalized children around the world. The research makes a contribution to and draws from 'Child Theology' (Willmer & White, 2006) which suggests a fresh reading of texts such as Matthew 18:1-4 as important for understanding the kingdom of God. This study encourages Romanian evangelicals and FBOs to further reflection on the Evangel in reference to categories of sin and the humanity of children; it is critical that FBO-church partnerships move beyond 'theological confessional assurances' that currently inform their actions and interventions with children.

FBOs sometimes claim that local churches are reluctant to respond to the most marginal children. This research challenges those FBOs to more consistent engagement with local churches, working together in the process to clarify theological rationale in their partnership. FBOs and churches in Romania and elsewhere must work with realistic horizons of expectation when they pray 'thy kingdom come, *on earth* as it is in heaven' as they embrace suffering children. If it is true that children in crisis serve as a type of 'barometer' for dysfunction in society, then the response of evangelical churches to children can serve as a barometer of their willingness to engage with their society.

This study raises questions about FBO 'managerial missiology' and its implications for churches and children. By giving first-person voice to Romanian pastors and leaders of local FBOs, the research is offered as a contribution to Romanian evangelicalism that is still emerging from its communist past. The findings and analysis generated in a local context provide specific missiological suggestions that may have application in neighbouring countries. The study will be useful for comparative purposes with others from post-communist Eastern Europe and Russia.

Organization of the Chapters

The book is divided into the following eight chapters. Chapter 2 frames the research problem and introduces the two faith communities that came together in Romania in the early 1990s: evangelical FBOs from the West and existent Romanian evangelical churches. I examine FBO concepts of intervention for children and missional assumptions of FBOs and discuss Romanian evangelicalism before 1990. In Chapter 3, I discuss the specific socio-cultural factors that put children in crisis in Romania before the end of communism and describe the situation for children encountered as Western FBOs arrived in the early 1990s. In Chapter 4, I describe the methodological paradigm and methods that include: initial sampling, preliminary and in-depth interviews, case criteria and selection, use of grounded theory and cross-case comparison in analysis.

Intercultural Studies. The Malaysian Baptist Theological Seminary in Penang is offering a two-year Masters course in 'holistic child development'.

Chapters 5 to 8 present the central categories, combining findings from Phase One, Two and Three. Chapter 5 examines the perceptions, operative assumptions, and factors that influenced FBO response to children; this is followed by a similar analysis of the churches in Chapter 6. Chapter 7 analyses FBO and church descriptions of outcomes with theological reflection on conversion and moral formation. I investigate how FBOs use the terms 'holism' and 'transformation', suggesting that 'transforming' children invites caregivers to embrace tension and discontinuity as pointers to the grace of God which regards all human actions as limited but integral to the partnership of God with humanity. Chapter 8 presents the core category for the study as a heuristic device to analyse the factors that hinder or enable partnership with a closing reflection of a 'child in the midst' of FBO-church collaboration. Chapter 9 concludes the study suggesting a pedagogical model that integrates action and theological reflection. I make several recommendations both for FBOs and Romanian evangelicals as they continue working together for children. These recommendations will require fresh attention to the Evangel in creative, imaginative, and truthful ways.

Chapter 2

FBOs and Romanian Evangelical Churches: Coming Together in 1990

Introduction

This study examines practice and partnership embedded in two different faith communities that came together in Romania: evangelical FBOs from the West and the existent Romanian evangelical local churches.[1] Each of these communities had different traditions and histories that gave meaning and value to their particular forms of living and 'elements that were essential for carrying out their practices' (Swinton & Mowat, 2006:21). Understanding these elements is crucial to addressing factors that either hinder or enable FBO-church partnerships in 1990-2004.

This chapter introduces these two streams of evangelical activity and how they converged in Romania. Central to the argument is the investigation of the relationship between incoming FBOs and indigenous Romanian evangelical churches as revealed in their actions for children in crisis. Before discussing the contextual factors that lead to the crisis, I introduce the problematics and tensions that serve as background concerns.

I begin with a brief definition of 'church', followed by a characterisation of the FBOs that came to Romania in and after 1990. The discussion includes reference to the larger global problem with children in difficulty, the development of evangelical FBOs in recent times, and missional assumptions of child-focused FBOs that influenced their expectations of Romanian churches. In reference to 'assumptions,' I follow Schein's definition: 'when a solution to a problem works repeatedly it comes to be taken for granted. What was once a hypothesis, supported by a hunch or value, comes gradually to be treated as a reality' (1997:21).[2] These sorts of basic assumptions are also described as 'theories in use' that guide behaviour and tell group members how

---

[1] Of the various meanings associated with the term *evangelical*, 'the theological meaning is primary, derived from the Greek word *evangelion* meaning message of salvation through the atoning work of Christ' (Bloesch, 1978:7). In the West, the descriptive term 'evangelical' (lower case) in common usage, means 'of the gospel', referring to both the theology of the New Testament evangelists, apostles, and prophets and the theology 'newly discovered and accepted by the Reformation of the sixteenth century' (Barth, 1992:5). Evangelical (upper case) is applied to any aspect of the movement beginning in the 1730s (Bebbington, 1989:1).

[2] Schein's discussion on 'assumptions' follows an explanation of 'espoused values' (Argyris & Schön, 1978). All group learning ultimately reflects someone's original values; 'someone's sense of what ought to be as distinct from what is' (1997:19).

to perceive and think (Argyris & Schön, 1978).[3] The second section of this chapter provides a characterisation of Romanian evangelicalism and churches that emerged before and after the communist era (1947-1989) and an overview of interaction with the West in the turbulent period of the early 1990s. Familiarity with this historical context is necessary to understand the expectations churches brought to the Western FBOs discussed in Chapter 6.

'Church' as Used in this Study

I approach FBOs and local churches as a reflection of Romans 12:4-5 recognizing that there are many expressions of love and service in the Body of Christ.[4] Because I do not intend to set out an 'either/or' dichotomy between the acts of love and service of FBOs and local churches, I will clarify what is meant by the terms 'local church' and Church.

Community and what the church is called to be

Barth recommends using the word 'community' rather than 'Church' as the Word of God dwells in community (1963:37). The church is the community (*ekklesia*) called to be the living interpretation of God's story, the hermeneutic of the gospel (Newbigin, 1989:222).[5] The Church is composed of people, a community of covenant and commitment to one another within God's covenant with all (Rom. 15:7; Col. 3:12-13).[6] In describing the nature of church, Volf says the church cannot always be defined by looking at what the church is in a given context; rather we must look at what the church is called to be (1998:10-11). 'A central theological reality is that the Church (local and universal) is uniquely equipped to be the locus of mission to the community and world because it is essentially missional by its very nature' (Engel & Dryness, 2000:4). A church is born through mission and lives by mission (Bosch, 1991:373) because to participate in mission is to participate in the movement of

---

[3] 'Theory in use' is differentiated from 'espoused theory' as the words used to convey what is actually done or what we want others to think we are doing - the fit between the two is called 'congruence' (Argyris and Schön, 1974:6-70).

[4] Paul in Romans is describing the how the body of Christ is held together. His parable of the body is applicable to both churches and FBOs as visible expressions of the living Christ. Barth notes: 'The Body in the parable is therefore neither the sum of it particular members, not the consequence of their individual action. The Body confronts the members, establishes them, and makes them ONE (1968:443).

[5] See also Newbigin's *Foolishness to the Greeks, The Gospel in Western Culture* (1986). The Church was not a society offering personal salvation for those who joined but rather it was called *ekklesia* from the beginning, claiming the allegiance of all citizens called to deal with the public affairs of the city (1995:16).

[6] See also Meeks' analysis of the urban social world of Paul. Meeks examines four possible structures: household, the voluntary association, the synagogue, and the school (2003:84).

God's love toward people, since God is the source of love, life and, mission (*missio dei*).[7] 'It is not the church that has a mission of salvation to fulfill in the world; it is the mission of the Son and the Spirit through the Father that includes the church, creating a church as it goes on its way' (Moltmann, 1993a:64).[8]

The church as the medium of the kingdom of God

The biblical vision and hope of the church is in the kingdom of God. The church is simultaneously the message and the medium expressing the fullness of the reign of Christ (Engel & Dryness, 200:74). The kingdom of God is already and not yet, immanent and transcendent. It is broader than the church as a visible organization; although the visible church is one of the most important manifestations of that kingdom in this world (Bright, 1995; Ladd, 1996; Padilla, 1985). The church is not the custodian of the kingdom but the kingdom is the orientation, the goal and purpose of the church (Jones, 1972:35). The kingdom of God presses the church beyond its present frontiers; the church is constantly moving towards a future that is described in Rev. 21:1-22:5; Isa. 65; and Lk. 4:18-19.[9]

It is significant to the argument that Jesus Christ left behind a *visible* community. Scripture holds out a hope found in what God has done in Christ, creating a new community 'being built together to become a dwelling in which God lives by his Spirit' (Eph.2:23). His church is both 'of this world' and 'of the world to come'; heaven and earth meet in the *local church* with all its humanity, unpredictability, ambivalence, messiness, vacillation, and earthly reality concomitant in representing Christ's mission in a fallen world. Local churches are grounded and function in local geographic communities.

---

[7] I acknowledge that I am only skimming over the tops of a very significant field of missiology and ecclesiology. Bosch links *missio dei* with *missio ecclesiae* (1991:370-73) and notes that Barth developed his ecclesiology in terms of 'the missionary nature of the church…the church is not the sender, but the one sent. Its mission (its being sent) is not secondary to its being; the church exists in being sent and in building itself up for the sake of its mission' (Barth, 1956:725) quoted and translated by Bosch (1991:372).

[8] See also Moltmann (1994:2) and Küng (1976:114-44).

[9] The contrast between the church and the kingdom of God is infinite and confronts us with the ambiguity of our situation. Paul speaks of the mystery of God (Rom. 11:25) and it 'follows that the whole relationship between God and man as set forth in the church is a mystery … the divine mystery of consolation in despair, of exhortation to hope, stands in direct opposition to all those final human words … to all those riddles which we propose' (Barth, 1968:413).

Evangelical FBOs and the Wider Global Situation Concerning 'Children in Crisis'

Evangelical FBOs are working around the world collaborating with governments, NGOs, national church structures, local churches, and individuals to address the needs of children in crisis. UNICEF uses the term 'children in extremely difficult situations' and estimates that about one billion children worldwide are deprived of any semblance of a normal childhood, facing poverty, war, and AIDS (UNICEF, 2005).[10] Statistics concerning children in crisis are often used by both secular and faith-based charities to elicit donor compassion and can be mind numbing, delivering incriminating facts with little sense of how these issues are interconnected or how one should respond. The following was compiled from an evangelical source:

> Malnutrition and starvation kill some 35,000 children under the age of 5 daily. There are estimated to be more than 100 million street children worldwide, some 1.5 million children are infected with the AIDS virus, between 100 million and 200 million are ensnared in child labour. At least a million children are prostitutes or trafficked worldwide, and about 2 million children die annually because they have not been immunized against preventable diseases. Between 1984 and 1994, 1.5 million children died in wars, 4 million were disabled, and 12 million lost their homes (Kilbourn, 1996).[11]

However, children do not come to us as quantitative statistics but as individual human beings in need of love, concern, and adult care. It may be more helpful and moral if we take the view that one child needlessly suffering abuse, neglect, or pain should be cause for our concern and action.

Brief historical background of evangelical FBOs

The Christian movement has been caring for widows and orphans since the time of Christ. God's concern for the alien, the outcast, and the helpless is

[10] What constitutes a 'normal childhood' is a legitimate question. I cite UNICEF's annual report. Of the 2.2 billion children in the world, UNICEF estimates that 1.9 billion live in the developing world. One billion of those children lived in poverty and were deprived of at least one of seven amenities that UNICEF regards as basic rights: shelter, water, sanitation, schooling, information, health care, and food. UNICEF's *State of the World's Children* (SOWC) is an annual publication available at www.unicef.org/sowc07 (accessed March 2007). The global needs of children in crisis are well documented in other places see Global Action for Children available at http://www.globalactionforchildren.org/ and Global Movement for Children available at http://www.gmfc.org/ (both accessed November 2010).

[11] Phyllis Kilbourn provides a categorisation for 'children at risk' widely used by FBOs: street children, sexually exploited children, children in conflict, child labourers, the girl child, and children with HIV/AIDS. For a faith-based perspective concerning children at risk see also Viva Network which posts a helpful overview: www.viva.org. See additional links and papers at the author's website: www.prevetteresarch.net.

central to Biblical ethics in both the Old and New Testaments (Exod. 22:22-24; Duet. 10:8; 14:28-29; Duet. 24:17-22; Lk. 7:11-17; Lk. 21:2-4; James 1:27). Evangelical activism on behalf of children in crisis began in late eighteenth century as industrial societies created commercial enterprises as children were regularly exploited for cheap labour (Cunningham, 2005:128-31). Later Lord Shaftesbury started 'ragged schools' to convert [potential] criminals to Christianity' (Besford & Stephenson, 2003:145).[12] Missionary societies of this time were concerned with Christianizing the children of their converts; child-focused programmes were not their primary concern although they did support institutional education or health care. Romantic models of childhood of the nineteenth century (Bendroth, 2001)[13] gave way to the secular materialisation of childhood in the twenty-century (Sims, 2006).[14]

Intervention for children in difficulty increased significantly through the work of modern mission agencies and FBOs. Children in crisis became a greater focus in Western cross-cultural mission in the 1900s. While there is adequate literature concerning the construction of the modern concept of 'childhood' that has informed modern FBO practice; I will argue that these assumptions have become so intrinsic to Western FBOs that they are rarely critically evaluated.[15] Bunge (2001a) brings together contributions from contemporary scholars who interpret how previous theologians have understood Christian obligations to children.[16] This book represents a new field of study that evaluates contemporary FBO practice in theological perspective.

---

[12] See Cunningham (2005:138-40) for critique of the philanthropy of the 19th Century. Some argued that the ragged schools of London contributed to, rather than diminished, the crime rates. Cunningham's analysis reminds us that what at the time may appear to be 'good social policy' for children can go very wrong.

[13] Bendroth examines Bushnell's legacy and states that sentimental attitudes towards children 'were in many ways, social and theological products of the nineteenth century' (2001:495) see also Cunningham Chapter 6 'Saving the Children, c.1830- c.1920 (2005:140-61).

[14] See Sims (2006): *An Evangelical Theology of Liberation for Affluent American-Evangelical Children* and his section on Bushnell's theological anthropology of children. Sims critiques Bushnell's theological anthropology of children as 'a lack of a critically self-conscious awareness of capitalist enculturation of desire and relationality'.

[15] The discussion of the modern construction of 'childhood' is important and I refer to perceptions of childhood as the Enlightenment thinkers defined them: Locke's *Tabla Rasa*, Blake, and Rousseau's 'noble savages' [*Emile*, 1762] to the present day. See also Bunge's introductory essay (2001a) concerning Ariès. This French scholar suggested in *Centuries of Childhood: A Social History of Family Life* (1962) that childhood is a comparatively recent invention specific to certain cultures at certain times in their history. Bunge and her contributors analyze Ariès' view, arguing that people of faith and theologians have not always regarded children as 'miniature adults or adults in the making' (Bunge, 2001:12; Traina, 2001:103-33).

[16] See Bunge's work with Francke (2001b:247-78), Heitzenrater on John Wesley (2001:279-99), and Berkus on Jonathan Edwards (2001:300-28) for historical analyses of sin, salvation and care for children. These theologians influenced their modern

Care for children and child rights as an emerging discourse

In the twentieth century, there were growing expectations in the West that the modern state would provide for children; this was enshrined in laws, education, and healthcare (Cunningham, 2005:161-71).[17] I begin the discussion that follows with the 1924 'Declaration on the Rights of the Child' drafted in response to the widespread destruction of WWI and the devastating impact the war had on the children in Europe. Eglantine Jebb, the founder of Save the Children played a key role in drafting this document, informed by her Christian beliefs and outraged at what war and international politics had done to children caught up in the conflict (Stephenson, 2003:52). The U.N. founded UNICEF in 1946 with the subsequent adoption of the document in 1959 as the first global treaty that focused exclusively on children.

UNICEF recognized the question of large-scale political order and sought to make the world 'safe for children'.[18] International efforts turned to economic development and poverty alleviation schemes took into account the needs of children. The United Nations ratified the Declaration of Rights as the Convention on the Rights of the Child (CRC) in 1989. The CRC 'by its advocacy became an agent for changing the widely held view that children were objects of international human rights law, they are now regarded as subjects of rights' (Stephenson, 2003:53).

Discussions on child rights, while giving great impetus, challenge, and intellectual credibility to agencies providing care for children (both faith-based and secular), were by no means congruent among evangelical FBOs that arrived in Romania in the 1990s.[19] Evangelicals have to 'reckon with the profound differences between affirming rights as inherent in the independent being of the creature on the one hand, and rights as intrinsic to the relation with

---

counterparts by linking their theology and activism. Also see *Celebrating Children* by Miles & Wright (2003:143-63,175-207) for additional essays on history of evangelical childcare.

[17] Cunningham (2005) calls the 20th Century the 'century of the child' citing Ellen Kay's book of the same title (1909). He demonstrates that the idiom 'save the child' was of utmost political and social significance at the turn of the century and Kay's book became a best seller as the phrase became commonplace in the Progressive era of the United States (1995:171).

[18] See David Sims (2006) and his remarks on President Hoover's real but problematic concern for the child, typical of the period.

[19] Discussions concerning children's rights and the CRC are debated and sometimes contested in the evangelical community. The United States still has yet to ratify the CRC and many FBOs from America are not comfortable with 'rights based language'. Recent publications underscore this point: Ennew & Stephenson (2004) *Questioning the Basis of our Work: Christianity, Children's Rights and Development;* Stephenson (2001) *Children's Rights: Has Anyone Got it Right?;* Valdez (2002) *Protecting Children: A Biblical Perspective on Child Rights.*

God on the other' (White & Willmer, 2006:10). Before 1990, FBOs engaged in little critical reflection (Schön, 1995)[20] concerning 'rights-based language'.[21]

FBO conceptual categories for children – nurture, nature, sin, and conversion

It could be argued that in contemporary Western culture, the carefree, safe, and secure child is the one who happily consumes and has all she needs. Contemporary FBOs tend to compare the image of the carefree Western child with the child from Africa or Eastern Europe who suffers abuse or deprivation. The child in the modern West is confronted with choices and options unimaginable as little as 50 years ago. 'In the early 1900's, reformers and philanthropists were deeply imbued with the romantic notion that childhood should be happy, the best time in life' (Cunningham, 2005:161). Our constructs of childhood today have taken these presuppositions to unbalanced extremes as children are seen as 'abnormal' if they do not enjoy the privileges and bounty of consumer capitalism, see Sims (2006)'. Normal children' are depicted in promotional literature as laughing or being schooled, whereas those on the streets or in abject poverty are sometimes depicted as 'abnormal' (Besford & Stephenson, 2003:148). Conceptual categories for children in difficulty are shaped by developments in both secular and faith-based arenas; evangelicals had a voice in the process but the input is mixed (Noll, 1994).[22]

Western FBOs reflect the struggle in contemporary evangelicalism to balance nature (genetic) vs. nurture (environmental), following the work of Fowler (1981) or Coles (1990) who argue that faith follows a process similar to human growth and development. Evangelical FBOs seem unclear on whether to celebrate children or entertain fundamental doubts of their human nature. Activist developmental or programmatic agendas often minimize discussions on theology and sin (White, 2003:47-51).[23] A discussion of children who have

---

[20] Schön defines reflection as when the practitioner 'allows himself to experience surprise, puzzlement, or confusion in a situation that he finds uncertain or unique; he reflects on the phenomenon before him and on prior understandings that have been implicit in his behaviour' (1995:68). See Chapter 4 for my use of Schön's *The Reflective Practitioner* in this research.

[21] While I acknowledge the importance of the discussion on 'child rights,' I note that in 5 years of field research, I heard only three FBOs in Romania talk about 'rights based programming for children' and no Romanian evangelical churches advocated 'child rights'.

[22] Noll's title and theme: *Scandal of the Evangelical Mind* is relevant to this discussion. Noll does not address the needs of children in crisis, however I suggest that evangelical FBOs working with children should consider his critique concerning evangelical tendencies to avoid critical integration of science and faith.

[23] White provides a concise review of theoretical frameworks in child development that inform the nature/nurture debate.

become sociopaths living in the streets and sewers of Bucharest or killings in American school hallways casts this dichotomy in sharp relief.

FBOs have adopted a vocabulary that addresses the needs of the 'whole child', bringing into their practice the cumulative work of developmentalists such as: Hall (1846-1924) and Gesell (1880-1961), early founders of child study, Freud and Erickson's socio-emotional development theories, Piaget's (1932), Kohlberg's (1981), and Donaldson's (1978) cognitive development theories, and Bronfenbrenner's ecological theories (1993).[24] These theories describe child development as a dynamically integrated system where the child's mind, body, physical and social worlds guide the mastery of new skills.[25] The adoption of child development theory has enabled FBOs to incorporate within their developmental framework spiritual and eternal dimensions of childhood and by so doing, they may have avoided a critique of the secularizing tendencies inherent in this thinking. While child development theory and literature is important, Western FBOs often assume it offers what is 'in the best interest of children', yet in most cases, it has been not been subject to a critical theological analysis. Stephen Plant (2003) suggests that some British FBOs have placed their faith in progress and human well-being to such a degree that a 'secular eschatology' has replaced confidence in Christian eschatology.

The question of a theology of mission for children

Given these observations, I raise a question: to what degree does a theology of sin, grace, redemption, forgiveness, resurrection, and eternity matter for church, child and mission? Is it assumed that the 'Evangel' is fully understood as it informs FBO or church action on behalf of children? The theological legacy of Augustine, Calvin, and the Puritan approach to 'original sin' and the 'need for children to be saved' is reflected in the vocabulary of some who are the focus of this study. In the middle ground are those who, like Buckland (2001:29-45), take issue with Augustine and suggest a more modernist, humanist, and Pelagian view that God has given children the capacity to

---

[24] This American psychologist emphasised the importance of studying development in-context by proposing an 'ecological systems theory' of development where 'ecology' refers to the various environmental settings which the child experiences. The contributions of social science and psychology concerning children and their development are influential but often overshadow theological approaches to childcare. See White (2003b:48-51) for a summary of the literature with applications for faith-based care.

[25] For discussion of human development based on a theological understanding of the image of God and its relational implications see Balswick *et al.* (2005) *The Reciprocating Self: Human Development in Theological Perspective* and Loder (1998) *The Logic of the Spirit: Human Development in Theological Perspective.*

choose.[26] This view is problematic, as adults working in evangelical FBOs understand that a child's capacity to choose responsibly is fragile and uncertain.[27] Western evangelicals have laboured over the 'age of accountability' (Issler, 2004:54-71). They hold a high view of the child's status before God (Zuck, 1996; White, 2001). Some FBOs have set aside the older idioms such as original sin, adopting 'participatory language' and 'child spirituality' (Nye, 1998; Ratcliff, 2004); others address 'structural sins' (Wink, 1992, 1998; McAlpine, 2002). Theologians such as Barth, Moltmann, and Gundry-Volf[28] have enlarged contemporary theological views of children. The reader cannot assume their scholarship was embraced by the FBOs that came to work in Romania in the 1990s.

These theological and developmental discussions have taken place in an open society over many years, influencing and texturing interventions offered by Western FBOs. In Romania, on the other hand, debates about human development and mission to children were nearly nonexistent before 1990. As I began my research, I hypothesized that theology was a nominal concern for FBOs that came to Romania in the 1990s.[29] I will examine the divergence of opinion in FBO-church partnership as to what is 'in the best interest of children'. On one side are theological questions of sin, conversion, atonement, life in Christ, and perspectives of eternity (concerns from above) and on the other are human welfare and developmental needs of children, psychological, social, and physical (concerns from below). Subsquent chapters explore the degree of meaningful integration of the two sides guiding FBO or church practice.

Does theology matter to FBOs? My response is that theoretically it should. I will explore how mission to children influences both practice and theology and

---

[26] On Augustine's views concerning children see Strotz (2001) and on Calvin see Pitkin (2001); it is my position that FBOs should not so quickly brush aside the work of Augustine or the reformers on original sin and children as sin must be taken seriously. The question of original sin may not be a core interest to modernist, liberal minded child advocates, but as we shall see, it is a very real concern for evangelicals in Romania.

[27] Evangelicals believe that all human choice and intellect is to some degree influenced by sin and fallenness. We invest years in raising children with no guarantees that as adults they will live responsibly. We should remain sceptical of views that place human choice above the leading of God's grace.

[28] For Barth's treatment of children and family see Werpehowski (2001), and Moltmann's 'Child and Children as a Metaphors of Hope' and Gundry-Volf are found in the January 2000 *Theology Today*, this volume was dedicated to issues concerning children and youth.

[29] I was not alone in this opinion. In interviews with others from World Vision, Compassion International, and the Fuller School of Intercultural Studies, I learned there is a growing consensus that theology has had little direct impact on the programme agendas of FBOs until the late 1990s. I based my hypothesis on 15 years of field experience in Southeast Asia working with children and FBOs before coming to Romania.

vice versa. White integrates child development with theological insights in a helpful five-fold typology (2003a:123-6). He suggests that children of all ages have five basic needs which must be satisfied in order for them to develop as healthy effective members of their social, cultural, and spiritual context. 1) Security – a safe place and reliable attachments; 2) significance – to be valued and given meaning; 3) boundaries – at spiritual, emotional, and cognitive levels children need reliable concepts of right and wrong; 4) community – Christ calls us to live together in trusting and protective relationships, and 5) creativity – freedom to express wonder and the child's internal world. In varying measures, Western FBOs, whether they articulate these theoretical constructs in their mission practice or not, brought these assumptions with them to Romania. [30]

Descriptions of FBOs that Came to Romania – A Brief Taxonomy

Hundreds of organisations and ministries have emerged in the last 50 years to serve the increasing needs of children in difficulty around the world. Since 1950, the growth in this sector has led to 'increasing competition for resources in a highly restricted environment' (Crocker, 2001:2). The increase in entrepreneurialism and organizational structure has brought increasing scrutiny from overseeing agencies, donors and foundations, clients, the media, and the public at large (Kearns *et al.*, 1994). I created a taxonomy to describe FBOs that came to Romania in the 1990s and were willing to work with local evangelical churches. The majority of these FBOs came from North America but not all.[31]

The 'professional or full time' child-focused FBOs

In the years after WWII and the Korean War, American evangelicals became much more visible and generous in international mission and concern for children in crisis.[32] In 1950, Dr. Bob Pierce, associated with Youth for Christ,

[30] For additional discussion on perspectives of child development in contemporary faith-based care for children at risk see: Greener (2003), Tompkins (2002, 2003) and other contributions in *Celebrating Children* (2003:13-215). By way of comparison, this book has a number of chapters on child development and very few concerning theology and children.

[31] FBOs came to Romania from many Western nations: U.S.A., Canada, Scandinavia, U.K., and Germany. However, the majority of the FBOs working with Romanian evangelical churches were from North America. I include in the case studies FBOs from Sweden, U.K. and a church-based FBO from Germany. Bosch notes that following Edinburgh (1910), the 'American were doing more of everything' and cites Ralph Winter's 'Twenty Five Unbelievable Years, 1945-1969' (Winter, in Latourette 1971:507-33) as evidence of the American hegemony in recent mission history.

[32] The exponential growth of American mission outreach in the last 50 years is the subject of other studies (Wilson & Siewert, 1986). As an American missionary embedded in both practise and research for the past 20 years, I acknowledge that we

became the founder of World Vision International (WVI) when he started a child sponsorship programme to help children orphaned by the war in China and Korea.[33] WVI became the largest evangelical faith-based relief and development agency in the world; they were one of the few to work legally in Romania before 1990.[34]

Soon, other large non-American, child-focused agencies, described as 'the professional child-development sector' grew out of the energy, optimism, and capital reserves of the Western evangelical sub-culture (Harder interview, 2002).[35] Some of the larger and more recognized FBOs in this category are: WVI, Compassion International, Christian Children's Fund, Tearfund (U.K.), Kindernothilfe (Germany), Dorcas Aid International (Netherlands), and The Stromme Foundation (Norway).[36] European and American FBOs adopted and modified shild sponsorship models. Whitall (2002:14-5) evaluates 'child sponsorship' noting it has brought tremendous financial resources to the 'professional FBOs'.[37]

These FBOs typically have working partnerships with national evangelical alliances in the countries where they work and identify with the World Evangelical Fellowship; most are signatories to the Lausanne Covenant of 1974.[38] The Western led mission movement gathered momentum in the 1980s reflecting the growth of the Western economies and their willingness to engage

---

Americans bring our largesse and generosity and our limitations, ignorance, arrogance, and human faults. As the communist era was ending in Romania, I suspect that many American FBOs were not attuned to these limiting factors as they might have been.

33 I discuss World Vision Romania as a case study; according to their published information, WVI now works in more than 90 countries with a global staff of 20,000 across the globe and 'affect the lives of 100 million world-wide', see: www.wvi.org (accessed November 5, 2010) also see 'Colossus of Care' (Stafford, 2005)

34 World Vision began work in Romania in 1977.

35 Before the research in Romania, I interviewed key leaders in the large child-care organizations based in Colorado Springs, Chicago, and Los Angeles. I am indebted to Dr. Ken Harder, then programme development specialist at Compassion International, for his help in connecting me to a number of agencies and key leaders in the U.S.A.

36 This list could be expanded and I only list these for reference. Not all these FBOs work exclusively with children at risk.

37 The 2009 Annual Report states World Vision 'raised US$2.575 billion in cash and gifts-in-kind. With the addition of a small amount carried over from the previous year, it was able to spend US$2.634 billion on activities around the world' Online report at www.wvi.org. See also World Vision Journal *Together* April-June 1989, 'Child Sponsorship: Getting to the real questions'. I return to discuss 'sponsorship and dependency' in Chapter 5.

38 While child-focused FBOs were represented at Lausanne 1974, there were no tracks or workshops dedicated to children. In subsequent Lausanne Congresses in Manila 1989 and GCOWE, Seoul the issues of children at risk were not featured as plenary sessions or main working tracks (Brewster, 1997) evidence that the 'child at risk' was still not a central concern of the Lausanne process. This changed in 1998 and a track for children was developed in Capetown at Luasanne 2010.

with marginalized children. The collapse of communism in Eastern Europe provided additional opportunities for FBO expansion.

The denominationally based child-focused FBOs

The denominational mission agencies of the 1900s had aimed at individual conversion, church planting, and social transformation through 'three main types of action: evangelism, education and medicine' (Beaver, 1970:26-7). These agencies gained cross-cultural experience in training pastors, building schools, churches, hospitals, and orphanages in Latin America, Africa, and Asia. They worked with women and children when men were not as responsive to evangelism. Education provided an effective force for the liberation and social uplift of women, many of whom would start working with children in crisis in the 1970s and 1980s.In the last 40 years, there is a widening demarcation in the size and scale of ministry between the British/European mission agencies and the North American ones. The Church Missionary Society (CMS) and Baptist Missionary Society (BMS) had missionaries working with children around the world, but they did not develop large, internal, child-focused FBOs within their denominational structures.[39]

Building on this legacy, denominational missionaries and local Christians compassionately responded to children suffering in urban and rural poverty through educational programmes, social assistance, and health care; in many cases linked with the indigenous national or local church of the denomination (Hodges, 1976).[40]

In the 1980s, denominational mission agencies began allocating missionary personnel and financial resources to international child-care services, but work with children was not 'seen as a priority' (Brant, 1996:104).[41] These FBOs are

---

[39] Many Western mission agencies had been working in Africa and Asia for more that 100 years. Examples of ministries that grew from the North American denominations are Compassion Internatonal and Latin American Childcare, affliated with the Assemblies of God. The International Mission Board of the Southern Baptist Convention set up the Lottie Moon Fund in honour of one of their missionaries who served in China from 1872-1912.

[40]The term 'indigenous church' has been used in missiology for the past 130 years. Hodges' book of this title (1976) is based largely on earlier work by Roland Allen (1962) who enlarged the 'three self formula' of Venn and Anderson. For additional treatment on the use of the term 'indigenization' in protestant mission history with application to indigenous theology, see Bosch (1991:448-50).

[41] Brant states, 'I think our missiological thinking had been based on church growth models that said we had to reach the opinion makers – the 'important people' (1996:104). I recorded similar statements in interviews with denominational leaders from the West and a review of denominational publications. Most of these interviewees indicated that the denominations saw care for children in crisis as a 'side issue' to the main task of evangelical mission, described in the literature as 'reaching people with the gospel of Jesus Christ'.

differentiated from the first category, as their missional focus was not specific to care for children in poverty or relief situations (not that they are unprofessional in practice). Denominational agencies were more likely to use the term 'parachurch' when referring to 'professional FBOs' reflecting their commitment to local/national church partners. In this category, I include the faith-based mission sending agencies (Fieldler, 1997). Examples are the Overseas Missionary Fellowship (now OMF), the Salvation Army, the Church of the Nazarene, the Assemblies of God, the Southern Baptist Convention, the Sudan Interior Mission, the Evangelical Free Churches, and the humanitarian mission departments that were started by many other denominations (Hardiman, 2006).[42]

The independent and 'younger' FBOs of the 1980s

Increasing globalisation and mobility shaped the decades leading into the 1990s (Korten, 1990). The emergence of a 'global youth and media culture' gave evangelicals in the West impetus for new variations of church and mission to care for children in crisis. The 1960s through 1980s witnessed the growth of the worldwide Charismatic movement and Pentecostalism in the developing world, a 'religion made to travel' (Dempster *et al.*, 1999).[43] Combined, these cultural and religious trends gave the child-friendly FBOs an injection of fresh energy from a younger generation of Western evangelicals and missionaries from the Global South (Jenkins, 2002).

An example is Youth with a Mission (YWAM), founded in 1960 'to get youth into short term mission work and give them opportunities to reach out in Jesus name' (Rawlins, 2001).[44] Forty-five years later, YWAM claims to have

---

[42] See Hardiman (2006) *Healing Bodies, Saving Souls: Medical Missions in Asia and Africa* for treatment of the history of medical missions from the late 1800s – 1960s. He examines aspects of the modern mission era where, for the most part, 'soul and body care' are left side by side as medical care became first a way of doing mission by showing compassion and civilizing and later more contentious as missionaries were drawn into local politics.

[43] It is difficult to define the independent Charismatic movement as it grows rapidly, changes in character, and is increasingly non-aligned with denominational Evangelicalism. Peter Hocken defines the Charismatic movement as 'outside the historic churches, is here called non-denominational, as a convenient label that is neither pejorative nor inaccurate. Non-denominational Charismatic Christianity refers to all groups exhibiting Charismatic characteristics (practise of spiritual gifts), and a post-conversion experience with the Spirit that have not yet acquired (and are often determined they will not acquire) the determinate structures of the denomination (1991:221).

[44] Quote is from the YWAM website www.ywam.org (accessed November 5, 2010): 'our many ministries fit into three main categories: evangelism, training and mercy ministry. We are currently operating in more than 1000 locations in over 149 countries, with a staff of nearly 16,000.' Rawlins' PhD thesis explores YWAM's growth and

over 5,000 full-time missionaries, with 25 working in Romania. . There are ten YWAM 'bases' in Romania, over 500 annual short-term volunteers, many of them young Romanian evangelicals. Younger FBOs with names like Pioneers, New Frontiers, and Helping Hands have sent hundreds of younger, less experienced missionaries to work intentionally with children and youth in crisis.[45] Many of these young adults have chosen careers in international service, in social work, medicine, and economic development – with scores coming to Romania and Eastern Europe.

Latin, South American, and Korean Pentecostal churches experienced rapid numerical growth in the 1980s.[46] In the early 1990s, Koreans, Argentineans, and Brazilians sent cross-cultural missionaries to Romania who had witnessed the influence of evangelical care for children in their home countries and started similar projects to work with Romanian institutionalized and street children.

Much of this new FBO activity was initiated independently of the older denominational agencies and the professional FBOs that had developed standards, training, and organizational depth. These new FBOs were directed by younger leaders, many lacking experience in theology, missiology, and working with local/national churches (Miller, 2003:7-10). Where they lacked experience, they usually relied on enthusiasm and pragmatic activism. The Viva Network estimates there are as many as 110,000 full-time workers and 20,000 ministries to children worldwide (Guthrie, 1998:89).[47] The combination of enthusiasm, eagerness to serve at children, lack of serious missiological preparation and connectedness to local or sending churches added to the misunderstandings that emerged in Romania in the early 1990s.

---

expansion. Many have assumed that YWAM was simply a 'short term mission agency' but this is no longer the case. YWAM has been a model for many of this sort of 'younger FBO'.

[45] The names of many of these younger FBOs working with children are indicative of their independent thinking and spirit in mission: Hope for the Nations, Children's Relief Network, Action International, Pathfinders International, Kids Alive International, AGAPE Children's Ministries, and Arms of Jesus Children's Mission, Canada.

[46] Petersen (1996) documented the growth of *Piedad* (Latin American Childcare) an indigenous childcare agency based in El Salvador that spread throughout Latin and South America, which was largely supported by the indigenous Pentecostal church.

[47] Viva began in 1995, the agency does little actual hands-on work with children, rather seeking to coordinate and network the hundreds of agencies that do. I asked the CEO how Viva arrived at this 'estimate' – hard research or anecdotal accounts? He published this answer, 'after four years of research the Viva Network is still trying to establish the actual size of what we have termed "the Christian community of outreach to children at risk". Although no one knows the exact extent of nature of Christian outreach to children at risk, everyone agrees that it is, although amorphous, massive' (McDonald, 2003:153).

FBOs and Missional Theory in Romania

Western FBOs are not monolithic and offer a combination of operational missiology[48] and management models in responding to children in crisis. Those that arrived in Romania in the early or mid-1990s started child-care projects with optimistic and pragmatic intervention strategies. They had resources, manpower, expertise, experience, influence, and other organizational capacities (Johnson & Ludema, 1997).[49] Some believed that since Romanian communism had ended in the execution of the dictator Ceauşescu following the 'Revolution by Candlelight' (Bultman, 1991), there would be openness to evangelical Christianity resulting in rapid growth in the number of churches and freedom to respond to children who had suffered so drastically in the state institutions. Below, I briefly describe four influential missional theories identified in both literature and personal observations that influenced FBO operational assumptions and actions in Romania.

Church Growth missiology and influence on FBOs working with children

The 'church growth movement' influenced many FBOs, described above as the 'denominational FBOs'. Church growth was introduced in missiology after McGavran, published his book *Bridges of God* in 1955.[50] Church growth championed a renewed focus on salvation from above, a soteriology with emphasis on the vertical dimensions of the gospel (repentance, conversion, radical life change).

> Salvation is a vertical relationship…which issues in horizontal relationships… The vertical must not be displaced by the horizontal. Desirable as social ameliorations are, working for them must not be substituted for the biblical requirements of/for salvation (McGavran, 1973:31).

---

[48] By the term 'operational missiology' I mean that every FBO (and church) has theological or biblical presuppositions and assumptions (Schein) that guide and influence their practise and interventions with children. Operational missiology can be very complex, as is the case of a large FBO like WVI, or as simple as a guiding statement such as: 'Jesus loves children and does not want them to suffer.'

[49] In findings and analysis, I discuss specific FBO (and church) operational capacities, which I define as their competence to do something useful for children. I based research questions concerning 'operational capacity' on the premise that evangelical FBOs and churches are quite effective at getting themselves into situations close to people's problems.

[50] In 1962, several missiologists joined McGavran in California to create the Fuller School of World Mission, bringing a cross-discipline approach, including mission theology (Ladd, 1974; Glasser, 1976), the history of the church and modern missions (Winter, 1981a, 1981b). The school later offered graduate training in cross cultural anthropology (Kraft, 1979, 1990; Heibert, 1978, 1987), sociology (Wagner, 1976), strategic management (Dayton & Fraser, 1980), and leadership.

Church growth advocated 'planting' new churches and mission structures. This scheme influenced Western FBOs that started dozens of new foundations to work with children in Romania. Church growth also suggested that churches should be started in 'homogeneous people groups' with attention to ethno-linguistic and sociological variables that define these groups; children at risk have been described as 'target groups' in church growth literature.[51] The church growth movement gained influence in the North American FBOs after the Lausanne Consultations of 1974, 1980, and 1989.[52] In the 1980s, Louis Bush launched the 'AD 2000 & Beyond Movement' and spread the idea of the '10/40 Window' that promoted the planting of culturally relevant churches in the area of the world which was least evangelised.[53]

This language of 'unreached people groups' and '10/40 Windows' was later taken up by evangelical denominations and professional FBOs working with children, including WVI and Compassion International.[54] Myers (1992) addressed a group of mission executives and described the global situation of children and introduced what he called the '4/14 Window' to describe the age range in which most people in the world made decisions to come to Christ. This idea was elaborated by Brewster (1997) who described 'children as an unreached people group' and raised no questions about the validity of the

---

[51] Early church growth theory was shaped by McGavran's work in India where he observed that Indian Christians were segmented 'horizontally by caste' and he began to think about how people made decisions to come to Christ in social groups – thus the term 'people group thinking'. It is acknowledged that the 'church growth movement' borrowed from the work of British missiologist Roland Allen (1962a) *The Spontaneous Expansion of the Church and the Causes that Hinder It.* McGavran was criticised for his lack of theological sensitivity outside the Fuller and 'Church Growth' community.

[52] Doug Birdsall, chair of the Lausanne Movement, is examining how the Lausanne Movement, the AD 2000 Movement, and INFEMIT (International Fellowship of Evangelical Mission Theologians who launched the Oxford Centre for Mission Studies) interacted or conflicted with one another in the 1980s. Birdsall's research indicates that the North American church growth movement had different operational assumptions and theologies than those coming from the developing world and tensions between the movements led to a response from those who advocated 'transformation *as* mission'.

[53] Church growth missiologists had determined there were still 3 billion people or 17,000 'unreached' people groups based on their definitions of 'evangelized' and 'unreached'. The terms 'reached and unreached' open a set of problems that go beyond the scope of this discussion. For advocates of 'church growth' missiology, it is assumed that if someone has not had the opportunity to hear and understand a culturally relevant gospel message, they are 'unreached' with the gospel. For the history of the AD 2000 movement and discussion about the '10/40 Window' see http://www.ad2000.org/ad2kbroc.htm (accessed October 11, 2010).

[54] To those unfamiliar with the geography of Southern California, I note that the Fuller School of World Mission located in Pasadena, CA, is a ten-minute drive from the international offices of WVI in Monrovia, CA. Several of the adjunct professors at Fuller were PhDs employed by WVI and there was a natural blending of ideas, especially in the 1980s.

concept, the underlying mission pragmatism, or how these ideological concepts might be informed or critiqued by theology or alternate views of mission with children. Brewster noted that the church growth movement had absorbed some of the energy formerly dedicated to building schools for children in poor countries. He described children as 'strategic' to the goals of missions and church growth.[55] Monsma (1996) and Brant (1996) employed similar themes of mission to children.[56] This approach raises a question to be explored in these pages: does God see children as a 'target group' who are instrumental to his purposes or alternatively might children act as pointers for FBOs and churches to learn something fresh of *mission dei*?

Many of the denominational FBOs that came to Romania had absorbed the idioms of church growth, especially those from North America.[57] The denominational FBOs coming from other countries had shifted their attention to church-based programmes to minister to children (Mullinex, 1998). This set up concomitant FBO expectations that Romanian local churches would be willing to implement these types of programmes. While church growth missiology espoused ministry to 'unreached peoples' by starting new churches, it did not make poverty alleviation, community development, or advocacy for children in crisis integral to FBO strategy. As a result, work with children ran on 'two tracks' – one prioritizing the vertical dimension of the gospel (from above) and the other addressing horizontal dimensions of human welfare (from below).

The influence of 'church growth' missiology was treated as 'background data' in this study. Care was taken in fieldwork to not label the cases as 'church growth FBOs' but slogans such as 'reaching Romania for Christ' were noted. The Western FBOs had many untested assumptions about implementing church growth in a post-communist Orthodox country (Volf, 1996b).[58]

---

[55] In 2009, Louis Bush shifted his attention from the '10/40 Window' to the '4/14 Window'. For information on this 'movement' see www.4to14window.com. One cannot help but speculate what the next 'window' will be for this brand of evanglical missiology.

[56] One is struck with the activist and objectivist tone towards children. Children are described as targets for mission enterprise, strategic in reaching the world with the gospel. The authors fail to ask if children might teach the agencies of the nature of God or the kingdom, indicating, in my view, a theological 'blind spot' in their missiology.

[57] A positive outcome of the church growth movement was an increasing awareness of contextualization and sensitivity to cross-cultural communication (Heibert, 1983; Hesselgrave, 1991).

[58] More will be said to critique this approach of 'winning Romanian to the Christ' as Romania is a Christian country culturally – Orthodox. I present evidence of those who came to Romania to preach the gospel to Romanians yet knew little about the historical Christian tradition of Romania. Volf discusses the problem in the 'Fishing in the Neighbours' Pond' (1996b).

'Integral or holistic' missional influence on FBOs that work with children

Paralleling and sometimes at odds with 'church growth missiology' in the 1970s and 1980s was a missional theory described as 'holistic or integral mission' (Sugden, 1997a; Lingenfelter, 1996; Yamamori & Padilla, 2004).[59] Bosch provides a historical overview (1840-1970's) of the relationship between 'soteriology' and 'humanization' terms he understands as 'service to soul' and 'service to the body' and have 'impregnated Protestant missionary thinking ever since' (1991:315-403; 315).[60] Holistic mission advocates that in order to carry out God's mission, the church can neither focus its activity exclusively on saving souls nor on worldly human progress, it must do both.

> The central aim of the Great Commission is make disciples, which includes simultaneously practicing love and righteousness that is, upholding justice. The tendency to narrow mission down to personal, inward, spiritual, and heavenly concerns makes a travesty of the gospel, yet this tendency is not far from much of modern evangelism (Bosch, 2003:181).

Samuel, Sugden, and colleagues (1999) sought to integrate proclamation, evangelism, church planting, and social transformation into a seamless whole of Christian mission. Advocates of 'holistic mission' challenged the assumptions of church growth missiology (Sider, 1999a) emphasizing 'transformation' for human societies, addressing structural and personal sin, and defining ethical obligations of Christians living within the rubric of the kingdom of God. Sugden follows Samuel in critiquing dualism in church growth:

> ....a basic division persists of a key theological divergence among contemporary wholistic ministries between a wholistic ministry based on Kingdom theology

---

[59] Depending on the source the term is spelt 'holistic' or 'wholistic' and they are used interchangeably. I will keep to 'holistic' for continuity but include the 'w' if used by a printed source. I am proceeding with caution, as words like holistic and integral should not be used without testing and exemplification – they are often emotive and propagandistic. For a brief critique of *Mission as Transformation* (1999) see the review by Willmer (2001).

[60] Bosch examines the major missionary paradigms from the first century to present; his thesis is that the Christian faith is 'intrinsically missionary' based on *Missio Dei*, see especially his chapter 'Mission in the Wake of the Enlightenment'. It should be acknowledged that long before Bosch published his book, WCC and its many ecumenical councils had promoted 'holistic' thinking. Bosch drew on ecumenical work in 'mission as mediating salvation' (1991:393-402), he examines the traditional views and suggests a move to a more 'comprehensive view of salvation'. The current evangelical discussions owe much to these ecumenical councils of 1940s-1970s such as the Bangkok report (CWME 1973) 'Salvation Today'; see Bosch (1991:384; 397-99; 457-61). Evangelicals have not always been forthcoming in acknowledging their spiritual debts to their ecumenical cousins.

> and a church growth theology based on two mandates, one for evangelism and one for a Christian duty in society to be salt and light (1997a:21). [61]

Holistic mission became more influential in evangelical dialogue following the Lausanne debates of 1974, 1980, and 1989.[62] The language and idiom of 'holistic mission' is preferred by child-focused FBOs like WVI who developed their core competencies in the delivery of community-based poverty alleviation programs serving marginalized children (MacLeod, 2000). These FBOs respond to the social, physical, and developmental needs of children, arguing that 'holistic care for children includes evangelism but it is broader than simple conversion' (FBOL#2, 2003).[63] However, this statement hints at bifurcation if the eternal questions of God do not interpenetrate the theory of 'holism'. The term 'holistic mission' sometimes leaves human and eternal questions 'side by side' with limited reflection on God's action and freedom.

By the late 1980s, these FBOs and other 'professional child-focused agencies' were defining their mission agendas for children within holistic frameworks as in these statements:

> World Vision is a Christian relief, development and advocacy organization dedicated to working with children, families and communities to overcome poverty and injustice.
>
> The purpose of Tearfund is to serve Jesus Christ by enabling those who share evangelical Christian beliefs to bring good news to the poor by proclaiming and demonstrating the gospel for the whole person through support of Christian relief and development.[64]

---

[61] The quote is from *Gospel, Culture and Transformation* (1997a) a reprint of the second half of Sugden's dissertation *Seeking the Asian Face of Jesus*. .

[62] In 1989, the *Manila Manifesto* stated, 'We affirm the urgent need for churches, mission agencies, and other Christian organizations to cooperate in evangelism and social action, repudiating competition and avoiding duplication...We affirm that God is calling the whole church to take the whole gospel to the world. So we determine to proclaim it faithfully, urgently and sacrificially until he comes' (LCWE, 1989: Affirmations 14, 17, 21). In 2010, differnces between the advocates of church growth and holistic mission are not as pronounced, but in the 1970s - early 1980s,when the divide between social concern and traditional evangelism was more intense. For a concise treatment of evangelical consultations and conferences that helped shape the movement see introduction in Samuel & Sugden's *The Church in Response to Human Need* (1987:vii-xii).

[63] I developed a numeric code for all the interviewees and the practise of referencing with a letter/number designation: FBOL=FBO Leaders, Pas=Pastors, FBOS=FBO Staff, Interviewee who did not want to be identified=I, all the interviewees are further identified by a unique number. The primary role of the interviewee was assigned as it concerned the purpose of the research - see Appendix D.

[64] These mission statements were taken from websites of both FBOs: www.wvi.org and www.tearfund.org (accessed April 2005).

Professional FBOs extended their commitment to holistic mission to others through public media and publishing.[65] Myers abridged the biblical narrative and developmental theories that have guided WVI in *Walking with the Poor* but few pages were specifically dedicated to implications for children (1999b:64-5;142; 181-92).[66]

We will examine the term 'holistic' as it specifically entails working with local churches in Romania, asking how FBOs define 'holistic' if they never become an integral part of a community in the ways typical of local churches. 'Holistic mission' is not a *fait accompli* in the Romanian context. Western FBOs use this language but that does not mean that FBOs are in consensus when they say they are carrying out 'holistic mission'.[67]

The use of missional structures by FBOs working with children

Mission structures can be analysed and interpreted in a number of ways: mission organizations, mission societies, sodalities, voluntary associations, and so on. These entities are often conceived to empower the local church but often operate independently of local or national churches. Historically, modern FBOs have been shaped by Carey's argument in 1792 based on the commercial trading companies of his time that Christians should use 'means' (voluntary societies) to spread the gospel. Voluntarism in the modern mission era has created hundreds of these entities (Bosch, 1991:327-34). Some use the term 'parachurch' to describe structures used by FBOs to carry out their mission.[68] I use the term 'faith-based organization' to designate a structured organizational entity that is autonomous from the local church.

---

[65] MARC promoted WVI's philosophy of holistic child-care and community transformation, known as Area Development Programmes (ADP) MARC resources include: Bradshaw, 1993; Jayakaran, 1999; Kilbourn, 1997; Ram, 1995; Voorhies, 1996. Tearfund UK is also a good source of literature for FBO practitioners; see www.tearfund.org/ research for downloads (accessed July 2007).

[66] I have interviewed Bryant Myers on two occasions; he described the evolution of WVI since 1970. Myers was hired in 1974 to help develop the emerging relief and development arm of the ministry and recalled that there was an intentional effort at WVI to move into 'development'. He described this as a reaction to the lack of sophistication the agency had discovered in working with local and national churches in the Global South.

[67] Some North American mission agencies contine to question the use of the term 'holistic mission', see the debate between Myers and Hesselgrave in Evangelical Mission Quarterly (1999a:278-87).

[68] The term 'parachurch' is used widely for mission structures that are something other than local churches and most FBOs in this study are examples of this sort of structure. The FBO/parachurch may be connected to a denominational mission agency representing many local churches in the sending country or a large child sponsorship agency, advertising for child sponsorship in the supporting churches of the home country.

> Organizations rely on structure: the system of task and authority relationships that control how people coordinate their actions in use resources to achieve organizational goals. Structure is shaped by the organizations mission, vision, and strategy and also by its culture and values (Rosenfeld & Wilson, 1999:291).

God's people in every generation utilize organizational structures to meet their needs and to serve others; modern FBOs are examples. Western FBOs are accountable to both donors and overseeing boards and offices. Some FBOs attempt to work in partnership with indigenous national or local churches, some more successfully that others. Too often mission structures reflect cultural values that conflict with the message of the gospel reflecting 'a structural hangover' from commercial models (Engel & Dryness, 2000:46).[69] 'These social vehicles or servant structures are created by the church for many purposes' (Snyder, 1975:164). Kraybill elaborates:

> These are the social skins, the servant structures, which the church creates to do its work but they are not the church, or the kingdom ... The church is composed of the people who respond to the reign of God. Servant structures or skins are then created by the church to accomplish both its internal and external mission objectives (1978:189).

Some Western FBOs have adopted the terms 'modality' and 'sodality' as proposed by Winter (1981c) and Mellis (1983), where the former represents 'a more stationary nurturing community, broader in scope and with greater permanence (the local church), and the latter a small community of highly mobile people.[70] Brewster (1997), Myers (1994) and Ward (1995) argued for the validity of child-focused 'sodalities' as delivery vehicles for faith-based care.[71] Stanley observed that evangelicals have generally 'been quite pragmatic in their use of structure' (2003:41)[72] which is evident in the structural approaches to childcare FBOs imported to Romania.

---

[69] Engel & Dryness point out that there are inherent dangers in Western organizational structures that yield to the 'implications of the premise of secular strategic planning, which are informed by rational thinking, informed by the rigor and logic of the scientific method that will inevitably lead to solutions for the problems that have always beset humankind' (2000:86).

[70] I refer to Winter's two-structure argument here as I found it in FBO literature and interviews with leaders of FBOs prior to starting the field research. Winter bases his argument on history not theology. I acknowledge that 'modality and sodality' are flat and simple categories and problematic. Winter has been critiqued for a very shallow reading of Paul and his New Testament 'apostolic bands' which he called 'sodalities'.

[71] For a useful discussion of 'modality and sodality' in youth work in modern Britain, see Ward (1995:36-39). I will return to this discussion in the analysis of the cases as I discuss the use of structures by FBOs in Romania.

[72] Stanley develops five dimensions that set the boundaries within which evangelical mission structures take their forms: Communitarian-Institutional, Voluntarist - Ecclesiastical, Denominational-Non Denominational, National-International, Unidirectional–Multidirectional (2003:39-46)·

As with developmental welfare of children, church growth, and holistic mission, assumptions about the appropriate use of the structures and voluntarism had become embedded in Western evangelical missional practice by 1990. This must be compared with the Romanian experience: a dominant State church, little history of voluntary societies (Saulean & Eupure, 1998:8-10), and no opportunity to develop 'parachurch' structures under communism.[73] The question of structures required further missiological reflection (Kraybill, 1978:190).[74]

Western FBO structural responses to children were increasing in the 1980s–1990s; this knowledge affected the research. A point of inquiry was to determine if the Western FBOs evaluated the appropriateness of their organizational structures in the Romanian context. I sought to understand how the structural approaches the FBOs brought to Romania enabled, empowered, or hindered local churches to address the needs of children in difficulty. The questions in Table 2.1 served as background reflection to the actual interview questions.

Table 2.1 Questions concerning FBOs use of structure to assist children

1.	Did Western FBOs assume that certain structures that had worked in other places would work in Romania?
2.	What were the types of structures suggested by the Western FBOs to the Romanians? Did the FBOs consider they might create dependency on the West?
3.	Does the creation of new structures increase competition for resources? Especially if the local church does decide to assume responsibility for the needs of children in need?

These questions led to theological reflection: do organizations and structures reflect life as seen in the teachings of Christ? Does leadership in decision-making promote servant-minded discipleship? Do the structures enable people

[73] There is no juridical separation between the Romanian Orthodox Church and State in Romania. This is especially problematic for American evangelicals who have not had to work within the complexities of a State church. This is in contrast the British evangelicals who have faced a much longer organizational tension in learning to work alongside the State church (Bebbingon, 1989).

[74] Kraybill points out in *The Upside Down Kingdom* that the kingdom of God transcends the church in two ways: it existed before the church and will exist after the church. His discussion (1978:189-90; 303-308) raises a caution concerning FBOs that adopt the structural patterns of the surrounding culture that do not reflect the values of the kingdom of God. 'The kingdom has visible social and political characteristics both in the body of believers who declare Jesus as King and in the structures they create to accomplish the mission of the kingdom. Furthermore, since the organizational patterns and structures are viewed as human creations, and not seen synonymous with the kingdom itself; they are less easily defined' (Kraybill, 1978:190).

to serve one another or do they encourage the acquisition of power and status? (Samuel, 1981:50)

Management methods, models, and influence on FBOs

The missional approaches described above entailed specific management, partnership, and organizational methods. [75] These were embedded in the operational assumptions of FBOs, especially in their deployment of personnel and resources to open local FBOs or partner with Romanian local churches. Concerning an earlier period in the twentieth century Stanley writes:

> … the increase in scale and institutional commitment appeared to require increased dependence on secular models of corporate organization. By the 1920s, the denominational missionary societies, especially in the U.S.A., had become big business, relying explicitly on the methods of secular corporations to manage the whole complex enterprise (Stanley, 2003:42).

Modern mission partnership principles were developed by Venn and Anderson in their famous ‘three self’ formula to which ‘British and American mission gave assent from the middle of the nineteenth century until World War II’ (Beaver, 1970:200; Bosch, 1991:288-97; 307).[76] Contemporary mission partnership literature (Kraakevik & Welliver, 1992; Rickett, 2002; Taylor, 1994) suggests that Western FBOs should listen carefully to their national counterparts. We will explore to what degree this sort of listening was evident in FBO and local church partnerships in Romania.

The end of communism in Eastern Europe provided a new set of challenges for the Western FBOs. The FBOs were full of confidence from years of work with children and experience gained in difficult contexts; added to this were idioms like ‘win and reach’, ‘holistic agendas’, ‘the whole gospel to the whole world’, and reliance on project management strategies deployed in the developing world. This was exacerbated by the sense of triumph of Western

---

[75] For instance, see Crocker (2001) who profiled a number of North American agencies working in relief and childcare including his employer Compassion International, which sponsors over 400,000 children worldwide. Also see Barnard (2004) Chapter 2 of his PhD thesis for how organizational literature is used by FBOs and mission agencies.

[76] The goal of mission was to create self-reliant Christian communities on the ‘mission field’. This meant starting and encouraging churches that would be ‘self-governing, self-supporting, and self-propagating’. The goal was to build the church from the bottom up. Ecumenical missiology made much of this, see Bosch’s discussion on Tambaram Conference of the IMC in 1938 (1991:295). He quotes this from the report: ‘An enterprise, calling for expensive buildings, western trained leadership and duplication of much of the equipment, paraphernalia and supplementary activities that characterize the church in the West, is beyond the supporting power of the average Asiatic community’ see footnote 4, Bosch (1991:529). This quotation is directly applicable to Romania in the 1990s. Church growth advocates this principle, but the focus on growth and numbers can create an ‘inverse effect’.

capitalist values over communism, promoted in the governments of both Prime Minister Thatcher and President Reagan. This set up a 'very complex cross-cultural challenge to be managed, not just Western-Romanian cultural differences, but Western capitalist-Romanian post-communist differences'.[77] Some additional generalizations need to be made at this point concerning management methods embraced by the FBOs.

Most FBO leaders from the West have training in organizational management and rely on it for problem solving.[78] There is extensive literature on NGOs, management, and organizational development that flows from management schools that evangelicals have adapted in various ways (Collins, 2001; Senge *et al.*, 1994; Drucker,1990; Argyris, 1990).[79] Pattison raises an important concern about mixing management and mission:

> Perhaps the most worrying aspect of the uncritical adaptation of popular management ideas and techniques within religious groups is that it may be a symptom of the kind of overall assimilation that will leave churches [and FBOs] unable and unwilling to stand out against problematic cultural norms and values. The model of the market and all that goes with it, including management, is a very clear and simple way of understanding the world and relationships – that is why it is so powerful ... (1997:165).[80]

This study demonstrates that working in post-communist Romania in the 1990s, was anything but 'clear and simple'. Change was both continuous and discontinuous,[81] it was very difficult to plan or develop programmatic responses with simple assurances, especially for FBOs working with Romanian marginalized children.

---

[77] Thanks to Haddon Willmer for this insight in a personal conversation.

[78] It is fair to ask if the international FBOs function like multinational corporations in scope and scale. Measurement, management, marketing, and promotions follow the lead of the so called 'free market'. See Collins (2005*) Good to Great and the Social Sectors*. In the West, leadership and organizational studies have recently shifted focused on servant leadership and power sharing (Greenleaf, 1977).

[79] Engel & Dryness discuss the uncritical adoption of strategic planning stating, '… it is a deeply ingrained cultural value for Americans that any problem carefully analyzed and understood can be appropriately addressed and (usually) solved (2000:69). Samuel Escobar coined the term 'managerial missiology'.

[80] Pattison goes on to analyze the American experiment: 'this position is similar to that which American denominations created in the last century. The groups needed to recruit a substantial number of volunteers. To do this they had to compete in a kind of spiritual market place, using the techniques of business and management. The result was that they successfully perpetuated their existence. However, they lost the capacity to be critical of the mores of American business and society' (1997:166). See also Eskridge and Noll (2000) who concede that the blending of management and business acumen helped strengthen denominational Christianity in the U.S.A. that could be extrapolated to the child-focused FBOs that grew out of those denominations.

[81] I define this term as a period time that is marked by interruptions, full of unconnected elements, without sequential order or coherence in form and meaning.

Concerning management and mission, Samuel and Sugden ask several questions relevant to Romania: does promotion, marketing, and sloganeering undermine more relational and long term evangelism? Are national churches turned into distribution centres for resources that the FBOs supply, especially if FBOs ignore local capacity and resources? Does multinational management pull away the most qualified leaders from the churches to the lucrative salaries offered by FBOs? And, what role does competition for donor resources have in the FBOs' ability to stand with marginalized children? (1983:152-55) [82]

Some FBOs have developed sophisticated systems of measurement and evaluation for child-focused impact assessment. Western FBOs have emerged in a culture that takes statistical and objective measurement seriously and demonstrate their bias in how they discuss evaluative criteria.[83] Total Quality Management (TQM) is mentioned in some FBO literature. Faith-based social service and research has been mainstreamed in the United States (Johnson *et al.*, 2002).[84]

I am not arguing that we jettison organizational stewardship of FBOs; wise management and governance have a role in systematic delivery of faith-based care for children. If FBOs bring management theory with them as a matter of pragmatic reasoning; do they do so with critical internal assessment and is it subject to theological analysis? What are the *limits* inherent in management theory in a given cultural situation when working with the gospel and children at risk? Should FBOs be more concerned about categories of certainty or categories of fidelity to Christ, and are they compatible? To answer these questions, I will explore in the case studies management models used by the FBOs and address 'problems and possibilities in measurement criteria'.

A commitment to begin a foundation or partner with other organisations also entails a discussion of personal power (Hagberg, 2003). Abuse of power can lead to misunderstanding between leaders of FBOs and pastors. The management assumptions of FBOs illuminates that efficiency is important and may be connected to impatience in working with local churches in Romania. While it is reasonable to assume that Western FBOs benefited from the adoption of management models before coming to Romania, questions will be raised concerning operational humility; skills involved in listening and dialogue. To what extent do FBOs retain their sense of divine calling to

---

[82] The article was carried in *IMBR* as: 'Mission Agencies as Multinationals' and was written to address concerns in India in the early 1980s.

[83] See Dayton & Frazer (1980), Engel & Dryness (2000) as much Western contemporary missiology focuses on measurable goals, precision, predictability, control - all associated with modernity.

[84] Johnson's *Objective Hope* presents a systematic review of nearly 800 faith-based studies, including a core group of 25 evaluations of effectiveness in FBO services. Based upon the quantity and quality of existing literature, the authors concluded that though the overall body of work shows generally favourable findings, most areas of FBO service '... have not been the subject of serious evaluation research' (2002:21).

children and the compatibility of management in living faithfully to God, the scriptures, and the community?

Romanian Evangelicalism – The Local Partner

Romanian evangelical churches are a localized expression of the body of Christ. I turn now to discuss evangelical beginnings and factors that shaped the historical development and persecution of the churches before and during the communist time. This provides contextual background for explication of Romanian evangelical practices that were carried into the 1990s (Chapter 6).[85] Secondary literature from Romanian sources informs discussion of evangelical identity and practice. A brief overview of Western evangelical intervention in the early 1990s serves to introduce partnership dynamics.

Figure 2.1 Romania Circa 1990

[85] Since I could locate almost no literature to describe Romanian evangelical work with children before 1990, I focus here on developing a picture of evangelical movement, churches and believers leading up to 1990.

Romanian Christianity – Orthodox heritage

Historical Christianity has played an important role in shaping the history and cultures of the Balkans and Romania. Romania is said to have embraced Orthodox Christianity in the first half of the first millennium; some maintain that the Romanian people chose 'the Orthodox Byzantine rite, rejecting both the policy seeking to spread Catholicism and, later, in the sixteenth century, the Reformation' (Eliade, 1943:15). With the schism of the Western and Eastern Church in 1054, Romania became a disputed territory between the Church of Rome and the Church of Constantinople. The Orthodox Church became dominant in the Middle Ages, with Catholics having some influence in what is now the Transylvanian region. The Reformation in Western Europe was spread into Romania by Lutheran communities, especially to the German cites in the West.[86] Protestant communities were well established when this region came under the rule of Hapsburgs. The study of Romanian history, Orthodoxy and Protestantism has been covered in other sources (Eliade, 1991; Pope, 1992a).[87] Orthodoxy is an integral part of Romanian social and political identity; evangelicalism must be understood against this backdrop.

Evangelicals arrive in the late 1900s

Evangelical communities began to appear in Romania at the end of the nineteenth century with the coming of the Baptists.[88] Baptist church work continued to grow in the interwar period, notably in Basarabia in the Northeast (Popovici, 1989). Brethren missionary work began in Bucharest at the end of the nineteenth century with the arrival of E.H. Broadbent from England and

---

[86] In Transylvania, 'the Saxons founded seven fortified cities, or *Siebenburgen*, all masterpieces of provincial baroque architecture' (Kaplan, 1994:171). For perspective on the cultural difference between Eastern and Western Romania (Transylvania and Oltania) immediately after the fall of Communism, see Kaplan's *Balkan Ghosts* Chapter 9. Kaplan makes reference to the influences of the Enlightenment on Western Romania and the noticeable difference in the two regions: 'Transylvania has its high Middle Ages, cathedrals, Cistercians, a whiff of its Baroques, its Enlightenment – the historical ages that made Europe … that did not exist in Russia or in [Eastern] Romania, Moldavia, Wallachia, Bessarabia, Bulgaria, Serbia, Macedonia, Albania, Thrace, Greece, and the Ukraine' (Kaplan, 1994:149).

[87] For additional sources on Romanian history and religion see Boia, 2001; Scarfe, 1988; Keppeler, 1996; Walter, 1988; Gillet, 2001.

[88] Dorin Dobrincu, historian at the Institute of History, Iaşi, Romania has begun work on a complete history of Romanian evangelicalism; he writes in an email, 'a thorough and integrated history of the evangelicalism in Romania has not been done, it was not possible prior to 1989 for obvious reasons: the ideological control of the state-party, lack of contact with Western evangelical historical research communities, and the original sources were not available'. I interviewed Dobrincu in Iaşi and he sent me a number of references and documents that shaped this section of the chapter.

Francis Berney from Switzerland (Ionescu & Oprea-Teodorescu, 1994).[89] Pentecostal communities began immediately following WWI as missionaries came from the West (Şandru, 1992) though some claim the Pentecostal movement began without the influence of Western missionaries (Ceuţă, 2002). While Pentecostals arrived after the Baptists and Brethren, their movement spread rapidly, especially in Banat, Crişana, Transylvania, Bucovina, and northern Moldova.[90] The evangelical communities became geographically concentrated in the West and Northeast with a smaller concentration of churches in the Southeast.

Growing tensions with the Orthodox majority: 1918-1938

Evangelicals were impacted during the interwar period (1918-1938) when cultural, political, and religious elements established the Romanian Orthodox Church as the dominant religion of the nation.[91] The constitution guaranteed religious freedom and conscience, yet some articles contradicted this (Dobrincu, 2003). The slogan of the extreme right, 'to be Romanian is to be Orthodox' appeared in the 1930s, and was enshrined in public memory.[92] During this time evangelical churches and other minority religious groups came under increasing legislative discrimination. After international intervention, the Baptists and the Brethren obtained from the State official status as religious associations, but persecutions against evangelicals were common (Dobrincu, 2001:8-9).[93]

Despite persecution, evangelicals refused to renounce their faith and many were condemned to severe punishment, jail terms with hard labour, and others to concentration camps. Taloş notes that in the 1930s, evangelical churches increasingly 'preached Christ crucified' (1998:32). The internal resolve of the

---

[89] For additional information on the Brethren movement in Romania see Măceşaru (1997) and on the Baptist movement see Bunaciu & Bunaciu (1997).

[90] The history of the Pentecostals in Romania is found in several sources, a brief but fair treatment is from Codreanu (2002). Dr. Ian Hall who lives in Romania, believes that indigenous Pentecostal communities began prior to WWI. See also Şandru (1992) and Andreiescu (2001). Several sources listed in the bibliography are in Romanian, to assist in my research, I had relevant sections translated for comparison with sources written in English.

[91] For a confessional-theological framing and terminology specification with direct reference to the Romanian situation in this period see Ţon (1988:6-7, 81-82.).

[92] This was a period of nationalism that embraced the Orthodox religion, led by Corneliu Zelea Codreanu. He founded the 'The Legion of St. Michael, the Archangel' (later transformed into *Garda de Fier* 'The Iron Guard') that became a political movement and represented a sort of neo-pagan nationalism that gained greater momentum under communism. See Christian Romocea's doctoral thesis (2007).

[93] The official status of 'religious association' meant that the Baptist and Brethren were granted some protection by the Romanian constitution; Dobrincu says this only afforded them 'minimal rights'.

evangelical churches was stiffened and prepared in some ways for the persecutions that were to follow under communism that reinforced what was described as a 'martyr culture' (Dobrincu, 2001).[94] This shaping of the Romanian evangelical 'mind' is important as it indicates that the churches of the 1990s had lived with more than 60 years of pressure and restrictions (Keppeler, 1996). [95]

WWII – 1989: Communism and Impact on Evangelicals

Immediately following WWII, the Baptists, Brethren and Pentecostals were recognized as 'official' denominations and gained the status as legal *cults.*[96] With the strengthening of communism in the 1950s, the churches came under increased scrutiny of the State and the *Securitate* – the Romanian equivalent of the KGB. Communism attacked all Christianity, especially evangelicals who were viewed as out of step with the new Marxist order for society.

Nicolae Ceauşescu became the First Secretary of the Romania Communist Party in March 1965 and was named President of the Republic for life in March 1974. This particular form of communism, known as '*Ceauşescuism*', was to dictate the country's course for twenty-five years (Treptow, 1997).[97] He brought with him his own brand of communism based upon an elaborate 'personality cult', blending Marxism and nationalism and eschewing outside interference. Both Orthodox and evangelical leaders were monitored, churches were closed, and pastors were imprisoned. There is evidence that the Orthodox Church collaborated with the Party to secure its place as the official state church (Deletant, 1999:62-3). Evangelicals claimed to maintain a strict separation of church and state (Negruţ, 2000:102-10).[98]

---

[94] Dobrincu explains 'martyr culture' as 'a willingness to die, but more importantly, our identity was shaped to be stalwarts and expect the worst from the Orthodox majority' (Personal email, 2005). In the context of this exchange, he noted that this mentality did not help evangelicals learn to cooperate with the Orthodox Church after 1990.

[95] See Keppeler's PhD thesis (1996) *Beliefs and Assumptions about the Nature of the Church and its Leadership: a Romanian Case Study*, which traces the history and the contemporary influence of the Lord's Army.

[96] The word *cult/cultul* (cult/the cult) means a denomination legally recognized by the State; the word does not have the same meaning as the word has in the West for Christians. The word *sectă/secte* (sect/sects) designates all religious groups that are not officially recognized by the Romanian State. The term *sect* has taken on pejorative meaning and is used to discredit the members of the non-recognized religious groups.

[97] For a good annotated bibliography from American and European social science research on Romania's recent communist period see Popa & Horn (1994) *Ceauşescu's Romania.* Sources in my bibliography from the Centre for Romania Studies in Iaşi were located with the help of Dobrincu and Manastireanu.

[98] For an analysis of the relations between the State and the evangelical denominations in Communist Romania see Gillet (2001), and Ţon (1996). Just before this book went to press an important book was released in Romania: *Redemption Memory*

Many evangelical leaders, such as Richard Wurmbrand[99], a Lutheran Pastor from Bucharest, Simon Cure, a Baptist, and Constantin Caraman, a Pentecostal, were sent to Romanian gulags or imprisoned. Wurmbrand wrote *Tortured for Christ* (1967) still read in Romania today by young leaders who have grown up since the revolution.[100] Wurmbrand's writing, speaking, and the marks of the prison life on his body, gave him influence in speaking on behalf of the persecuted church in the East raising the awareness of Western Christians concerning the church in Romania and Eastern Europe.

Evangelical identity as shaped by communism

Believers or *Pocăiți* (the Repenters)[101], as evangelicals came to be known during this period, were forced to register all churches and members with the State. Those who refused were labelled as enemies of the State or anti-communists. The believing communities had means of identifying one another as there was constant suspicion of infiltration by the *Securitate* agents via informers.[102]

> It has always been our understanding that evangelical witness is dependent in a great measure on certain type of spirituality of the believer. Committed evangelicals called themselves believers and not simply Christians to make a distinction from the nominal Orthodox in the state churches (Bunaciu, 2003:1).

(*Răscumpărarea memoriei,* 2010) by Vasilica Croitor, this is the first Pentecostal historical assessment of the influence of Communism on the Pentecostal Union.

[99] Wurmbrand was converted in 1938 after studying in Moscow; he ministered to Russian soldiers in Romania and started his 'underground ministry'. In 1965, long before Solzhenitsyn presented his testimony to the West concerning the Russian gulag, Wurmbrand presented his to the U.S. Senate's Internal Security Subcommittee. In April of 1967, Wurmbrand formed 'Jesus to the Communist World' (later named 'The Voice of the Martyrs') working initially with and for persecuted Christians in Communist countries, later expanding its activities to help persecuted believers wherever they may be found.

[100] See also (Dobrincu, 2005) 'Richard Wurmbrand's tours in Great Britain and their International Echoes 1968-1972' presented at British-Romanian Symposium, New Europe College, Bucharest, 4-5 April 2005, Romania and Britain: Relations and Perspectives from 1930 to the Present.

[101] The word *pocăiți* according to the Romanian *DEX* is 'a person who repents, a follower of a Christian cult which came from Hungary around the year 1860 who considers repentance above other virtues, a follower of any of the religious Christian cults and a sectarian' (1998). It is derived from the verb *a (se) pocăi* which means 'in Christian rituals, to confess sins, to repent and to try to get forgiveness through fasting and prayer, to manifest sorrow, to have remorse, to repent for a bad deed or a mistake' (DEX, 1998).

[102] This insight comes from interviews with believers who endured the constant scrutiny of the *Securitate* and articles that appeared in church magazines following the fall of Communism.

Church worship and liturgy became more significant as evangelical identity was shaped around the idea of 'true believers'. Printing of religious material was forbidden and believers risked being condemned to prison and hard labour if caught smuggling Bibles, books, tracts and literature. Churches preached against 'carnality and worldliness' and personal piety meant obedience to scripture, prayer, and regular fellowship with other believers. Eschatological hopes focused on the bodily return of Christ or escape from the present world.[103] Education for pastors was restricted; the Baptist and Pentecostals had Bible schools but only a small number of students were admitted each term. Higher education and promotion in the workplace was restricted for the *pocăiţi.*

Work with children and youth was monitored by the State. Churches did not baptise any child until they were 16-18 years old and evangelism of children and youth outside the church was prohibited.[104] Sunday school classes and Christian education in local churches were limited. This lack of freedom to work with children would have consequences for the FBOs that arrived in 1990 with the assumption that Romanian churches would be willing to work with children in difficulty.

The term 'Evangelical' as it came to be understood in Romania

The term 'evangelical' is not widely used in Romania.[105] Although the term has historical roots in Protestant countries, 'its usage and connotations in the Romanian context has not so much to do with theological categories, although these can by no means be excluded [sic], as with unwritten mentalities and practices' (Neagoe, 2003:4). Evangelicals might have been labelled as *Pocăiţi* by their Orthodox neighbours, but if asked to identify themselves, they used the term 'believer' or said they were Baptist, Pentecostal, and so on.

Under the communist government, The Romanian Ministry of Cults made a distinction between Protestant and Neo-Protestant *neoprotestanţi* (evangelical cults); believers did not use this term.[106] Officially recognized were the

---

[103] I base these comments on interviews conducted with pastors in Romania who lived under the communists. Suspicion of the 'world' was a common theme when these men discussed their views toward the State. Protests against the government did occur, but I was told that the average 'believer' in Romania had little knowledge of this. Most believers were concerned with 'getting along with life in this world' as best as possible, more important was being 'saved to be ready to go to heaven'.

[104] I will discuss the implications of these restrictions and theological positions of Romanian evangelicals in Chapter 6. In brief, evangelicals did not baptise anyone who was not able to understand the consequences of faith and repentance.

[105] Evangelicalism is a global and amorphous movement; attempts to define it and histories are found in the literature concerning identity and praxis, see Bebbington, 1998; Wells & Woodbridge, 1975; Noll *et al.*, 1994 and Noll, 1994:7-10. See also, (Reid *et al.*, 1995), especially the chapters 'Evangelicalism' and 'New Evangelicalism'. See my earlier note on the Evangel.

[106] Referring to the situation in Romania, Pope observed the ambiguity of the terms:

Baptists, Seventh Day Adventists, Pentecostals, and the Christians According to the Gospel and the Romanian Evangelical Church. In this study, I use the term 'evangelical' to include those churches that identify themselves with the Romanian Evangelical Alliance (Pope, 1992b).

Religious liberty and the rise of protest movements in the 1970s

After a visit to both China and North Korea in June 1971, Ceauşescu led his regime through a 'mini-cultural revolution' modelling his regime after Mao and Kim Il Sung. Atheist propaganda was reintroduced with renewed vigour including proposals for 'political-ideological activity, with Marxist-Leninist education of party members and all working people' (Deletant, 1999:119). Nicolae and Elena Ceauşescu solidified their hold on power and strengthened their cult of personality.[107]

Evangelicals offered a range of reactions to new violations of liberty and faith. Some believers would have nothing to do with the State or overt opposition.[108] Other denominational leaders reacted and spoke out for religious liberty and freedom of conscience. Baptist pastor Iosif Ţon was the key leader of this initiative.[109] This protest movement of evangelicals began in the fall of 1977, led by The Romanian Committee for the Defence of Religious and

---

'protestant/neo-protestants', by including the evangelicals, the free churches, the fundamentalists, and the sects in the latter category (Pope, 1992b). In personal interviews when I asked Romanian pastors about this term, I was told, 'this is a term the communists gave to us because they did not have a good way to label us' (Bochian interview, 2006).

[107] For more on the emergence of the personality cult see Heitmann (2001), thanks for reference provided by Danut Mănăstireanu. Mănăstireanu is active in evangelical and Orthodox dialogue; he became a key dialogue partner for this research project.

[108] Şora commented on collaboration by the Orthodox: 'the churches were opened, but in the same time they were kneeling. The silent treaty between the State and the church hierarchy was "give me a free hand and you pretend nothing happened". The Church moved in the area that concerned strictly the souls of men. It was tolerated because it didn't bother in any way what the Communist order was doing. That is how the Church survived.' Interview source from Dobrincu (2003:8).

[109] Among those who joined him were Pavel Nicolescu, Radu Dumitrescu, and Aurelian Popescu (Baptist), Constantin Caraman (Pentecostal), and Silviu Cioată (Brethren). Ţon, who had studied theology in Oxford in the early 1970s, returned to Romania. In 1973, he wrote an important paper entitled *The Baptist Doctrine on the Church*. A number of copies were sent to England, where the last part was printed as a brochure under the title *Whoever will Lose his Life* (first in English then in Romanian) in connection with the situation of the Baptist churches in Romania including the interference of the State in the religious activities. The paper was then shortened to a letter, at the initiative of Vasile Taloş. Fifty pastors signed the letter. It was handed to the registry of Ceauşescu. It was the first time that a large group of pastors directly exposed the persecutions that the Baptist churches had been put to under Communism; see Ţon (1988) and Sabou & Ghitea (2004).

Consciousness Liberty (Dobrincu, 2003).[110] The denunciation of human and religious liberties escalated and attracted the attention of Western human rights activists.

Consequently, in the late 1970s and early 1980s, Romanian evangelicals began to receive increasing support as religious freedom became more important for Western evangelicals. American President Carter received Ceauşescu in Washington after the country had achieved most favoured nation (MFN) trading status believing that the Romanian churches were receiving more fair and just treatment.[111]

As Romania slid into economic chaos in the 1980s, persecution of evangelical churches increased. Funderbunk, a staunch conservative and practising Baptist, served as the U.S. ambassador to Romania in the 1980's. He openly supported Romanian evangelicals, he resigned as a sign of protest against human rights violations and lack of support from the State Department (Kaplan, 1994). American President Reagan later described communism as the 'evil empire'. These events provide clues to how the Western (especially American) evangelicals and FBOs came to perceive their counterparts in Romania, these persecuted brothers and sisters took on something of 'super saint' persona.

Increasing alliances with the West

The oppression of religious freedom led to an increased number of alliances and partnerships with Western evangelicals during the 1980s. Significant evangelical leaders were able to travel outside of Romania to the U.K., Europe, or the U.S.A. as students, pastors, and speakers.[112] Some used the opportunities abroad to discuss the deteriorating economic situation and treatment of evangelicals with their colleagues in the West and arrange for Western guests to visit Romania. *Religion in Communist Lands*, edited by the Keston College Research Centre, raised awareness for British evangelicals (Scarfe, 1976).

---

[110] The Romanian is: *Comitetul Român de Apărare a Libertătii Religioase şi de Conştiintă – ALRC;* Dobrincu (2003) is an important resource with a detailed account of the evangelical struggle of religious liberty and persecution of the Romanian evangelical churches in this period.

[111] Ceauşescu also took notice of the religiosity of Carter that probably meant nothing more than a weakness. See 'Contempt for Jimmy Carter' and 'Baptist Disinformation for Carter' (Pacepa, 1990:219-21). Pacepa details the infiltration of the Carter administration by the *Securitate* and the successful placement of agents within the Baptist church in America.

[112] How these and other individuals got permission to travel out of Romania remains a subject of some controversy. Some were accused of 'collaboration with the authorities'; others had family members that were willing to pay or had influence. I interviewed 46 Romania pastors only one admitted to me that his father had been willing to make 'compromises' to help him study outside of the country.

Cities, towns, and some churches in Western Europe began 'twinning' or partnering with Romanian villages that were being systematically destroyed by the State in order to facilitate the policy of rapid industrialisation (Deletant, 1999:153-55).[113]

Increasingly in the second half of the 1980s, Western evangelicals began to utilize FBOs for sending Christian aid and evangelism materials into Romania. These FBOs varied in size and capacity and included the following activities: Bible couriers, humanitarian aid, and student evangelism. Campus Crusade sent 'volunteers' to study the Romanian language and befriend Romanian students. Preachers, teachers, and some denominational leaders came from Europe, Scandinavia, and the Untied States. After an earthquake destroyed many old buildings in Bucharest in 1977, World Vision became more active as a Christian relief agency in the 1980s. The Western FBOs and Romanian evangelicals were largely unaware of the growing crisis in Romania with institutionalised children, little direct aid was sent to address the needs of children except for that sent to provide material relief for families living in poverty.[114]

The end of the communist era – December 1989

The last years of the 1980s were difficult for all Romanians, not just evangelicals. In an effort to eliminate all the national debt, the country was exporting a huge per centage of its national output. TV footage from the time shows Ceauşescu inspecting displays of meat, vegetables, and produce that were actually props made from polystyrene. Food lines grew longer and the discontent of the Romanian population escalated.[115] Across Eastern Europe, communism was falling from favour and the Romanian dictator had grown increasingly out of touch with reality.[116] The revolution in Romania began in

---

[113] During the 1960s, the regime began planning for urban and rural systematization; the plan was put into full effect in the late 1970s, see discussion in Chapter 3. This plan also included demolition of hundreds of churches (Orthodox, Catholic, Evangelical), historical monuments, and buildings (Deletant, 1999:151; Cernat *et al.*, 2004:106-12). Almost all villages situated in close vicinity of larger towns or cities were affected by this policy.

[114] The child institutions were maintained by the State and were off limits to all foreign visitors. I discuss why the local churches had so little knowledge of the children living in the State institutions in Chapters 3 and 6.

[115] For a insightful firsthand account of daily life for the average Romanian in the last years of the communist era, see Cernat *et al.* (2004).

[116] Analysis emerged in the late 1990s that Ceauşescu had lost control of the apparatus of the State and was living in an increased vacuum of information. When he was 'rescued' on the roof of the Senate Building and flown to a mock trial, it is likely that some of his own Party officials had arranged his capture and were dispensing with a now defunct relic of the Cold War, see Siani-Davies (2005). It has been suggested that he was sacrificed with the complicity of the *Securitate* so the leaders of the communist

Timişoara in mid-December 1989 with the protest of a Hungarian Reformed pastor, Loszlo Tokes who was threatened with imprisonment by the *Securitate* (Colson, 1992:51-62). On Christmas Day, Ceauşescu and his wife, Elena, were executed by a firing squad in a small town near Târgovişte, about 40 km west of Bucharest.

Summary of the impact of the communist years on evangelicals

During the communist era, evangelism, church planting, and social activities of the church had been severely restricted. A number of evangelicals left Romania, especially in the 1980s, contributing to a network of Western connections and relationships. Bunaciu observed that there were several distinguishing characteristics of the evangelicals in the communist time.[117]

> a) First, the church was seen as an alternative community, which involved two main features, separation from the world (which was both theological and sociological), and a strong sense of identity. This contributed to the church's tendency to look inward as opposed to outward as any form of social engagement had been prevented by the State.
>
> b) Secondly, the believers' understanding of their situation was that suffering gives meaning to the service of God; there was no such thing as 'cheap grace'.[118]
>
> c) A hope in the future as a way to overcome the present, this eschatological expectation was not merely escapism but gave believers a horizon of hope in what could have been a hopeless situation.
>
> d) Finally, the policy of the communist government to limit theological (clerical) training meant that the church relied on the lay leadership of the local church, which strengthened congregational leadership (Bunaciu, 2003).

Education of clergy for churches was virtually nonexistent as only several selected individuals were allowed to study in the small seminaries operated under State oversight. At the end of the communist era, there were only 160 trained ministers for the 1200 Baptist churches (Mănăstireanu, 1998a:2).

Churches had been destroyed, new building construction was forbidden, property was confiscated, and yet the Romanian evangelical church survived

---

party could stay in control.

[117] This series of comments is my paraphrase taken from an interview and a paper from Dr. Otinel Bunaciu, who became a dialogue partner. He earned his first degree at Regent Park, in Oxford in the late 1980s, and returned to Romania after the fall of communism. He earned his doctorate in theology and church history at the University of Cluj, Romania.

[118] It may be that the Romanian evangelicals attributed 'a value to suffering it does not deserve, and fell into the ancient Christian mistake of thinking persecution does the church good' (Willmer email, 2006). It is the grace of God in Christ that builds the church.

and, in certain areas of the country, grew numerically, a testimony to their resolve and resourcefulness. In 1989 there were approximately 1000 Pentecostal churches with 150,000 believers, 1200 Baptist Churches with 100,000 baptised believers with and an additional 200,000 adherents. There were at least 200 registered Brethren churches with 50,000 members and about 100,000 adherents (OCI, 2001).

Romanian Evangelicalism and Encounter with the West in the 1990s – Overview

With the collapse of communism, evangelicalism entered a new phase in its development. After many years of atheistic propaganda, there was apparent openness to the gospel as people showed a genuine interest in learning about spiritual matters. The following factors were identified from secondary literature and interviews as contextual background for the examination of FBO-church partnership in reference to children in crisis. I provide a general overview of activity in the early 1990s that includes mission agencies; some of these did not come to work with children.

A sudden influx of mission agencies concerned with evangelism

Romanian evangelical churches retained a tenacious faith and were looking 'forward to the next world.' However, churches had learned to survive 'in the present world', and they had certain expectations of Western evangelicals after years of repression. Churches lacked financial resources, buildings, and material resources. Alternatively, Western FBOs had known economic, social, and political freedom; they had resources for mission and organizational initiatives. Western mission agencies and FBOs rushed into Romania to help strengthen the existing and impoverished evangelical churches; most did so with the stated intent of 'taking the gospel to Romania' (Negruţ, 1999b:10).[119] Ţon noted, 'there was a rush of hundreds of organizations from the West to do mission here' (1993:3).

It became commonplace in the West to affirm that 'Eastern Europe is a mission field ... the opportunities are now to reach Eastern Europe for Christ' (Davies, 1991:17). Few of these mission agencies published research to indicate they had analyzed the impact forty-five years of communism had left

[119] I analysed the mission statements and printed literature of 98 Western FBOs and found this phrase in some form was used in 60 per cent of those documents. As pointed out earlier in this chapter, this sort of sloganeering, 'reaching, winning, taking the gospel' became very common, especially with those mission agencies that were connected with the Lausanne Evangelical Movement and the Church Growth Movement; the terms reflect some of the language of Lausanne and Evangelicalism in the 1980s and early 1990s). This sloganeering is perplexing as Western FBOs intended to 'take the gospel' to a country that had many centuries of Christian tradition.

on the overall social, economic, and religious outlook of Romanian evangelicals.[120] Western FBOs set about actively seeking cooperative national partners and establishing Romanian registered foundations and associations. Chapter 5 will analyze FBO expectations and the creation of a new FBO childcare sector.

Lack of coordination between Mission Agencies and FBOs

After decades of restrictions, it was possible to build new churches, bible schools, and training institutions, and begin humanitarian foundations. FBOs offered, as part of their mission strategy, ministry to institutionalised children or those turning to the streets for survival. It is difficult to measure the impact the media had on Western FBOs and their donors concerning the needs of Romania's poor and children.[121] The influx of foreigners and foreign aid proved impossible to coordinate or control. As one NGO director observed, 'new charities sprung up like dandelions in wet grass'. The free-for-all in aid distribution caused confusion and an overlap of efforts (Swartz, 1994). NGOs and FBOs from the West were not required by the Romanian government to collaborate with one another, and a general atmosphere of entrepreneurialism prevailed.[122] This created further tensions with local churches concerning responsibility for children in crisis and will be discussed in Chapter 6.

Freedom and spiritual openness encouraged ad hoc partnerships

Freedom to travel both in and out of Romania increased contact with evangelical churches and leaders from all over the world. As Christians in Romania were able to openly work with Western partners, FBOs sought out Romanians who could facilitate ministry and their agendas.[123] Geographically,

---

[120] One exception to this statement would be WVI who published articles indicating that post-communist Romania provided unique challenges to evangelical mission (Horner, 1991). These articles focused on the medical needs of the country.

[121] See the archives of both CNN and BBC available online and the BBC documentary *The King of Communism* aired Nov.17, 2003. I give additional space and treatment to this issue in Chapter 3.

[122] While gathering background material for this book, it became clear that something of an *invasion* had occurred in Romania in the early 1990s. I compared this in conversations and interviews to the 'Oklahoma Land Grab' when settlers in America were able to drive their schooner wagons out into the plains of Oklahoma and claim their new territory by placing four flags at the corners of their new 'property'. It seemed that many NGOs and FBOs were racing to get their 'stakes in the ground' before others claimed their share.

[123] Some published accounts are available but it appears the activity itself far outnumbers the published material. OCI Romania estimated that at least 50 mission agencies arrived in Romania between 1990 and 1992. OCI is Romanian based research group that monitors numbers of FBOs, evangelical churches, and believers and posts its

the Western and central parts of the country (Banat, Crişana, Maramureş and Transylvania) had longer cultural-religious association with Western Europe. Evangelical churches were not as established in southeastern Romania (Muntenia, Oltenia and Dobrogea). FBOs gave individual missionaries and project managers the freedom to develop evangelistic strategies to assist existent evangelical churches. The Western cities of Timişoara, Arad, Oradea, and Cluj were more accessible and received more FBO attention and benevolence in the early 1990s.[124]

The Baptist Union, Brethren Church, the Pentecostal Union, a part of the Lord's Army movement, and a group of Lutherans from Bucharest founded the Romanian Evangelical Alliance in March 1990. Vasile Taloş served as the first president followed by Paul Negruţ. The Alliance pledged to work together more effectively in the areas of evangelism, church planting, Christian education, and in defence of religious liberty (Gibson, 1993). The outcomes of this alliance in the early 1990s were more cosmetic than substantial as interdenominational cooperation was difficult in the post-communist context where suspicion and lack of trust were prevalent in both church and the larger society (Bunaciu interview, 2003).

New tensions with the Romanian Orthodox Church

As Western missionary activity increased, it brought new tension between evangelicals and the Orthodox Church. Most conflict arose from perspectives about evangelism and proselytism.[125] The Romanian Orthodox Church reclaimed dominant status in religious affairs of the country as the official state church. In the 2002 census, the Orthodox Church registered 18,817,975 members (86.8 per cent of the population). The public press was not always favourable towards evangelicals who reported infractions on their religious liberty in education, civil administration, and denials of building permits for new churches.[126] Some of this opposition came from local priests who did not welcome evangelical activity in their area (Bunaciu, 1997).[127] These strains

research online: www.oci.ro (accessed February 2010).

[124] A glance at a map reveals that the major highways from Western Europe come into Romania near both Oradea and Timişoara. Many of the relief agencies arriving in Romania in the early 1990s simply saw so much need in the Western part of the country they did not continue on further into the interior. This in part helps to explain how so many FBOs were able to establish offices and programmes in Transylvania.

[125] For perspectives on these tensions see Maxwell, 1995; Mănăstireanu, 1994; Gheorghiu, 2003; Volf 1994.

[126] There is strong social pressure from family, friends, tradition, and from politics to be affiliated with the Orthodox Church. Those who have been raised in the Orthodox tradition tend to remain Orthodox.

[127] These problems are particularly prevalent in the rural area where many Romanians have a predominately agrarian mentality and the society is characterized by a reduced

reinforced negative attitudes in some evangelicals who saw the Orthodox Church as an adversary and not a friend. This factor is examined as it concerns intervention for children and collaboration.

Statistical growth of the evangelical churches 1989-2004

Evangelical activity increased steadily in the years 1989-2004. In 1992, the first official post-communist nationwide census counted 380,086 evangelicals (1.7 per cent of the population). In the 2002 Census, the number increased to 440,000 or 2.4 per cent of the population. In 2005, OCI estimated the total number conservatively at 500,000, based on their definition of evangelical.[128] *Operation World* ranked Romania with the fourth highest number of evangelicals in Europe (Mandryk, 2010:701). The Pentecostal Union reported in 2004 to have over 2,500 churches, the Baptist Union over 1000, and another 1500 evangelical churches were claimed by the other evangelical groups: Charismatic, Evangelical Free, Adventist, Brethren, etc. bringing the total to over 5000 churches. OCI (2004) listed 360 locally registered FBOs and associations. Most were directly supported or worked in partnership with Western FBOs that assisted local partners in evangelism, church planting, leadership training, discipleship, literature production, and ministries that were focused on children.

These numbers are typical of ‘church growth’ studies; they quantitatively serve to establish that following 1989 Romanian evangelicals experienced a ‘dynamic’ partnership with Western FBOs and mission agencies. The statistics represent a significant amount of activity and investment in a country that struggled through the 1990s as one of the poorest countries in Europe crippled by years of economic mismanagement.[129] To date, little quantitative or qualitative research has been carried out to measure sociological, economic, or political impact resulting from amount of ‘church growth’ nor to answer the

---

civic sense, which retains many ideas incongruent with a democratic society, including religious intolerance.

[128] Given the decline of Romania's overall general population in the same period, which was 4.87 per cent, evangelicals took this as sign of church growth and ‘God’s favour’ (Downes interview at OCI, 2003). I reserve judgement on this statement but include to illustrate that ‘numerical church growth’ is important to Romanian evangelicals. For a more complete and updated listing of evangelical church activities see OCI website: www.oci.ro, which in 2010, claimed there are more than 6,000 evangelical churches.

[129] World Bank (2004) reported that 20 per cent of the population (5 million people), primarily concentrated in the rural areas of the country, were still living under a subsistence level; with 12 per cent unemployment and the G.D.E. per capita at 30 per cent the EU average. Romania joined the EU in January 2007 and the economic situation is improving. Current economic statistics are available online at www.worldbank.org.ro_(accessed March 2008).

central research question concerning what enables or hinders FBO-church partnership for children.

Summary

The chapter described two faith-based communities who came together in Romania in the early 1990s. Western FBOs and Romanian local churches developed in different contexts and histories. Both communities claim to be evangelical Christians, but their assumptions of responsibility to God, church, mission, fellow believer, society, and children in crisis were in many ways incongruent. These contextual factors establish the problematics that form the background to investigate FBO-church partnerships and joint action for children in crisis.

The first half of this chapter briefly examined Western FBO work with children in crisis, perceptions in child rights, welfare, and development. Three types of FBOs 'professional, denominational, and independent' were described as being influenced by the missional theories of church growth and holistic mission, use of structures, and managerial missiology. Western FBOs had initiative, resources and willingness; they brought missional assumptions with them to Romania in 1990 as they responded to the needs of Romanian churches and children. Questions were raised about theological objectives of FBOs, especially how these influence actions toward children and partnerships that remain faithful to God, the scriptures, and the community.

The second half of the chapter provided a description of Romanian evangelical beginnings, persecution and experience in the communist era. Romanian evangelicals entered the 1990s with a commitment to the local church and a belief that their suffering gave meaning to their service to God. The evidence from statistical church growth studies indicates that FBOs encountered apparent openness of Romanian pastors and churches to work together, but tells us little of how mission with children was understood. FBOs responded in a time of economic crisis that created severe difficulties for Romanian families, churches, and children. FBOs and churches came together in the rapidly changing social context of post-communist Romania.

This study does not address every missiological problem associated in East-West partnership particular to Romania. I will focus on one aspect: 'What factors have enabled or hindered international and local FBOs and Romanian evangelical churches to cooperate effectively in ministry with children in crisis in the time frame 1990-2004?' This chapter has established that mission to Romania presented unique opportunities and challenges to both FBOs and the existent indigenous evangelical churches. It will not be helpful if this discussion becomes pejorative or ideological concerning method. FBOs and churches will be treated as compatible missional structures and as organizational expressions of the Body of Christ (Romans 12:4-6). Having established the research problematic and context, I turn now to examine the factors and causes that precipitated the crisis for children in Romania and why the FBOs responded to that particular situation.

Chapter 3

Social and Structural Factors With Outcomes for Children in Romania

Introduction

The crisis for Romanian children has been the subject of much academic interest over the past 17 years. The institutionalised children and the failed policies of the Romanian government have been the subjects of documentaries, dissertations, books and numerous studies on abandonment and adoption.[1] My purpose in this chapter is to answer the question: 'What were the socio-structural factors in Romania before and after 1990 that contributed to the crisis for children?' Thc answer informs the subsequent discussion of factors influencing FBO-church partnerships that responded to the children. I withhold theological and missiological commentary until Chapter 5-8 and keep primarily to a social, economic, and structural analysis.

When I began fieldwork in 2003, I asked a number of FBOs if they had done any research on the social or structural factors that led to the childcare crisis. Only three FBOs answered in the affirmative. Romania is a particular version of the modern state, shaped by specific conditions. The problems for children in Romania were dire but not completely unique, modern states and societies often abuse their most vulnerable members (Cunningham, 2005:135-50).[2] I do not intend to present a moralistic or superior stance toward the Romanian situation, rather to examine the specifics of this context. The assumption of many Western FBOs and mission agencies entering Romania in the early 1990s was that the communists had taken control of Romania by force, which was not the case.[3] A university professor taking part in a medical

---

[1]I review several in this chapter see Groza *et al.*, 1999; Zamfir, 1997; Jigau *et al.*, 2002; Ryan & Groza, 2004; Ames & Carter, 1992; Dickens, 1999; Dickens & Watts, 1996.

[2] See Cunningham's analysis of children's home and the treatment of children in modern institutionalization in England and Wales. Bernardos is highly respected in U.K. today, but at one time they shipped children to Australia (2005:138, 148-50). One could cite Nazi Germany, Cambodia, and Sudan, any number of countries that demonstrate the modern nation states have been guilty of mistreating and abusing children.

[3]I heard these comments several times in field interviews. For discussion, see Deletant (1999), especially: 'Introduction, Path to Power of the Romanian Communist Party and Chapter 1,'Soviet Domination and the Communist Dictatorship' (1999:55-62) for a description of the rise of communism in Romanian and the subjugation of the Romanian Orthodox church. Many Westerners (especially Americans) entering Romania in the early 1990s, expected Romanians to see the communist system as a failure. What Westerners failed to recognize is that most Romanians had been born and raised in

research study recalled his motivation for joining the communist party to obtain an academic position. 'At the time communism was a utopic, albeit vague, concept that attracted many people seeking equality' (Morrison, 2004:170).[4] I offer the research in this chapter to both FBOs and churches, especially those that tend to criticize the Romanian state for its treatment of children, with little attempt to actually understand how these policies came to influence the current situation and the long-term efforts that will be required to bring about systemic change.

Ceauşescu's Romania and Social Policy

To begin, I briefly examine two socialist policies that had influence on the childcare crisis that evolved between 1966 and 1990. In Ceauşescu's Romania, social scientists concluded that the 'conditions among children were a direct consequence of government social policy' (Zamfir & Zamfir, 1996:1).

The socialist government – systemization

The communist governments of both Gheorghiu-Dej (1947-1965) and Ceauşescu gave Romania more than 40 years of relative political stability. The carnage that resulted in WWII affected most of the population; the communists took power with the backing of the Soviet Army in 1948. The country was rich in natural resources and Romanians were ready for a government that would provide jobs, security, and housing. Basic survival was the primary need of much of the population.

Gheorghiu-Dej began a period of industrialization and solidified the communist power structures in the government. Industrialization of the country occurred at the expense of the agricultural sector and rural lifestyle, but the process was gradual. Ceauşescu's rise to the head of the Party was characterized by his ability to manipulate his opponents and consolidate personal power at the expense of the central committee (Deletant 1999:104-16).

Ceauşescu implemented a more radical policy of systemization (*sistematizare*) to hasten the implementation of a new urban and industrial society. Individual farms were put into the state collectives; historic rural

---

system that provided free education, job security, and 45 years of peace. 'For the Americans, any sign of a Romanian's adherence to the old communist mentality was devalued' (Dickens & Groza, 2004:481).

[4] Morrison worked as an anthropologist on a joint Romanian and American research team to understand the opinions of people in Hirlau, Romania concerning institutionalised children. This team was a joint partnership between WV Romania, Dr. Barbara Bascomb, and Case Western University. They studied how deinstitutionalisation would affect bonding between residents of the orphanage and the family units they had formed.

villages were razed relocating greater numbers of peasants to the cities where they were moved into hastily and shabbily constructed large apartment blocks. This policy dismantled the older neighbourhoods in the cities and disrupted the extended family networks in the villages by forcing relocation into the blocks. 'In 1950, 78 per cent of the population worked in agriculture; by 1977, that number was reduced to 35 per cent' (Robilla, 2002:78).[5] Relocation of the population served two purposes: move the population close to the new factories and to make it easier to control and monitor the people. 'In general, the structural change of the Romanian society through the enforced urbanization process caused a series of social mutations, aimed at destroying and flattening the traditional social structure' (Saulean & Epure, 1998:8).

Securitate – control and function

Ceauşescu was obsessed with monitoring the lives of the Romanian people.[6] He understood that to control the population he would need a much more extensive security apparatus. He transformed the existent secret police, the DGTO,[7] and into the feared *securitate* which eventually employed one million people in a far-reaching network of informers involved at every level local and national (Groza *et al.*, 1999).[8] To get a good job required party approval and *securitate* screening. Reporting on fellow workers and members of your family to the 'block and street committees' was expected of everyone, including children, all phones in the country were bugged, offices were watched, teachers were required to report on the activities of their students.

---

[5] Deletant notes that, 'Over 11 million people (most rural families) were resettled from private houses in about 7,000 villages to cheap low quality apartment blocks and apartments in 550 standardized 'agro-industrial centres' (1999:151).

[6] For a more detailed description of the workings of the *Securitate* see Pacepa (1990). Pacepa served as the former head of DIE – *Departamentul de Informaţii Externe* (Foreign Intelligence Service), until his defection to the United States in 1978. He states, 'When Ceauşescu came to power in 1965; the Romanian security forces had one central and eleven regional KGB-designed electronic monitoring centres and five central mail censorship units around the country. The DGTO had, as of March 1978, ten central and 248 peripheral automated electronic monitoring centres, plus over a thousand 'portable' units covering small towns, vacation resorts, and the picturesque, historical monasteries favoured by Western tourists, as well as 48 mail censorship units' (Pacepa, 1990:132).

[7] General Directorate of Technical Operation which had been developed to control domestic population through interceptions via microphones, and mail censorship (Pacepa, 1990:128).

[8] Victor Groza is a Romanian/American professor at the Mandel School Social Science, Case Western Reserve University. He and his colleagues made a number of trips in and out of Romania throughout the 1990s. He written on the condition of the institutions and extensively documented international Romanian adoptions. For access to papers and research see http://msass.case.edu/faculty/vgroza/articles.html (accessed December 2010).

> You couldn't trust anybody. My parents always told me that every other person is a *securitate* person. Even your brother would report on you. You had a world inside your mind and that is where you kept it (Groza *et al.*, 1999:12).

Breakdown of trust in Romanian society – implications for children

When I moved to Romania in 2002, I recognized similarities from working in post-communist Cambodia: social fragmentation and suspicion that permeated social interactions and interpersonal ties in the community (Dickens & Groza, 2004:478). It is difficult for those who have not lived under constant surveillance or oppression to understand the impact this way of life can have on normal individual relationships, loss of trust in neighbours, community, and the larger society (Kligman, 1998:15).[9] In Romania the capacity for creating social capital (Putnam, 1994; 2000), civil society (Saulean & Epure, 1998), and factors that make social cohesion possible, were systematically undermined by the intrusion of the government into private life.[10] 'One of the strategies employed by the communist regime was social atomization, i.e. the intentional sowing of mistrust at all levels of society, that made the spontaneous creation of volunteerism, and general cooperation in the community very difficult' (Bates email, 2005).[11]

It is not my intention to demean the Romanian people or their national pride; the details and tragic outcomes of this period in Romania history can be found in numerous sources.[12] It is widely agreed by observers that, 'no country in the Eastern bloc [was] as uncompromisingly Stalinist in its economic and social policies and methods as Romania' (Bacon, 1984:162). For Ceauşescu, 'power was not a means; it was an end'.[13] The intrusion of the state, the loss of trust in neighbour and general society had deep implications for families and children.

---

[9] Kligman's book title, *Politics of Duplicity* is based in part on this factor in Romania life. She states, 'In Romania, domination of the public sphere functioned through widespread participation in the productions of lies; Romania's socialist edifice was constructed on false reports, false statistics, deliberate misinformation and false selves as well (1998:15) She goes on to discuss *dublare* – a Romanian word that roughly means division in two or split personalities (1998:265).

[10] Social capital is defined by Putnam as 'stock of active connections among people; the trust, mutual understanding, and shared values and behaviours that bind the members of human networks and communities and make cooperative action possible. It also includes the social networks and the norms of reciprocity and trustworthiness that arise from them. In that sense, social capital is closely related to what some have called civic virtue' (2000:19).

[11] Dana Bates is director of New Horizons Foundation see www.new-horizons.ro (accessed November 10, 2010).

[12] There are dozens of studies, papers and books concerning the life and times of Ceauşescu and his legacy in Romania, see http://www.Ceausescu.org/ceausescu_texts/ (accessed November 10, 2010).

[13] This quote was taken from Eric Fromm's introduction to George Orwell's *1984*.

I turn now to discuss policies of the socialist state that led to the crisis for children and the outcomes that continue to impact childcare practice in present day Romania.

Socialist Policies with Long-Term Effect on Families and Children

There were many factors inherent in the socialist system that eventually contributed to the childcare crisis; these affected not just families with children but every aspect of Romanian life and society (Robila, 2002).[14] These policies are described as 'structural' in the literature: economic factors, employment, the role of women in the workforce, the juxtaposition of the state to the family, the demographic policy to increase the size of the population, the ban of abortion, and the institutionalisation of children (Zamfir, 1997).

Economic factors

After a short period of economic growth, between 1950 and 1969, the Romanian economy experienced a state of decline that became much more dramatic by the end of the 1970s. Zamfir, refers to this as a 'structural crisis' which he identifies with the state controlled economy, the bureaucratic apparatus, and the socialist ideology. He refers to this as a type of super industrialisation with 'distorted price controls, irrational and arbitrary leadership, lack of articulate macro-economic vision, and the incapacity to bring the state economy out of crisis' (Zamfir *et al.*, 1994:3). Initially the state had promised benefits to all its citizens: guaranteed jobs, pensions, free education and health care services, cheap and relatively abundant housing, highly subsidized basic goods and services, welfare benefits, including child allowances and scholarships. These promises evaporated with the continued decline of the economy throughout the 1970s, largely attributable to the fiscal mismanagement of the government that became mired in corruption.

Romania exported most of its low-priced agricultural crop and manufacturing, paying a revenue tax to the Soviet Union. State revenues were not reinvested in the infrastructure and the local economy. In the 1980s, Ceauşescu began spending vast sums of money on building projects in downtown Bucharest like the monolithic presidential palace. Albania aside, it became the poorest country in the communist bloc (Groza *et al.*, 1999). Wages and salaries were kept low and fixed at almost equal values; doctors, nurses, labourers; teachers were earning equal salaries.[15] In 1974, it became illegal to

---

[14] See Robilla's PhD dissertation, *The Impact of Financial Strain on Adolescents' Psychological Functioning in Romania* used to locate several studies cited concerning poverty in Romania.

[15] Policymakers preferred to appeal to egalitarianism in time of misery. Differences in wages and salaries were quite small. 'It was thus stipulated by law that the highest wage

spend foreign currency on western medical literature (Horner, 1991:14). All goods, even basic food items, were allowed to become progressively scarcer.

Socialist ideology of work and implications for women

In order to build a new Romania, all citizens were expected to contribute to the building of socialism and the state. This axiom served as a mandate to mobilize the adult population, but it had consequences because 'all citizens were formally categorized as productive or non-productive members of society' (Kligman, 1998:24).[16] This mandate for all to work redefined the role of women in the society. The government actively promoted the role of women in the work force and Ceauşescu proclaimed they were equal to men in the society.

> Women equally participate now in the entire social and economic activity, in the leadership of all the fields of activity, in accordance to their capacities and possibilities... for ensuring the wellbeing, and increasing the level of civilization of the Romanian people (Ceauşescu, 1980:24-5).[17]

The socialist system, in theory, promised women an equal place in society and in the workplace, reflecting the Marxist ideology that women will contribute to the new order as heroes of the State. 'Women should occupy leading positions, according to her capacities and possibilities. There is no difference concerning her political and intellectual capacity' (Ceauşescu, 1980:16).

In addition to being productive in the work force, women were encouraged in their patriotic role of motherhood. Within this responsibility, education of the children was considered critical so that the children would grow up to honour and respect the state. The state enforced the ideology that mothers had a solemn duty to ensure sure that their children were brought up in the true spirit of socialism.

> The Romanian people have always honoured the woman-mother ... One of the most important duties of women as mothers and educators is to devote

---

could not exceed the lowest wage by more than factor 5.6. For example, the wage of a general manager of a large enterprise was only three or four times higher than the lowest wage ... food production was firmly oriented toward export, through which hard currency could be obtained. All food that could be exported was taken from internal markets. Imports were drastically reduced ... hidden unemployment emerged and grew' (Zamfir & Zamfir, 1996:4-5).

[16] Kligman's *The Politics of Duplicity: Controlling Reproduction in Ceauşescu's Romania* is one of the most thorough, she details with extensive annotation the dark period especially for Romanian women between 1966 and 1995.

[17] For this and other quotes from Ceauşescu (1980) the translation was provided by Anca Cristina Constantin (2000). For a complete bibliography of his speeches concerning women and reproductive rights, see Kligman (1990:333).

> themselves to rearing the young generations in the spirit of ardent patriotism, respect and appreciation for the glorious past of our people, and desire to dedicate their entire lives to the development of our socialist country and the communist ideals (Ceauşescu, 1980:26).

Since women were the natural bearers of children, the state recognized its obligation to help women as they contributed to the economy. Various forms of social assistance guaranteed maternity leaves and childcare facilities. These benefits were designed as positive incentives and to assure the state of women's contribution to the labour pool. As a consequence, the state began to take on more responsibility for nurturing and care giving normally assumed by women in the home. Despite the promise of gender equality in the socialist system and the legislation of women's rights as workers, state policy often conflicted with their natural role as mothers. 'This contradiction in women's roles as both workers and (re)producers helped to blur the distinctions in the public and private spheres of daily life' (Kligman, 1998:26).

Socialist ideology of family

Elevating the role of women in the workplace also had an impact on the way men understood their roles in the home as fathers and husbands. The traditional Romanian family is patriarchal; the role of the father was usurped by the socialist state to legitimize its rule over the population (Zamfir & Zamfir, 1996).[18] The nationalization of all property and the banning of abortion, explained below, challenged the family's reproductive rights.

> … in fiat, the state assumed the paternalistic role in society. As a result, citizens were treated as 'if they were children who benefited from the care or neglect of their parents, and particularly from the wizened guidance of the '*pater familias*' (Kligman, 1998:30).

The state became the father and caregiver of the people. Ceauşescu was called the 'father of the people' in print, media, massive rallies, and in all public gatherings. Heredity played an important role in the socialist state; it was important to know one's family heritage as this played an important role in determining the status of a good socialist citizen.[19] The family was juxtaposed,

---

[18] The family type was patriarchal in that the husband and his family connections determined kinship lines. However, the Romanian woman has always had strong influence in the home and community; she is usually the one who will discipline the children and maintains 'order around the house'.

[19] The party made family background, *origine sănătoasă,* (healthy origin) important for work, placement, and service to the state. 'A healthy family history did not contain priests (especially Uniate or Greek Orthodox ones), landowners, relatives abroad, former political prisoners, or divorced members' (Kligman, 1998:32). A public myth was created around Ceauşescu's life and family origins. He was celebrated as the son of hard working farmer, when in fact he came from a very poor family. His father was an

if not subjugated to the state under communism, which resulted in a 'diminished sense of personal accountability for children' (Burke, 1995:21). The state's influence on the family had implications for all Romanians, including evangelicals. I note that no pastor of a local church or FBO participant in the study acknowledged the influence of the state on the role of fathers in local churches.[20]

The Socialist plan to increase the population of Romania

One of Ceauşescu's primary goals was to increase the size of the labour force. Some have argued he wanted to build a Romanian military to match the Soviet Red Army, but this seems unlikely (Deletant, 1999:108-11).[21] In order to have a malleable labour force, the government needed an obedient population. The *securitate* was strengthened to ensure that the population could be controlled. Also the government reduced the number of indigenous 'non Romanians'- gypsies, Hungarians, ethnic Germans, and Jews (Groza *et al.*, 1999:13).[22]

Demographic policy that led to increase in natality

After WWII, natality (live birth rates) fell sharply, poverty that was widespread in the country. Abortion was legalized in 1957 and offered at a small fee. Most families at this time had no more than one or two children. The situation continued in the years 1956-1966. By 1966, Romania had one of the lowest fertility rates in the world (Zamfir & Zamfir, 1996:16).[23] The high cost of raising a child became a factor in the size of families. Those families that could afford a better standard of living had smaller families; those with large number of children could afford very few material options, both parents were working. Since wages were set by the state, new attitudes began to emerge concerning children. Children became a source of economic stress on families, each

---

alcoholic. Some scholars suggest that his need to project himself into the role of 'father of the nation' was engendered by his own questionable family heritage.

[20] I will return to this discussion when I address the Romanian family and evangelical church in reference to children in Chapter 6.

[21] While it may be true that Romania had dreamed of repatriating Soviet Moldova, the Banat region of former Yugoslavia, and parts of Bulgaria that had been taken away in the land settlements of the WWI and WWII, it is more certain that the government wanted the nation to become an economic and industrial power.

[22] For two decades, Ceauşescu sold citizens of ethnic descent abroad for $5,000 to $10,000 per head creating a cash fund to use at his discretion. There were a significant number of ethnic Hungarians living in Transylvania.

[23] 'A pronounced decline in birth rate occurred: from 25.6 live births per 1,000 inhabitants in 1955, it dropped to 14.3 per 1,000 in 1966. By 1965, the birth rate had reached 1.91 per 1,000, the second lowest rate in Europe, higher only than Hungary, where the birth rate was 1.81' (Zamfir, 1996:16).

additional child becoming a greater strain on already low income (Zamfir, 1997: 17).

'In Romania, the demographic policy (*politica demografică*) was explicitly politicized for the purpose of building socialism' (Kligman, 1998:9). Planned and managed economies depend on a stable workforce so control of population demographics was a common socialist policy. The Ceauşescu regime would give new meaning to the term demographic policy and introduced new laws with direct consequences for children.

Official banning of abortion: decree 770/1966

As birth rates fell throughout Eastern Europe, governments sought ways to boost the birth rate. The solution that Romania took was unique in the region; in 1966, the government introduced an official ban on abortion with the infamous 770 Decree.[24] Since the government considered population growth essential, the response was to simply ban abortions and the use of all contraception available at the time. The policy was applied with no room for compromise on the part of the women or families.

> By legislating reproductive behaviour, the state intruded into the most intimate realm of social relations. This radical alteration of social relations and the organizing structures of everyday life was a primary objective of the development strategies promulgated by communist planners' (Kligman, 1998:22).

The draconian measures ranged from obligatory medical checkups to punishments involving fines and imprisonment.[25]

> To encourage women to have more children, financial benefits increased with each successive birth. In addition to violating women's freedom of choice and reproductive rights, the money received did not adequately cover the cost of supporting any children, leading to further economic deprivation (Morrison, 2004:170).

---

[24] The 770 decree read in part, 'The practice of abortion is both an antinational and antisocial act, and an impediment to the normal development of our population. It is necessary to introduce the most perfect order and discipline with respect to the application of the existing laws and regulations pertaining to the interruption of pregnancy'. Decision of the Political Executive Committee of the Central Committee of the Romanian Communist Party cited in Kligman (1998:42)

[25] Women under the age of 45 were rounded up at their workplaces every one to three months and taken to clinics where they were examined for signs of pregnancy, often in the presence of government agents. Women, who did not have children, even if they could not, paid a 'celibacy tax' of up to 10 per cent of their monthly salaries Women who miscarried were suspected of arranging an abortion. Some doctors resorted to forging statistics. 'If a child died in our district, we lost 10 to 25 per cent of our salary. But it wasn't our fault: we had no medicine or milk, and the families were poor' (Breslau, 1990:35-6).

Some steps were taken to support families with children such as a special tax on childless couples, up to 20 per cent of their income. Zamfir claims these support measures were generally perceived by the public to be 'token signs of the position of the government rather than serious initiatives' (1996:15).[26] As expected, birth rates began to rise steadily but studies by the state showed that the rates began to return to previous levels due in part to illegal abortions, poverty, and deteriorating health care for mother and newborn, especially for those not privileged by the party. By 1973, the total fertility rate had dropped back to 2.4 children per woman from a high of 3.7. In 1967, the number of unwanted children began to steadily rise.[27]

Figure 3.1 Selected religious sects – families with six or more children; in per centages of the relevant population group (Zamfir & Zamfir, 1996:23)

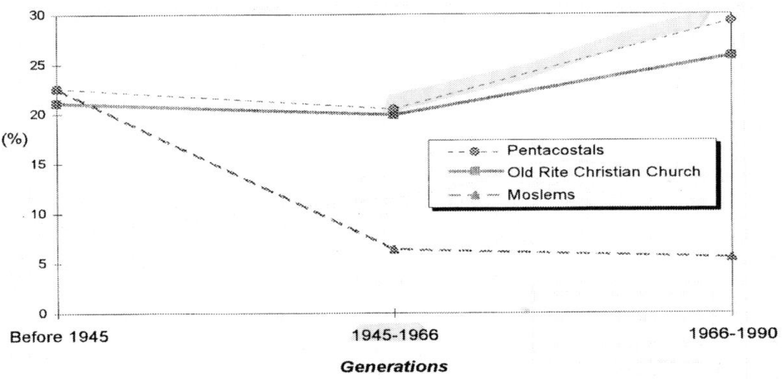

There were exceptions to the fall in birth rates, notably among the gypsies and the 'members of religious sects' and in some geographic regions like the Northeast where there were many poor and isolated villages. These groups and regions had historically encouraged large families (See Figure 3.1).[28]

---

[26] For insight into lives of women under the communist regime, see the documentary, 'Diamonds in the Dark', directed by Olivia Carrescia in which archival footage and interviews relate the women's struggles for survival under Ceauşescu. 'The chronic lack of heat and electricity, and the long lines for crumbs of food, were just some of the burdens borne by women. Professionals, students, factory workers and farm workers; all were obliged to take part in pro-Ceauşescu demonstrations, take care of home and family, and produce more children for the regime' (excerpt from *Diamonds in the Dark*, 2000).

[27] Kligman argues that 'the poorest women were especially vulnerable to abortion-related complications and as a result were more likely to become maternal mortality statistics' (1998:8).

[28] Zamfir labels the sects as 'Pentecostals and the Old Rite Christian Church, a traditional sect that separated some centuries ago from the Russian Orthodox church and was established in Romania' (1996:23). I include this diagram as it confirms field observations in my research. I visited many Pentecostal families that had more than 8 or

Increase in the numbers for unwanted children

By 1974, the government redoubled its efforts at to ensure that planned and centralized reproduction matched expected outcomes. This had the effect of increasing the number of unwanted children and children born in poor families who were by the late 1970s facing chronic economic stagnation. Due to continued illegal abortions, infant and maternal mortality continued. In 1984 the party ordered each family to produce at least five children with continued taxation approaching 30 per cent of income. Popescu noted: 'mothers of more than five were declared *hero mothers*, paid a state allowance, and given priority in housing' (1997:110).[29]

The intention of the state policy was to increase the population from 23 million to 40 million; penalties against abortion were stiffened to include imprisonment or being put to death. The number of unwanted children steadily increased, many being born to poor families that could not afford illegal abortions or the added burden of more children in the home. The solution put forward by the State to care for unwanted children was institutions, orphanages, and hospitals. The following factors have been identified as factors in the rise of child abandonment (Zamfir & Zamfir 1996:22-9; 50).

1. As income declined and the cost of living escalated in a worsening economy the result was a reduced interest in adopting children.
2. Adoption carried a social stigma; the children available for adoption were seen as bearers of negative traits of their parents.
3. Socialism had reinforced the preference for centralized organization and had created a pathological distrust of the private lives of individuals, thus the state was perceived as a solution for all problems.
4. Most of the abandoned children were born in poorer families with no other option for income and they were encouraged to leave the children in the institutions – the state knew best how to care for children.
5. The number of illegal and botched abortions contributed to an increase in maternal mortality and this contributed to abandonment.

---

9 children. Pentecostal churches in Romania regularly taught their members in the communist era that a large family was a sign of 'God's blessing'. I suspect this is an example of the sacralisation of the state policy and that further demographic research into the size of Pentecostal families would indicate that the birth rates have markedly declined since the mid 1990s, despite the continued teaching that 'children are a blessing from God'.

[29] Groza adds to this: 'However, the policy actually said that mothers with 10 or more children were
"hero mothers", similar to taxation, there were regional differences in how policy was articulated and enacted' (1999:19).

The Institutionalization of Children under Socialism

The Romanian state began opening childcare institutions at the end of WWII and continued to build these institutions throughout the next 45 years.[30] As the economy deteriorated and the state enforced the pronatalist policies a crisis developed for children at risk from poverty, abandonment, physical and mental disability, or ethnic origin. Thousands of children were abandoned in maternity hospitals and then placed by the authorities in orphanages. Families that could not afford to care for their existing children would simply abandon new ones at the hospitals on delivery (Johnson *et al.*, 1993). Children were placed in institutions for other reasons: a physical or mental disability, family dysfunction, poverty, repeated hospitalization, and juvenile delinquency. However, once a child was placed in an institution, it was almost impossible to reverse the decision. Since abandoned children were not evaluated on any level, the people who ran the institutions rarely recommended that children return home (Kligman, 1998:225-29).

Before the systemization policy had weakened the social fabric of the country, families had been able to turn to neighbours and extended family to help with when extra care for children was required. Policy and propaganda were effective in convincing families that the benevolent state should care for children when the family could not. When Ceauşescu was finally ousted in 1989, it was estimated that between 90,000 to 120,000 children were living in 600-700 childcare institutions and 16,000 children a year were dying of treatable illness (Groza *et. al.*, 1999; Triseliotis, 1994).[31] The government did not keep statistics on the per annum rate of child abandonment in Romania before 1990; however, FBOs and NGOs estimate the number between 9,000 and 12,000 a year (Kligman, 1998:95).[32]

In the early 1970s, significant resources were allocated to childcare institutions as the state was obligated to provide care for children. Families

---

[30]Abandonment and institutionalisation are not recent phenomena in Romania or elsewhere. Institutions to house children have been used in Europe since the fifteenth century (Cunningham, 2005:148). Kligman addresses the role of the Catholic Church in Italy in the role of institutionalisation for abandoned children. In the aftermath of WWII there were homes for orphans and abandoned children across Europe that were nothing like the ones that many now associate with the 'orphanages of Romania'. The conditions in the institutions of the communist era are unique in the Romanian history of childcare.

[31] Though unofficial estimates are as high as 170,000. The 1990 number of 100,000 is an estimate. More reliable data was gathered by the Committee for the Protection of Children in 1992; see *UN Convention for Child Rights: the Current Situation in Romania*, (1994). In 1991 there were 92,000 children living in institutions. Most researchers conclude that the exact number will never be known with any certainty.

[32] Kligman notes that abortion statistics from the 1980s were better documented. 'In 1983, for every child born there were circa 1.5 abortions … The fact that 742,000 women were registered as pregnant in 1983 invalidates certain attempts to justify reduced natality in terms of the state of health conditions' (Kligman, 1998:95).

were assured that children would be properly cared for, but conditions deteriorated rapidly. There are a number of factors that contributed to the dismal conditions that developed in the institutions and were reported so widely by the Western media in the early 1990s.

The shadow economy and theft of resources intended for children

The chronic economic crisis in Romania was eased somewhat by a 'non-formal economy' or shadow economy. This involved corruption, regular theft from state institutions, and many 'off the book' enterprises. When legal resources such as wages, pensions or state services were inadequate, the illegal economy made up the difference. Children in the state institutions were at a distinct disadvantage as they depended on resources that came only through state channels.

It became widely accepted that the state's resources could be used for one's private benefit.[33] 'Institutional staff members frequently stole food, clothing, and health care products that had been allotted to children' (Zamfir & Zamfir, 1996:29). The economic crisis contributed to the siphoning funds away from social programmes. Despite the official ideology, children in the institutions were not priorities for the state as they presented no threat and could not complain about their conditions. Allocations for maintenance of the buildings and facilities were never adequate. Staff in the institutions received very low wages contributing to lack of morale, and theft was seen as legitimate compensation. Staff training was inadequate and there were chronic shortages of medicine (Dickens & Groza, 2004:472).

Lack of specialized training and medical models for child care

Training and specialization in the social sciences was abolished in Romania in 1969, and sociology and psychology were removed from the universities of in 1978 (Zamfir *et al.*,_1999).[34] All social problems were solved through administrative, bureaucratic, and political mechanisms based on the ideology of the human system with power vested in the state. Since there were no trained

---

[33] As reflected in the Romanian proverb, 'They pretend to pay us, we pretend to work'. It became common to use whatever resources were at hand. When asking how far the gratuity of the state extended, I was told 'as far as you could go and not be caught'. I also heard similar comments from Romanian evangelical Christians who would not admit to these practices but said that 'everyone they knew' was involved is some form of 'shadow economy'.

[34] 'In 1952 the university level degree [in social work] was reduced to a post-high school degree, and in 1969 it was completely abolished by the communist regime since the ideology at the time considered social work training as useless based on the premise that the communist state is not confronted with social problems' (Zamfir & Zamfir, 1995:35).

social professionals, programmes such as crisis intervention, family foster care services, domestic adoption, or home-based care did not exist. When institutionalized children became ill, hospitals could refuse to treat them since they had no family identities. It was common for gravely ill children to remain in the institutions and receive no medical treatment. Visitors to Romania in the early 1990s reported seeing small burial grounds behind the institutions since the children had no family to claim them and no identity therefore could not be buried in 'holy ground' (Groza *et al.*, 1999:34).

All the institutions for 0-to-3-years-old operated as orphanages or *leagăne* under the authority of the Ministry of Health. The directors were medical doctors; the only trained personnel were one or two underpaid nurses or aids. They frequently resembled hospitals for the terminally ill. The other women who worked in the institutions usually had only a high school degree as nursing training had been greatly reduced in 1976 (Horner, 1991:14). The average child to caregiver ratio was one aide (*infirmiere*) to every 25 children, which made it impossible to give the children much in the way of personal care. Children were often forced to spend all their time in bed as there was no space allocated for play, or for intellectual, or developmental activities. The medical model in the institutions gave one primary obligation to the doctor and staff: 'keep the children alive', therefore psycho-social care was not provided. Even in homes for older children, the only activity conducted by the trained staff was medical care.

> Ironically, the emphasis on a medical approach to the problems of children rather than on the creation of socially and emotionally stimulating environments was responsible to a great extent for the deterioration in the state of health of the children and significant delays in their physical and psychological development' (Zamfir & Zamfir, 1996:31-2).

Classification and selection of children

Once children reached the age of three, the children in the orphanages were divided into two or three groups for further 'treatment'.

NORMAL CHILDREN

Normal children could pass an assessment by a physician. With no training in child development, the criteria used for placement was uncomplicated: if the child could walk, talk, masticate, use the toilet, and had no physical difficulty or defects then she was 'normal'. These children were sent to training schools where they lived in group home environments, were fed, clothed, sheltered, and received some form of education. Few gypsy children were judged normal. 'Discrimination against gypsies resulted in their overrepresentation in the orphanage system. They were as likely as children with disabilities to be sent to dystrophic centres simply based on their ethnicity' (Morrison, 2004:171). The 'normal' children were under the guidance of the Ministry for Education until the age of 18.

MINOR HANDICAPPED CHILDREN

The second group had minor handicaps. These were the children who were deaf, blind or had problems that were considered to some degree to be 'salvageable'. These children were sent to what were euphemistically described as 'special schools or hospitals'. They may have been called special but they were not as well supplied as normal schools. These children were also under the Ministry of Education (Groza *et al.*, 1999).

UNSALVAGEABLE CHILDREN

The third category were children diagnosed with physical, medical, or other problems that were considered too severe for a normal life and were sent to a dystrophic centre, an institution for the 'irrecoverable' considered to be unsalvageable. These were children 'from whom God seemingly had looked away' (to borrow a phrase from Romanian poet Mircea Dinescu) and were placed under the direction of the Ministry for the Handicapped. They were labelled as 'non-productive' in a society ideologically based on production, and condemned by Darwinian notions of fit and unfit (Kligman, 1998:322).

This category included those with legitimate mental and physical disabilities and children with minor conditions that could have been easily corrected such as having large or malformed ears, crossed-eyes, or club feet. Because, these children had been neglected in their early years, rarely picked up, held or spoken to, they experienced poor muscle development and physical coordination. 'Many of these children were subsequently misdiagnosed as disabled and sent to an orphanage for the irrecoverable' (Morrison, 2004:171). It is believed that the main purpose for sending children to these homes was to hide them away, reinforcing the myth that Romania did not have any social problems or handicapped children.[35]

---

[35] Sadly this legacy continues in Romania. In 2006, there were two televised reports concerning the conditions of handicapped children in Romania. Disability Rights International found children with disabilities hidden and wasting away, near death, in Romania's adult psychiatric facilities. A report released by DRI, 'Hidden Suffering: Romania's Segregation and Abuse of Infants and Children with Disabilities,' describes teenagers weighing no more than 27 pounds. 'Some children were tied down with bed sheets, their arms and legs twisted and left to atrophy. Despite Romanian government claims that it has ended the placement of babies in institutions, MDRI found infants languishing in a medical facility so poorly staffed that the children never leave their cribs. Many of these children have no identity papers. Officially, they do not exist.' From http://www.disabilityrightsintl.org (accessed November 15, 2010).

The conditions in the institutions

To say that the institutions that served as homes to the thousands of Romanian children were poorly maintained and managed would be gross understatement. The three-tiered system resulted in different standards for the institutions. Some were better maintained than others, but this might be a case of comparing bad to worst. Studies in the early 1990s of the institutions for older children found that staff ratios ranged from 8:1 to 35:1; children received the minimum of personal interaction with adults (Johnson & Groza, 1993). For the children in the worst institutions, no educational or recreational programming was provided. Parents of babies in the institutions were only allowed to visit one hour a week and were not allowed to hold the child; they were only allowed to sit by the bed.[36] As children became older, they had to entertain themselves as best they could and learn to defend themselves against the more aggressive children. Sexual abuse was suspected between staff and children and children with other children.[37] The institutions lacked hot water, soap, washing machines, linens for the beds; children wore and slept in constantly soiled bed and clothes. In addition to a lack of running water, sewer systems were either inadequate or did not exist.

The effects of institutionalization on children were first documented by Chapin (1917); subsequent studies in child abandonment (Bowlby, 1973; 1998) have provided theoretical frameworks for research into these issues in Romania (Johnson & Groza, 1993; Johnson *et al.*, 1993).[38]

Summary – How institutionalised children were understood under socialism

Curtis suggested that children in the institutions came to be understood under communism as a product of the specific ways in which the discourse surrounding children was manipulated by the socialist system (2004). Four main ideas emerge concerning 'the institutionalised child' in communist Romania:

---

[36] No data is available on the number of children in the institutions that had a living parent. The majority of the children were not true orphans. It was common for the parents to keep one or two children at home and abandon those born later, especially if the children showed any defects.

[37] I make this observation from interviews in Romania and personal experience growing up in an orphanage. Threats were commonplace to make sure we did not talk about abusive treatment to other adults.

[38] I trust that future scholars will join these in assessing to what degree faith-based interventions have assisted in rebuilding the lives of institutionalised and abandoned children. Romania's national crisis with children continues; many people of faith, both Evangelical and Orthodox are engaged in providing care for thousands of children. To date, little has been done to empirically document faith-based interventions.

1. The institutionalised child, as a child in need of protection, was understood as different from the 'norm', devalued and strongly stigmatised.
2. Children who suffered from any kind of handicap were most devalued, being seen as unproductive members of society (Burke, 1995).
3. Parents were encouraged to place all disabled children in institutions at birth and to 'forget about them' (Lansdown, 2003).
4. Institutionalisation of children served to reinforce the construction of 'otherness', or 'abnormality', and the need to separate the child from wider society, a practice which in turn fortified the institutionalisation policy (Curtis, 2004:39).[39]

For the average Romanian, children in the institutions 'were never publicly spoken about … they didn't officially exist, no one spoke about them, their rights or their conditions' (Curtis, 2004:22).[40] The state refused to address the underlying structural issues that led to the abandonment of the majority of Romania's 'unwanted' children and identified the children themselves as a *social problem* to be removed (Burke, 1995). Since the State had taken upon itself the mandate to solve all social problems; the responsibility for unwanted institutionalised children was removed from the families or parents (Zamfir & Zamfir, 1996). When families did place children in orphanages the children became the property of the state and very few records or information were kept about the child's family, the children easily became lost in the system (Groza *et al.*, 1999). The Romanian medical community that took responsibility for these abandoned children knew they were not a government priority.

> In 1989, the total government health care budget for 'developed' Romanian's 25 million people was $7 million – or 28 cents per capita. Which could be compared to 'developing' Uganda's 56 cents per capita or the United States' $2000 per capita'(Horner, 1991:14).

The Situation for Children in Crisis After 1989

Following the death of Ceauşescu, Romanians experienced renewed hope and expectation for their country. Rid of the despised dictator, a new government

---

[39] Thanks to Phillipa Curtis for dialogue and sharing her research, *Under the Influence, Local NGOs and Discourse in Post Communist Societies* (2004). She did her field research in Romania and studied one FBO working with children at risk. Curtis helped me locate several sources cited and suggested I contact Heart of the Child, that I included in the case studies.

[40] Most Romanians claimed they had no knowledge of these homes; they were kept hidden from the public, state properties were off limits to the general public. In the case of the homes for handicapped children, one medical doctor said she was told these homes did 'not exist' because Romanian scientists had done away with such primitive diseases. I will return to this question in Chapter 6 in discussing how Romanian churches and pastors perceived the child in crisis.

was to be formed with a restructuring of the economy and state political apparatus. 'From incomplete revolution to entangled revolution, from popular uprising to coup d'etat, an impressive number of interpretations have been given to what happened at the end of 1989 in Romania' (Neumann, 2001:21).[41] The expectations and anticipation for quick change in Romania proved to be short lived and soon gave way to disappointment and renewed cynicism toward the government (Cernat *et al.*, 2004). The following issues provide the socio-economic background shaping FBO-church response to children in the years 1990-2004.

Poverty and economic decline following 1989

In much of Central and Eastern Europe, poverty increased after 1989. The Romanian state and economy experienced chaos and dysfunction.[42] The fiscal crisis worsened as the state enterprises and ex-party members and *Securitate* privatized holdings. This was followed by a collapse of the national currency, the Lei, with rapid hyperinflation.[43] In April of 1991, food prices soared 200-600 per cent as the government faltered in creating a market economy. These developments did little to alleviate the crisis of children still languishing in the institutions scattered all over the country.

In Romania, the proportion of children living in poverty in 1990 was 4.4 per cent and by 1994 these figures had increased to 37.5 per cent (UNICEF, 1997). Reductions in public services, health care, education, and social provision had disproportionately serious effects on children and families; child poverty rates increased one-and-a-half times more than the overall poverty rates (Carter, 2001). Romanian economic output did not increase significantly, real wages and employment lagged behind. The rapid decline in the economy impacted poor families and infant mortality rates increased rapidly, despite an overall

---

[41] There is widespread suspicion that Ceauşescu was eliminated by an internal coup. For analysis of the many interpretations of the 'revolution' in December 1989, see (Neumann, 2001). See also the French Romanian documentary *Requiem for Dominique* and the BBC documentary, *Ceauşescu: Behind the Myth* an investigation by Richard Behr (1995).

[42] The transition period following the 1989 revolution proved to be extremely difficult economically for most Romanians. A World Bank study on the distribution and affects of poverty between 1989-1994 found that the poverty rate in 1989 was 3.7 per cent while in 1993 it had increased to 20 per cent (1997:10). 'Poverty declined somewhat by 2000, but was at 28.9 per cent in 2002, above the 1995 and 1996 levels' (World Bank, 2003:6).

[43] In 1989 one U.S. dollar was equal to 14.92 *lei*. The depreciation reached a peak in 2002 when \$1 = 33,055 lei. These are the average annual exchange rates, as established by the National Bank of Romania, available at http://www.bnr.ro/ (accessed April 2004).

fertility drop between 1991 and 1993 (UNICEF, 1997:12).[44] In *For a Child Centred Society*, Zamfir (1997), stated that 50 per cent of the total number of children living in the poorest families represented 30 per cent of the total child population. In the period between 1990 to 2000, 70 per cent of Romanians indicated that their incomes were barely sufficient or insufficient to cover necessities and were dissatisfied with their earnings (Robila, 2002).

By reintroducing abortion in 1990, Romania hoped to reduce the number of the abandoned children. Though the number of newborn children was reduced by 38 per cent between 1989 and 1996, the number of abandoned children increased (Roth, 1999:30). Immediately following the elimination of the infamous 770 abortion decree, the number of legally performed abortions for women aged 15-49 years skyrocketed: 992,265 abortions were performed in 1990; 450,000 abortions each year during 1991-1996, and 223,914 additional abortions in 2003.[45]

Increasing numbers of children institutionalised between 1989-1995

There could have been as many as 120,000 children living in institutions in 1989. That number declined in 1993 to 73,000 largely due to international adoption. It is estimated that between January 1990 and July 1990 over 10,000 children were taken out of Romanian by international adoption agencies that promoted the idea that one could *save* a child by adopting her. In many cases this was done with dubious legality and with almost no assessment of the children's needs (Groza *et al.*, 2003).[46]

> Couples flooded into Romania almost immediately after the December 1989 revolution with a view to adopt children from the 'orphanages'. Rapidly in their wake came representatives of adoption agencies, and a thriving network of taxi-drivers, interpreters, lawyers, hotels and sundry middlemen appeared, catering to this growth industry. A governmental Romanian Committee for Adoption was established in early 1991 as a focal point for potential adopters from abroad, but was rapidly overwhelmed (UNICEF, 1997:76).

Kligman detailed how corruption and inefficiency enabled both Romanians and Westerners involved in 'saving children' and trafficking in babies. She cites a Romanian official:

---

[44] In this same report UNICEF stated that about three quarters of the child population in Romania were living in families with lower incomes and half that number was living in poverty (UNICEF, 1997:25).

[45] The total number of the legal abortions by women aged 15-49 years old between 1990-2003 was 6,483,177 (INSR, 2004a:16).

[46] A number of health, behavior and developmental concerns have been raised about international adoptees, particularly children from Romania. See Groza & Rosenberg, 2001; Ames & Carter, 1992; Johnson *et al.*, 1993.

> … the child is the object of a traffic in money and goods … in which Romania citizens as well as foreigners participate, whether we are talking about the natal or adoptive families, or intermediaries…It is as though potatoes were being sold at the market' (1998:230-1).

The numbers of children aged zero to three years living in institutions rapidly increased by as much as 45 per cent between 1990 and 1993. By 1994, UNICEF estimated the overall numbers had increased to over 98,000 children.[47]

Hundreds of children continued to be abandoned at birth by mothers who could not afford to care for their children. The director of an FBO working with abandoned babies in Bucharest the past eleven years described a typical scenario.

> A mother will show up at the hospital without any official government papers, she is usually 'from out of town' or gives no local address; a single mother with several children. She delivers the baby but does not give the baby a name and leaves the hospital within 48 hours leaving the child in the care of the nurses. There are no social workers to track down the mother so the child is left in with no official legal status, the child cannot be adopted because the child is not legal under Romanian law. This baby is officially nobody's child (FBOL#72, 2006).

Some hospitals would keep these abandoned babies for up to three months and then they were placed in an institution. Throughout the 1990s, this scenario was repeated in many hospitals in the large cities all over the country on a regular basis.[48] Children who were 'disabled' in any capacity were also placed in institutions with regularity; many were 'disabled' due to lack of psychological or emotional support in the first months of life.

International response to the child crisis

When the Western childcare professionals, media, FBOs, and NGOs arrived in 1990, they were 'shocked' at the conditions they discovered at the hospitals, institutions, and orphanages. Western moral superiority may not have been the most helpful response.[49] The worst conditions were found in the homes for the

---

[47] 'In these institutions, about 24 per cent of the children are under the age of eight, 20 per cent were nine to eleven, 31 per cent were 12 to 15, 19 per cent were 15 to 18, and about 6 per cent are over the age of 18' (Groza *et al.*, 1999:36).

[48] This scenario is not as common in 2006 as it was in the 1990s, but continues. I interviewed a number of NGO and FBO leaders who shared similar stories and served on the governing board of an FBO that works with both mothers and abandoned babies.

[49] In the introduction to this chapter, I said we should use caution in judging the situation for children in Romania. In Chapter 2, I discussed the assumptions of Western FBOs concerning child development and the 'nature/nurture' debate. Western FBOs came to Romania from societies that long ago went along with the 'children's rights revolution'. When they encountered Romania and the institutions became suddenly

'unrecoverable' children. Images of children rocking back and forth, some chained to cribs, children who were restrained – either physically with straps or chemically through tranquilizers – and others resembling survivors of concentration camps were documented and sensationalized in documentaries such as ABC's '20/20' 'The Shame of the Nation'.[50] Children were left lying in cribs, not stimulated or moved for most of the day. Crying was ignored as policy and necessity.[51] I interviewed a number of Western and Romanian Christians who visited the institutions when they were first opened to the public in 1990; the following comment is typical.

> I had never seen anything like this, the children were being kept like caged animals, they were not permitted to leave their rooms, and some could not leave their beds. The smell was horrible, nothing had been properly cleaned, sheets and bedclothes were soaked with human waste. The people who were in charge, stood around drinking coffee and smoking cigarettes, no one seemed to care about the children. The saddest were the babies and the very young children, they were never be picked up, some just would lie and stare at the ceiling, I did not know if they were in a trance or coma (FBOL#19, 2004).

Groza provides a physical description of an institution he visited in 1991:

> The orphanages were colourless, shockingly quiet and devoid of any of the usual visual or auditory stimulation that children usually receive from bright colours, pictures, and displays. Walls were painted in dark browns, to hide the dirt. It seemed as if the entire building was sucking the souls of the children, and perhaps the staff that worked there. There were no toys. There was no exercise or exposure to the outside. Most children were below the twentieth per centile for height and weight compared to normally developing children and grossly delayed in motor and mental development. While official data were not available, some staff said that mortality rates in the winter could reach 40 per cent (1999:33-34).[52]

The media coverage of children in the institutions generated an international response from public and private foundations, and governments. Foreign assistance 'poured into the country filling the reopened spaces of civil society' (Kligman, 1998: 227-28). By 1992, approximately 400 NGOs were registered

---

visible, they were 'shocked' and felt superior. As will be demonstrated, this sort of thinking easily leads to mistakes in understanding concerning the 'other side'.

[50] This is the ABC News Programme 20/20. Interview with Barbara Walters and Hugh Downs October 19, 1989.

[51] I worked with several FBOs currently assisting hospitals in Bucharest where babies are abandoned. Staff nurses did not respond to the cries of an abandoned child. When asked why, the nurses respond that they are too busy with 'children who have parents' and the abandoned children need to learn to comfort themselves as soon as possible since they have no parents.

[52] See *A Peacock or a Crow? Stories, Interviews and Commentaries on Romanian Adoptions* (Groza, *et al.*, 1999) especially Chapter 3 'Dickens, Boys Town or Purgatory: Are Institutions a Place to Call Home?' which provides a poignant first-hand description of life inside the institutions in the early 1990s.

in Romania providing humanitarian assistance, personnel, training, and technical assistance (Dickens & Groza, 2004:471).[53] Child protection laws written in the 1970s were inadequate to monitor or regulate this activity.[54] Analysis of NGO activity in the 1990s indicated a lack of coordination on behalf of these agencies resulting in much replication of effort (Dickens & Groza, 2004).[55]

HIV/AIDS in post-communist Romania – impact on children

The first AIDS cases were diagnosed in 1985 but 'knowledge about it was firmly and deliberately repressed by the regime (Kligman, 1998:221). The unchecked spread of the disease impacted the rising number of institutionalised children. In 1990, health officials and others encouraged parents to institutionalize their AIDS-infected children. As one medical doctor recounted, the disease was not well understood:

> The tragic thing about the spread of this disease is that mothers brought their children for immunization or medical care because they loved them, and in receiving that care they were infected …The parents wanted the children at home; but people were afraid of the disease and didn't understand how it spread … The longer any child is institutionalized, the greater the chance of contracting an infection (Watkins, 1995:13).[56]

As early as 1990, the Centre for Disease Control reported human immune deficiency virus (HIV) in the infant/child population (Hopper, 1999). In the same year, the incidence of pediatric AIDS ran second only to the number of cases reported in the U.S. (Groza *et al.*, 1999). Romania in 1990 had 54 per cent of all pediatric HIV infections in Europe (Watkins, 1995).[57] The hospitals

---

[53] International assistance came from many sources both from governmental and private such as the European Union (EU), USAID, UNICEF, Save the Children, numerous schools of social work from the US, the U.K. and other Western countries, and a whole range of smaller NGOs and FBOs that sprang in the aftermath of the worldwide publicity in 1990.

[54] The Romanian state laws concerning child protection had not anticipated the 'invasion of philanthropy' from the West; for historical comparison of conflict between the state and philanthropic agencies see Cunningham (2005:154-57).

[55] The article I refer to is 'Empowerment in Difficulty' published in *The Journal of International Social Work*; the authors identify some of the problems caused by reactive, crisis-oriented international intervention, and then describe developments in child-welfare policy and provision in Romania up to 2000.

[56] WV Romania operated an HIV/AIDS programme in Constanţa in the early 1990s described in the WV journal, *Together* (1995). In that article a medical doctor describes how Romanian doctors in Constanţa had no idea of the disease or how to treat it when they first encountered it – AIDS was a 'forbidden' disease under the old regime. At one point 50 children were dying each month.

[57] Experts are not sure how the virus entered the country but suspect it might have been introduced by foreign students and Romanians returning from work abroad in Africa as

and institutions of Romania had very poor screening of blood supplies before 1990; the reuse of syringes and un-sterilized medical instruments was common during 1987-1991 that led to thousands of newborns and infants becoming infected. The outdated practice of giving adult blood to children was ended in 1991 (Bohlen, 1990).[58]

As a result there were 3,372 recorded cases of AIDS in December 1994. Specific to Romania is the distribution of these cases; of the individuals who had AIDS, 236 were adults, and 3,136 were children and teenagers. Zamfir reported that by 1995, 1,157 individuals had died of AIDS since 1985, 87 were adults, and 1,070 were children or 92 per cent (1996:30-31). By March 1995, 438 more children had died. Romania continued to have the highest HIV infection rate for children in Europe indicating the difficulty in controlling its spread (UNICEF, 1997:48).

After 1994, there was an increase of HIV/AIDS incidence among young adults, resulting largely from heterosexual sexual transmission (UNICEF 2004:7). In 2001, the Ministry of Health declared HIV/AIDS a national health priority and developed a plan for universal access to treatment with the purpose of extending access to medicines for people living with HIV/AIDS and to increase the quality of the treatment. In 2002 a law was passed to grant free treatment and supplementary nutrition to people with the disease. In 2005, the governement implemented a new strategy to contain the virus and focus on prevention, especially among young people and vulnerable groups. Progress to treat HIV/AIDS in children continues in partnership with the U.N., the E.U., NGOs and FBOs.

Street Children – Categories for a New Phenomenon in Romania

Studies consistently demonstrate that one of the most important indicators of the quality of life for children is the risk of abandonment. 'The lack of a family environment can generate several problems in socialization that represent multiple risks for the healthy personality development of a child' (Zamfir & Zamfir, 1996:33). In the 1990s, many children who had been emotionally neglected in the orphanages moved into the public square of Romanian life.

The institutions and orphanages became increasingly overcrowded and the quality of care deteriorated. The command economy was dismantled before social support and educational systems were implemented to accommodate the growing numbers of children in the institutions. Consequently, there were

---

Ceauşescu had established trade channels with leaders of non-aligned African governments.

[58] Western media also took notice of the AIDS issue in Romania, publishing heart-wrenching stories such as: '*Romania AIDS Babies: Legacy of Neglect*' and '*Fight Against AIDS Lags in Romania*' in the New York Times. Kligman also discussed this issue with references (1998:221-24).

thousands of 5-to-17-year-old children with uncertain futures due to the lack of long-term planning for their integration into the school system (Morrison, 2004:172). Children began to run away from the institutions, and the medical staff at the orphanages did little to prevent their leaving as the runaway children were often the most difficult to discipline and difficult to control (I#5, 2003). This created a new crisis for children as they turned to the streets for survival.

> The term *street children* is problematic as it can be employed as a stigmatizing label; one of the greatest problems such children face is their demonization by mainstream society as a threat and a source of criminal behaviour. Yet many children living or working on the streets have embraced the term, considering that it offers them a sense of identity and belonging. The umbrella description is convenient shorthand, but it should not obscure the fact that the many children who live and work on the street do so in multifarious ways and for a range of reasons – and each of them is unique, with their own, often strongly felt, point of view (UNICEF, 2006:40). [59]

The exact number of street children [globally] is impossible to quantify, but it is likely to number in the tens of millions or higher, some estimates place the figure as high as 100 million. It is likely that the numbers are increasing as the global population grows and as urbanization continues: 6 out of 10 urban dwellers are expected to be less than 18 years of age by 2011 (Kilbourn, 2005).

By late 1991, there were hundreds of children living on the streets, sleeping in the train stations, the parks in the summer, and in the underground system of sewers in the winter. Children ended up on the streets for a number of reasons.

> According to the information offered by Romanian officials, more than half of the children began living on the streets by leaving the family, while another 25 per cent ran away from institutions and orphanages with only a third of them originating in Bucharest. Poverty, alcohol, domestic violence and physical abuse were the major causes that caused these children to leave their families (Groza, 1999:86)

In 1995, over 20,000 children were estimated to be on the streets in Bucharest (Costin Sima & Cace, 2003).[60] Several definitions have been put forward to clarify the term, 'street children' as this from the Inter-NGO Programme for Street Children and Street Youth:

---

[59] See www.unicef.org/sowc06 'The State of the World's Children 2006: Excluded and Invisible' (accessed November 15, 2010).

[60] These numbers vary depending on the source; I heard in personal interviews with street workers that the numbers in the mid 1990s went as high as 30,000. The FBOs were some of the first Western organizations to work with street children; I located a number of FBOs that came to Bucharest expressly to work with these children. The publication cited, *The Street: Between Fascination and Slavery* was published by UNICEF when the numbers of street children in the cities was declining.

> Street children are those for whom the street (in the wide sense of the word: i.e. unoccupied dwellings, wasteland etc.) more than their family has become their real home, a situation in which there is no protection, supervision or direction from responsible adults (Ennew, 2000:14).

Cockburn defined street children as 'those who have abandoned their homes, schools and immediate communities before they are sixteen years of age, and have drifted into a nomadic street life' (1991:13). FBOs have been especially active in working and writing about them (Kilbourn, 1997; Kilbourn & McDermid, 1998; Anderson, 2000). Five of the eleven cases chosen for this research provided programme interventions for street children. I discuss three categories that describe Romanian street children.

Children in the street

The most visible and marginal group are called *children 'in' the street*, what UNICEF calls children with *no* family contact. These children are under 18, they live permanently on the streets, have no address, no connection to family or adult guardians. These children live entirely by their own wits; each child providing his/her own material and psychological support. In Romania, most of these children had run away from the orphanages. They made their way to the major cities, particularly Bucharest; conductors on trains usually let them ride for free. They found a new home living in organized gangs or by simply finding a group that would accept them. The *Gara de Nord*, Bucharest's central train station, became a magnet and night shelter for these children. Others lived in underground tunnels excavated for the city water and steam heating mains. FBOs and voluntary agencies began to set up halfway houses and shelters where the children could find a meal and someone who offered concern (Dobrisan & Kachelmyer, 2002).

After spending most of his adult life working with youth in crisis in other countries, a FBO leader came to Bucharest in 1992 to work with street children. He said that the street boys he tried to help in Bucharest were some of the most dysfunctional he had encountered in 30 years of work. He associated their emotional detachment to abandonment, life in the institutions, and constant abuse living on the streets for more than two or three years (FBOL#37, 2004).[61]

---

[61] This individual worked with street boys in Bucharest from 1992-2004, moving the boys from *Gara de Nord* to a home he established in Târgu Mureş in Transylvania. After 12 years of this work, he was beaten and robbed in this home by some of the boys that he helped and he shifted his attention to working with gypsy children. He expressed deep frustration experienced working with the boys and his lack of apparent success.

Children of the street

The second classification *children 'of' the street* describe those with occasional family contact. These are children who have at least a living relative or parent but the children are so alienated from them that they rarely see them. This became the largest group in Romanian cities. These children spend a variable amount of time on the streets, a day to a week at a time. They often came from abusive home situations. They can go home, but life on the street is preferable to regular beatings from alcoholic fathers.

> Their initial experience is that life on the streets, though difficult, is more bearable than life with their families. They enjoy the freedom, and the lack of family tensions, and the streets generally provide them enough excitement, camaraderie and material subsistence to seem preferable to their bad family situations. Generally, their family links deteriorate as they become more involved with 'street culture'. Some of them work at legitimate jobs, but the majority drift into whatever offers some income, whether it's selling flowers or drugs, shining shoes or stealing, begging or prostitution (Jones, 1991:4).

NGOs and FBOs interviewed in this study estimated that 40 per cent of the children in their programmes had homes and families, but the children would only go home when life on the streets became too difficult, as in the worst days of winter.

Children on the street

The final group are known as *children 'on' the street*, or children with continuous family contact. These children live with at least one or both of their parents, or some other adult relative, and work in the streets to provide some family income. These children do not attend school during the day and usually come from extremely poor families and unstable homes. This category best describes the many Roma (gypsy) children who are working in the streets of Romania and Europe.

> The children drop out of school and are free to roam the street. In Romania, public education up to the eighth grade is compulsory and in theory is provided free. But there are mitigating factors that cause children to opt out of the system, the costs of school supplies, teachers often demand bribes; ethnic children (Roma) face discrimination and are not given places in the school (FBOL#9, 2004).[62]

These children should have been in school but instead they joined the swelling population of street children.

---

[62] Dr. Otinel Bunaciu is the president and director of Project Ruth, an FBO working with gypsy (Roma) children in Bucharest. I will be discussing this FBO in more detail as a case study in the field research. I discuss the Roma situation in Chapter 5 & 6. For specific studies on the Roma of Romania see Achim, 1998; Fonseca, 1995; Jigau *et al.*, 2002.

Street Children – irretrievable damage or restoration?

Romanian street children learned to survive as best they could. Social workers said the children had 'as good a chance' of survival on the streets as they had in the institutions where mortality was far higher than the rest of Romanian society (FBOL#53, 2005). Street children faced constant harassment from the public, aggression from older more experienced kids, police, and the courts. Children rounded up by the police were put in institutions for juvenile offenders where they faced harsh discipline with few rights. Once released from custody, they would return to the streets where violence and mistreatment were the norm.

Children and youth on the streets became more susceptible to drug abuse and violent crime (Cantwell, 2005:10-11). Throughout the 1990s, drug abuse escalated, street children could be seen carrying glue bottles and plastic bags, they would inhale the styrene fumes by placing a small amount of glue in the bag, which was known as '*huffing aurolac'*. Most of the children became hooked on these substances that helped to ease hunger pains and dull emotions.

> Substance abuse rates are proportionately higher among marginalized youth, street children and children of minorities (particularly gypsy children), and the use of drugs can be a gateway for involvement in drug trafficking and other criminal activities and opens the door for many of these children into the world of organized crime and prostitution' (UNICEF, 1997:49).[63]

Once children are established on the streets, they have a low probability of returning to normal home life. The street child is exposed to sex, abuse, and a negative socialization process that destabilizes their personality (Suico, 2000; Derbyshire, 2001).

> Most writing about ... young people living on urban streets ... assumes, even insists, that they live in disorganized, illegal misery. They are described as psychologically and irretrievably damaged, unable to form relationships as the children that they are and definitely destined for emotional, social, and economic failures as the adults they will become (Ennew, 1994:409).

This idea of the street child as 'always in misery' has been challenged by those investigating the attempts of children to reconstruct lost families and create self-supportive networks (Aptekar, 1988; Ennew, 1994). One study in Bucharest by Fulbright scholars interviewed 130 children living on the streets and surveyed a number of NGOs to determine what street children understood of their rights and their perceptions of the role of both the government and NGOs. The authors concluded that street children have definitive opinions about how these agencies should understand their situation and help them find a voice in society (Flanigan & Nicholas, 2003) .

---

[63] See the studies by Stoica-Constantin *et al.* (2000) and Ennew & Stephenson (2004); both investigate the extent and frequency of consumption, kinds of drugs used, and categories of teenage consumers.

I will examine several cases where FBOs and evangelical churches worked with street children and explore how faith-based interventions were designed and carried out in various methods of collaboration. I will challenge the idea that street children are 'irretrievably damaged, unable to form relationships' with evidence that children can be restored to emotional and social health. At this point in the discussion, it is important to comprehend the difficulties and challenges presented by street children to these organizations and churches.

Reform Process in Child Protection: 1997- 2005

Despite the legacy of the social, economic, and institutional crisis for children, some progress on child welfare was made in the early 1990s. Social work courses were taught again in some universities and became full degree programmes by 1994 (Zamfir, 1996:9-10). Prototype programmes were established to prevent further institutionalisation, to assist the reunification of children with families, and to promote in-country substitute family care. The Romanian Orphanage Trust, a British NGO, helped to underwrite these programmes at the county council level (Dickens & Watts, 1996). A government National Committee for Child Protection was founded in 1993 but was short on detailed targets. In 1997, major childcare legislation was introduced and the Department of Child Protection (DCP) was established, requiring all sectors in Bucharest and county councils to establish social service departments for children and families (Dickens & Groza, 2004:474).[64]

Laws to regulate international adoption

After the chaos of the unregulated international adoptions in the early to mid 1990s, in August 1997, the Romanian government issued two emergency regulations[65] (*ordonanțe de urgență*) concerning adoption and child protection (numbers 25 and 26).[66] Emergency Act no. 25, (article 1) introduced the expression 'child in difficult circumstances' (*copil aflat în dificultate*) and stressed the right of the child to protection from community and state when his/her life within family context was not possible. Emergency Act no. 26 gave

[64] For more complete details of the 1997 and subsequent child care reforms, see Dickens (1999) and Roth (1999).

[65] The difference between a law (*lege*) and an emergency regulation (*ordonanță de urgență*) depends on the body (Parliament and Government respectively) issuing them. Constitutionally, the Parliament is entitled to issue laws and to approve them through debates and by vote. The Government, however, can issue a specific regulation that will have a similar power when put in practice; this avoids debates and votes that would normally proceed when these reach the parliament.

[66] These two legal actions were the first to establish legal precedents on children in at risk situations, up until that time, laws written in 1977 had regulated the process (Dickens & Groza:2004:474).

equal rights to both Romanian and foreign couples/citizens to adopt Romanian children.

The Romanian Adoption Committee was established as the official governmental body certifying valid adoptions with specific procedures concerning the terms of approvals and certifications in order to adopt a child. However, this law still allowed foreign adoption agencies to earn points by investing money and resources in regional services and then using these points to 'buy babies as a baby trafficking charter' that led to further abuse and corruption in the Romanian adoption system.[67] New legislation was passed in 2000 in an effort to control what continued to be a lucrative business, 'by 2000, more than 3,000 babies were sent abroad at a cost of up to £30,000 a child' (Traynor, 2005:17). Adoption laws were modified again in late 2005 to ban international adoptions.[68]

Laws to promote the rights of the child

A further turning point was 2001 when child welfare became a government priority, with support and pressure from the E.U., emphasis was placed on reintegration of children living in institutions with families, creating a foster care system, and establishing alternatives to residential care for unwanted children. New legislation was adopted in 2004 (Law no. 272/2004) regarding protection and promotion of child's rights. A government agency was established, National Authority for the Protection of Child Rights (NAPCR).[69]

The law acknowledged the rights enlisted in the U.N. Convention on the Rights of the Child (Salvaţi Copiii România, 2002).[70] Legal protection was

---

[67] Between 1994 and 2000 there were over 15,000 adoptions of children in Romania of which 10,000 were international. Additional legislation was passed in 2003 helping to reduce these numbers: 279 out of a total number of 1,662 were international (Groza, 1999).

[68] Romania continues to suspend all international adoptions after a contentious debate between the European Union and some other Western governments that were in favour of continuing the international adoptions. In order for Romania to join the European Union in 2007, the EU insisted it ban international adoptions. See 'Romanian Hails Orphanage Success Story' article printed in the Guardian Newspaper http://www.guardian.co.uk/international/story/0,,1656707,00.html (accessed November 15, 2010).

[69] The website http://www.copii.ro/ is the official site of the National Authority for the Protection of Child's Rights and posts updates concerning child focused legal reform in Romania.

[70] There is no uniform position within the faith-based community as to how to apply The Convention on the Rights of the Child (http://www.unicef.org/crc/) to their work. World Vision Romania was the only FBO in the case study that referred to the CRC in their programme planning. I cite the use of the CRC by the Romanian government to demonstrate that 'rights based language' has become part of the current childcare discourse in Romania.

extended to all children wherever they were with parents, separated or abandoned, in school or in the labour market, within the country's borders or abroad, handicapped, or with behaviour problems. The child protection laws for the first time imposed sanctions on parents who mistreated or exposed their children to threatening situations. The law now requires social workers, medical professionals, and teachers to report cases where suspicion of abuse in the family is present.

This new legislation addressed the mistreatment that had been found in the institutions. Stativă (2002) found that although the frequency of abuse and violence in institutions had dropped in 1999-2000, almost half of the institutionalized children (48 per cent) confirmed physical abuse or beating as a punitive practice. The same study showed that 47 per cent of parents frequently use physical beatings as a punishment measure. A number of related findings indicated an alarming tendency toward violence in schools and the presence of drug use in schools, (UNICEF, 2001). Institutionalization for children under new laws has been recognized as a temporary measure; including severely disabled children (Buzducea, 2005:95).

Reduction of the number of children remaining in institutions

According to the NAPCR as of 2005, there were almost 4.7 million children (0-18) in Romania of whom 2.2 per cent are under the auspices of child protection authorities. In 2003 there were 42,777 children living in institutions, 76 per cent of them between 10 and 18 years. By the end of 2005, over 170 large child institutions had been closed, with 31,107 children living in 1,407 placement centres and 43,783 children had been placed in foster families or enlarged families. [71] Placement of children in foster families has not been without problems with allegations that that some families have taken in children to receive financial assistance offered by the government and European Union. Child welfare reform has been incremental and a painful process for both children and child advocacy groups. Attitudes toward institutionalized children have been difficult to change in the general population. Child abandonment continues in Romania (UNICEF, 2006).[72] Statistics only tell a fraction of the story; as in Chapter 2 concerning church growth statistics, these numbers do not answer the central research question. Living and working in Romania taught me to adopt a generous scepticism when reading statistical reports from the government, the E.U., UNICEF, NGOs, or FBOs as child studies frequently

[71] The new placement centres were to house no more than 8-10 children. NAPCR claimed 1027 public centres were home to 25,808 children and 380 private centres, including FBOs, were home to 5,299 children.

[72] This report was published as 'The Situation of Child Abandonment in Romania 2005' and can be downloaded at http://www.unicef.org/romania/ (accessed November 15, 2010).

promoted agency agendas. The research required personal visits to FBO, NGO, and government facilities for children. Some were reasonably maintained and children were receiving 'adequate attention', others were outstanding examples of childcare that demonstrated high levels of commitment to child and practice.

Summary

In the early stages of research, I learned that most FBOs and churches did not give an adequate account of recent social and structural factors impacting child welfare in Romania. This chapter addressed the question, 'What socio-structural factors led to the crisis for children in Romania before and after 1990?' To think critically and objectively about the structural causes of childhood pain, neglect, or abuse is a complex emotional and intellectual task. Ceauşescu's 'politics of duplicity' (Kligman, 1998) had significant influence on family welfare in Romania. The socialist restructuring of society before 1990 continues to influence concepts of community, family, and child. Trust was systematically undermined in society. Evangelical churches were to some degree insulated from the state policies described in this chapter. However public discourse surrounding the abandoned or institutionalized child and expectations of the state in caring for abandoned children had long-term negative consequences with significance for this study. How these factors influenced the response of local evangelical churches to children in crisis is discussed in Chapters 6 and 7.

In the interest of contextual research, this chapter engaged with specialists in the human and social sciences who conducted child welfare studies in Romania.[73] I describe this in subsequent chapters as the view '*from below*'.[74] In order to address the central research question, 'What factors hinder or help FBO-church collaboration?' it was necessary to explicate the structural factors that shaped the current situation for children. Ceauşescu and his government's policies towards society and children are offered as evidence of one modern state's attempt to remake an 'unredeemed world'. The intention was not to vilify Romania's past but to investigate the factors that influenced FBO-church response to children in crisis in the 1990s. International and national efforts

---

[73] To date, very little evangelical sociology or child impact studies have been done in Romania concerning children in crisis. One hope in publishing this study is to encourage others to do so.

[74] I observe there is a non-material or transcendent perspective that is often edited out in this sort of narration. This chapter has intentionally not included 'the view from above'. I will bring this into the analysis in later chapters. I will establish the importance of bringing together 'from above' and 'from below'. I argue that evangelicals must learn to think more concretely about the nature and workings of the physical world, the character of human social structures like government and the economy and how they affect the lives of children (Noll, 1994:7).

have resulted in child protection and reform in the years following 1997, however much work remains to be done.

Western FBOs came to Romania from societies which long ago went along with the 'children's rights revolution'. When they encountered Romania's institutionalized and street children, they were 'shocked' and felt compelled to respond. This sort of thinking easily leads to mistakes in understanding. In Chapter 5, I examine perceptions and expectations of FBOs from the West. Some came to 'save' children through adoption, others came to 'save' souls, and others came to 'save' children from pain and suffering. The children who became the object of their mission and interventions were born in the late 1970s and 1980s – they were called *decreţei* (children of the decree). Many of these children were the result of structural policies; they grew up in the institutions and on the streets. Others grew up in fragmented, dysfunctional families; they learned in the 'shadow economy' that bending the rules made survival possible. Some of these children were labelled as 'unsalvageable' and treated as irrelevant. I contend that despite whatever a government, a law, or a policy may mandate, every human child is of infinite value to God and acts as a pointer to His kingdom.

Some FBOs lacked cultural understanding, certain skills, and experience. Their sense of their own social history concerning child welfare was in many cases weak and unexamined – as evangelicals in the West have also made use of political and social agendas to shape the lives of children. When governments, NGOs, FBOs or churches use children for their own purposes and do not respect children for their own sakes, they risk engaging in religious or social engineering, attempting, like Ceauşescu to mange the future via children.

I will now explicate the methodology and methods followed throughout the study.

Chapter 4

Methodology and Methods

Introduction and Overview

This chapter describes methodology and the combination of methods used to gather and analyse data. The research plan was designed to follow two main phases of fieldwork in order to answer a central research question. Since there were no existent study on FBO-church collaboration in Romania, the first phase was exploratory and conducted from February 2003 through November 2004 – 22 churches and 35 FBOs were visited. I conducted 60 interviews with leaders of churches and FBOs, created a typology to describe FBOs, and defined a set of categories and characteristics of both FBOs and churches that were working in partnership. A set of criteria was identified to select 11 cases from 98 FBOs working with children. The second phase began in November 2004 and continued through August 2006 combining case study methods, 33 semi-structured and 23 open interviews with participants from the cases. Grounded theory and cross-case comparison were used as primary methods in analysis. A third phase of work combined missiological and theological analysis in explanation building.

Choice of Qualitative Methodology and Methods Used in the Study

The field research design followed 'reflective design', the methodology progressed in the course of work (Schutt, 2001:206). I used a mixed-method approach (Drisko, 2004)[1], primarily qualitative with limited quantitative methods to validate and verify research findings.[2] Qualitative research is referred to in social science as interpretive or descriptive research (Denzin & Lincoln, 2003:3-4)[3] and involves the collection, study, and analysis of

---

[1] My study started with snowball sampling and survey research, moving to case selection and the development of in-depth interview guide, case visits, and practitioner participant research.

[2] Schutt differentiates between the two methodologies: 'quantitative research is typically taken to be exemplified by the social survey and by experimental investigation', while 'qualitative research tends to be associated with participant observation and unstructured, in-depth interviewing' (2001:17). '.

[3] Qualitative research is defined by Denzin & Lincoln as 'a situated activity that locates the observer in the world. It consists of a set of interpretive, material practices that make the world visible. These practices transform the world … At this level, qualitative research involves an interpretive, naturalistic approach to the world. This means that qualitative researchers study things in their natural settings, attempting to make sense of,

empirical materials, it is phenomenological, inductive, explanatory, and process oriented.

The primary qualitative methods used to generate and collect data were standardized open-ended interviews (Patton, 1987:112), intensive in-depth interviews (Lofland & Lofland, 1995:18-19; 78)[4], recording and logging field notes, examining relevant documents, and multiple case studies. A number of interpretive methods were employed: personal observations with memos to accompany interview transcripts, case study write-ups, and follow-up interviews to clarify emerging themes. The primary approach chosen to analyse the interview transcripts was a strategy for generating empirically grounded theory (Glaser & Strauss, 1967; 1987). Appreciative inquiry and cross-case comparison was also used in analysis of the findings. 'It is common for researchers to use more than one method' Blaxter & Tight (1984:84). However, it is important when combining methods to ensure that data gathered by one practice be analyzed carefully with respect to the limitations.

Epistemological and theological perspectives

I acknowledge that an evangelical theological interpretation influences my study of human relationships, human development, and organizations. I integrate insights from theology, missiology, child development, and organizational development in the argument (Swinton & Mowat, 2006: 32-7).[5] I turned to qualitative research methods as a systematic way to examine a specific phenomenon: FBO-church partnership concerning children. While these methods were useful in generating and collecting data, I did not rely on social science as authoritative in the final analysis. Loder influenced my thinking in adopting an integrative approach to theology and social science, he cautions that 'functionalism, structuralism, and empiricism can bracket the person of the investigator ... for the sake of objectifying the findings and meeting the canons of the empirical test ... ' (Loder, 1998:xi).[6] All research and

---

or interpret, phenomena in terms of the meanings people bring to them' (2003:3-4).

[4] Lofland & Lofland (1995) define intensive interviewing as a qualitative method that involves open-ended relatively unstructured questioning in which the interviewer seeks in-depth information on the interviewee's feelings, experiences, and perceptions (:18).

[5] See Chapter 3 in *Practical Theology and Qualitative Research*. The authors make an argument for the use of social science research in studies of practical theology with a helpful discussion on how practical theologians understand the concept of biblical revelation and Christian realism (2006:37).

[6] In *The Logic of the Spirit, the Human Spirit in Theological Perspective*, Loder devotes the first three chapters to his methodological integration of theology and human development. His argument is that both are necessary but that human sciences reflect a perspective 'from below' (following Pannenberg) and that God's work with human beings originates 'from above', which he describes as a 'relational unity' (1998:13). Loder adopts Barth's Christology and Torrance in his theological argument (1998:30-4).

inquiry takes place from within some interpretive paradigm, a basic set of beliefs that guides actions (Padgett, 2004:4).

Realist Christian perspective

In qualitative research the observer is an irreducible part of any study of social reality. I approached the study from a personal perspective and experience, an Anglo-American, evangelical/pentecostal missionary. I think and write from a critical realist Christian perspective, a term I borrow from Jones & Yarhouse (2000).

> We are [Christian] critical realists, which means that we believe that there is a real world out there where it is possible to know and know truly (hence, 'realism'), but we also believe that our theories and hypotheses about that world, and our religious presuppositions and beliefs about reality, colour and shape our capacity to know the world hence, 'critical realism' (2000:15).

This sort of Christian realism claims that we can know something of the world, but 'our claims are modest due to our limitations, finiteness and proclivity towards distortion' (Carson, 2005:117). I hold a theocentric view of the natural world and recognize that my evangelical understanding and perception is influenced by personal belief, experience, culture, and background. The 20 years of cross-cultural missionary experience I brought to this research enabled me to better recognize personal presuppositions.[7]

Integration of spirituality in the research

I assume that evangelical faith-based interventions can be distinguished from other approaches to work with children. The study draws from a theological framework believing 'God intends certain things for children' based on particular interpretations of scripture.[8] As followers of Christ we seek to understand and live within God's kingdom, but we often fall short in our interventions with children, and in our research endeavours. The research process itself was a spiritual exercise. Mahar writes about the 'potential role of spirituality in conducting field research,' his premise is that 'self, beliefs and experience are related in such a way that *depth* applies to each equally in field research'. Mahar developed a particular method for processing 'spiritual

---

[7] I recognize the limitations of my powers of observation and interpretation, recognizing 'blind spots' does not remove them.

[8] As an evangelical, I interpret the Bible as the revealed Word of God and believe that all human beings are created in the image of God (Genesis 1:27-8). The implication of John 1:14, 'The Word became flesh and made his dwelling with us' is critical to my understanding of scripture and line of inquiry and will be further explicated in the course of the argument.

reflection' of a number of research students working in Cuba and illustrated it with a model as in Figure 4.1.[9]

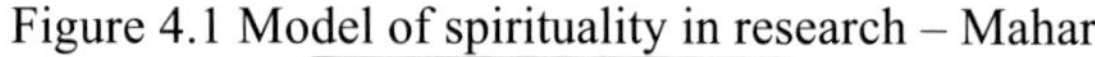
Figure 4.1 Model of spirituality in research – Mahar

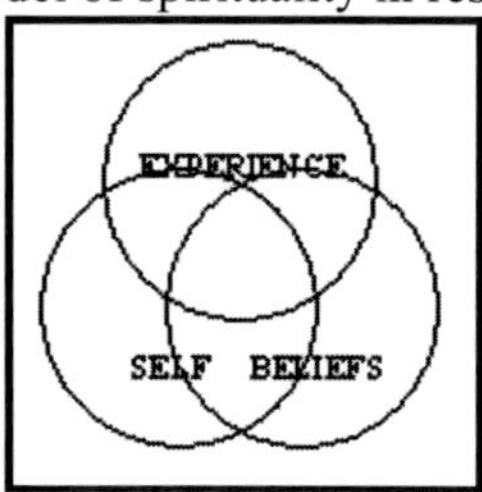

Five years of field research deepened my awareness of self, belief, and experience in a specific context, represented in Figure 4.1. The methodology required a constant reiteration of reflection and action, visiting projects, interviews, conversations, write ups, return visits to projects for additional reflection, prayer, reading, and writing. Prior to this study, I approached project management as an interventionist seeking to solve problems or assist suffering children. The six years invested in research integrated my intellectual, spiritual, and practical perceptions.[10] Bogdan & Biklen argue for the necessity of self-reflexivity in research.

> Because you are so central to the collection of data and its analysis, and because neither instruments nor carefully codified procedures exist, you must be extremely self-conscious about your relationship to the setting and about the evolution of the design and analysis (1992:121).

I agree with Adams, who in exploring the spiritual formation of the researcher comments, 'more holistic [integration of academic and spiritual] scholarship encourages me to live out who I am becoming – to pursue knowledge in action that gives direction to my values' (2006:13). I found that structured research created a space for both inquiry and spiritual reflection.

Definition of Researcher Role – Observer or Participant

An initial objective was to collect empirical data from the participants and projects that would be central to the description and interpretation. In the

---

9 Mahar writes as a Christian researcher, concerning the model: 'It is important to emphasize that this is meant as a practical model rather than a philosophical model. Epistemologists can argue if any experience can exist outside the self. It also may be questionable if beliefs can exist outside the self'.

10 I will refer in later analysis to the influence of Parker Palmer, Annie Dillard, Herni Nouwen and others on both my interpretation of the data and personal reflections on how the research process shaped my analysis and spiritual growth in research.

course of the study, I became aware of personal values and assumptions as well as those of the participants.[11] The research was both a theoretical and practitioner exercise, it was an attempt to understand and analyse issues I had experienced as an embedded participant. Strategies were followed in the research design to identify misunderstanding and to maximize credibility (Padgett, 1998).[12] In the first phase of research, I struggled with definitions of the terms 'participant-observer' (Mason, 1996:61-8). With two of the cases, I had an institutional role. I developed a participatory relationship with four others acting as observer, trainer, facilitator, and evaluator (Schutt, 2001:270-73).

Limits to researcher objectivity

Throughout the first two phases of research, I was engaged in both full-time missionary practice and part-time research and writing.[13] I conducted fieldwork from 2003 to 2006, allocating specific days of each month to visit research sites, conduct interviews, scheduling return trips to the projects as a observer/researcher, and when asked, as consultant. In some cases, it was difficult to define to what degree I was a participant and to what degree I was an observer.[14] Patton describes why researchers need to get close to their subjects.

> Qualitative inquiry depends on, uses, and enhances the researcher's direct experience in the world and insights about those experiences. This includes learning from empathy ... Empathy develops from the personal contact with the people interviewed and observed during fieldwork ...(1990:56).

According to Strauss & Corbin (1998), familiarity with the field of activities is a necessary condition for generating theory within a complex problem area. My practitioner expertise with children was an important asset in the inquiry. However, familiarity can cause problems if objectivity is not sought.[15] Direct engagement with both practice and research created a new sense of 'empathy'

---

[11] 'All researchers take sides, or are partisans for one point of view or another. Value-free interpretive research is impossible' (Denzin & Lincoln, 2003:23). These authors also argue that qualitative research can make no objective claims to reality, as 'constructivism' is all there is. In response, I suggest that we can provisionally know certain things, which are truthful, albeit in limited and fallen ways.

[12] Examining bias or personal perception requires ongoing vigilance, not eliminating them but remaining aware of their impact on the study (Mason, 1996:55-6).

[13] 'Missionary practice' means I was employed as full-time denominational missionary, carrying out regular work responsiblities while working on doctoral studies.

[14] I was unsure to what degree I was conducting 'etic' research and to what degree I was becoming 'emic' These terms are used in anthropology to describe cultural 'insider/outsider' perspectives (Hiebert, 1983:50-4).

[15] Strauss and Corbin (1998) claim that objectivity consists of: the ability to achieve a certain degree of distance from the research materials and to represent them fairly.

in my perception of the issues faced by FBOs, churches, children, project leaders, and staff. I did not try to maintain a neutral 'passive observer', nor was this the best role to adopt, particularly as the level of suspicion and distrust in Romania is quite high. I needed to gain confidence and trust from participants. Neuman describes this process as an 'access ladder' describing how levels of trust and time in the field are proportional (2000:353). Research settled into a blended role of observer and practitioner; asking reflective questions while participating in the activities of the projects.

Insights from 'The Reflective Practitioner'

In the struggle to find a balance for participation, distance, and objectivity,[16] I found guidance in Schön's (1995) '*The Reflective Practitioner'*. He provides a useful vocabulary for advocates of 'practitioner research' and critiques 'technical rationality', defined as:

> The view of professional knowledge which has most powerfully shaped both our thinking about the professions and the institutional relations of research, education, and practice – professional activity consists in instrumental problem solving made rigorous by the application of scientific theory and technique' (2003:21).

In his often-quoted topographical metaphor Schön distinguishes the 'hard ground' of empirical research with the 'swampy lowlands' where practitioners deal with real human problems and concerns.[17] Both of these approaches were useful and appropriate in this study. I worked with both empirical data and 'messy human situations'. I set out to conduct research that was rigorous and grounded in the context. I learned to practise the discipline Schön refers to as 'reflection in action' (1995:54). Drawing on a reserve of 'tacit knowledge', I recognized that there were submerged nuances of FBO-church collaboration that I had taken for granted prior to conducting structured research. The

---

[16] As is common for a novice researcher, I had the assumption that 'research' *required* a certain distance and objectivity. I assumed it would be inappropriate to bring my previous missionary experience and knowledge of project management into the research, but realized that it could not be eliminated. Therefore I chose to make it an explicit process of self-reflection and critique.

[17] The original quote reads: 'In the varied topography of professional practice, there is a high, hard ground where practitioners can make effective use of research-based theory and technique, and there is a swampy lowland where situations are confusing "messes" incapable of technical solution. The difficulty is that the problems of the high ground, however great their technical interest, are often relatively unimportant to clients or to the larger society, while in the swamp are the problems of greatest human concern... (1995:42). See also Atkinson & Claxton (2003) *The Intuitive Practitioner: On the value of not always knowing what one is doing.*

research process itself became a process of 'thinking about doing while doing', learning while in the midst of performing research and working with children.[18]

Phase One: Mapping the Research Terrain

Phase One was designed as a means to gain entry into the FBO and Romanian church context. This involved identifying FBOs, churches, pastors, and other leaders through a series of interviews and a preliminary analysis of the information collected. While it is convenient to discuss the research design in terms of specific blocks of activity, in actuality the fieldwork emerged and evolved over time and followed the recursive elements common to reflexive qualitative research.

Phase One of fieldwork began in February 2003 and was completed in November 2004. In that time, 550-600 hours were invested in preliminary discussions with key informants, interviews, inspection of written documents, writing summaries and ongoing review of personal observations about the situation as I discovered it (Mason, 1996:60-66). This procedure was an effective means of acquiring a working knowledge of the issues central to the study. I describe in chronological order the procedures and methods followed illustrated in Figure 4.2.

Figure 4.2 Methods used in Phase One

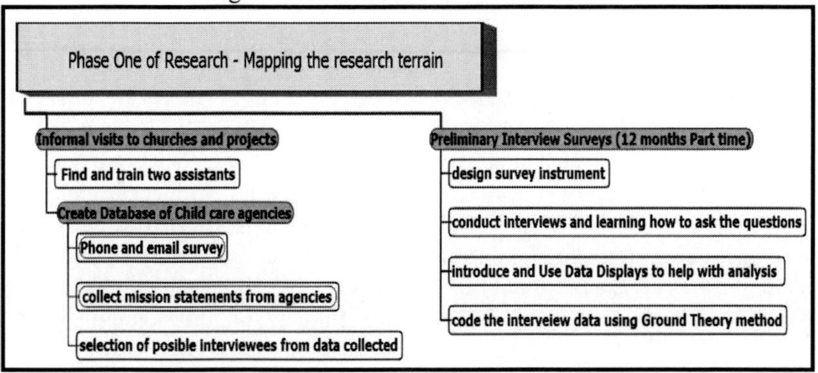

[18] Padgett (2004a) discusses the issues in the research/practice debate as some are concerned that reflexivity can produce endless self-absorption. When researchers become partners with practitioners does this weaken empirical research? The issue is also discussed by Mason, 'if you wish to conceptualize *yourself as active and reflective* in the process of data generation, rather than as a neutral data collector [then you must] analyse your role in the situation' (1996:41f).

Creation of database and initial survey of FBOs and churches

Before conducting guided interviews, I spent several months making informal visits to churches and FBOs to gain a working knowledge of the situation. In January 2003, I hired two Romanian research assistants. I felt it important to involve Romanians in the study as minimal work had been done to understand or document Western faith-based interventions.

The first task was to create a reliable database of FBOs and agencies working with children in crisis. One Challenge International (OCI) was a primary source as they maintain a database of most evangelical agencies working in Romania with a subcategory listed as children/youth. A search of the OCI database[19] was compared with databases from World Vision Romania, the U.S. Embassy,[20] and Cleaford Trust U.K., and Pro Child Romania.[21] Ninety-eight agencies were identified that were self-described as 'working with children'. It was unclear to what extent these FBOs were working in collaboration with churches or specifically with children in crisis.[22] Mission statements or ministry objectives were collected from the 98 agencies. The database was updated throughout the study.

A phone and e-mail survey of 59 FBOs was conducted to determine: a) types of children being assisted, b) types of interventions provided, c) types of partnership with local churches in their area, and d) willingness to be interviewed in a preliminary survey.

Preliminary interview survey of FBOs and partner churches

The next step was a purposive selection of FBOs and churches for interviews. Using responses from the phone survey, a sub-database (n=35) was created. This list included FBOs both large and small, churches with independent projects, and three FBOs that said they did not work with local churches. I decided to interview at least 15 FBOs or churches from this list that fit Rubin's three guidelines for selecting informants when designing a purposive sampling strategy: the informants should be 'knowledgeable about the cultural arena or situation or experience being studied [children in crisis], they should be willing

---

[19] The OCI database of Romanian Mission Agencies website: www.oci.ro lists over 360 agencies.

[20] The U.S. Embassy list is a list provided by USAID, and was published on the U.S. Embassy website www.usembassy.ro (accessed June 2003). It listed 117 agencies.

[21] The ProChild database listed 37 agencies; this was a partnership of Romanian NGOs working to share information and to provide support for improving the lives of Romanian children, youth and families. It was founded in 1999 to provide a formalized network of non-governmental organizations working in the field of child welfare in Romania; it ceased to exist in 2006.

[22] Our database was created in Microsoft Access and provided the name of the organization, short description, mission statement, vision statement, contact person and information, web address, and type of ministry the FBO is carrying out with children.

to talk, and they should be representative of the range of points of view' (Rubin & Rubin, 1995:66). Also, the sampling was designed to include the main geographical areas of Romania: Banat, Transylvania, Muntenia, Dobrogea, and Moldova, see Figure 4.3.

Figure 4.3 Project and church locations chosen for preliminary interviews

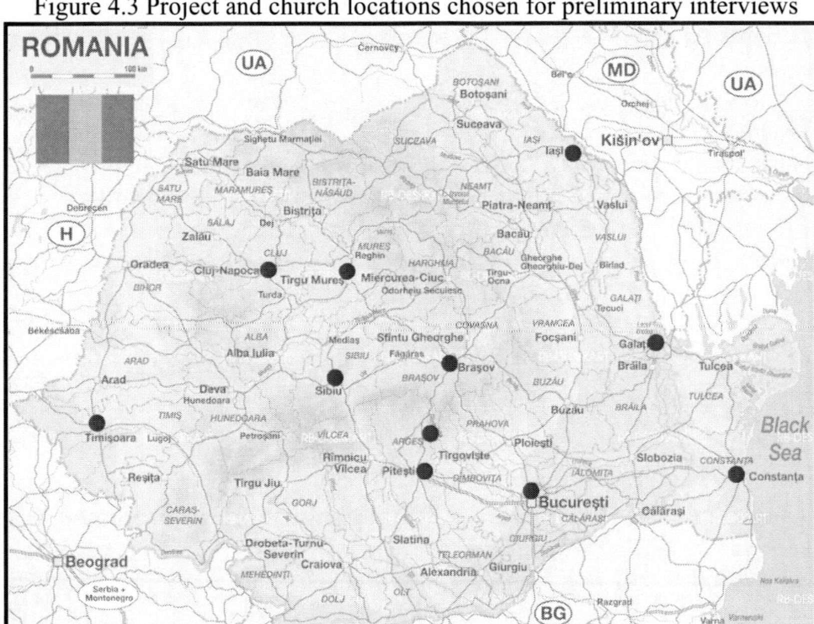

A preliminary survey questionnaire was designed and used in a guided interview format titled 'Preliminary Survey of Child Agencies in Romania'. The interview asked 23 questions concerning five subject areas (see Table 4.1).

Table 4.1 Types of questions included in the preliminary interview survey

1)	Programme description: History of the programme, recipients, ages, background and needs of the children, staff training and reasons for starting the programme.
2)	Partnership Issues: Nature of the partnership, who makes decisions concerning programmatic interventions, how does this organization work with the local church or a denomination?
3)	Programme goals and Evaluation: What are the goals of the programme; how are the goals evaluated, how do you define success in your work?
4)	Finances: What per centage of your work is financed from outside Romania, who are your primary financial partners and do you receive financial support from any governmental sources.
5)	Future issues: What are the primary barriers and problems the FBO faces, what do you see as the primary opportunities?

The first interviews took place in July 2003 and continued through November 2004; all were conducted at the FBO project location or local church. The first 15 interviews began to produce recognizable patterns of data. Allowances were made for 'snowball sampling' (Schutt, 2001:134-35) [23] and additional FBOs and churches were selected for interviews. I learned I was the first to conduct research on FBO-church partnerships in Romania; asking questions about FBOs, churches, and partnerships' required sensitivity and patience.

The interview questions were intended to be straightforward, but when asked, 'how do you work with a local church' a FBO interviewee might take 30 minutes to explain 'how it was difficult it is to work with domineering Romanian pastors' (FBOL#8) or a Romanian pastor would need to describe how 'Western missionaries just did not understand the situation in Romania' (Pas#9). In some cases, it was necessary to spend 30-45 minutes with the interviewee talking about rationale for research. Questions were asked in such a way that the participants were given a conceptual framework and vocabulary to better engage with the issues under study and grasp the basic direction of the research.[24]

Collecting and organizing data from the preliminary interviews

In the initial interviews I experimented using a micro-recorder but learned that most Romanian participants were more open, relaxed, and conversation was more constructive if interview notes were recorded using short hand and a memo pad.[25] All interviews were conducted with at least one research assistant present to assist in taking notes, if translation was required (5 cases) then I had two assistants present, one always recording the conversation with pen and paper.[26]

As soon as possible after the interview, tapes or notes were transcribed and reviewed for errors with study participants. The interview transcripts were typed into MS Word™. Additional personal memos and observations were

---

[23] This technique allows the researcher to identify one member of the population and speak to him or her and ask that individual to identify others in the population and speak to them and so on; in this way the sample 'snowballs" in size.

[24] Throughout the study, assurances of confidentiality were given to all participants, due to sensitive nature of some of the information. Permission was asked to use the names of the organizations. An Excel spread sheet was created to keep all data on interviewees but names are not published in this book.

[25] The first year I was in Romania, I assisted a researcher from the University of Southern California who relied on a micro-recorder. One interviewee explained later that the procedure felt like an interrogation, a distinctly uncomfortable situation in a post-communist country with fresh memories of the *Securitate* who were very effective in 'bugging' almost every office and place of work.

[26] A Dictaphone was only used if the interviewee gave permission.

written in the margins of the documents.[27] Miles & Huberman note that 'write-ups usually add back some of the missing content; raw field notes stimulate remembering things' (1994:51). I learned this was invaluable in writing up field notes. Briggs also comments on limitations in working with interviews and the importance of safeguarding reliability and validity (1986:23).

Preliminary coding of the transcripts and thematic arrangement began as soon as possible after the actual interview (see below for application of grounded theory). Ideally, coding and memos should be written the day after the interview, as the data can grow 'cold' if not given some preliminary work. Only two of the selected FBOs refused to be interviewed, in one case the specific objection was, 'if this is an "investigation" of our agency, then we don't want to be interviewed, we have a long history of *Securitate* investigations and we don't see why there should be any more' (FBOL#8, 2003). After this comment, I removed the term '*investigation*' from my introduction to any FBO or church.

By November 2004, 60 interviews had been completed using the preliminary survey instrument. I also conducted open interviews with a number of FBO leaders, denominational leaders, pastors, and student workers about attitudes towards children. The latter were recorded as field notes and combined with the interview survey interviews for a total of 82 sources as displayed in Table 4.2.

Table 4.2 Categories of participants in Phase One

Pastors	11
FBO Romanian directors	27
FBO Romanians also serving as pastors	12
FBO Western directors	17
Missionaries	2
Denominational officials	3
Students	10
TOTAL	82

Lessons learned about trust in interviewing

Skill in interviewing was a gradual process. Some of the interview questions were more relevant to FBOs than churches. Romanian pastors had a better understanding of congregational life, they were less familiar with terms like 'para-church or FBO'; these terms were modified to 'Western mission groups.' Terms like 'evaluation' and 'outcomes' had to be explained as 'what do you consider as success?' The preliminary survey was an effective method to gain a

[27] Thanks to a tip from Don Ratcliff, I set up my Word documents to leave a wide blank column (2.5 inches) to the right of the actual interview transcripts for additional memos and notes.

working knowledge of FBO and church agendas in childcare; this was critical for second phase of research.

Visiting churches and projects resembled an ethnographic study where the goal is to understand a culture or social context from the insider's point of view and make inferences from what people say or the way they act (Spradley, 1979:4-8; Hammersley & Atkinson, 1983). The guided interviews were conducted as 'exploratory'; and indicated the need for connectivity and relationality with research participants. Trust and communication between FBO and church leaders was a more important issue than I had foreseen. Not all interviewees were willing to discuss underlying issues concerning partnership.[28]

Data Displays and Grounded Theory and as Methods of Analysis in Phase One

Analysis in Phase One began with collecting and organizing the data, writing memos, coding, and thinking about what how interviewees understood the questions. Once recognizable patterns emerged in the data, I began using 'data displays' defined as 'an organized, compressed assembly of information that permits conclusion drawing and action' (Huberman & Miles, 1994:11). Data displays included visual charts, diagrams, and schematics. A series of data displays was produced at the conclusion of Phase One to visually describe casual connections in the interview data (See Appendix C).

Applying grounded theory

Here I put forward a 'working definition' of what is known as grounded theory (henceforth GT) in the literature.[29] The term was originally used in 1967 by Strauss and Glaser and describes a qualitative method to discern the patterns of meaning embedded in a given text or set of data. GT allows the researcher to develop theory or core categories that are derived inductively and 'grounded in the data'. The approach is not a specified, step-by-step plan but rather a method of analysis that seeks to generate theory from raw data through a recursive process. GT is also known as 'constant comparison' which means that the ideas that constitute the theory are developed and refined throughout the course of the research (Oktay, 2004:24).[30]

---

[28]Interviews sometimes turned into what felt like 'long therapy sessions' as there had been a great deal of misunderstanding between Western and Romanian partners in the early to mid 1990s.

[29] I say 'working definition' as there are many applications of GT in the social sciences. It should be noted that 'grounded theory' is not a new science or technique. People have been reading texts and interpreting events from those texts for many centuries. For discussion comparing GT to biblical hermeneutics see Seale (1999:103-104).

[30] GT was applicable to this research as it allows flexibility to form new concepts in

GT was particularly well suited to a study of local interactions between churches and FBOs. GT is an interpretive inquiry that orients research to everyday understandings and accepts human subjectivity as part of the process (Strauss &Corbin, 1998). This was relevant as many of participants were responding to questions based on their subjective knowledge of children and ministry.[31] GT is not without its critics and limitations that are summarized by Seale as: a) grounded theorizing is an inappropriate methodology for certain types of research problems, such as long-term historical processes b) there are legitimate objections to the narrow analytic strategy imposed by a heavy reliance on coding as a first step, and c) the equation of coding with grounded theorizing and the imposition of singular interpretations can be forced by the analyst (1999:101-104).

Coding procedures used in the study

In Phase One and the case studies, I followed a coding procedure to analyse transcripts of interviews and literature published by the FBOs. This procedure established linkages between concepts and then integrated them into higher order analytic categories. The preliminary survey interviews were analysed to identify a) types of factors that contributed to or hindered FBO-church partnership and b) the categories to be used in case selection.

Coding began with 'open' or 'descriptive' coding, selecting key words, phrases, or ideas from the interviews that required little interpretation. These may also be labelled as pattern codes, which are more inferential and explanatory (Miles & Huberman, 1994:57). In Phase One this resulted in 100+ open codes. Coding progressed to more abstract levels, known as 'axial coding', where text segments were integrated into working categories and concepts establishing linkages between code and categories, asking questions of causality or if the codes contradicted one another. The third step is known as 'selective coding' that involves 'joining the narrative categories into a working understanding of the target phenomena and arriving at one or several core categories that represent the central category' (Strauss & Corbin, 1998: 107; 161). I did limited selective coding in Phase One since I was not looking for a central category at this stage. Table 4.3 is an example from Phase One with five open codes from two interviews. A process memo written at the time explaining the rationale follows the table.

---

working with the data and comparing those to previous data and emerging ideas, moving from data through reflection and to theory. It requires being alert to the data and subject matter as the study progresses as generalisation and systematisation emerge (Glaser & Strauss, 1967).

[31] I was assited here by Robert Barnard relied on GT in his PhD thesis, 'An Examination of Dysfunctional Behaviour in Christian Evangelical, Mission Organizations and Strategies for Resolving the Consequences of Dysfunctional Behaviour' (2004).

Table 4.3 Example of coding from Phase One

Open Codes	Questions of causality	Axial Code
Acceptance-rejection Not our problem They (West) have the money We don't have the resources Salvation begins at the house of God	Who is responsible? Children as threat or....Children as opportunity? Fear or realistic limits?	Possible motivations for working together or engaging with children

The open codes were taken from two interviews with pastors who were working in limited collaboration with FBOs; they were reticent to commit church resources to working with street children. The axial code chosen (motivation) indicates there may be some causality and inference: does the street child present a threat to the ongoing ministry of the church or to its own children; does the church truly lack the resources to deal with so complex a problem (which may show wisdom on their part not to get involved), does the church see an opportunity for extending love and grace but have reasons for not doing so at this time? I label the axial code 'motivation' since it is becoming apparent that both FBOs and churches have different motives for engaging with street children and not all of them seem altogether altruistic (personal process memo, October 2004)

An established coding procedure aids in identifying abstract assumptions, biases, variations, general patterns, and key categories (Miles & Huberman, 1994:61).[32] The primary analysis objective in Phase One was to identify continua and criteria for selection of cases. The key axial code identified was the 'means or methods' used in FBO-church collaboration, that is, how intentional is the partnership.

The analysis of Phase One was necessary for clarifying some of the theoretical and practical boundaries of the study: How FBOs and churches understood and defined partnership; there were many conflicts concerning control of projects. FBOs used the terms 'holistic or transformational' with little reference to churches; Romanian pastors did not use the terms. FBO and churches had different assumptions about intervention with children; some churches were taking an interest in children without FBO help. A number of

[32] It can be argued that coding itself is a subjective experience; it does depend a great deal on the perspective of the person doing the coding and the questions being addressed in the research. I did not treat the coding as the last step in analysis, it is important to keep in mind the 'whole picture' from any interview or case and allow the coding to be part of an integrative process. Coding should not dictate what can be inferred from an interview or case, it is a tool for looking at the data from another perspective.

FBOs had decided not to work with local churches. The findings from Phase One were written up and later integrated in Chapters 5-8.

Selection of Cases for the Study – Phase Two

Phase One provided access to a number of potential projects (n=35) to consider as case studies. The following discussion includes rationale of case study, the analytical categories developed for case selection, a short description of the cases chosen in chronological order, and an explanation of additional methods used in the analysis.

Overview of case study as method [33]

Findings in Phase One produced little evidence that the FBO-church partnerships had been developed with a clear pattern or theory guiding childcare practice or collaborative strategy. What was emerging was a largely entrepreneurial approach to partnership.[34] In Phase Two, I used a multiple case comparative study (Stake, 1995; Yin, 1984; 2003) as it had advantages over single case design. Yin notes that multiple cases require the development of certain skills and can provide a rich theoretical framework (2003:46-7). I hoped that this method would strengthen the findings by replicating pattern matching.[35] Case study methodology has been carried out in High-Risk youth Programmes (Yin, 2003), so the method was a good 'fit' for this research. If the time is limited, Stake (1995) suggests that case selection offers the opportunity to maximize what can be learned if cases selected are willing subjects; this too was applicable as I was dependent on the willingness of the FBOs, churches and participants. Finally, a good instrumental case does not have to defend its typicality (Yin, 2003:13).

Criteria and categories used in case selection

In order to define the criteria for case selection, key categories and nine axial codes from Phase One were displayed as a data display.[36] The six primary and

[33] In locating the literature on case study as method, I relied in part on Tellis (1997), outline available at http://www.nova.edu/ssss/QR/QR3-2/tellis1.html (accessed November 17, 2010).

[34] This *ad hoc* approach was due in large measure to the unregulated nature of childcare services; (the Romanian government did not set up laws until 1997 to regulate child services) and the sheer number of agencies that entered Romania to help children.

[35] Campbell & Stanley (1963) described 'pattern-matching' as a useful way to link data to the propositions. Pattern matching is a situation where several pieces of information from the same case may be related to some theoretical proposition.

[36] I made extensive use of the computer software *MindMapper*™ in creating data displays.

three secondary axial categories or *continua* are itemized in Table 4.4. Table 4.5 provides a one or two sentence description of each category.

Table 4.4 Continua used in defining criteria for selection of cases[37]

A.) Methods of collaboration between FBO and the church Ad hoc Collaboration------------------------------------Intentional Collaboration
B.) Types of children in individual project Gypsy -------street children ----------institutional----------disabled---------------others
C. The extent of guidance offered by the FBO Firmly guided partnership----------------------------------Loosely guided partnership
D. Ways that trust has been developed or neglected in the partnership. Trust seems to be marginal-----------------------------------Trust seems to be strong
E.) Types of interventions being carried out in the projects Primary spiritual interventions-----------------------Physical or social interventions
F.) Variations in language of intervention: faith (biblical) versus child development Faith Language ---Child Development Language
Secondary Categories that were used as criteria in selection:
G.)Methods primarily used to monitor and evaluate the project Formal/written Evaluations-------------------------non-formal or verbal evaluations
H.) Extent of theological/biblical language in FBO work with children Intentional Theology ---Incidental Theology
I.) Types and kinds of caregivers at the specific project Volunteers from local church----------------------------------professionals from FBO

Table 4.5 Explanation of each continuum

A. Methods of collaboration between FBO and the church
This was the central category, discussed in all preliminary surveys. I discovered a range of collaborative strategies: ignoring one another or experiencing conflict, limited partnership, FBOs supplying financial assistance, churches and FBOs in close collaboration.[38]
B. Types of Children in the projects
While not technically a continuum, selected cases were working with different types of children. Some children came from extremely poor church families, others had left the failed state institutional system to live on the streets; others had run away from abusive homes.
C. The extent of guidance offered by the FBO
FBOs developed both firmly and loosely guided partnership with local partners, by this I mean that some FBOs closely monitor and oversee the activities of the church/local partner but in other cases the church/local partner decides what is best

[37] It should be noted that the chart is a visual aid. The categories enabled case selection but the FBOs are not monolithic and demonstrate variance on each continuum, not all cases selected can be plotted on every continuum, and not all cases demonstrate variance at every level.

[38] No cases were selected in which the FBO had completely bypassed working with the church, these do exist but were not relevant to the research inquiry. My designation of 'limited' implies there is at least some recognition of the role of the local church; however in some cases it implies very limited cooperation.

for the children with little input from the FBO.
D. Ways that trust has been developed or neglected in the partnership
Trust was mentioned in 90 per cent of Phase One interviews. Several FBO directors reported they felt the pastors wanted to 'control the ministry agenda' to children, others expressed concern that churches had little tolerance of children in crisis. Case selection helped answer the question: what issues have led to misunderstandings with FBOs and affected the question of trust?
E. Types of interventions being carried out in the projects
FBOs provided a range of interventions; taxonomy was created to differentiate spiritual and physical/social interventions. Case selection sought clarification of rationale for the types pf interventions provided, special attention was given to the terms: conversion, holistic, transformational, and moral formation in case selection.
F. Variations in language of intervention: faith versus developmental language
Cases were selected to explore implications of faith language (conversion and spiritual change) vs. child development (human psycho-social change).[39] I sought to understand if working with the Romanian authorities influenced language of intervention.
G. Methods primarily used to monitor and evaluate the project
Phase One established that the assumptions of the founding FBO or church had a significant influence on how project evaluation was conceived and implemented. The following questions were asked of the cases to better clarify this category: Who is the evaluation for, is this for the donors and sponsors, the child in the programme, the church, the local community, who are the primary stakeholders?
H. Extent of theological/biblical language in FBO work with children
This continuum is a subset of Continuum F and was labelled after beginning Phase Two. This continuum served to identify variation within the cases as to how leaders and project staff used the Bible to talk about God, the kingdom of God, and salvation of children, personal transformation, and social concern.[40]
I. Types of Caregivers
Phase One identified variations in the preparation, calling and training of the personnel working with children. Cases were selected that relied on volunteers, full-time employees, professionals, and church-based workers.

Exploratory work with the cases

Case selection followed a sampling procedure that would produce contrasting results and sufficient cross-case data to analyse the factors shaping FBO-church

[39] Concerning this bifurcation, in Romanian evangelicalism there is a strong dichotomy between faith language (the language of knowing God, living for Christ, Christian living) and language associated with human/child development (psychological development, social concerns of child and family). This continuum emerged as a stronger and more central category in the subsequent case study analysis.

[40] All the FBOs and churches have operative theologies, they may or may not articulate these views but thinking and talking about God is important in faith-based work with children, family, and community.

partnerships.[41] Since no prior theory was being tested, seven cases were designated as 'representaive'. I visited each case a) to gain better knowledge of the specific case b) to set up case study protocols with project managers, and c) to locate additional cases or churches that might provide additional descriptive variation.

At the onset of Phase Two, I planned to spend up to two weeks at four cases and then examine a 'shadow case' of each type. I tentatively selected four cases (from the original seven), which represented variation on the continua and methods of FBO-church collaboration. I intended to do observation, interviews, and participation with the 'actors' taking part in the study (Zonabend, 1992).[42] It became clear that I would not be able to invest several weeks at each project. There were a number of extenuating factors: increasing responsibilities in personal work, emerging information that childcare projects were not especially 'open' to outsiders spending extended time at project locations, lack of access to key people in projects due to their schedules, and the realization that 'suspicion of evaluators' could limit my interaction with key participants.

After additional interaction with the seven selected cases, two were dropped; one experienced problems in senior management and the other proved too remote for useful repeat visits. Since spending extended time at a few cases was not an option, I added six based on the selection criteria for a total of eleven FBOs: four in Bucharest, one in Piteşti, three in Galaţi, one in Braşov, and two in Sibiu to enrich the cross-case analysis.

Descriptions of cases selected

I provide an intentionally short description of each case, in the order chosen, collaboration method with partner church, and primary intervention with children. Each case and relation to the nine continua in Table 4.5 is discussed in subsequent chapters.

1. *World Vision Romania* – Largest FBO in this study, self-described as Christian humanitarian agency. Uses various models of collaboration with local church but the country director stated that evangelical church partnership was not the primary agenda of the FBO. Describes interventions as 'holistic and transformational.'
2. *Mission of Mercy Foundation* – A local FBO with one international partner (Mission of Mercy – U.S.A.). Project funding, management, and operations are independent of local churches, but works in limited

[41] Case study research does not require a minimum number of cases, nor prohibit the random selection of cases. Individual cases are not a sampling unit like different units in a survey.

[42] Participants in research studies of this type are sometimes referred to as 'actors'. I chose not to use the term in interviews with participants but on this definition the 'actors' in this study were the pastors, FBO leaders, staff, volunteers, children, and other colleagues.

collaboration with Baptist and Pentecostal churches in Piteşti. Primary intervention: educational assistance for poor and Roma children.

3. *City of Hope Foundation* – A local FBO with one primary international partner (Children's Relief Network) supported by a number of Western churches. City of Hope worked locally with one or more 'contemporary' churches.[43] Primary intervention: rehabilitation of street children.
4. *Light and Life Foundation* – A local FBO with two international Scandinavian partners. Limited local church collaboration, the Romanian director is a senior pastor of a local Pentecostal church, he is also a lawyer. Primary intervention: moving children from institutions to group homes and street shelters.
5. *Project Ruth Foundation* – A local FBO started by a Baptist church in the *Ferentari* district Bucharest, the poorest area of the city. Initiated when a Western missionary asked the Romanian pastor to assist Roma children living near the church. Primary intervention: formal education for Roma children.
6. *Mission Without Borders Romania* – A large FBO located in Sibiu, has affiliate offices in eight Transylvanian counties and a network of international donors. Primary intervention: mobilising volunteers to assist institutional children, works with what it describes as 'holistic church based' approach.
7. *Ţoar Foundation* – A local FBO in Sibiu (Western Romania) has several international partners. Initiated by leaders in local Brethren churches after long relationship with Child Evangelism Fellowship, U.S.A. Primary intervention: provides family style foster care for children from institutions.
8. *Centre for New Life* – A local FBO started in a 'non- traditional church' in Braşov,_Transylvania, and partners with CRY-UK. A German pastor moved to Romania just after the revolution in 1989 and started this charismatic church. Primary intervention: drop in centre for street children and Roma families in surrounding villages.
9. *Galaţi Cluster* – Three cases were selected in this city, the three have close collaboration with one another but work independently and in diverse ways with local churches.
   a. *Heart of a Child* – A medium-sized social service agency, received funding from USAID, World Learning and SERA. Recognized in Romanian press for excellent social work with children from institutions, poor families, and abusive homes.
   b. *Word Made Flesh* – A medium-sized local FBO connected to international partner agency that works in community based care

[43] I will discuss the types of evangelical churches in Chapter 6; the 'contemporary' church has made a break with the legalism and narrow fundamentalism of the more 'traditional' churches of Romania.

with Roma families and children. Self-described as 'church among the poor'.

c. *Bethesda Foundation* – small local FBO with limited outside assistance. Provides home for street children and children leaving institutions.

Data Collection and Work with Cases

The eleven cases provided primary data for the main phase of the study. Each project was visited a minimum of two times, none more than four. Data was collected through observation, semi-structured interviews with FBO directors, staff, administrators, church workers, volunteers, some children,[44] and participation in training forums at the FBOs.

A case study protocol (Yin, 2003:64)[45] was designed; it combined a semi-structured interview guide and case analysis tool.[46] In November of 2004, a pilot case was selected (Mission of Mercy) and three working days were invested with this case experimenting with the protocol. I realized the case protocol was too detailed, as it required a minimum four hours to address the interview questions.[47] I shortened the protocol and divided it into two parts: the interview guide and a 'case study analysis tool'. The latter was used as a means to verify and compare findings in subsequent case analysis write-ups (Miles & Huberman, 1994:76-8). The case analysis tool included the categories and sub-questions in Table 4.6.

Table 4.6 Case analysis tool categories

1.	Origins and type of organization, affiliation, structure, and departments.
2.	Partnership strategies and methods of collaboration with local churches.
3.	Budgeting and resources for programme, staff training, child services; that is, who assumes responsibility for the operation and management of the programme.
4.	Vision, goals, activities and types of programmes, target audience; how do international and local partners contribute to programme interventions.
5.	Evaluation and impact of programme activities, responsibility for measuring the outcomes of the programme.
6.	Perceptions of the FBO and the programme in the local community, if the

[44] Access to children in the projects varied. In some projects it was limited, as the policy of the FBO did not permit observers to interact or question the children. In cases where I was a practitioner, there were opportunities to spend time with the children.

[45] Yin recommends the use of case-study protocol, as part of a carefully designed research project should include: an overview of the project, field procedures, questions and a guide for the report (2003:64).

[46] The case analysis tool was designed using relevant literature in child development, organizational studies, and data gathered in the pilot study.

[47] Yin (2003:84) points out that inquiry in pilot cases can be intentionally broad and then narrowed as the study progresses.

	local church was a partner how did the partnership impact the community's perception of the church?
7.	The influence of the donor organization on the local programme, on the church and on the children in the programme.
8.	How did the FBO and church describe the child in crisis, what was the understanding of the needs of the child.
9.	In what ways did the FBO and church rely on 'operative theology' in shaping partnerships or interventions for the child?

Mission of Mercy as a pilot case study

The pilot study involved three visits for interviews and participant-observer time with staff, director, and children. A semi-structured interview guide was based on categories listed in Table 4.6. The interview guide facilitated systematic data collection (Weller & Romney, 1988).[48] Questions led the interviewees through a discussion of their participation and experience working with church and FBO, how both FBO and church contributed to the task of providing care to children at risk, evaluation of impact, and spiritual change in children. The semi-structured interview guide is attached as Appendix B.[49] I interviewed two pastors in the same city as the pilot case. This served to test the interview guide and modify some questions. For instance, when asking the questions: 'As you think of the local church and children in crisis, what are some benefits you believe the church can offer to children? What about the FBO?' Both Pastors asked for explanation of the rationale and line of questioning. I explained I was not arguing for or against FBOs or churches but trying to find how they worked together. In this city, FBO-church tensions preceded my arrival and thus required my explaining and asking questions in such a way as to not alienate the interviewees.[50] Feedback during the interviews was very important in 'learning how to ask' (Rubin & Rubin, 1995).

Application of appreciative inquiry (AI) in interviewing

The foregoing example demonstrates why sensitivity was important in interviews. I adopted aspects of the 'appreciative inquiry' approach (AI)

[48] Systematic data collection refers to systematic interviewing where each informant is asked the same set of questions Weller & Romney (1988). This approach is contrasted with open-ended interviewing where subjects give long explanatory answers to a variety of different questions and the researcher follows lines of interest in the questioning (1988:6).

[49] There were two separate interview guides used in the study (one for churches and one for FBOs). I have combined them in Appendix B.

[50] The situation in this city was not unique. I learned that a number of Western FBOs had 'bypassed' the local church in establishing their outreach to children. These pastors were suspicious that I was trying to build a case 'against the local church' in favour of the FBOs.

developed by Cooperrider & Srivastva (1987) in interviewing.[51] AI is a process of valuing, the act of recognizing the good in people or the world around us; affirming past and present strengths, successes, and potentials; to perceive those things that give life to living systems (Hammond, 1996:7). AI represents a dialectic approach in a move away from rationalistic, mechanistic, problem-solving frames that are common in much organizational research. AI takes into account aspirations and hopes for the future in translating these conversations into reality. A central assumption of AI is that dialogue and language creates much of the reality found in organizations; see Hammond (1996) for concise treatment and application. AI utilizes a '4-D' cycle; it has been used extensively in organizational development and evaluation.[52]

Most relevant to my inquiry, was the first part of the cycle that seeks to 'discover' or identify the organizational processes that are working well. Knowing what little I did of the Romanian church and Western FBO experience, I chose this line of inquiry to avoid being mired down in long discussions of problems in FBO-church partnership'.[53] I developed an initial line of questioning that sought to draw out positive learning experiences. The participants were asked to describe significant achievements or encouraging factors in partnership. Later in the interview, questions were asked concerning weaknesses in partnership, but these questions were predicated by dialogue appreciating what the FBO or church had learned from each other. I cite an example from an early interview in Bucharest (2004).

> My question: Can you tell me what positive lessons you have learned from the local churches?
>
> FBOL#11: At first we had a number of disagreements; they were quite legalistic about the kids. They did not want them to come to church when they were high on glue or dirty.
>
> My response: But do you think they might have had some good reasons for saying for that?

---

[51]Originally developed at Case Western University as a method of working with and understanding organizations See http://appreciativeinquiry.case.edu/ a 'worldwide portal devoted to the fullest sharing of academic resources and practical tools on Appreciative Inquiry' (accessed November 18, 2010).

[52] I did not utilise the entire cycle as I was looking for responses to 'discovery' level questions. The other D's in the AI process are: *Dream* – the envisioning of processes that would work well in the future. *Design* – planning and prioritising the processes that work well. *Deliver* – the implantation of the proposed design. See Myers' discussion of AI in *Walking with the Poor* (1999b:173-79).

[53] I intentionally selected the majority of cases where positive factors in partnership could be explored. This does not mean that I avoided difficult issues and discussions that arose in the interviews; AI allowed a more positive framing of the overall interview process.

FBOL#11: I guess so, but we had already decided that the kids needed a safe place to go and to learn the Bible.

My response: Now as you think about it, can you look back and see that there might have been things that both you and the churches could offer the children?

FBOL'11: Yes, in time we learned a lot more about working things out with the churches.

My response: Would you explain some of those lessons for me as you see them now?

AI was also useful in discussions concerning 'spiritual' interventions for children, especially when FBOs and churches held divergent positions in reference to faith and programme outcomes. By keeping the interview process intentionally 'appreciative' constructive dialogue was encouraged with pastors and FBO leaders who disagreed on 'who most deserved the help' and avoided eliciting defensive responses.[54]

Continuing field work at case locations

Cases studies continued on a part-time basis from November 2004 – April 2006, the sequence is diagrammed in Figure 4.4.

Figure 4.4 Sequence of Case Studies 2004-2006

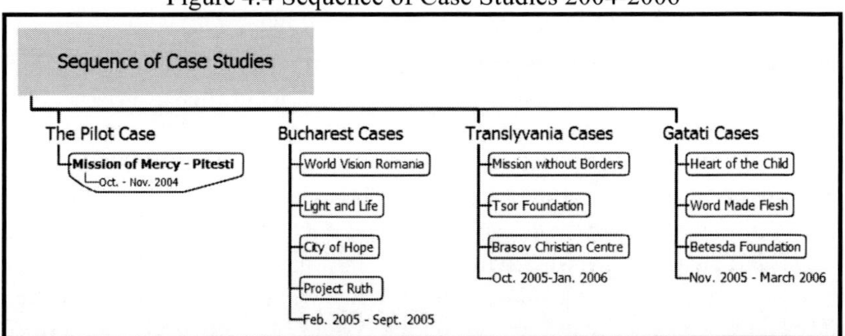

In early 2005, four cases in Bucharest were studied and compared with the pilot case.Each case demonstrated different methods of working with local churches and offered varied programme interventions for street children, institutionalized children, and Roma children. In three cases I met funding partners from the West.

In interviewing, I learned to take time to dwell on specific issues that were relevant to the specific case. The first interview questions were open-ended to elicit narratives, stories, and descriptions of experience. Each interview usually

[54] This subject of 'who most deserved help' is discussed in Chapter 5 and 6.

required two hours to complete. After interviewing the project director, I would meet staff members, followed by observation of the physical facilities, activities with the children, and a walk through the surrounding community.[55] Documents and records were collected at the projects including: files on children, letters to sponsors and donors, minutes of meetings, written reports of events, internal organizational charts, audits, and public press reports (Stake 1995, Yin, 2003).[56] Case visits were conducted one day at a time, giving time for reflection on the transcripts, documents, coding, and write-ups. As the study progressed, I scheduled follow-up discussions with study participants at conferences, workshops, in their homes, and churches to review or correct their comments from interviews. As case write-ups were completed, participants reviewed them for accuracy.

At each project location, interviews were conducted with pastors of affiliated local churches to understand their role in the partnership and to compare their ideas with those of the FBOs. On several occasions, the pastors accompanied me to the projects after interviews for more interaction. In the case of *Project Ruth*, the FBO director was also the pastor of the local church. I was careful to allow FBO leaders and pastors to give independent feedback and suggestions. I chose not to share corresponding interview data with each side, as I felt this would have influenced responses.

Insights learned in case inquiry – allowing for fluidity

The preceding paragraphs may give the impression that interviewing pastors, FBO leaders and people who work with children was a linear process, it was not. Interviewees had their 'own story to tell' and case visits and interviews often grew into animated discussions that were instructive as to the best way to ask questions to bring out the narratives of partnership. After completing ten to twelve interviews, I knew the questions well enough to 'skip forward or back as needed'. The interviewees would sometimes jump ahead in their comments to questions that were listed last in the interview guide – such as spiritual care or evaluation – then return to 'hot button' issues as the interview progressed. For example, I became increasingly aware of a dichotomistic approach to psychosocial needs of children held by FBOs on one side, and eternal concerns

---

[55] I was given a walkthrough tour of almost every facility and project but not all, in some cases photography was allowed and in others I was asked to not photograph children to protect their dignity and privacy.

[56] The amount of documentation from each case was by not uniform. Some FBOs like World Vision and Heart of the Child had extensive documentation, internal records, conference proceedings, pending project proposals, and personnel records. Other projects had very little other than case records for children and the odd internal publicity reports sent to donors. Some cases said they could not share internal documents without express permission from their international governing board.

for children held by pastors and churches on the other. I took additional time in the interviews to explore these perceptions and labelled them '*Side A*' and '*Side B*' in the analysis.[57]

Interviewing required keeping conversations focused on the core topics yet allowing for spontaneity and fluidity. As I gained experience and insight in interaction with the participants, the study became more dynamic. By learning to ask reflective questions such as: 'how does your faith affect…' in the first half of the interview (concerning partnership and organizational issues) responses were enhanced in the second half of the interview concerning outcomes in the lives of children. Responses to the interview questions took on a 'thicker', more detailed nature (Patton, 1990). Field notes and personal memos were important and substantial in the process.

Additional cases and summary of interviewees

Three more cases in Transylvania were studied in the second half of 2005. *Mission Without Borders* worked with dozens of local churches, training, and mobilizing volunteers. The *Ţoar Foundation*, partnering with local Brethren churches, served as a locally sustainable model for foster care. [58] *Centre for New Life*, (ACVN) was a founded by an independent charismatic church; however, when they began work with street children the FBO experienced opposition from more traditional evangelical churches in the city. The final cluster of cases was located in Galaţi on the Danube delta. *Word Made Flesh* worked in the poorest part of city serving extremely poor families and children and was intentional in the use of theology to guide FBO practice.[59] *Heart of the Child* started as a NGO in the early 1990s and provided a number of exceptional social service interventions. In 1999, both founders became evangelicals and chose to make 'faith-based care' a priority.

At the conclusion of the casework, 56 interviews had been conducted, 34 of those using the interview guide, the youngest participant was 22 and the oldest was 70+. Three FBOs were led by women, the rest by men; many of the senior staff and programme mangers were women. The gender mix in the interviews

---

[57] I mentioned some of my assumptions in the introduction. It is important to acknowledge preconceived positions in qualitative research. My prior experience led me to believe I could find a number of cases that would help me build an argument for 'holistic church-based ministry'. The interviews and subsequent analysis illuminated the wrong assumptions I held about 'holistic ministry' in Romania.

[58] I use the term 'sustainable' to mean owned and sustained by a local community. The *Ţoar Foundation* was originally founded in the early 1990's when members and families from local churches visited state orphanages and institutions in their area and decided to bring the children into their own homes, offering a very 'sustainable' model of child care.

[59] I include a number of quotes from this case in the analysis. This FBO demonstrated an intentional effort to think creatively concerning theology and children.

was approximately 60 per cent men and 40 per cent women. Interviewees filled different roles in the organizations: teachers, administrators, health care providers, and consultants. Children were also informally interviewed; their comments were recorded as field notes. Table 4.7 provides a catagorisation of interviews that were conducted. A chart of all interviews identified by their interview number and organization is attached as Appendix D.

Table 4.7 Categories of interviewees during second phase of research

FBO directors/managers	15
FBO Leaders also serving as pastors in local churches	13
Staff/volunteers at cases	10
Pastors not working at FBOs	9
Missionaries working at projects	4
Professors/consultants/others	5
TOTAL	**56**

Defining the boundaries of case selection and inquiry

Before moving to methods of analysis, I mention defining boundaries and limits in case selection. I located several FBOs that were not working with churches but did excellent work children in social service delivery. To compare variables such as importance of church collaboration and spiritual vs. psychosocial care, I interviewed two of these directors. Both felt that the special needs of traumatized children were served better by the FBO. Their responses were noted and pushed me to think more carefully about the integration of 'service to the soul' and 'service to the body' (Bosch, 1991:392).[60] I considered including an FBO written up in the *Journal of International Youth Foundation*.[61] The FBO had been recognized for creating 'service learning clubs' for youth in an economically depressed area of Romania, but worked primarily with Orthodox churches with no partnerships with evangelical churches. This case was considered a 'boundary defining case' and was not included in the study. On the other hand, I located *Ţoar Foundation* later in study, and since it represented close collaboration with Brethren churches and contradicted some of my earlier findings, it was added

[60] See my earlier comments in Chapter 2 concerning 'holistic mission' pp. 40-42. The findings from the cases indicated that FBOs and churches were dividing missional tasks between human social welfare (from below) from their concerns with ulimate reconciliation with God through Christ (from above).

[61] See Thorup & Kinkade (2005) 'What Works in Youth Engagement in the Balkans' at the website of the International Youth Foundation. The section of this report concerns *The New Horizons Foundation*, Lupeni.

as a selected case.[62] Throughout the fieldwork, it was necessary to remain faithful to the selection criteria to avoid case overload. Eleven cases proved sufficient as research categories became 'saturated' and the cross-case analysis had become conceptually dense.

Analysis of the Case Study Data

Case analysis was a reiterative process of thinking about the participants, interviews, coding of data, asking questions of the emerging data, and follow up visits for elaboration and verification of findings. Analysis of case data involved examining, categorizing, tabulating, and recombining qualitative data. Yin suggests developing an overall analytic strategy and employing specific techniques in the analysis (2003:109). I present some of the analytical methods that were followed but point out these were not always sequential.

Explanation of case pairing

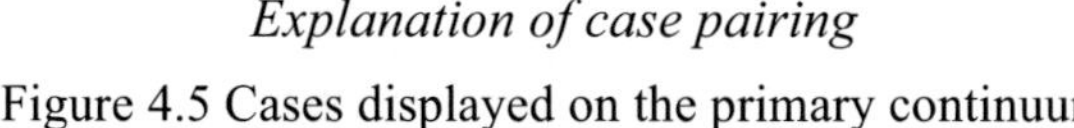

Figure 4.5 Cases displayed on the primary continuum

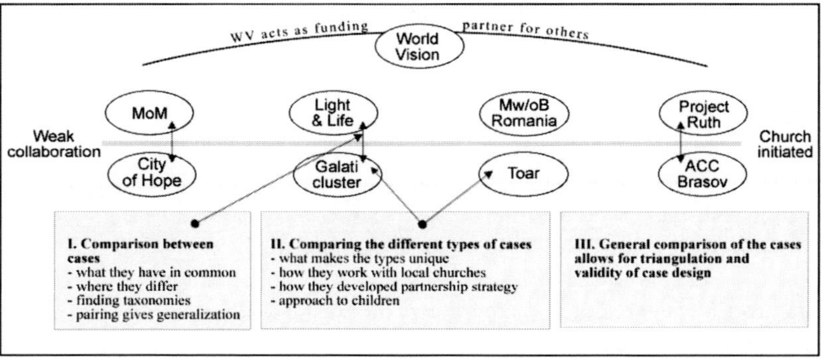

Using data displays, I plotted the cases on several continua; Figure 4.5 illustrates the cases displayed on the key continuum.[63] The horizontal alignment identifies those on the left who worked in limited collaboration with churches and those on the right initiated by a local church. The vertical pairing

[62] I was beginning to conclude that all the churches working directly with children were a) relying on funding and help from the West to operate or b) the local churches had not been successful in encouraging their own members and families to open their personal homes to children form the failed institutions. This foundation contradicted both those assumptions and was a welcome addition to the overall study.

[63] In the subsequent chapters, I arrange the cases on the different continua, the data displays are simpler that this illustration. Thanks to Radu Suteu for his help on this and other graphics.

of the cases indicates similar collaboration with local churches. World Vision is placed above the line for the reasons described above.[64]

The three boxes below the names of the cases point out (i) that comparisons were made between the pairs identifying commonality, differences, and pairing leading to generalization (ii) comparing across the cases identifying types and means of building partnership strategy and ministry outcomes and (iii) a general comparison of all the cases provided triangulation, and evidence supportive of a degree of external validity (Yin, 2003:106).[65] The paired cases varied in their methods of meeting the needs of children and other continua allowed for further comparison. While the case selection did not produce 'maximum variation', it does provide adequate differences to enhance the external validity of the data in the study.[66] Each case was treated individually, analysis was done to answer the central research questions and offer suggestions to improve practice and evaluate programme changes (Patton, 1987, 1990).

Labelling the cases as 'types'[67]

Project Ruth and *New Life Braşov* were labelled as near 'ideal church-based cases', both demonstrated that international FBOs can work closely with church initiated projects.[68] *Mission Without Borders*, *Word Made Flesh*, and *Ţoar Foundation* were labelled as a 'unique collaboration cases,' as they demonstrated intentional strategy to work with a variety of local churches and sought local church input in programme design. They varied in scale and funding but had similar programme goals. *Light and Life* and *Bethesda Foundation* are examples of 'typical Romanian directed cases', where FBO Romanian leaders and local pastors worked in collaboration. Most funding came from Western sources, expertise and human resources are shared by FBO and church, and Romanians made the programmatic decisions. *City of Hope*

---

64 *World Vision Romania* is labelled as a funding partner based on this statement, 'We work in limited ways with local evangelical churches, but this is only a fraction of what we do in the country, we help a few churches with their local projects' (LFBO#16, 2004).

65 The need for triangulation arises from the need to confirm the validity of the processes. In case studies, this can be done by using multiple sources of data such as interaction with participants, interviews, and observations (Yin, 2003).

66 I submit that the cases selected were a representative my sampling of FBOs working in Romania (n=98).

67 I have adopted the typology: 'ideal case', 'unique case', and 'typical case' from qualitative research literature (Yin, 2003:41-6; Miles & Huberman, 1994). See Ratcliff's web pages on Qualitative Research for resources on case labelling and types http://www.don.ratcliffs.net/professional.htm#qual.

68 My label of 'ideal' reflects a delimitation of the topic. As stated earlier, I am not arguing for or against the FBO or the church as the 'best method' for childcare – both are necessary.

and *Mission of Mercy* are 'typical Western funded types', representative of Western FBOs that initiated and funded local programmes, operated largely independent of local church ownership. The eleven cases represent different evangelical denominations (see Table 4.8); most are found in urban contexts. *Ţoar Foundation* is rural, and all are partnering in some capacity with foreign FBOs. This range of case variation was intentional to maximize differences between the groups and to add to the generalization of the data or 'external validity' (Schutt, 2001:197).

Table 4.8 Denominational Affiliations of FBOs

Affiliated with Baptist Union	**Affiliated with Pentecostal/Charismatic**	**Affiliated with Brethren**	**Independent or Interdenominational**
Project Ruth *Bethesda –* Galaţi	*Light and Life* *City of Hope* *New Life – Braşov*	*Ţoar Foundation*	*Mission of Mercy* *Mission w/o Borders* *World Vision* *Word Made Flesh* *Heart of the Child*

Interaction with the cases – impact on both analysis and the researcher

The methods used in this study were fluid not fixed. Field interaction required curiosity, sensitivity to people and places, and analysis requiring sensitivity to the data and learning to 'draw distinctions between literal, interpretive and reflexive readings of the interviews' (Mason, 1996:54). Because of the prolonged nature of the study, my conceptual framework changed, the cases became more decipherable.[69] I discovered there were 'mysteries and contradictions that did not fit into the emerging coding system' (Miles & Huberman 1994:62).

Analysis was 'reflexive' as I was 'drawn into' the case studies and the inner workings of the FBO-church partnerships as they often overlapped with my responsibilities as a mission leader.[70] Analysis required a) development of interviewing skills with study participants, b) critical reflection on my interpretation of the data, and c) interaction with the cases. Earlier, I cited Schön's 'swamp analogy' and as the case studies progressed I refined my role

---

[69] Prolonged study, over several months or years, is one assurance of a degree of internal validity (Schutt, 2001:196). I was not conducting experimental or 'causal research' but the prolonged nature of the fieldwork (4 years) did provide opportunity to modify and test the conceptual framework and analysis.

[70] For instance, I would speak one week in a local evangelical church and afterwards engage the host pastor in conversation about Western FBOs or problems with 'outside' influence. The next week I would be advising an FBO in the study how to work more closely with the churches where they were having difficulty.

as a 'reflective practitioner' working in the 'lowlands'. As a primary research instrument, I noted the changes I experienced in process memos.[71]

Coding and application of GT to case analysis

Since there were two distinct phases of field research, I integrated the findings from Phase One, the categories in Table 4.4, with new codes and categories that emerged in the cases until the data was not contributing any significant new information. This is known as 'theoretical saturation' in GT, 'the categories should be continually tested and revised until they are able to embrace the data accurately' (Strauss & Corbin, 1998:143).[72]

All the case interview transcripts were printed and assembled in large ring notebooks, yielding 300+ pages single-spaced text. Also included were the printed documentation gathered from each project and websites for each case were searched and printed. Interim case summaries or *vignettes* (Miles & Huberman 1994:77-81) were written for eight of the cases.[73] Each notebook was arranged to display one or two cases. Initially I conducted the coding procedure without a computer program as marking up the notes by hand with coloured pens helped me intuitively identify ideas and concepts more readily. I worked through all the transcripts at least twice, following the coding process as axial codes were identified. All codes and categories were written in margin notes.

USE OF ATLAS.TI IN ANALYSIS

As the bulk of data accumulated, I realized a computer program would allow me to better manage the documents and transcripts with easier tracking of codes, related quotes, and cross-case synthesis. All the text documents were later converted to .rtf files and entered into the ATLAS.ti software program (Barry, 1998) in order to develop an analytical code tree.[74]

---

[71] I kept 'process memos' in a number of ways, one of the most helpful was writing and filing emails to research colleagues and comparing what we were learning. I set up folders in MS Outlook to keep these and other memos at the end of the study; I created at least 30 separate folders with hundreds of memos and emails.

[72] The analysis progresses to identification of analytic categories and guiding themes. Coding and recoding are over when this phase of analysis has run it course, or the categories are 'saturated' and sufficient numbers of regularities emerge.

[73] 'A vignette is a focused description of a series of events taken to be representative, typical, or emblematic in the case you are doing. It has a narrative, story-like structure that preserves chronological flow and that normally is limited to a brief time span, to one or a few key actors, to a bounded space, or to all three' (Miles & Huberman, 1994:81).

[74] I brought into ATLAS.ti all the codes that were already marked by hand and used the program to track and label these codes and their associated quotes. ATLAS.ti is extremely flexible; reviews are available online as the product compares with with NUD-IST and NVivo.

EXAMPLES OF CODING

Over 320 open codes were marked in the case transcripts. A *code family* (axial code)[75] would thematically integrate 30 or 40 open codes such as: 'church as community', 'children find safety', 'provides a family', 'we have human resources', and 'children learn of Jesus'. These particular codes were clustered under 'church-based interventions.' I would adjust the categories, linking together concepts and properties cross-checking with other codes and cases. Additional code families were identified to explain the data such as: 'church's use of means to meet needs', 'FBO use of means to meet needs', and 'church's perception of needs'. Table 4.9 illustrates how open codes were integrated into one of the 16 code families. [76]

Table 4.9 Identification of Code Family: 'FBO use of means and interventions'

Examples of open codes from the interview transcripts (taken from a list of 45 open codes)	**Code Family (Axial Code)**
• Offer specialized skills to meet the needs of children • Education, feeding, counselling • Encourage participation of child in project • Specialized workers brings professionalized work • Working through the community as a means to ministry • Christian ethics and social concern • Vision/Calling • Decisions to act are usually analysis based • Volunteer and paid staff are both used • Much more focused on the use of means and structural response	**FBO use of means and interventions to meet needs of children** ↑ **1) Professionalised and structural** **2) Contextual approach** **3) Organizational competencies** →

In this example, 45 open codes were integrated into the three subcategories: professionalism and structural approach, contextual approach, and organizational competencies which in turn became 'FBO *use of means*' to meet needs of children.

---

[75] ATLAS.ti labels axial codes as 'code families'; a term that I feel better embraces the nature of this research. This program allows the researcher to mark quotes and codes first, then return to all codes and merge them into code families.

[76] I should point out that coding is not intended to be perfect science. It relies on the skill and perception of the researcher; the intuition and insight that one brings to the coding process. I do not take it as self-evident that a particular interpretation can be made of this data; rather I have attempted to 'continually and assiduously chart and justify the steps through which the interpretations were made' (Mason, 1996:150).

Cross-Case Synthesis in selective coding

The next step was 'selective coding' or identification of the core categories (Strauss & Corbin, 1998:143-45). In integrating the 16 code families into more analytical themes, I looked for patterns that emerged throughout the cases considered as a whole. This involved a different sort of reflection than working with single cases. I developed new interpretive questions to put to the data; itemized in Table 4.10.

Table 4.10 Interpretive and theoretical questions of case data

1.	How do both the FBOs and churches perceive children? As they talk about meeting their needs or their participation, how do they describe faith, God or the Spirit in providing care for children in these ministries – can I discern 'operative theologies'.
2.	In describing their interventions, what themes can be identified in these areas: spiritual, social, emotional, physical? How do FBOs or churches use social science or child development theories?
3.	Do either the FBO or churches have fresh ways to describe their understanding of faith, theology, and doctrine? Are they just going on past assumptions or established 'confessional assurance'?
4.	In FBO activities to assist churches and local partners are there themes that demonstrate motive for assistance of church-based programmes; do they support training in theology or child studies?

I worked to identify causality, continued searching for variables, relationships, similarities and contradictions between the code families, recording notes in analysis memos.[77] In order to integrate the 16 code families into four selective categories I created a wall mounted visual matrix of the data. Atlas.ti can create 'code family networks,' these were printed and pasted together on large flip charts.

In this manner, all 16 code families were examined with their respective codes, quotations, and case names in one place.[78] Figure 4.6 further illustrates this process where four code families were integrated into the first central category: factors that contribute to how FBOs think and respond to children at risk: 'interventionist and specialized responses', discussed in Chapter 5.

---

[77] This example illustrates my query into financial motivations: 'what is the causality factor of the financial incentive (in the child sponsorship programme) offered by this particular FBO? I am not sure the church would have started the programme on its own if those finances were not available. What other factors might explain why the church or FBO starts a programme; does this show up in other cases where the financial incentives differ (analysis memo, July 2006)?

[78] As a visual learner I found printing and displaying network views on office walls a helpful exercise as it allowed a better visualization of all categories. Using colour pens, code families were clustered into the four central categories.

Figure 4.6 Selective coding illustrated

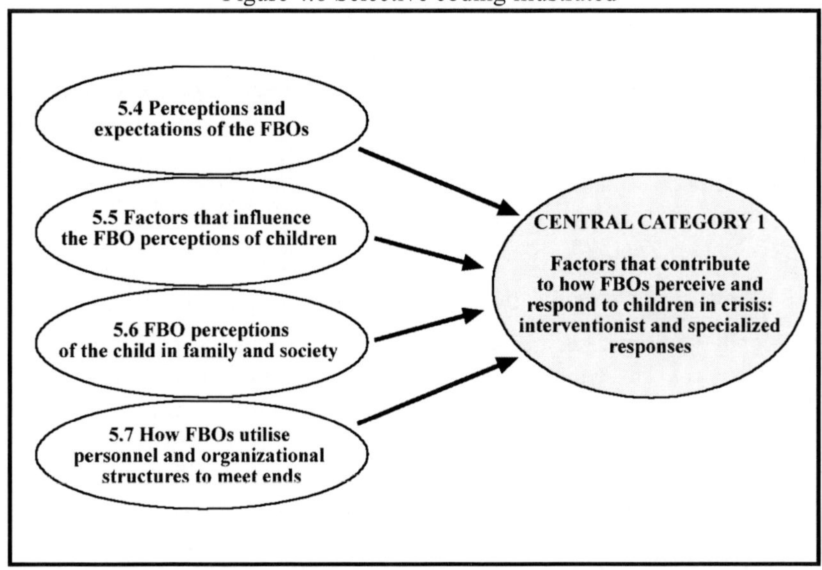

The 16 code families and integrated into four central categories of the study:

1. Factors that contribute to how FBOs perceive and respond to children in crisis: characterized by interventionist and specialized responses.
2. Factors that contribute to how local churches perceive and respond to children in crisis: expressed in embedded communities of faith.
3. Factors that most influence desired outcomes in lives of children: conversion and social concern in tension.
4. Factors that facilitate working in partnership leading to the core category: embracing tensions in partnership for children.

Explanation building as missiological synthesis

The identification of the central categories provided the means to embrace and describe the complexity of elements, properties, categories, and variables that typify the sorts of churches and FBOs that responded to children. The third or final stage of analysis involved a more holistic approach to the cases, beyond simply examining connections between the codes and categories. This is referred to as 'explanation building'[79] and involved a missiological synthesis of the factors that influenced FBO-church collaboration and their responses to children in crisis (Yin, 2003:120).

[79] Explanation building is a type of pattern matching and relevant to explanatory case studies; it is helpful in hypothesis generating process or to develop ideas for further study (Glaser & Strauss, 1967).

Findings of the study were integrated with insights from theology and missiology by theoretically placing a 'child in the midst' of FBO-church partnership. The third phase of research involved a re-examination of the selected categories for evidence (or lack) of integration of eternal concerns for children (from Above) and human and earthly concerns (from Below) which resulted in an analytical critique of 'holistic mission'. This analysis informed the development of the central or core category (Strauss & Corbin, 1998:146)[80] and contributed to revising propositional statements and inductive analysis.

Towards a Central Category of Working Together for Children

A secondary objective of the study was to suggest a core category or 'theory' generated from the data that would enable closer cooperation of FBOs and churches in delivery of care for children. In an effort to define 'efficacy in partnership' I induced that FBO-church collaboration was best described as a combination of 'missional tensions'. A heuristic lens illustrates the core category, which is labelled: 'embracing tensions in partnership for children' (Figure 4.7).

Figure 4.7 Embracing tensions in FBO-Church partnership for children

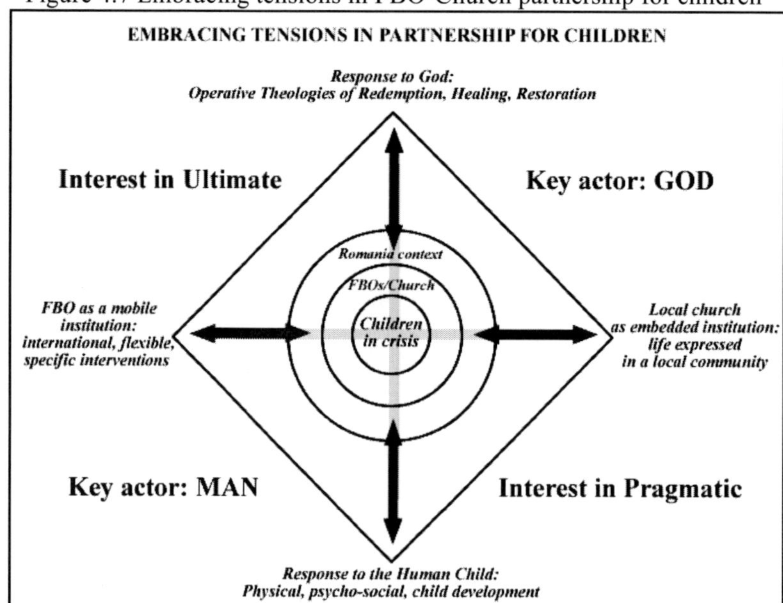

[80] The core category should represent the main theme of the research describing what the research is 'all about'.

The core category is further explained as: delivery of faith-based care for children in crisis requires embracing tension and demonstrating meaningful integration of eternal concerns (response to God) with human concerns (physical, psycho-social, structural). Care for children may be expressed through embedded local communities and specialized FBOs. Children in crisis serve as a theological and missiological pointer. The core category assumes that there are many valid childcare interventions, projects, methods of collaboration, and ways of sharing Christ's love with suffering children. Using the core category and heuristic lens, I shifted the analysis from examining the specific factors contributing to partnership to examining theological assumptions that had been largely unexamined by either FBO or church. The elements that led to the central category are explicated in the chapters that follow.

Summary

The methods described in this chapter were followed to describe and analyze complex socially embedded phenomena and to answer the question: What factors have enabled or hindered partnership FBOs with Romanian evangelical churches in reference to children in crisis? The methodology was primarily qualitative and employed a 'mixed-method' approach carried out in two phases, 116 individuals from churches and FBO were interviewed. Phase One was conducted as exploratory research, 22 churches and 35 FBOs were visited in a preliminary survey that provided data for case selection criteria. Eleven cases were studied in Phase Two, 33 semi-structured interviews provided additional data for analysis.

The research relied on participant-observer methodology as it was determined 'getting close' to research participants was critical to data generation and collection. Limitations and strengths to qualitative research were noted in the chapter. I do not take it as self-evident that only one interpretation can be made of this data, rather I have attempted to 'continually and assiduously chart and justify the steps through which the interpretations were made' (Mason, 1996:150). Social science methods such as grounded theory and case study were integrated with theological and missiological analysis. The research methodology served as an example of integration of 'from above and from below' (Loder, 1999:7-12).[81]

---

[81] Loder's methodological paradigm described by Loder as 'from above and from below'. 'From below' means from the standpoint of human science and experience and 'from above' means from the 'standpoint of God's self-revelation in Jesus Christ in whom it is disclosed what God means by humanity in relationship to what God means by God' (1998:4).

Chapter 5

Factors that Influence How FBOs Respond to Children in Crisis

Introduction

FBOs were analysed as one side of the partnership equation. This chapter examines the factors that contribute to how FBOs perceive and respond to children in crisis, characterized as interventionist and specialized responses. I also answer a secondary question: what were the expectations of the Western FBOs of Romanian churches when they came to work with children? FBO expectations are integral to understanding factors shaping partnership with churches. To introduce the discussion, two phases of activity are described that created a new FBO sector in the 1990s. This is followed by perceptions and expectations that FBOs hold of local churches and communities where they serve, factors that influence FBO perceptions of children in crisis, FBO theological and developmental perspectives, and how FBOs utilize personnel, and organizational structures to meet ends.[1]

The Creation of a New FBO Sector in Romania

Two distinct periods of time were identified that shaped the engagement of FBOs with children and churches. The first, 1990-1996, was characterized by 'reactive, crisis-oriented international interventions' (Dickens & Groza, 2004:470), largely unregulated and at times chaotic. Financial and human resources to assist children were poured into Romania with inadequate understanding of long-term outcomes or cooperation between FBOs and NGOs.[2] Interviews with FBOs indicated that most worked independently of one another and pursued individual agendas. Marginal FBO effort went towards rebuilding a sense of responsibility for children local churches or though the extended families. Evangelical FBO activity may be interpreted as a

---

[1] FBOs in this study were directed by both Western and Romanian men and women. All the cases have connections with funding partners in the West.

[2] For a historical and contemporary analysis of the Romanian nonprofit sector see Saulean & Epure (1998:2-10). The non-profit (NGO and FBO) sector was revived after the collapse of communism. The authors define the nonprofit sector as consisting of 'a network of diverse organizations'. The structure of this network can be captured through a set of criteria, as put forward with a 'structural-operational' definition consisting of five components: organized, private, self-governed, non-profit distributing, and voluntary (Saulean & Epure, 1998:12).

subset of the overall NGO response to the childcare crisis described in Chapter 3.

Legal issues and FBOs

Romanian laws in the early 1990s were unclear as to the exact ways in which foreigners could own property or register foundations. FBOs began operating in a country that had experienced five decades of state control restricting civil society and virtually forbidding voluntary associations (Saulean & Epure, 1998:6-9).[3] After 1990, repressive state legislation was in many ways replaced by corrupt authorities; crime rates rose as consumer capitalism coexisted with state socialism. Mafia-like structures replaced the once-feared *Securitate* – creating a sense of societal anomie. One description of the social context that emerged in Central and Eastern European countries was, 'post-communist society is an example of post-modernism in the raw' (Bretherton, 1996:2).[4]

Interviews were conducted with Romanian legal specialists who assisted Western FBOs with official registration in the early 1990s. Existing laws, still in effect from 1924 and 1973, had not anticipated the incursion of foreign agencies. The National Department of Child Protection (DCP) was begun in 1993, and laws to regulate foreign adoption were not passed until 1997 (Ordinance Nr. 25 and 26).[5] As FBOs came to 'reach or help children', an unintended outcome was the creation of a new FBO sector, largely independent and unsupported by local evangelical churches. Trained first as a lawyer, a Romanian FBO director working with street children in Bucharest described how FBOs went about this process.

> The early 1990s was a time when there was a legal vacuum in Romania. Work could be done with the city hall but child protection schemes were not clearly defined. In the early 1990s local churches did not have what we call *a juridical personality*. The local churches got their legal standing through their relationship with the recognized cults [Baptist, Pentecostal, and Brethren]. Local churches could not purchase facilities or get official approval for childcare projects. The churches were not forbidden by the government to work in their own buildings but they were not prepared financially or legally to operate

[3] Romanian civil society had been gaining strength in the interwar period (1918-1938) with support of the French who helped Romania put in place new legal frameworks for voluntary and civic organizations. The communist period was a 'step backward in Romanian civil society and the voluntary associative movement in general' (Saulean & Epure, 1998:9).

[4] FBO leaders who came to Romania in 1990-1991, many with years of international experience, said that dealing with Romanian civil society was an exercise in frustration: corruption was endemic, bureaucracy was like a 'negotiating a twilight labyrinth' (FBOL#3, 2003).

[5] The fact that it took Romanian civil society seven years to adopt these laws was due in part to the substantial income derived from adoptions that went to government officials who oversaw the process.

> projects – nor did they have a great interest in doing this. The focus for most was to find donations to support the local church. Westerners assumed it would be easier to register new foundations to care for these children (FBOL#9, 2004).

Laws did not prohibit FBOs from working directly with churches; it seemed more expedient for a foreign FBO to work unilaterally to register a foundation or association.[6] FBOs were required to register foundations to deliver social services. They sought advice, some helpful and some untrustworthy, from Romanian lawyers, civil authorities, and evangelicals from local churches.[7] As an immediate consequence most local churches and pastors were bypassed, Western FBOs registered local affiliates who remained accountable to Western donors and foreign sponsoring organizations.[8]

Early indications of partnership tensions

Misunderstandings began to surface in the early 1990s. Church and FBO cooperation concerning childcare at that time was reported as problematic with FBOs recording little documentary evidence.[9] One could ask why the Romanian church should seek a partnership with a foreign FBO or, why the FBO should work with the church? Bunaciu made this observation concerning ‘unhealthy partnership dependencies’.

> Before the revolution, we had Western guests visit our churches who knew we were a persecuted church. These pastors and guests would tell us that they could see that the Lord was with us and that he was keeping us faithful and strong. After the revolution some of these same guests must have felt that since freedom had come we needed material help from the West. I think this has weakened our

---

[6] According to the law, an *association* ‘is a convention through which several persons put in common, on a permanent basis, their material contributions, their knowledge and their activities, in order to achieve a goal with no pecuniary or patrimonial benefits.’ By contrast, a *foundation* is defined as ‘an act by which an individual or a legal person makes up a patrimony, distinct and autonomous from his own and devotes it, generally on a permanent basis, to the achievement of an ideal public interest purpose’ (Saulean & Epure, 1998: 6).

[7] Whether the international FBOs understood the implications of this action or were simply taking the quickest route to establishing a local office is open to interpretation. The ‘haste to begin something’ added to the general sense of discontinuity that surrounded the evangelical churches.

[8] I will return to this topic in Chapter 8 under ‘*religious opportunism*’ on behalf of FBOs and local advisors.

[9] Phase One interview transcripts contained many anecdotal accounts of such problems, when asked to produce written documents or analysis none were provided. Obviously, promotional literature edits out misunderstandings between partners.

> churches spiritually as now we are looking more to our Western friends than we are to the Lord for our financial needs (personal interview, 2004). [10]

Romanian church leaders (Mănăstireanu 1998a: 1998b; Taloş 1997; Bunaciu, 1999; Negruţ 1999b) critiqued the influx of FBOs appealing for evaluation of the evolving situation. Ţon (1993) described cross-cultural problems in partnership. Some Western observers noted that church growth statistics were influential, as the press for 'numerical growth' fed the rationale to begin more projects (Downes, 2001:40). Evidence is inconclusive but similar factors may have shaped reports on the numbers of children being brought into FBO projects.

Volf provided an appraisal of the tensions between Western and Eastern ways of evangelism that was reflected in FBO delivery of care to children.

> A good way to describe the situation in Eastern Europe today is to say that yesterday's dreams have turned into today's nightmares. This holds true not only in politics and economy but also in church life. One need not be an expert in Eastern European Christianity to know that at the very centre of the religious turmoil are the issues of mission and proselytism (1996b:28).[11]

In Chapter 2, I addressed missional assumptions of Western FBOs noting that many Western personnel had acquired some level of missiological competence prior to coming to Romania. As tensions escalated, it was not clear how the Western FBOs went about establishing dialogue with local partners. This led LeBreche, a veteran missionary in Timişoara, to design a doctoral research project to understand ethnocentrism and cross-cultural value conflict between Romanian and American missionaries (2007).[12]

Limited reflection on the place of the child in FBO expansion

Few Romanian or Western analysts dealt specifically with the question of how children might inform missiological or theological discussions. This omission seems unusual given that many Western FBOs came to assist children and youth in the 1990s.[13] I held an assumption in early research that FBOs had a

---

[10] Bunaciu also said that it had become common in some churches to refer jokingly to the 'fifth gospel' i.e. 'the gospel according to the sponsor' or the new golden rule, 'he who has the gold rules' (Interview, 2004).

[11] Volf goes on to analyse the 'problem' in his article, 'One way to put it is to say that what Protestants (mainly of the evangelical kind) consider to be [objects of] legitimate mission Catholics and Orthodox (whom I will refer to as established churches) consider to be illegitimate and culturally damaging proselytism' (1996b:29). The issues Volf is addressing became especially contentious when allegations emerged that FBOs and churches were proselytizing children.

[12] LaBreche's thesis, *Ethnocentrism and American Evangelical Missions in Romania: Research into Cross Cultural Value Conflict and its Causes* (2007) investigates tensions between Romania church leaders and American missionaries.

[13] I reviewed 86 FBO promotional pieces produced for fund raising. For comparison and

predisposition towards action and pragmatic[14] intervention based on the four missional assumptions described in Chapter 2. The child was an object of mission but not a significant point for missiological reflection. The perceived needs of children were such that dozens of projects were started with little field research. FBOs came, as one interviewee said, ‘like a foreign invasion force’ (FBOL#47, 2004).[15]

The second period of FBO work, 1997-2004, was marked by more nuanced discussions of international partnerships. Some disillusionment and cynicism between FBOs and local partners remained. This was mitigated by maturation and self-examination on both sides. The positive findings are largely a reflection of this latter period. By the end of the 1990s, with the help of USAID, a network of NGOs, FBOs, and private volunteer organizations was established called *ProChild Romania*. The original agenda of ProChild was to create a forum for the foundations to discuss issues central to their mutual concern for the well being of children.[16] The president and several of the founding members were from FBOs. According to one individual, over time the agenda of the meetings changed from talking about programmatic responses to how ProChild could work as an advocacy forum to speak on behalf of children to the Romanian government. Divisions arose in the meetings and the founding president resigned as he felt the ‘original agenda was being skewed by secular NGOs’ (FBOL#16).[17]

Central Category 1 – Factors That Contribute to how FBOs Think and Respond to Children in Crisis

The remainder of this chapter integrates findings and analysis that led to identification of Central Category I summarized in the statement: *interventionist organizations and specialized responses*. The axial categories

---

analysis of the parallel situation in Russia during this time frame see Penner (2003), Elliott (1996), Ham (1996), and Harris (2000).

[14] I use ‘pragmatic’ here to mean ‘a practical, matter-of-fact way of assessing situations or solving problems’ rather than the technical philosophical sense.

[15] As of this writing (2010), the situation has improved; World Vision and OCI stand out as examples of Western FBOs doing research on the needs of Romania evangelicals and children.

[16] The organization was founded to bring together American child welfare organizations with Romanian NGOs. USAID facilitated the first meetings to help find ways that NGOs and Private Volunteer Organizations could cooperate with the Romanian government. It is no longer active.

[17] The ProChild narrative reflects some the realties faced by FBOs in dialogue with NGOs. The FBOs were concerned for faith, children, advocacy, and social care, and some of them had tried to involve local churches in the meetings. However the network did not have a clear role for the ‘faith-based’ sector and conflicts emerged concerning the role of *faith* in the public sector.

were derived using cross-case analysis and grounded theory; (Figure 5.1) and used as section headings in the text. Comments from interviews with FBO leaders and Romanian pastors inform the discussion as they elucidate perceptions and expectations both of and from FBOs.

Figure 5.1 Central Category 1 – Factors that shape FBO response to children

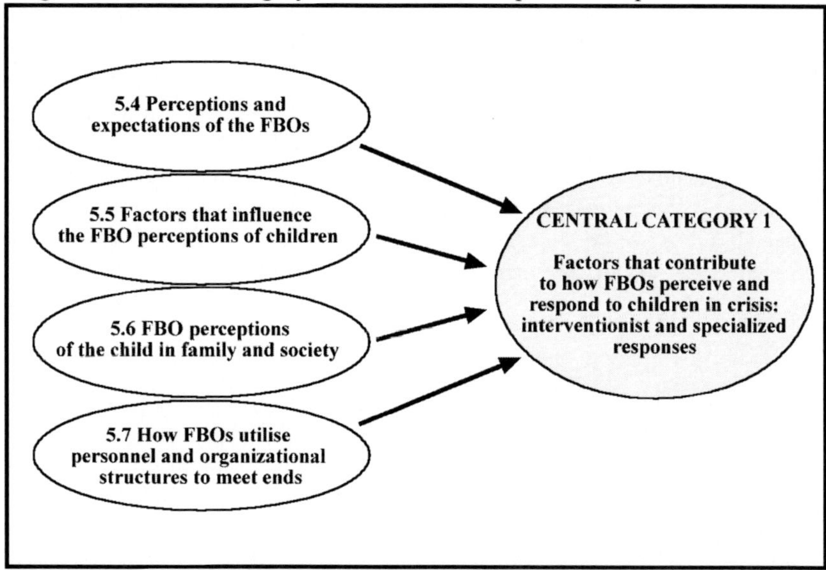

Unless otherwise stated, the term 'FBO' is used specifically to refer to those FBOs that participated in this study and 'church and churches' refers to those churches working with the cases either in partnership or close proximity. Table 5.1 provides the abbreviations of the cases used in the text.

Table 5.1 Cases and abbreviations used in the text

Name	Project Locations	Abbreviation
World Vision Romania	National – 20 counties	*WV Ro*
Mission of Mercy	Pitesti and Bucharest	*MoM*
City of Hope Foundation	Bucharest	*CoH*
Light and Life Foundation	Bucharest and Gradestea	*L&L*
Project Ruth Foundation	Bucharest, Rosiori de Vede	*Ruth*
Mission Without Borders	Sibiu and Transylvania	*MWB*
Ţoar Foundation	Sibiu County	*Ţoar*
Centre for New Life (Asociatia Centrul Vietii Noi)	Braşov County	*ACVN*

Heart of the Child (Inima de Copii)	Galaţi	*IDC*
Word Made Flesh	Galaţi	*WMF*
Bethesda Foundation	Galaţi	*BF*

Perceptions and Expectations of the FBOs

The findings demonstrate that Western FBOs had operational and organizational ends in mind and their missional assumptions[18] were not always congruent with Romanian evangelical subculture. Three assumptions are examined below: a) that children in crisis deserved church care and attention, b) that local evangelicals would be willing to partner with the FBOs, and c) that local churches would take up the FBO agenda. For a data display of this problem see Appendix C (pending final edit).

FBOs expectations of Romanian churches

FBOs leaders stated that in the early 1990s, the churches were either not able or unwilling to work directly with children in crisis. FBOs listed as contributing factors, 'local churches lacked capacity in resources, training and finances', 'they were inundated by the needs of their own members and families', 'were not interested', or did not feel that the children in crisis 'were their immediate priorities' (FBOL#5,#10, 2004). A Baptist professor explained the lack of training in their faculty and noted that 'social work' was not a priority.

> Most pastors don't have the knowledge or skills to do technical social work; they lack ability and theory. This sort of training was never provided to the church or universities under communism and it is still not included [2003] at our Faculty as part of theological training. Our seminary separates the two, theology and sociology are seen as different subjects, they are not integrated (I #3, 2003).

To operate projects, FBOs from the West needed facilities, appropriate staff, church partners, or local collaborators. Newly arriving FBOs with limited knowledge of the local context held untested expectations of the churches such as: willingness to send volunteers, provide funds, and take moral ownership of new projects. When expectations originated in a Western 'home office' unfamiliar with the local situation, they caused dissonance for local staff and directors.

> Our home office didn't really understand what was needed in Romania, they expected that we could find funding for the children but it was not available in

---

[18] Since cases were selected to represent a cross-section of FBOs, their missional assumptions are varied. For instance *WV Ro* has a high commitment to 'holistic mission' as described in Chapter 2, whereas, a church-based FBO like *Ruth* had a higher commitment to 'church growth'.

> local churches. We are willing to do our part but their expectations of us were not realistic, they did not understand the economic reality here (FBOL#18, 2004).

Since local churches were hesitant to offer volunteers, Western FBOs began to hire the best people they could to work in their projects.[19] Occasionally, potential employees were referred to the agencies from local churches. In other cases, they responded to advertising, or they met children on the streets and responded on their own initiative. FBOs began foundations as organizational vehicles for childcare in the absence of a functioning evangelical social service sector. Two Western FBO directors stated that local churches would 'not assume the task of caring for children who were not already attending those churches'. A Romanian working with Roma children in Oradea explained that foreign FBOs did not take the time needed to understand the local situation.

> Many evangelical churches are made up of poorer and undereducated people [certainly not all]. It was amusing to me that the Western agencies were seeking help from the local churches. Romanian churches were crowded with our own families and children, many with more than 5-6 children. It seemed unfair that the Western agencies would have asked our churches to help them in caring for street [and institutionalized] children. After all, the Western churches had much more money than we did and they came here to help the street children (FBOL#20, 2003).

I take up the case of the church's perception of FBOs and children in the next chapter as it further illuminates this dissonance. Six cases demonstrate more realistic expectations of churches based on experience or persistence in dialogue and relationship building; they are examined below.

FBO perceptions of local pastors as gatekeepers

In Phase One interviews, both Romanian and Western participants suggested that I not ask the question, how does a FBO work with a local church? 'This is the wrong question to ask. You should ask how the FBO *works with the pastor*' (FBOL#11, 2004). A Romanian FBO leader took this to another level, 'I believe that many pastors would prefer to shut down everything that they cannot control, or at least refuse to be involved in the work' (FBOL#10, 2004). Romanian pastors are extremely busy people; it is common for a pastor to be responsible for eight or nine churches simultaneously, overseeing elders and deacons, who are personally accountable to the senior pastor. The 'pastor as gatekeeper' influenced perceptions and actions of Western and Romanian

---

[19] The term *volunteer* was used repeatedly in interviews with leaders of Western FBOs as in, 'it was difficult to find people to volunteer.' Romanians explained that this term had very negative connotations left over from the communist era where people were expected to 'volunteer' for the state that was a euphemism for 'being assigned or conscripted to a task for the regime'.

leaders of FBOs.[20] A Romanian working with street children was frustrated with what he termed 'authoritarian pastors'. He made this comment:

> These authoritarian pastors are one reason that I do not work closely with Romanian churches. The programme we are doing with street children would need to be under his control and we don't want that. I want the programme to be led by our staff who know the children on the streets (FBOL#12, 2004).

This was not an isolated finding; misunderstandings with local pastors came up in 60 per cent of FBO interviews. The use of authority in FBO-church partnerships was treated as a factor in analysis, that is, hierarchical church leadership contributed to partnership tensions (Heuser, 1999:139-40). Noting that many young adults from local churches were working in the FBOs, I inquired why pastors allowed them to work with outside agencies. A Western FBO director offered this explanation.

> The pastors want to build patron-client type relationships; if [church] young people are working with a foundation, salaries and financial help will eventually come back into the church. Also there is an information gap, and we live in a society of distrust. By placing someone *inside* a foundation they might learn what they are doing (FBOL # 37, 2004).

This response indicates how suspicion influenced partnership; FBO leaders could become as suspicious as their church counterparts. *WMF* sought to cooperate with local pastors in Galaţi, demonstrating a willingness to work within limitations while at the same advocating change on an incremental scale (Schein, 1997:305-306).[21]

> We believe in building our ministry from the 'bottom up not from the top down,' we want to be as close as possible to the children and community. Strong pastors who are the primary decision makers lead many churches here; they usually control what is going on in the church. Our approach is to become active members in local churches, as we earn the trust of the pastor; we invite him to see what we are doing. Our staff and volunteers come from the churches with the pastor's blessing (FBOL#60, 2005).

If we allow that FBOs encountered 'gatekeepers', eight cases decided it was in their interest to cooperate with the pastors and churches, the remainder felt that working independent of the church was more 'effective'. Only one case

---

[20] I acknowledge that 'pastoral control' occurs in many evangelical churches; there are pastors in the West who fit this description. Pastors as 'gatekeepers' will be addressed in Chapter 8 after considering the Romanian church perceptions in Chapter 6.

[21] Schein notes that if younger organizations are not under too much external stress, the culture of the organization evolves in small increments by continuing to assimilate what works best over the years. 'Such evolution involves two basic processes: general evolution and specific evolution (1997:305).

(*WMF*) gave evidence of intentional theological reflection on spiritual authority, citing Phil 2:5-14 (FBOL#60, 2006).[22]

Which children most deserved FBO assistance

Western FBOs emerged in an evangelical subculture deeply influenced by outcomes of modernity, that is, secular science aids in finding solutions for social problems and provides categories of rational certainty (Seel, 1994:291-92). As described in Chapter 2, contemporary Western constructions of 'child and childhood' bring together Christian, secular, humanist, romantic, scientific, and developmentalist paradigms in a puzzling matrix – ascribing moral and individual worth to children as an outcome of their humanity.[23] It is sometimes convenient to forget that not many years ago children in the West were suffering from abuse in workhouses and forced labour in factories (Cunningham, 2005:140-53).[24]

FBOs focused their attention on the most traumatized children in the institutions and on the streets, believing that the conditions for children called for rapid and specific interventions. They offered psychosocial, physical, and spiritual assistance stating this was 'in the best interest of the children'. A review of FBO mission statements and internal documentation revealed mixed theological and organizational motives. Four FBOs questioned the local church's lack of response; one went so far as to say that the local churches were 'unsympathetic' to children on the streets.[25] Five FBOs said pastors wanted assistance for children in their churches before they would agree to help children on the 'outside'.

---

[22] Spiritual in this reference is within a Christian and evangelical framework. In the remainder of this chapter, the word 'spiritual' is a theological category, reflecting Christianity's affirmation of a world of spirit/Spirit, in which God's eternal Word coexists with a material world (Jn. 1:1-3).

[23] Cunningham (2005) examines how these diverse threads of discourse have shaped our modern views of children. He analyzes the Western construction of 'childhood' within both the private and public spheres of life, arguing that beyond the influence of family and intimate human relationships, 'childhood belongs to public life, both in the sense that public policies toward children were articulated and often implemented, and in the sense that childhood played a part in economic, social, and political life of communities' (2005:202).

[24] Historical evidence shows that children were often treated badly or cruelly (by today's standards) based on what was taken at the time to be good social and economic science.

[25] I refer in this sentence to a case that asked they not be named. One FBO leader went so far to say that Romanian pastors were guilty of 'sinning against God' in their attitudes toward street children (FBOL # 32, 2005).

DOES THE DICHOTOMY ENCOURAGE REFLECTION ON FAITH?

This argument, comparing children in the churches with those outside, indicated a dichotomist and distrustful approach, doing little to encourage faith-based dialogue concerning 'who deserves FBO care'. It is evidence, in my view, of a Western evangelical 'myopia' concerning the *child in the midst* (Matt. 18:1-3) in light of the kingdom of God (White & Willmer, 2006). It might have been more helpful to ask, 'how does the child in crisis act as a *pointer* or sign to both church and FBO?' I will raise this question at several points in this book, as I argue the *child in the midst* offers a point of reflection for missional practice.[26]

Working with children in trauma is a long-term restorative process, with limited guarantees of success or certainty of outcomes. This either/or approach was a minority opinion and these cases demonstrated scarce effort to research or understand Romanian evangelical perceptions concerning children. The comments indicate a weak understanding of the 'body of Christ' where the bond of peace calls for unity (Eph. 4:2-6) where the stronger can learn from the weak (Rom. 14:1-2).[27] Some FBOs failed to appreciate that the local churches had a 'working knowledge' of the context that the newly arriving FBOs did not. Local pastors understood their church adherents; they also knew firsthand that street children could be dangerous, unpredictable, and required more care than they could realistically provide.[28] FBO expectations to provide rapid intervention and resultant misunderstanding indicated a lack of: listening, theological dialogue, and 'organizational learning' (Britton, 2005:11).[29]

ALTERNATIVE EXPECTATIONS FROM FBOS TOWARDS CHURCHES

A more hopeful example of FBO expectations of the church came from a FBO working with children living in the institutions.

> Western agencies arriving in the early 90's needed to understand that most local churches lacked the capacity to get involved with the most trumatised children. Churches were struggling to find the resources to take care of their own children

---

[26] In Chapter 8, I further develop this metaphor, as the child serves as *a theological pointer* in the central category of this study.

[27] See Sugden (1997b:28-9), children at risk are the focus in this issue of *Transformation*, Sugden argues that partnership in Christian mission is not a matter of pragmatism but the nature of theological reality concerning God's call to the church.

[28] The discussion in the text is drawn from four specific cases. Eleven FBO Western leaders in Phase One reflected similar attitudes; these expectations were evidence that 'managerial missiology' (Chapter 2) was a contributing factor - versus listening to children, listening to partners, or listening to the Biblical text.

[29] Britton points out that partnership can be interpreted to be 'coercion under a different name', but it also can also mean participation, shared ownership, and capacity building. Partnership provides an important setting for organizational learning, defined as: 'individual and collective learning in an organization context that results in changed organizational behaviour' (2005:56).

> and it was only reasonable that they would be concerned for their members and families (FBOL #3, 2003).

A list of terms generated from interview data to summarize FBO expectations from local churches ranged from pessimistic – 'the church is ecclesio-centric' [focused on the church to exclusion of the community], 'not responding seriously to the needs of abused people and children', 'too concerned about getting people saved', 'they just want to start more churches',' tend to discriminate against street children and gypsies' – to positive – 'the church is the best place to bring children who need restoration', 'demonstrates great compassion for children in need', 'God's family can provide the security and safety the children need'. Eight of the selected cases were committed to working with churches, as one FBO director observed, 'what churches lacks is experience – not concern and love for suffering children' (FBO#23, 2005).

This range of FBO perceptions was traced to the presence or absence of several factors: prior experience in Romanian evangelical churches, sensitivity to wider theological resources, willingness to set aside agendas in order to listen to one another, willingness to examine FBO assumptions and perceptions, intentional research on the issues at hand, and commitment to working through difficulty in partnership (Sookhdeo, 1994:53-4; McKaughan, 1994:74-5).[30]

Expectations of FBOs to provide assistance in social work

The 11 cases demonstrated a range of collaboration strategies with local churches and Romanian childcare authorities. All FBOs registered with the local Department of Child Protection (DCP). Three of the cases (*BF*, *CoH*, and *ACVN*) began their work with minimal research; the founders of these FBOs described 'a definite call to work with children'. *WV Ro* and *MWB* were working in the country prior to the revolution and demonstrated a more informed understanding of the chaotic social service sector that emerged following 1990.[31]

All cases described expectations of financial, material, or social service assistance from Romanian churches. This was more prevalent in the early 1990s when optimism for radical change was high and many held expectations

[30] Cross-cultural partnership requires relationships that 'are entered into and maintained, adapt to changing situations, will give and receive, involve mutual accountability, are open to correction, and face the explicit weaknesses of each other' (Sookhdeo, 1994:54).

[31] WV Ro has the largest financial, institutional, and organizational resources of any FBO in Romania.

that NGOs and FBOs would resolve the myriad of problems associated with children in crisis.[32] This comment is typical:

> In our experience, Romanians had the idea that Western money and assistance would be able to solve most of the social problems. This attitude is still prevalent but not to the same extent as it was in the early 1990s, reality has set in (LFBO #10, 2004).[33]

It was evident that church expectations of assistance were met to some degree by FBOs willingness to intervene (Dickens & Groza, 2004). Three cases said they made little assessment if FBO activity would 'disempower' the initative of local churches.

UNREALISTIC EXPECTATIONS LEAD TO DIVISION OF LABOUR

The perception that foreign FBO and NGO intervention could quickly resolve social problems set up idealistic and unrealistic expectations creating a division of labour between churches and FBOs. A pastor made this remark about FBOs in his city: 'The Western agencies have the expertise and resources to *fix* the problems [for children], and they know what should be done, we should let them handle this' (Pas#3, 2004). This pastor's comment implies that 'problem children' were perceived as someone else's problem, namely the FBO's.

I label this 'unrealistic' as the problems associated with children are never '*fixed*' in totality; even when brought through a restoration process, children will still act and live as fallible human beings. They can be cared for and counselled, but resolving the larger structural or societal problems that affect children often results in partial success in the short-term. FBO leaders did not differentiate expectations for change in the short-term versus long-term as applicable to 'transformation'.[34] Obviously, children change, but they live their lives experiencing change as a constant, demonstrating the 'transitory' nature their humanity. Children in all times need adult care, love, and protection.

Depending on their willingness and resources, FBOs provided social assistance setting up a pattern of dependency on Western resources (Araujo, 1994:119).[35] A more measured FBO response would have required less action

---

[32] Marius Radu, a political historian, made a similar comment concerning the changes in post-communist Romania: '... we developed an attitude of servitude under the communists, leading to asking for things all the time. This coupled with the paternalism of the Party led to a lack of personal and societal initiative that was carried over into our unrealistic expectations of Western partners' (personal conversation, 2003).

[33] After an initial period of high expectations for change in the early 1990s, cynicism became more prevalent in the general population. Ex-members of the communist party controlled the first elected government after the revolution.

[34] See Chapter 7 for interrogation of the terms 'transformation' and 'holistic' as used by the FBOs. .

[35] The number of FBOs is one indictor; fifteen FBOs listed church financial dependence as a 'hindrance' to their efforts to mobilise churches – only three acknowledged that the FBOs might have some responsibility for this situation.

at the onset, possibly providing space and time for theological and missiological reflection with local partners (Vencer, 1994:101-10).[36] Activist and pragmatist agendas were normative for the selected cases. Most local churches continued to see the child in crisis as a 'non-church' issue and went on coping with their own internal problems, content to let the FBOs carry on with their agendas. The perceived FBO-church division of labour did not provide opportunity for 'shared organizational learning' (Britton, 2005:13).[37]

POSITIVE OUTCOMES FROM FBO SOCIAL ASSISTANCE

FBOs developed a range of social assistance responses that went beyond their projects. *MWB* trained local DCP personnel, for many this was their first formal training in child social assistance. *WV Ro* organized national conferences to bring churches, FBOs, and NGOs together to discuss needs of children in Romanian society (2000).[38] Other FBOs offered collaborative models of care for institutionalised children and poorer church families. *MWB* expressed awareness for the concerns of church partners.

> As an FBO we have to be reliable, especially when we are asking the church to get involved and we put the church name or people into a project. Remember if something goes wrong with the [DCP] authorities, the church is still going to be there if the FBO leaves the area. The church is rooted in a community; it has to take responsibility if the FBO creates moral or financial problems (FBOL#70, 2006).

CoH, *MoM*, and *BF* set up independent social service programmes: street drop-in centres and homes for homeless boys and girls. *Ţoar Foundation* enlisted local Brethren churches to take children from institutions into church member's homes.[39] Expectations of social assistance were discussed in committee meetings and agreements were made that included input from FBO, local church, families, and children demonstrating models of communication that included the concerned constituencies (Butler, 1994:22-3).

---

[36] Vencer describes how problems emerge when mission agencies start programmes or systems that are too expensive for the local partner to eventually take over. He calls this a 'misuse of infrastructures' (1994:107).

[37] See Senge *et al.*, (1994) on the 'learning organization'. Britton describes how some organizations 'consider learning as something not to be encouraged but more like a crime' (2005:13).

[38] These first conferences were held in 1993 and 1995. Then in 2000, WV Romania organized two major follow-up conferences, targeting all Christian churches: Orthodox, Catholic, Reformed, Lutheran, Evangelical, Adventist etc. (1) In June 15-16, 2000, the conference, 'Following Christ in Everyday Life' was held at the Palace of the Parliament with more than 1000 participants. (2) In November 6-9, 2000, in Iaşi, a similar conference was held and over 700 participants from all Christian churches attended.

[39] *Ţoar Foundation* had a longstanding relationship with Child Evangelism Fellowship, an American organization that has worked in Eastern Europe prior to the 1990s.

Community and DCP perceptions of the FBO

The local community generally held FBOs in positive esteem. Positive perceptions were evidenced by newspaper reports, recognition from civic and health officials, and DCP.[40] The FBOs were responsible for establishing protocols with the local child protection offices.

> Our agency has a good working relationship with the community and childcare authorities [DCP]. We have been recognized for providing professional services; the city hall gave us the use of our current location to use for the next three years (FBOL#25, 2006).

IDC was recognized for service to 1000+ children in Galaţi in national social service publications. Curtis used *IDC* as a primary case study concerning the public discourse surrounding the institutional child and NGOs (2004). *WV Ro* brought medical doctors and psychologists to provide training for national DCP staff. 'We began offering training to DCP in 1997 as they were very under resourced; this helped us build our credibility with the government and community' (FBOL# 70, 2004). Public child welfare institutions continued to be under resourced into the late 1990s. FBOs engaged in rebuilding social service capacity by assisting local service providers.[41]

> Our staff and volunteers have an influence on the ethics and practice of staff at the institutions. The state employees at the orphanages often comment that we seem very committed to these children. The staff of state orphanages are underpaid and under trained; they usually don't take these jobs because they have a desire to care for the children, they just need the work (FBOS#10, 2006).

Interviews with DCP employees confirmed that evangelical volunteers were kind to the children at the institutions, 'we have learned by observing their actions and are impressed by their commitment' (I#4, 2004). This finding indicates a positive reversal to reports from Western academics who visited the institutions in the early 1990s and cited negligence of children (Groza *et al.*, 1999:14-16). FBOs deserve recognition for service provided to DCP and demonstrating Christian social concern. The question still remains: 'what factors hindered or enabled FBOs to engage the church in this process?'

Not all community perceptions of the FBOs were positive. Three cases experienced opposition from the local leadership of the Orthodox Church based on suspicion that evangelicals were using childcare projects as a cover for

[40] I interviewed civic officials connected to six of the eleven cases, newspaper and public sources were considered as supporting documentary evidence. Three of the FBOs did not have a strong relationship with DCP in their region. Reasons given for this were: DCP did not want to work with evangelicals, corruption in DCP, and local civic relationships were not as important as caring for children in crisis.

[41] Terms like social service capacity, stakeholder interest, and capacity building, while common in the literature, were not normally used by FBO personnel in the interviews (*WV Ro* was the exception). I use these terms as they are applied in social science literature (Eade, 1997; Johnson & Ludema, 1997).

proselytizing minors.[42] Evangelical – Orthodox tension is associated with geography; cases in Galaţi, Bucharest, and Southeastern Romania reported more opposition than the projects in Transylvania.

> Because we are associated with an evangelical church, the Orthodox priests have preached on several occasions against us. Unfortunately we have learned that many people are opposed to us, not because of the work we are doing for the children, but because we are evangelicals (FBOL #62, 2005).

Also cited were occasional problems with local DPC officials, usually from the refusal of the FBO to pay bribes or offer gifts.[43] Corruption was listed as one of three primary hindrances to FBO delivery of care in the initial survey from Phase One.[44]

Factors that Influence FBO Perceptions of Children in Crisis

Four categories were identified as specific factors influencing FBO perception of the child in crisis: recognition of the specific psycho-social, educational, physical needs of children; effectiveness in delivery of interventions; donor perceptions of the FBOs; and perception of contextual needs. These subcategories inform how needs were assessed and criteria used to respond to them.

Recognition and addressing the specific needs of children

All the FBOs stated that spiritual, physical, and social needs should be addressed. Only *WV Ro* specifically used the language of 'child rights'. After completing Phase One of the study, mission statements of 98 agencies were analysed for frequency of terms concerning types of interventions provided by FBO as summarized in Figure 5.2.[45]

---

[42] The Orthodox Church is only one aspect of any Romanian community; its opposition should not be perceived as the opposition of the entire community, although, in some cases, its influence is prominent and can lead to violent acts when used as means of intimidation. See 'Nine Baptists beaten by Orthodox in Romania' (Bunaciu, 1997).

[43] Bribery or 'gift giving' goes beyond the scope of this discussion, but it is an integral part of Romanian culture of granting 'favours'. For instance, it is a normal expectation, when seeing a doctor, to bring a gift of cash in an envelope. Failure to do so can result in receiving less that adequate treatment. For more on the cultural nuances of 'hospitality' see Richmond (1995) and LeBreche (2007).

[44] From the responses of 34 FBOs in Phase One, the three primary causes of 'child welfare problems in your location' were: 1) corruption at local or national level, 2) children not seen as important by society and church, 3) poverty of families and children.

[45] The mission statements were obtained by one of following methods: a) phone calls to the individual agencies b) accessing the data at the agency website or c) access to published information or from data obtained from OCI Romania that continues to keep

Figure 5.2 Interventions described in mission statements

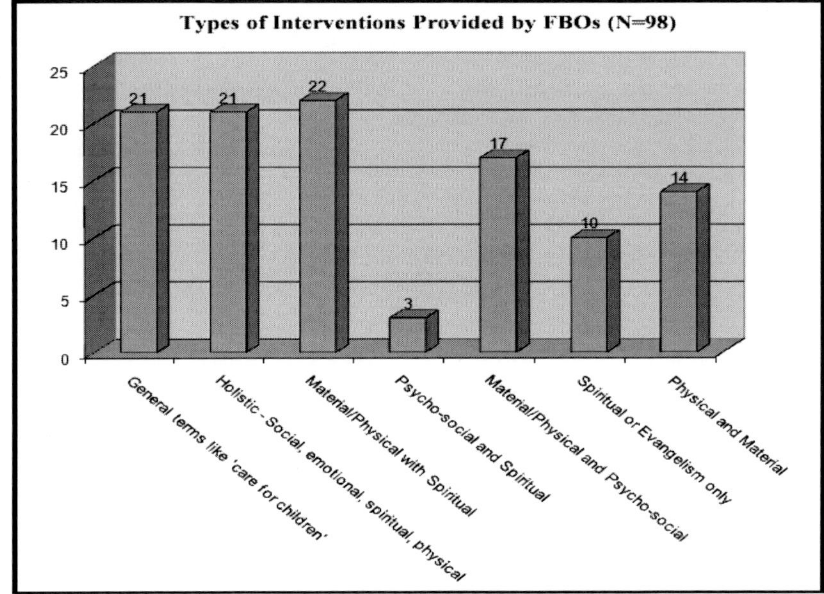

This analysis categorized interventions and sought to determine if the FBOs had any agreed upon standards of best practice.[46]

It was determined that while the FBOs demonstrated a variety of interventions, there was no common denominator of 'best practice' or standard in delivery of care. Mission statements listed combinations of interventions including: physical, emotional, material, psychological psycho-social support, education, holistic, spiritual formation, life change by knowing Jesus, behavioural change, and character development. Since FBO mission statements used imprecise language, a typology was created grouping responses into three categories.

The first category made spiritual care a priority over physical or psychosocial needs, stating that while the latter are important, they were secondary to 'spiritual' care for children. This group used explicit Christian language labelling interventions as learning the Bible, prayer, living in a Christian community, discipleship, counselling, child evangelism, and summer camps. The second category provided some combination of community health or training programmes for parents, psychosocial, physical, educational

---

an updated database of over 320 Christian agencies, organizations, and associations working in Romania.

[46] In addition to the types of interventions offered by the FBOs, also identified were the recipients or target groups, the intended outcomes of the ministry/programme, and the use of explicit Christian language in delivery of care to children.

programmes, and spiritual care. The FBOs in this category used the terms 'holistic care' or 'transformational development' (Currie & Commins, 2001; Byworth, 2003) in interviews or documents, the terms were used to describe a variety of interventions.[47] The final category emphasised social, physical, and health care as their primary interventions, with limited reference to 'spiritual' interventions.[48] Based on this typology the cases were plotted on continuum E as described in methodology and Figure 5.3. Special attention was given to the terms, 'salvation, conversion, holistic, transformational, and moral formation' for comparison with data from churches.[49]

Figure 5.3 Continuum of interventions being carried out in the projects

Prioritize spiritual interventions--------------------Prioritize human/social interventions
BF, CoH, ACLN, L&L------Ruth, MoM, Ţoar, WMF------ MWB -------WV Ro, IDC

RESPONSE TO ABUSE AND ABANDONMENT

Both pastors and FBO leaders recognized that FBOs provided 'specialized care' for children. 'The child living on the streets or sexually abused at a young age requires a different set of interventions than the child that has grown up in an extremely poor village and never received formal education' (FBOL#55, 2005). FBOs used the terms 'abused, marginalized, poor, exploited, and suffering' to describe children. Street children were described as more difficult to assist than those living in state institutions. These children had been totally dependent on the institutions, once they turned to the streets they resorted to crime and gang activity to survive.

> Street children have almost a reduced sense of personal identity and worth; they were constantly pushed down by the system. Personal initiative was taken away from them. They don't how to deal with authority or how to respect other people (FBOL#28, 2006).

FBOs stated that trauma and abuse could be alleviated if children learned personal dignity and self-respect (Kilbourn, 1997; Greener, 2003:128-30).

---

[47]WVI has developed a specific definition of 'transformation'. Other FBOs used 'holistic and transformation' however these terms have been adopted by FBOs they lack clarity – they are used so widely and include so many approaches to childcare that is difficult to define 'holistic care' at a field level. The assumption is that if one combines physical, psychosocial, and spiritual the outcome is holistic.

[48]An example of this type is Bethany Children's Services (not included in the case study but in Phase One). The director of this local foundation reacted to the term 'faith-based'. She said they preferred to think of their work with children as being 'professional and based on good social work practice' not based on faith.

[49] The cases are arranged on this continuum according to interview responses, programme descriptions, and programme design.

IDC and *WV Ro* employed staff psychologists and trained evaluators; offering a range of programme interventions. Several of their programmes qualified for funding from USAID and World Learning. Their project managers referred to current Romanian research in family and child abuse (Zamfir, 1997; Muntean & Roth, 2000). *IDC* provided interventions for women at risk of abandoning their children (Curtis, 2004). *WMF* and *CoH* worked with children suffering 'attachment disorder' (Bowlby, 1973; 1998; Granqvist & Dickie, 2005:197-210).

> We deal with dependency issues regularly in the lives of the children we know. The more fundamental issues are attachment disorders, lack of life skills, and lack of behavioural development. When we concentrate on the behavioural and attachment issues, the children begin to do better in school and begin to acquire life skills (FBOL#60, 2005).

Children with 'attachment disorder' experience difficulty bonding with other children, adults, and caregivers. Romanian institutionalized children who have been adopted into Western families have been the subjects of Western studies (Chapter 3).[50] Evidence of successful reintegration and treatment for abused children was found in FBOs that located Romanian families who were willing to provide emotional support over many months.

WHAT IS IN THE CHILD'S 'BEST INTEREST'?

FBOs stated they were working in the 'best interest of children.' Of course, churches also might claim to act in the best interest of children, but the problem is there can be different interpretations of 'best interest' as seen in this comment from an FBO director.

> Sometimes the church does not understand what is in the 'best interest of the child'. Churches don't take the time to understand the needs of traumatised children. We need to understand why they ended up on the streets and what they are feeling. It is important that children learn about dignity and respect for themselves and others; we want them to learn something about honesty and hope, learning to trust others, authority figures, and care givers (FBOL#55, 2005).

When asked to clarify what was meant by the 'best interest of the child', the director explained that the FBO provided 'safety, shelter, emotional care, and spiritual help'.

I do not dispute that children should receive adequate care; my questions concern how the FBO integrates 'physical' and 'spiritual' interventions in the 'best interest of the child'? Does the FBO assume these are integrated in practice, what knowledge of 'spiritual' informs this statement? This FBO offered no evidence that children had been participants in the process of

---

[50] On the other hand, there are very few published research accounts of faith-based interventions for these children in Romania; this study suggests it is needed.

programme design (Gourley, 2003:89-90: Johnson *et al.*, 1998) or criteria used to determine 'best interest'. The FBO implies the church does not understand the child's difficulty but fails to recognize that the church may respond in other, possibly just as helpful ways. It is doubtful that FBO personnel have personally experienced the conditions of children living on the streets. Pursuing a more open line of inquiry might persuade the FBO to examine its internal assumptions and confident assurance that it is providing for the 'best interests of children'. I will return to this discussion after considering the perceptions of the church in Chapter 6.

Efficacy in delivery of specific interventions

FBOs demonstrated capability to provide specific interventions; in so doing they developed expertise with specific groups of children. FBOs were concerned with 'measurable outcomes' based on programme interventions. Interventions were designed ins response to 'felt needs'. It should be noted that secular planning models and rational thinking can lead us to assume that outcomes can be programmed and measured. But faith and grace from God are gifts not commodities; a gift cannot be measured only accepted. But measurement is also a characteristic of stewardship. I return to 'problems and possibilities in measurement' in Chapter 7.[51]

> We want to know how we can help the children most effectively, if they need attention for abuse in an institution we need to know how to meet that need, or if from a broken family then we can help them find family contacts. We try to understand what circumstances have affected the child if we are to respond and be effective (LFBO#38, 2006).

Small local FBOs often began offering basic services such hygiene training or tutoring. Programmes developed capacity over time and interventions became more specialized. Children were given shelter from street life, substance abuse was treated, families in poverty were given assistance, children from institutions were placed in foster care; education and tutoring were offered. *MoM*, *IDC*, *WMF*, and *Ruth* assisted children from extremely poor families, who often took children out of school at a young age.[52]

---

[51] See discussion in Chapter 2 on managerial missiology. There is always a danger in faith-based work yielding to the underlying assumptions and categories of modernity and certainty (Sampson *et* al., 1994; Seel, 1994; Plant, 2003).

[52] Poverty is one cause, not the only factor in school truancy. Parents will opt to keep a child at home to assist with farming. They may not be able to afford school supplies, uniforms, shoes, and clothes. In extreme cases, the child is sent outside the home to work, beg, steal, or work in prostitution; this is not the case with the majority who drop out of school. For studies on poverty in Romania, see Zamfir & Zamfir, 1996; Carter, 2001: Jigau *et al.*, 2002; Robila, 2002.

> Poverty in Galaţi has forced many children to abandon education in favour of working to assist the family with income ... The primary social constraints consist of: illiterate parents and older siblings, inability to pay school fees and social marginalization of the teachers and better-off children... In November 2001, at the beginning of this project the statistics of the Scholar Inspectorate of Galaţi indicated an alarming increase in overall levels of school abandonment. IDC began to assist 96 children that dropped out of school (before the 8th grade). With a little help we can help them continue (FBOL#25 & FBOL#60, 2006).

The Roma people face discrimination in the public school system, some send their children to beg in Western European cities (UNICEF, 1997; Fonseca, 1995). *Ruth* addressed the needs of neglected Roma children and employed certified teachers (accredited by the Ministry of Education) and counsellors to work with Roma families. Staff members openly discussed discrimination against Roma families and attitudes in public education.[53] The Ministry of Education recognized Ruth School for its contribution in furthering education for Roma children and curriculum design.

The cases provided evidence that the FBOs were engaging on multiple levels: individual, familial, and societal[54] but in a largely uncoordinated effort. A rough estimate of the children assisted by the eleven cases in this study is well over 40,000.[55]

Before proceeding, I note that while FBOs worked towards effective social service interventions, little evidence provided thus far demonstrates a meaningful integration of programmatic response to human needs with 'spiritual' care. FBOs used the word 'spiritual' in various ways but offered little theological explanation as to what this word meant for the child. The interventions described above are commendable and demonstrate what I refer to as 'Side B – from below', that is, human actions that address legitimate physical and psychosocial needs. I will continue to examine if these interventions are meaningfully integrated with '*Side A*' – the action of God towards the child.[56] I am establishing that a 'tension' exists between the two

---

[53] The issue of discrimination toward Roma (gypsies) is important and I discuss it in subsequent chapters.

[54] Or to use Bronfenbrenner's language of ecological systems theory: the FBOs attempt to engage the *microsystems* (direct personal contact, experience and interaction like parents and family), the *mesosystems* (links between the microsystems like schools or community), the *exosystems* (what the child does not experience directly but still affect her like parents work or faith) and the *macrosystems* (poverty, wealth, neighbours, and the wider culture).

[55] This must remain a rough estimate, as the FBOs had a number of projects that are caring for children on a part-time basis and a drop-in basis.

[56] Concerning this bifurcaton see earlier discussion in Chapter 2, also see Bosch (1991:397-399). This is not merely a distinction in idea or theory, but it is embodied in parties, movements, within historical Christianity and is a theological, practical, ecclesiastical discussion in missiology.

sides. As described, they sit side by side and require more theological and missiological explication, we will also need to consider the perceptions of the churches to address these questions.

Donor influence on perceptions of FBOs and children

The FBOs relied in varying degrees on foreign donor contributions that contributed to perceptions and expectations. A common form of financial assistance came through child sponsorship. Sponsorship is a complex issue in Christian childcare, with arguments for and against as sponsorship sets up a range of expectations (Stephenson, 1997).[57] I examined four cases that relied extensively on child sponsorship, each using a different method: *MWB*, *WV Ro*, *MoM*, and *L&L*. Space does not allow an in-depth analysis of each method. On one end of the spectrum is *WV Ro* that relies on a broad-based Area Development Programme (ADP) aimed at assisting the community, family, and child, the sponsored child is 'represented in the community' (Cookingham, 1989:12-15).[58] On the other end of the spectrum is *MoM* that insists on connecting one specific sponsor with one individual child; children may not have more than one sponsor. Sponsors provide financial assistance for Roma and poor children at the *MoM* educational centre.[59] The objective in sponsorship is to 'connect' a sponsor in the West with a child through prayer, letters, communication, and giving.[60] Whatever the model, sponsorship sets up donor expectations for the FBO concerning delivery of care for children that in turn influences perceptions in the local community. FBOs have an 'image' to safeguard with their donors; their integrity is open to public scrutiny.[61]

---

[57] See also Stafford (2005). Borstein explores 'the intimate and personal relationships encouraged by sponsorship and the political economies within which they are situated, which include jealousies, desires, and altered senses of belonging' (2001:1).

[58] 'World Vision childcare projects will enable children to be healthy according to established national standards, to participate in some form of appropriate education, and to receive an appropriate form of spiritual challenge or nurture … projects will address the physical, social, psychological and spiritual needs of poor children with particular attention to addressing the causes of those needs, and incorporate the principles of World Vision's development ministry to the maximum extent possible' (Childcare Policy Standing Decision) in Cookingham (1989:12).

[59] All children in the *MoM* programme have an individual sponsor in the U.S.A. The sponsors receive an annual progress report, letters, and a Christmas card from their sponsored child.

[60] Each FBO in this study had a different method to 'connect' donor and child. The word 'connect' is taken from interviews where the FBOs described the attempt to link the donor and child in some sort of relationship.

[61] Abuse of child sponsorship has led to a number of investigative reports and documentaries. For an academic assessment of ethics and sponsorship see Crocker (2001).

FBOs used sponsorship to assist children both in and outside the churches. Romanian churches had no experience with sponsorship before 1990. Ruth developed a local church-based child sponsorship model but relied on a foreign office to manage contacts with the donors in the West. Donors expect financial accounting of resources given to the child, which influences local administration of the project. Two cases said the donor office was 'out of touch with field issues' (LFBO#18 & FBOLS#8, 2005). Sponsorship requires organizational capacity in local and international offices to manage profiles and inform donors; not a capacity typical of small FBOs or local church. The following statement demonstrates how donor expectations influenced a local FBO when it shifted its programme focus, moving children from group homes to foster family placement.

> We had sponsors for all the children in our group homes; some [sponsors] were willing to continue when children moved to foster families, others were not. We lost support for the group homes but also individual children. This created internal problems; we had not foreseen this policy change [required by the government when new laws required group homes be downsized and children be relocated to foster care] (FBOL#38, 2006).

Donor expectations can influence a local FBO to increase the number of children in a project, especially when the directive comes from the funding agency. 'We were running short in our operational budget; we were told [by the U.S. office] the solution was to add more children to our sponsorship list' (FBOL#18, 2004). Crocker raises a legitimate ethical concern when he warns against the *'prostitution of poverty'*, that is, when FBOs use the pain of suffering of a child to generate sympathy or funding on behalf of children (personal interview, 2002).[62] The challenge for FBOs relying on child sponsorship was to avoid becoming 'donor driven', remaining faithful to children and families in the local context, and faithful to the gospel (Srinivasagam, 1994:40).[63]

Perceptions of the structural and civic factors that impact children

FBOs engaged with local government, civic authorities, and state institutions. This interaction was coded as 'structural factors' influencing FBO operational objectives. FBOs follow patterns common to philanthropic societies, 'they are not utopians or revolutionaries, and they work with the grain of the economic, social, and political structures of their times' (Cunningham, 2005:138). *IDC*,

---

[62] At the time of this conversation, Crocker was the director of International Programme Development for Compassion International in Colorado Springs. He now serves with the international mission of the Nazarene Church. See also his paper 'Organizational Integrity and Ministry Success' (2002).

[63] Finances are an area that typically causes friction between donors and recipients. This is discussed more fully in Chapter 8.

WV Ro, and *WMF* stated that factors such as corruption and state policy contributed to child abandonment, institutionalisation, and poverty with residual impact on families and children. These cases demonstrated reliance on social science,[64] espoused 'holistic' ministry,[65] and were part of a larger international network. *WV Ro* has made shaping public policy towards children an organizational objective. The national director stated:

> WV Romania does not define itself as a parachurch, rather as a Christian development organization that works with the church locally and globally. *WV* works for strong partnership with the community, the majority of the partnerships are community driven. As an NGO, WV works to engage the government and civil society, we believe that serious systemic change can only happen by working with the government and public policy (LFBO #2, 2003).

This ubiquitous language is unique to *WV Ro* among the cases; this statement reflects an ambitious agenda for social change, seemingly devoid of theological suspicion.[66] No other cases were this 'optimistic' in their objectives working with Romanian civil society. There were other FBOs who maintained a hermeneutic of *theological suspicion* they were careful to place too much trust in human systems (even faith-based ones). Barth is helpful on this point:

> The church must remain in solidarity with this world of 'dry bones'; but it must be a church that has set its hope on God only. When the church embarks upon moral exhortation, its exhortation can be naught else but a criticism of all human behaviour, a criticism that moves through every one of the 360 degrees of the circle of our ambiguous life' (Barth, 1968:428).

Smaller FBOs with less organizational and financial recourses engaged the public sector at more modest levels. The founder of *CoH* described work with city officials when they negotiated the use of property as a day-shelter for street children:

> To the city officials [Sector 2, Bucharest] street children were a problem they didn't want to discuss and were interested in covering up. They promised us the use of a building only after they were publicly embarrassed when another NGO did not use the facility as promised. It was 7-8 years [after 1990] before the government took any serious action on behalf of street children. Poverty and institutionalisation was only part of the explanation for the problem. We dealt with a great deal of government corruption and police brutality (LFBO#28, 2003).

ACVN and *BF* set up centres for street children and faced criticism that were 'evangelical sects out of step with Romanian society' (FBOL#63, 2005). Another FBO leader described a 'poverty mentality' that she equated with

---

[64] This was verified through examination of the FBO training resources and linkages to universities in addition to conversations with staff and directors.

[65] 'Holisitc mission' was used by these three cases, albeit each FBO used the word to describe a range of interventions.

suspicion in society and lack of vocation, or 'marred identity' (Christian, 1999:139-40).[67]

> We have to deal with economic poverty and lack of resources faced by the children. But we also deal with a different 'poverty mentality'; by that I mean there is more to poverty than lack of material resources. There is emotional and spiritual poverty in some of the communities where we work. For instance, there is suspicion and lack of trust that affects the people, which makes it even more difficult if we are trying to explain something like, 'God loves you' (FBOL#44, 2005).

Four local FBOs (*BF*, *ACVN*, *Ţoar*, *L&L*) described 'societal or structural' factors as less important, giving more weight to spiritual aspects identified as 'sin', 'fallen people', and a 'world that is at enmity with God'. This latter group: a) was started in close cooperation with local churches, b) used a 'literalist' hermeneutic with scripture, and c) was more concerned with children coming to Christ than making a change in social structures. This was noted as differentiation between 'structural factors' and 'spiritual factors,' further evidence of 'above and below' logic operative in the cases.

Child welfare and legal reform: influence on FBOs

Childcare reform laws passed in 2002, and 2004 mandated the closure of state orphanages; these legal changes required that FBOs work more closely with local DCP offices.[68] The laws required the reintegration of children with parents, relatives, or foster families. *IDC*, *MWB*, and *Ţoar* argued this not always been in the 'best interest of the child', especially if placed in homes where they were not wanted.[69] Depending on the strength of the relationship with DCP officials, FBOs found themselves negotiating a delicate balance with government representatives and new foster families.

> The forced closure of the institutions and the subsequent reintegration of children into homes that may not want them leaves us with many questions. We

---

[67] I compare this with Jayakumar Christian's analysis in *God of the Empty Handed* and his assessment of poverty as 'marred identity' where the poor lack of self respect and lack a sense of 'vocation', which Christian argues as a factor in human marginalization greater than economic poverty.

[68] See earlier discussion in Chapter 3 for description of these laws that were passed to reform child welfare.

[69] Observers inside and outside Romania questioned the rapid adoption of these laws, especially since Romania had little experience with structures of foster care and child social service. Children were sometimes placed with relatives, especially uncles, aunts, and grandparents who may or may not have had the resources to care for them. The 'foster homes' were hastily set up and immediate suspicions arose that some foster parents were taking the children as a means to take advantage of the funds provided by the European Union. Questions about foster care have historical precedents; see Cunningham (2005:150-52) and White (2002).

> have seen situations where a child is forced to return to a bad situation – for example taking a young child to a grandparent that is not interested in her. Remember that the social workers [DCP] are not always concerned with helping children find a good family, now they will see them as children they just need to 'move on' (FBOL#70, 2006).

FBOs offered assistance in screening foster families and monitoring of the children placed in foster care. FBO staff visited the child and family on a bi-monthly basis. *CoH* developed a programme strategy in which project personnel were encouraged to legally adopt or foster children.[70] This type of faith-based engagement is exemplary of sustainable, practical efforts to care for the human and pragmatic dimension of childcare (Side B). None of the FBOs addressed the issue of foster care might as a theological or missiological question.

FBO Theological and Developmental Perspectives of the Child [71]

FBOs have both scriptural and developmental assumptions that guide their practice; they demonstrated acceptance, tolerance, and compassion of children who are often stigmatized by the larger society.[72] The following section differentiates theological (biblical) perspectives of the FBOs from perspectives specific to child welfare and development. The cases were plotted based on interview and document analysis concerning their use of biblical language (conversion and spiritual change) vs. child development language (human psychosocial change) as displayed in Figure 5.4. (Continuum F in methodology)

Figure 5.4 Variation in language of intervention: biblical and developmental

Biblical Language --Child development Language
BF, Ţoar -----ACVN-----Ruth, CoH, L&L----MoM---MWB, WMF ----WV Ro, IDC

[70] I provide a case vignette of one of these families in Chapter 7 and Appendix F.

[71], I am not attempting in the analysis to examine the data as a 'systematic theologian'. I am seeking to hear with an ear towards 'what the Spirit might be saying to the churches and FBOs'. In this and subsequent discussions of 'theology', I have adopted the term '*operative theology'* to best describe what is said and done in the name of God by the interviewees.

[72] Chapter 2 noted that from the early 20th century, Western missionaries and FBOs have been influenced by modern conceptual categories for children on the margins. FBOs came to Romania with embedded assumptions of what they consider to be a 'normative child and family'. This study found little evidence that FBOs had engaged in critical self-analysis on their views of children and family.

I sought to understand if working with the Romanian child protection authorities influenced language of intervention. I conclude this section with questions concerning the term 'holistic'.

Theological categories in reference to children

FBOs made several assertions about God's concern or love for children.[73] Only two FBOs (*WV Ro*, *WMF*) produced documentary evidence that they relied on theological reflection to inform their practice (McAlpine, 2002; Chronic, 2006). FBO personnel gave biblical references concerning children and family, I used the terms 'biblical and theological' as synonymous in coding. Descriptions of biblical rationale for work with children were arranged on a secondary continuum with 'intentional theology' at one end, and 'incidental' at the other.

UNCONDITIONAL LOVE AND CHILDREN AS GOD'S IMAGE BEARERS

In speaking of God's concern for children, the terms used most frequently across the cases were 'unconditional love' and 'recognizing the image of God in every child'. This quote is representative of the 20+ references in the transcripts.

> God's *unconditional love* for children hasn't changed ... His love never ceases. God's work with children should be done through people who have surrendered to the love of God. God rescues the abandoned, restores the abused and makes a home for the forgotten (FBOS #5, 2006).

God's 'unconditional love' was not clearly defined by interview participants; I understand it as 'God's love, which penetrates all roles, expectations, and worldly valuations in pursuit of the genuine good of a person in their irreplaceable identity,' (Werpehowski, 2001:399).

In Galati, *WMF* works in the poorest neighbourhood focusing on Roma families and street children. The director stated it was critical to include the family in sharing God's love with children. This is supported by research in other contexts (Miles, 2003a:33-5).[74] In an area where alcoholism and family dysfunction are prevalent, *WMF* describes its ministry as 'biblical compassion by immersion or working "incarnationally" in the community' (FBOL#60,

---

[73] I labelled this category as 'theological,'' but in fact, the word 'theology' was rarely used in the actual interviews. I worked through the interview transcripts and coded references to the Bible, God, the Holy Spirit, salvation, and so on as indicators of 'operative theology'.

[74] See Miles on the role of family in caring for children in crisis. He reviews the social science literature (2003a) and notes contradictions with scriptural guidelines for parenting and families.

2006).[75] A ministry centre acts as a hub of activities for families and children; *WMF* encourages their project staff to live for a time in the homes of their host community to better understand family dynamics.[76] *WMF* considers the local church as integral to demonstrating God's compassion to families and children.

> God wants these children to be able to live in safety, to receive some kind of education, experience a loving environment and family, learn the possibility of respect and care. As we say here '*băgare de seamă'* which means to notice someone and treat them as a friend. There would be no way to bring long-term change without the input of the church in this community (FBOL#60, 2006).

FBOs also stated that children are God's image bearers Gen 1:26-27; 9:6 (Dempster, 1999:48; McConnell, 2007). The Latin term *imago dei* was used by two cases; others said that children had intrinsic worth because they were 'created in the image of God' (Gundry-Volf, 2000:470; Moltmann, 1993b:216-20).[77]

> It is of the highest importance that we recognize the image of God within each child. We want children to understand how God sees them. Of course many of these children have a very poor self-image since they were not valued in the institutions – it takes lots of work to help them see the image of God within their hearts (FBOL# 64, 2006).

When FBOs used the term 'created in the image of God,' they did not expound on sin, fallenness, or the nature of childhood other than to acknowledge children needed to be 'led to Christ' or 'given a chance to receive Jesus'. I took this as evidence that 'theological anthropology', that is, reflection on humanity's image bearing, sin, conversion, forgiveness, salvation, reconciliation, redemption, and formation (Loder, 1998:5)[78] was incidental to

---

[75] See Grigg (1990:51-66) who worked with the urban poor in Metro Mania and popularized the term '*incarnational approach'* which he meant as 'living with and at the same level as the poor'. Grigg's work was informed by the work of Latin American theologians, Padilla (1984) and Costas (1986).

[76] Asking project staff (both Romanian and Western) to live in the homes of poor families was unique to this case. *WMF* asks that every long-term staff member make a commitment to living for a period of time (a month or longer) with a family in the community.

[77] In *God in Creation* (1993), Moltmann provides a biblical exegesis of the 'The original destination of human beings – *Imago Dei'*; commenting on Gen.1: 26-27, 'Human beings come into being, not through God's creative word but out of his special resolve. The word that precedes the resolve is addressed by God to Himself. It is a self-exhortation; in a resolve, the author of the resolve acts on himself first of all' (1993b:217).

[78] Loder argues 'for human uniqueness as openness to the world' and speaks of the person as 'a spiritual being … no longer subject to its drives and its environment' but 'free from the environment'... spirit is the principle that may be opposed to a naturalistic view of life and contravenes in evolution. Human openness to the world and self-transcendence is what Pannenberg (1985), calls "exocentricity" and in this one word he designates the human spirit' (1998:5-6).

FBO work. It was assumed the children needed Christ, but FBO participants did not develop the implications of the redeemed child 'in Christ'. This was noted as a lack of meaningful theological integration with physical or social interventions.

GOD'S LOVE FOR CHILDREN AS EXPRESSED THROUGH FAMILY

The interview guide was structured so that questions about spirituality and theological themes could be discussed at the end of each interview.[79] The professionalized FBOs, *WV* Ro and *IDC*, used phrases such as 'family systems' and 'children are a product of family environment' more frequently than references to scripture or God. However, 70-75 per cent of the respondents in other FBOs answered questions concerning programme interventions by referencing biblical texts; explaining their work was based on 'God's love and concern' for children and families.

Cases working in close collaboration with local churches (*Ţoar*, *WMF*, *Ruth*, and *ACVN*) consistently referred to God's intentions for both child and family. I wrote in a process memo: 'God's concern for children is used as frequently as God's concern for family, yet only six of the selected cases actively seek to place abandoned children with families.' The Romanian interviewees were more consistent than Western respondents in referencing God's love for children expressed through family.

> Success for us means offering God's unconditional love to the children; we want to be a Christian role model for the children. We try to provide the necessary steps like education, social skills – we do this so that the children can somehow integrate back into a family. You cannot completely take away the pain these kids have known on the streets; placing them in a family environment is our goal (FBOL#61, 2004).

Those FBOs working closely with churches were more likely to suggest that the families in the churches could provide care for children (see Chapter 6).

LOVE AS CONVERSION OR GIFT?

I asked the FBOs to explain the connection between 'unconditional love' and their attitudes toward conversion or children attending a particular church (Scott & Magnuson, 2004:448-50).[80] No FBO made conversion a prerequisite

---

[79] This was intentional, the first two-thirds of the interview was an inquiry into partnership and organizational questions. I intentionally did not want to bring theological debate into the interview process having learned in Phase One that there were some important theological differences between the churches and FBOs.

[80] See author's 'Do we need to Convert Them?' (available at www.prevetteresearch.net) This essay examines conversion as gift or exchange. There are many faith-based programmes that operate from the perspective of 'economy of production and exchange', that is, the goals for young people (behaviour change, spiritual development, and social skills) are treated as a type of production. The programme director, staff, and caregivers provide certain interventions and skills with the expectation of a set of

for a child to receive care or programme assistance. *Ruth*, *BF*, *CoH*, *L&L*, and *MoM* said conversion was important: 'we want to bring children to faith', 'help the children live for Christ', 'teach children to share their faith with their friends and family', and 'bring the children into local churches'. Others described love as simply a 'gift' from God. I took this to mean a gift 'outside the economy of production and consumption, distribution and exchange …the gift remains radically transcendent to the determinations of reciprocity …' (Schragg, 1997:140).

> To live out the gospel means to offer the gift of unconditional love, not just evangelism. We feel that meeting physical needs is showing love to the children in ways that they can understand. We know we don't have to force children to come to any particular church; our objective is to offer them love as a gift from God (FBOL# 25, 2006).

FBOs embraced a vocabulary of biblical values and took the Bible seriously, but 'confessional assurances' had not been critically examined in responding to children. Most biblical reflection was loosely organized and coded as 'unintentional theology'. It became evident in the latter stages of analysis, that the FBOs, while acknowledging 'God's love for children', gave little attention to what their activities with children might teach them about God Himself or if their practice and methods might benefit from more critical theological evaluation. Children were valued; response to their human suffering was legitimated by occasional references to scripture. FBOs closely connected with churches were more likely to express concern for sin, God's grace, and judgement, but this was not a primary topic in FBO responses concerning child and family. As will be discussed in Chapter 6, questions of sin and salvation were primary concerns in the churches.

FBOs perceptions of the developmental needs of children

Interviewing childcare workers was at times emotionally painful; they expressed meaningful experiential knowledge of the children in their care. Many shared their frustrations working with the deplorable conditions of the institutions, in hospitals where mothers abandon their babies, in poor Roma villages with subzero conditions in the winter, rescuing children forced into begging or stealing. These insights provided a unique window into FBO perceptions of the human dimension of intervention.[81]

---

outcomes and a spiritual 'product', that is, conversion.

[81] Limitations of space prevent the inclusion of the many narratives that were crucial for my personal understanding of the cases and the people involved. One woman who had worked with abandoned babies and children for a number of years showed me photographs of the conditions of the hospitals when she first started there in 1993. The people leading projects to assist children deserve a second volume of research.

Beyond biblical references, FBO personnel expressed practical and common sense perceptions of societal and familial influences on children. These were pastors, nurses, social workers, educators, and young leaders from Bible schools who worked full time in childcare. To understand frames of knowledge underlying FBO assumptions, personnel were asked about reading and exposure to child psychology or development. Less than 35 per cent of all FBO personnel had academic training in social work.[82] Two individuals had post-graduate training degrees in child-related studies. Less than 30 per cent of Western participants were conversant with child psychology (Piaget, Erickson)[83] or faith development (Westerhoff, 1976; Fowler, 1981), none had read Hay and Nye (1998) or Loder (1998).[84] Depending on the reader's perspective, this may not be a negative finding, as child development theory *per se* can be questioned in a critical evangelical argument. I acknowledge that modern 'child-development categories' have been influential in Western FBO responses to children, whether explicitly acknowledged or not.

The 'professional' FBOs have largely adopted human development theories as the dominant background discourse in faith-based childcare; theological 'espoused values' are secondary in their published documents (Currie & Cummins, 2001). Denominational FBOs tended to discuss child welfare in a medical terms rather than psychological terms.[85] Regardless of education or exposure to literature, the directors and senior staff listed the following as primary social/familial factors impacting children: 'institutionalization, poverty, alcoholism, abuse of women in the home, family dysfunction, violence towards children, abandonment in early childhood, lack of attention in the family, and degrading social conditions for children'. These were coded as 'perceptions of the human side of the childcare.'

Perception of the Relational Needs of Children

In coding the transcripts, I noted 35 references to 'relational needs of children in crisis.' Almost without exception, caregivers spoke of the importance of

---

[82] This number is based on all FBO participants in both phases of the research, 27 of 78 respondents.

[83] Piaget theorized that interaction with the environment impacts the structural potential of the psyche producing intelligence, language, moral judgment, and imagery (to mention a few of his categories of behaviour). The FBOs did not make extensive use of terminology one finds in child development literature. See Loder who discusses the influence in child development of interactionist and behaviourist psychologists (Freud, Erickson, Jung, and Skinner) (1998:18-26).

[84] These latter texts, *The Spirit of the Child* (1998) and *The Logic of the Spirit* (1998), are influential in the current academic conversation concerning child development, and child spirituality. Many, perhaps most, subsequent research studies have made use of Nye's definitions of 'spirituality'.

[85] 'Child health and welfare have been medicalized in the West since 1920; it has served as powerful argument for extending the role of the state in health and welfare generally' (Cunningham, 2005:176).

spending 'relational time' with the children. I asked a programme manager with staff and administrative responsibilities how she evaluated progress in the children who were staying at their night shelter.

> I spend part of every Wednesday with the boys, several hours if I can … for me this is the best way to get to know about their experience and determine how we can help them…I was asked by a government [DCP] employee, 'Why do you spend so much time with these street children?' My answer was, 'I want to demonstrate the love of God to them' (FBOS# 8, 2005).

The cases demonstrated a variety of relational methods: role-play and games, drama, sports, singing competitions, camping, and hiking.[86] Referring to relational support for teenage youth (14-17 years), an FBO leader made this observation:

> Children on the streets lack a sense of personal worth and value. Their day-to-day existence is dangerous and their deepest needs are relational, they need someone to show them something other than usury and abuse (FBOL#55, 2005).

Loder notes that teenagers are making a major transition in life development 'with the disequilibrium as intense as any other since birth, which means they want to hold on and let go and need a transitional object such as a mate or best friend' (1998:206).[87] A boy at a drop-centre who was addicted to huffing *aurolac* (glue) said, 'these are our only friends not living on the streets, we come [to the centre] because we know we will find someone who will listen to us' (personal conversation at L&L, 2005). A FBO director said daily work with street children had deepened his dependence on God, but did not expound on what specifically he had learned of God in the process.

> I don't believe there is anything I have done in my life that has taught me more about human relational needs and ministry than giving my life and time into children on the streets. This relational commitment has given me a much greater dependence on God and His love for me and the children (FBOL#28, 2004).

Relational support in faith-based care provides children with security, significance, and boundaries, necessary for restoration. This serves as a theological pointer to the covenant love of God seen in the '*I-Thou*' relationship of the child's eternal significance (White, 2003a:124).

---

[86] An excellent tool and resource used with street children to encourage listening to verbal and non-verbal expressions is the '*The Big Green Bag*' developed by Filipina psychologist Gundelina Velazaco with funding from the Pavement Project; see http://www.sgmlifewords.com/usa/en/index.php.

[87] Concerning adolescence, Loder adds: 'Because the theological potential of this stage is emerging as each one senses the underlying void that is opening up and as each moves out into an unknown future to which she is biologically, socially, and culturally destined. Adolescent youth sense with greater comprehension than ever before the truth about human existence: it comes to nothing, in and of itself it comes to nothing' (1998:207).

EXPERIENTIAL KNOWLEDGE VS. TECHNICAL KNOWLEDGE

The majority of the Romanian FBO personnel learned what they knew of 'child development' experientially working with children over an extended period of time.[88] They did not acquire explicit 'technical knowledge' from a university or formal study of child, family, and social systems. They acquired their 'tacit' skills and knowledge in the 'swampy lowlands' of everyday practice (Schön, 1995). [89] The efficacy of their experiential 'know how' was recognized and praised by public health officials. Four FBO staff members had first-hand experience of family abuse in their own homes (alcoholic and abusive fathers in each case). One staff member lived on the streets prior to recovery through an FBO (Dobrisan, 2002); many staff members had friends who had grown up in dysfunctional homes and institutions.

FBO workers are effective at getting themselves 'close to people in pain'. A number of men and women in their early 20's said they had spent enough time with orphaned and street children to see themselves as 'big brothers and sisters'. Their supervisors confirmed that shortage of funds often necessitated FBO staff working extra hours. I heard few complaints about the additional work; instead it appeared to be a 'badge of honour'. I am not commending the FBOs for contributing to overwork; staff burnout and compassion fatigue are indicators that an FBO is neglecting the caregivers (Wright, 2003:340-43).[90] These practical and human experiences informed FBO perceptions of children and provided much of the data FBOs were using to develop their programme interventions. [91]

Only WV Ro had adopted a formal child protection policy for staff and children. I gave four local FBOs resources on 'child protection' and was

---

[88] Usually two to three years; the experiential knowledge I describe here could be enriched by interaction with child development literature just as it might be enriched by theological reflection. Many Romanian FBO personnel were relying on experiential knowledge and 'operative theology' learned in the churches.

[89] The terms 'explicit and tacit' used by Schön are usually attributed to Polyani (1966) where explicit knowledge is expressed in words and numbers using written and verbal means and tacit knowledge is highly personal and hard to formalize, making it more difficulty to communicate with others. See Britton (2005:44) for a summary of the terms and how they are applied in organizational learning.

[90] In a field memo I wrote: FBO workers and staff are much like the pastors of Romanian evangelical churches: they give themselves to incredibly long hours of work, they do not ask for help or time off as this is seen as 'un-spiritual' and they exhibit something of a 'saviour complex'. Caring for those who provide care is becoming a more established practice in Western evangelical churches. See Browning (1987) on providing member care.

[91] I suggest that Western FBOs and Romanian churches have much to offer one another in developing a critical and reflective evangelical 'mind' concerning children. This becomes more pressing as standards for childcare in Romania are being improved, and childcare issues are complex. Evangelical FBOs have been working at 'frenetic pace' allocating little space for collective organizational learning or research.

incredulous that Western funding partners had not implemented policies or rules for screening staff.[92]

Combining theological and societal perceptions of children – is this holistic?

The findings indicate that FBOs demonstrate theological and developmentalist perceptions of children in their speech and action, but to what degree are these perceptions meaningfully integrated? The phraseology in the interviews implies (or states explicitly) that if an FBO addresses the spiritual, psychosocial, physical, and emotional needs of children, this constitutes 'holistic mission' as in this definition:

> Holistic mission is a frame for mission that refuses the dichotomy between material and spiritual, between evangelism and social action, between loving God and loving neighbour. Holistic mission is the life of Christians passionately pursuing their relationship with God by seeking to be more like Christ, and who, because of their life in Christ, are passionately sharing the good news (Myers, 1999b:286-87).

It is my view that mission with children should be 'holistic' but it is difficult to achieve. The FBOs who are committed to it and proclaiming it may not wholly succeed. That being the case, it is useful to examine how it is lived and worked out in practice. FBOs hold ideas of sin, fallenness, and the action of God's grace towards children on one side and the impact of a dysfunctional families and social systems on the other. How do FBOs integrate their eternal concerns for God and child with their practical concerns for the human child? Clearly, they are concerned for both, stating that the love of God is instrumental in their pragmatic programme interventions. FBOs have made a contribution to breaking down prejudices that exist in Romanian society toward children, especially towards institutional children and the Roma, what Saunders calls 'ministry from the margins' (1997).[93] Given the findings thus far, the term 'holistic mission' with children needs more testing and assessment. For instance, how does the term 'holism' incorporate the local church embedded in the life of the community it serves? To what degree have FBOs meaningfully integrated divine and human concerns; is '*holistic language*' patching up where more missiological reflection may be indicated?

---

[92] I do not accuse the FBOs of negligence. But those purporting to care for them can abuse children. Abusers may try to join the staff of childcare programmes to gain access to children. .

[93] Cheryl Sanders advocates inclusion of both women and children in ministry (1997:163-79) she articulates a 'theology of inclusion and to establish inclusive practices and multicultural perspectives that harmonize with the gospel we preach and honor the Christ we proclaim' (1997:10).

How FBOs Utilise Personnel and Organizational Structures to Meet Ends

Mission structures used by FBOs are typically organized around a specific set of tasks and may or may not be localized in the long-term sense. Eight of the cases used the term 'parachurch'.[94] *WMF* resists the term, citing Bosch, 'because church and mission belong together from the beginning, a church without mission or a mission without church are both contradictions. Such things do exist, but only as pseudo-structures' (1991:372). I now will examine personnel, management and FBO use of organizational structure – factors that are very much of this present world. The following were identified in the data as important subcategories: motivation to serve children, sense of calling, preparation of FBO personnel, mobilizing volunteers, and organizational competencies.

Motivations and organizational values to serve children

Christian organizational structure is shaped by internal values as FBOs are 'expected to honour, nurture, and promote specific moral and spiritual ideals as those ideals provide particular inspiration for their service' (James, 2004:13). There are tensions as FBO organizational values and motives do not always coincide with church organizational values. Earlier I described how donor perceptions influence FBO expectations that impact motivation. Beyond financing projects and providing services, the cases expressed concern their projects 'reflect the values of the kingdom', which they named most frequently as 'compassion for the vulnerable', 'ethical and accountable work', and 'providing opportunity to grow in Christ'. Four cases (*WMF*, *MWB*, *Ţoar*, *Ruth*) said organizational objectives included 'strengthening the local church to provide care for children in need'. *WV Ro*, *L&L*, *CoH*, *MoM*, and *IDC* were motivated to 'provide community-based social services' and direct interventions to children in crisis. The following subcategories describe individual staff motivations.

A SENSE OF PERSONAL 'CALLING' TO WORK WITH CHILDREN

The most recurrent organizational category in the transcripts was individual commitment of personnel working with the FBOs.[95] Eighty-five per cent of the participants made references to a personal call such as being 'called to hurting

---

[94] I am not being pejorative of the FBOs in using the term 'parachurch'. This term implies that the local church has a specific role in which pastors or priests serve the spiritual needs of the congregation. Christians may work as Christians outside of the church sphere, but that is '*para*' [alongside] the church.

[95] I interviewed 116 individuals; only 22 were not working directly with children. I am indebted to these men and women not only for their contribution to my study but even more so to the high level of dedication and commitment they have given to children in Romania.

children'.[96] Individual calling was not a specific interview question, but when asked, 'how or why did you become involved in this work', the responses were patterned: 'I was called to it', 'called in my church by the Lord', 'I heard a news report that touched my heart', 'I made a trip to Romania and felt called to come back', and 'I felt God wanted me to give my life to this'. If asked to explain 'calling' in more detail, the interviewees described subjective feelings such as a special direction from God, usually in the form of feeling a deep compassion for children in crisis. These responses had a 'mystical' or transcendent quality; interviewees tended to discount objective factors in personal anecdotes. Only 12 interviewees said they specifically prepared to work with children based on reading or technical knowledge.[97]

Participants did not expound on the theological nature of 'calling' that is sometimes identified with the spiritual gift of serving (Acts 6:1-4; 1 Cor. 12:28; Rom. 12:7; 16:1-2). The gift of serving is sometimes understood as a divine enablement or endowment to accomplish practical and necessary tasks that free up, support, or meet the needs of others (Palmer, 1993). Evangelicals typically interpret 'enablement' to mean if one is called to a task, God will enable them, that is, 'His demanding call depends on His enabling grace' (Bloesh, 1978:199). I defined 'calling' in this study as an inner sense of divine initiative, a belief that God directed an individual to a specific task and imparted a personal sense of responsibility.

On a more objective level, 18 Western personnel learned of Romania's problem with street children or orphans via the media – documentaries, newspapers, or TV. They stated this gave them awareness but was not a primary motivation for coming to Romania. The following statement by a woman who left a nursing career in the U.S.A. to work with abandoned babies is representative.

> When I came [for just a week in 1995] I did not intend to stay long. But the longer I stayed the more I could not get the children out of my mind and heart and I knew I wanted to commit long-term to working with these children. I needed to know that God was calling me to this place…I now know God called me to this work and I will stay until he directs me elsewhere (FBOL#72, 2006).

In a process memo, I referred to certain responses as the 'God card' meaning that some respondents were so convinced of God's direction; it was problematic to ask for a more logical explanation. Some FBO directors were not screened for professional competence with children before opening projects – four Western and four Romanian evangelical lay-people had no prior

[96] This 85 per cent response represents the eleven cases and survey interviews in Phase One.

[97] I was asked to consult with several of the FBOs concerning delivery of care for children and staff development. See Parker Palmer's *To Know as We Are Known* (1993) and *Let Your Life so Speak* (2000) as both books give fresh perspectives on 'hearing the inner voice of vocation and calling'.

experience managing a childcare project.[98] Interview transcripts contained 23 references to experiential 'sense of God's call to manage or start a project'; which I labelled as' reliance from above in organizational practice'.[99] Assurance of personal calling was to some degree a reflection of faith 'being sure of what we hope for and certain of what we do not see' (Heb 11:1), and also a Kierkegaardian 'leap of faith'.[100] 'Sense of divine calling' was noted as a primary motivation for individuals working in extremely difficult circumstances (Miller, 2003:10-11).[101]

Activist and Individual Agendas: Minimal Cross-Case Collaboration

Given FBOs are led by people with a personal sense of faith and calling, it was not surprising to find individual agendas across the cases. FBO work was activist in orientation (Bebbington, 1989:10-11); as a consequence organizational collaboration between FBOs was minimal.[102] The FBOs were entrepreneurial; programme planning was often described as 'responding in faith when children needed help'. When asked, 'How does faith inform your organizational work?' responses were as varied as the cases. Nine project personnel said their faith in God's direction 'strengthened their resolve' to continue in very difficult circumstances. Five others said faith had 'given us hope' that they felt was important to pass on to children. No FBO said 'faith' had led them to work in closer cooperation with other FBOs or local churches. Individualist agendas were characteristic of both Romanian and Western managed FBOs.

I looked for evidence that 'faith-based' organizations were concerned about working together as a means to demonstrate how the 'entire body of Christ' might more faithfully represent the gospel in practice. The best example of

---

[98] Evangelicals historically have relied on voluntarism from the laity. The FBOs in this study reflected a degree of anti-clerical activism.

[99] See James (2004) as transcendence or spirituality in 'organizational leadership' is an emerging field of study. As with many of the responses in this section, there was little theological explication from research participants.

[100] As in the sense that 'human reason is up against something it cannot think' (Loder, 1998:11); I observed that many evangelical FBOs and their staff take this 'leap of faith' approach rather than making the longer and more troublesome journey of discerning, listening, and learning before coming to their field of service.

[101] Following Rudolf Otto, Donald Miller, in a study of emerging churches in the Global South, identified a similar transcendent factor in the leaders of churches that he referred to as '*myterium tremendum*'. 'Leaders …believe in a divine presence that is active in the universe and that can be encountered' (2003:10).

[102] Bebbington argues that from the late 1700s to present, evangelicals have been active in all manner of ministerial activity; conversion of the lost and church work is a primary activity. Care for children has also been an historical 'mark' of evangelical social concern. Notably 'collaboration' is not one of Bebbington's 'marks' of evangelicalism. Many American FBOs come from different denominational backgrounds and find it difficult to collaborate in their own country, much less in a second culture.

cross-case collaboration was in Galaţi where three FBOs (*WMF*, *IDC*, and *BF*) shared both programmatic and managerial responsibility. *MWB* in Sibiu demonstrated the most consistent effort to work with all denominations of local churches.

PROFESSIONAL BACKGROUND AND TRAINING OF FBO DIRECTORS

FBO personnel live and work in the 'immanent realm' where organizations and children face the worldly realities of paper, pencils, personalities, bureaucracy, and management problems. Practical secularity is required to manage an FBO, including some form of accountability and assessment. Training in organizational development (OD) and management were discussed with each case. Evans observes that Western NGOs have a longstanding interaction with OD and depending on perspective, 'it was in the NGO world that OD became a science or art' (2002:5).[103] Eight directors stated management training for their staff and personnel had become an organizational objective since the founding of thc FBO.[104]

WV Ro, *MoM*, *IDC*, had the organizational capacity to employ management personnel.[105] Three Romanian FBO directors gave up professional secular careers and said their skills were useful in 'managing' ministry. Florin Ianovici worked as a legal advisor to his denomination, he helped a Norwegian FBO that became involved in dubious property acquisition. He stated his original obligation was only to help the FBO out of a legal dilemma; he had no intention to work directly with children. In the course of the legal negotiations, the Western FBO asked him to become the director of the local FBO; he declined the offer three times. He explained how his professional skills led to his 'calling'.

> I felt I had some obligation to help the children. The legal situation was very precarious and the Western agency was in jeopardy. I was seeking God's will for the children. I turned down offers to work in a law office to stay with L&L. I think the key that opened my mind was learning that I could be a servant of the Lord by serving children in a professional way (FBOL#9, 2004).

---

[103] For studies in OD, see Argyris, 1990; Ashkenas *et al.*, 2002; Perrow, 1970 and Burke, 1994. Most FBO directors were not trained in technical OD theory but Western management models influenced their organizational practice. See Engel & Dryness (2000:55-82) Chapter 3, 'What's gone wrong with the harvest?' for enlargement on the shortcomings of managerial missiology.

[104] As of this writing, FBO personnel have better professional preparation than was available in the 1990s. Social science and management training are now offered at most universities. There are still no courses offered in the Romanian seminaries integrating faith, management, or social science. Those wishing to study missiology usually come to the U.K. or America (Mănăstireanu, 2006).

[105] The annual budget of WV – Romania in 2005 exceeded the annual budget of the five smaller cases in this study.

Ianovici later completed his PhD in Romanian law, challenging the hegemony of the European Union legal system that he felt was out of touch with Romanian culture and family. This case demonstrated how a Western partner can contribute to increased professional capacity and critical thinking about children in a local FBO. The FBOs are matched with the professional background of each on-site director in Table 5.2.

Table 5.2 FBO directors and professional background

WV Ro – PhD Business ethics	*MWB* – Pastor and District leader
MoM – Romanian Medical doctor and Nurse	*Ţoar* – Pastor of Brethren church
L&L – Romanian Law degree	*ACVN* – Psychology – undergraduate
CoH- Romanian Law student, Bible school graduate	*IDC* – Social Science – undergraduate
Ruth – PhD theology – U.K.	*WMF* –MA Theology – U.S.A.
BF – Church elder and engineering degree	

Mobilizing Volunteers

The smaller FBOs lacked adequate financial resources to employ skilled professionals; they relied on mobilizing volunteers from local churches. Their stated aim was to 'attract people of very high commitment that value building personal relationships with children' (FBOL#39, 2005). Western FBOs also recruited volunteers from their home countries to assist in their projects; a typical length of stay was one or two years. MWB was successful at mobilizing dozens of volunteers from local churches; however, this proved more difficult for other FBOs in the study.[106] I followed an appreciative inquiry approach (Hammond, 1996) as *MWB* invited me to visit partner churches and interview staff and pastors. I sought to learn how FBOs had changed the negative discourse surrounding 'volunteering'. A summary of those factors identified from this and the other cases is displayed in Table 5.3.[107]

Table 5.3 Factors that help mobilize local volunteers

1. MWB first trained a team of coordinators, whose primary role was to recruit and train volunteers from local churches. The coordinators were encouraged to get to know pastors before contacting any young people in the church.
2. FBO personnel were instructed to listen to the interest levels of the volunteers.

[106] As some of these better-funded FBOs had financial resources, I surmised they were not as 'internally motivated' to mobilize volunteers.

[107] All the cases had expressed interest in mobilizing volunteers; some did so more effectively than others.

The FBO was willing invest time in listening; the goal was to learn what the volunteers were interested in doing and what they envisioned as a positive way to get involved.
3. The coordinators were given instruction in how to build positive relationships with local DCP authorities in order to gain access to the children's homes and institutions.
4. FBOs sought the pastor's endorsement when young people from a local church were interested in visiting children in the orphanages. If the pastor asked for help with the children in his church, the FBO helped to organise activities for those children. This brought credibility to the FBO.
5. The FBO understood the importance of motivation for volunteers, and camps, outings, and activities were organised for volunteers as well as for children receiving care.
6. The FBOs had a desire to 'cross the line from just a feeling of sympathy for the children to really doing something practical for the children'. It is a thin line from 'we were forced' to 'we want to do this.' The key for MWB was finding how to motivate and empower the volunteers (FBOL#70, 2006).

Organizational competencies and management modalities

The term faith-based *organization* implies the use of systems, boundaries, and competencies. An organization is a combination of people (social systems) and knowledge (information systems), giving it a certain structure and culture. Three functional dimensions of an organization achieve its programme goals: governance, management, and implementation (Burke, 1994). Organizations are not just simply people and their institutions, 'they also include the spirituality at the core of those institutions and structures' (Wink, 1998:4). I discuss organizational models and factors that influenced competence and collaboration.

METHODS FBOS USED TO BEGIN ORGANIZATIONS

As stated earlier, FBOs encountered a labyrinth of official bureaucracy in the early 1990s resulting in a new 'FBO sector'. The selected cases pursued a number of methods to obtain official registration.[108] Four primary strategies of project initiation were identified and the cases were typed as examples of each. The method used to begin an FBO was judged to be a factor influencing partnership with local churches.

1. *WV Ro* and *MWB* had an official presence in Romania prior to 1989; they were registered under existing laws but had to re-register in 1990. They had gained sufficient managerial competence and employed national staff that understood the legal system and local authorities. *WV Ro* had worked with the

[108] In Phase One, I identified 18 FBOs that experienced problems in the official registration process. Five simply bypassed the system and worked unilaterally, they were active in the early 1990s but were forced to comply or cease operations by 2000 as laws were strengthened.

Romanian Orthodox Church and *MWB* with Baptist churches in Transylvania. These FBOs were categorized as '*performative*' as they had the structures, skills, and capacities required to perform reasonably well in the transition of the early 1990s (Roxburgh & Romanuk, 2006:45). Performative organizations, while having capacity and assurance, do not always thrive in the midst of discontinuous change as defined in Chapter 2; these organizations are often not prepared to make changes in management or organizational style due to past successes. These FBOs relied on partnership models they had proven in previous experience and sought church partners with established qualifications.

2. *L&L* and *MoM* were examples of Western FBOs with international experience in other contexts. They were represented by a Western spokesperson(s) with a desire to begin a project and who felt God was 'leading' them. Experience in Romanian language and culture was limited. In both cases, direct exposure to children in crisis influenced the FBO to act in the present. 'Something had to be done, the situation was terrible' (FBOL#7, 2003). The Western representative had stakeholder support from the donor organization and located a Romanian partner, either in a church or through a registered denomination, to establish a foundation.[109] These FBOs were categorized as '*reactive*' since they were reacting to the crisis and began projects with little research or understanding of the local context. Reactive organizations 'experience diffuse confusion, conflict, anxiety in the face or relenting episodes of crisis without end' (Roxburgh & Romanuk, 2006:48).[110] These FBOs developed partnership models that were typically based on short-term agendas, some church partnerships ended in disappointment for both sides.

3. Romanians initiated *CoH*, *BF*, and *IDC* with little or no outside support. The founders were between 24-30 years old, had college educations, and spent time with children living on the streets. They started work with only three or four children, who were described as 'friends'; children were not referred to as 'clients'. The '*visionary founders*'[111] located Western partners who were willing to finance operations; this enabled the organization to add staff and

---

[109] The results of this approach were mixed; in the case of *L&L*, as described above, the Western partner became involved in a malicious and unsustainable partnership that was terminated in order to continue.

[110] In the first phase of research, I identified 18 of these 'reactive' organizations; they were the typical models for Western-led FBOs. I described them in field notes as 'both activist and anxious' as they were constantly responding to crisis situations and using the 'God card' to explain their organizational rationale'. I concluded that this anxious activity had contributed to the lack of dialogue between FBOs and churches. In Argyris' terms, this was a 'single feedback' loop that never sought to ask 'how or why' questions of operational agendas or theological assumptions of the child.

[111] The 'founders' of these FBOs may not describe themselves as 'visionary'. This term is adopted from leadership trait theory, which identifies capacity, achievement, responsibility, participation, status, and situational alertness as necessary traits for effective leaders, for discussion on trait theory see (Bass, 1990).

programme interventions. The Western FBOs supplied funding, additional human resources, training, and linkages to other organizations. These locally founded FBOs eventually provided care for hundreds of children and were categorized as '*emergent* or *experiential*' characterized by creativity, innovation, energy, and 'the bringing forth of new forms of mission as the organization enters, listens to, and engages the community' (Roxburgh & Romanuk, 2006:41). These FBOs partnered with local churches that were open to change and new models of ministry, these churches were also labelled as 'emergent'.

4. Local churches in Bucharest, Sibiu and Brasov started *Ruth*, *Ţoar*, and *ACVN*. Two pastors described these FBOs as an '*extension*' of the church to provide social services to children.'[112] The pastors were instrumental in instigating the projects; two admitted that initially they were reluctant to 'help children that caused problems for the community' (LFBO#9 & FBOL#17, 2004). The churches represent three denominations: Baptist, Brethren, and Independent Charismatic; each created a structure to give oversight and administration to the FBO. These FBOs were typed as '*transitional* or *bridge* FBOs' as they represented a transition from a type of church that was hesitant to assist children to one willing to discover new ways of being God's people serving children on the margins.

GOVERNANCE AND ORGANIZATIONAL STRUCTURE

FBOs rely on models of governance, defined as the overall leadership of the organization, usually involving a director or board concerned with the long-term issues such as mission, strategy, values, policies, and goals (Carver 1997). Governance is especially important to 'performative' FBOs that are concerned with donor accountability and organizational sustainability. Every case used some type of organizational chart; typically a hierarchical model, with the director or governing board at the top.[113] The 'emergent and transitional' FBOs were less concerned with external governance and hierarchical structure. FBOs developed both firmly and minimally guided partnership with local partners, that is, some FBOs closely monitor the activities of the church/local partner and in other cases the church/local partner decides what is best for the children with little input from the FBO. The FBOs were plotted on a continuum in Figure 5.5 (see Continuum C in Methodology).

[112] Yach explained: 'the statutes for our church did not allow us to set up a home for children. We checked the laws and found an old law (1921) that would allow us to set up our own association as an 'arm' of our church. The foundation offers focus and specialization and we view it as *extension of* the local church' (FBOL#38, 2006).

[113] Foundations and associations are required by Romanian law to have an oversight board within the country.

Figure 5.5 The extent of guidance offered by the FBO

Firmly guided partnership*----------------------------------*minimally guided partnership
WV Ro, MoM-----IDC-------- L&L—CoH—WMF----------ACVN, Ruth-- Ţoar, BF

FBOs on the left rely on Western styles of governance, with layers of internal management. *WV Ro* conducts semi-annual internal and external auditing done by professionals. *IDC*, smaller in scale, submitted to an external audit conducted by World Learning and USAID; this facilitated receiving assistance to build organizational capacity but did not help *IDC* become more 'holistic'.

> We have been successful in getting support for designing our programmes and social interventions from World Learning. We feel we have had good management training; we have been able to send our staff to learn skills in social work and programme oversight. However, none of this training has helped us with learning how we can evaluate spiritual work with the children in our programmes (FBOL#61, 2005).

The FBOs plotted on the right of the continuum use governance structures that enable the local church to make programme decisions with minimal input from a foreign FBO and are rarely, if ever, subjected to external auditing. The local FBOs (middle group) depend on relationship and flexibility with their governing boards. A director stated, 'our organizational structure is built on relational trust which means we must have respect for one another, without it we cannot work together' (FBOL#60, 2006). L&L partners with two Scandinavian FBOs and also described 'governance' in relational terms.

> In our meetings, we take time for dialogue and brainstorming, our personal relationships are close. We are financially accountable to [Western donors] but in programmes for the children we have asked the board to trust our judgment … I feel we often learn new things with our board and they appreciate our need to make decisions based on local knowledge (FBOL#55, 2006).

Some experiences with Western governing boards have been less positive, tensions developed over issues such as what types of management models are best suited for Romania and whether or not Western money dictates the direction of a project. Cross-cultural misunderstandings have arisen concerning control of programme and staff, resulting in the resignation of at least one director (FBOL#28, 2006).[114] The challenge for FBOs is to remain faithful in honouring God while not falling into the trap of 'managerial missiology'. I will

[114] LaBreche (2007) showed that conflicts between American and Romanian evangelicals were usually the result of value conflicts. For instance, the values considered most important for Americans were honesty, servant attitude, and stewardship; the values most important for Romanians were church fellowship, family relationships, and codes of conduct in church.

return to trust in governance in Chapter 8 as I analyze organizational tensions that influence partnerships.

FACILITIES AND STRUCTURES FOR CHILDCARE

The variety of programmes described above logically required physical locations for providing care. FBOs built or purchased a variety of physical structures to help children: drop-in and night shelters for street children, foster and group homes, school buildings, vocational training facilities, and renovated apartments for older youth leaving institutions. The facilities are the 'hardware or physical structures' needed by the FBOs; however, physical plant and property are expensive. The vast majority of the funds for facilities came from foreign funding sources as Western FBOs directed hundreds of thousands of pounds into buildings.[115] This amount of money being directed to children's projects set up competition with Romanian churches that were also trying to raise money for new church buildings. A research memo illustrates the point:

> On the day I first visited the Ţoar project in a small village in Western Romania and saw the family homes for children I was impressed with the sustainable nature of the project. This was probably because the day prior I had visited another project about 100 miles to the south where the FBO was building a £200,000 'Christian home for children'. This home was to provide housing for 30 children coming out of a Romanian state institution that was being closed. The FBO had done almost nothing to involve families from local evangelical churches (four in this town) and seemed to be substituting one institutional response (albeit Christian) for a secular on. It was this and other field research experiences that confirmed my developing hypothesis that Western FBOs were not doing all they could to engage the local churches in delivery of care to children (March, 2005).

Summary

This chapter has described factors that influence *FBO perceptions of children in crisis* in Romania. FBO responses to children were characterized as interventionist and specialized. In order to answer the central research question concerning FBO-church partnership, it was necessary to investigate as an independent variable FBO expectations of the Romanian churches and local context. A new FBO sector was created in Romania in the 1990s; this produced both positive and negative experiences for international FBOs and local church partners. FBO expectations were not always congruent with evangelical churches as mission to children in crisis was a new endeavour for both sides of the partnership. Western donors influenced the perceptions and actions of

---

[115] I estimated cost of the properties and facilities for the 11 selected cases, the average project spent £100,000-£150,000 on buildings, and in two cases this amount would be tripled. Exchange rates of £1 = $1.61 average between 1990-2004, most large projects were factored in dollars.

FBOs, as did the local communities. FBOs demonstrated they could work with the grain of the economic, social, and civic structures of the evolving Romanian child welfare system in the 1990s. FBOs were expected to provide social assistance; some expectations were unrealistic concerning Western expertise and resources.

FBOs experienced a difference of opinion with some local churches about which children deserved care. This was one of the factors that exacerbated divisions in labour between FBO and church. Some FBOs decided to bypass local churches; others took time to listen, dialogue, and collaborate. In evaluating FBOs response to specific needs of children, missiological questions were raised about what is 'in the best interest' of a child and measurement criteria. I suggest there are potential problems in reliance on categories of certainty, especially in work that requires faithfulness to God and children who have been traumatized or abused.

The FBOs operate with theological assumptions based on their understanding of God's unconditional love and God's image borne by every child. I argue that they tend to lay these eternal concerns '*side by side*' with their perceptions and actions aimed at meeting the physical, developmental, and psychosocial needs of children. I questioned the degree of meaningful integration. The term 'holistic ministry' as used by FBOs has generated questions. FBOs are not embedded in communities in the ways typical of local churches, thus the term 'holistic' requires further examination as a practical expression of mission and as a factor in FBO-church partnership.

FBOs have utilized personnel, structures, management, and governance to accomplish their organizational ends. I concur that good management practices are essential to childcare, but suggest that these factors must be carefully considered in faith-based work with children if they are not to become mere instruments of 'managerial missiology'. FBOs must ask themselves how their managerial and organizational methodology honour God and does the framework of management do justice to mercy and grace of God, and if so, how?

I now turn the discussion towards an analysis of similar factors that influence local churches.

Chapter 6

Factors that Influence How Romanian Chuches Respond to Children

Introduction

This chapter examines the factors that influence Romanian evangelical church perceptions, interactions and responses to children in crisis. Addressing the FBOs and churches as independent variables provides the analytical framework to examine factors that hinder or enable their collaboration. The secondary research question: 'What were the expectations local churches had of the arriving FBOs?' is also addressed.

I begin by describing the term 'local church' as used in Romania and identify five characteristics of church life and practice that had been reinforced under communism and carried into the 1990s.[1] These characteristics influenced church perceptions and responses to children and became more relevant as FBO activity increased throughout the 1990s. This is followed by expectations churches had of FBOs, perceptions of the child and family, perceptions of children in crisis, and the churches' use of means to assist children. I quote pastors, FBO leaders who work in churches, and church members as primary sources.[2] I acknowledge that the research involves a limited number of churches.[3]

The analysis led to a second central category summarized in the phrase: 'embedded communities concerned with faith and repentance' (Figure 6.1). As in Chapter 5, the axial categories are used as section headings in the text.

'Local church' as used by Romanian Evangelicals

No one definition of 'local church' emerged in the fieldwork. Pastors and FBOs use the word *biserica* but rarely define what they mean by 'church' beyond reference to common texts (Acts 8:1; Eph. 3:10; 3:21 5: 20-29).[4]

---

[1]Unless otherwise noted, the word 'church' refers specifically to evangelical churches in Romania. This includes Baptist, Pentecostal, Brethren, Charismatic, and independent.

[2] In many cases, pastors of churches were working with a small FBO and were coded as FBOL. In Phase One, 12 pastors were interviewed who were working with FBOs; in Phase Two, 13 of the 29 FBO leaders were also serving as pastors.

[3] It was impossible to visit every church in Romania. This research established that in the mid-1990s, the majority of the churches in Romania were not working with children in crisis. The numbers increased in the late 1990s.

[4] 'Church' is assumed in normal conversation to mean 'a local church'. The Orthodox Church also uses the word *Biserica* to mean a local church and national church. For a

Denominational identity, as in 'Baptist church' or 'Pentecostal church' is important to pastors and church adherents.[5] The following terms were used to describe local churches: 'Bible believing', 'independent', 'traditional', or 'legalistic'; these are imprecise terms but were accepted as vernacular definitions. Evangelicals prefer terms that separate them from the dominant state Church; the most frequently used modifier was 'believing' church.

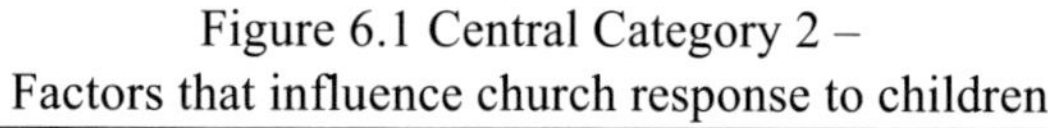
Figure 6.1 Central Category 2 –
Factors that influence church response to children

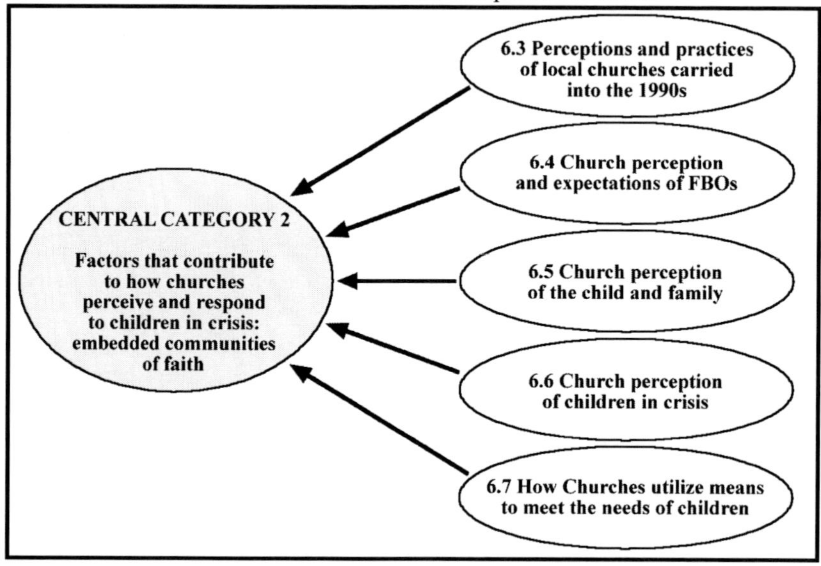

Evangelical churches in Romania are congregationalist in structure. They follow the historical legacy of the 'Free Church' tradition.[6] In addition to the Word, the sacraments of communion and water baptism, and the gathering of God's people, they emphasise two other conditions regarding the presence of

---

discussion of how Orthodox ecclesiology differs from Protestant, see Volf (1994; 1996b), Staniloae (1980:122-35), and Stricker (1998:145-54).

[5] Some would argue that there is no systematic evangelical ecclesiology, see Stackhouse (2003) *Evangelical Ecclesiology: Reality or Illusion?* It became evident in fieldwork that little intellectual investment had been made in the early 1990s to develop a fresh approach to ecclesiology in Romania. Negruţ later issued a Trinitarian challenge in this direction (1999a).

[6] See Volf (1998:127-37) Chapter 3, 'The Ecclesiality of the Church' especially his discussion on 'Where is the church' (:130-33) in which he develops the historical construction of the Free Church movement quoting from John Smyth and other English Separatists. Free church models were further developed by Anabaptists and brought to Romania by German Baptists in the 19th Century (Chapter 2).

the Spirit of Christ in a church: obedience to Christ's commands and 'biblical organization of the church' which is, in theory, Christ's dominion realized through the entire congregation (Volf, 1998:131-32).

Perceptions and Practices of Local Churches Carried into the 1990s

In the communist era, evangelicals lived the ideology that the Christian faith was best expressed in the role of the suffering church, believing that their suffering was part of their service to God.[7] There was a longing to see the church free from oppression; redemption and hope in Christ were sustaining beliefs. 'Taking adult baptism in the communist era was linked to an oral pledge to live a life free of sin; this was an oath of allegiance and taken very seriously' (FBOL#16, 2004).[8]

After 1990, leaders who had resisted State control of the church – Cure, Wurmbrand, and Ţon were considered heroes of the faith. The Bible continued to be read and preached in churches, literally interpreted. Evangelicals embraced a fundamentalist and federalist concept of atonement provided for all humanity in the work of Christ on the cross.[9]

> [Believers] placed heavy emphasis on the literalness of Christ's action on the cross. God the Father literally took all the sins of mankind and placed them on His son on the cross, and the blood that was shed on the cross-washed those sins away (Sabou & Ghitea, 2004:12).

---

[7] As noted in Chapter 2, it is a mistake to attribute to suffering a value it does not deserve. I note that some degree of 'martyr mentality' (Dobrincu) was influential in the churches as the FBOs arrived. See Ţon's PhD thesis: *Suffering, Martyrdom and Rewards in Heaven* (1996).

[8] Concerning water baptism, if people did come to a church and were converted in the 1980's, it was difficult to receive water baptism as government restrictions on churches were enforced. As a result, for several years, there were no official converts to the church, just 'registered members'.

[9] I asked a Romanian seminary professor (Baptist) to elaborate on his understanding of 'evangelical theology'. He referred to a number of conservative American theologians among them Donald Bloesh. According to Bloesh, conservative evangelical theology stresses the 'moral regeneration of the will over rational and spiritual insight; crisis over process; God's gracious initiative over man's religious quest; the service of God's glory over the fulfilment of the self, scriptural norms over cultural mores; biblical proclamation over rational apologetics; the cross as substitution over the cross as moral ideal; and, the historical particularity of the revelation of Jesus Christ over the general wisdom and experience of the religious community'(Bloesh, 1978:14). Romania evangelicals who received theological education would probably concur with these statements. However, I note that this summary is simplistic and offers false dichotomies and oppositions that bracket the Evangel in categories of 'certainty'. This sort of theologizing is common in conservative Romanian churches and Western denominational FBOs and does not encourage open dialogue on meaningful integration of human and divine concerns for children.

The churches looked to an eschatological horizon linked to the second coming of Christ to claim his church, 'life has many problems but one day we will receive our eternal reward, this world is passing away' (Pas#4, 2004).[10] Conversion, adult baptism, and regular church attendance (as many as four times a week) were marks of a 'true follower of Christ' (I#2, 2003). Pastors used the following terms to describe their churches and members: 'reverent, faithful, holy, prayerful, worshipping, loving, stubborn, small, insignificant, restricted, persecuted, separate from the world, pious, waiting for heaven, and anticipating the rewards of Christ'. On one level, FBOs and churches shared a common evangelical 'language' and set of ecclesial assumptions. However, a number of factors were identified, particular to the Romanian evangelical 'mind,' that shaped understanding of its role in society with implications for children in the 1990s.[11]

Definitive sense of community – separation from the 'world'

Churches retained a 'stronger sense of community than their non-believing neighbours as the believers were committed to church fellowship and to supporting the needs of their members in times of need' (Pas#12, 2006). Persecution generally brought more resolve and strengthened the cohesion of the congregations (Barbosu, 2004:4).[12] Activities of worship (preaching, prayer, communion, baptism) were practised in the local church and possibly in the home but not with the wider community. As a result, the local churches looked inward; salvation begins 'at the house of God' and tended to be like spiritual 'islands' (Moyle, 1999:26).[13] Church members sacrificed financially and built their own facilities; people in the Timişoara Elim church built a

---

[10] The Romanian evangelicals stand firmly on the hope of a future in Christ and in the company of their spiritual forebears. 'Although they be pilgrims upon earth, yet they confidently hasten onwards towards the place that which is beyond all heavens, guarding their future heritage peacefully in their hearts (Calvin quoted by Barth, 1968:153).

[11] I am borrowing this usage of 'mind' from Mark Noll (1994). See Chapter 6, 'The Intellectual Disaster of Fundamentalism (:109-39). Noll provides a useful analysis of the situation in American conservative evangelicalism that has application to developments in Romanian evangelicalism during the 1990s. '[Fundamentalist] Evangelicals look for simple and understandable gospel, the gospel is not complicated, anyone can understand it … evangelicals tend to stress the dangers of the world, take comfort in spiritual piety, centrality of evangelism and conversion to faith in Christ, and expectation of the end of time when Christ returns for His church' (1994:115).

[12] Before 1990, church meetings were held as many times as permitted and others were held in secret. There was more religious freedom for evangelicals in Transylvania but 'everything was monitored by the local *Securitate*' (I#3, 2003).

[13] This is not a pejorative statement, the churches and believers were restricted to a limited social space; they were like 'little seeds who for the sake of Christ accepted narrowness' (Willmer email, 2005); they had lived life as 'hidden in Christ'.

building to seat over 2,000 people largely with funds from the community (Pas#2, 2003).[14] After 1990, churches continued to meet several times a week, and this 'sense of cohesion and community' gave the churches resolve to begin evangelism, as they understood it, in their communities.

Deeply held pietistic values but few contextualized theological resources

After 1990, Romanian evangelicals retained a commitment to personal and corporate piety. Churches trusted Christ for personal conversion and the gift of grace to lead a 'victorious life in Christ' – a life possible after conversion but not before as sin and the fallen nature must be reconciled in the new birth experience (Jn. 3:3). The local church was the trusted social institution for spiritual life. There were virtually no voluntary structures outside the local church for ministry. 'Legalism, narrowness in church doctrine and theology with restricted forms of worship had become common especially in the rural areas' (Barbosu, 2004:6).[15] I described this in field notes as 'hardening of theological and ecclesial categories'.[16] Theological resources for pastors were limited; many owned nothing more than a Bible. Much of the theological training had been done through sermons, sharing of books and pamphlets and informal gatherings.[17]

Mănăstireanu critiqued East-West partnership providing an emic view of theological education (2006).[18] He raised two primary concerns: the shortage of adequately trained pastors and the need for a more contextualized evangelical theology appropriate to the Orthodox religious context. Some theological schools lacked serious academic standards and uncritically imported theology

[14] In Bucharest, Providence Baptist Church expanded its church by digging and building a new basement which they then proceeded to refill with dirt to pass inspection with the local *securitate* and then dug out the dirt for meetings (FBOL#16, 2004), further evidence that churches had initiative and local resource.

[15] In Romania, legalism has been a 'label' used in various missionary and theological circles to describe one of the weaknesses of the evangelical church. Legalism is 'the ethical religious theory that prescribes an excessive conformity to a religious code by which one may earn or secure his salvation' (Barbosu, 2004:5).

[16] My term has two axes of concern. I found a clear division in the pastors on the subject of legalism. One group was deeply concerned about holding to 'biblical faith'. They worried that Western ways would 'weaken or dilute' the faith of believers, a concept in which there are positive elements concerning Western offerings. The other group tended to be younger or better-educated Romanian pastors who saw the legalistic categories as a hindrance to growth and liberty in the Spirit of God.

[17] Ţon and several others who left Romania before 1990 were instrumental in having a number of theological books from Western sources translated from English and sent back to Romania.

[18] Bible schools in the early 1990s stressed a dogmatic, literal reading of scripture, which resisted historical or higher criticism. Honest intellectual debate was not encouraged in church sermonizing or theological education.

teachers and disputes from the West.[19] With study abroad an option after 1990, many capable emerging evangelical scholars left Romania for the West (Mănăstireanu, 2006:7).[20] I interviewed seven seminary professors, and as of 2008, no undergraduate training was available concerning 'church, child, and mission' either translated or from a Romanian source.

Pastor as primary leader and spiritual authority

The senior pastor was responsible for decision-making, spiritual authority, and leadership. In theory the churches were congregationalist, but in practice, the lead pastor was often 'in charge of everything' (Pas#2, 1994).[21] In most cases he was the sole decision maker and questioning his authority was seen as 'unfaithfulness to the church' (Pas#11, 2006).[22] In cases where pastors were responsible for several churches, each church had elders and deacons but ultimate authority rested with the pastor. Constant work and activity left little energy for pastors to give to personal spiritual development or to their immediate family. Pastors were dedicated to the local church(s), convinced that their energy and spiritual energy should be given to the 'people of God' (Shawchuck & Heuser, 1993:23).[23] Western FBOs that wanted to work with

---

[19] For example: 'proponents and teachers influenced by the Free grace movement, came to Romania under the communist regime, some working under the umbrella of organizations such as Campus Crusade for Christ or Biblical Education by Extension. After 1990, there were dozens of Western theological imports: ... such as, hyper-Calvinists, seeker sensitive [sic], also brought with them elements characteristic to their own indigenous theology ... not well received by the Romanian evangelicals' (Barbosu 2004:6).

[20] Official statistics between 1994 and 1999 estimated almost 115,000 Romanians emigrating, the great majority of them less than 40 years of age and with university and/or professional training. Mănăstireanu has kept a database of 60+ Romanian evangelical scholars who have been awarded PhDs (many in systematic theology), well over half that number are teaching in schools outside of Romania.

[21] Pastoral authority was a theme in many interviews, mentioned by FBO leaders, eight pastors, Bible school students, and FBO personnel; the factor is discussed at several places in the analysis.

[22] I acknowledged in Chapter 5 that pastoral authority is not unique to Romanian pastors; their Western counterparts are just as given to overwork and control. What is unique to Romania is the socio-cultural understanding of leadership (*conductator*). Some have attributed the Romanian dictatorial style of leadership to a 'Balkan mentality', which allows leaders to use shame and intimidation especially with deviant cases. Also mysogynism is prevalent in the Balkans and is evident in Romania church leadership and ideas concerning women in the church. Vulnerability is seen as weakness and personal struggles are not to be shared in public, see Boia (2001) and Deletant (1996).

[23] Shawchuck and Heuser have done extensive research on American congregations finding that many churches are 'over managed and under led' (1993:23). A pastor

both children at risk and local churches had to work either with, around, or under these pastors.

No formal theology of social concern but implicit faith in action

Before 1990, churches did not develop an intentional theology or liturgical language of 'social concern', in part because communist ideology had claimed that a socialist state had no social problems. It was only after the revolution that some pastors learned the term 'social gospel', often from a fundamentalist missionary from the West (FBOL#23, 2004). Church life and energy was focused on saving souls not resolving social problems, an attitude reinforced by the 'dualism of spiritual and worldly life' (Moyle, 1999:18-19).[24]

Believers maintained a distrust of the 'world' on theological grounds: *contra mundum* – against 'worldliness', usually translated as *pofta lumesti* (worldly desires), believers were taught to avoid the sin of 'mixing with the world'.[25] This theological category had complex implications for evangelical values and church life and created tensions between church and the 'world', much beyond dress and personal preferences.[26] 'We take unto ourselves the protestation against the world as it is' (Barth, 1968:155).[27] In some churches, the holiness tradition became more entrenched in both doctrine and practice after 1990 as a reaction to perceived 'worldliness' and Western influence. Many believers had been denied a university education, resulting in further social and economic

---

leading eight to ten churches at some point ceases being a pastor and becomes a manager.

[24] This became an important factor when analysing the evangelical church's response to children in crisis, especially those from the institutions. Evangelicals, like most Romanians, understood these children to be responsibility of the state, see Chapter 3.

[25] In the New Testament, the term world (Gk. *Kosmos*) has three basic meanings: 1) the earth or the created order; 2) the nations, the human community; 3) the ways of fallen humanity, alienated from God and his truth (Wells 1994:37). I am using the third meaning, as in, 'the collective expression of every society's refusal to bow before God, receive his commandments, or to believe His Christ' (1994: 39).

[26] Churches did not teach cultural relevance, they remained suspicious of what was 'worldly' (materialism, TV, music, videos, dress) and best kept out of the church. The conservative evangelicals forbid drinking alcohol, smoking, dancing, jewellery and make-up, no rings, or candles (a reaction to Orthodox liturgy) and playing cards.

[27] See Barth's work on Rom. 5:3-5 where he writes, 'We affirm the negation which says that we are creatures and we see clearly (Rom. 1:20). We are able to take to ourselves the protestation against the world as it is (Rom 8:19-20) for we recognize that we stand under judgement, and we love the Judge, because He lets it be known that he is not to be identified with the god of this world (Barth, 1968:155). Barth is not representative of Romanian evangelicals and I am not quoting Barth to support their position. Barth has proved helpful in analysis, thus I quote his early work from Romans at several places in this research.

isolation.[28] This sense of 'separation from worldliness' has been described as 'evangelical Gnosticism' (Miller, 1999:45). I am not convinced this is an accurate description of Romanian believers. On *Side A* (concern for God and eternity) evangelicals said they should live holy lives separated unto God, not be stained by the 'world'. But on *Side B* (life in the present world) every evangelical I interviewed expressed concerns about family, their children, community, and life *in this world.* I argue that believers are 'not suicidal Gnostics hurrying to get out of this world' [29] as they marry, raise families, work hard, want their children to get a good education, are hospitable people, and honour God by serving others (Petersen, 1996:112-16).[30]

Evangelicals typically lacked social capital in community affairs and avoided the circles of civic power.[31] In the early 1990s, there was little exchange of information between the evangelical churches and the media, institutions of formal education, and emerging child protection authorities. It remained difficult in the early 1990s to change the church's language of social concern; Romocea suggests that evangelicals could be a voice for change.

> Evangelicals tend to reduce social reality to its vertical, individual aspect that refers to the relationship among church members and with God, with no bearing on implications for the wider society...This is sad especially because these churches, with their inherent autonomy in regard to cultural identity and nationalist ideology, may serve well as agents for social change (email, 2004).[32]

I argue that churches were becoming agents for social change in the 1990s. As will be demonstrated, one of the outcomes of engagement with children in crisis has been to enlarge evangelical social concern, what I label in this analysis as 'social holiness for children' (adopting Wesley's term). Implicit in their faith and life in Christ was a Spirit-inspired concern for their neighbours and home communities. Generosity and social concern was practised with little formal instruction. The Orthodox community was suspicious and labelled believers as '*sectants*', in response they responded (in most cases) with

---

[28] Evangelicals under communism were denied access to many fields in university education, engineering was open to them and as a consequence I interviewed 15 pastors who had degrees in engineering. Levels of education for pastors had influence on partnerships with FBOs.

[29] Thanks to Haddon Willmer for this phrase (personal conversation, 2005).

[30] Petersen answered similar questions and allegations concerning social concern in his study of Latin American Pentecostals, arguing that Pentecostals had an implicit theology and praxis of social concern, see also Martin (1990).

[31] I am using Putnam's term as he defines social capital (2000:19). Evangelical 'social capital' was built with members of the church and larger believing community; however evangelicals do not describe their communities with this term.

[32] Romocea completed his PhD in 2007 *Church and State: Theology and Continuity of Orthodox Religious Nationalism in Romania.*

kindness, prayer, and concern for families and individuals with whom they had daily contact.[33]

Compromised moral situation

After years of monitoring by the *Securitate,* the churches (with all Romanians) were living in a society of suspicion and lack of trust (Kligman, 1998:215).[34] Totalitarianism had been based on adherence to rules and regulations. This influenced evangelical ways of thinking and living in the both the sacred and secular. Believers attended church regularly where the Bible was taught with absolute certainty; sin, repentance, and holiness were expounded as literal, not intellectual or complicated categories.[35] Believers returned to their daily lives surrounded by disinformation and ethical ambiguity. In Romanian society, moral boundaries were not defined as 'black and white' but by a hundred shades of 'grey'. Romanians learned new ways to 'bend or negotiate the rules,' jokes from the former era still had resonance: 'they pretend to pay us, we pretend to work'; 'the fish rots from the head' (Richmond, 1995b).

One must be careful of over generalizations in reference to a people and culture. All human societies have moral shades of grey. The capitalist West has its own variety, though Western evangelicals seem less willing to acknowledge their moral ambiguities. I regularly heard these proverbs in my work with Romanian evangelicals. Some have also argued that Romanians have a latent sense of fatalism engendered by both culture and history (Boia. 1997). As a Westerner 'looking in' with a pragmatist and optimistic view of present and future, I observed that Romanians tended to be 'critical, suspicious, and hard nosed realists'. They also demonstrated a remarkable ability to accept their cultural ambiguities with humour and patience.

Conformity had been reinforced by the state (and church); diversity and innovation were discouraged, and few challenged the system. A vocal

---

[33] I travelled to many churches and stayed in the pastor's homes as a guest. I observed on several occasions pastors and their wives taking food to neighbours who had less than they. I took note that 'social concern' does not always happen in a formalized framework; what I saw might be termed 'operational social concern'.

[34] There was a sharp distinction between the public and private spheres of an individual's life/identity under communism; totalitarianism reinforced the split of private and public self. 'People were manipulated by the system, but they also manipulated the system, creating an entire edifice based on false reports, false statistics, and deliberate disinformation in order to survive' (Kligman, 1998:215).

[35] This statement is something of a paradox. On the one hand evangelicalism has theological roots in European pietism and conversion and repentance are not simple intellectual categories. Evangelicalism took shape long before WWII and was shaped by these precedents. However in Romania, pastoral education was greatly reduced under the communist regime and pastors were cut off from those historical resources, resulting in the presentation of a gospel of narrow categories, emphasising repentance and obedience to scriptures.

evangelical minority protested officially, choosing to reject the authority of the state over the church. Less publicized were those believers who practised their faith quietly rather than risk persecution of their families and loved ones. The 'compromised moral situation' engendered a willingness to work 'around the system' while others resorted to duplicity to survive (FBOL#4, 2003).[36] Corruption and abuse of power in society were endemic; it is naïve to think this did not influence churches and pastors.[37] A number of church leaders were compromised by *Securitate* as informants and were removed from leadership after 1990. Others were able to find Western sponsors and continued in leadership, feeding church divisions and suspicions.[38] As discussed in Chapter 5, FBOs that were anxious to establish childcare projects, sometimes worked with compromised local partners who were practised in managing the 'complexity' of the Romanian legal system.

> We [evangelicals] had been waiting and praying for freedom. We listened to Radio Free Europe in our homes, we had expectations that our Western brothers and sisters would eventually come and bring us help. Unfortunately, this led to a lack of initiative for some of our leaders and created opportunism in others. Many of us did not know we had these options (I # 3, 2003).

The quote demonstrates the church's limited 'horizon of expectation' and assumptions of what might be possible. I will analyse the question of religious opportunism in Chapter 8.

Church Perceptions and Expectations of FBOs

Church expectations of the FBOs did not happen in a vacuum. Western FBOs had made trips to Romania in the 1980s and some Romanian pastors had

---

[36] I recognize that human societies and governments - both in the East and West - are given to manipulation and abuse of power. This analysis does not expunge the Western FBOs from duplicity, but it is fair to argue that Romania had endured a systematic form of state corruption that found expression in social and religious life.

[37] Romanian leadership/power structures are very hierarchical and date back to the *Boier* (feudal lord) of the 1800s. Ironically these power structures were to have been levelled by Ceauşescu and communism: the ownership of private properties was supposedly abolished and the majority of the big property owners (*marii proprietarii*) – were put in jail. The same was applied to businesses that had been privately owned for generations and were nationalized. However, the communist party reinforced these indigenous hierarchical power structures (Balcanu, personal conversation, 2005).

[38] Unlike Eastern Germany where Stasi Files were opened to public, the Romanian Securitate files were not made public. In March 2006, historian Marius Oprea announced the official opening of the Institute for the Investigation of Crimes of Communism. Since then files have been released to several evangelicals contributing to the research. They learned for the first time that friends or pastors of churches had been infromers (Cruceru (2007). Collaboration with *Securitate* was widespread, it is doubtful that a full accounting will ever be brought to light. Vasicia Craitor's *Redemption Memory* (2010) is a start in the right direction.

established their own networks. In the early 1990s, dozens of newly arriving Western FBOs actively sought out church partners (see Chapter 2). Findings from Phase One revealed the term 'child in need' carried a different meaning for church leaders than for FBOs. FBOs assisting street children were sometimes criticised by pastors for 'wasting church resources' or 'taking good people out of the churches where they were more needed' (FBOL#28, 2005). Nine pastors faulted the FBOs for 'bypassing the local church' by not first assisting the poor children and families who were members of the churches. Interview analysis yielded three primary factors that shaped these perceptions of FBOs: evangelical identity and fragmentation, change brought about in evangelical ideology in transition to an open society, and financial expectations of the churches of FBOs.

Evangelical identity and fragmentation between churches

Before 1990, evangelicals had been denominationally divided with limited means of building trust and collaboration. The three main groups (Baptists, Pentecostals, and Brethren) had communication with sister churches but little cooperation between the denominations; what did occur was based on relationship or friendship.

> Before 1990, I don't think we ever met together as pastors from our city from the different churches [across denominational lines] didn't think it was important and in some cases the Baptists accused us [Pentecostals] of 'taking away their members' (FBOL#43, 2005).

When FBOs arrived, church leaders expected Western personnel to learn the Romanian language and culture. Many did not, Ţon appealed for missionaries to come who were willing to make a long-term commitment to serving the churches (1993:2). It was also expected that FBO personnel would acquire 'competence' in the evangelical subculture; churches did not change their practices to accommodate FBOs.

> One needs to contextualize himself in order to be effective … in Romanian this means a double contextualization – accommodating not only to the secular culture but also to the Romanian church subculture. The churches from some areas of the country [Moldova] are extremely legalistic and do not accept outside ways easily (Barbosu, 2004:4).

Bulzan authored the first study of Romanian evangelical identity (2005).[39] He stated 'there is no coherent picture of how far evangelicals have moved

---

[39] 'The Status of the Evangelical Movement in Romania' was funded by in part by World Vision. Bulzan led a team of researchers who surveyed over 1200 evangelicals to understand what sense of identity existed, what united and divided them, and their attitudes towards politics, society, and civic causes.

towards a common identity over the past 15 years' (2005:1). Dobrincu elaborated on the impact of sectarianism:

> The legalism, the anti-intellectual spirit in the churches, the resistance towards some of the essential elements of modernity (i.e. appreciating a critical spirit, rationality, civic responsibility, etc.) are powerful streams of influence in the evangelical churches (Dobrincu email, 2004).[40]

Fragmentation worsened as FBOs imported their models of church, theological divisions, and denominational structures. Childcare FBOs were a part of the process; many unknowingly contributed to the divisions. Taloş called both evangelical and Orthodox churches to greater unity:

> In times of economic, political, and social distress, Romanians often find hope and trust in the church. This is why it is imperative that Romanian evangelical churches set aside feelings of animosity and work together to bring salvation, renewal and restoration to the Romanian people (1997:21).

FBOs saw the lack of cooperation and assumed the divisions in the churches were over minor issues, such as worship styles, music, clothing, and outward forms. Few invested time and resources to adequately understand historical and social factors shaping evangelical identity.[41] Rogobete, a Romanian political scholar, analysed the question of Western and Orthodox (Eastern) identity, but pastors and FBO leaders working with children have largely ignored his work.[42]

Changes in evangelical ideology in an open society

The churches and believers were caught in a vortex of socio-cultural change arising from a number of factors: adapting to the economic fallout, changes in general society for which they had no roadmap, a sense of dislocation, and marginalization as a religious minority (Downes, 2001:37-9; Roman, 2003). One middle-aged pastor expressed a common frustration, 'it was better for us under the communists, at least then we knew what to expect' (Pas#5, 2004).

---

[40] Quote from an questionairre answering specific questions, he adds, 'I think that the Romanian *Pocăiţi* are less evangelical and more like the American fundamentalists, even though this term is used only by those who had strong contacts with the American fundamentalists, especially the Baptists from the Southern Convention, the Dallas-like dispensationalists or the apocalyptic Pentecostals' (Dobrincu, 2004).

[41] Seventy per cent of FBO leaders said they had assumed the reason the churches were not working together was they 'disagreed over church [internal] issues'.

[42] Rogobete's paper, 'Morality and Tradition in Post-Communist Orthodox Lands: on the Universality of Human Rights with Special Reference to Romania' was presented at the American Political Science Association. Rogobete contrasts identity in the West that is based on individual rights and values ascribed to individual worth with identity in the Eastern tradition which is linked to ethnicity, religiosity, and national identity (2003:12; 15-16).

Before 1990, following Christ entailed becoming a member of a persecuted community with significant implications for how one was to live out their faith. The shift to an open society, the influence of the West, and 'consumer choice' changed the ideology of taking an oath of allegiance to Christ and belonging to a local church.

> [Following Christ and church membership] now became one of many possible options and did not carry the same stigma as before. There was still opposition from the Orthodox Church to be sure, but nothing of the scrutiny and suspicion of the communist state (FBOL#64, 2005).

Kusnierik, suggested that churches were not prepared for the complexity of the so called 'free market' of post-communist Eastern Europe (1996:1). It is questionable if the church could (or should) have been 'prepared' for the invasion of the West, but there is no denying the scale of change that swept into Romania after 1990. With the coming of a 'market economy,' evangelicals were unprepared to adopt their message and seek a 'market share'.[43] I hypothesize that one reason the American mission agencies were so influential with Romanian evangelicals was their expertise in 'marketing' the message of Christianity. As one American missionary put it, 'it is all about the market, which is the measure of success' (FBOL#4, 2003).[44] An Australian observed how leaders were adapting to the changes of the early 1990s.

> I know some leaders who did significant things before the Revolution have adapted quickly, continuing their ministry in ways relevant for the new conditions, while the others are still puzzled and did not know what to choose from the multitude of opportunities offered to them' (FBOL#3, 2003).

Some churches shifted from a confessional ideology to adopting a programmatic or strategic (market) approach. Churches started by Western missionaries appealed directly to younger (age < 20-25) Romanians offering 'charismatic worship services', as in the case of Brasov Christian Centre (*ACVN*).[45] In the communist era, it was possible to talk of a willingness to suffer for a faith that was not negotiable. For the generation that had lived by

---

[43] The 'free market' is certainly an oxymoron as nothing is 'free' in the capitalist market. The transition in Romania (1990-1994) was acute and impacted all phases of life. Under the communist system, economics, politics, and society were centralized by the State; after 1990 each sector acted independently. Whilethe evangelical church had a limited role under the communists, it accepted its role as a 'confessing and believing church'.

[44] Marketing companies (Leo Barnett, StarCom, and MTV) invested in research and profiled the emerging youth market, flooding the country with music, clothing, and products designed for a 'global youth culture'. See also Rubatos (2004).

[45] One usually thinks of Pentecostal churches as places of enthusiastic worship. The Romanian Pentecostals did not clap, sing loudly, or promote 'enthusiasm'. These 'new charismatic' churches were very attractive to younger Romanians who had grown up in the 'legalism and control' of the 'more traditional' churches.

these principles the shift to an open society was difficult, as illustrated in this anecdote from a pastor in Cluj.

> My father walked many miles to visit all the people in his church; he was harassed, arrested and once severely beaten. When some Western missionaries met him and saw that he had to walk they said, 'you need a car.' Today in the church we have many young people that don't have to pay the price my father did; they can get jobs working for the Westerners. I wonder if these young people will learn to believe, pray, and have the commitment my father had (Pas#6, 2004)?

Aspects of their faith had been tested under communism and religious dogma had been concretized but evangelicals were not equipped for competition that came with a market economy and FBO entrepreneurialism. By the late 1990s, evangelical churches were one of many new options for young people; described as the 'Pro TV generation' (Cotrau, 2003).[46] FBOs offered jobs to Romanians who could speak English and help with their agenda, creating additional suspicion in churches, 'our loyalty was constantly questioned due to our close links with foreign organizations' (FBOL#43, 2004).

New childcare projects and churches were being started 'on a regular basis' throughout the 1990s. In Phase One, 60 per cent of FBOs said 'starting a childcare foundation' was a higher priority than dialogue with pastors about societal changes affecting the churches. Church growth slogans such as 'all of Romania must be reached with gospel' (OCI, 2001) did little to encourage constructive FBO-church dialogue.[47] A frequent response from pastors was 'they [FBOs] will do what they came to do' (Pas#5, 2004).

Financial expectations of churches led to dependency

Tensions developed when churches expected material and financial assistance to be sent through the church and FBOs chose instead to directly assist children. These expectations had been set in motion in the 1980s as agencies brought in Bibles, medical relief, and other 'underground support'. Throughout the 1990s, churches experienced increasing economic adversity caused by the

---

[46] Pro TV and Pro Media are the commercial names of the largest media concern in Romania, owned and operated by controversial businessman with connections to the old *Securitate*, This network was one of many that began offering Western style programming to Romanian youth in the 1990s.

[47] I contrast this with Newbigin's model: evangelism means persuading people, but it does not mean proselytizing them (1995:121-23). This agenda to take 'the gospel to Romania' is verified in literature from dozens of FBOs and mission agencies. One is pressed to ask, 'what gospel did they have in Romania after nearly 15 centuries of Christianity?'

devaluation of the national currency (lei) and inflation.[48] A thriving underground economy accounted for up to 40 per cent of the GNP.

Expectations of foreign financial assistance fuelled the infusion of capital, resulting in competition for funds. By 1994, this had turned into a flood, signalling to churches that 'our Western brothers and sisters want to help us' (Pas#1, 2003) creating a cycle of dependency on foreign assistance.[49] Financial sustainability means that a church can support itself without outside assistance and is a theoretical principle in both missiology and community development (Allen, 1962; Roseland *et al.*, 1998).[50]

Negruţ said 'projects' had become the marks of missiological correctness, whether or not the 'projects' were relevant for Romania; 'what is missing on both sides [West and East] is a theology of the church and mission that overcomes ... the legacy of Western individualism and Eastern European collectivism' (1999b:22).

I am suggesting that children provide missiological clues; they are not simply objects of missional concern. Ţon questioned the emphasis on quick results with little appreciation for long-term sustainability in mission partnerships. [51] In some cases, local city officials criticized Romanian churches for making unfulfilled promises which had been predicated on FBO funding (Ţon 1993:5) [52]

Many FBOs lost sight of the basic principle that 'God expects his people to use the resources they have no matter how meagre (Phil 4:12-19)' (Engel & Dyrness, 2006:73). While much of the assistance was given in a genuine spirit of Christian compassion, aid was not always distributed wisely; creating problems for churches that focused on 'brick and mortar projects'.[53] I include

---

[48] Robila (2001) examines this impact on the poorest families and psychological functioning of adolescents. The average net salary per capita in 2000 was 40£ (a 39 per cent increase over 1998), the rate of inflation was 45.7 per cent in the same period.

[49] Economic dependence is discussed here as it affects the sharing of power in organizations and has implications for FBO-church childcare.

[50] I surmised that most of the Western FBOs would have understood 'in principle' the validity of a local church supporting itself in ministry; how they worked this out in actual practise and partnership is another matter. See Bonk (2003) *Mission and Money: Affluence as a Western Missionary Problem.*

[51] When power and decision-making lie with the organization outside the country, and not with the local indigenous churches, this undermines their ability to manage their own affairs. Too often mission agencies act as promotion and distribution centres that bypass the national or indigenous church (Samuel & Sugden, 1983:154-55).

[52] See the debate that ensued from this article in letters to the editor in EWC&MR and *Missionary to Romania Criticizes Western Short Term Evangelism* (Byrd, 1993).

[53] That is, building of large and expensive edifices that were in excess of the current and foreseeable needs. A visitor to Romania today will find many a number of expensive church buildings and educational facilities that represent this phase of giving in the 1990s.

two responses that describe financial expectations. The first is from a Western FBO director with 13 years experience and 'wiser' through the process:

> I think our agency has created something I call the 'evangelical elite'. In every town and village where we sent significant aid there are now these highly influential families that have 'distribution power'. They were the ones who received and distributed the aid; they became the powerful families in these places. I think we understand now where we went wrong but there were so many requests from churches for help, we just got in 'over our heads' (FBOL #3, 2003).

The following is my paraphrase of a conversation with a Romanian working with children; he witnessed the unhealthy expectations of Romanian churches (and FBOs) in the early 1990s.

> I believe you [Westerners] unknowingly used the weaknesses of the Romanians to accomplish some of your goals when you came to our country… [he described a Romanian style of leadership that is controlling and culturally conditioned]… you hired that type of person to manage your work. The word we use to describe this sort of person is *şmecher* [a con artist] … At the same time we took advantage of your good will. You were naïve, you came with great expectations. I could not believe the way the Western missionaries talked, all the things they said they would do. We could see that [foreign workers] were not very interested in understanding how our churches worked... So we worked with you to make sure you got what you wanted, and at the same time we got what we wanted (Confidential interview, 2004). [54]

These quotes are atypical; the both interviewees honestly confront a difficult area – financial mismanagement and their part in it. In interviews about financial support, there was no mention of theology or how a 'child in the midst' might point churches or FBOs towards faithfulness to God in actual practice. Children were an object of programmed intervention, they were rarely asked to speak back into the process (Miles, 2003b:97). Financial assistance did reach thousands of children, but the sustainability of these projects was a secondary or tertiary concern (Dickens & Groza, 2004).[55]

Church Perceptions of the Child and Family

Pastors were asked to discuss ministry to children in their churches and attitudes towards children in general before discussing children in crisis. The

---

[54] In a similar interview, a pastor commented on Western missionaries with 'options': 'I was shocked at all the options the Americans had in their approach to ministry. We had no such thinking; they seemed to be able to make unlimited choices while we had been living in a straight jacket for most of the past 30 years. When you are tied up like that for so long you forget you even have arms' (FBOL#32, 2005).

[55] See Chapter 3. This was a problem for both NGOs and FBOs; the difference is the denominational FBOs and mission agencies had decades of historical precedents that should have informed their practise in Romania in reference to churches.

findings are reported separately below. No set of categories can completely describe how the churches perceive children.[56] I examine those categories which best embrace the data from the interviews: theological perspectives of children and how children are perceived as part of the church and family. I present a continuum of ministry responses and conclude with external factors that influence church perceptions.

Theological perspectives of children

I did not find that churches were engaged in 'critical or systematic' theology with children, instead I describe what follows as 'operative' or 'irregular theology' (Barth, 1963:47).[57] Three primary subcategories were discussed: the nature of sin and need for salvation, Gods love and grace, and children as 'a gift from God'.

Perceptions of conversion: saved from sin

Romanian pastors hold a high view of sin, forgiveness, and the biblical centrality of redemption in Christ. The influence of 'original' sin on all children is taken seriously as all are born 'in Adam', and sin is passed along to every member of the human race, several pastors quoted Romans 5:12-14. Pastors stated categorically they believed that children needed to be 'saved from sin' or 'rescued from sin by the cross and blood of Jesus Christ'.[58] Romanian doctrine on original sin and redemption is rooted in Anabaptist/Baptist heritage, conservative Brethren, and the holiness influence on Pentecostals (Bulica, 2004:271).[59] In the interviews, one pastor referred to Augustine, two to Luther, but most stated their positions with no theological

---

[56] I am relying on interviews with local pastors to get their perceptions of the place of the child in the family and church. I interviewed several Romanian seminary professors to fill in what data was lacking from the pastors.

[57] Barth's term 'irregular theology' is helpful in this context; next to the 'official theology' of the churches and the academy there is the 'irregular theology that appears in sermons, pamphlets, letters, and other non-official expressions of the church such as sermons and conferences' (Barth, 1963:48); also see Maachia (1999:11).

[58] Barth said that 'sin is the possibility that union between God and man may be broken' (1968:246); however, most Romanian pastors would change the word '*possibility*' to '*reality*'. Pastors were uniform in their responses that all have sinned and fallen short of the glory of God.

[59] None of the pastors went on to explain how they understood the effect of conversion on original sin, other than to say children would be 'saved'. I gathered from the interviews, conversations with pastors, and listening to their preaching that conversion did not eliminate the flawed nature of humanity implicit in the doctrine of original sin. See Chapter 7 for discussion of 'conversion as outcome'.

exposition. The pastors held uniform views on humanity's sinful condition (Stortz, 2001:78-80; Bendroth, 2000:495-96).[60]

Bendroth explores the unease in contemporary theological circles with the concept of 'Adamic Sin' and suggests that the modern theological landscape has become more 'complicated' since the middle of the 19th Century, as theologians have struggled to come to terms with the many 'moral contradictions' of childhood. In so doing it could be argued in rebuttal that the West has simplified its view of sin and children and handed it over to the optimistic educational and welfare process of the secular state. In the West there has been a sliding away from the difficult spiritual and intellectual struggle to address sin in both children and adults. Romanian evangelicals have not followed this path and are still engaged with the questions of sin, many times at variance with the views of Western FBOs

Children were rarely baptised before 16-18 years of age (FBOL#12, 2004), the most common explanation was they had not reached the age of moral maturity to understand water baptism (Issler, 2004).[61] Water baptism follows instruction in scripture, confession, and personal repentance. 'Wc teach and believe in God's sovereignty, he will save all who come to him in repentance; but young children are not able to understand the consequences of their sin' (Pas#8, 2006). When asked about spiritual condition of children before coming to Christ, pastors responded that children (all human beings) are 'dead in trespass and sin' until they are 'reborn' from above (John 3:2-3).

Some Western FBO leaders dismissed theological convictions of pastors concerning conversion and salvation as 'simplistic' or 'extremely narrow' (FBOL#18, 2004). I suggest it would be more helpful to understand it as a serious point of theology held with conviction that needs greater theological explication. Children can be regarded as 'both sinful creatures and moral agents' (Bunge, 2004:46).[62] Bunge encourages a 'broad and complex view of children' (:44). She develops a four-part rubric to explain how the Christian tradition has understood 'children as sinful creatures and moral agents':

> 1) Stating that children are sinful implies they are born into a world that is not what it ought to be; there are many factors mitigating against children and causing them harm. 2) To say children are sinful means they carry out actual

[60]See Storz (2001:88-94) for discussion on Augustine's understanding of Adam's transgression and the nature of the human being. Augustine's views on original sin are influential in Romania by way of reformed theology (via Luther and Calvin). See Bendroth in 'Children of Adam, Children of God' (2000) .

[61] I identified very little published material in Romanian sources about age of accountability. Views of 'believer's adult baptism' have been disseminated by Baptist theological doctrine: 'it is generally recognized that Baptist theology in Romania has been under the influence of both Protestantism and Anabaptism (Bulica, 2004:270). Most Baptist theology was transferred to Romania from European Baptists with little cultural modification or sensitivity to the Romanian context (Dobrincu, 2001).

[62] This theological view is supported in Scripture (Genesis, Psalms, and Proverbs).

> sins; they are moral agents who act in ways that are self-centred and harmful to others. 3) Young children and infants are not as sinful as adults and need to be treated with tenderness and care. 4) Since children are sinful, they have also been viewed as equals in the eyes of God that has helped breakdown barriers of race, gender, and class (2004:46-7).

The pastors hold a theology that deals with conversion in terms of sin and atonement; it is not mixed with secular caring and welfare terms prevalent in the FBOs. However, when pastors speak of sin, they should be careful to address sin as revealed in the light of God's grace and forgiveness (Rom. 5:15-17).[63] Romanian pastors have yet to debate questions of 'nature vs. nurture' typical of Western concepts of childhood (Cunningham 2005). Pastors would disagree with a definition of sin, put forward by Loder that may be more acceptable to Western FBOs:

> ...sin is to be understood as the pervasion or turning inward of the human spirit, producing internal conflict, anxiety, and self-destructive behaviour. The failure of persons to create and compose lived and liveable worlds may be studied in the human sciences as adaptation failures – disintegration of groups, societies, and culture (Loder, 1998:29).[64]

Pastors did not use the terms 'holistic', 'child rights', or 'well-being' as theological categories.[65] At this juncture in the argument, the divisions between '*from above*' and '*from below*' stand in sharp dichotomy.

THE LOVE OF GOD AND 'GIFTS FROM THE LORD'

Secondly, pastors used biblical language concerning God's love and ultimate intention for children (Matt. 18:3; 13-14; Mark 10:13-14). There was agreement with the FBO perception that God's love and grace should be extended to all children and that the church should bless and receive children. The ultimate solution for the child's life was found in redemption and love of Christ. The phrases 'God's love, God's forgiveness, or mercy for children' were used by 95 per cent. Pastors differ from FBOs concerning the role of the church in providing ministry to children. Pastors claimed that the church is better equipped for providing 'spiritual nurture, evangelism, and discipleship' than providing programmes for children who have experienced physical or

---

[63] Barth commenting of Rom. 5:15 '... sin is shown forth as the power, which reigns, within the closed circle of humanity. Nevertheless, its power is bounded by the freedom of God, of God Himself, and of God alone ... it has no other boundary'. It is required of us that we explicate sin in light of God's grace and mercy (1968:257).

[64] I find legitimacy in both the theology of the Romanian pastors and Loder's approach to the human spirit. Human sin, fallenness, and separation from God have been reconciled in the work of God in Christ. This is God's grace and mercy towards children and humanity. At the same time, as a Pentecostal, I favour a wider approach to understanding the nature of the human spirit as advocated by Loder.

[65] Only two pastors were familiar with the U.N. Convention on the Rights of the Child, eight pastors had heard the term 'holistic'.

emotional trauma, an area in which they acknowledge FBOs make a significant contribution.

A third theological perception was 'children are a heritage or gift from the Lord' (Psalm 127:3). This is an ancient concept in Scripture (Gen. 30:11; 20-22; 1 Sam. 1: 11; 19). Children come from God and belong to God; they are sources of joy and blessing, gifts to both parents and the community (Thomson, 1996; Samuel, 1996:11). Pentecostal, Baptist, and Brethren pastors said that children are a sign of God's favour; Pentecostals teach that large families are the will of God for believers.[66] Biblical attitudes toward children were also influenced by the theological education of the pastor, denominational background, what a pastor thought children could comprehend of God, and openness to learning from children.

Church and family influence on the child

The communist legacy influenced the church's perspective on what responsibility it held for child evangelism and assisting families with the task of raising children. As one pastor described it, '[Before 1990] we could not invite children from the villages, any evangelism with children who were not born to parents in the church was illegal' (FBOL#38, 2004).[67] Another explained why his church did not prioritize ministry with children.

> Ceauşescu's government wanted the children to belong to the 'Pioneers'. Before the revolution we had to be very careful about activities with children in the church as informers watched us closely. I don't think we neglected the children but they were not our main concern (FBOL#40, 2004).[68]

On the one hand, when FBOs gave direct assistance to children in crisis, pastors argued that the '*local church must come first*' in delivery of care to children. On the other hand, churches tended to prioritize ministry to adults over children. When asked about this, pastors argued from the logic that if there were no local church, then there would be no believing families or adults,

---

[66] This is also true in other legalistic churches. Pentecostals are taught that sex is only for procreation and there is an increased blessing for more children. I speculated in my field notes that Pentecostal churches had sacralised the decree from the government that Romanian women were to have at least five children. The paradox often struck me between the serious and sombre atmosphere characterizing church services versus the complete disappearance of solemnity outside of church – laughter, joy, and celebration surround most social occasions – especially weddings. No doubt, there is some 'duplicity' as believers have read the Song of Solomon.

[67] A few churches had Sunday school programmes for children prior to 1990 and held summer camps. 'It took us a while to realize after the revolution that we could share the gospel with children outside our churches' (Brethren Elder, 2004)

[68] Three pastors discussed the implications of the communist State's control of the society and influence on the Romanian family described in Chapter 3. Other pastors did not seem to recognize this when they discussed families in their churches.

therefore children who came to Christ would have no place for grounding in the faith. Since pastors had a marginal understanding of the 'parachurch structure', the local church was their primary reference point. 'How can a child come to Christ and be meaningfully discipled outside the local church?' (Pas#6, 2004).

Pastors maintained that the Christian family was a fundamental unit of the church or as Chrysostom put it, the 'little church' (Guroian, 2001:64).[69] Godly parenting and raising responsible children are expected outcomes in the lives of believers.[70] Parental authority rests in 'a divinely appointed spiritual mission to carry out and mediate a promise of grace to one's children' (Werpehowski, 2001:395). Romanian families are generally nurturing towards young children. Children under seven or eight years of age are usually not a concern for the pastor or church; they are the responsibility of the parents.[71] I found little evidence that ministry to children, youth, and family had been critically examined in seminaries or churches in the 1990s. Much remains to be explored in historical theology and implications for children in Romanian evangelicalism (Osmer, 2000; Bunge 2004:42-53). Only three pastors had studied early child development. Twenty-four pastors had obtained baccalaureate degrees or higher in theology (biblical studies), none in human or social studies. Given that Romanian evangelicals have a better grounding in theological studies, a logical place to advocate for future child scholarship might be in theology or mission with children.[72]

Methods used by both churches and FBOs in providing ministry to families were questioned by a pastor of large church and director of a local FBO:

> I think that many FBOs working with children are *treating the symptoms* but *not the roo*t of the problem. We need some of them to help us [pastors and churches] understand how to better serve our families. Our families are held together by 'cultural glue' but our churches simply make assumptions about the role of husband and wife towards children (FBOL# 9).

---

[69] See Guroian (2001:64) 'The Ecclesial Family', he cites Chrysostom's homily on Eph. 5:22-23 'If we regulate our households [properly] … we will also be fit to oversee the church, for indeed the household is a little church. Therefore, it is possible for us to surpass all others in virtue by becoming good husbands and wives'.

[70] This of course has historical precedence in the theology of Luther, see (Strohl, 2001:134-44), and others since the Reformation; see Pitkin's scholastic assessment of Calvin and children (2001:160-90).

[71] The majority of the pastors said the primary responsibility of the church is towards adult members, and adults shape the spiritual lives of children. 'Children are to obey their mothers and fathers, they learn about faith in the home, we feel parents have a responsibility to oversee their children (FBOL#9, 2004).

[72] Research helped to illuminate that Romanian evangelicals have yet to access their theological heritage concerning children, see 'Historical Perspective on Children in the Church: Resources for Spiritual Formation and a Theology of Childhood Today' (Bunge, 2004).

Since 2002, a discussion has emerged in the churches that more must be done to help families know how to disciple their children. The economic situation in urban areas is creating an upwardly mobile middle class and many urban churches still are using methods appropriate to pre-1990 Romania.[73] The rush to join the middle class is putting pressure on both parents to work outside of the home and consumerism is creating a highly competitive economic situation. National divorce rates have doubled since 1999 (INSR, 2005).

Reflection on theological assumptions and values

Romanian pastors and churches prioritize conversion to Christ; this is a transcendent category and eternity with Christ is a central assumption in church life. In this framework, before children have 'spiritual value' and can be formally discipled in the church, they must become followers of Christ. Spiritual care for children is moved to an older age than in the West; the unspoken assumption may be that younger children are 'spiritually undervalued' in the church before they make a decision for Christ. However, evangelical churches value family and assume the believing family will 'nurture children and prepare them for repentance'. This leads the FBO to ask a legitimate question, 'what about the children who have no parents (believing or otherwise)?' FBOs went directly to children on the margins who were 'outside' the reach of the local church families.

It may be possible that Romanian churches keep alive the idea of the nurturing believing family and local church in ways the Western FBOs do not, while FBOs are able to create programmatic responses to children in crisis that Romanian churches have not envisioned. I looked for evidence in the cases that FBOs combined their gifts in caring for marginal children with those of families in local churches. I will explore these findings in Chapter 7 and 8. Churches are communities where families are linked together over the long-term, they represent several generations located in one place, and they are *embedded* in community life. Unlike FBOs, churches do not exist by hiring personnel or organizational contracts; their social care is long-term and delivered through family networks. Where FBOs are bound by organizational parameters that limit their bonding with local communities, churches are not. Churches may practise a narrow form of spirituality, but their social care goes much wider. 'They don't just add spiritual care to social action, but they are socially active in ways that FBOs can never replace' (Willmer email, 2005).

---

[73] Before 1990, church members were not economically 'upwardly mobile'. For a historical parallel, see Bendroth's 'Children of the Middle Class' (2000:499-500). She argues that the rise of a middle class in America in the 1800s created a new construct of childhood: 'children became objects of parent's devotion, and since they had no economic function children were in a sense the … projects of their parents' (:500).

Continuum of responses to child ministry

In 1990, Baptist, Pentecostal, and Brethren ministry with children varied church-by-church, not denomination-by-denomination. The majority of the churches had some programme for 'youth' (14-22 years) but ministry to young children (three to ten) was limited. Churches with programmes for younger children were the exception. Traditional churches[74] combined children and adults in the same services. When questioned, pastors said church services were to be 'holy and reverent'; children should learn this sitting with their parents. Rural churches were comprised of lower income families; it was common for Romanian Pentecostal families to have eight to ten children.[75] A pastor in a medium-sized city, a church of 400 members, expressed a common perspective.

> After the revolution we started a Sunday school for the children, we only had few adults interested in working with the children. Missionaries have told us we should do more for children, but we don't think putting too much attention on children is important in our church (Past#6, 2004).

In Phase One, churches working with children in any capacity were classified on the following continuum:

I<-------------------o---------------------o-----------------------o---------------------o---------->I

'Traditional' Children are recognized	Provide some age appropriate teaching Children need moral instruction	Very proactive with strong focus on children

On the left, traditional churches recognized children as part of the family; care for children did not require serious effort from the pastor and was not a specific area of ministry. These pastors often said they lacked physical space for separate ministries to children. This seemed in contradiction to their conscious choice to build new church buildings that had large sanctuaries and little space for classes or other activities for children.

Moving towards the middle were churches that continued with most of the worship characteristics of the traditional churches but implemented ministries of religious and moral education and training for teachers. This group would

---

[74] Pastors used the term 'traditional' to identify their churches, meaning they retain the following worship formulae: church is a place for reverence and holiness, men and women do not sit together, women cover their heads, men lead all prayer and ministry, the church does not use drums or guitars in worship, and a focus on prayer and preaching. 'Traditional' would be used to distinguish this type from the 'open or free churches' that have been started since 1990.

[75] See Chapter 3, social research indicated that Pentecostals and Gypsies (those referred to as sects or minorities with strong natalist tendencies) were the fastest growing minorities in the country under the communist regime (Zamfir & Zamfir, 1996:23).

also acknowledge that children are capable of faith and choosing Christ at an earlier age than 16.[76] This comment is typical of this category:

> We see all men, women, and children [in the church] as children of God and all need some form instruction in God's word. [You from America] have developed many ministries focused on families, women, children, youth, etc. This has not been a high priority in our churches but we are starting to do it (Pas #7, 2004).

Pastors said that the majority of church resources should be focused on adults since they support the work and activity of the church by their efforts and tithes, evidence that children have little 'voice or influence' in the church (Velasco, 2003:76-7).

On the right of the continuum were churches that actively support ministry to all ages of children, described as 'bridge churches' in Chapter 5. They provide age-appropriate education; allocate human and financial resources for children, and the majority work with a Western FBO.[77] These churches provide Sunday and music programmes, use creative teaching such as puppets and songs, and organize ministry to children in the community. The Brethren churches in Sibiu are representative of this group. In the 1980s, Johann Iach worked with Child Evangelism Fellowship (CEF) from the U.S.A. and trained churches how to teach children about Christ. His son started *Ţoar* and spoke about his father's influence:

> My father had a deep appreciation for Sunday school and Christian education, I remember him teaching all us music and the Bible since I was just a very small boy. I know that some of my love for children came from him. He learned a great deal from Paul Kaufmann [American founder of CEF] who would visit Romania and our churches and teach about the importance of ministry to children (FBOL#38, 2004).[78]

External factors that influence church perceptions of children

The Romanian government monitors all religious activity in the country; the officially registered 'cults' are accountable to the Department of Religious Affairs.[79] Since 1990, a number of independent churches have been registered

---

[76] These churches would expect children to attend Sunday school and church activities, but the church would not be significantly involved with their lives outside church.

[77] This category of churches was found in every denomination; they had mostly positive partnerships with FBOs. Three of these churches were selected as specific case studies: Providence Baptist (*Ruth*), Brethren Sibiu (*Tsor)*, and Brasov Christian Centre (*ACVN*).

[78] CEF writes and translates a number of materials for children. The primary focus of the ministry is 'evangelism' for children with little emphasis on physical or psychosocial ministry.

[79] Concerning the term cult, see Chapter 2. In the opinion of some evangelicals, the Romanian state overly *constrains* religious activity, which I believe is an overstatement. In late 2006, a new, controversial law was passed in Romania restricting the right of religious associations to receive the same rights and protection accorded the 'official

as religious associations and are also accountable to the government for religious activities, including work with children.[80] The Romanian government delineates the religious work of a local church from the charitable interventions of FBOs. Tensions with the Orthodox Church and Western funding were identified as two 'external factors' shaping evangelical church perceptions of children.

ORTHODOX TENSIONS WITH EVANGELICAL CHURCHES CONCERNING CHILDREN

I have noted the tensions between evangelicals and the Romanian Orthodox Church concerning proselytizing. Where these inter-faith tensions are most pronounced (as in Galaţi or the Southeast), the question of a local church providing anything beyond spiritual and religious instruction for children exacerbates the strain. Churches have a longer history and experience with Orthodox leaders than FBOs and exhibit deeper sensitivity to these struggles. The slightest hint of impropriety on behalf of evangelical churches elicits criticism in the media, including accusations of overt proselytizing or scandals involving children.[81] These reports mix suspicions with fact and demonstrate that the Orthodox Church carefully guards its role in safeguarding spiritual care of children. This climate of religious suspicion means that evangelicals are cautious with starting activities that invite more censure.

Both evangelicals and Orthodox maintain that the spiritual care of the family and children is the responsibility of the 'church'. Ion Peia, a Baptist pastor in Bucharest, served on the World Vision board and commented on the ecumenical conferences mentioned in Chapter 5.

> We need [this type of conference] to bring churches together in dialogue around the issue of the child. In our conference held in 2000, the sins of the nation were discussed in 10 areas. A great spirit of repentance and new relationships between [Orthodox and evangelical] leaders were born. We need to find areas of common concern to address the problems of children and families (FBOL#16, 2004).

WESTERN DONOR INFLUENCE ON CHURCH-BASED PROGRAMMES FOR CHILDREN

Earlier I discussed financial dependency on Western support; this had consequences for church perceptions of children. Four churches said that

---

cults. Romania joined the EU in 2007, religious laws are designed to monitor religious activity; setting limits is a task that falls to the state in Europe. The official cults are registered with the department of Religious Affairs.

[80] Examples are: Calvary Chapel, Evangelical Free Churches, Assemblies of God of Romania, and scores of other independent churches.

[81] I collected a file of newspaper articles from Romanian dailies and Orthodox literature that accused evangelicals of a number of scandals including misappropriation of funds, sex with children, and adultery of pastors.

donors in the West had unrealistic expectations that children who receive financial help will gladly attend a local church.

> These donors want to see the children [they support] attending the church; they want pictures with the children singing, reading the Bible. We have to respect this perspective. Personally I am not comfortable when they ask us to send photos and reports as not all the children we help want to come to church (FBOS#8, 2005).

In this case, the donor organization (from the U.K.) was controlling and capitalist, as the provider of the funds assumed they 'owned the project'. This sort of mission 'imperialism' (Sanneh, 1989:112)[82] occurs when those with 'the wealth, knowledge, and power…are those who control' (Costas, 1986:6-7). In Phase One, 13 churches said they received foreign funds for children. All churches receiving FBO financial support acknowledged that donors influenced their perceptions of what they should be doing to help children. No church was asked by the Western donor to explain the local context, local church history, or religious attitudes toward children. This raises questions: is the donor's intention to empower the church to learn faithfulness to both God and child or is the donor more interested in controlling outcomes with children? To what degree do Western FBO missional management assumptions relegate control to the local church as it concerns the 'child's best interest'? The answers to these questions will be considered in examining factors that influence mutual accountability in Chapter 8.

Church Perception of Children in Crisis

I turn now to discuss how churches perceive and understand the specific task of ministry to children in crisis. Given the view of pastors examined thus far, it might be expected that local churches would approach troubled children in the manner of a family taking in a dysfunctional foster child. I asked pastors to describe how they had accepted the challenge to cross social boundaries to reach the children, to define what constituted concern for these children, and lessons learned. I also explored motivations unique to churches, and how churches utilize human and spiritual resources to meet needs.

How the churches learned about children living in institutions

Systematic research changed many assumptions I held about local churches and FBOs. I had wrongly assumed that churches in the communist era had

---

[82] Sanneh is responding the elements of Western culture that came together in colonialism and mission in *Translating the Message*. I extrapolate these historical antecedents to the situation in Romania as much of the FBO activity has been bound up in confidence of the West and its trust in pragmatism and capitalism as a basis for its 'proclamation'.

knowledge of the situation inside the state orphanages. However, the living conditions for children in the institutions were not public knowledge; only employees of the state had internal access.[83] International media reports in 1990, seen by FBOs in the West, were simultaneously broadcast by Romanian news services, 12 pastors said they learned about the conditions inside the institutions through public media.

> I remember when I first heard about it ... There was an orphanage not more than ten kilometres from our village and we knew it was there. We [all Romanians] began to understand what had happened under the communists with the children at about the same time. I felt ashamed that we had not known about what was going on inside (FBOL#38, 2006).

Pastors and medical doctors in the churches said they had no knowledge that care for children had deteriorated to such a degree. When I asked if women from the churches sent their children to these homes, pastors denied this, but given the numbers involved, it seems likely to have happened. I concluded from this feedback that pastors and churches, like the FBOs, became aware of the crisis for children after 1990; however, their responses were altogether different.

Crossing boundaries to work with children in crisis

I provide three vignettes from my fieldwork to illustrate some of the barriers churches crossed in responding to children in crisis. In Phase One, I recorded eight similar accounts.

John[84] grew up attending a Pentecostal church. His father was a pastor. He started working with street children in Bucharest when he was 20 years old. When he asked several pastors to help him do something for children; one told him: '… those children are like the Jebusites [an enemy of Israel] in the house of God, you should leave them alone.'

> So after that I decided to do something on my own, I found a few friends [from local churches] that shared my interest and we started helping the children, we only found a couple of pastors who were interested, but it took a while to convince them we were serious (FBOL#28, 2004).

---

[83] It would be inaccurate to say that people had *no* knowledge of the institutions as housing blocks surrounded some. Most were built on the outskirts of the cities but even there, the buildings were visible to the public. What was invisible to the public was the daily treatment of the children. A Romanian remembers: 'somewhere among the blocks there was an orphanage of children under four or six years old. Clusters of children clutched at the railing, emanating a fetid urine smell… the women passing by took pity on them and gave them *grisina* [biscuits] (Cernat *et al.* 2004:284).

[84] Name has been changed.

In Turgu Mures, I interviewed an American who had worked with street children in Romania since 1993 (Dobrisan & Kachlemyer, 2002).[85] When he was giving sandwiches to the street children at the *Gara de Nord* (Bucharest Train Station), he had a similar experience with a local pastor and recorded those comments in his journal.

> I know you give the street kids food and have heard what you are doing in the *Gara*, buying clothes and other things. Why are you doing this? What right have those children to this kind of attention? They are dirty, they steal, they are immoral, they are parasites on society -- and you are helping them? My own children were in want growing up and did not have suitable clothing. Why should you buy clothing, better than what I have for my own children for a filthy street child? (FBOL#32, 2004)

Kachlemyer believed that 45 years of communism had restructured Romanian thinking to the point that many had become immune to the suffering of children and others on the margins.

Hermann Meier moved to Brasov[86] from Germany just after the collapse of the Berlin Wall in 1989, and when he tried to work with 'traditional churches', he encountered similar opposition. He started a new church using contemporary music to attract university students and non-churched youth. 'The traditional churches told us we were using *worldly methods*. They said that our church should be more "holy" if we wanted to change people's lives' (Pas#16, 2006). Meier realized that the traditional churches were not working with children or youth on the streets, so the university students in his church started a drop-in centre. The pastors told Meier that indigent youth were a danger for the church and he was crossing 'religious boundaries' (Noll, 1994:121).[87] 'I was shocked that the Romanian pastors held such a negative perspective about working with troubled youth and children' (Pas#16, 2006). To corroborate his story, I interviewed two of these pastors who said, 'bringing these things into the church [rock music, concerts and inappropriate dress] are not pleasing to God … [as for the street children] they are dangerous and cannot be trusted' (Pas#11, 2006).

These accounts raise questions: Why were local pastors so reluctant to respond? Is it because street children were indeed a menace and the church needed to keep them out – or is something missing in this narrative? While

---

[85] Kachlemyer helped Catalin Dobrisan escape a life on the streets and write this book about his experiences. Before coming to work with street boys in Romania, Kacklemyer worked for 24 years in the U.S.A., Mexico, and Latin America with street children. He said working with Romanian street children was more difficult than other places as the children did not bond with caregivers.

[86] Brasov is home to a university and an important cultural centre in Transylvania. The ideology and identity of students was shifting dramatically the 1990s.

[87] Noll (1994) observes that evangelical fundamentalists are most controlling and reactive in times of cultural or societal turmoil. This is especially true of dispensationalists who want to be protected from the tumults of their day.

some approach a child in crisis as an 'opportunity to show the love of God', did these Romanian pastors demonstrate an 'awareness of limits'? Has the experience of the reluctant pastor taught him that life in Christ is a limited proposition rather than a 'covenant partnership with God' (Barth)? On the surface, this truncated spiritual approach to 'outsiders' of the pastors seems as short sighted as the FBOs that were critical of these types of churches in Chapter 5.

These narratives seem to contradict the Spirit of Jesus who is crucified 'outside the gate' to redeem what is rightfully His (Costas, 1984).[88] It has been suggested that religious communities need boundaries or 'plausibility structures' for social identity (Berger, 1967:45-51)[89] and that people prefer to become Christians [and remain so] 'without crossing racial linguistic, or class barriers' (McGavran, 1980:223).[90] But an unwillingness to learn from the humanity and pain of children is not a meaningful pointer to the good news of God in Christ and limits both churches and FBOs in expressing the inclusive love of Christ and *missio dei*.

I see potential for two axes of learning from children in crisis. Starting again in Matt. 18:1-3 when Jesus placed a child in the midst of the disciples – on one hand he offers the disciples the opportunity to learn of the Father and of the kingdom – theological categories. On the other, he offers the disciples the chance to learn a new way as a social organization – human categories. The disciples had been arguing about greatness as a prerequisite to leading in their immediate peer group. The compassion of Christ leads the church to crossing social divisions.

Thankfully, the narratives above were not a complete account of churches working with children in crisis. While acknowledging there were churches that for one reason or another did not respond, the cases provided evidence of factors that enabled a more positive response from churches.

---

[88] Costas' thesis is that Christ set the example for the church 'outside the gates'. Jesus spent most of his ministry away from the religious and political power of Jerusalem, living and dying outside the gate. The narrative of the gospel does not validate mission done from the political centre to the periphery of society.

[89] Berger argues from a sociologist's perspective that all religious communities need boundaries to maintain power, that faith communities are social structures. They need 'plausibility structures' that are communities of communication and interaction among members, having clear boundaries between insiders and outsiders. If internal communications weaken and boundaries are routinely crossed, religious faith and identity weaken (1967:45-46).

[90] McGavran is credited with the term 'homogenous unit principle' that was influential in church growth literature. Building as well on social science research, McGavran spoke of homogeneous units in human society, be they linguistic, ethnic, economic, or educational as the means by which people joined together to make group decisions (1980:225). See *Bridges of God* (1955) 'people become Christians fastest when least change of race or clan is involved' (1955:23). Those who argue for holistic mission have soundly critiqued this argument; see Padilla (1983:285-302).

Accepting the challenge to work children in crisis

Even though churches were hesitant, I identified several that initiated childcare projects with little FBO assistance. To begin such a work, however, pastors needed a rationale for working with children, especially if they perceived them as dangerous or threatening.

WHAT CONSTITUTES CHURCH CONCERN FOR A CHILD IN CRISIS?

In Chapter 5, I cited FBO leaders who alleged that churches were reluctant to work with children in crisis. Only two said they discussed their conclusions with pastors. When I asked pastors to respond, they said they *were* concerned about children (and adults) who were 'outside the church'. Their concern was grounded in 'bringing the lost to faith in Christ and helping them to live for Christ' (Pas#7, 2005). Another said 'it makes little sense to give out sandwiches if they are not given a chance to know about Jesus' (Pas#11, 2006).

In reviewing transcripts, it was clear that pastors were adamant about offering eternal life through Christ; to the degree that it sometimes seemed wider social concern was unimportant. I coded these and similar comments as '*Side A* –concern for eternity with God'. I struggled to better understand their logic, which I was beginning to consider 'docetic in outlook and gnostic in method' (Noll, 1995:123). A Romanian associate discerned my frustration and a criticism I made about pastors and offered this insight.

> Yes, we have a deep concern for redemption, atonement, and salvation and in making these things personal and appropriate to each Romanian. Most of the Orthodox do not take these things 'seriously'. Our reaction to Orthodoxy might be one of the contextual answers when asking why we are so adamant about salvation and preaching the Gospel (Pas#11, 2005).

This comment caused me to pause and put the concern 'for salvation' in a broader historical category. Since the late 1700s, evangelicals have been concerned about 'real Christianity' (Wilberforce)[91] especially when they perceive the majority church is not taking the gospel 'seriously'. Indeed, the pastors were primarily concerned with the 'vertical' dimensions of the gospel (Wells, 1994:41).[92] What was not fully appreciated (by a number of FBOs) was that the church does not stop with conversion; they invite people into

---

[91] I refer here to Wilberforce's book first published in 1797, *A Practical View of the Prevailing Religious System of Professed Christians in the Higher and Middle Classes in This Country, Contrasted with Real Christianity*. The title makes it hard to miss the point, Wilberforce, the Methodists, and the Clapham circle were convinced that the Anglican clergy and state church of their day were not preaching or living 'real' Christianity.

[92] Vertical implies a hope in God and future life in heaven, it also implies in this context, less attention to the present world. For an exposition of 'in the world but not of it' (1John 2:14-15) see Wells (1994:39-44). His interaction with Barth and Bultmann is helpful on this point.

encounters with Christ in the midst of their ordinary human experience. They then continue with the task of nurturing, spiritual formation, and creating believing communities, an expression of 'social holiness' that includes God's concern for children in crisis. It is God who leads and accompanies His people in expressing compassion and concern for those on the margins, even when their attempts may not appear 'holistic'.

THE IMPORTANCE OF DIRECT PERSONAL CONTACT WITH CHILDREN

'Social holiness' was demonstrated when believers personally engaged with the children in institutions, the streets, in hospitals, and in the poorest communities. This required churches to cross religious and social barriers (Curtis, 2004).[93] Pastors spoke of their initial experience as both a struggle and an opportunity to express their faith; they were leading their congregations into unknown territory asking them to accept children who were seen as society's outcasts.

Providence Baptist in *Ferantari* had almost no experience with the local Roma community, other than to avoid it. When this church was founded (1950s), the neighbourhood was made up of working class families. In the 1970s–1980s, many were moved from their homes into apartment blocks in the city centre and Roma clans moved into the area. Romanians do not trust or normally associate with gypsies (Achim, 1998:179).[94] Roma children are often undisciplined and crime rates are significantly higher in their communities (Zamfir & Zamfir, 1993:217-22). Pastor Bunaciu described his own feelings:

> I didn't know or understand much of the gypsy culture; I considered them rough Romanians. When we started to work with them I noticed the illiteracy and I noticed that they smelled bad, but this is not a 'gypsy smell'. I now see it as the smell of grinding poverty; we would all smell this way if we didn't have access to hygiene (FBOL#17, 2004).

A local church can offer values, community, communion, opportunity for growth in Christ, and socialization. Once Bunaciu became convinced that the Roma children should be connected with his church, it became a process of gaining the support of the church members.

> We started inviting the children to come for food and tutoring help as well as our evening services. It was a struggle; the elders thought it was dangerous.

---

[93] Curtis examined the negative discourse in Romanian society concerning the children from the institutions. She demonstrated that children from the institutions were a social stigma; they were never spoken about.

[94] Achim argues, 'their [gypsy] present condition is rooted in their historical past. Their inferior social status, their separation from the general population, discrimination from the majority population, their distinct way of life may all be traced back to their long years of servitude (1998:179. Fonseca's ethnographic study (1995) of gypsies in Europe is important. It is hard to convey to the uninitiated the deep sense of prejudice that the average Romanian holds against the gypsies. Gypsies were often the objects of vilification in popular television and newspapers.

> Eventually the regular members began to see that we could do something and accepted the children – grudgingly at first but more willingly over time (FBOL#17, 2004).

In *Sibiu*, when Brethren churches first took food and clothing to children in orphanages, they were distressed by the living conditions. They continued to visit on a regular basis, eventually inviting children into believer's homes on weekends. Despite receiving assistance from the church and foreign foundations, life for children in the institutions was not improving and they lacked trained staff.

> '… the state employees did not appear to care about the children. We realized we could do something to improve their lives, we were not experts but we know the love of God and we were determined to share this love with the children. We opened a family style home for them … members of the church worked as house parents (FBOL# 38, 2006).

I asked several church members who volunteered at orphanages and drop-in centres (none of whom had previously worked with institutionalized children) about their experiences. This exchange demonstrates how personal contact shaped perceptions of children.

> I met these children on the streets and found out they were living in the underground sewers; at first they frightened me (I#8, 2005).
>
> BP: what helped you to overcome your fear?
>
> Over time I learned they were just children who needed attention so I offered to visit on weekends.
>
> BP: Did you feel like you were qualified to help, did you have any training?
>
> No I did not know what exactly I could do to help, but I knew I could do something; God helped me offer myself to these children. After a number of months, I had lost most of my initial fear (I#8, 2005).

Pastors and church members did not deny feelings of fear, uncertainty, and lack of confidence in initial stages, but consistent personal contact with the children and staff at institutions changed their perceptions and responses. The churches maintained a distinction between members and non-members, but no pastors described children as 'beneficiaries' – a phrase often used by the FBOs. 'Churches exist because families and people believe in God and want to belong; they give the church life. Working with these children we have learned that they need of the love of God' (Pas#6, 2004). Bonding and personal time spent with children in crisis was evidence of the Spirit moving the church to wider mission in the community. *Koinonia* in the body of Christ is demonstrated by the breaking down of human and societal divisions. The church (*ekklesia*) is 'called out' of families, societies, and nations; it is called to give ultimate allegiance to the Triune God. (Meeks, 2003:85).[95]

EFFORTS OF CHURCHES TO UNDERSTAND CHILDREN IN CRISIS

A pastor of a traditional Pentecostal church explained that people in his church were not ready to accept 'dangerous' children in their worship services. The church had been established for many years and members had little comprehension of problems associated with children from institutions, 'we thought they were someone else's problem, we didn't create it so we weren't very responsive to it' (FBOL#33, 2004). Rather that accept the status quo, he encouraged a few members of his church to volunteer at a street drop-in centre.

> They [believers] had no way to relate to the children they saw on the streets. At the ministry centre they got a chance to meet the boys and share stories, [the believers] were more comfortable in a controlled setting. Later some of the men started teaching the boys work skills (FBOL#33, 2004).

Pastors expressed realistic concerns for safety of church members. Workers from the churches visited the orphanages and occasionally invited children into the church. 'We did not understand why or how we should bring these children into our churches' was a comment in several interviews. The pastors were not being uncharitable, they believed the church should be a holy place and they knew the children did not know how to behave in church services. Children raised in institutions had few 'social boundaries' and have proved challenging for the best trained social workers. Children who have grown up without forming meaningful attachments are sometimes known as 'trust bandits' (Magdid & McKelvey, 1987:13-14).[96]

This led to problems with stealing and violence toward 'normal' children in the church, even toward adults who were leading classes. The situation was more volatile when street children were brought into the churches (Anderson, 2001:30).[97] Most of the street children had run away from institutions or abusive homes where they typically experienced violence, physical abuse, and emotional trauma that continued on the streets. Most street children were addicted to glue and, in the late 1990s, heroin was becoming increasingly available (Radu, 2003).

---

[95] 'Therefore all other allegiances are subverted and reconfigured. The church gives a new sense of belonging that relativizes other bonds' (Meeks, 2003:85).

[96] Magdid and McKelvey describe the character profile of a disturbed child: 'a lack of ability to give and receive affection; self-destructive behaviour; cruelty to others; phoniness; severe problems with stealing, hoarding, or gorging on food; speech pathology; marked control problems; lack of long-term friends; preoccupations with fire, blood, or gore; various types of learning disorders; a pathological type of lying' (1987:13-14).

[97] Only a handful of churches were able to integrate street children into a 'normal worship service'. See Derbyshire (2001) and Anderson (2001) for practical tools on working with restoring street children.

In some cases, street children were asked to leave and not come back. Other churches demonstrated acceptance and patience, sometimes at personal risk to pastors and members.[98] Bucharest International Church encouraged street children and youth to attend their services; they often disrupted the services, took money out of the offering, and stole from adult members. I was involved with this church as a teaching pastor and became acquainted with a number of these children. A former gang member said, 'finding people who treated us like we actually mattered and showed us respect was influential in my decision to leave the streets and change my life' (I#9, 2006). Local churches can teach children self-esteem through affirming their worth and value, inviting them to participate in ordinary activities (Greener, 2003a:44).[99] Street youth in this particular church learned they were valuable to both God and their church-based caregivers.

Six churches gave reports of integrating children into church-based programmes. All were intentional from the beginning in finding families in the church that agreed to 'host the child' when she visited. This finding parallels evidence presented in Chapter 5, as FBOs also learned that family support was critical for intervention with abandoned children. Churches recognized that restoration would take time and did not treat the children as a 'problem to be solved'. Most pastors admitted they had no training in working with the 'emotional trauma' associated with institutional life. Christ invites believers into situations that are at times unmanageable and chaotic. This is inherent in the nature of the gospel: 'it never promises without threatening, it never begins without ending something, it never gives gifts without also accessing harsh costs' (Brueggemann 2001:84).

Motivation of the church to work with children at risk

Pastors, church members, and volunteers were asked to explain their motivations for working with children. I do not discuss responses that closely parallel the findings from FBOs (as in references to 'personal calling') but focus on findings unique to churches.

---

[98] In one case, teenage boys from a local street ministry centre physically assaulted a young child of a pastor. Kachlemyer, mentioned earlier, was also physically assaulted in his home by several street boys who had received his help and assistance. Work with troubled children and youth requires more than a passing interest or commitment. The 'faith-based' component has been explored through studies of Teen Challenge in the U.S.A. (Johnson *et al.* 2002) and opens possibilities for further study in Romania.

[99] Greener cites literature concerning child resiliency that encompasses three general categories: individual qualities; qualities of the child's environment; and social/interpersonal skills, simply summarized by Grotberg (1995) as 'I am', 'I have', and 'I can'. Children who are high in self esteem, 'I am', have confidence in approaching new situations and are better at refusing to accept negative messages about themselves.

BIBLICAL INJUNCTIONS AND PRACTICAL MOTIVATIONS

When asked, 'what motivates you to help children?' the most frequent responses were references to biblical injunctions, 'the Bible tells us to help widows and orphans in need' (James 1:27), 'we are to care for fatherless children, little ones' (Isaiah 1:17; Matt. 10:42; 18:6-10; Mark 9:42; Luke 17:2).[100] Pastors quoted specific texts concerning the 'the compassion of Christ for the lost or hurting people' (Matt. 9:36; Mk.1:41). Compassion in a biblical sense means 'pain and hurt are to be taken seriously, that the hurt is not to be accepted as normal … it is an abnormal condition for humanness' (Brueggemann, 2001:88).[101] Church motivations (like FBOs) were pragmatic and activist, 'we had to do something, the children were suffering' or 'we saw them on the streets and we offered help.' Pastors with more biblical education made a distinction between theological and sociological motivation.

> We have a biblical obligation to show [children] the love of God; my understanding of the New Testament shapes this perspective. Peter and Paul both tell us to remember the poor. I would think this is a basic mandate for any Bible believing church – not to forget the poor. God's approach to the poor is first theological, not sociological (Pas#15, 2006).

Churches understood the practicality of improving the living conditions of the children living close to the church.

ENCOURAGEMENT FROM COLLEAGUES – QUESTIONS OF FINANCIAL SUPPORT

Four pastors attributed their personal motivation to encouragement from Western missionaries or guests in their churches. Visitors saw the children in the streets or institutions and discussed it with their Romania hosts, suggesting the church could make a difference. 'Swedish visitors helped me to see street children differently and told me that God could use our church do something for them' (FBOL#69, 2006). In each case there was a prior relationship built on mutual trust. Pastors admitted that without personal trust they would have been hesitant to accept the advice (Rickett, 2002:74-77).[102]

Pastors reported that attitudes and motivations to work with children began to change in the late 1990s. After the initial period of intense FBO intervention

---

[100] See Miles for a useful discussion of 'widows and orphans': 'Being an orphan in ancient times meant deprivation of support, of legal standing, and becoming vulnerable to those who would exploit the weak' (2003b:38).

[101] The characteristic Greek word for compassion is *splagchnoisomai* which means 'to let one's innards embrace the feeling or situation of another … Jesus takes the pain and suffering of marginal ones and embodies it in his own person and history' (Brueggemann, 2001:89) See also Nouwen *et al.* (1983:11-23).

[102] Effective partnerships depend on the 'prior question of trust'; studies indicate there are three kinds of trust in partnership: trust in *intentions*, trust in *competency*, and trust in *perspectives*. 'Trust happens in a partnership when both parties are convinced that there is equal concern for the well-being of the ministry that is shared between them' (Rickett, 2002:77). See Chapter 8 for more on trust in partnership.

(1990-1997), churches took a greater interest in starting projects.[103] Some suggested that this motivation was simply a way to gain access to finances flowing into the country to support childcare projects from Western donors. 'It seemed to me that churches were more interested in getting access to easy financial help, we could see that the West wanted to help children' (Pas#14, 2006).[104] While reasonable to believe that churches learned that Western donors would support projects for children, this sort of accusation is difficult to substantiate. It does, however, reflect a truncated understanding of the work of the Spirit in leading churches to discover new ways of living out the gospel. The church is successful in being a sign of the kingdom, 'to the degree the Spirit makes it so' (Myers, 1999b:39).

Other motivational factors were: increasing interaction of the churches with children in crisis over several years, prayer resulting in expectations for change, an emergent generation of younger leaders with greater awareness of social responsibility, FBO staff and volunteers from the churches inviting others to contribute, and the slowly improving economic situation of the churches.

How Churches Utilize Means to Meet the Needs of Children

Churches rely on means and interventions that are intrinsic to a community of local believers. Pastors were asked to describe the resources they found most appropriate for responding to children in crisis. Their answers yielded three categories: a) the utilisation of human resources, b) expressions of grace, forgiveness, and mercy as interpreted by church, and c) discipleship and character formation.

How churches utilize human resources to meet needs

Churches have a resource that is essential (maybe most essential) to faith-based care for children – people who know and love Christ. Some pastors acknowledged their churches lacked financial resources; none said the church lacked 'human' resources.[105] The churches most likely (7:1) to respond to children in crisis provided specific ministry for young adults (ages 18-27)

---

[103] Based on empirical evidence gathered in Phase One, the number of church-bases childcare projects roughly doubled after 1997.

[104] Note that this comment came from a Romanian who was suspicious of his own colleagues. This is the sort of 'internal suspicion' that had become embedded in the collective psyche. Comments of this nature were made by both Western and Romanian participants. Suspicion and trust existed in dialectical tension.

[105] As stated in the introduction, I hold the assumption that human resources are grounded in the local church. I also hold the conviction that God sustains all creation and can use any part of his creation as a means to extend his kingdom.

before and after 1990.[106] These individuals wanted to do something practical for the children living in their immediate neighbourhoods. They started with basic interventions: teaching children basic hygiene, visiting institutions, giving sandwiches to street children, and reading to children who could not read. 'Our young people read the Bible, understood the implications of Jesus teaching, and then acted in faith and obedience' (Pas#14, 2006).[107] Through preaching, teaching, prayer, worship, and community the churches were shaping the minds and hearts of young believers who responded to the social and psychological needs of children.

Training in social services was not a requirement for participation; however, being faithful to the local church was. The churches were quietly laying the seeds of a new expression of God's Spirit as they nurtured families and young people in the love of Christ.[108] Several new Bible schools were started in the 1990s; as part of class assignments, students visited orphanages, engaged with street children, and gypsies.[109] The students returned to their home churches, involved their friends, and found local resources. As church projects expanded, they recognized the need for trained or specialized people to assist in the work and partnerships with FBOs emerged. 'We worked together to locate qualified people who could provide training for our members' (Pas#15, 2006). Churches did not offer experts but people who were 'concerned for the health and safety of the children and were willing to spend time with the children as an expression of Christ's love' (Pas#8, 2006).

The churches in Transylvania sent dozens of young people to work in orphanages. As this gathered momentum, they brought a new sense of purpose and energy back to their churches.

> God was working with the young people from our churches, as they got more involved with the children; more people prayed for them and started helping

---

[106] Before 1990, many of the Baptist, Pentecostal, and Brethren churches had 'youth groups'. Youth were active in Bible studies, singing, prayer, and some evangelism. This segment of the Romanian evangelical church was 'ready for mobilization' at the fall of communism. By 2010, there were several national youth networks, national youth conferences, and summer camps. See: 'The Development of Youth Ministries in the Romanian Pentecostal Union: Peniel Ministry Case Study (Lucian, 2007).

[107] The willingness of young evangelical people to start something new to advance the kingdom is by no means unique to Romania; this has been evident from the Moravians and Methodists to the modern student mission movements (Howard, 1981:21-22; Ward, 1995).

[108] In Chapter 8, I explore an 'unintended outcome' of FBO partnership with local churches, evidenced in the expression of compassion that emerged from local churches in these young adults.

[109] Before 1990, only two official 'faculties' were allowed to train potential pastors. The newer schools have been criticized by Mănăstireanu (2006) as offering shallow and uncritical theology. Nevertheless, the schools attracted hundreds of students in the early 1990s and many of the students were asked to work with children and youth on the streets.

> them with summer camps and ministry. It changed our perspective towards the institutions and gave our churches a new enthusiasm for ministry (Pas#14, 2006).

Four of these 'young people' went on to pastor churches or direct FBOs; they remain active in childcare and ministry. Young women from the churches were especially willing to volunteer; several became senior staff at local FBOs.[110]

The phrase used most frequently by pastors to describe individuals who worked with children was, 'they have a gift (or heart) for this work' (Rom.12:6). A corollary emerged from the data: if church members (especially young adults) were a) prayerfully encouraged to become involved, b) given the chance to work with children as an expression of their Christian faith, and c) the pastor encouraged the process then human resources were increasingly available. The process was not instantaneous; it required patient, intentional nurture over a period of months (sometimes longer). It was an expression of the transcendent love of God in Christ (*from above*) visible through local church body (*here below*). It was evidence that the kingdom of God 'appears among the oppressed, the poor, the powerless, the children, turning the status quo of human value systems upside down' (Moltmann, 2000:599).

Expressions of faith and grace as an intervention for children

Pastors stated that belief in God should be practical; churches should be concerned about people who do not know Christ.[111] Faith is invisible and non-historical; it is the 'point at which life becomes death and death becomes life in Christ; and by its operation we are dissolved and reconciled unto God' (Barth, 1968:151). When asked to describe faith in action, four pastors referred to the parable of the 'good Samaritan' (Luke 10:25-37).

> What we believe about God needs to find expression in the way we live. We work with street children as a practical expression of God's love from our church. We call it 'good Samaritan theology', which means we have an obligation to help those we meet who are in need (Pas#14, 2006).

Brueggemann notes that the Samaritan by his action 'judges the dominant way by disregard of the marginal … [the Samaritan] replaces the numbness

[110] UNICEF (1997; 2004; 2007) and human development studies (Overland & Koenig, 1998; Zamfir, 1996) continue to emphasize the importance of empowerment and education for women in reducing risk factors for young children. Male pastors lead churches in Romania; but much of the volunteering and socialization of children is done by women. The traditional churches tend to restrict the role of women in public worship; this is changing with more socially progressive churches.

[111] . It was noted in coding the transcripts that pastors often connected personal faith, piety, and holy living with sharing their faith and serving others, expressions of social concern at a local level.

with compassion' (2001:90-91). [112] Churches described spiritual interventions as: 'offering the love of Jesus', 'the grace of God', and 'faith in God's love for us.' Evangelicals believe faith is a gift from God based on grace, not something acquired by human effort but requiring a human response to the love of God. Faith is not fundamentally a developmental phenomenon. 'If faith is a human response to God's grace, it must be rooted in God ... [faith] is working both from the bottom up and from the top down' (Loder, 1998:31).

Church caregivers used the words 'grace', forgiveness', and 'acceptance' 55 times, and interchangeably, the words were coded as 'a primary means of providing spiritual care for children'. Other phrases used less frequently were: 'extending God's hand to children', 'demonstrating the kindness of God', and 'offering love as a gift'. I summarized a reflection on this language in a field memo.

> Grace, love, Godly kindness, forgiveness, and acceptance are core values for the church-based spiritual care. Churches also offer discipline and structure to children, but this rests on the provision of acceptance and love. Grace is not a 'mystical concept' to the churches. They mean that God accepts the children as they are and churches want to demonstrate this in their work (December 2005).

GRACE AND DEVELOPMENTAL GAPS IN THE LIVES OF STREET CHILDREN

A pastor and FBO director shared the following reflection on the importance of grace in bringing healing to children from the streets.[113] He discussed how children of different ages responded to spiritual intervention.

> In our experience, younger children [up to 8-9 years] are more open to spiritual concepts like grace and love, they are like a sponges; full of joy and excitement in their relationship with God. With teenagers things are more difficult, they don't accept the image of a 'heavenly father' – especially if they have had an abusive father at home; they have accumulated a lot of bitterness from the experiences in their lives. Traumatized children have difficulty understanding why bad things happen to them and in their teen years they exhibit more volatility and anger. Showing grace and acceptance to these children is very important (FBOL#25, 2005).

He then described his understanding of the spiritual, emotional, and physical needs of children coming off the streets. He suggested 'grace' could be applied

---

[112] Space does not allow a thorough discussion concerning theology of the 'good Samaritan'. As with many references to biblical texts in these quotes, the pastors are not speaking as systematic theologians but they have accepted the Bible as the 'Word of God'. For an Old Testament exegesis of supporting texts that were familiar to Jesus audience, see Dempster (1999:44-52). For insights into the socio-cultural context and historical setting of the parable see Bailey *Through Peasant Eyes* (1983:33-56).

[113] This individual had some training in pre-law, a four-year Bible school education, and no formal training in child psychology or child development. What follows in this account I discern to be 'practitioner' knowledge gained from ten years working on the streets with children.

as a spiritual 'intervention' as he had observed developmental gaps between their *biological age*, their *experiential age* (what they had personally experienced), and their *developmental age* (cognitive and socio-emotional). These 'ages' or stages of development are either accelerated or delayed depending on the abuse and trauma the child has experienced (Greener, 2003b:126-30).[114] I present his model as Figure 6.2.

Figure 6.2 Model of Grace as intervention

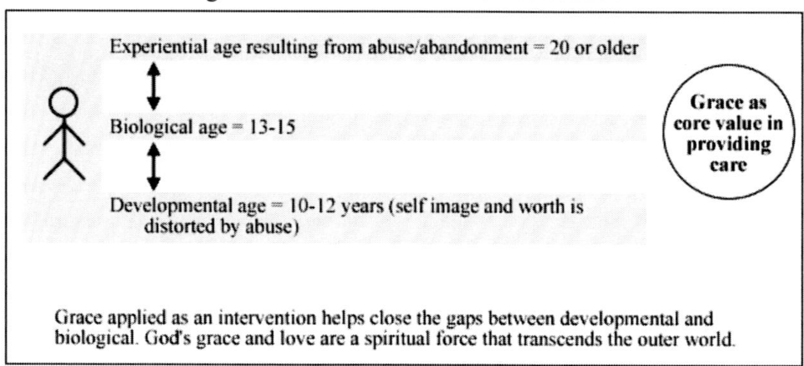

He explained 'grace which closes the gaps' as God's grace and love that is a spiritual force that transcends the visible world.

> Children are accepted and forgiven by God no matter what has happened to them, they can know they are forgiven based on the grace and gift of God. We can demonstrate this to children as we depend on His grace and mercy (FBOL#28, 2005).

This is a poignant insight gained through years of practical experience (working below) and dependence on God's mercy (from above). This reliance on 'grace' goes much further than simply accepting the experiential age and trauma and helping a child stay out of trouble. It suggests that some recovery of 'lost years' might be possible in the grace of God. The developmental 'age' and humanity of street children has been distorted by abandonment and abuse. 'We apply liberal amounts of grace, forgiveness, and acceptance in those areas where we see the biggest gaps' (FBOL#28, 2005). Grace in a practical sense meant praying with the children, sharing scripture, encouraging them to accept

---

[114] Concerning child trauma, Greener explains, 'An experience is defined as traumatic if it overwhelms the child, dramatically and negatively disrupting the stability of the child's inner world' (2003b:127). It is telling to compare Greener's analysis of trauma (through the lens of developmental psychology and neurophysiology) with the account of the FBO worker in Romania. They approach the childhood trauma from two different frames of knowledge: Greener relies on development science and the pastor is looking almost wholly to God's transcendent grace – a theological approach. Both are people of faith. What is needed is a way to bring the two perceptions into dialogue so they might meaningfully inform one another.

the past, helping them understand forgiveness for their abusers, and including them in a community of support. Without grace and forgiveness, children have a difficult time moving beyond their trauma, as do all human beings (Arendt, 1958: 236-43).[115]

GRACE THAT ALLOWS ADMISSION OF VULNERABILITY

Grace as a spiritual intervention was also described as 'vulnerable grace'. A pastor and FBO leader described the struggle many Romanian believers have with 'vulnerability'. I paraphrase his comments:

> Most believers have imposed on themselves [or others have imposed on them] 'high holy standards' and they believe they have to live under these. There is real pressure in our churches to live a holy life. The result is that we feel guilty when we fail to maintain these standards. But I believe it is important that we make space for *being vulnerable*, this is important for us. We don't often speak about our weaknesses. The grace of God allows us to do this...
>
> It has been a challenge teaching our staff to be vulnerable, but this is important if we want the children in our programme to be honest with us. It is impossible for anyone to be completely holy and perfect. I want our staff to *admit to weaknesses and to give that permission to others*. I say to our staff, 'never follow or completely trust someone who will not admit to being lame'. I refer here to Genesis 32 when the Lord made Jacob lame. If we admit *we are vulnerable and need God's grace*, children can learn to respect us and we can create and build a meaningful relationship with them (my paraphrase and emphasis FBOL#55, 2005).

I had only two conversations like this in four years of field research. Romanian pastors are reluctant to discuss vulnerability. This pastor is not describing a 'weakness' that shirks personal moral responsibility but a biblical dependency on God's grace. 'Neither is there any creature that is not manifest in his sight: but all things are naked and open unto the eyes of him with whom we have to do' (Heb. 4:13; 4:16; 12:15). Admitting to faults, weakness, and mutual need of grace is one way to demonstrate to children that caregivers are also vulnerable in the eyes of God (1Cor. 1:27-9). Jesus placed a child in the midst (Matt.18:2) of the disciples to remind them that receptivity, vulnerability and openness are the ways of His kingdom (Nouwen, 1990).[116]

---

[115] Arendt discerned that forgiveness was Jesus' most enduring action, 'The discoverer of the role of forgiveness in human affairs was Jesus of Nazareth' (1958:238). If a society does not have an apparatus for forgiveness then its members are destined to live forever with the consequences of any action (Brueggemann, 2001:85).

[116] For discussion on vulnerability in the form of the 'Wounded Healer', see Nouwen (1990: 79-90; 1994) and Miles & Houlihan (2003:202-203). Suffering children may remind us of our weakness and suffering. Children who have suffered can contribute to the healing of others, in spite of their own suffering.

GRACE AS MEANS TO CARRY ON IN DIFFICULTY

Grace was also described as a means of coping with the frustrations, difficulties, and disappointments working with challenging children. These children, especially those over 12, require intensive emotional commitment from the caregiver. Behaviour ranges from violent, abusive, and manipulative to unresponsive, often directed at the caregiver (Magdid & McKelvey, 1987:53-6). Since few church-based caregivers had prior training in psychology or social care, they relied on spiritual resources for emotional support. This was most frequently described as 'help from the Holy Spirit' and 'the grace of God' (Rom. 5:3-5).[117] Is perseverance in the face of adversity possible because in

> 'some other way or other we have penetrated the reality of and meaning of the occasion, because we have seen through it … No! *We do not know it, but we know our ignorance*. But God knows it; and we believe, and dare to know because God knows. We know that for us, it is impossible to know the power and meaning of the tribulation in which we stand' (Barth 1968:155-56, my emphasis)

Church as 'community and family' was also a source of support, 'I have learned to depend on God's grace and the support of my pastor and church, I would have given up long ago without these' (I#5, 2004).

Churches that were operating childcare programmes were required to work with the local DCP and civic authorities. The leaders and staff were subject to constant inspections and requests for financial 'favours'. 'God's grace helped us to cope with the unethical and corrupt system. God gave us the energy to go on in our work despite these pressures' (FBOS#8, 2006).

Personal spiritual formation and discipleship of children as means

Pastors and church members were asked 'what practical methods are used to help a child in crisis recover and have a normal life?' The responses fell in three categories: 1) provide an opportunity to live in a Christian home or family setting 2) find a local church that will accept them and 3) offer the child personal spiritual formation, that is, learning to live as a follower of Christ.[118] The pastors did not suggest organizational or institutional responses, as did some FBOs. They did not elaborate on methods for younger children other than

---

[117] Romans 5:3-5: 'we also rejoice in our sufferings, because we *know* that suffering produces perseverance; perseverance, character; and character, hope. And hope does not disappoint us, because God has poured out his love into our hearts by the Holy Spirit, whom he has given us'.

[118] Of course these responses do not help the child who does not find a family or church home. I have shown that many FBOs placed children in group homes and alternative facilities. The children would often live in one of the facilities provided by the FBOs and attend a local church on Sunday with supervision from the FBO.

to say it would be best if they were placed in a caring Christian family. This may indicate a blind spot, as pastors assume children who are too young to understand conversion will to be raised by believing parents. The first two responses may indicate inadequate understanding as pastors assume children who are too young to understand conversion will be raised by believing parents and churches are willing to accept difficult children. These interventions are appropriate for children from more normal settings but do not address the special needs of a child coping with extreme trauma.

Concerning spiritual formation, the churches are situated in a Christian tradition that views children as 'developing beings who need instruction and guidance', preparing them for the time when they can make a meaningful decision for Christ cf. Duet. 11:18-19, 31:12-12; Prov. 22:6; Ish.38:19; Eph.6:4. Because children are 'on their way' to becoming adults, they need nurture, guidance from adults who can help them develop morally, intellectually, and spiritually' (Bunge, 2004:48).[119] Discipleship involves instruction in scripture, learning to obey its commands, learning respect adults and others; it begins with a right relationship to God and results in right relationships with other people. Following Christ and learning to live by commands of scripture should result in 'life transformation' or *metanoia* – what genuine conversion implies. Discipleship and living for Christ is not mere talk in the churches, as we shall see in Chapter 7. Spiritual formation is seen as the primary means to develop the character of children.

Summary

This chapter has described factors that influence perceptions and expectations of local Romanian churches. Churches were treated as an independent variable in the research and were characterized as 'embedded communities of faith'. The findings and analysis provide the 'other half' of the inquiry needed to address the central question concerning factors that hinder or enable FBO-church partnership.

Evangelical churches carried into the 1990s perceptions and practices developed in earlier times of repression that had both limiting and intensifying consequences, especially in the shaping the church's commitment to pietistic values. Church perceptions of FBOs were shaped by shifting evangelical identity in the chaotic 1990s, challenges created by the transition to an open society, and financial expectations that led to degrees of dependency on Western finances. The evangelical churches demonstrated commitment to God, scripture, family; they had not typically engaged in discussions of child welfare common to Western FBOs. Churches prioritize conversion, or service to the

---

[119] Children in evangelical homes are given 'good enough parenting' for the most part. Abuse does happen, but it remains a taboo subject in the churches. This is changing as Romania society and evangelical ideology adapt to the changes of the last 17 years.

soul, over service to the body. Pastors and churches hold seriously to a theology of grace, repentance, and conversion for adults and older children. Children are expected to be nurtured in the 'little church' or Christian family. Spiritual care for children is shared between family and church, but family is the primary socializing unit. Evangelical churches are sensitive to historical tensions with the dominant Orthodox Church in ways FBOs are not.

Evidence was examined as FBOs alleged that churches were reluctant to respond to children in crisis. Churches provided legitimate reasons for their concerns; some decided that FBOs were better equipped to handle difficult children – others crossed social and religious boundaries to express practical interventions. Church-based care was enabled by personal contact with children and intentional efforts to understand the situation; not always appreciated by fellow evangelicals. Pastors and church-based caregivers were not motivated by formal training in social services, but by their understanding of scripture and a willingness to improve the lives of children, which I termed 'social holiness'. Throughout the 1990s churches took on more responsibility; FBO partnerships were not always prerequisites for church-based projects. Questions concerning donor influence were discussed as Western FBOs provide both positive and negative incentives.

Churches offer an essential ingredient in faith-based care for children: believers in Christ who offer themselves in love and service. Churches described grace, mercy, forgiveness, and the love of God as essential interventions to meet the needs of children. Grace was described as means to meet developmental gaps, an invitation to vulnerability, and provision to continue in the face of adversity. Pastors admit to ongoing challenges integrating children into the spiritual life and community of the church. Church-based care has been a progressive spiritual exercise, resulting in wider social responsibility. The traditional churches remain hesitant to respond to complex childcare issues such as abuse, abandonment, and family dysfunction.

The following chapter will examine outcomes as a factor influencing FBO-church partnership.

Chapter 7

How Churches and FBOs Describe Outcomes in the Lives of Children

Introduction

Chapters 5 and 6 analysed the broad differences between FBOs and churches as they worked with children in the 1990s. In this and the following chapter, I integrate the findings and analysis from both FBOs and churches. Before discussing the specific factors that enable partnership in Chapter 8, it will be necessary to examine how both FBOs and churches perceive, evaluate, and measure outcomes in lives of the children. Churches and FBOs have overlapping and differing expectations, especially concerning what they deem 'successful outcomes'.[1] FBOs and churches differ as well on how outcomes are to be measured or whether they can be measured. Since outcomes shape FBO-church partnership they will be considered in some detail.

Figure 7.1 Central Category 3 – Outcomes Conversion and social concern

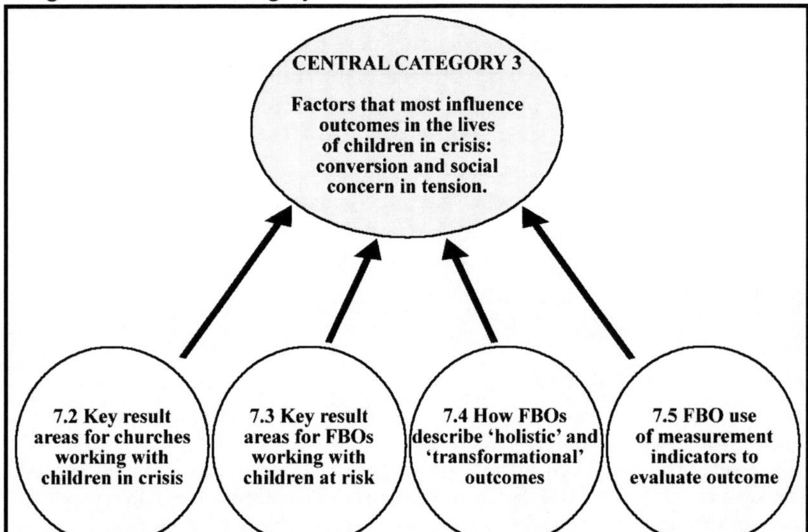

[1] I will not be assessing the efficacy of faith-based interventions in this chapter; that research awaits future endeavours. This chapter points in that direction. Research has been done in the West on the *impact* of faith-based programmes (Johnson, *et al.*, 2002), but to date, this has not taken place in Romania.

To begin, I clarify the terms 'child development' and 'spiritual change' as used in the remainder of the study. These terms, if not delimited, can lead to confusion in analysing FBO-church partnerships. This is followed by an examination of key result areas (KRAs) identified in interviews with pastors and church workers and how they evaluate outcomes. The second half of the chapter provides a similar analysis based on interviews with the FBOs. The terms 'holistic' and 'transformational' were frequently used by FBOs, churches rarely use these terms. I offer a theological critique that suggests more meaningful integration of human and divine concerns for children. The chapter concludes with an evaluation of possibilities and challenges in faith-based outcome measurement. Cross-case comparison led to the third central category, which was identified as: 'conversion and social concern in tension' (Figure 7.1).

Clarification of the term 'child development'

Before discussing outcomes, a short clarification on 'child development' will strengthen the argument. In Chapter 2, I discussed FBO conceptions of childhood, suggesting that recent child development theories have been incorporated into assumptions of the spiritual dimensions of childhood.[2] In Chapter 5, I argued that most FBOs in Romania adopted a 'child intervention' discourse (Cunningham, 2005) with little critical theological or missiological analysis. Children and child development bring inherent questions to a discussion of outcomes. What will become of children, where are they going? Much of modern child development theorizing is concerned with understanding and managing outcomes in the lives of children; about the impact of programmes, parents, and interventions. Romanian churches are concerned for outcomes in children but they do not conceptualize or describe this in terms of 'child development' typical of FBOs.[3]

I reviewed a number of definitions of 'child development' from FBO documentation; the following is representative:

---

[2] For additional resources on child development beyond those already cited see Kail, 2000; Myers, 1996; Edwards, 1996; Cohen & Chetley, 1994. More specific to Western FBOs are new courses such as 'Holistic Child Development' offered by Baptist Theological Seminary in Malaysia in partnership with Compassion International. For additional resources see: http://www.hcd-alliance.org/resources (accessed December 2010).

[3] Romanian pastors did not use the term 'child development' but they are concerned about outcomes, religiously defined. They ask serious questions about the nature of the child's soul, both for today and tomorrow. As I will discuss, they do not always ask these questions in adequate ways, not because they lack Western child development wisdom, but because their theology is narrow and at times devalues the humanity of the child.

> Child development is a process of change during which a child is able to reach *his/her unique God-given spiritual, physical, mental, emotional and social potential.* The development of each of these dimensions should be promoted simultaneously, through interaction with his/her environment, and should be viewed as a continual lifetime process (Stephenson & Glover, 1998:6, my emphasis).

This definition raises questions. Concerning 'unique': does this usage encourage individualism to a dangerous degree? And does this definition burden the child with an overbearing expectation, or requirement, to reach an alleged potential that may lead to anxiety and competition. I would argue that 'unique' can lead to the kind of human anthropological expectation that conditions the child for anxiety about her potential rather than affirming her special covenant with God, which does not depend on her performance or reaching a certain 'potential'.[4]

Does 'God given ...potential' in this statement affirm that child and human development is dependent on the gift and grace of God? Human beings become human in being called by God (Barth, 1960).[5] From a theological point of view, the goal of child development is for the child to live in relationship to God and other human beings (Putman, 2007:67).[6] Child and human development are dependent on the freedom of God to be for us not against us. God in Jesus Christ desires to be both 'humanity's partner and omnipotent Saviour' (Werpehowski, 2001:387). Tomkins suggests there is no 'blueprint' for child development that is suitable for every situation; rather we must 'consider a menu of approaches including: spiritual life, nutrition, health, intellect, emotion/behaviour, and social awareness' (2003:165-67). There are other issues that could be raised here, but I point out in that much of contemporary child development theory tends to bracket theology and what God expects of the actual child.

There are gaps in mission literature concerning theology, conversion, and child development[7] that are reflected in missiological perception and practice in

---

[4] Much Western child development theory seems to assume that uniqueness is somehow connected with 'godliness'. Children and youth in the West demonstrate increasing anxiety that shapes much of their self-perception.

[5] In this I follow Barth's later writing. He clarified his view of human existence encompassed and constituted by the free grace of the One who wills to be with humanity as seen in Jesus Christ: 'The God who speaks with man in promise and command. [God's humanity] represents God's existence, intercession, and activity for man, the intercourse God holds with him, and the free grace in which he wills to be and is nothing other than the God of man' (Barth, 1960:37).

[6] A theological awareness recognizes that we live our lives not so much as 'utterly different from everyone else' but we derive meaning in our lives from relationships with others. Jesus offers the invitation to us to say 'no to self'; he does not call us to us to independence but dependence on grace and community.

[7] Beyond Bunge see White, 2003a; Willmer & White, 2006; Thatcher, 2006; Issler, 2004 and Hendricks, 1980.

Romania. Hendricks raises an important point: 'if by "development" one means an inevitable, non-varying pattern by which every child must develop and does naturally and invariably, the gaps … are serious' (1980:231). And if conversion is a relationship with God that is qualitatively different from other experiences and 'does not build on any previous experience of a child, then the gaps … [may be] uncrossable [sic]' (1980:232).

Developmental science seeks to provide a general pattern of how children learn, think, internalise, and act; it cannot regulate and predetermine how children will function in every area of their lives. If child development is understood as a studied description of how children experience and relate to reality, then it may be helpful in evaluating religious experience, but it has limits in explaining the eternal aspects of a child's relationship with the ontological 'otherness' of God (Nye:2004:103).

Clarification of the term 'child spirituality', 'spiritual change' and conversion

Spirit, spiritual, and spirituality can also be ambiguous words.[8] A key ambiguity is that 'spirit' is seen as both *part of* the human being and as a name for something *beyond* human being.

> For the Spirit searches all things, yes, the deep things of God. For what man knows the things of a man except the spirit of the man which is in him? Even so no one knows the things of God except the Spirit of God (1 Cor. 2:10-11).

Here Paul acknowledges that 'spirit' is naturally a part of human being, and a source of power other than human – the 'Spirit' of God.[9] Loder notes that the human spirit is the 'driving force in human development that separates humanity from the rest of nature' (1998:4); his *Logic of the Spirit* is an in-depth study of the relationality between the human spirit and the divine Spirit. Too often, the human spirit and divine Spirit are pulled apart by modern theories of child spirituality. Ratcliff notes that there are divergences regarding how 'spirituality' should be defined within particular religious traditions (2004:9).[10]

---

[8] Christians 'designing and analysing studies of children's spirituality might differ substantially on the interpretation of personal salvation and inherent sinfulness as a bridge to be crossed before valid spirituality can be spoken of in children. Likewise different approaches to worship, payer, symbol, and sacrament as adults will … shape perceptions of children's spiritual strengths and limitations' (Nye, 2004:103).

[9] See also Ezekiel 36:26-27, 26 'I will give you a new heart and put a new spirit within you; I will take the heart of stone out of your flesh and give you a heart of flesh. I will put My Spirit within you and cause you to walk in My statutes, and you will keep My judgments and do them'. 'Where God is to dwell God must have a habitation' (from Andrew's Murray's *Spirit of Christ*, originally published in 1888:17).

[10] This is true within evangelicalism, leaving aside other faith traditions. Ratcliff (2004) has edited a useful volume with contributions from social scientists, theologians, psychologists, and practitioners. See also Cavalleti (1992) and Berryman (1995).

Some Western and Romanian evangelicals talk of God's Spirit doing God's special work in regeneration and sanctification as though there is no human spirit in the child. This view limits the humanity of the child; but in order to work with the child in crisis, FBOs and churches must attend to both the child's capacity to receive from God and the child's natural human capacity. Social scientists and psychologists argue that spiritual experiences can include a sense of transcendence through experiences of beauty or nature.[11]

Models are evolving for describing 'spirituality' as an innate human capacity, recognizing that even very young children have capacity to respond to spiritual nurture and moral teaching. Hay and Nye (1998) note that in order for children to speak of their experiences, they rely on the religious vocabulary provided by their families and culture. It is suggested that child spirituality encompasses being self-aware, self-directed, aware of 'otherness' – all of which may be mystical, immaterial, and ill-defined (Ratcliff, 2004:8; Nye, 1998). Nye states that that the child's spirituality is 'an unusual level of consciousness or perceptiveness relative to other passages for that child' that is relational, as 'this was often in the context of how the child related to things, especially people including themselves and God' (1998:237). The central category of her thesis at Nottingham, U.K. was identified as 'relational consciousness' built on three fundamental categories of children's spiritual experiences: 1) awareness sensing 2) mystery sensing and 3) value sensing (1998:129-140).[12] Children and youth who have 'spiritual' experiences may not have religious vocabularies to express or articulate their encounters with mystery or the numinous: that which is beyond them. This may be true if 'spiritual' is defined as 'mystery sensing' but lacks clarity if 'spiritual' is interpreted in a theological sense.

This chapter examines specific evangelical concerns embedded in both Western and Romanian perceptions of 'spiritual change' in children. Unless stated otherwise, I use the term 'spiritual change' as a theological category, reflecting Christianity's historical affirmation of a world of spirit/Spirit in which God's eternal Word coexists with a material world (John 1:1-3). Christian spirituality encompasses 'the relationship, union, and conformity with God that one experiences through one's reception of the grace of God and a

[11] For additional discussion concerning troubling dreams or visionary encounters, experiences of altruism and kindness or compassion see Coles (1990). This is part of the human capacity of the child, but it is also the habitation where God seeks to dwell. The discussion of transcendence in children when linked to spirituality leads to additional ambiguity, as there is no one definition of transcendence. Transcendence is sometimes used to refer to human being as in 'self-transcendent personality' or it may refer to the transcendence of the one God.

[12] For a summary and further exposition see Ratcliff (2004:8-10) and Nye (2004:93-7).

corresponding willingness to turn from sin to God' (Tyson, 1999:1), which according to Paul means, 'to walk according to the Spirit' (Rom. 6:1-19).[13]

Evangelicals do not deny that young children can have experiences that are preconscious or nonverbal, as when a baby forms attachment with its mother or is denied the bonding experience (Berryman, 2004:29-33).[14] Children learn to make decisions at a very early age. A child can also make a conscious decision to follow Christ, but this is a 'spiritual experience' or 'conversion' of a fundamentally different degree as grace and faith are given to the child as the free gift of God (Hendricks, 1980:233). In an evangelical sense, conversion occurs when a person is awakened by God the Holy Spirit and responds to God the Father's acceptance of them through the action of God the Son. 'It involves the turning from a destructive pattern of existence to a redemptive pattern. This re-orientation has affective (practical and action-orientated) aspects and cognitive (mental) aspects' (Hendricks, 1980:233).[15]

Key Result Areas for Churches Working with Children in Crisis

To understand outcomes and key result areas, pastors and church workers were asked to describe how they understood change in the lives of children and if change was measured in any way. Analysis of responses was coded into three subcategories: spiritual change in the life of the child, behavioural change, and change that impacts the family. The subcategories best embraced the 54 open and five axial codes from the transcripts.[16] Findings reflect input from pastors willing to work in some capacity with children in crisis. Of 36 pastors/churches in this survey, 18 churches 'allowed' the children from the FBOs to attend

---

[13] Christian spirituality is always rooted in the experience of God in Jesus Christ The witness of the New Testament has several emphases: In the synoptics—discipleship is following Jesus; in the Johannine writings—union with Christ through love (I Jn. 4:13ff); in the Pauline epistles—new life that is available through union with Christ's death and resurrection (Rom 6); in Hebrews and I Peter—Christian life is a pilgrimage 'looking to Jesus the pioneer and perfecter of our faith' (Heb 12:2) who has left us 'an example that you should follow his steps' (I Pet 2:21) (Tyson, 1999:1-2).

[14] Berryman explores the nonverbal communication system of children, comparing 'iconic and indexical referencing' (2004:32). See his discussion on brain functions in children (limbic brain, neo-cortex, left and right hemispheres of the brain). He posits that silence, intuition, mystery, and nonverbal communication are activities of the limbic brain that are interpreted and verbalized in higher brain function (:33-34). On brain functioning and emotional sensory patterns in children, see May & Ratcliff (2004:149-66).

[15] Conversion involves personal cleansing, forgiveness, reconciliation, and renewal 'in order to become a participant in the works of God' (Bosch, 1991:488).

[16] Not every interviewee shared the same information; the pastors were more likely to spend time talking about behaviour change in children, than why they should come to Christ. Assumptions about conversion were intrinsic to their expectations.

services, and six intentionally cared for these children, the latter group worked closely with FBOs.[17]

Spiritual outcomes in the life of the child

In response to the question: 'What is the most important outcome you would like to see in life of a child?' Ninety-five per cent of pastors said children needed make a decision to follow Christ; the terms 'repent from sin' and 'come to Christ' were the most common phrases. Pastors did not elaborate on what constitutes 'sin' for a child, which was not surprising given the theological perspectives concerning 'original sin' discussed in Chapter 6. Variation was noted concerning the age a child could be held 'morally accountable'.[18] Only four pastors said children could make a meaningful decision for Christ before fifteen years of age. Missing in these accounts was an adequate response to the children who came from dysfunctional families and institutions who had experienced sin and mistreatment at the hands of others. The majority of pastors and churches had yet to come to terms with dysfunctional families who are 'outside the church'. Pastors generally remained 'socially distant' from institutionalized or abandoned children.

My inquiry did not press Romanian pastors to explain their views on issue of eternal destiny of infants or very young children (Issler, 2004).[19] Romanian pastors discussed their convictions about child conversion with limited theological or missiological reflection, continued evidence that assumptions were guiding practice. After analysing the interviews I concluded, 'pastors

[17] I cannot verify that these numbers are a statistical representation of all churches in Romania, from my qualitative observations, I can make an informed estimate that this is an optimistic projection. By some estimates there are between 4,000 and 5,000 evangelical churches in Romania in 2009. Reliable statistical data concerning church-based care for children is currently unavailable.

[18] The Bible says nothing about the 'age of accountability'; this is a historical theological argument. Concerning Anabaptist views of children and age of accountability see Miller's work with theology of Menno Simons as it concerns children (2001:198-206). Barth rejected the hereditary transmission of sin that would rule out a human agent's responsibility for the evil one does or becomes (CD IV/I:500). For additional commentary and other references on Barth concerning original sin and baptism see Werpehowski (2001:391-94). See also Moltmann's discussion, 'At once God's image and a sinner' in *God in Creation* (1993b:229-34).

[19] See Issler 'Biblical Perspectives on Developmental Grace for Nurturing Children's Spirituality' for theological arguments that children are a special class in the kingdom of God, especially his comments on theological affirmations of developmental distinctions (2004:60-62) and a useful table (:62) that weighs the theological evidence and historical Christian views of dying infants going to heaven. Issler suggests that God has 'set up a special third category for children who have not yet reached the developmental milestone of an age of moral adult discernment' (2004:55) which would also include those who may never reach that milestone due to a mental disability.

rarely question their views about children and salvation, these are *espoused values* or theories resting on traditions – not critical thinking. [20]

CONVERSION AS A SPIRITUAL PRIORITY

Pastors hold adamant convictions concerning 'all are born with a sin nature' (Pas#5, 2005). Sisemore (2004) argues the way original sin is understood will impact how human nature is understood, as well as how children are perceived. He builds from the biblical text, through Augustine and Calvin, to the Puritans, focusing on Jonathan Edwards as the last bastion of this tradition in America. His argument is relevant, as Romanian understanding of original sin in some ways causes them to underestimate the value of young children. Romanian pastors show kindness to children but said all true 'spiritual change'[21] considered as outcome is controlled and shaped by the Word of God to which Christ is central. Romanian evangelical perceptions of sin and children have not been subject to the revolt against Calvinism that has characterized Western childcare since Bushnell (Bendroth, 2001:359-63).[22]

I interviewed four Romanian theologians[23] who affirmed that seminaries and denominational traditions teach a federal theory of sin and a literalist interpretation of scripture. Concerning sin and salvation for children, one said:

> The average Romanian evangelical pastor feels the most important spiritual step is to lead people to accepting Christ. We treat salvation for children as we do for adults; they are lost [in trespass and sin] and need Christ as their personal saviour (I#2, 2003).

Convictions concerning individual sin and personal salvation were so rigidly held that to question a pastor's theological rationale immediately shut down the flow of the interview.[24]

---

[20] As pointed out in Chapter 5, that the same is true of FBOs, they rarely question their views of humanitarian social concern or child development theory.

[21] 'Spiritual change' is my term or shorthand for the pastor's use of 'saved', 'born again', and 'repent'.

[22] Bendroth examines the 'problems of the sinful child' as Bushnell's critics were concerned that that he had all but abandoned the possibility of childhood sin. 'By Bushnell's time Calvinism was on the defensive as Methodism that emphasized human ability, and Unitarianism, that emphasized human rationality, seemed to fit the new order far better than an Augustinian understanding of the corporate human guilt of Adam's original disobedience' (Bendroth, 2001:359). It is interesting that the American scholars in Bunge (2001) have left Reinhold Niebuhr out of their accounts in addressing questions of sin and society.

[23] Background of these participants: PhD from UK and PhD from Cluj, - Baptists, PhD from Bucharest and Sheffield, UK - Pentecostals.

[24] I did not ask pastors to explain how they acquired their biblical understanding of sin in children and subsequent need for redemption. Later in analysis of the interview data, it became more evident that pastors had acquired their convictions from traditions handed down in sermons and in the denominational seminaries, which had served as their primary means of theological reflection, referred to earlier as '*irregular theology*'.

Romanian evangelicalism has been influenced by and resembles fundamentalism of the late nineteenth and twentieth centuries that reacted to the changes of modernity, rational ideals, and rejected more open readings of scripture (Noll, 1994).[25] 'Theological categories' concerning conversion of children/youth were 'hardened' in reaction to the changes in society after 1990 (Chapter 6), which were perceived as 'threatening or worldly'.[26] Child spirituality and 'relational consciousness' (Nye) has not been discussed in Romanian churches.

Limitations to Conversion as a 'Private Transaction' and Two 'Sidedness'

Outcomes with children that go beyond conversion and discipleship have been peripheral to evangelical theological reflection in Romania.[27] The essence of Romanian pietism is the primary interest in personal salvation. This is problematic in that it limits 'salvation' to nothing more than a 'private transaction between a child and God and that this can become an accomplished, dated event' (Trueblood, 1970:21). The humanity of children (*Side B*) as a theological category was bracketed as eternal destiny and personal conversion are prioritized. The strength in this position is that eternal life in Christ (*Side A*) is taken seriously.

I looked for evidence that evangelicals were moving in a constructive direction integrating *Side A* and *Side B*. This was found in limited measure where churches were engaging with children in crisis; these churches were grappling with the needs of traumatised children and recognized the inadequacy of one-sided formulae for conversion. It is not the understanding of human nature as fallen that is problematic in the churches, but deeper reflection and critical thinking is needed. I suggest that Romanian pastors could be 'more explicit in ruling out possible misinterpretations that diminish the fundamental humanity of children' (Pitkin, 2001:190). In the majority of cases, eternal concerns, those 'from above', dominated the logic of pastors; human development of children was rarely mentioned, even as a 'spiritual' subset of conversion.

Variations on Conversion as Outcome

Church perceptions of children and sin give some clue to the general acceptance by Romanian pastors of 'church growth' missiology, with its

---

[25] One of the consequences from the dogmatic kind of biblical literalism that gained increasing strength towards the end of the 19th century was a 'reduced space for academic debate, intellectual experimentation, and nuanced discrimination between shades of opinion' (Noll, 1994:124).

[26] I frequently heard sermons in the churches lamenting the influence of the 'world' on Romanian youth, children, and families. The younger and better-educated pastors were making an attempt to engage with these cultural shifts.

[27] Bunge (2001a) and White (2001) argue this has also been true in the West, see earlier notes in Chapter 2.

emphasis on 'salvation as a vertical relationship' (McGavran, 1973:31). Western missionaries working with churches gave a similar rationale for treating children as 'lost without Christ'. The typical Romanian evangelical church had little experience in dealing with children recovering from trauma or abuse. The pastors did not address questions of structural or societal sin 'against children' in any interviews.[28] I discuss two methods observed in 'leading children to Christ' and different expectations of outcome.

In the first, children from the streets or FBO programmes were taken to a typical evangelical church. They were encouraged to participate in normal church-based activities; evidence of the division of labour between FBOs and churches.[29] Churches used discipline in the form of setting behavioural boundaries. They were quick to give the children a set religious vocabulary and teach religious formula for 'experiencing salvation'. The prescribed method was to explain to the child her need for conversion, present the gospel in some format (story or illustration), offer the child the opportunity to repent and follow Christ, pray with the child, and then expect the child to follow Christ and the teachings of the Bible. This method represents a 'transactional approach' (Scott & Magnunson, 2005:449), that is, children were encouraged to 'exchange' their sins for a new life in Christ.

This is at best a 'hopeful' and at worst a 'magical' approach to children in crisis, assuming that once a child 'has made a verbal confession of faith' then right action and behaviour will automatically follow. Romanian pastors are right to an extent. The gospel is good news to those who believe, and the seed of the gospel provides new life, but 'quick fix' approaches can foster an irrational faith that breeds 'unthinking practice, insensitivity, and impatience with human being' (Willmer, 2005).[30] To insist that children in crisis receive the 'gospel' in pre-packaged ways may be damaging to their long-term recovery (Scott & Magnuson, 2005:450). It was observed that these churches rarely questioned their method of 'gospel presentation'. This was further evidence of uncritical confidence in assumptions and confessional assurance of

---

[28] In holistic mission, societal and structural injustice is discussed by Myers (1999b:27-30; 77-78); Christian (1999); Linthicum (1991:106-110) and Wink (1992). For a recent evangelical treatment of the child in society see Chapter 4 'Child Well-being in Society' in McConnell *et al.* (2007:133-159). This book, *Understanding God's Heart for Children: Towards a Biblical Framework* is a collection of papers and essays presented at the 2006 Cutting Edge Conference in the U.K.

[29] As explained in Chapters 5 and 6, the churches have accepted that FBOs are willing to operate programmes for the children that provide programmatic response to specific needs. I am not arguing for this as a 'best practice' but describing what currently exists. The churches believe they are better equipped to lead children to Christ and discipleship, which is directly linked to church attendance, while FBOs go about the work of good 'social work' with children.

[30] Email comment from Willmer.

'good news for children'.[31] It is difficult to raise questions in evangelicalism about what is the 'Evangel' especially when evangelicals are sure they have the true gospel and outsiders are the ones who are not true to the Evangel. This phenomenon is certainly not limited to the Romanian context and is evident in the historical development of Evangelicalism as there are tensions between what the Evangel is and what is our Christian or *churchly version* of it'. [32]

A second approach was observed in churches working consistently with children in crisis. These provided spiritual input in church activities as a continuation of their daily programmes. They demonstrated patience, took time listening to children and their life histories, and did not insist that children become believers as a first step. They were more sensitive to the trauma of children, who were welcomed and received by the believing community, not primarily as subjects to be converted. Responding to pain and pain-based behaviour is a primary challenge for churches and FBOs (Anglin, 2002). A church can demonstrate acceptance and love while at the same time provide security and boundaries for children. These churches practised an essential kind of love and kindness – gift giving, the kind of love described by Paul in 1Cor.13:4-7:

> Love is patient, love is kind. It does not envy, it does not boast, it is not proud. It is not rude, it is not self-seeking, it is not easily angered, it keeps no record of wrongs. Love does not delight in evil but rejoices with the truth. It always protects, always trusts, always hopes, and always perseveres.

This is the love that originates in the heart of God and accompanies us in our humanity in the person of Jesus Christ. It is this love that brings healing and opens in adults and children the possibility of transcending our brokenness and trauma. These churches did not minimize conversion as a 'spiritual change' but they took a more patient approach to the humanity of the child and the requirements of the gospel.[33]

Reflection on Conversion as Priority

In analysing this data, I asked the question: 'Does the priority of conversion point the pastors or churches in new theological directions concerning the

---

[31] In the language of Argyris and Schön, this is an example of 'espoused theory' with little reflection to match it to 'theory in use' (1974:6-7). In this situation, pastors say, 'we are introducing children to Christ', an 'espoused theory'. Pastors were not asking themselves if the 'theory in use', what they have been habitually doing over the years, might require more in-depth reflection on faithfulness to God in sharing Christ with children.

[32] I also interviewed a number of Western missionaries working with children who held similar views; they assumed they had 'the gospel' and were 'bringing the gospel' to Romania. Such an approach limits asking questions of central assumptions.

[33] This sort of movement will have long-term consequences, as evidenced in some forms of British and American evangelicalism where conversion is one of many possible outcomes.

child's humanity or their practical faithfulness to God?' When Jesus places a 'child in the midst' (Matt 18:2), he offered the disciples to opportunity to see His kingdom in fresh ways; the child is an invitation to listen with attentiveness to the call of God in Christ (Moltmann, 2000). I found more evidence that churches wanted to convert children than willingness to receive children in crisis in wider ways. In a few cases, church workers told children their life situations and problems were the result of their personal actions or they were 'conceived in sin'. This is arguably a sin against the children (Moltmann, 1993b:230-31). I am not abdicating personal responsibility in children, what I am questioning is the accusation that a child ends up on the street as a result of her personal actions.

This raises an important question in child theology: 'Is God *for* the child or is God *against* the child'. Does God see the child as a covenant partner or as a being who is 'steeped in sin from his birth'?[34] There were exceptions: churches working closely with troubled children did not minimize the fallen nature of children nor did they *accuse* children of sin or their situation. These churches looked realistically at the factors that had put these children in crisis; they saw the children in their humanity not as passive objects of mission or evangelistic endeavour. These churches were open to share with the children the story of our common human situation: all are flawed and imperfect, all have sinned, all need the saving grace of God – they did not keep this truth from children.[35]

Jesus teaches that children may be *sinned against* (Matt. 18:6). Children in this study have been sinned against by society, by failed institutions, and those who deny the human value of children. These children carry these sins in themselves; they have to live with not only what has been done to them but

---

[34] No churches in the study were asking these sorts of questions, so I raise them here. See Moltmann (1993b) Chapter 9: 'God's Image in Creation: Human Beings' especially his historical discussion of justification in Reformed Theology. 'The Protestant doctrine of sin is part of the doctrine of justification, and has nothing to do with a pessimistic view of sin or with the denial of creation' (1993:231). Moltmann elaborates on the historical foundations of this doctrine and the alternative positions: 'Flacius Illyricus was the author of the notorious thesis that sin is the actual substance of the human being who has not been born again' (1993:231).

[35] I first began to interact with this line of thinking when Professor Willmer presented a paper 'Child Theology' on sin and children at Cutting Edge, DeBron, Netherlands in 2003. I had been working with children in crisis for 15 years but had never taken time to reflect on how children might be 'sinned against' by interventionist childcare agendas. In these paragraphs, I am drawing on insights from personal participation with the 'Child Theology Movement' over the past few years. See the 'Child Theology Consultation in Cape Town South Africa' Feb. 2004 at www.childtheology.org (accessed December 2010). The Cape Town consultation examined how the child falls short of the glory of God, how the child is sinned against, how the child is held in the grace of God in Christ, and how the child is given responsibility to move forward. The consultation adopted this approach from Willmer's article 'Christology, Atonement and Forgiveness' (2001b).

what they have done. My assessment was the majority of the churches, pastors, and seminaries were basing operational values on conventional evangelical assumptions; few questioned how children were 'sinned against'. The purpose for having an adequate doctrine of sin is not that a charge can be brought against children that will accuse them, but that both pastor, church, and child can 'recognize what they have shared in, what they have become and what world they are a part of' (Willmer, 2003:7). Salvation and sin were typically treated as narrow personal categories, but 'salvation' is always aimed at 'overcoming sin (whether personal or structural) which is the great disorder within this world that tries to frustrate the work of God' (Bosch, 1993:183).

How churches evaluate spiritual outcomes

Pastors were asked how 'spiritual change' was evaluated; responses were based on visible evidence of conversion as in attitude towards scripture.

> We look for evidence of a new heart in children, this is fruit of the Spirit – if children have God's life in them they will have a certain hunger for God and his Word. We teach the Bible so they will have the Word in their hearts [here he quoted Psalm. 40:10] (Pas#8, 2006).

Spiritual fruit (Gal. 5:22) was mentioned in several interviews. Pastors gave a number of examples that were combined with other common indicators of 'a changed spiritual life'; frequency of use is noted in Table 7.1.

Table 7.1 Outcome indicators of changed spiritual life (from pastors)

Showing respect for God and the church	12	Obeying parents and teachers	7
Learning to pray	10	Learning to sing or play an instrument	4
Reading and memorizing the bible	9	Feeling accepted by the other children	3
Regular attendance in church or in Sunday school	8	Getting along with others	3
Gal. 5:22 love, joy, kindness, peace children gain self respect	7	Trusting others	3

These findings are indicative of the higher value churches place on outward behaviour, respect for church, participation in church life, prayer, and scripture reading (LeBreche, 2007).[36] Conversely, those mentioned less frequently, feeling accepted by other children and trust, are indicative that factors intrinsic to children's emotional health may have less value than visible signs of

[36] This finding was compared with LeBreche's research (2007). In his survey of 50+ Romanian evangelical leaders, they listed external rules, behaviour [holiness], and showing respect in worship services as their core values for Evangelical subculture.

repentance. Seventeen churches used written records as indicators of change in children: mainly attendance and scripture memorization.[37] Churches working in partnership with the FBOs had some form of Christian education, usually a Sunday school. One pastor acknowledged, 'just counting the children in Sunday school [as an indicator of success] is not really adequate, we need to do more to understand them' (Past#14, 2006).[38]

Behavioural and Moral Change as Outcome

Churches exercise moral authority in the lives of children. Pastors draw on biblical authority that gives shape to the Christian community. Concerning scriptural authority Hauerwas comments, 'it shapes a community ... without it; claims about moral authority of scripture make no sense' (1981:55). Furthermore scriptural authority and a community shaped by scripture only make sense if they are true to the character of God.[39] Behaviour change was mentioned in every interview, conditioned on the age of the child and what could be expected at that age. I had two in-depth conversations with pastors concerning how values and belief influence behaviour. Pastors showed more interest in discussing behaviour change linked to moral actions (Nucci, 1997) [40] than value formation.[41] Churches seek to socialize children into their moral community; they value observable behaviour, which their internal moral reflections have caused them to affirm (Covaleskie, 1996:1).[42]

A seminary professor and pastor explained the significance Romanian evangelicals assign to 'repentance with evidence of changed behaviour'. He

---

[37] The remaining churches did not feel written records were important. The child usually came to church with family or FBO personnel; these pastors were content if a child from the streets or orphanage 'did not cause any trouble'.

[38] The majority of the churches (24/46) made some form of investment in training Sunday school teachers and recognized the importance of providing age-appropriate Christian education.

[39] See Hauerwas the 'Moral authority of scripture and community' (1981:59-64). With reference to Romanian churches working with children: 'Authority is the means through which a community is able to journey from where it is now to where it wants to be. It is set on its way by the language and practices of tradition, but while on its way it must often subtly reform those practices and language in accordance with its new perceptions of truth' (1981:63).

[40] Moral development is an important category in Western education; see 'Synthesis of Research on Moral Development' (Nucci, 1997).

[41] Values are linked with search for meaning, trust in life, and affirming ideas of value or worth expressed in feelings of delight or despair (May & Ratcliff, 2004:149).

[42] In 'Moral Reflection and Moral Education,' Covaleski suggests, ''... we should bring the young into a [moral] community so that they are properly and seriously normed into it, but in such a way that does not preclude their engaging in moral reflection as adults. However, we note that moral reflection is done against the background of an existing moral consensus' (2003:2).

inferred that behavioural expectations applied to both adults and children old enough to make a decision for Christ.

> We live in a morally compromised society where everyone claims to be a Christian, therefore for someone to become a 'believer' [*pocaiti*] is a very serious step in our way of thinking. When someone has decided to follow Christ, then his or her outward life should change. We don't look for mystical signs; we have seen enough of that in the Orthodox Church. Our pastors look for behavioural change; these are more obvious in adults...This [logic of behaviour change] informs what we expect in the lives of children, once they are saved they need to start living more 'holy' lives. This may be why we hesitate to baptise children until they are 16 years old (Pas#7, 2003).

The expected behavioural changes reflect both conservative values in evangelicalism and conformity expected in the churches: 'As children grow in their walk with the Lord, they should demonstrate improved moral character' and 'as they grow in spiritual maturity they should be willing to witness to what the Lord has done in their lives' (quotes from pastors, October, 2006). Also mentioned were change in moral attitudes resulting in concern for others: 'showing kindness', 'responding positively to authority', 'obeying their parents', 'giving to other children', and 'show respect to caregivers'. This is evidence that pastors acknowledge children as 'moral agents' (Bunge, 2004:47).[43] Few comments were made concerning how 'behavioural change' might lead children to know more of God's love or the riches of the gospel; children were expected to learn scripture and obey its commands. The lower value assigned to 'search for God and ultimate meaning' can partially be explained in the assurance that once a young person becomes a follower of Christ, the 'search for ultimate meaning' has come to an end and obedience to Christ and the Word provide individual value and worth.[44]

EVALUATING BEHAVIOUR AND KRAS AT CHURCHES

The primary means of measurement for behavioural change was through participation in programme activities and observation of children. A staff member of a local FBO worked regularly with Roma children who attended her church commented:

> We want to know if the Christian input they receive at church has an impact on their lives. I have worked with many children from the surrounding [Roma]

---

[43] Bunge makes the important distinction between moral choice, the capacity for the child to accept responsibility for harmful actions (actual sins), and those behaviours which equate a child's physical and emotional needs or early developmental stages as sins. 'Actual sin' against others or oneself is rooted in the human 'state of sin' and a failure to centre life on God in Christ (2004:47).

[44] Romanian evangelical piety is demonstrated in Bible study, prayer, and corporate worship. I often observed children and adults engaged in these activities together. Evangelicals seemingly have little time for 'spiritual retreats' or 'higher life workshops' so faith is expressed in obedience and holy living.

> community and have seen that their lives do change as the come to know God. They are different from the other children; their behaviour [she mentions dishonesty and stealing] begins to change (FBOS#6, 2005).

Caregivers attributed change in behaviour to the work of the Holy Spirit, the Word of God, and connection with the believing community, families, and church. A pastor observed street children coming to his church from the drop-in centre.

> The children in the programme that attend our church are different than those hanging around on the streets. A change comes to the children through the Holy Spirit and the Word of God. We encourage them to be involved in ministry with other children, caring for others is evidence of a changed life (Pas#14, 2006).

Overall, churches have yet to develop complex methods of evaluation for children; in the most positive cases they are still learning how to integrate dysfunctional children into regular activities. Four churches with staff and volunteers serving at the FBOs were considering using some type of evaluation criteria. I discuss *Ruth*, *ACVN* and *Ţoar* below in analysis of FBO outcomes. I modified a programme quality assessment tool developed by Greener and used it to evaluate key result areas (KRAs) when visiting church-based programmes assisting children in crisis.[45] Five areas were examined: learning environment, routine and guidance in classes, behavioural boundaries, adult child interaction, and parental/caregiver involvement.

The survey indicated that children were expected to change or conform in outward behaviour; pastors and teachers had limited access to resources on moral formation in children and youth. Teachers demonstrated high levels of personal concern for children from dysfunctional backgrounds. The survey indicated that church-based training in 'moral formation' could provide opportunity for teachers and children to learn more of ethics and human freedom.[46]

---

[45] All the churches in this mini-survey were operating some form of child ministry (Sunday Schools, summer camps, or midweek classes/activities). The children from FBOs or institutions were included in these activities. Churched did not operate separate programmes for children in crisis.

[46] As part of my research and work responsibilities, I visited and taught an introduction to ethics in seven Romanian high schools (ages 14-19). When the students were asked to define the difference between morals (what we do that indicates our knowledge of right and wrong) and ethics (a system of what is held to be morally true) less than ten per cent of the students understood the difference. Ethical education in the Romanian school system is still recovering from the abolition of formal instruction in 'ethics' during the communist era.

Societal change and influence on believing families – outcomes for children

Pastors were asked to discuss expected outcomes in reference to the influence of believing families. The Romanian family is not as individualistic as the West, extended families are important to the church and Romanian social structure (Zamfir, 1997; Groza et al., 1999). Extended families were likely to attend one church (Keppeler, 1996).[47] In the early 1990s, Romanian pastors had confidence in the congruence of believing families and the local church as mutually reinforcing social institutions, despite earlier efforts of the State to undermine family solidarity. Confronted with social dissonance (Chapter 6), the churches sought to resist change in the ways they understood: dogmatic preaching, enforcing traditional practices in church life, and warning about 'worldly desires' (Downes, 2001:40).[48] Some believing parents sensed they were losing moral control over their children's lives as media and popular culture became more influential. [49] Provision for children's 'spiritual safety' was mentioned as an outcome; believing families were the best way to ensure this 'safety'.

Willingness of pastors to discuss family dysfunction, problems, or inadequacy in ministry was proportional to their education and knowledge of family systems.[50] The majority of pastors had no training in pastoral care for families or counselling.[51] Over the duration of the study, I noted changes in pastor's comments and attitudes toward family. In 2002, few would acknowledge that believing families had internal problems. By late 2006, ten interviewees said that believing families were having difficulty coping with changes in society.

---

[47] This statement is still largely true in rural churches but is rapidly changing in urban settings. When Keppler did his research in Romania (early 1990s) the extended family structure was still locally intact. Since the late 1990s, Romanian families have become more separated and mobile, with young adults frequently moving to the West, Bucharest, or other large cities in search of better employment opportunities.

[48] Downes suggested that churches in Romania had difficulty responding to the changes in society that she attributes to: influence of media, political pressure from the EU, foreign corporations, economic pressures, changes in demographics as the population aged, child abandonment, secularization of society, and loss of Christian values (Orthodox and Evangelical).

[49] I attended 15 regional or national youth rallies and events (2002-2007). The topics for sermons and workshops were dedicated to holy living in the face of cultural change and resistance to 'immoral youth culture' as seen in MTV and popular media.

[50] For instance, pastors in Timişoara, Cluj, Oradea (Western Romania) were more open to discuss family and possible dysfunction; pastors with education outside Romania were markedly more honest on this subject.

[51] There is abundant literature on pastoral care… for families see May *et. al,* 2005; Strommen, 1998; Strommen & Hardel, 2000; Browning *et. al.*, 1997). Formal studies on pastoral care for families and care for children have received little attention in Romanian Evangelical seminaries and Bible schools.

These factors influenced church's willingness to work with children in crisis. For those churches that did offer help, families were integral to faith-based outcomes. After 15 years leading a Romanian church, a German pastor made this observation concerning outcomes in families relevant to children.

> The families in our church are like social networks, if one person has a job, they try and get their family members a job, there is much more loyalty in the families here than we have in Germany. One measure of success at our church is observing how a family changes over time. We have learned not to think about individuals but the entire family, which we see as a resource for children in our city (Pas#15, 2006).

Church support for families working with children in crisis

Intentional efforts to assist troubled children resulted in outcomes in children's lives, in believing families, and in the churches. Since social services were limited; churches offered emotional and spiritual support to both children and the families assisting them. 'The family has the most potential of any institution for providing for children's basic needs and for shaping their spiritual and moral lives' (Bunge, 2007:83). Capitalizing on family networks, churches provided relational support to children with no connection to their natural families – where sin had disrupted the child's most important relationships (Putman, 2007:67).

Pastors described intentional care for the family (believing or not) as both intervention and outcome, as when a family decided to live for Christ or care for a child in need in the name of Christ. Believing families provided mentorship, service, and compassion to children living in poverty, dysfunctional homes, or socially marginalized situations (FBOS#5, 2005). Roma children from the Ruth School participated with young people from Providence Church in service projects around *Ferantari*. These activities had positive social influence on Roma children with reciprocal impact on church families who were involved. Churches offered children exposure to singing and the gift of music as families participated in corporate worship. Educational classes at churches brought together children from believing families and children from streets; this gave street children a sense of accomplishment, which in the long-term could 'help them discern their vocation' (Bunge, 2007:61).[52]

---

[52] I refer to Bunge's ten 'best practices' for nurturing the moral and spiritual lives of children within the context of family in this section: 1) reading and discussing the bible and interpretations with children; 2) worshipping with a community and carrying out family rituals of worship and prayer; 3) introducing children to good examples, mentors, and stories of service and compassion; 4) serving together and teaching financial responsibility; 5) singing together exposing children to spiritual gifts of music and the arts; 6) appreciating the natural world and cultivating a reverence for creation; 7) educating children and helping them discern their vocations; 8) fostering life-giving attitudes towards body, sexuality, and marriage; 9) listening and learning from children;

In Chapter 6, I suggested that Romanian evangelicals might have kept alive the idea of local church in ways that FBOs have not. This statement is based on evidence that churches encouraged families to receive children in need. New child protection laws mandated that all children from institutions be placed in 'family situations' by 2007. This led to increased childcare activity by churches and reintegration of children into believing families.[53] I asked 14 pastors, 'How do you compare family influences and church influences on a child's spiritual growth?' All stated that the family had more spiritual influence on the child than the church.

> The church is a supplement to the spiritual growth of the family. We understand repentance, faith, and following Christ to be an individual decision but the family can help reinforce and affirm this decision. We believe that the deepest spiritual changes will be developed in the family (Pas#8, 2006).

I located 10 churches that were actively involved in providing homes for children coming from the institutions. All the FBO personnel were active members of evangelical churches. There is another side to this narrative: hundreds of evangelical churches did nothing to connect believing families with children in need. One is left to imagine the impact if FBO activity had given more attention to believing families as partners in care for children.

CHURCH, FAMILY, CAREGIVER, AND CHILD – A SYSTEM OF CARE

Figure 7.2 Systems Model of the Church, Family and Child at Risk

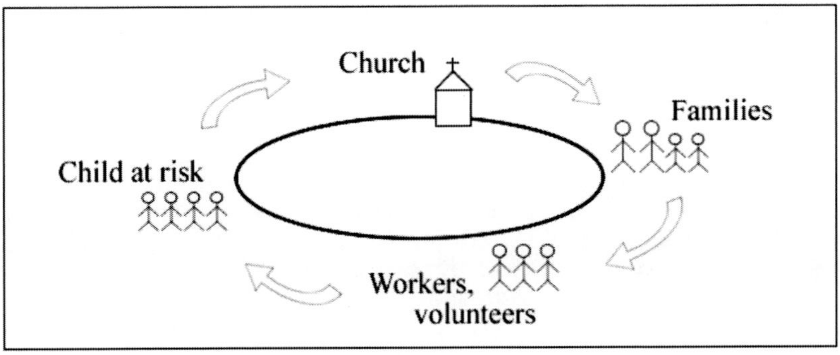

---

and 10) taking up a Christ-Centred approach to discipline, authority, obedience, recognizing that in the Christian tradition parental authority is always limited (Bunge 2007: 59-63). To some degree, each of these 'inputs' is offered by believing families in Romanian churches.

[53] While the laws did not go into effect until January 2007, changes were noticeable in 2004; those FBOs that were building homes to house more than eight children were forced to adjust their plans.

I selected one church to represent those working intentionally with troubled youth. Two in-depth interviews were conducted to ascertain how families, volunteers, and youth in this church worked with children in crisis. The pastor described an integrated model linking intervention and outcomes. I present it as a graphic in Figure 7.2; the human components of the church impact one another as is described in systems theory[54] whether applied to churches, families, or organizations (Shawchuck & Heuser, 1996:53; Schein, 1997:247-48). The model also reflects the 'micro-meso' components in Bronfenbrenner's ecology theory (1993).[55]

The pastor affirmed that while believing families have greater spiritual influence on their natural children; their spiritual influence can be passed on through 'mentoring' to young workers in the church who in turn work with children at risk (Clinton & Clinton, 1991).[56] Love for God and others as a 'fruit of the Spirit' is demonstrated in families (Gal. 5:12); this cycle impacts the church, the workers/volunteers, the pastor, and the surrounding community. 'It is like a healthy circle the church can nurture the family but the family and the child on the streets should have influence on the life of the church' (Pas#15, 2006). The church provides the relational network for tangible expressions of the love of God (Myers, 1999b:50).[57] Caring for street children offered opportunities to learn forgiveness and tolerance.[58] 'Whoever welcomes one of these little children in my name welcomes me; and whoever welcomes me does not welcome me but the one who sent me' (Mark 9:37). Jesus declares children his representatives in society (Moltmann, 2000:599).

A CASE STUDY OF CHURCH-FAMILY SUPPORT FOR A CHILD FROM THE STREETS

How does a local church practically support a family responding to a child in crisis and what is a realistic outcome? I met Ionuţ and his parents, Catalin and

---

[54] 'Systems theory views organizational components as being interrelated – both interdependently and inter-dynamically, each part depends on all the other and change in one causes changes in all the others. A church or congregation can be viewed as a total entity; its components are not seen in isolation' (Shawchuck & Heuser, 1996:53).

[55] See Chapter 2, fn. 24 for discussion of Bronfenbrenner's ecological theory of development for children.

[56] Here, mentoring involves the commitment of an individual or family to coach or care for another member of the church. Clinton defines mentoring as a 'relational experience in which one person, the mentor, empowers another person, the mentoree by the transfer of resources' (1991:3). See Stanley and Clinton (1992).

[57] We sometimes overlook the centrality of the biblical narrative that is 'ultimately about relationships and restored relationships' (Myers, 1999b:50). Myers argues that relationships must be restored in four dimensions: relationship with God through Christ, just relationships with ourselves and our community, loving and respectful relationships with others – those unlike us and sometimes our enemy – and relationships with creation and responsibility for our earth.

[58] See Chapter 6 concerning 'crossing social barriers' to work with marginalized children.

Olti̧ta, at Bucharest International Church in 2002.[59] The mother shared with me the story of her adopted son's trauma. I include the entire interview and case vignette as Appendix F, providing here the more important elements.

The birth mother, not yet 21, worked in a gang that specialized in prostitution and theft. Ionuţ was abandoned at three years of age to the gang. He was repeatedly sexualized and traumatized, suffering from malnutrition and probably attachment disorder. The gang left Ionuţ sick and covered with lice at a local drop-in centre where Olti̧ta worked with other street children. She says he had the look of 'feral child, wild and crazy not like a normal child'. With a new baby girl to care for, Olti̧ta and her husband decided to take Ionuţ into their home on a short-term basis. After two months, which she described as 'almost impossible', she felt God was asking her to raise this boy. The family spent the next four years restoring this child to some form of normalcy.

> The first year with Ionut was the most difficult of my life … we felt this was something God was asking us to do … God showed us how to live through the days, it was just a matter of daily persistence and faith and we had support from our church and believing friends. I don't think anything else got me through this, people prayed for us, the church stood with us and offered to help …The church and our faith in God were our primary resources.

This child from the streets was brought into a Christian home with very few social support resources. The case offers theological clues as to how children in crisis facilitate bearing witness to Christ in this 'yet unredeemed world': sacrificial giving, hope in the love of God, and impossible possibilities. This child was 'sinned against' in horrible ways, and Ionuţ carried these sins into the presence of God, his new family and their church; all shared in his human suffering. Olti̧ta and her family put their hope in Christ even though they had no guarantee that Ionuţ would come through his ordeal a normal child; evidence that faith frequently includes categories of uncertainty.

> There is no calm or merry freedom from hurt in those who hope for, but who do not yet possess redemption. Security is not anticipated and redemption occurs in the midst of upheaval and amid the chaos of unredeemed humanity (Barth, 1968:156).

Key Result Areas FBOs Working with Children at Risk

FBOs and pastors expressed some of the same outcome expectations such as spiritual growth and behavioural change; I will not discuss those that overlap with little variation. For instance, two FBOs: *BF* and *Ţoar* stated that the primary outcome for children was 'a new life in Christ'. To ascertain if certain terms were used by FBOs, I supplied as talking points four domains identified from literature on 'child well-being': resilience, social skills, character change,

[59] Names of family used with permission. I worked with this family for five years and they have graciously allowed me to include their 'story'.

and dignity (Ben-Arieh, 2000:15-17).[60] Interviewees were asked to describe outcomes in whatever terms they best understood them. As with church outcomes, I also examine evidence of untested assumptions (espoused theories) in FBO descriptions.

FBOs use a range of terms to describe 'spiritual' and human outcomes

Where pastors had been almost unanimous concerning conversion as a priority, FBOs offered a range of outcomes, citing none as a priority. Those mentioned with greater frequency were: 'spiritual renewal', 'personal character', 'moral change', 'awareness of personal worth and dignity', 'responsibility', 'transformation', and 'holistic'. The language indicated a more humanitarian[61] or 'child friendly' understanding of general outcomes; however, in analysing the responses, I noted that some were ill defined and lacked clarity.

For instance, FBOs used the phrase 'unconditional love of God' in talking about spiritual interventions without clearly defining expected outcomes (Chapter 5). The following statements were abridged from documents and interviews with *IDC*[62] and are typical of FBO outcome statements. I noted references to both eternal and human concerns.

> We know God loves the children unconditionally. Most of these children have little real experience with this kind of love. For abandoned children we believe God intends for them to have protection, acceptance, and that they should be received with love. We want children:
>
> - To be aware of the world & of themselves
> - To be aware of their purpose in life
> - To develop a strong character
> - To know they are accepted and have value (worth)
> - To know they are loved
> - To experience salvation
> - To have a family – as a reflection of God's purposes
> - To have an advocate in Romanian society

---

[60] In '*Beyond Welfare: Measuring and Monitoring the State of Children—New Trends and Domains*', Ben-Arieh explicates the shift in thinking that has taken place over the past twenty years in child welfare. 'Moving from the enabling/risk factors domains of survival to well-being, and especially to the life skills … has been the result of the shift from 'negative' to 'positive' which, in turn, led to the shift from traditional to new domains' (2000:237).

[61] This is not a pejorative usage of 'humanitarian'; I argue that eternal and human concerns must be integrated but require more missiological/theological reflection on the inherent tensions. I do see a wider reading of 'spiritual' as a possible source of confusion in Romanian evangelicalism.

[62] This FBO, *Heart of the Child (IDC)*, is directed by Romanian women and provides a variety of programmes for children. The FBO started as an NGO in 1995 but become faith-based when the directors became evangelicals through the influence of Western evangelical childcare professionals.

(Personal interviews combined with documents from *ICD*, 2006).

These statements demonstrate a combination of terms and outcome expectations. 'Character' crosses over to moral formation and invites the question, based on what ethical framework or authority? 'Salvation' is usually a theological term, but the FBO documents provide no explanation, so one could ask if salvation means 'saved from danger and exploitation' or does it mean 'saved by the action of God in Christ and, if so, to what end?'

Tensions in FBO-church partnership arose when FBOs uncritically combined language of outcomes such as: 'spiritual change', 'value formation', 'shaping society for children' and 'God's kingdom', but did not make clear to local churches how they intended to accomplish their goals. Pastors advocated a narrower hermeneutic concerning salvation, FBOs tended to stress a wider or more 'comprehensive view of salvation' (Bosch 2003:183-84).[63] In most cases, the theology was 'informal' and 'social' outcomes were randomly mixed with 'spiritual' outcomes. I first discuss outcome categories identified from FBO documents and transcripts that were linked to 'spiritual change'.

Moral formation as an outcome

Both FBOs and pastors state that behaviour change in children is an outcome connected to 'spiritual change'; there was consensus from the FBOs that conversion was a part of the process. However, FBOs allow for a gradual process in conversion where spiritual change can also mean 'moral formation' that produces behaviour change (Coles, 1990:23).[64] Ninety per cent of the FBO respondents identified 'character change' as an important outcome and connected it to moral formation. The interview transcripts contain 16 references to 'character' in children as in this statement.

> We are working for *character formation* in the lives of the children, we look for changes in attitudes and how the children treat one another, how they respond to authority and their values, are they honest, do they show concern for others (FBOL#70, 2006).

Local and smaller FBOs were more likely to use non-specific categories to define moral outcomes: 'children are making progress in getting free of the

---

[63] Bosch (1991:104-08; 215-17; 297-300; 2003:183-90) argues for a comprehensive understanding of salvation. 'When salvation becomes simply personal and religious, it is a reality for those individual souls who are saved from the world. But this view of salvation is closer to that of the Greek thinking than the message of the Bible. For the Greeks, *sōtēria* meant being saved from physical life: salvation from the burdens of material existence' (1993:183).

[64] Psychologists speak of 'stages of moral development' that is children's growing capacity to analyze complex moral issues, sort them out, and think about them using various ethical or philosophical points of view. Coles is a recognized authrority, see *The Moral Intelligence of Children* (1998) and *The Moral life of Children* (2000).

streets … they are learning to trust one another and us, and show signs of spiritual progress' (FBOL#58, 2005). FBOs were making a needed and important contribution in confronting moral formation in troubled youth as integral to faith-based care (Winship & Reynolds, 2003).[65]

Unlike churches, FBOs focus intentionally on children who do not have families, are traumatised, live with fractured emotions, and have anti-social personalities (White & Wright, 2003:117-18). *CoH*, *L&L*, *BF*, *ACVN*, and *Ruth* attributed their understanding of outcomes concerning 'character and value formation' to daily interaction with dysfunctional children who were lacking in 'normal values'. These FBOs referred to practical experience, not reflection on child development or 'developmental assets' (Search Institute)[66] as means for assessing outcomes. FBOs and children were active participants, each bringing an individual life experience to the situation (Greener, 2003a).[67] Evidence of FBO grassroots participation and learning experience served to de-mystify the process of faith-based outcome measurement in the Romanian context. The delivery of care for children in crisis was undertaken with faith and stewardship, but moral outcomes were never completely predictable.

Affirming Children in Moral Choice

FBO leaders consistently stated that intentional interventions were necessary to affirm children in making moral choices (Blakeney & Blakeney, 2004).[68] Several FBOs provided similar accounts of moral problems associated with street and institutionalized children; responses from four directors were combined in this paraphrase:

---

[65] At the 'Independent Sector 2003 Research Forum: The Role of Faith-based Organizations in the Social Welfare System' in Washington, D.C., a number of papers were presented. Winship and Reynolds examined the role of religious practice in strengthening moral values in teens.

[66] Search Institute has created a chart: '40 Developmental Assets'. The chart provides an 'at a glance' view of categories and definitions that have been identified as 'building blocks of healthy development that help young people grow up healthy, caring, and responsible'. See www.search-institute.org/downloads/#40assets (accessed November 2010).

[67] Development is not something that just 'happens' to children nor is it the FBO that 'develops the child'. 'Children are not passive recipients of life events, but active players who bring individual characteristics to and past personal experiences to every situation, making every child's personal experience a unique one within a general child development framework' (Greener, 2003a:40).

[68] See *Delinquency: A Quest for Moral and Spiritual Integrity* for review of contemporary literature on the connection between adolescent misbehaviour and 'spiritual' development (in the wider sense of this word). 'Spiritual awakening, religious calling, and spiritual/religious commitment are more common in adolescence than at any other time of life' (Blakeney & Blakeney, 2004:373). In the social science literature of this genre, the researchers seek to understand how spiritual convictions and spiritual connections (personal and in community) alter negative trajectory with youth at risk.

> When children came to us from the streets and institutions, they would lie without a second thought; they had learned to do this for survival ...they would steal and fight; this is just the way life for them on the streets and in orphanages... The children really have no understanding of how to follow rules... We have to teach them the meaning of right and wrong, you would be amazed at how distorted their ideas of right and wrong are... We work with them and try to help them understand what it means to have a conscience ... Anyone coming to work with us needs to understand the background of the children and their problems (combined from FBOL#28; #38; #55; #62, 2006).

These are honest reflections concerning the child's humanity and their problems not filtered through the language of academic psychology or child development. The children described have spent most of their lives on the margins of Romanian society, living with no moral guidance or parental care. They entered faith-based programmes who offered acceptance and a willingness to work with them 'where they were' (FBOL#18, 2004). 'Acceptance' was labelled as an important intervention (Chapter 5); it was evident that FBOs could 'receive' these children in ways that local churches could not. The FBOs were not encumbered with the concerns of a localized faith community; they were free to act in the present.[69] This has bearing on the overall argument as the domain of 'locality' has influence on partnership and mutual accountability.

'Moral formation' was labelled as an axial code to describe outcomes in children learning to choose right from wrong. The habitual patterns of seriously troubled children and youth (teens), fighting, stealing, lying, running away, 'are structurally and functionally related to predictable disturbances in moral reasoning. Resistant patterns of moral misbehaviour act out unresolved moral claims of caring, autonomy, fairness, and truthfulness. Troubled young people get stuck because they rely on *either* thinking or feeling; *either* self regard or other regard' (Blakeney & Blakeney, 2005:377). I interviewed only three FBO practitioners who had formal training in rehabilitation of 'street youth'; others learned while working with children and youth Interviewees who described the process of 'moral formation' used the following terms most frequently; numbers represent occurrences in transcripts (Table 7.2).

Table 7.2 Terms used to describe moral formation (FBOs)

Learn personal respect and self-worth before they would respect others	13
Overcome their addictions to lying and stealing	10
Control their temper and anger and not respond in violence	9
Not abuse other children, property, or one another	6
Learn to be honest and trustworthy	6
Learn how be role models for other children	4
(Compiled from interviews with FBO leaders and staff).	

[69] The FBOs have freedom to come and go, they can specialize and reach a 'target' audience. Local churches are 'embedded' in the sense that they belong to the local community with obligations to families and neighbours.

AFFIRMING DIGNITY AND PERSONAL WORTH

Two FBO leaders offered documents written for their staff on the importance of teaching children the value of self-respect (FBOL#28; FBOL#32). Dignity was used interchangeably with 'personal worth' and 'respect for self and others'. Children need assurance that they are valuable as human beings, not because of achievement or failure, but who they are in God's sight; 'their significance is based on the mercy of God' (White, 2003a:124). Outcomes concerning personal worth or self-esteem were mentioned by every FBO and coded as psycho-social outcomes as in, 'we want children to learn stability; we want them to learn to value life, to do this they need understand they have personal worth' (FBOL#38, 2005).[70]

Where churches considered 'conversion, respect for scripture, church, and prayer' as outcome indicators; FBOs encouraged 'self-respecting sociality' (Werpehowski, 2001:398) and valuing one's neighbours as integral to spiritual and moral formation. Both churches and FBOs mix theological assumptions with conventions of moral behaviour. FBOs hold different theological values than those represented in the churches. FBOs stated that a child's worth is intrinsic to God's love and acceptance; they did not explain how human worth and human sin were reconciled in their expectations of outcomes.[71]

The FBOs did not state explicitly that they acknowledged the freedom of children to make wrong choices, but their comments revealed tacit recognition that human interpersonal freedom, whether for or against one's fellows, is intrinsic to understanding 'freedom for God'.[72] The FBOs referred to God and scripture as the foundation for asking children to make moral changes; it was assumed the Bible required a code of conduct.

> When children face difficult choices, the Bible gives guidance for better living and guides them morally and ethically. Faith in God will also help them with family issues and we pray that God will be their support throughout their lives and that they will learn to help others (FBOL#25, 2005).

PERSONAL RESPONSIBILITY AND SOCIAL SKILLS AS OUTCOMES

WV Ro and *MWB* produced internal documents used to guide their moral frameworks concerning children (Macleod, 2000); these were published outside Romania for affiliate international offices.[73] *MWB* worked primarily

[70] Only three FBOs (*WV Ro, WMF,* and *IDC*) used the term 'psycho-social' as an outcome indicator. This word is used frequently in the literature on child development. The coding simply helped me to arrange words and phrases for cross-case comparison.

[71] This 'difference in values' will be examined in Chapter 8 as it influences partnership between FBOs and churches.

[72] Werpehowski is following Barth when he says human freedom 'entails a divine permission for obedience to the divine command but it is bounded by creaturely limits' (2001:398). See also *Humanity of God* (Barth, 1960).

[73] Heather MacLeod leads World Vision's work on advocacy for children with an emphasis on child protection.

with children living in institutions, 'emotional support' was noted as a primary programme intervention. The expected outcome was helping children learn personal responsibility – linked to moral outcomes.

> Learning personal responsibility is very important for a child raised in an institution; this is connected to their sense of self-worth. We want to help the children develop a positive self-image, the mentality of many children from the institutions is they are rejected and have little worth. We feel the best solution is to give them emotional support and acceptance with the love of Jesus (FBOL#27, 2005).

Development of social skills was mentioned by FBOs working with older children (14-18 years), especially those making a transition to independent living. FBOs often placed children from institutions into a small group home in their early and teen years where they were taught basic life skills: personal hygiene, cooking, cleaning. When they reached 18, they had marked difficulty taking responsibility for their lives (FBOL#68, 2006).[74] Social and vocational skills meant the difference in successful transition from FBO care.

Five of the eleven cases connected self-worth, self-image, dignity, and personal responsibility to a provision of 'acceptance in the love of Jesus'. They did not explain how this integration was to be accomplished but expressed no doubt it would. Moltmann is more specific on this point: 'the presence of God makes the human being undeprivable and inescapably God's image… The dignity of human beings is unforfeitable, irrelinquishable and indestructible, thanks to the abiding presence of God (1993b:233). The underlying assumption in these comments is that God will act; it was loosely explained as God's action on the will and soul of the child.

> Children in this culture have some vague ideas about Christ and God, but for most of them religion is just icons and dark churches. We hope that the children will have a life-changing experience with God; we want them to know and experience the love of God. This happens when God touches their soul and the Holy Spirit opens their heart to understand. This is something we trust God to do, and we want to create the best environment for this to happen in their lives (FBOL#25, 2005).

It became apparent in cross-case comparison that basic assumptions concerning 'faith in God's willingness to act on behalf of hurting children' were generally held as *fact*.[75] FBOs spoke of God's intervention in moral

---

[74] This research is concerned with children and youth under 18; however, many of the FBOs faced the question of transitioning youth from programmes to 'life on their own'. The institutions created a disempowered and 'powerless child' who had little sense of cause and effect.

[75] As quoted in Chapter 2: 'In fact, if a basic assumption is strongly held in a group, members will find behaviour based on any other premise inconceivable' (Schein, 1997:22). This was true in some degree of all FBOs, but the church-based FBOs spoke

formation with the same confidence that churches spoke of God's willingness to save children from sin. Congruence with 'espoused' theology and childcare 'theory in use' was assumed, not examined through critical reflection (Argyris and Schön, 1974:6-7). The interviews gave little variation at the level of deeply held assumptions of the Evangel. FBOs were working within conventional evangelical precedents, the Bible serving as the ultimate guide for right behaviour; few FBO resources were allocated for formal study on moral formation, theology, or ethics.[76]

Maintaining 'healthy' scepticism in moral formation

Street and abandoned children would come repeatedly to drop-in centres or shelters and returned to the streets and their regular habits. The word 'resilience' was not well understood by Romanian interviewees. When I explained resiliency as 'ability to cope with difficult and stressful situations' (Greener, 2003b:42), several respondents laughed and said, 'that is not something we need to teach them, every child that comes off the streets or a broken home has learned to cope with difficulty' (FBOS#6, 2005).[77] Such local knowledge engendered a certain 'healthy scepticism' in the local FBOs concerning how to monitor and evaluate moral change in children. FBOs accepted the child's immediate situation, trauma, dysfunction, and humanity while at the same time believing that the child is entitled to grace, forgiveness, and the gift of God in Christ. FBO success in effecting change was directly proportional to a willingness to manage, welcome, and engage this tension.

Concerning 'managing, welcoming, and engaging' tension', I draw insight from both theology and organizational theory. Theology lives with dialectical tensions: Christology, God with humanity, and God's kingdom as future – God's kingdom as present, God as resurrection life – God as crucified, God's judgement – God's grace. Also organizational theorists embrace change theory as central to understanding the life of a learning organization (Senge *et al.*,

---

more openly of God's action for children. On the other end of the continuum (*World Vision* and *IDC*) there was more commitment to programmatic interventions.

[76] With the exception of *WV Ro* and *WMF*, the other FBOs were under-resourced in these areas. Their budgets did not allow for research in theology, ethics, or evaluation criteria – their primary purpose was to care and intervene on behalf of the children.

[77] 'Resiliency' is one of the terms in childcare literature I found to be an imprecise tool. It is defined as 'the capacity to spring back, rebound, and successfully face adversity'. Street children, orphans, and children in poverty have developed a range of coping mechanisms; they survive in a world where most 'normal' children would be lost. Greener says the goal of the childcare worker is twofold: a) eliminate unmanageable stress when possible and b) promote resilience in children so they are better able to cope (2003a:44).

1994; Mintzberg, 1994). Willingness to 'welcome, manage, and engage' tension is essential faith-based work with children in crisis[78]

FBOs demonstrated a willingness to persevere with the children in spite of their 'fallen ways'.

> We have children who come to our centre and they go to every NGO and FBO in this part of the city. They know how to act when they are here and they return to their old ways when they are back on the streets. They are experts at *şmecherie* [conning or trickery]. For instance we had some children that would come and say they had 'repented' but we knew that they had just learned to say the right words... (FBOL#11, 2004).[79]

Since FBOs maintained regular contact with children, they were able to observe their behaviour over extended periods of time. It was common for a child to continue in this pattern for many months with no observable behavioural change. Behaviour could be switched on and off, and children learned how to take advantage of the benefits provided by the FBOs, typical of children with attachment disorder or 'trust bandits' (Magid & McKelvey, 1987:12).

As children became more trusting of caregivers, they would slowly ask for help or become more involved with programme activities. When FBOs have hidden agendas in their programmatic interventions, such as dogmatic or conversionist expectations, these are easily perceived by children in crisis who have learned that most adults either do not care about them or want something in return. All children have an intense early warning awareness that is developed for their self-protection; this is heightened in children who experience abuse (Greener, 2003b).

> Any hidden agendas or interventions may be counter productive for the children [in crisis], their families, and the institution. This includes the danger of a secondary religious aim to proselytize, which can fragment and divert efforts toward the best interests of the children or families (Scott & Magnuson, 2005:454)

Awareness of their 'natural suspicion' may serve as another theological pointer in working with children in crisis; they invite caregivers to embrace their pain and discontinuity. 'We must not delude ourselves, there are no moral actions, such as love, or honesty, or purity, or courage which have rid themselves of the *form of this world*' (Barth, 1968:434). I am not advocating that childcare workers treat children as objects worthy of suspicion, rather

---

[78] I develop this more fully in Chapter 8 as a core category in this study.

[79] In the West, we have become acquainted with 12-Step recovery programmes like AA (Alcoholics Anonymous). These programmes advocate taking one 'day at a time' and the importance of personal willingness to admit powerlessness in the face of addiction and recognizing an outside power can help. This interviewee was basing her comments on a child's willingness to change in reference to the 'conviction of the Holy Spirit' concerning personal sin.

children in crisis reflect God's grace in Christ which regards all human actions as limited, creaturely, and worthy of unmerited mercy.

Throughout, I have made note of the culture of suspicion and lack of trust in Romania. Here I am connecting with an earlier quote from Barth (Chapter 5) concerning the dry bones of this world and an appropriate theological 'suspicion'. 'When the church embarks upon moral exhortation, its exhortation can be naught else but a criticism of all human behaviour' (Barth, 1968:428). I argue that children 'already in crisis' are theological pointers; they are speaking to us in God's language. This can serve as a corrective force when FBOs tend towards managerial missiology or assume programmes can 'fix' a child in crisis.

Further reflection on moral formation and FBOs

In their attention to moral formation, FBOs demonstrated concern for the wider structural issues that impact the lives of children. In recognizing the complexity of the forces that have shaped and damaged children, they were cautious about conversion a primary objective.[80] For the pragmatic and interventionist evangelical caregiver, this is an important point: a child's human experiences often occur outside the structures and training of organized religion (Ratcliff, 2004). For children in crisis, much of what they 'know' has been filtered through painful situations. The FBOs work with an ethical tension: in the present, the moral compass of the children has been seriously compromised; yet FBOs hope for moral change in future. This hope does not depend on 'the moral capacity of children in crisis to change their lives' (FBOL#60, 2005); it rests on the hope hidden with God in Christ.

> Indeed if the truth be told, [we] ... are always restless in tribulation. But our hope is of a different kind; for it is the hope of faith. This does not rise and fall as ours does. Its *nerve centre lies not in human capacity*, but in the capacity and purpose of God (Barth, 1968:157) my emphasis.

The hope for a child's recovery of conscience or 'moral compass' rests on living through and embracing the present; it is dependent on the hope of the kingdom of God that transcends the abuse and sin that has been inflicted on children. 'The being of a child is defined in the justification and final judgement of God' (Willmer email, 2005). Signs of the kingdom were evident in the FBO caregivers who remain committed over months and years to the task of reshaping a child's moral life. This commitment raises questions: How

[80]The FBO caregivers acknowledge that children are human beings with many normal and natural needs like play and imagination. When the spirit of a child is arrested by the Spirit of God, we need a careful use of language; see Loder's comments on Helen Keller's experience of learning the sign for water at the well. 'She did not merely learn a sign she learned the power of signing, and implicitly of language as a whole' (1998:28-9).

long does the FBO plan to intervene, what happens if and when the FBO leaves? Do FBOs plan to support the child's moral formation in Christ in the long term? Is it reasonable that FBOs will stay committed to children for 16-18 years? I will return to these questions in considering factors that enable FBO-church partnership in Chapter 8.

How FBOs Describe 'Holistic' and 'Transformational' Outcomes

In Chapter 2, I discussed the missional terms 'holism' and 'transformation'. Samuel defines transformation as:

> … [enabling] God's vision of society to be actualized in all relationships, social, economic, and spiritual so that God's will may be reflected in human society and His love experienced by all communities especially the poor (Samuel & Sugden, 1999:frontpiece).

Sugden (2003:70-6) provides his understanding of 'transformational development' and relevant publications since Lausanne 1974. He suggests the argument of priority concerning evangelism or social action in mission was resolved 'to a certain extent' by the term 'transformation' and hinged on different views of humanity.[81] Evangelism approached individuals as autonomous and social action as persons in relationships (2003:71).

In Chapter 5, I argued the term 'holistic' by FBOs required more assessment. Both terms were used by several FBOs, but there was almost no cross-case consensus on meaning.[82] As a result of this finding, it was necessary to test usages of 'transformation' and 'holistic' throughout the study; this became more important in analysis of outcomes.

How WV Ro uses the term 'transformation' to describe outcomes

World Vision International (*WVI*) has done more than any FBO in this study to develop an 'integrated framework for transformation' which includes holistic development, child survival, valuing and protecting children, children as participants in the change process, and includes responsibilities and

---

[81] *Mission as Transformation* (1999) is one many publications from the Oxford Centre for Mission Studies. See also Samuel (2002) and Sampson *et al.* (1994). While Sugden may be correct on some levels (international and Lausanne) concerning the resolution of tension between 'evangelism and social action', this should not be assumed in the Romanian evangelical context.

[82] This finding surprised me; only four of the FBOs in Phase One, used the term 'transformation' in the sense defined by Samuel. The word 'holistic' had more resonance but it too was used incidentally. I observed tension and little meaningful dialogue between traditional evangelical churches who advocated the priority of conversion and advocates of 'transformation' like World Vision. This was an early clue to which mission agencies and FBOs had been more influential in shaping church perceptions of children.

involvement of parents, communities, and governments (Currie & Commins, 2002:24).[83] Myers argues that 'transformational development' outcomes are relational and spiritual (1999b:11; 13-15); his theological rationale is grounded in narrative approach to scripture (1999b:20-56). *WVI*'s framework and policy define this as a process 'through which children, families and communities move towards wholeness of life with dignity, justice, peace, and hope' (Byworth, 2003:100).[84]

In an internal working paper, 'Spirituality of the Child' (2002), McAlpine put forward a model advocating the 'child' as the focal point of a three-sided triangle: ADP, church, and family. While *WVI* has extensive published resources on 'transformational' care for children, I identified only three FBOs (all with Western partners and well-funded) and three evangelical churches conversant with *WVI*'s version of 'transformation'.[85] *WV Ro* operates limited partnerships with evangelical churches; their work is concentrated in area development programmes (ADP),[86] national health care, and partnership with the Orthodox Church. In those places where they partner directly with evangelical churches, the outcomes of *WV Ro* projects included:

- Increasing the role of Christian education in children's lives
- Assistance to churches in times of natural disaster (floods)
- Training in prevention of child neglect and assisting mothers at risk
- Working with older youth from orphanages in learning life and vocational skills

---

[83]The report of the 'Children in Ministry Working Group' *Focused Especially on the Well-Being of Children; An Integrated paradigm for Transformation* (2002), is the result of three-year global study to define WVI philosophy concerning the place of children in the WVI area development paradigm. The document draws extensively on current secular research in child well-being and public policy discussions.

[84] In the article, 'World Vision's Approach to Transformational Development: Frame, policy, and indicators,' Byworth discusses five domains of change: restored relationships, well-being of children, empowered children, transformed systems and structures, interdependent communities that lead to 'community based and sustainable' transformational development (2003:103).

[85] See sources in the bibliography as evidence that WVI has done much to further the discussion of 'transformational development' and children in the international arena. *WVI* distanced itself from local churches as the agency professionalized in the 1980s-1990s; see *Strengthening our Bridges* (2002).

[86] Area Development programmes are long-term (two to three years) community development projects operated in 11 geographical regions. WV Ro personnel establish relationships with the community assess needs, work with the community to prioritize needs, and develop the projects. All planning is done with the input of locals willing to be involved. In most ADP programmes, the Orthodox church of that community serves on the local steering committee. For this reason, evangelical churches have been slow to participate, see Chapter 6 – Orthodox tensions.

- *WV Ro* made financial contributions to Ruth School which has resulted in integration of Roma children into mainstream society (data from WV Romania, Annual Report, 2006 and interviews).

WV Ro influence on local evangelical churches

I interviewed two WV Ro national directors and staff and board members; they estimated that 50-60 evangelical churches had received direct financial assistance (FBOL#16, 2004). In my evaluation, *WV Ro* was working with a much broader social and 'transformational' agenda than most evangelical churches in Romania were able to meaningfully comprehend. Through participation in national conferences, pastors engaged with *WV Ro* on an informational level: they resonated with calls to national repentance concerning social sins (Downes, 2001:41). The majority of pastors I interviewed saw *WV Ro* as a 'humanitarian organization more concerned with social concerns than leading people to Christ' (Pas#2, 2004). This corroborates the FBO-church tension described in the findings; magnified by the scope of the *WV Ro* programme base.[87]

While *WV Ro* is making a significant contribution to community faith-based child care and influencing public policy concerned children, I found little evidence their commitment to 'transformational development' had been significantly adopted by local evangelical churches.[88] I would argue that World Vision functions much like a Christian UNICEF in Romania; they have international and national influence, depend on managerial missiology, and admit, 'we find it difficult to relate to the needs and interests of small local congregations' (FBOL#16, 2004). This might be explained by the rationale expressed by a former national director:

> World Vision is not a church-based agency we are a development agency, we have the budget and manpower to carry out this type of development agenda … We believe we have a mandate to bring the churches, the NGOs, the FBOs and the secular bodies together for the sake of children – advocacy is a key core competency in our transformational framework (FBOL#2, 2003).[89]

---

[87] The annual expenditures in 2006 were $6,696,179 in cash and $20,399,483 gifts in kind (Total = $27,095,662). Of this amount, $342,378 or less than two per cent was spent on 'Christian Commitment programmes'.

[88] The statement reflects the limits of my research. I determined in Phase One that it would beyond my scope and resources to study evangelical churches, FBOs, and Orthodox churches. The Christian Reformed World Relief Committee of Romania uses 'transformation' in much the way *WV Ro* does. The residual tension between Evangelical and Orthodox Churches impact WV Romania's influence, a factor *WV Ro* willing embraces.

[89] I will allow this comment to speak for itself. I prefer the language of Philippians 2 to this sort of aggrandizement. *WV Ro* has had five national directors since 1990; each brought a different personality to the position. My impression in this interview was that

WV Ro distributes financial help or gifts in kind to local evangelical churches, they have a more difficult time transferring their theory of transformation, as churches remain suspicious of 'worldly systems' they can not understand or explain within their biblical hermeneutic.[90] I turn now to examine how other FBOs use the terms 'holistic and transformation'.

How other FBOs use 'transformation' to describe outcomes

The local FBOs and church-based FBOs (*ACVN; BF, Ţoar*) used transformation in less ambitious ways than *WV Ro*.[91] None had formalized definitions; the word was used to describe spiritual conversion, providing security and safety, recovery from family dysfunction or trauma, community work, education, and holistic ministry. There were 30+ references to 'transformation' in the transcripts, what follows are specific examples. Every FBO in this study used the term 'transformation', in most cases referring to a number of outcomes. My point is to demonstrate that no single 'definition' of transformation was identified in this study.

Linking Security and Sociality to Spiritual Transformation

FBOs understood that children needed a place of acceptance and safety in order to make changes in their lifestyles. 'Without security there can be no safe base for exploration, relationships, play, and development ... without it dysfunctional mechanisms develop that prevent the child from experiencing love' (White, 2003a:121).

> We want children to know they are safe and accepted – this fits within our thinking about transformation. We are cautious about being too aggressive with spiritual things [explains conversion as coercion]. Children need to know that they are going to be protected; this is part of spiritual care for children (FBOL#60, 2005).

WV Ro was acting in the role of a successful multinational corporation and local churches were 'incidental' factors in their national agenda. *WV Ro* hired a new national director in 2006; who indicated she would be more sensitive to national evangelical concerns.

[90] This is not an argument that churches have 'gained all the wisdom needed from biblical texts'. I established earlier that theological resources for churches and seminaries have been limited, largely influenced by denominational agencies. The discussion raised questions: should *WV Ro* begin investing in training pastors to understand their transformational developmental frameworks? Is this theory of transformation sustainable in local churches (Wallace, 2002:133-37)?

[91] Where *WV Ro* acts as a multinational FBO on a 'macro scale', the local FBOs are 'micro' FBOs and are much closer to local communities. They are not synonymous with local churches in that they have the freedom to come and go, but they tend to rely more on local human resources. The distinction is important concerning 'scale of impact'.

CoH and *L&L* said offering a 'safe spiritual atmosphere' including protection from abuse was necessary for 'personal transformation'. These FBOs were not involved in community-based transformation schemes. Children leaving the institutions or streets had little experience with caregivers who made them feel secure; many had experienced abuse in their families or from adults in the institutions. 'When we talk to these children about the love of God, it must be done in a way that helps them understand His protection and security, this is a key to their transformation' (FBOL#51, 2005).

FBOs worked with their respective local DCP offices seeking approval for projects. City officials changed their opinions when the FBOs said they could help 'transform street children into better citizens'. The city offered *L&L* a building, 'I think they wanted to see if we were serious, they did not believe we could help the kids who were causing them so much trouble' (FBOL#28, 2005). *ACVN* and *BF* closely linked 'transformation' to personal evangelism. Since street children tended to be sceptical of overt proselytizing, a FBO director commented, 'they cannot be sold the gospel as a gimmick or offered spiritual help as a quick fix solution. We aim at "transformation" in their hearts and attitudes towards the gospel' (FBOL#28, 2005). Transformation was frequently labelled as personal spiritual process as in this statement.

> The ultimate 'transformation' in the lives of children is that they understand what it means to have a God-committed relationship. This is a spiritual process, we can't just give the children Jesus like a piece of bread, they have to come to know him and it is a process of spiritual transformation (FBOL#18, 2005).

When FBOs found churches unwilling to work with children, they described the outcome as a 'transformation of church attitudes toward children on the streets' (FBOL#28, 2004). Spiritual transformation for abused children was also described as 'continuous conversion':

> We are trying to help children recover from abuse, transformation starts when they begin to see themselves as having worth and dignity. This process usually takes months, and then if they come to Christ, they continue to go through 'transformation' as they learn to put on Christ (LFBO#58, 2005).

Community Organizing and Group Homes as Transformation

WV Ro's ADP programme was described as 'community development'. Linthicum makes a distinction with community organizing 'which is a process where people of an area organize themselves to "take charge" of their situation and thus develop a sense of being a community together' (1991:31). Community organizing has the the following characteristics:

> [It is] relationally based on the development and maintenance of one-on-one contacts out of which mutual risk and trust grow. It is pragmatic and acts locally doing what the community says needs doing. It looks for actions that are 'doable' where members of the community can experience success in the early stages of action' (Linthicum, 1991:32).

This definition was more applicable to local grassroots FBOs outcomes working with child and community.

FBOs described obstacles in 'transforming' local communities in which children and families find it difficult to imagine a better future. *WMF*'s approach was described in Chapter 5 as 'serving with the poor' (Chronic, 2006; O'Callahan, 2004). 'We celebrate community with each other because in community we find the greatest potential for discipleship, service, and growth (*WMF* Lifestyle Celebration #4).[92] *WMF* seeks to provide a 'spiritual community' for poor children, their families, and project personnel, thus enabling 'local transformation'. Community service is an important component. FBO personnel work closely with families, but the *WFM* 'community' is not synonymous with the neighbourhood; the director when confronted with lack of visible success described it as a supportive framework:

> … after years of relationship, some children are still on the streets, still on drugs, or worse. There are those 'success stories' who are now back where they started … I encourage myself by looking at 'our community' which has grown over the years both in maturity and size. Truly, there are a number of shining spots that have been forged in the community of ministry among the poor (Chronic, 2005:18).

The directors and staff of *BF* live in 'group home' situations with boys and girls from the streets. They discussed the importance of 'community' as demonstrated in their extended families.[93] The leaders said 'spiritual transformation' required both time and relational boundaries. Successful group homes require consistency on the part of caregivers and continuity in the 'community' (Anglin, 2002).[94] *BF* hopes all children in their care will make a declaration of faith in Christ, acknowledging that children from dysfunctional backgrounds must first learn trust and experience a sense of belonging. 'Our home-style environment allows children opportunity to live a more normal life; the children can attend school, and interact with other children. In this way we

---

[92] The spring issue of 'The Cry' (2005), online journal of *WMF*, describes a number of approaches this ministry takes in working with community transformation. See http://www.wordmadeflesh.org/learn/read/

[93] This is a small Baptist FBO uses conventional conversionist terminology to describe spiritual outcomes; the use of transformation here could be exchanged with conversion. When they found that street children were not being given care by the local government, they purchased two small houses to raise a number of the children in what they describe as 'our little community'.

[94] In a study of group homes, Anglin (2002:64) identified 'congruence' as an important element of successful care for children and youth. He identifies three major properties of congruence: 'consistency, reciprocity and coherence'. For additional discussion on Anglin's finding with application to group homes, see Scott & Magnuson (2004:444-50).

can help them learn how to reconnect with community life' (FBOL#62, 2005).[95]

EDUCATION AS TRANSFORMATION

MoM works with families whose children need social assistance and help in school. Their actions are aimed at transforming perceptions held by community members. They help parents make homes emotionally safer places for children by encouraging parents to become more involved in their child's education (Tomkins, 2003:170).

> Families tend to see themselves as needy and poor, they don't see what they can offer to others or their children … there is a deep spiritual need in community, we see our role serving the children as 'transforming' the spiritual poverty we see around us. By assisting children, we impact families and encourage them to get more involved with their children and community (FBOL#18, 2005).

FBOs providing educational assistance considered completion of course work or improvement in schoolwork a transformational outcome. In Project Ruth, the children live with their natural families, attend school every day, and participate in some weekend activities. Several Roma children have gone beyond the primary grades (Grades One through Eight) to finish high school, a major accomplishment for children from this community.[96] Roma communities often ostracize families who put children through formal education, considered breaking clan traditions (Achim, 1998:191-92).

> For children from poor families, graduation from the 8th grade is difficult [high school is usually not considered for Roma children]; acquisition of learning skills is an important outcome. It is very difficult to get a job or professional training without at least eight grades. For children who do not finish high school, we help with connections to vocational training (FBOL#18, 2004).

Educational outcomes and changes in children impact the larger community. From its base in the local church, *Ruth* offers assistance to community members: accessing public health care, ministry to mothers suffering violence or abuse, and serving as an advocate for Roma education in the Romanian Ministry of Education. 'We are slowly having impact on this entire community,

---

[95] White has written extensively on residential care and alternatives; his family operates Mill Grove in East London, which has been a home to family and children for three generations. See White (2002) 'The Ideology of Residential Care' and articles posted at http://www.childrenwebmag.com/c/articles/in-residence (accessed December 6, 2010).

[96] Many Roma children often do not start school until they are 12 or older; this means they never attend high school. Approximately 40 per cent of eight-year-old children have not attended school or have stopped; only 50 per cent of children between the ages of 7-10 attend school regularly. The number of girls not completing eighth grade is significantly higher than boys; only 4.5 per cent of adults have attended high school or college (Zamfir & Zamfir, 1993:215-16).

I don't know if I would call it 'transformation' [like *WV Ro*] but we are slowly shaping values in the Roma community about children' (FBOL#64, 2005).[97]

Ruth personnel were asked why educational outcomes were important to a church-based FBO. They replied that education provides children a sense of worth and value. The school headmaster said education equips children to discover their life potential; faith was an 'important' factor, but she did not expound how faith and educational outcomes are integrated.

> Our teachers are evangelicals, their faith is important, as is giving hope and encouragement along the way. Education means that the children will have an opportunity to get some form of employment, but it also gives the children a sense of worth, that they can accomplish something meaningful (FBOS#5, 2005).

HOLISTIC OUTCOMES DESCRIBED AS TRANSFORMATION

In its international journal, *WMF* published this statement, 'our objective is to redeem the whole person toward the redemption of society. We seek to be agents of holistic transformation, desiring to facilitate the realization of regeneration, restoration and reintegration of the poorest of the poor' (O'Callaghan, 2003:1). *MWB* partners exclusively with evangelical churches and described holistic transformation as a process of 'planting spiritual seeds leading to eventual maturation of spiritual life' (FBOS#10, 2006). Social care is shared by both FBO and church. Once children are connected to local churches, FBO personnel continued to maintain a relationship.

> When we talk about spiritual outcomes – we are talking about transformation. We are not responsible for converting these children. We want to plant spiritual seeds in their lives like hope, love and trust. We believe this will result in 'spiritual fruit' (FBOL#70, 2006).

MWB developed the acrostic: SEEM [Spiritual, Educational, Emotional and Material] to describe holistic outcomes in the lives of children. The project manager said the FBO had developed this acrostic first as an evaluative framework.

> We have tried to understand the child as a 'whole' being, with needs that are social, physical, emotional, and spiritual. Our ultimate goal would be reaching children and people for Christ; we want to do that in a way that touches the child, family or community. This acrostic came out of our work to define what we wanted to evaluate in children (FBOS#10, 2006).

The SEEM framework is an outcome of practical experience and in dialogue with their local partners. They did not collaborate with other FBOs using

[97] The Ruth School does rely on some foreign funding; the local church is providing human resources and initiative to lead the project. Community organizational activities for social change in Roma neighbourhoods have received little research attention. The Roma maintain strong clan and family allegiance but internal values often work against 'organizing for social betterment' (Zamfir & Zamfir, 1993:217; Fonseca, 1995).

similar multi-dimensional evaluation frameworks. 'We use the SEEM framework to evaluate our overall ministry. Our knowledge has come from coordinator feedback, volunteers, and others that work directly with the children' (FBOS#10, 2006). This supports evidence presented in Chapter 5 and 6 that non-professional Romanian childcare workers acquired 'tacit knowledge' in local practice.

I combined a number of statements from the transcripts to summarize additional ways the FBOs described 'holistic outcomes' resulting from specific interventions:

1. Providing social services for children – the outcome is to help children with social reintegration with their families and back into Romanian society.
2. To contribute to the spiritual and moral renewal of Romania by presenting the Gospel in a practical way, though street evangelism, assistance for orphans, formal education, moral, and spiritual development
3. Providing spiritual and material help i.e. food, medicines, clothing that results in improved living conditions for the children, both in health and hygiene whether they are still in the institutions and they are living in foster families.
4. Provide psychosocial care for children, who have been abused, are affected by violence or trauma – to help restore these children to spiritual wholeness and to help the children escape the cycle of violence.
5. Provide assistance on advocacy issues that concern children: child rights, adoption issues, laws regulating child services, work to influence government structures – the outcome is improved policy and public services for children.

(Developed from FBO literature and interviews with FBO directors 2005-2006)

Table 7.3 provides an overview of terms used by FBOs to describe transformational outcomes ordered according to frequency of use in transcripts. The frequency of responses should not be equated with value or importance as a final assessment of FBO outcomes.

Table 7.3 Terms used by FBOs to describe transformational outcomes

Spiritual Change (undefined)	14	Community-based transformation (as defined by FBO)	6
Moral or character change	12	Maturation of spiritual life in Christ	5
Change of heart or Experience the love of God	10	Holistic Transformation (as defined by FBO)	5
Awareness of personal worth- dignity	9	Educational Outcomes	4
Spiritual Change – conversion	8	Changes in family structure	4

Awareness and respect of self and others	8	Security, safety, and protection	4
Development of social skills and personal responsibility	7	SEEM	1

Reflection on 'transformation and holistic mission' with children

> I beseech you therefore, brethren, by the mercies of God, that you present your bodies a living sacrifice, holy, acceptable to God, which is your reasonable service. And do not be conformed to this world, *but be transformed* by the renewing of your mind, that you may prove what is that good, and acceptable, and perfect will of God (Rom. 12:1-2).[98]

I am not being pedantic in listing the uses of the word 'transformation'; the research demonstrates that as a descriptor of outcomes, the term is dependent on the usage or definition of individual FBOs. This means 'embracing open questions, tensions, and some confusion, while at the same time remaining honest' and trying to sort out meaning (Willmer, 2001:1995).[99] There is no single accepted definition of 'transformation' in the Romanian evangelical context; there is diversity, ambiguity, hope for change, and practical demonstrations of love – signs of God's kingdom. Included are theological ideas, mixed with categories of social change, and human concerns.

'TRANSFORMATION OR TRANSFORMING' – WHAT HORIZON OF EXPECTATION?

One is tempted to combine these varied concepts and conclude the resultant bricolage represents 'transformation' for children. Before taking that leap, I will consider several questions that inform my position. First, to what degree is 'transformation' as described by the FBOs actually a completed and accomplished work? Might it be more honest to speak of 'transforming' rather than 'transformation' that seems to imply a complete change of system or order? What realistic horizon of expectation in Christ best describes the goals and expected outcomes of the FBOs? Secondly, after 15 years of FBO and church intervention, there is limited evidence that transformation for children approximates the freedom from suffering and evil promised in the kingdom of God as shall be revealed in 'a new heaven and new earth' (2 Pet.3:12; Rev. 21:1). I found more evidence of 'not yet' than 'already finished' as FBOs and churches were working largely in isolation of one another and many thousands of children continued to need assistance.

---

[98] Barth in his exposition of this passage inserts in his translation the phrase 'not to fashion yourselves according to the present form of this world, but according to its coming transformation' (1960:424, footnote 1). In this reflection, I follow Barth's thesis that the 'coming transformation' of the world is brought about in the action and will of God; human beings are participants but not the ultimate actors.

[99] See Willmer's 'Transforming Society Or Merely Making It' (1995).

The FBOs demonstrated in a measure what God has 'already accomplished in Christ' in redeeming the humanity and spiritual lives of children; this should not be trivialized. Their engagement with children in crisis reveals an important theological reality 'the already in the kingdom and in Jesus is not the wholistic transformation of the world or humanity … the already in Christ includes [much] pain and suffering' (Willmer, 2001:194). FBOs (like churches) acknowledge dependence on God and grace; the transformation the Bible speaks of is dependent on the mercy and action of God. 'We have found the world a great, unsolved enigma; an enigma to which Christ, the mercy of God, provides the answer' (Barth, 1968:427). This is revealed through the cross, especially as it concerns caring for children in crisis.

> The cross points to a choice between addressing pain and suffering from the perspective of order and management by taking control of the public sphere, or building covenant communities which embrace pain and pay the price through their own suffering … The cross makes possible a new reconciled humanity [and community] (Eph. 2:18-22) (Sugden, 2003:73-4).

It is highly unlikely that social policy and improved FBO or NGO management will completely eradicate the problems that children continue to face in Romania. The cross points us to the finality of death, the great '*Krisis*' or 'great disturbance' (Barth, 1968:424)[100] and its ultimate solution in Christ's death and resurrection. This should not be misunderstood as a retreat from suffering and evil.

There are some who would say the presence of suffering is confirmation that the world is bound for destruction and would retreat from addressing personal and social evil. But by no means should the church or FBO passively endure all suffering as it awaits the final consummation. There is some suffering that is irremovable – such as incurable disease, but we identify what is irremovable in working to remove what is. 'Far from being an experience of imperfection and evil that cuts us off from the love of God (Rom. 8:38-39), suffering is experienced with Christ (Phil. 3:10-11); it is a channel of his resurrection life (2 Cor.4:7-18) a means of overcoming the powers of evil (Rev. 12:11)' (Samuel & Sugden, 1987:147).

FBOs and churches must continue to watch, pray, and act in the knowledge that God establishes what is rightfully His. Concerning the outcomes described above in the lives of children, their families, and community, I hesitate to evaluate the actions of FBOs as 'transformation' as a high claim for their present achievements. Rather I interpret these outcomes as 'critical anticipatory signs' and 'pointers' towards the kingdom of God, which is both present and coming. These are vital actions of obedience, faith in God, prayers for change;

---

[100] Barth's exposition of Romans 12-15 confronts the 'problem of ethics' in a section he calls the 'The Great Disturbance', saying that human behaviour must inevitably be disturbed by the thought of God' (1968:424).

they do not allow space for or resting or boasting. All human actions are tentative, subject to God's glory.

> Within the limits of the great and general 'building' on which we are engaged, we do no more than arrange demonstrations; we can act only so to provide significant signposts and witnesses to the glory of God. Whether our actions do in fact serve His glory must be left entirely to his decision, precisely because their purpose is the service of his honour (Rom 2:6) (Barth, 1968:431).

HOLISTIC MISSION AND THE DISTURBANCE OF GOD

Following this proposal, I comment on the term 'holistic'. I am arguing for a meaningful integration of what is *from above* (God's purposes) with that which is *below* (human concerns for children) in FBO-church collaboration. Outcomes have been described as meeting the physical, emotional, and spiritual needs of children, redeeming whole persons and communities. Some take it as fact that God will intervene for children in crisis but do not specifically explain how or why.

Commenting on World Vision's measurement and evaluation of transformational change, Byworth concedes that much remains to be learned about 'the place of spirituality in a community's sense of hope, and what impact this will have on participation and sustainability' (2003:101). Indeed, 'faith, hope, and love' were criteria established by Paul as ultimate outcome indicators (1Cor. 13:13). Byworth's comment underscores my point: much of the FBO language about holistic change tends to leave 'spirituality' or salvation in Christ, which engages with eternal life with God, *on one side.*[101] On the *other side* is the validity of caring for the humanity of the child, addressing hunger, abuse, or need for family, what some described as 'Samaritan theology', helping children make it through another day on earth.

While churches may be willing to talk of salvation as a priority, FBOs rarely do. Evangelical FBOs have not given up on eternity, but how does eternal destiny affect their 'Samaritan practice'? Jesus speaks of eternity with God and care for suffering neighbours as integral and serious to life in His kingdom; he refers to children as a way into the kingdom and to 'His way of doing things' (Matt: 18:1-3). In analysis of outcomes, it was evident that neither churches nor FBOs have put extensive resource into sorting out such questions. Values and central assumptions remained unexamined and 'confessional assurances' shaped descriptions of outcomes. FBOs tended to use language of faith and God on a 'spiritual' level and went on with programmatic interventions aimed at bettering child welfare in practical secularity that they called 'holistic'. How does this 'holistic activity' interface with the eternal God? Some said it was

---

[101] Language for eternity with God is various; the point is that for salvation to mean anything worthwhile it must take into account the demands of God on the human situation. If left to assumptions and no critical evaluation, then the message of God in Christ is bracketed, not informing the totality of FBO action for children.

experienced in prayer, others in times of 'divine intervention'; few explained how reflection on God or the Evangel shaped their 'holistic agenda'.

God does not remain 'bracketed' on His side of the equation; God in His freedom goes beyond our predictions and our reasonable expectations. The cross 'articulates God's odd freedom, his strange justice, and His peculiar power' (Brueggemann, 2001:99). God surprises and disturbs; this is one of Barth's points in his exposition of Romans 12:1-2.

> Once again we are confronted with this sidedness of the whole course of our human existence.... our life and will and acts are brought into question. For the freedom of God, the 'Other sidedness' of His mercies, means that there is a relationship between God and man, that there is a dissolution of human 'this sidedness' and that a radical assault is being made upon every contrasted, second, other thing (1968:427).

Children in crisis provide another theological clue at this point: FBOs (and churches) must do the best they can, taking reasonable action, thinking creatively, at times taking risks caring for the whole child, but they should remain open to what they cannot plan or predict of God in advance. Children who have been traumatized are experts at upsetting established theories, organized programmes, and methodical caregivers; they constantly surprise, challenge, and disturb, in so doing they speak (or shout) the language of God. Faith-based care entails openness to the prodding and judgment of God, sensitivity to the experiences and pain of children living in a fallen world. God is not limited by 'holistic' agendas; most children who have been severely traumatized will always carry the scars of their experience.

Here I take some issue with those who predict that children can be '*completely restored* to wholeness'. All children (and human beings) carry signs of both wholeness and brokenness; sin is a present reality and any 'holistic' agenda that does not give a reckoning of sin, falls short in describing the life in the kingdom. The balance is found in the walk of faith that places trust in God's sustaining love and His unlimited freedom. Any account of holism offered by the FBOs must take into account God's freedom and disturbance, God's 'gift of pain' (Yancey & Brand, 1999). FBO personnel acknowledged the power of faith to sustain them in especially difficult circumstances. They discussed narratives of sacrifice, pain, and disappointment. I suggest that these narratives of disappointment and frustration should be included as 'holistic outcomes'[102]

This suggests another question: how does 'holism', as put forward by the FBOs, account for the death and burial of God in Christ? Brueggemann sees in the crucifixion of Jesus 'the ultimate act of criticism in which Jesus announces the end of the world of death ... and takes the death into his own person.'

---

[102] For a piercing study concerning the Christian faith and the problem of evil and pain see Ulrich Simon's *A Theology of Auschwitz* (1979).

> The criticism consists not in standing over against but in standing with; the ultimate criticism is not one of triumphant indignation but one of passion and compassion that completely and irresistibly undermines the world of competence and competition (Brueggemann, 2001:94-5).

FBO Use of Measurement Indicators to Evaluate Outcomes

FBO leaders were asked how they recorded and measured outcomes in childcare. Who was the evaluation for – donors, children in the programme, the church, or the local community?[103] Answers were dependent on several factors: value the FBO placed on measuring outcomes, requirements of the local DCP, requirements of the foreign donor organization, and value the FBO placed on evaluation criteria. All the FBOs used some mechanism to monitor outcomes; some more robust than others. FBOs acknowledged that written measurement indicators have value and should be used, but they were not discussed as a critical operational component. FBOs were generally more conscientious than churches in using some form of written measurement. Based on this analysis, the cases were plotted as displayed in Figure 7.3.

Figure 7.3 Methods primarily used to monitor and evaluate the project

Formal/written Evaluations-------------------------------non-formal or verbal evaluations
WV Ro- IDC----MoM MWB Ruth---WFM -- L&L CoH ------ACVN Ţoar ------BF

The professional childcare FBOs (*WV Ro* and *IDC*) used formal evaluations.[104] They relied partially on secular funding, had professional staff, and established means of monitoring and measuring outcomes with children.[105] Programmes receiving government (SIDA, DFID USAID) or NGO (World Learning, SERA) funding must meet managerial standards, as donors require evaluative criteria and measurement indicators including: child and family profiles, health records, family records, community records, economic or community impact studies. Wallace observes that local churches and small

---

[103] As stated in the opening of the chapter, my intention was not to assess or measure efficacy in faith-based interventions in Romania. Only one question in the interview guide was asked about measuring outcomes, my purpose was to ascertain if it was being done at all and, if so, how it influenced FBO-church partnerships.

[104] Byworth (2003) provides a schematic overview of WV's process of measuring 'transformational development'; he describes domains, indicators, definitions, data sources, and measurement process. His discussion on 'transformed relationships through care for others' and 'emergence of hope in communities' is relevant to church-based work. I found no evangelical churches using these criteria.

[105] *IDC* acknowledged that they have received help in shaping these measurement criteria from SERA (a French-Romanian NGO). WV Ro and IDC had both undergone an external 'performance audit'.

FBOs do not usually understand the implied management style of 'project cycles, the use of logical frameworks, strategic planning, and formal evaluation procedures' (2002:135). These FBOs differentiate publicly funded programmes from direct religious assistance, which includes assistance to churches. Professional international FBOs were more concerned with 'evidence based transformation' than local FBOs (Belshaw, 2002:89).[106]

MoM and *MWB* kept individual 'progress updates' on children; these were used to report to local DCP and individual sponsors of children.[107] *Ruth* maintained educational achievements, other FBOs monitored progress in social skills, maintained health records, family evaluations, and general activities. These FBOs were not receiving government funding; support came from churches, individual donors, and FBOs in the West. Standards for evaluation were determined by each project; the funding partners set guidance for sponsorship reporting. *WMF* evaluation was done in accordance with their 'community based approach' to childcare.

> We keep a file for each child but evaluation is done in reference to our impact on the community. We evaluate changes in child, family, and community, for instance we might ask 'is the community more hopeful about prospects for their children' (FBOL#60, 2006)?

Western partners entrusted the evaluation criteria to the national directors and staff of *L&L*. Measurement indicators were developed in consultation with local DCP. *L&L* designed and implemented standardized evaluation criteria that were adopted by other childcare projects in Bucharest. This FBO served as an example of contextualized outcome measurement – based on local economic, social, and political realities. *L&L* was invited to contribute to a national forum on childcare, and the director served on the mayor's local advisory council to National Authority for the Protection of Children.

Church-based FBOs maintained few written records on individual children. The primary means of monitoring progress was personal involvement or relationships with children, relying on non-formal and verbal evaluations; in most cases church-based workers knew every child by name. Measurement criteria was left to the discretion of the church or local FBO and included evaluation of progress of children in tutoring programmes, grading Bible

---

106 See Belshaw (2002) 'Towards Evidence-based Strategies of Transformational Development', he asks what is necessary to identify and implement effective strategies for transformation and suggests gathering three types of knowledge: 1) evidence of impact, 2) cumulative evidence about best practices and 3) evidence about the institutional configurations, management systems, and financial systems.

107 Child sponsorship as a method of support was discussed in Chapter 5. The typical 'progress report' contained a short personal history, family (if applicable), age, sex, health, current hobbies or interests, and participation in programme activities.

correspondence courses, activity at summer camp, attendance records from literacy classes or Bible studies (Mullinex, 2000).[108]

Possibilities and challenges in faith-based outcome measurement

Analysis pointed to both possibilities and challenges with measurement indicators and criteria. FBO records contained physical data, psychological outcomes, and behavioural changes. Research on FBO outcome measurement in capacity and effectiveness remains 'very young and underdeveloped …entailing a sharp learning curve' in the West (Fischer, 2003:2).[109] With the exception of large, well-funded multinationals such as *WV Ro*, it is even less utilized in Romania and invites further study.

Activist and interventionist FBOs have helped hundreds of children; to date very few impact studies have been undertaken. Community faith-based social services are a promising area of study in Romania; local FBOs are positioned to shape the discussion. Most Western partners have been slow to encourage local FBOs to engage with civic society, *L&L* demonstrates this can happen with local initiative. FBOs share common concerns for 'dignity, self worth, and moral change' with NGOs. FBOs could begin by learning from secular studies (Harty *et al.*, 1996).[110]

FBOs measure what they value and believe they can influence. This research has identified 'faith in Christ' as an important intervention and outcome. But how does one measure 'faith', especially since it is recognized as a gift from God and cannot be produced by human effort or engineered? Here I have more questions than answers. There is a need for clearer understanding of the role and character of faith in respect to programme services being offered. Can faith be considered a programmatic factor as in the use of prayer and scripture as elements of the programme? To what degree does faith influence the programme environment, the staff, the children involved?

---

[108] As described earlier in this chapter, church-based evaluation criteria were still being considered when I was conducting research.

[109] Fischer discusses how the design and implantation of outcome measurement approaches from secular literature can be effectively adapted to FBOs and their programmes. Drawing on the United Way (a large U.S. charity) logic model framework, he addresses the practical issues of surrounding the development of measures and methods.

[110] Beyond studies cited concerning 'transformational development', there are a number of web sources available to assist FBOs in this process. See 'Performance Measurement Toolkit' available for download at http://www.nationalserviceresources.org/ (accessed, December 6, 2010). See also Hudson Institute's 'Faith-based Ministries Code of Conduct' which includes a statement focused on evaluation: 'We commit ourselves to credible and objective evaluation procedures and to maintaining clear and documented participant records so as to facilitate proper assessment of programme performance' Sherman (2003:2).

FBO leaders stated it was important to improve work with children while learning to better know and love God. 'The identification of specific outcome expectations enables programme staff to make explicit the operational theory or assumptions of the programme' (Fischer, 2003:6). Extra focus here may encourage FBOs to think more critically about their expectations of 'God's concern for children', critique the use of holistic as a 'catch all' phrase, and encourage reflection on participation with local churches. Outcomes in human service interventions are directly linked to the quality of programme personnel. As discussed, few FBO personnel have specific training in psychology or child development, but these individuals bring a specialized disciplinary background to the children they serve, namely a deep commitment to Christ and His love for children. This characteristic should be more fully explored and understood in assessing programme outcomes.

Making space for unpredictable outcomes

Resident in possibilities for measuring faith outcomes are inherent challenges. Is faith in Christ equivalent to 'self-esteem' or 'relational consciousness'? Concerning the 'disturbance of God', to what degree are FBOs operating with open awareness of God's freedom? If space is allowed for unpredictable and disappointing outcomes, should they not be included in measurement criteria? I did not find a FBO that listed 'disappointment, setbacks, and reversals' as an outcome indicator. Yet these are evidence of work and life in a 'yet unredeemed world'. A biblical eschatological framework means making space for the 'already' of pain and sacrifice as an outcome indicator.[111] 'When men are slowed down, disappointed, and discouraged … this slowing down is only from the Good' (Barth, 1968:432) this confronts us with the knowledge that only God knows what is a meaningful service in His honour.

Programme outcomes entail a discussion of evidence, measurability, and certainty; however, work with children in crisis pushes both FBO and caregiver to categories of fidelity. For instance, caregivers offer love and consistent companionship with difficult children (an intervention); to what degree can an outcome such as *koinonia* in Christ be measured? There are children who do not fit neat categories of measurement; there are those who 'completely … undermine the world of competence' (Brueggemann, 2001:95). 'The kids in our programme are hardened street kids and they come to us with a "don't measure us" mentality' (FBOS#8, 2006). Faith, hope, and love are central to the language of faith-based work with children. Can these qualities be reduced to quantifiable 'measurement criteria'? I continue this discussion in Chapter 8 and argue that faith-based care also involves embracing discontinuity and

[111] See Plant (2003) concerning secular eschatology vs. biblical eschatology in FBO expectations.

tensions as church and FBOs continue learning to respond to 'human and divine concerns' in meaningful ways.

Summary

This chapter integrated findings and analysis of outcomes as described by churches and FBOs. These factors contributed to their understanding of partnership. Perceptions and expectations of outcomes differed in important areas and influenced ability and willingness to collaborate. The terms child development and spiritual change required further clarification. In this study, 'spiritual change' it is grounded in the experience of Jesus Christ. In examining outcomes, it was determined that both churches and FBOs rely on certain 'confessional assurances' based on their understanding and confidence in God's love for children.

Pastors and churches hold that the primary outcome in work with children is conversion, that children find 'new life in Christ.' However, there are limitations when salvation is considered a 'private transaction' as this may bracket the humanity of children. Prioritizing individual conversion has not encouraged churches to consider the implications of structural or societal sins against children. Some churches have moved beyond transactional methods of conversion; they provide acceptance and love as a free gift within boundaries and protection, while nurturing children in faith. An adequate doctrine of sin is necessary, not to accuse children but in order to confront pastor, church, caregiver, and child with God's grace, mercy, judgement, and covenant. Pastors value the child's participation in corporate church life; moral authority is grounded in scripture. The primary means of outcome measurement in churches is participation and observation. Church-based care was described as an 'integral system' as families and church youth offered support and homes for children in crisis resulting in reintegration as an outcome. The story of a specific child offered a theological marker to bearing witness to Christ in pain, suffering, and uncertainty.

FBOs use a variety of terms to define outcomes, combining physical and psycho-social with concern for God and eternity. However, ambiguous statements about 'saving' children were confusing to churches. FBOs are making an important contribution in Romanian childcare; moral formation was discussed as an integral outcome. Dignity, self-respect, personal worth, and responsibility enable children to learn who they are in the sight of God and their fellows. Children in crisis invite caregivers into mutual participation with uncertainty and discontinuity, a theological pointer to the grace of God which regards all human actions as limited but integral to God's partnership with humanity.

FBOs use 'transformation' to describe outcomes. Does this term describe a realistic horizon of expectation for work with children when the 'already' of their present situation includes much pain and suffering? If so, should 'transformation,' as an outcome, include space for uncertainty and recognition of what is 'not yet'? FBO outcomes are signs of the coming kingdom, demonstrations of obedience and faith; they act as markers not ultimate indicators. Considering 'holistic', which claims to integrate human and divine concerns; to what degree is the freedom of God bracketed? God disturbs and surprises. Terms like 'holistic' can become 'catch-all phrases' covering up where more theological and missiological reflection is required. Holism should take account of the unpredictable nature of God and the constant challenge of pain and unrealized expectations. Holistic childcare entails the participation of a believing community living through the full range of human experience.

FBO measurement of outcomes is non-standardized, the multinational FBOs are more likely to use evidence based criteria. Local and church-based FBOs use a range of methods from individual profiles to educational assessments. There are possibilities for future faith-based measurement studies in Romania especially concerning the impact of a believing community on the moral formation of children and youth. The identification of outcome expectations could help FBOs be more specific in clarifying their theological and holistic assumptions in programme delivery. Challenges include recognizing those aspects of faith-based work with children which resist measurement. Faith itself is a gift from God and not humanly engineered. Measurement in faith-based work should take account of categories of pain and disappointment as well as God's faithfulness and freedom.

The integration of FBO and church descriptions of outcomes prepares the way for the final phase of the study – an analysis of partnership factors and the core category: embracing tensions in FBO-church partnership for children.

Chapter 8

Embracing Tension in Partnership: Factors that Enable Churches and FBOs to work together

Introduction

Chapters 5-7 have analysed the perceptions, assumption, activities, and outcomes that characterized church and FBO collaboration from 1991-2004. Evangelical care for children in crisis continued to expand through this period with minimal research or reflection on factors that were shaping the collaborative process. I turn now to the task of integrating the three central categories: 1) FBO interventionist and specialized response to children, 2) churches as embedded communities concerned with faith and repentance and 3) conversion and social concern as outcomes in order to answer the central research question:

> What factors have enabled or hindered international and local FBOs, mission agencies and Romanian evangelical churches to cooperate effectively in ministry with children at risk in the time frame 1990-2004?

Following the research plan, I identified a fourth central category – factors that facilitated working in partnership. This became the core category of the study: 'embracing tensions in partnership for children'. This chapter will analyse the tensions and factors that influenced FBOs to encourage empowerment (Cowger, 1994)[1] or dependency with local churches. I begin with a short discussion integrating the cases, followed by an explanation of the core category and a heuristic lens.

A Description of the Cases Arranged in Four Quadrant Model

The findings from the cases were synthesized to facilitate 'explanation building'. Several data displays were utilized in the process of identifying the core category. A four-quadrant model was created by arranging selected axial codes and key phrases from the transcripts on a vertical and horizontal plot with the cases arranged in one of four possible quadrants. Taking account of

[1] Cowger offers six basic principles of empowerment at the micro level, they include: 1) an understanding of the potential capacity of the people and systems with a view to what both can be in the future. 2) The principle of self-determination joined with the belief that people have the capacity to solve their own problems. 3) Focus on strengths and resources as well as problems and deficits. 4) Recognition of the universality of social conditions. 5) A developmental perspective, including a public policy component of change. 6) Recognition of the community context of change (1994:262-64).

variables on the continua (see Table 4.4) and induction analysis of the transcripts, the cases were plotted in a four-quadrant model – Figure 8.1.[2]

Figure 8.1 Four-Quadrant Model

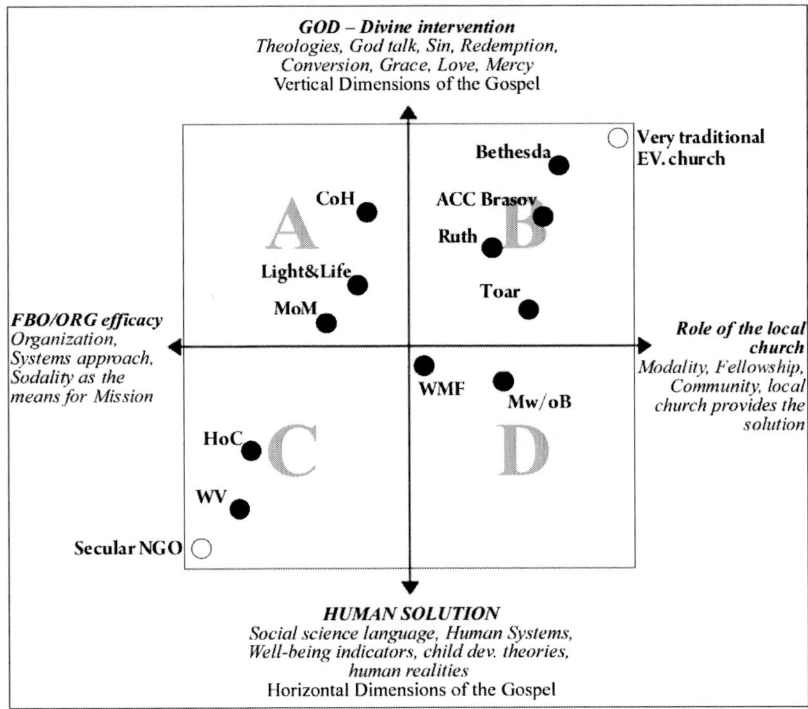

The vertical axis describes what I have referred to as *Side A* – God's ultimate intentions for children, redemption, conversion, and vertical dimensions of the gospel and Side B – human solutions and interventions, social sciences, child development, and human realities. In other words, who is ultimately responsible for actions on behalf of children? These are held in tension; the evangel of Jesus Christ includes both the vision of faith and the

[2] This arrangement of cases on this 'four-quadrant model' was a method of synthesizing a large amount of data in a visual matrix. To validate the representation, I discussed the 'four quadrant diagram' with several study participants (at least one representative from each quadrant) who confirmed the diagram was a useful representation of the dynamics we had discussed in interviews. The case descriptions that follow in reference to the four-quadrant model are intended to enable the reader to understand the case synthesis and inherent 'tensions' to be discussed in the chapter. Where appropriate I refer to cases by their Quadrant letter.

truth of science (Torrance, 1984:x-xii). Chalcedonian Christology implies an interpenetration of the human and divine revealed in Jesus Christ.[3]

> Because the divide between the human and the divine is humanly unfathomable, it must be crossed by the act of God, but the argument from above is that this has already been done in the paradox of God's becoming fully human while remaining fully God in Jesus Christ (Loder, 1998:12).[4]

The horizontal axis describes structural or organizational means to help children in crisis representative of FBOs and local churches. The cases were plotted in representative quadrants with descriptions as a means of focusing the analysis on factors that facilitate partnership. Diagrams have limitations and this model is not to be read as a static representation of the cases; they are dynamic organizations, changing with time and circumstances. I am not arguing that one quadrant or case should serve as the 'best' example of FBO-church partnership.[5] I am using this model to demonstrate an interpretation of variation in partnerships.

Quadrant A- Representative cases: MoM, CoH and L&L

The FBOs in this quadrant relied on independent organizational structures for the delivery of social services that were independent of local churches; placing priority on direct intervention for marginalized children. Projects began with little research in the local context; conflicts arose when FBOs questioned if churches had a genuine interest in 'these kinds of children' (FBOL#33, 2004).[6] FBOs recognized the local church as a 'participant', but did not consult the

---

[3] In *Transformation and Convergence in the Frame of Knowledge,* Chapter 6, Torrance argues from Barth's Christology that the natural order is not the context to understand God, but that the natural order must be understood in context of the revelation of Jesus Christ (1984:285-302).

[4] In discussing theological anthropology, Loder follows Barth when he comments, 'I take [Barth's] Christological position pivotal as God's revelation of what God means by "human" and at the same time what God means by "God" (1998:30). See also, Chapter 3 'Examining the relationality between the human and divine' (1998:36-42) where Loder integrates psychological theory with the theology of Pannenberg, Barth, and T, F. Torrance (Loder 1998:27). See discussion on page 308.

[5] When I began the research, I expected to make an argument for a particular case or model, assuming that efficacy in partnership could be reduced to a formula for success. I had planned to use an organizational argument that posits if the 'right factors, the right processes, the right people, the right agenda, the right strategy' were properly aligned then that case would demonstrate success (See Collins, 2005). I judge a significant outcome of the research to be a critique and alternative to this logic in favour of the central category of this study – 'embracing tension in partnership'.

[6] Recalling the discussion in Chapter 5 concerning methods followed to initiate a project, these cases were labelled 'reactive as they experienced confusion, anxiety in episodes of crises. The description here takes into account that all the cases have 'matured' since their inception and are now functioning in a 'non-crisis mode'.

church on design of programme interventions or management. Interventions were directed towards a specific group of children, often termed a 'target group'. Outcome indicators included spiritual and psycho-social with priority on spiritual outcomes (Chapter 7). The leaders and staff of the FBO attended local churches. These FBOs hired evangelical staff if possible; they were initially hesitant to hire Orthodox Christians.[7]

Quadrant B – Representative cases: Ruth, BF, Tsor and ACVN Brasov

These FBO were initiated and registered as foundations by local church partners; staff and volunteers were members of the church.[8] Church members continued involvement after the FBO hired additional staff. They were described as the 'social arm' of the church to carry out ministry on behalf of children. The church partner was described as a community of believers in a specific locality. Pastors and church elders shaped the work of the FBO; young adults and families were encouraged to engage with children in crisis. Churches met the needs of their poorest members as well as children who were occasionally perceived as 'possible threats'. The life of the church was central to the project. Providing Christian care and bringing children to faith in Christ was prioritized over shaping public policy or advocacy. Care for families in the church was an important factor in church life and provided a system of care for children.

Quadrant C – Representative cases: WV Ro and IDC

These are highly organized FBOs with specialized delivery of service and care for children.[9] They have multiple international partners, internal/external management structures, and local boards of governance providing financial oversight. Partnership with evangelical churches was secondary to programme delivery to children; churches may or may not be involved in the 'community

[7] Membership in an evangelical church was not a prerequisite for employment. The situation has been changing since 2002 as FBOs have had to professionalize to work within the guidelines of new Romanian child protection laws. MoM hires teachers from both Orthodox and evangelical backgrounds, recruiting the most qualified people.

[8] Described as 'transitional or bridge' cases in Chapter 5, I used the term 'emergent' to describe those cases that were started locally by Romanians with little or no outside help from foreign organizations. In the case of *CoH,* soon after starting its work with street children, the FBO received attention from Western donors and began to receive most of its financial resources from the U.S.A.

[9] These were typed as 'performative' organizations in Chapter 5; they typically have difficulty learning from smaller partners and lack flexibility in programme delivery and management methods. They rely on their international partners for assistance in programme design, auditing, and performance reviews. At the bottom left corner of the diagram, I have labelled a secular NGO, which would have many of the same characteristics but would omit 'faith' as programme intervention.

development' or social service programmes of the FBO. They have clearly defined mission statements, programme objectives, and are guided in their work by organizational, social, and human sciences. The terms 'holistic' and 'transformational' were used to describe programme interventions.[10] These FBOs stated that social service delivery should be done 'professionally' implying that skilled, trained professionals were better equipped to deliver social services; volunteers were well organized and accountable to oversight. WV Ro is involved in public policy work with the Romanian government and assists DCP offices in counties where they work.[11]

Quadrant D – Representative cases WMF and MWB

These FBOs functioned semi-autonomously but made participation with local churches a core programme component. The church was considered a primary vehicle to provide care for children; mobilisation and engagement with church leadership were priorities, programme interventions were designed in collaboration. The FBOs valued individual spirituality and piety and described social responsibility as 'Samaritan theology'. Understanding of familial risk factors was clearly demonstrated in this quadrant. Child abuse and abandonment were understood as family dysfunction. Interventions to assist children and families were coordinated with the churches. Social reintegration of children from the institutions into families or society was a primary programme outcome. Training programmes were established for members of churches to receive specialized training to work with abused or abandoned children.

The Core Category and Heuristic Lens

The four quadrant model displays partnership variations employed by FBOs and churches, each case and quadrant has inherent strengths and weaknesses, and each is a reflection of Roman 12: 5-6.

---

[10] As I have argued in Chapter 7, the terms 'holistic and transformation' are dependent on the definition of the FBO. I note that these FBOs were most dependent on secular management and community development theory and use these terms 'holistic-transformational' more frequently than cases in the other quadrants. I argue that holism should include some form of long-term residence in a local community. 'Mere intervention can never be holistic, because it never completely takes up residence with people living in a specific place, people in the wholeness of their lives' (Willmer, personal email, 2005).

[11] The 2006 World Vision Romania Annual Report states that only 7.3 per cent of programme funding comes from inside Romania. In discussion with the national director, he estimated that 30 per cent of giving (cash and gifts in kind) came from international donors (secular sources); the remainder comes from child sponsorship funds (usually individuals with faith-based motivations to support children).

> Let each one according to his gift, do it well, so there are many different things being done well, rather than badly, and doing it right is the product of the whole body, in the mercy of God's judgment which has not yet been disclosed to us. [12]

Figure 8.2 The Core Category as a heuristic lens

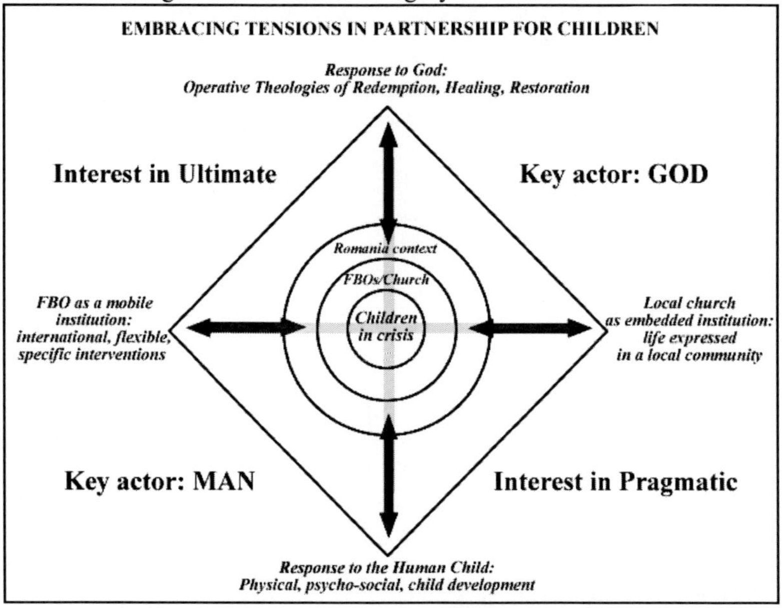

EMBRACING TENSIONS IN PARTNERSHIP FOR CHILDREN

Response to God:
Operative Theologies of Redemption, Healing, Restoration

Interest in Ultimate

Key actor: GOD

Romania context
FBOs/Church
Children in crisis

FBO as a mobile institution: international, flexible, specific interventions

Local church as embedded institution: life expressed in a local community

Key actor: MAN

Interest in Pragmatic

Response to the Human Child:
Physical, psycho-social, child development

The four-quadrant model, cross-case synthesis, and iterative analysis led to the identification of a core category for the study. In an effort to define 'efficacy' or 'what was working in partnership', I induced that FBO-church collaboration was more meaningfully described as a combination of missional tensions. This statement implies that partnerships involve tensions that can be understood because it is possible to identify and describe causal factors. I then labelled the core category: '*embracing tensions in partnership for children*'. 'Embracing' requires not ignoring or attempting to abolish tensions but working within them; whist living hopefully in God and honouring His intentions for children. I created a 'heuristic lens' as a graphic to frame the essential elements of the core category (Figure 8.2).[13]

---

[12] I am indebted to this phrasing of from Romans 12:4-6 to Prof. Willmer who sent this in personal email (July 2006).

[13] As in the explanation above concerning the four-quadrant model, I recognize that diagrams of this sort have limitations. I have relied extensively on data displays as they enable me to make conceptual what seems in the beginning abstract. A more helpful diagram might be three-dimensional with moving components in the graphic, but this goes beyond my ability with computer-generated data displays.

The core category is further explained by this statement:

> Delivery of faith-based care for children in crisis requires embracing tension and demonstrating meaningful integration of eternal concerns (to and from God) with human concerns (physical, psycho-social, structural). Care for children may be expressed through embedded local communities and specialized FBOs. Children in crisis serve as theological and missiological pointers, not simply as objects of mission or intervention.

Defining the core category assisted with two analytical tasks: providing an overall explanation of 'what the research is about' and a cognitive shift envisioning missiological suggestions for practice. The child in crisis both receives from and instructs partnership. Embracing tensions offers FBOs and churches a means to explore the nature of the gospel, evaluate perceptions, assumptions, and new possibilities in programmatic response to children in crisis.

I will explain several elements of the diagram that are enlarged in the chapter. As in the four-quadrant model, the vertical axis represents tension between God's divine action towards and response to human beings on one pole and human actions and responses towards God and children in crisis on the other. There are various theologies that describe how God deals with humanity; I have described what was found in the specific FBOs and churches.[14] The evidence suggests there are tensions in Romania between the 'evangelistic and societal dimensions' of mission directed to children (Bosch, 1991:401). Specific to this study is the child in crisis, pictured at the centre of the diagram located in a specific context. The vertical arrows indicate that God acts on behalf of children and children also point us to understanding God and his kingdom (Matt. 18:2-4); children are objects of human intervention but also inform those actions.

On the left of the horizontal axis are FBOs: mobile institutions, with international funding, flexible programmes, and specialized agendas. On the right are local churches embedded and expressing the life of Christ in local communities. In Chapter 2, I discussed the terms 'modality' and 'sodality' (Winter, 1981c; Mellis, 1983; Ward, 1995:36-39)[15] used by some participants

---

[14] For instance one could continue to compare any number or theological views of children: Barth, Moltmann, Rahner, Schleiermacher, see January issue of *Theology Today* (2000), or others in Bunge (2001) As discussed in earlier chapters, there has been minimal critical missiological or theological reflection in the Romanian evangelical churches or FBOs on alternative views of salvation, sin, or God's action in the child's frame of reference. I will make some recommendations in this chapter and in Chapter 9.

[15] Winter (1981c) argued that historical orders and movements such as the Franciscans, Jesuits, Moravians, and the Student Volunteer Movement were examples of 'sodalities'. Modalities were compared to the local church as they are stationary, offer continuity, longevity, a nurturing community, breadth, and basis for family care.

in the study.[16] The horizontal arrows indicate that tension exists between local churches and FBOs. They are mutually related to each other's purpose and objectives; both state they want what is in the 'child's best interest' and for the child to know Christ. They are usually 'semi-autonomous' in their decision making in relation to how they perform their respective tasks (Van Gelder, 1985).[17] Theoretically, both churches and FBOs relate to an agreed upon reference point (the authority of scripture and God) and work together to so that their actions for children will be maximized.

Figure 8.3 Tensions in partnership leading to the core category

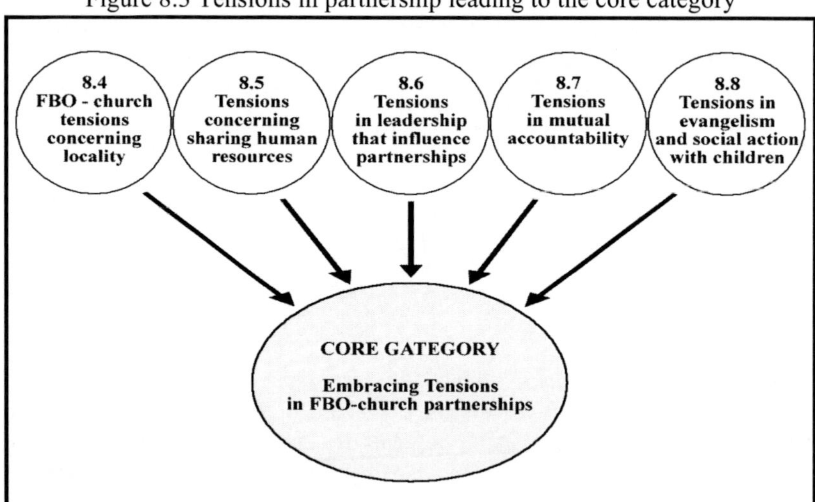

In Chapter 2, I asked the question 'Do structures enable service of one another or encourage the acquisition of status and power' (Samuel 1981:50). This chapter will explicate the factors shaping the tensions identified in the study that were judged to have the most influence on partnerships working with children.[18] I discuss how FBOs and churches understood the call of God to the

[16] I am not committed to these specific terms; see Stanley (2003) for others. I recognize that FBOs and churches operate as different types of organizational entities.

[17] Sodalities tend not to relate their purposes, goals, and objectives to modalities and need to take precautions. Modalities, on the other hand, tend to authoritatively dominate sodalities and need to take precautions. Neither sodalities nor modalities want to recognize a reference point beyond their own autonomy. Semi-autonomous decisions need to be informed by mutually related purposes (Van Gelder, 1985).

[18] As in each key category, I have had to limit my report to the factors that were deemed to be most influential. This is an inherent limitation in using GT or any coding scheme. In writing this chapter, I have drawn from findings in Phase One that informed Phase Two; the 11 cases were given more weight in the analysis. There are several problematic categories, especially concerning conflict in administration and leadership,

local church, shared human resources, resolved leadership tensions, learned mutual accountability and advanced together in expressing social concern for children. The core category and contributing factors is diagrammed in Figure 8.3.

FBO-Church Tensions Concerning 'Locality'

Tensions between local church autonomy and expectations of foreign FBOs were evident throughout the study. The idea of the 'indigenous church' has come under increasing pressure in the last 50 years as globalization has created more opportunities for mission agencies, local/national denominations, and local churches to participate in the direct international partnerships (Engel & Dryness, 2000:75).[19] Evangelicals in Romania share 120 years of history, are a recognized religious minority, and usually had their own buildings for worship. The concept of 'local church' was more clearly understood than 'faith-based organization'. Discussed here are ways that the FBOs recognized the role of local churches concerning children, tensions in locality, and willingness to examine assumptions and cultural values.

FBOs and the 'call of God' to the local church

Evangelical churches are 'embedded' in local communities; the term 'embedded' captures the essence of being an integral part of a surrounding whole. When pastors spoke about the 'call of God to the church', they referred to their sense of belonging and sense of locality. Commitment to locality is a tension in FBO-church partnership.[20] A pastor expressed a typical sentiment concerning foreign FBOs, 'they come for a time, but we know they will eventually leave' (Pas#13, 2005). FBOs recognized in principle that 'the church is the sustaining institution within communities of poverty, long after

---

where I did not have sufficient data or permission from the participants to bring into this discussion.

[19] Engel & Dryness argue that the missional nature of the local church has diminished in the last century because of the dramatic growth of 'parachurch agencies'. This has manifested in two particular ways: 1) efforts initiated by mission agencies with little accountability to the local churches and 2) mission agencies have fostered a superior-subordinate relationship in churches in receiving countries (2000:75). This was the case in much of the former Soviet Union and Eastern Europe in the 1990s. This study is limited to agencies working with children in crisis, but findings concerning 'local church autonomy and interdependence' in missiological perspective merit more research in Romania.

[20] See Chapter 6 for discussion on local church value concerning community. I identified 'locality' as a primary domain in the analysis as it came up in every interview with pastors. Churches were described as 'spiritual islands' (Moyle, 1999: 26), but it was important for FBOs to recognize how this sense of belonging to a local place gave the congregations continuity and cohesion.

the NGOs have departed, churches continue to serve' (WVI, 2002:7). FBOs are not embedded in local communities like churches; they make programmatic decisions as to when to come and when to leave. Open communication on this point was a factor influencing partnership.

When FBOs and local churches shared the same geographical space, they had to determine obligations of one for the other. Paul argues in Romans 14:1-2 that the stronger can learn from the weak (Sugden, 1997b:28).[21] Churches and FBOs both had 'strengths and weaknesses'; willingness to learn from one another meant openness to instruction and 'encountering the action of God' together (Barth, 1968:151).[22] Work with children in a specific geographical area required that FBOs remain sensitive to their motives as their actions were sometimes interpreted as a move to displace the church.[23] A determining variable that enabled partnership was the visible action of the FBO to affirm 'God's call to the church serving the local community' (Pas#7, 2004). Local churches commended *MWB* and *WMF* for this characteristic. As one director commented, 'we are tenaciously committed to working with the church, what we do with children makes little sense without their involvement' (FBOL#60, 2006). Churches were not dependent on FBOs for direction concerning their locality; they were present in the community when the FBOs arrived.[24]

Tensions and convergence of values in serving the local community

As discussed in previous chapters, Romanian churches and Western FBOs shared certain values such as a commitment to God and willingness to serve

---

[21] In Romans 14, Paul is addressing a division between those who called themselves 'strong in the faith', who were Gentile believers, and those who were 'weak in the faith', probably Jewish believers, who held to the traditions. His argument is that both sides can learn from each other; Paul bridges two cultures. This is applicable to Romanian churches and Western FBOs as they had much to learn from one another as they came together to serve children and represent God's body and grace.

[22] Both FBOs and churches were simultaneously engaged with an encounter with Christ. This may have been implicit, but partnership offers the opportunity to make the encounter 'explicit'.

[23] In smaller cities, where there were only three or four evangelical churches in a population of less than 100,000, pastors were more likely to make this sort of comment. Churches displayed a 'territorial' attitude when well-funded FBOs were able to open more visible projects than the local evangelical church in the eyes of the general public.

[24] To illustrate how international FBOs sometimes overestimate their influence: Evans, who works with Tearfund, recognizes that the church works at the 'grass roots'. He uses the metaphor of a human 'hand' to describe FBO and church relation. He describes FBOs as the 'wrist or knuckles' and local churches as the 'fingertips' (2002:12). This is a faulty image, in physiology wrists and knuckles usually 'control' where fingertips reach. But FBOs do not determine the location of a local church. FBOs may help to 'lengthen' the reach of the church in an instrumental way, but they rarely influence choice of location.

locally; if these values converged, partnerships were strengthened. Churches placed value on maintaining community, locality, and continuity. FBOs usually placed a higher value on bringing direct intervention to the child. This was identified as a tension between 'relational orientation versus task orientation' (Lingenfelter & Mayers, 1986:81-93).[25] Organizations, churches, and individuals, when dedicated to learning and intentional in efforts, will invest resources according to their values and priorities believing they can influence outcomes and ends (Schein, 1997:19-22). Conversely, low priority issues are usually considered 'not important enough' to spend time learning about, resulting in a 'we can't change it mentality' with a tendency to mystify rather than rationally understand.

Cross-case comparison found the majority of FBOs verbally endorsed the church's identity as a 'community of believers' in a specific place. However, when children were treated as an object of FBO intervention, it did not necessarily commit the FBO to working with local churches.[26] FBOs in Quadrant B and D developed programmes to empower churches to serve children in crisis. In these cases, child-focused programmes motivated churches to respond to wider needs of their communities, noted by FBOs and pastors:

> We have seen the churches grow in their understanding of God's calling to our community. In the beginning there were some who told us that helping children from the institutions was a waste of time and resources ... Caring for the children has changed our perspective of what we can do as a church; we have seen the changes in the lives of the children … This kind of work opens people's eyes to see possibilities they could not see before … We have seen what God does in the lives of suffering children and our church has received as much as we have given the children ... This experience has helped us to be more expectant of God (paraphrase of FBOL#38 & Pas#12, 2005).

It was inconsistent for a FBO to assert they were interested in the life and ministry of local churches (an espoused value) but neglect the church in programme design and operation. Statements from FBOs such as, 'the local church does not care about the children on the streets' (FBOL#7, 2003), failed to give a full account of God's Spirit expressed through His church despite the limitations of believing people. 'The church, like individual Christians, always exists between believing and unbelieving; the church's being is always the argument between them' (Willmer, 1999:14). FBOs' unwillingness to embrace the tension of 'believing and unbelieving' resulted in limited cooperation. Partnerships were better served when FBOs understood their theological

[25] Also see Labreche (2007) for analysis of this cross-cultural value conflict with reference to 'task oriented' Western (American) missionaries and Romanian evangelical pastors.

[26] I could not identify any network or FBO 'forum' that addressed the question of 'local church engagement'. World Vision's conferences had brought churches and FBO leaders together for one-time events, but no ongoing 'strategic network' was in place to bring together FBO and church leaders.

rationale was 'in the service they could give to churches, fulfilling those tasks [with children] that the churches saw as necessary but did not have the resources on a local level to accomplish' (Kirk, 2000:199).

Willingness to examine assumptions concerning community

Church assumptions of 'belonging' in a local community were often in tension with FBO readiness to enter a community to provide for children in crisis. Faith-based partnership required persistence in God's grace 'which is essential to its being grace, when that persistence is lacking, practice can be like that of the rational market' (Willmer, 1999:14).

WV Ro, *WMF*, and *MWB* defined their relationship to the church in writing: 'Our work calls us to relate to local congregations in the communities where we serve' (WVI, 2002:15). But policy documents, especially those written in international offices, have to be worked out in the local context. *WV Ro* prioritized community development and public policy working with civic leaders; their willingness to partner with Orthodox churches meant that some evangelical would not participate in their programmes.[27] *WV Ro* embraced this tension and continued with the ADP agenda.[28]

In the late 1990s, church-initiated FBOs (Quadrant B) grew in capacity and delivery of services to their communities (Chapter 6); they needed to find additional funding that brought tension between expectations of external donors and faithfulness to the local congregation.

> In order to create a robust organization, we required more structure, time, and finances than our church could provide. We have tried to stay true to our roots; we wanted to grow organically in the community. We do not want to become 'donor driven' but recognized the need for outside assistance (FBOS#6, 2005).

When FBOs set aside predetermined agendas and responded to a church's concerns, they demonstrated an 'appreciative' awareness (Hammond, 1996), acknowledging that God was already at work in the community through the church.[29] FBOs that continued to assume they did need not the support of local

---

[27] WVI's international study 'Strengthening our Bridges' (2002) recognizes 'local congregations', but in the Romanian context, their work with Romanian Orthodox churches sometimes put them at odds with evangelical churches. WV Ro continues to build bridges between Orthodox and evangelical leaders at the national level. At the local community level, especially in rural areas, suspicions remain high between evangelical pastors and Orthodox priests.

[28] I recognize that World Vision Ro has made a significant contribution to community development, human health services, and child advocacy. The Orthodox churches that have cooperated with them in ADP programmes have also grown in their understanding of 'holistic' mission. See comments in Chapter 7.

[29] The cases that worked in close cooperation with local churches and communities demonstrated what I described as 'appreciative' methodology, that is, they sought to discern what was happening in the local churches and capitalized on those strengths. See

churches were increasingly dependent on foreign funding by 2004; cases in Quadrant A represent this trend (FBOL#18; #28, 2005).[30] *IDC* operated for several years as a successful NGO before the Romanian founders joined an evangelical church. The organization began to make changes in programme interventions based on requests from local churches to include 'spiritual input'; this immediately created tensions with non-evangelical staff (FBOL#25, 2005) but indicated that the 'FBO' was willing to examine assumptions about methods of intervention as they participated in the life of the church.[31]

Collaboration required learning from FBO, church, and community, re-examining assumptions, 'remaining mutually open to correction, facing explicit weaknesses' (Sookhdeo, 1994:54), and honouring God. Contrary to some who said, 'it's all about the market, which is our measure of success' (FBOL#4, 2003); FBO-church partnership for children in the kingdom of God was not about gaining 'market share'.[32]

Willingness to embrace local culture and values

Missiology over the past 30 years has made much of contextualization and language acquisition in cross-cultural work,[33] to the degree that one would assume personnel from the West would have been proactive in these activities. This was not the norm for child-focused FBOs in Romania, especially in the early 1990s.[34] Partnership conflicts of this period were attributed to cultural

---

Chapter 4, Methods for description of 'AI'; also see (Myers, 1999b:176-79; Johnson & Ludema, 1997:71-77).

[30] The cases in Quadrant A (*CoH*, *MoM*, and *L&L*) continue their work with children. My comment is based on linear observations and interviews. I had access to these cases in my role as project director and witnessed first-hand how increasing dependence on Western funding allowed the FBOs to continue their programmes largely independent of local church ownership.

[31] I advised the directors of this organization to listen carefully to all stakeholders: the local churches, the members of their staff who were not believers and the families and children they were serving who were also not evangelical. This required learning 'managing competing interests' (Cooley, 2005) and dialogical skill on the part of the senior leadership.

[32] See my earlier comments in Chapter 2 and 6 about FBO reliance on managerial missiology. Here the comment and response concerning 'market' has to do with 'target audience', that is, a group of children or people 'who need the gospel'.

[33] There are several general sources on cultural studies listed in bibliography, see Geertz, 1973; Kraft, 1979; Hiebert, 1987; Lingenfelter, 1981; Sanneh, 1989, 1993; Hofstede, 1997.

[34] In Phase One of this research, more than half of all Western interviewees had not learned Romanian. This may be explained in part as many Romanian evangelical young adults learned excellent English after the fall of communism and worked with the FBOs, an experience reflected in my own personal attempts at language study.

misunderstandings (Ţon, 1993). FBOs from the West shared both locality and a *cultural* context with churches.

Value conflicts and solutions were observed across the cases. *WV Ro* and *IDC* worked with Romanians who had 'ascribed status', such as Orthodox priests and civic officials. Priests have more cultural status than 'evangelical pastors' who are often seen as out of step with Romanian mainstream religious life. *MoM*, *L&L*, and *CoH* included professional Romanians in their local management.[35] In Galati, Western and Romania leaders jointly represented *BF, WMF, and IDC*; they collaborated closely with churches seeking to shift attention to the child in the context of community. Western personnel (missionaries) worked with 'local church networks' and encouraged churches to initiate *Ruth* and *ACVN*.

Rubatos researched the post-communist Romanian business environment to educate incoming E.U. personnel of cultural organizational and work values. 'Romanians have a weak institutional collectivism but a strong small group collectivism ...they rely extensively on informal networking' (Rubotos, 2004:64).[36] Romanians tend to be sceptical of external 'institutions'. Local churches are small group 'collectives' immersed in their own evangelical subculture. 'It was a failure of many foreigners to appreciate Romanian cultural values or see them as a strength; this undermined efforts at working together to achieve lasting change' (Dickens & Groza, 2004:481). I induced from participant-observation and comparison with other research (LeBreche, 2007) that Western FBOs had better success in partnership when they worked through the social networks of churches and extended families that served as a natural bridge to learning cultural values concerning community and children.

FBOs at times failed to take into account their 'achievement oriented identity', that is, prestige is attained and integral to organizational and personal self-worth. Western FBOs valued the sense of accomplishment found in setting up new projects and assisting significant numbers of children. On the other side of partnership, Romanians sometimes failed to acknowledge their 'status oriented identity' – prestige is ascribed, personal connections are particularly important (Lingenfelter & Mayers, 1986: 99-101). Romanian churches deferred to the pastor as the primary decision maker and rarely challenged his status and authority. Children have low 'identity status' in Romanian culture.

Western FBOs that sustained resilient partnerships with churches acquired cultural competency and language skills. FBO directors said the average time

---

[35] These were Western funded FBOs, Western interests in 'achievement and task orientation' meant local church input was not a primary concern, especially if churches were perceived as unwilling to take up the *task* of childcare. These FBOs hired 'informed' locals who were capable of carrying out programme objectives, a medical doctor, a lawyer, and a specialist in child social work.

[36] Rubotos is a Romanian evangelical doing graduate studies in the U.K., she offered a two-day seminar from her research to a group of Western FBO and mission agency leaders in Bucharest (2005).

required to establish a 'culturally relevant' partnership was a minimum of two to three years. These FBOs were characterized by long-term commitment of personnel, willingness to work through cross-cultural conflict (Elmer, 1993:178-82).[37] Most of the foreign FBO personnel from the eleven cases obtained these skills. [38] They understood that Romanian churches had confidence in being sent by Christ to children of their local culture.

> If the FBO refuses to learn and understand the culture and context, which includes how the churches understand that context, then yes, the church should be very careful of the FBO agenda. If the FBO is not willing to come alongside the church sharing the ministry, then the FBO will end up going it alone with little cooperation from the church (FBOL#64, 2005).

Tensions Concerning Shared Human Resources

The complexity of interactions between FBOs and Romanian churches accentuates the unpredictable nature of organizational partnership.[39] Organizations are collectives of people and sharing human resources led to both cooperation and conflict. FBOs recognized that people in churches were a critical component in programme delivery. Concomitant was the assumed willingness of local churches to offer human resources to the FBOs. Examined here are the factors that contribute to or hinder sharing human resources.

Recognizing and enabling local capacity

Pastors spent much of their time working with 'ordinary' daily lives of members who were seeking answers from God and the Bible (Willard, 1998:13).[40] The life of a local church is both 'dusty and divine' (Bosch, 1991:389); it requires that pastors commit to the body of Christ in the course of common human activity, celebrating birth, baptisms, transitions, marriages, and

[37] The challenge of cross-cultural conflict is important and deserves more attention than I have space to give it here. See Elmer (1993), especially Chapter 12. I highlight cultural values as a component of 'tensions' in partnership to assist children.
[38] By 2002, Western evangelicals began more serious reflection and scholarship on cross-cultural communication (Downes, 2004, LaBreche, 2007). When I arrived in Romania (2002), I observed a lack of serious engagement with Romanian culture and language on behalf of many Western FBO personnel working with children.
[39] Partnership includes a number of human and organizational system components that are dynamic and interrelated, the actions of one component in a system has some impact on all the other connected components (Britton, 2005:9).
[40] I use the term 'ordinary' following Willard's discussion on the word. God comes to us, he brings the 'Life' we hunger for in common ordinary ways (Jn. 1:4). 'Jesus came to our world through the back roads and outlying districts of one of the least important places on earth. Jesus lived and ministered for thirty years among socially insignificant members of a negligible nation … he did this to be with us, to be one of us, to arrange for the delivery of his life to us' (Willard, 1998:14).

showing solidarity in pain, sickness, and death. Few Romanian pastors adopted management models of church leadership from the West (Pas#11, 2005).[41] Pastors were asked for suggestions to help FBOs identify more closely with churches.

> We would ask them to remember where they started; most of the leaders of FBOs have experience in the church and know what that we are committed to serving the local fellowship. FBOs work hard to create organizations that in the end tend to separate them from the local church. It is important to stay close to the life of the church, to the lives of ordinary people (Pas#13, 2005).

Santos points out that everyday activity in a church creates an institutional memory that FBOs ignored to their disadvantage:

> Churches are the result of the historical process of learning solutions, which creates a set of behavioural patterns that enable them to reproduce the solutions in the future without the need to go through the whole difficult process again. This creates a *practical memory* that preserves solutions, although frequently and unfortunately without necessarily being aware of their origins, and generates a strong system of norms and culture (2004:208).

FBOs that acknowledged this 'practical memory' sought ways to work with pastors, equipping believers to engage with children in crisis. This required patience and remaining sensitive to limitations while valuing and respecting the human talents in the church.[42]

> The churches needed financial assistance but we worked hard not create financial dependency on our organization. We did help with material assistance where we could but at the same time we asked if the youth from the churches could visit the children in the institutions. We learned that the church was usually willing if we took the time to work together in programme planning (FBOL#70, 2006).

I adopted the term 'capacity building' to describe equipping individuals in a local church; that is preparing a church for engagement that enhances both church and the child's capacities and possibilities (Eade, 1997:60).[43] *WV Ro*

---

[41] Where churches and pastors in the West are usually conversant at some level with management or organizational thinking, the average Romanian pastor relies primarily on his knowledge of the Bible and his knowledge of the local community in leading the church. After 2001, 'leadership' organizations like John Maxwell's Equip (U.S.A.) came to Romania in increasing numbers to offer training in 'church management'. This has been difficult to critique as these organizations are well-funded and influential, repeating the same mistakes as those that arrived in the early 1990s to do evangelistic crusades and church planting.

[42] God uses the entire body according to His Spirit and chooses not just those who are trained for ministry. See Miller (2003:3-10) for discussion of 'equipping and releasing lay ministry' as a factor in the rapid expansion of churches in the global South.

[43] Capacity building is a common theme in community development. Eade (1997) gives useful guide to its source and usage. She acknowledges that the term is used so indiscriminately in contemporary development that a clear, meaningful definition can be

used this term in reference to community development; no other FBO used 'capacity' in reference to human resources in the local church. FBOs had to remain cognizant of the capabilities of partner churches and guard against paternalism. This involved empowering Romanians to use their own problem-solving skills to identify needs and specify responses and overcoming lack of confidence in local personnel (Dickens & Groza, 2004).[44] There is significant difference in building capacity and simply relieving needs (Rickett, 2000:4).

Mobilization of church 'laity' – potential for tension

Church volunteerism was proportional to FBO intentionality to include the church in programme design and outcomes, as observed in Quadrant D cases.[45] Churches and FBOs had to guard against manipulation of volunteers. Members from local churches employed by the FBO could undermine organizational integrity through misuse of finances or unfounded criticism. FBOs could misuse their influence to question a local pastor's authority.[46]

Foreign FBOs unintentionally undermined the initiative of local churches when they addressed community problems unilaterally. A pastor commented on this, 'It is important for our churches to understand that we *can* do something about children in this community; we need partners who encourage us to take more initiative' (Pas#12, 2005). This happened when church youth were given the opportunity to influence an institutionalized child's life and development or teachers and tutors from local churches gained confidence serving children while expanding their pedagogical skills.[47] Churches recognized the contribution of FBOs that made sustainability integral to their ministry objectives, as evidenced in *ACVN*'s partnership with CRY-UK at their drop-in centre for street children (Pas#15, 2005). In this case, CRY-UK joined with an existent local church project in Braşov after experiencing conflict with

elusive. I accept her working definition: 'strengthening people's capacity to determine their own values and priorities and to organize them to act on these' (1997:23); however, I add that human capacity is limited and dependent on the grace and command of God.

[44] Dickens and Groza found that Romanian social workers lacked confidence in their abilities, largely a result of the communist years that subjugated individual initiative and creativity in the work place. 'Many Romanians had insecurity about their abilities, for too long the state had told them what they needed, what was good for them and what they could and could not do' (Dickens & Groza, 2004:479).

[45] See discussion on mobilizing volunteers in Chapter 5 - case study of *WMF*.

[46] Manipulation of personnel was observed on both sides of partnerships. Cases were selected to avoid this behaviour as much as possible.

[47] Teaching in Romanian schools is largely done by 'rote memorization'. Tutors working for *Ruth* and *MoM* were given exposure to Western teacher training and instructional methods.

Bucharest DCP offices in the transition of a Western funded children's home to state control.[48]

Families from local churches – contributions to partnership

In Chapter 7, church and family were described as a 'system of care'; the church preserves a sacred attitude toward family while engaging in social formation. In reference to Figure 7.2, I now include FBOs that aligned their resources with existent 'church care systems' thereby increasing potential human resources. 'Love and acceptance by a believing family was an invaluable contribution to restoration and reintegration of our children' (FBOL#51, 2005).

In situations with severely traumatized and institutionalized children, nine FBOs said progression towards recovery was much more likely if the child was placed with a family from a local church (see Appendix F). FBOs did not describe child placement specifically as a 'theological or sociological' activity. However, placement with a believing family demonstrated integration of both '*Side A'* and '*Side B'*: a) the action of God for the suffering child (James 1: 26-27), b) security for the child and a place of safe and reliable attachments in a family, and c) a believing community offering trusting and protective relationships (White, 2003a:124).

> We try to give the children a connection with families through our local church partners. This not only benefits the child but it strengthens our connection to the church. The church is the essential link (FBOL#54, 2005).

It was difficult to place older children from institutions in full-time residential care. FBOs relied on families from churches to take these children on outings, offer counsel and friendship, and at time refuge and protection. 'Most of the children we help are under constant threat on the streets, we ask families to just provide a space for an afternoon where they will be safe' (FBOL#40, 2004). Based on the evidence, holistic outcomes as described by FBOs in Chapter 7 were in most cases dependent on contributions from families in local churches (Moffitt, 2003:237).[49]

---

[48] CRY-UK (Care and Relief for the Young) is a U.K. faith-based charity; they worked as a funding and training partner at the Casa Robin Hood children's home in Bucharest (1996-2001). The project was established to train Romanians in a Western model of care for institutionalized children.

[49] Moffitt is the founder of 'Harvest', an organization enabling churches in the U.S.A. to partner directly with 'southern' churches in Christian development. He argues that 'holistic development' is the mission of the local church and provides a case study of a high school and church from the U.S.A. partnering with a local church in the Dominican Republic (2003). There are problems inherent in this model if Western local churches assume they have solutions they can import to their partners in the East or South see (Engels and Dryness, 2000:109-230).

Church and FBO combined care for staff and personnel

Work with children in crisis is psychologically stressful for the caregiver. Providing daily care for abusive, violent, or emotionally unresponsive children taxes the human resources of 'spiritually' dedicated individuals.[50] FBO-church partnerships had some obligation to walk together with volunteers and staff who experienced 'compassion fatigue'.[51] Partnership involves 'sharing in each other's suffering as Paul describes in 2 Cor. 1:7, which is 'the fellowship (*koinonia*) of Christ's sufferings' (Phil. 3:10; Gal. 6:17; 2 Cor. 4.8-12). The churches offered emotional and spiritual support for FBO personnel through prayer and fellowship with other believers. 'Care for the caregiver' was recognized as a contribution to the life and vitality of the FBO (Wright, 2003a).[52]

> [A large American FBO] recruited their staff and volunteers from the church. I observed people with too much responsibility, too much stress, and too much on their schedule. They end up frustrated and tired; they had little energy for their family or the life of the church. These people needed the spiritual care and nurture of the church (Pas#13, 2005).

FBO staff indicated that churches contributed to their emotional health offering 'stability', 'assurance', and 'spiritual support' (FBOS#7; FBOL#65, 2005).

> Work with street children is discouraging; some staff resigned when they saw little progress or change in the boys and girls after months of work. We encourage all our staff to attend churches that provide them with spiritual encouragement and understanding (FBOL#54, 2005).

---

[50] See Chapter 5 concerning 'calling' of FBO personnel and remarks on 'calling and enablement'. In 22 years of international work with children and youth in crisis, I have mentored or been responsible for dozens of individuals who came overseas to assist in our work. Many start with great enthusiasm, saying they are 'called by God'. Discouragement and frustration eventually take their toll and some return to their home countries in emotional crisis. FBO personnel turn to local churches in times of crisis for spiritual and emotional support.

[51] See World Vision, Washington Forum publication *Compassion and Fatigue* (1996) for resources, especially Baroness Cox's 'Embracing Compassion and Fatigue' (1996:64-72).

[52] Member care has received increasing attention by evangelical mission agencies in the last 20 years after numerous studies indicated that personnel returning home were experiencing emotional or family breakdown (O'Donnell, 1992, Taylor, 1997). People come into the caring professions and particularly care for children for many reasons. 'Many are consciously or unconsciously motivated by their own childhood needs. They may have needs for power and authority that were not appropriately met when they grew up. They may personally identify with children in difficult circumstances' (Wright. 2003a:340-45).

Local churches influenced self-perception of FBO personnel. Four FBO leaders said that appreciation from churches contributed to staff morale, another said churches provided a measure of FBO effectiveness.

> We want to know if we are acting as effective instruments in God's work; appreciation [from a church] is important to our organization. Affirmation is important to our staff. When people are discouraged in their work or faith, we rely on our connections with the churches as they give us a sense of connection with the Body of Christ (FBOL#25, 2005).[53]

This comment reflects a common tension experienced by FBOs (and churches) that valued efficacy and tangible results but lived in the 'not yet of the kingdom' serving hurting children. There was an underlying assumption in FBO-church partnerships that 'pain and frustration' could not be embraced as *normative* in ministry. Faith was linked to 'overcoming' or 'moving beyond the pain', indicating inadequate theological reflection on disappointment, puzzlement, and pain that accompany the promises of the gospel.

Where FBOs had limited contact with churches (Quadrant A and C), personnel expressed regret they were not affirmed by the church. Some 'do not really understand the meaning of community and communion until they feel deeply the pain of separation' (Kirk, 2000:202; Bosch, 1991:464-66). Given that many FBO staff did not receive formal training in managing personal stress, the church's contribution to their spiritual and emotional health was an important factor in long-term retention of personnel.

Character references and assistance from local pastors

With the exception of four FBOs (*WV Ro, IDC, MoM, and Ruth*), personnel were recruited from evangelical churches in the immediate area. FBOs relied on local church knowledge for recommendations and qualifications of personnel.

FBOs expressed varying degrees of appreciation for input from pastors, specifically: 'personal encouragement in difficult situations', 'advice on how to handle conflict with volunteers and staff', 'cooperation' and 'moral support'. In selection and placement of personnel, pastors provided character references. Individuals seeking employment with FBOs were observed in a faith community demonstrating their willingness to serve.[54] This was referred to as being 'proven in the local church' (Pas#9, 2005; FBOL#55, 2005).

---

[53] The personnel at FBOs (and churches) want assurance that their work in meaningful and has purpose. Christ leads the church to follow in the 'way of the cross'; God sometimes leads the church through joy and victory, but there is no avoiding embracing pain and frustration in caring for children in crisis. See Nouwen *et al.* (1983:89-101) concerning patience as a discipline that unveils false hopes.

[54] Ideally, FBO and churches would develop a child protection policy (MacLeod, 2003) that would require that the references from a pastor or local church be cross-checked

> We ask the church for recommendations for potential staff for our group homes. We want to know about [the applicant's] experience in the local church … Are they proven people, have they demonstrated a willingness to show love and concern for children (FBOL#38, 2006)?

The FBO-church contribution of 'people of proven character and compassion' to child social services was a valuable contribution in public institutions where state employees were often 'unmotivated' (Groza *et al.*, 1999:35). Romanian state child-welfare workers continue to lack training concerning emotional trauma of children.[55] Believers from local churches were intuitively sensitive to the bonding needs of these children.

> It was difficult to find qualified social workers, people who were both honest and deeply loved children. Our local University still doesn't offer a degree in social work. We prefer to hire people from churches that we can train because our experience is they are more dependable and genuinely care for emotional needs of the families and children (FBOL#61, 2005).

FBO programmes financed exclusively by external donors described more frequent personnel conflicts. Two cases described situations where Western management were asked to intervene in staff conflict.[56] Occasionally local churches were asked to serve as conflict mediators, evidence that church 'practical memory' (Santos, 2004) was supportive of FBO practice. FBOs that undervalued the resource of 'local knowledge' learned difficult lessons.

> We had a few experiences when people came from the churches and took positions with us as a 'political positions'; they came with mixed motives. They came to gain influence in the church or community, not because they were interested in helping the children (FBOS#8, 2006).

Four FBOs said long-term programme outcomes were influenced by the perseverance of volunteers from churches. MWB specifically cited 'personal piety and commitment to Christ in a local church' as qualifications for personnel. Three FBOs correlated 'holistic outcomes' with commitment of volunteers to God and faithfulness to the local church. Piety is essential to the church's role in shaping society and children.

---

with additional sources. In Romania, unfortunately, this sort of information was either limited or unavailable and the local church often served as the only method for 'background and criminality checks'.

[55] See discussion in Chapter 3 concerning the 'medicalization of child welfare'. Early child development is still a nascent area of study in Romanian universities; few DCP staff are trained to recognize that many developmental problems of children might be the result of social or family neglect.

[56] Churches and FBOs are like all human organization: personnel conflicts are a reality. There are ways to minimize conflict if the organization makes an effort to manage 'competing voices'. 'Romanians have not had much training in how to resolve conflict in work situations, the normal way is to internalize issues until there is a major 'blow up' (confidential interview, 2005). Barnard's PhD thesis (2004) is a useful reference to faith-based organizations concerned about training in conflict resolution.

> We sometimes hear that the church is afflicted with piety, but the real trouble is the piety is not deep enough! ... An important contribution would be the liberation of the term 'piety' from its present damaging connotations, reinstating it as a term of respect ... [what is needed] is a massive dose if we are to be a healing service to our generation (Trueblood, 1970:66).[57]

FBOs expressed appreciation when pastors informed church members of the children in their programmes. 'We need to motivate people to become involved. It is a great help to have this initiative come from the pastor...who communicates to the church the value of children' (FBOL#60, 2006).

Christians bring to children in crisis the *Agape* love of Christ (1 Cor. 13) which is not dependent on outcomes but on the action of God in Christ and through His Spirit.[58] Partnerships recognized, in principle, the importance of building up the body of Christ 'until we all reach ... maturity, attaining to the whole measure of the fullness of Christ' (Eph. 4:13), where each member is dependent on the gifts of others (Rom. 12:5). Adopting Paul's analogy of the body, partnership can be described as 'participating in the life of one another in a way that the needs of all are met' (Kirk, 2000:189).

Tensions in Leadership that Influence Partnership

Leadership[59] was discussed in every interview with pastors and FBO directors. The interviews contained 45 references categorized as leadership themes. Partnership is directly linked to questions of power, trust, and leadership.

> A truly mutual relationship cannot exist between two parties who possess unequal power. Power, principally, is the freedom and ability to make choices and act ... invested in things we possess: wealth, status in the community, knowledge, educational qualification ... gifts of leadership. Powerlessness is a lack of these possessions: a lack of assets or the inability to use them effectively (Kirk, 2000:195).[60]

---

[57] Trueblood wrote *A New Man for Our Time* (1970) at the height of the American civil rights movement and the War in Vietnam. American churches were polarized between the agenda of the left - social concern and the right - evangelical piety. He argues for cultivation of reverence and piety, engagement in public service, and intellectual integrity – necessary to hold the two sides together.

[58] Christians are made God's sons and daughters though Christ who gives the Spirit. God's life is lived by the Spirit of Love (*Agape*). '*Agape* is service of others, giving with no expectation of return; loving those who are both neighbour and enemy' (Mt. 5: 43-48) (Wolff: 2003:22).

[59] In terms of Biblical leadership, a leader is 'a person with God-given capacity, God-given responsibility who is influencing a specific group of people towards God's purposes for the group' (Clinton: 1999:694). For sources on leadership see also Greenleaf (1977); Heifetz (1994); Rinehart (1998); Mintzberg (2006).

[60] Kirk develops a biblical perspective of power concerning partnership: 1) Power is a reality and held by ordained rulers (Rom. 13:4). 2). The exercise of power is legitimate. 3) All power ultimately comes from God and is delegated (John 19:11; 2 Chron. 1:12),

FBOs and churches have different means of exercising leadership. Leadership and the use of authority can be examined in economic, social, bureaucratic, political, and religious relationships. When people speak of leadership or personal power in Romania, they are not speaking in hyperbole (Boia, 2001; Rubatos, 2004:22-3). The following categories concern leadership in reference to partnership, with the caveat that the situation in Romania is not static. This discussion integrates findings from all phases of research, as leadership variables were not limited to the 11 cases. I conclude this section describing a generational leadership transition currently taking place in the Romanian evangelical movement with reference to children and youth.

Overcoming leadership suspicions that remain from the past

Early in the research I assumed, with many Western observers, that the breakdown of trust in Romanian society was largely the legacy of communism and the intrusiveness of the state (Deletant, 1996; 1999).[61] I learned that actions of both FBOs and churches had at times further eroded confidence and mutual trust. Simply blaming the communist past does not account for misunderstandings in faith-based partnership in the 1990s.[62]

Western FBO leaders acknowledged their failure to analyse how suspicion and the 'compromised moral situation' would impact collaboration with churches. FBOs gained knowledge though experience, leading in some cases to competition for personnel. When asked to describe his agency's 'rush' to respond to children in crisis, an American FBO director responded: 'This was intensified by those who were anxious to respond quickly or lose their

---

the New Testament speaks of the power and authority of Jesus Christ in God's rule. 4) Power is easily corrupted, often to oppress others (Eccles. 4:1; Mic. 2:1-2; Jas. 5:1ff) and active through principalities and powers. 5) Power is transformed by Christ, the Gospel represents a reversal of the common view of power through the cross (1 Cor. 1:18; Rom. 1:16) (1999:195-96). For alternative study on 'power and powerlessness' as it concerns the poor, see Christian (2000:117-67).

[61] As discussed in Chapter 3 and 6 the communist system was dependent on top down authority that weakened local decision making capacity; this reinforced a cultural style of local leadership that was autocratic and hierarchical. Social relationships were influenced by the legacy of distrust and disinformation nurtured under Ceauşescu and the *Securitate*, which left a legacy in the society that allowed for both abuse and distrust of power (Deletant, 1996). Boia (2001) considered communism a system against human nature and humanity.

[62] In Phase One, most Western FBO interviewees said they had learned to 'cope' with Romanian leadership and organizational patterns, both secular and sacred. Romania Christians had endured one of the most oppressive regimes of the Eastern Bloc. For FBOs to ignore this influence on church leadership and faith-based partnership seemed in hindsight naïve; after reflection and research I consider this further evidence of untested assumptions and assurances.

opportunity' (FBOL#73, 2007).[63] Learning together and sharing responsibility were crucial factors in overcoming suspicion, a dominant cultural characteristic (Rubatos, 2004:32). Given the chaotic environment of the early 1990s, willingness to listen to one another in the early stages of partnership served as an indicator for successful collaboration in the second half of the decade.[64] It is not my intention to catalogue misunderstandings; however, the most frequently mentioned by both sides were:

- Resentment when FBOs neglected the needs of poor children in the church.
- FBO misrepresentation of willingness to distribute aid through local churches.
- FBOs did not want to be identified with only one local church.
- Unwillingness of local churches to cooperate with FBOs.
- Street children were unwelcome in local churches.

RELIGIOUS 'OPPORTUNISM' BY LEADERS ON SIDES

In the early 1990s, FBO leaders who were motivated by pragmatic or reactive agendas sought out facilitators who could expedite work and get things done in a 'Romanian way.' I referred to these individuals in field memos as '*religious opportunists'*; a less pejorative term might be '*religious realists*'.[65] On the Western side were entrepreneurial leaders who sought out local partners; projects were their priority. On the Romanian side were local facilitators who, while not always being recognized within their particular churches as people of integrity, 'showed remarkable insight in seizing the opportunity' in particular, 'they learned English and how to "market cooperation" to Westerners' (FBOL#73, 2007). They negotiated official channels, handled money, and advised Western decision makers. These leadership styles characterized

---

[63] See Chapter 2. This was common in Eastern Europe and the CIS (Deyneka & Deyneka, 1998; Brown & Brown, 2003; Penner, 2003). I did not find in these sources an adequate theological analysis of the 'anxiety' of the Western FBOs. I surmise that the 'fear' of losing opportunity was paradoxically embedded in Western optimism and superiority that accompanied the 'invasion' of Western FBOs.

[64] I base this statement on overall qualitative findings and observations not a statistical representation. In both phases of research, I surveyed 59 FBOs; of that number, the majority reported difficulties working with local churches. The 11 cases were selected, in part, because they had worked through the worst difficulties and persisted in 'making partnership work'.

[65] I use these terms hoping to avoid negative labels. All societies have early adaptors and innovators who facilitate change in culture and social systems (Pardes, 2003; Kotter, 1996). I am including both Romanian and Western FBO leaders in this reference. They were generally men over 45 years of age, with strong, controlling personalities, and usually recognized leaders in their organizations or churches. They made contacts with Western or Romanian partners prior to or shortly after the revolution. It is important to recognize that both sides contributed positively and negatively to collaboration.

Quadrant A partnership, particularly in the early stages. [66] I collected several quotations like this from a Romanian law student: 'I hesitate to admit this, but some of our leaders were not always ethical when they helped foreigners that were coming to assist them...' and this from a Western FBO: 'We were unprepared for the level of duplicity in the local culture' (confidential conversations, 2004). The evidence was consistent that FBOs and Romanian churches learned about mutual strengths and weaknesses through trial and error not concerted planning and dialogue.

Kraybill cautioned against the 'uncritical use of structures not appropriate to the local context' (1978:189-90). FBOs that relied on imported project models, managerial missiology, and free market methods remained obligated to Western donors and stakeholders. Western FBOs assumed Romanian leaders shared their values and ethics. A Romanian FBO director said this about his experience with a Western partner.

> [The Western FBO] was more concerned about collecting figures and numbers [referring to children and finances]. We rely on relationships and getting to know who we are working with. They did not seem as interested in taking time to know us or our problems (FBOL#40, 2004).

Leadership styles are usually culturally conditioned and situational (Hofstede, 1997). Given that FBOs were looking for partners and churches were looking for help where 'they could find it', the evidence indicates that at least some FBO and church leaders sought out and exploited personal contacts. In some cases there was waste of resources, loss of trust, and reaction on both sides. A Romanian who spent ten years working with street children made this observation:

> In the early 1990s nobody had a long-term plan for how we would work together, cooperation was not a priority. Western agencies were coming to our city and hiring people who were not reputable. I remember a pastor saying he was worried that these people would gain influence over the church (FBOL #51, 2005).

Acknowledging Romanian internal leadership conflicts

Leadership conflicts were not limited to Romanian churches and Western FBOs. Romanians directing local FBOs also experienced opposition from local pastors. A director assisting Roma teenagers said pastors undermined his attempts to work with a Western agency.[67] There can be a 'dark side' in

---

[66] This paragraph is a summary of a short paper I wrote in 2004, the first 15 interviews focused almost exclusively on 'who took advantage of whom'. I learned that this situation was a subset of the larger NGO experience in Romania (Dickens & Groza, 2004). The strengthening of laws regulating childcare activity after 1997 through 2004 helped to reduce much unregulated and spurious activity.

[67] When I would hear an account from a Romanian FBO leader of this nature, I would attempt to interview the local pastors; this was not always possible as some pastors

leadership that motivates a group or individual to be involved or oppose caring for children (McIntosh & Rima, 1997).[68] Control issues were observed mono-culturally and cross-culturally. Pastors were not always willing to accept that local Romanians could manage childcare projects or they assumed they should be consulted before a project was begun in their community.

> In the communist times, pastors [in the evangelical churches] served 'between' the people and the authorities. My interpretation of what happened in the 1990's is the pastors had a system that was working under Communism: they assumed they mediated between the authorities and the local people. When the Western FBOs arrived, pastors took it upon themselves to act as the mediators (FBOL#47, 2004).

For some Western FBOs, any sign of adherence to the older, more traditional, legalist church traditions was devalued; although, some Romanians, especially pastors, strongly identified with these traditions and considered them useful and worth maintaining. This included values of collectivism compared with individualism, strong family ties, and social protection.[69]

Embracing leadership tensions in times of transition

As churches negotiated the societal and cultural shifts of the 1990s, some leaders reacted to forces beyond their control and sought 'to justify their stand against the world' (Noll, 1994:115). Others were open to change, responded to children, and worked with FBOs. Pastors were said to have acted as 'gatekeepers' (Chapter 5). This is certainly not limited to Romanian evangelicals. Wallace makes a similar observation from Africa, 'at the level of local congregations there tends to be a hierarchical structure, where decision making is dominated by a pastor or a few prominent members' (2002:134). Unwise financial or material assistance from FBOs did, in some cases, create a 'local elite' who were not especially sensitive to the needs of marginal children.

Younger Romanians (age <30) working at FBOs expressed anxiety about excessive control of pastors.[70] A graduate student in psychology, working with

---

would not discuss individuals whom they considered *persona non grata* or if the pastor considered the individual 'unrepentant' - a term I heard used frequently to describe those who did not comply with senior leadership. These were noted as competition, jealousy, and rivalry – all signs of '*not yet*' in the Body of Christ.

[68] McIntosh and Rima (1997) examine several paradoxes of personal dysfunction found in a global survey of leaders. There are hundreds of studies in the West concerning children and abuse in churches, in foster care, in homes. An important contribution in Romania would be a culturally relevant guide for churches and FBOs concerning prevention of abuse. See Muntean and Roth (2000).

[69] I located a number of Romanian FBOs essentially run and managed by large extended families, sometimes bringing allegations of nepotism from Western donors.

[70] I worked closely with this age group during my research. Hidden and explicit

street children, made this observation, 'local churches are essentially control structures. The Baptist and Pentecostal Union have central hierarchies and bureaucracies but that's really not where the control is – it is the local pastors' (I#7, 2004).[71]

This individual may have not have fully appreciated that pastors faced suspicion from Orthodox priests and DCP; the activities of local and foreign FBOs had potential to make the situation worse. As partnerships matured in the late 1990s, FBOs became more sensitive to these factors; they exercised caution and took time to assess the church's concerns, including pastors in programme planning. Embracing tension in this decade of transition required understanding of cultural leadership patterns, clarification of responsibility at the local level, and sharing 'moral ownership' for projects (Rickett, 2004:46-47). A Western FBO director commented after ten years of experience:

> We learned the hard way the importance of listening to the local context. At first, our international office thought they had all the answers and gave us their agenda for our programmes. We have learned the value of local leadership knowledge that now informs our organizational practice (FBOL# 18, 2005).

Making the child in crisis an 'object' of intervention had potential to escalate apprehensions of Romanian pastors. Alternatively, when mutual concern for children served to bring the leaders of churches and FBO out of their entrenched positions, tensions were more hopefully managed.

TENSIONS WITH TRUST AND CONTROL IN LEADERSHIP

When the human weaknesses of individuals or organisations, such as abuse of power or need to control, are unexamined, conflict is a typical outcome (Kellerman, 2004).[72] Partnerships in the early and mid-1990s were derailed by

---

behaviour (outbursts of anger and resentment) had to be understood in the context of recent history, particularly the way social control had been exercised through fear and repression by the communists. 'Needing assistance but not wanting to be told what to do [by Westerners or older Romanians] led to leadership conflicts' (Dickens & Groza, 2004:484).

[71] This quotation needs further explication for those unfamiliar with Romania evangelical church leadership structures. As the interviewee describes, the Baptist and Pentecostal Unions are very structured hierarchies, I called them '*institutional evangelical silos*' in field memos. These church leadership patterns were reinforced under communism as all leaders were monitored by the state; to be recognized, churches were forced to register with their respective 'Union'. After 1990, the Unions continued to consolidate influence and control as much as possible. This was mitigated by the fact that local churches consider themselves autonomous and Romanians can be 'audacious mavericks' (Richmond, 1995b:134). Romanian denominational officials affirmed in interviews that the pastor was the primary decision maker in the local church.

[72] Leaders are like everyone else in the church. They/we behave badly for different reasons, and they/we behave badly in different ways. I found that neither Western nor Romanian leaders had given adequate consideration to the many ways that leadership can go terribly wrong. See Kellerman's *Bad Leadership: What It Is, How It Happens,*

lack of transparency in communication. Pastors understood their role as 'shepherds of the flock'; they had paid a price in previous times to carry this responsibility and assumed FBO resources should pass through the church. Western FBOs operated with the assumption they could act independently. When it appeared that a particular Romanian pastor would not facilitate their agenda, FBOs were free to find others who would. This set in motion a process where churches responded in kind and sought connections to other FBOs.

> [In the early 1990s] churches had difficulty working together or trusting one another. Individual churches were free to make agreements with outside agencies. Romanian pastors made arrangements with outsiders to start a project, but they were hesitant to work with other pastors on a project that they do not control (Pas#6, 2004).

These *ad hoc* or transactional partnerships[73] led to complaints from pastors that Western FBOs exercised control through finances. Leadership assumptions and values not openly discussed led to declining trust. In these cases, leaders on both sides had to re-examine their motives and readjust priorities in partnership or continue to operate independently of one another.

Leaders who valued collaboration made adjustments; they refocused on relationships of trust, reciprocity, and accountability.[74] Trust is created by actions and words, open self-disclosure, and sharing information that gives meaningful feedback, described by Dent as 'partnership intelligence' (1999:21-23). A 'high partnering quotient' values interdependence. With increased interdependence the need for trust rises proportionally (Rickett, 2002:76-77).[75]

Why It Matters: 'When leaders are unwilling or unable to control their desire for more, bad leadership will be the result. Greed is likely to be pernicious when it entails a hunger for power. Sometimes this results in little more than the leader's unwillingness to share power by, for example, delegating tasks and consulting with others. But in its more extreme form, a craving for power can be dangerous. It is not stretch to say that the root cause of totalitarianism is a leader whose need for control is all consuming' (2004: 20).

[73] I distinguish between 'transactional' and 'empowering' organizations and partnerships. Transactional partnerships are interested in trading people, power, ideas, training or resources that are usually vertical or top-down. An empowering partnership is more interested in leading people so that participants discover their human potential and the value of joint participation. See 'Fostering collaboration, promoting cooperative goals and mutual trust' in Kouzes and Posner (1995:151-77).

[74] This statement is reflected by the 11 cases selected for this study. To some degree, all these cases have made adjustments in their leadership styles over the past 13 years; they are treated collectively in this discussion as representative of learning to build trust in partnership.

[75] Rickett makes the point that different types of relationships require different degrees of trust. He uses a 'sliding scale' (2002:77) as the level of trust needed depends on the level of interdependence in a partnership. He also factors in cultural distance in this analysis. 'The need for more trust rises as the level of interdependence rises. The more

Trust holds a partnership together, it is established when partners safeguard each other's credibility and decide what gives confidence to each member. FBO-church actions of this nature created partnerships that more closely reflected the biblical values of unity in the Body (Eph 4:4). They moved beyond arguing about control, territory and 'which children most deserve care'.

The founder of Project Ruth discussed this as 'prior question of trust', describing an individual who established a long-term relationship with the church and earned the trust of the pastor before suggesting a pilot programme for Roma children. The Romanian director of *L&L* described working through conflict and learning to trust the Western FBO as a factor of 'vulnerability and recognition of grace and forgiveness, this is what holds us together' (FBOL#55, 2005).[76] Another director described a situation where his intentions were misunderstood and he felt he was judged unfairly by a foreign FBO, resulting in 'breach of trust' and loss of confidence on both sides of the partnership.

Moving Beyond Illusions of Control

In the 1990s, Western FBO overconfidence was coupled with a fear of losing opportunities. The 'fear' of losing opportunity was paradoxically embedded in Western optimism and superiority that accompanied the 'invasion' of Western FBOs. At the same time, local church confessional assurance provided some insulation from uncertainty about the future. These were leadership factors that resulted, in some cases, to FBO negligence of local partners and excessive control in churches. But leadership that builds trust 'is not as concerned with simply offering new ideas or proving their worth, as it is with facing the world with expectation and open eyes, exposing illusions and shadows' (Palmer, 2000:85-7). Palmer draws on the work of Annie Dillard in discussing how leaders have an unusual degree of power to project on other people and organizations their 'inner shadows' or their 'inner freedom'. This implies that leaders can help create the conditions under which people experience the organizational life of the church or FBO.[77]

---

the partners are dependent upon each other, the more they need trust. The further apart partners are in language and culture, the more they need trust' (2002:76).

[76] This particular FBO was a case study in a restored partnership; originally the Western partner had worked with a Romanian facilitator who legally jeopardized the FBO. Instead of leaving Romania, the FBO found a Romanian pastor that was willing to help sort their legal troubles. Over the next several years, the Western FBO and Romanian director collaborated on a number of projects. The Romanian director attributed their partnership to grace, forgiveness, and vulnerability.

[77] It is a mark of spiritual maturity when leaders, both in churches and in FBOs, create the space in their lives to understand the power of 'illusions'. When leaders are out of touch with their interior lives, as is often the case with anxious and driven personalities, their 'interior shadows or illusions' may unconsciously increase their power. Palmer discusses five 'shadows' that are projected from the lives of leaders: 1) Insecurity about

In varying degrees, the eleven cases selected for this study demonstrated that trust in FBO-church partnerships was possible.[78] The partnerships learned to differentiate between 'illusions' of control and matters of substance concerning the needs of children in crisis. The child, as a language of God, served to point the partnerships beyond the illusions of 'institutional security' or 'fear of failure' when partners acted in predictable and fallen ways. FBO and church leaders said they came to realize that partnerships were made stronger by dependence on grace and mutual trust. Leaders on both sides experienced some form of pain or loss; they chose to move beyond control and reaction. 'The substance and manifestation of forgiveness is the fullness and power of new and better life' (Willmer, 2001:27).[79] Recognition of forgiveness as a way forward in partnership was discussed as essential in the larger Romanian context of suspicion. Leaders moved beyond the misunderstandings of the past as partnerships were grounded in Christ.

> Leadership is called ministry precisely to express in the service of others that new life can be brought about ... rooted in God's self disclosure in history ... not because it is rooted in optimism against all the odds of human life, but because it is grounded in the historic Christ event ...(Nouwen, 1990:75-6)

Generational tensions in leadership

In the early stages of partnership, churches expressed uneasiness that 'our best young people were leaving to work for FBOs'. FBOs that respected these concerns worked with pastors to discern how volunteers and paid personnel could benefit both the church and the FBO. A generational shift in leadership began in the Romania evangelical movement in the 1990s; work with children in crisis was integral to the process. I identified a growing division between the younger (<35 years) leaders and their elders noting at least three demographic age groups in Romanian churches: the 'elders', the 'transitional generation', and the 'Pro TV generation'.[80]

---

identity and worth – wrapped up in institutional status, 2) battleground mentality 3) functional atheism, 4) fear of chaos, 5) denying death (2000:85-90).

[78] I will not attempt in this analysis to 'rank' levels of trust in the partnerships. Clearly some of the FBOs had stronger levels of trust with local churches as they made this a mission objective. But even in cases where there were problems with Western FBOs or local churches, all the cases demonstrated that they were willing to continue to work towards resolution.

[79] In 'Christology, Atonement and Forgiveness', Willmer makes the point that forgiveness is not simply 'a dropping of charges, it is not an empty freedom from the wrong done and from guilt as the ground of accusation and punishment', rather forgiveness is a forward looking and future constituting event, a new way of being' (2001:26).

[80] For research purposes I stratified Romanian evangelicals into three age groups. 1) The elders: those that were at least 40 at the time of the revolution and had already gained some level of influence in the churches under communism. 2) The 'transition

Many of the 'transitional generation' (both men and women) began working with Western FBOs in the early 1990s. As students, they pursued university education and careers in social work; by the late 1990s, they filled key managerial roles in local FBOs. The uncoordinated FBO activity of the 1990s resulted in a new group of leaders emerging and produced an unintended outcome described as an 'emergent strategy' by Mintzberg & Quinn (1995), as in Figure 8.4. [81]

Figure 8.4 Deliberate and Emergent Strategies

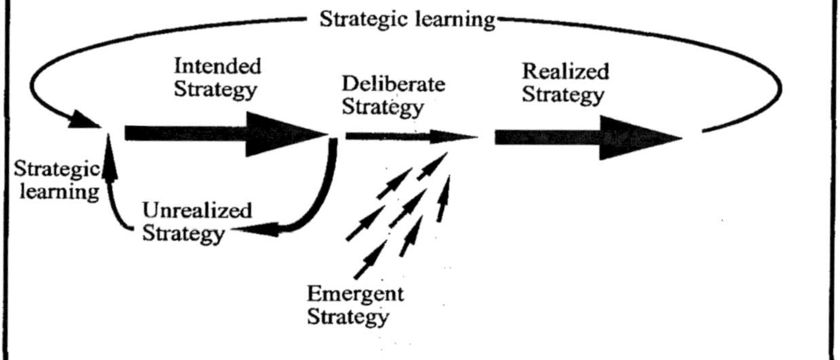

Deliberate and Emergent Strategies (adapted from Mintzberg & Quinn: The Strategy Process)

The primary FBO 'intended strategy' was intervention for children, described in Chapter 5 as 'creation of a new FBO sector'. The 'emergent strategy' was an informal association of hundreds of volunteers and staff who worked with children and took interest in the societal factors that put children at risk. In the absence of formal 'strategic learning', these young adults started new churches, formed their own networks and ministries, in a sense creating

---

generation' was between 20 and 35 at the time of the revolution. This group experienced the revolution with great hope and enthusiasm for change. The slow transition of Romanian to a 'democratic society' left this group with cynicism, but they are more analytical concerning the engagement of the church with the social issues. Finally there are those who were five to fifteen years at the time of the revolution. I refer to this age group as the 'Pro TV generation' as Pro TV is a popular television station that began broadcasting in Romania in 1995 to cater to the new and younger audiences (Chapter 6). Thanks to Cristi Soimaru for this last term.

[81] Mintzberg and Quinn introduced a model to explain their understanding of the reality of strategy development and made a distinction between planned and emergent strategy. The authors argued that strategy actually realized (implemented) by an organization is rarely exactly what was originally intended or planned. Some elements of strategy emerge from responses to opportunities and threats that organizations face as they carry out their work. For a technical discussion on this concept see Mintzberg (1994:356-67).

new strands of 'social capital' for children (Thorpe & Kinkade, 2005).[82] They questioned assumptions of their churches and denominations, especially concerning narrow views of evangelism and response to social issues.[83] Others moved to the West to pursue advanced studies in theology and pastoral care.[84]

These young adults were not trained scholars, they were activists: they initiated and led projects for youth, children, and the poor from local churches. The transition generation had largely positive contact with Western FBOs and contributed to the 'diffusion of innovation' and new forms of organization (Schein, 1997:363-64).[85] A faculty member from a Romanian seminary commented on this analysis:

> It is true that younger Romanian leaders are more willing to learn. They have been, and are now, more open to new ideas that have come from the West. In fairness to some of the older church leaders, they were not equipped to understand the rationale behind social programmes for children (Pas#9, 2006).

The transitional generation has come under some justified criticism from their elders; they have yet to prove they will avoid some of the pitfalls of the 1990s, especially the dependency on Western finances. Legitimate questions need to be raised if younger local FBOs are simply seeking to establish local presence and raise donations for children. Also of concern are the tendencies of 'younger' churches and leaders to uncritically import theological superficiality and franchise 'church brands' from the West.[86] This research indicates that

---

[82] Dana Bates created what he describes as 'service learning clubs' in Lupeni, Romania, one of the poorest areas in Romania and is currently researching connections with social capital theory and the theology of Dumitru Staniloae. See external assessment of Bates approach in 'What works in Youth Engagement in the Balkans' (Thorup & Kinkade, 2005).

[83] Social issues includes, but are not limited to, abortion (Romania has the highest rate in Europe), pornography through the media and internet, the situation of the Roma – especially children, trafficking of young women from Moldova and Ukraine through Romania, living conditions of the elderly and poor, and work in hospitals that continue to receive mothers who chose to abandon their children.

[84] See earlier comment on Romania scholars emigrating from Romania in Chapter 6. It should not be assumed that the traditional churches have widely embraced creative or imaginative theological scholarship.

[85] Schein's work concerns the learning culture in organizations and managing the contradictions of stability, learning, and change. See Howard (1981) for historical review of 'student power' in world mission that traces how young adults have shaped mission movements such as the Moravians, Methodists through the modern student volunteer movements of the last 50 years.

[86] A case in point would be the new charismatic churches following the model of Hillsong Church of Sydney, Australia, Calvary Chapel from the U.S.A., The Vineyard from U.K. and the U.S.A. I interviewed a disillusioned missionary returning to his country after 10 years in Romania who said, 'Many of these FBOs and mission agencies are "cloning" their brand of church and mission in Romania.

critical theological/missiological reflection may help inform their future activism for children.

Tensions in Mutual Accountability

Partnerships often fail when assumptions about the responsibility of the partners are vague, assumed, or not clarified (Araujo, 1994; Rickett, 2000:17; Sookhdeo, 1994:61). FBOs demonstrated secular practicality in governance, programme management, finance, and use of facilities (Chapter 5). The degree of willingness of FBOs to delegate and share accountability[87] with churches was a factor in collaboration. FBOs had an opportunity to help churches understand that managing ministry was both a spiritual and secular activity. The tendency was to veer toward one of two extremes, either being spiritually idealistic or pragmatically technique driven. A Romanian expressed his expectation of Western partners.

> We understand that Western organizations have to manage people and resources. We grew up with a system that put one person in charge and he told all the others what to do, but we expect sharing of responsibility [sic] with 'brothers' from the West' (FBOL#61, 2005).

Araujo notes that 'independence in the body of Christ is both an illusion and unbiblical' (1996:1). Three subcategories were identified: sharing responsibility in programme design, finances, and governance.

Sharing mutual responsibility for programmes and outcomes

A clear rationale for partnership should be included in an agreed upon mission statement or philosophy of ministry. The mission statements from the 11 cases included definable outcomes but did not delineate the responsibility of local church partners. *WV Ro, WMF*, and *MWB* explained this as a 'work in progress'. Romanian respondents said that Western expectations of accountability were poorly communicated in the 1990s.[88] Two local FBOs were constrained by their international partners to maintain primary accountability with Western donors:

---

[87] Accountability in its broadest sense is 'a willingness to place oneself under someone else's review and examination concerning one's motives, actions, and outcomes according to mutually agreed upon expectations, in an environment of good faith and mutual trust' (Araujo, 1994:121). Accountability is widely discussed in the literature on mission partnership; see Kraakevik & Welliver (1992); Dent (1999); Taylor (1994). I found no FBO-church partnerships using the literature cited.

[88] In the 1990s, churches and FBOs did not start out working together by first establishing 'clearly defined expectations of one another'. FBOs typically received a request from a local church for funding help, but mutual agreements and partnership agreements were largely ad hoc. Clarification of expectations and formal partnership agreements, if they were written, came after years of trial and error.

> Our funding partner in the U.S.A. requires that we maintain a connection with the children coming from the community and their sponsors in the U.S.A. We have 'connections' with local churches but we are primarily accountable to our international corporate office (FBO#18, 2004).

This approach limited open dialogue with churches, as the FBO was not seeking mutual accountability. Alternatively, *WMF* and *MWB* said local church 'ownership' of project outcomes was a central objective.

> Foundational to our mission is the belief that the local church provides stability to all we are trying to do. We believe that the churches will be working in Romania longer than our organization. So we have made this central to how we think about partnership (FBOL#70, 2006).

Viable FBO-church partnerships exemplify 'complementary partnerships' (Rickett 2003:23) where two or more organizations attempt to share complementary gifts and abilities to achieve a common purpose, in this case serving God, one another, and children.

'Ownership' or control is not the domain of either partner; neither Western FBOs nor Romanian local churches have all that is required to meet God's ultimate intentions for children. Faith-based partnerships share mutual responsibility and a common dependence on the Spirit of God (Taylor, 1994:246). A Romanian pastor commented, 'This idea of sharing responsibility has sometimes been difficult for us; working with [FBO X] has influenced my understanding of listening to others and to God' (Pas#12, 2005). Sharing responsibility and accountability with FBOs had a reciprocal effect as pastors passed what they were learning to the churches and children in their care. Two pastors were asked for suggestions to offer FBOs that would enhance church 'moral ownership' of projects.

1) We should share a common vision; we believe that God can give both the church and the FBO understanding and wisdom [referred to this as 'apostolic vision'].
2) There should be discussion on our biblical rationale – for instance, what each partner means when they say 'God intends'; do we agree on what the Bible says about the poor and children.
3) There should be open dialogue and listening; how they can the FBO apply their expertise locally, this should also include dialogue with other churches in the area.
4) Create a space for discussing what we have learned together – this does not happen enough (Pas#8, 2005 and Pas#13, 2005).

Embracing Tensions with finances

Funding is complex; local projects were often started dependent on foreign funding. 'The distinction between foreign control and foreign assistance can become very thin and confused' (Dickens & Groza, 2004:482).[89] Some FBOs offered the church a choice of following advice or losing funding. Disagreements over control of finances had potential to be manipulative and destructive, and created friction between FBO donors and church recipients. Both partners should understand the following concerns:

> Accountability by the recipient for the funds provided, caution when donors try to dictate unhelpful or unworkable terms, which undermine the local leadership of the project or demand data, or information that could be damaging to the work if made public (Srinivasagam, 1994:40). [90]

The cases demonstrated that Western donors did not always understand these issues. For instance, a recurrent theme was donor expectation of the local partner to assume a larger percentage of financial responsibility for the project than they were willing or able to do. Foreign donors were sometimes described as 'out of touch with local economic reality' (FBOS#9, 2006). Two international FBOs (Quadrant A) gave local churches minimal opportunity for input in project design. When Western FBOs created programmes or built facilities that had little chance of being locally sustainable, they were noted as a 'misuse of infrastructure' (Vencer, 1994:107).

In the cases involving child sponsorship, mutual financial accountability was especially important. Child sponsorship models have potential to undermine the initiative of poorer families who may be helped through other means to provide care for their children (Cookingham, 1989:13). Given the role of the Romanian state in usurping the role of the family during the communist era (Chapter 3), I specifically asked FBOs using child sponsorship models if they had considered the implications of child sponsorship. *WV Ro* said they had considered the issue but were dependent on child sponsorship for financing their community development programmes. No other FBOs had researched the

---

[89] Butler suggests, 'No area in partnership has more potential for problems than finances' (1994:11). The party supplying the resources often assumes that they must 'give an account' for financial investment. It is likely that the uncritical (some would say abusive) use of finances, by both Western and Romanians, in the early 1990s will never be completely resolved. I will use caution in this section with specific case reference names for the reason Butler suggests. I did not collect financial data from all the cases, as some said, financial data was not open to 'public access' The larger and professionalized FBOs receiving public funds made their financial data available through published annual reports.

[90] Jesus was concerned about the use of money – recognizing that human values and treasures are too often equated with material wealth. For discussion of donor accountability see Nouwen, (2004), *The Spirituality of Fund-raising:* 'Money and power go together. There is also a real relationship between power and as sense of self-worth' (2004:13). For discussion concerning money and evangelicals in recent North American history, see Elkridge and Noll (2004) and Stackhouse (2004) 'Money and Theology in American Evangelism'

situation or given it adequate consideration before establishing sponsorship programmes.

FBOs that valued local knowledge gave churches a voice in the process of selecting sponsored children. One local FBO was required by an international partner to maintain a certain number of sponsored children in their programme. This request was unrealistic given the transitory nature of the children in the community and the complexity of working with Romanian DCP authorities.[91] Had the international donor been in communication with local church leadership, they could have verified the feedback from the local FBO via triangulation of the data[92] and re-evaluated their request. International funds for child sponsorship were easier to acquire than the slower, more complex, and more patient means of working together with the local church to discover and utilize local resources (Mullinex, 1998). With the exception of *WV Ro*, FBO child sponsorship continues in Romania with little scholastic assessment or evaluation.[93]

Two church-based FBOs minimized their dependence on Western funds by creating culturally appropriate and 'economically sustainable' models of childcare (Roseland *et al.*, 1998). Project Ruth's approach to assist Roma children was described as a 'software solution' (LFBO#54, 2006).[94] The intention was to keep costs to a minimum by transferring a locally designed educational method to Baptist churches in Moldova. Ţoar reduced its dependence on Western finances as families of local Brethren churches opened their homes to children leaving state institutions (FBOL#38, 2004). It was important that both FBOs and churches did not lose sight of the basic principle that God expects His people to use the resources that He has made available to them (Phil. 4:12-19). Finances, like all kingdom resources, are dependent on connection with the Vine (John 15:5).

> When those with money and those who need money share a mission, we see a sign of new life in the Spirit of Christ. We belong together in our work because

---

[91] Western FBOs raising sponsorship funds are required to comply with financial and accounting oversight from their host country tax authorities. Foreign FBOs registered local affiliates who were required by Romanian law to provide an audited account of financial activity. These local FBOs were accountable for income in ways that local churches were not.

[92] Qualitative research methods sometimes rely on 'triangulation', a process whereby the data from several sources or methods is compared and measured against other data.

[93] In my view, sponsorship was not the best option for families from poor communities (especially the Roma).

[94] 'Software' is a metaphor for the knowledge gained in the *Ferentari* community serving Roma children. This method began with teaching hygiene and health classes, moving to remedial education, and then to a full school programme. The 'hardware' was described as the buildings, which local churches already had, and the classroom supplies, books, and physical necessities to operate the programme.

> Jesus has brought us together, and our fruitfulness depends on staying connected with him … (Nouwen, 2004:7).

Tensions in governance and management

Board governance is one way of insuring organizational competence in programme delivery (Carver, 2004).[95] Cooley (2004) refers to good governance as 'the management of competing interests' that I interpret as embracing tension in governance.[96] Six cases shared management and decision making with local churches and established mechanisms to communicate with key constituencies (FBO, church, donors, staff, and volunteers); the others operated as independent organizations.

Western FBOs (*WV Ro, WMF, MWB*, and *MoM*) registered local foundations as affiliates and were required by law to have Romanians serving on their boards. These individuals were not necessarily pastors of local churches. Shared management in FBO-church partnerships calls to mind Hofstede's (1997) findings concerning 'power distance', that is, the extent to that there is inequality between individuals in organizations and unequal distribution of power in institutions.[97] It can be argued that since Western FBOs were shaped by management cultures of relatively low 'power distance' and Romanian churches were hierarchical organizations, joint partnership required a steep 'learning curve' and commitment from both sides to intentionally share 'power' in management. This was verified by the cases. Westerners and Romanians acknowledged 'a fine line' between dependency and interdependency in managing projects.[98] Governance and organizational competence required attentiveness to both God and practical human concerns; too often, questions of what most honoured God in strategic decision making were peripheral to management discussions (FBOL# 61; FBOL #65, 2005).[99]

---

[95] See Chapter 5.7.3.2, I discussed governance concerning FBOs. Here I explore briefly how governance requires 'embracing tensions' in FBO-church partnership.

[96] Good governance is 'shared governance' which depends on boards that take seriously their role as a link and liaison with stakeholders. This means that trustees develop healthy relationships that promote open, two-way communication. (My appreciation to Dr. Robert Cooley for his notes 'The Exemplary Board' presented in his seminar on seminary governance in Charlotte, NC, 2005)

[97] For a discussion of conflict in culture and organizations see also Schneider & Barsou (1997:77-106) Chapter 4 'Culture and Organization'. The authors include a discussion of Hofstede's oft quoted findings on 'power distance', 'uncertainty avoidance'.

[98] I served as chairperson for three FBO boards in Romania. This statement is based on both research interviews and many 'off the record' conversations with Western and Romania colleagues concerning governance.

[99] In the case studies, only three of the eleven FBOs said that management was a means to discern God's intentions. See my earlier comments on managerial missiology and inherent shortcomings. Management practices were analysed as necessary and

Churches normally had 'boards of elders or deacons'. In Quadrant B cases there was regular communication between management structures of the church and FBO. Cases in Quadrant A relied on a 'facilitator' (Butler, 1994:28), usually a Romanian, effective in listening to both the church and FBO. *L&L* served as an example: a Romanian pastor and lawyer acted as liaison to the Western FBO while on the board of the Bucharest Department for Child Protection. His input shaped the policy of the FBO and direction of ministry to hundreds of abandoned youth. *MWB* maintained a commitment to transparency in shared management with local churches. The Western FBO brought resources and expertise; the church partners assisted with local knowledge and contextually appropriate response to children.

In two cases, Western FBOs made promises to churches through their international boards that were not kept. 'The church needs to have wisdom in working with Western partners in a shared ministry, not all the Western organizations can be trusted' (confidential interview, 2005). FBOs that invited members from local churches to join in board discussions demonstrated willingness to receive input from local stakeholders. Effective partnerships are a process, not an event.[100]

Tensions in Evangelism and Social Action with Children

In Chapter 7, I discussed how FBOs use the term 'holistic' to describe spiritual, physical, and social outcomes while avoiding some of the theological effort required to work out a more meaningful integration of eternal and human concerns. Both FBOs and churches spoke of the need to find common ground and discuss the biblical basis for partnership but neither suggested a fresh look at 'holistic mission' for children.

On one side of the partnership equation, evangelical churches were committed to an unwavering pietism. They were hesitant to examine the nature of the Evangel (as they knew it) and implications for children in crisis. The church's primary point of departure with FBOs was emphasis on priority of conversion; working to change or better society for children was a secondary concern.

> Evangelical churches hesitate to be involved in social programmes that have no evangelistic component, the primary role of the church is to be salt and light,

---

important, noting that most secular management practices are rarely put to any real theological 'test'.

[100] The average time in the 11 cases to establish 'shared governance' was two years. Two FBOs were still not sharing governance with churches after more than ten years working in Romania.

> and to be that light, people have to come to hear the gospel and come to faith in Christ' (Pas#4, 2004).[101]

On the other side, FBOs were entrenched in 'holistic' missional assurances. They used biblical phrases such as 'the kingdom of God' and emphasised the ethical responsibility to care for the human needs of marginalized children and families. FBOs were committed to activist and interventionist methods as 'children were suffering; we had an obligation to help them' (FBOL#58, 2005). But in order to carry out this activity, FBOs required the sort of evangelism that calls people to be servants of the King and His kingdom.

> The people who think that evangelism is dead or is fully incorporated into the acts of justice and mercy would do well to think again. How is the fire of social sensitivity to be sustained and replenished? The Christian is a person who regardless of the century in which they live, knows the answer; the way to become ignited for social justice is to approach the source' (Trueblood, 1970:104).

FBOs assumed they too had an adequate understanding of the Evangel to carry out their agendas.

Mission to children must embrace this tension that can otherwise lead to 'becoming submerged in social ethics and relativizing the person of Jesus Christ' (Bosch, 1991:398). To what extent has FBO-church collaboration enlarged evangelical social awareness? What are the specific FBO-church contributions to children from institutions and those marginalized by Roma ethnicity? Several hopeful signs were identified in FBO-church partnerships that provided evidence of God's Spirit integrating human and divine concerns and God's actions in bringing FBOs and churches out of their mutual assurances. The following factors demonstrate that FBOs and churches have witnessed to the wholeness of the Evangel in explicit and implicit ways.

Overcoming social barriers through partnership – embracing the 'other'

As FBO-church partnerships responded to street and institutionalized children, Roma, and others 'outside the gate', they encountered resistance overcoming social, religious, and cultural barriers. Two enabling factors linked to partnership were identified. The first was 'mutual acceptance' – including children, FBOs, and local churches.

> The most important thing we offer these children is acceptance. We do this because every child is created in God's image and we learn about the nature of God as we care for children. Our understanding of God's acceptance of children informs our thinking as we partner with churches, we are one Body (FBOL#28, 2004).

[101] I have argued earlier that the churches are engaged in 'social holiness' by nature of their common life in the wider community. My point here is that churches prioritized evangelism not that they completely neglected social responsibility.

The second was 'mutual response, each according to their gift'. The abandoned child and those ostracized by society brought together the gifts of the local church and FBO as an expression of the Body – a Christological reality (Rom. 12: 4-6a). Paul goes on to say 'welcome one another, therefore, just as Christ has welcomed you …' (Rom. 15:7).

Barth commenting on Rom. 12:5, argues that the Body is not the individual men and women of the church.

> … not the mass of individuals, not even a corporation, a personified society, or a totality, but The Individual, The One, The New Man (1Cor. 12:12-13). The One, this Body of Christ, is what confronts us in the parable of the body and the problem of the "other" in the fellowship of believers' (Barth, 1968:444).

I take Barth's Christological emphasis as helpful in thinking about partnership; the Body of Christ is not divided. In this manner, the combined work of FBOs and churches is taken up in a Christological argument rather than an instrumental or 'organizational one. This helps to overcome the question of modality-sodality often used as a rationale for FBO and church mission and division of labour.

Miroslav Volf has made an important contribution to our understanding of 'otherness' and reconciliation; he defines 'embracing the other' as '… the will to give ourselves to others and "welcome" them, to readjust our identities to make space for them, [this] is prior to any judgement about others, except that of identifying them in their humanity' (1996b:29).[102] I am applying Volf's definition of 'embrace' to the core category. God makes it possible for FBOs and churches to embrace tension and one another. God embraces the child in crisis and the limited human actions of the caregivers.

Throughout the 1990s, Romanian churches were redefining their religious and social identity; marginalized children offered them the opportunity to 'embrace the other' and enlarge their definition of evangelism as they participated in the social life of suffering children and their communities. The churches continued to evangelize, form, and inspire people through preaching, teaching, and worship. Believers were people with social understanding who lived in the 'ordinary world' raising families, working and interacting with neighbours. Churches have influence 'because they form people who think and pray … using distinctive language: repentance, forgiveness, renewal,

---

[102] Embracing goes beyond the household of faith, but it is clear that believers have an obligation to embrace one anther. An enlargement of otherness with reference to Christology comes from Barth's additional comments on the 'Body' in Rom. 12:5. 'It must be fellowship that is encountered in the community: but this means an encountering of the OTHER in the full existentiality of his utter OTHERNESS. In the neighbour, it must be the ONE who is disclosed. … Fellowship is the ONE which lies beyond every 'other'. The ONE, the INDIVIDUAL, is therefore not one among others, not a cell in a larger organism, but simply the HOLY ONE - *sanctus* (Barth, 1968:443 emphasis in original text).

reconciliation' (Willmer, 1999:15) all of which are a resource to the wider society.

FBOs often acted as 'first responders' providing triage in an emergency situation. Churches that became hospitals of social healing joined them. Together they sought out and embraced the child on the margins, they took risks together responding to street or institutionalized children, and they learned mutual dependence on God and one another, at the same time increasing their social presence and influence in the community. Social action and wider influence were a product of embracing God, Christ, one another, and the child.

Facing discrimination against Roma children

MoM, WV Ro, IDC, WMF, Ruth, and partner churches went against social and cultural norms responding to Roma children. Roma children were treated as outcasts by the larger society; people in their neighbourhoods expected little of them.

> Even Roma parents really don't expect much of their children; they are not expected to do well in school. We know that demonstrating acceptance and concern is foundational to our witness to Christ. Our church is now seen in this neighbourhood as both a house of worship and a place that provides education and community service to Roma children (FBOS #6, 2005).

In the 1990s, discrimination and social justice were rarely discussed in evangelical churches, especially since the Roma population were viewed with open suspicion and mistrust.[103] Ten years after beginning Project Ruth, Bunaciu continued to confront discrimination in his church and other locations where they were opening schools:

> I continue to see prejudice in our churches concerning gypsies and children from very poor backgrounds. The gypsy population that lives around our church is involved in crime. The average church member finds it hard to trust the gypsy people as a whole. There are still some people in our church that are not happy to see 160 gypsy children running in the backyard. However, they recognize the progress we have made; we are changing the image people hold of the Roma (FBOL#64, 2005).

---

[103] I hesitate to label this as 'Romanian cultural blindness to discrimination' as all Romanians do not share it. In 2001, the mayor of Piatra Neamat was forced to cancel plans to construct a ghetto to house the Roma of his city. The planned compound on the site of an old chicken farm would have incarcerated local Roma behind a high wall, kept them under police surveillance, and forced them to work.

Local churches, acting in Christ's name, received rejected children and challenged discrimination and social prejudice (Adeney, 2003:96-7).[104] The Roma child 'in the midst' of a gathered congregation was a sign of God's good news for the poor. FBOs and churches shared responsibility for educating believers about the needs of marginalized children. As they responded, churches gained understanding of the problems and causes. 'Our [church] members had typical *pocaiti* mentalities towards gypsies. To be inclusive we had to break down the discrimination from within' (Pas#7, 2005).[105]

Overcoming ethnic intolerance towards Roma children was evidence of renewed 'hermeneutic of social concern' (Petersen, 1995) in Romanian evangelicalism. In the early 1990s, the typical evangelical church did not go out and invite the children on the streets, in the institutions, or Roma to come in; this was left to the FBO. Intentionality in partnership to welcome children into the family of faith integrated the church's concern for the child's eternity with FBO concern for their human and social development. 'Social justice' was reintroduced into the language of local churches in part through the lives of marginal children (Wall, 2003:109-23).

Care for abandoned children: Agape expressed in practical sociality

Chapter 6 established that church volunteers did not begin their work with an explicit psychological understanding of the emotional trauma experienced by children abandoned in the institutions; rather, they had an implicit biblical understanding of the pain of sin, separation from parents, and God. FBOs and churches caring for these children learned they were not a 'problem to be fixed' but children in need of relationship, compassion, and the love of Jesus. Communion lies at the root of this kind of compassion: *cum-patire* means to suffer with someone. [106]

Romanian state policy for almost half a century had encouraged parents to hand over their unwanted babies to the state; women in poverty continued to consider child abandonment an acceptable option (FBOL#50, 2005). Several

---

[104] See Adeney's discussion on 'Christ transforms culture: culture as a fellowship of creative deviants' and his suggestions working within worldview, concepts, and values (2003:96-8).

[105] A 'typical *pocaiti*' mentality is usually understood in Romanian evangelical culture to mean a person who believes in external holiness, attending church three-four times a week, and is concerned with strictly obeying the Bible, as they understand it. The 'typical *pocaiti*' does not discuss social justice as social systems are fallen and wicked. God redeems people not social structures.

[106] To be moved with compassion' appears 12 times in the gospels and always refers to Jesus or His Father. Jesus is the concrete expression of divine compassion in our world. 'His response to the blind, the lepers, the widows, and all who came to Him with their suffering flowed from the divine compassion that led God to become one of us' (Nouwen *et al.*, 1983:16).

maternity hospitals in Bucharest had as many as 30 abandoned babies in one ward with as few as three nurses. FBOs, which had been started by Western women, invited Romanian women from local churches to visit these hospitals on a regular basis. They provided support for nursing staff; they held and cared for infants who were otherwise only picked up when the nurses had time for them. Romanian families adopted some of these children and their home churches began similar ministries to mothers and children in their own communities.

The 'humanization of God' or the 'incarnation of the logos' is demonstrated in God becoming a baby (Moltmann, 2000:592).[107] Abandoned babies in Romanian maternity hospitals brought FBO-church partnerships into an encounter with the eternity of God expressed in a human infant. As followers of Christ, it was in the spiritual DNA of both FBO and church to care for the abandoned and suffering; as they opened their hearts and their homes, God released His *Agape* in them, expressed through practical sociality and divine love (Mangalwaldi, 2003).[108] FBO confidence in God's willingness to rescue abandoned babies and to help children recover from trauma and abuse was matched by the church's confidence in God's willingness to give these children knowledge of his eternal life (*Zoe*).

Building social networks for older children

Older children from the institutions found it difficult to trust caregivers, a mentality reinforced if they lived on the streets for any length of time. Both FBOs and churches reported that social reintegration of these children (ages 15-18) was especially difficult; they did not fit standardized programming and were threatening to normal families. The agreed upon method of initial intervention was personal interaction and follow-up.

> There are no assurances that our work with these children would actually turn out as we have planned. Rehabilitation of older street children was a question of daily interaction, stewardship and faith; there were no guaranteed results (FBOL#58, 2005).

Church volunteers joined FBO staff visiting the streets and institutions; interventions followed a progression from sporadic visitation, to regular

---

[107] 'The creator of heaven and earth divests God-self and becomes lowly in the Christ child or the so-called "baby-Jesus". The grand theology of the ancient church called this mystery the "humanization of God" or the "Incarnation of the logos" but it begins very simply, in a manner intelligible to every child, by God becoming a child and in this child's redemptive reign of peace. What a mystery a child is' (Moltmann, 2000:592).

[108] Mangalwaldi demonstrates in his essay how Christ's compassion was a prophetic compassion. Christ's compassion grew out of a 'prophetic insight into the social and theological *causes* of suffering. In his response Jesus went to the root of human misery', he addressed that longing in humanity for connection with the Love of God (2003:193).

visitation, to working alongside DCP and government employees, to cooperation with other social service agencies, to setting up nationally recognized programmes for child reintegration and recovery from heroin addiction, such as Teen Challenge Romania.[109] In this process, both FBO and church members gained access and influence in government institutions and health care programmes. Community and civic leaders acknowledged the positive impact on youth who were seen as 'dangerous or threatening'. Churches were no longer 'spiritual islands' as they engaged in 'socio-structural' work in the public and civic sector.

FBOs looked to tradesmen and homemakers in local churches to provide vocational training and life skills as youth made the transition to independent living. A common collaborative approach was to rent a small apartment for several teenagers. FBO staff and church volunteers lived with them and taught them to function outside the institutions. Workable alternatives in residential care depended on FBO-church collaboration (White, 2002).[110] Six FBOs attributed success in reintegration to cases where older teenagers became part of the social fabric of a church or youth group. Given the shortage of trained social workers in Romania, local churches provided stable individuals, peer groups, positive social values, families, and larger social networks.

Cooperation in training for specialized assistance

FBOs recognized that there had been limited teaching in the churches on social responsibility or child-welfare in the 1990s. Rather than accept the idea that FBOs were better equipped for social work and churches for evangelism or discipleship, FBO-church partnerships offered training in the churches with opportunities for practical experience.[111] FBOs made training and resources relevant to local churches by investing time and energy in listening carefully to what God was saying to the churches about what they considered their 'spiritual and evangelistic' obligations towards their neighbours. This meant

---

[109] City of Hope serves as one example of this progression: men and women from the FBO and local churches worked with street children in the 1990s. By 2000, these street children had become 'street youth', many joining gangs after becoming addicted to glue and heroin. There were no programmes for these 'older street youth.' A leader from CoH, saw this need and established a nationally recognized drug rehabilitation programme, Teen Challenge Romania. This programme provides street intervention and full-time residential care for young men.

[110] White argues for a multiplicity of approaches to residential care in answering those who would say that every child must be placed in a 'family' (2002:231-242) There are many models of residential care being 'tested' in Romania with little theoretical reflection: residential group homes, foster families, extended families, hostels, and schools.

[111] Training was usually offered for anyone interested. Younger adults who were regular in church attendance, took part in youth activities, and were willing to do volunteer work showed the most interest in these training courses.

'spending time at church prayer meetings to discern what the churches were praying for and why' (FBOL#60, 2005), a practical application of 'appreciative inquiry'.[112]

FBOs provided seminars to both DCP and churches in child welfare and emotional development. Churches were used as venues for short-term training opportunities including educators, child psychologists, medical doctors, physical therapists and neonatal specialists. Western FBO staff attended local churches; they invited local believers to take part in training seminars. Together, FBOs and churches demonstrated that evangelicals were willing to engage with children in crisis in informed and child-friendly ways. Tensions had to be managed in sharing faith without proselytizing or treating children with paternalistic attitudes.

Theological and Missiological Reflection on Embracing Tensions in Partnership

This study of FBO-church partnerships has demonstrated that evangelical responses to children required more than a 'gospel of sin management' that simply called for their conversion for a 'life in heaven' or readjusting questionable social systems for 'life in the present'. The Evangel offers life in Christ who fully embraces the 'already and not yet' (Willard, 1998:42).[113] FBO-church partnership is an expression of the love of God for humanity and children. I have suggested that FBO-church partnership requires exchanging categories of certitude, entitlement, and privilege for categories of fidelity, relationship, and mutual embrace (Brueggemann, 2005).[114] Following Jesus Christ to work with children or youth in crisis, invites, pulls, and pushes FBOs and churches into deeper *koinonia*. Children can serve to reorient FBO-church partnerships to future possibilities in their love and relationship to Christ. I set out here several pointers in this direction.

---

[112] Listening to how people pray and what they pray for is an effective way to gain insight into their hopes and aspirations. There are more 'formal ways' to perform listening exercises with churches, see Johnson and Ludema (1997:89-140).

[113] In his notes on this section of his argument concerning a 'gospel of sin management', Willard cites the language of Barth 'an absorption of Christology into soteriology' and goes on to say, 'there [can be] an entire loss of Christological concern in the preoccupation with personal salvation or that of shaping society (Willard, 1998:403).

[114] I draw on a comment in a lecture given by Brueggemann when he addressed a group of 'emergent' leaders. FBOs and churches both have a hunger for certitude but the gospel is not about certitude. The Gospel requires that followers of Christ constantly surrender in faith. Certitude is a flat and mechanistic category whilst fidelity is a relational category. 'We must acknowledge our thirst for certitude and recognize that if we had all certitudes in the world, it would not make the quality of life any better because we must have fidelity. We face in church ministry a constant confusion of those categories. Fidelity is like having a teenager in the house – we never get it settled for more than three minutes, we have to keep negotiating' (Brueggemann, 2005).

'Embracing the cross' in partnership

Partnership occurs in community, this is a secular fact. For FBOs and churches it needs a more precise Christian form. A Christian community lives in and exists in fellowship and partnership with God in Christ and therefore lives in obedience to the work of God in Christ, which includes and centres on the cross. As Villafane notes '... the cross frees us up to enter into legitimate and authentic mutuality— true *koinonia'* (1995:10). The 'way of the cross' calls both church and FBO to live in the company of Jesus in the way of his kingdom.[115] The 'cross' in Paul's influential presentation, not only makes clear who God is but teaches Christians how to live together in fellowship. Paul address the divisions in the church in Corinth by reminding his readers of the 'power of the cross for those who are being saved' (1Cor. 1:10-25; Phil. 2:5-11). The gospel as professed in the churches and FBOs in this study makes much of 'the cross', which implies a reversal of the common view of power that is redefined in the light of the crucifixion of Christ.[116] Concepts of power, control, and mutuality are especially relevant with regard to children. Power is understood in the gospel as resistance to the temptation to dominate (Phil. 2:5-6). Children rarely dominate adults or compete with adults for control or power in organizations, yet a critical look at ourselves and our organizations 'reveals that competition, not compassion, is often a main motivation in life' (Nouwen *et al.*, 1983:19). FBOs and churches are tempted to become immersed in all sorts of competition.

When FBOs and churches offered care to a child in crisis, they were 'given up' as the child's pain became the centre of their attention. FBOs and churches took a step *towards* the kingdom when they left behind their organizational or confessional assumptions to embrace outcast, excluded, ignored, or marginalized children (Wolff, 1993:110).

A 'child in the midst' as a pointer in partnership

What does God intend when he places a child in the midst of FBO-church partnership? In Matt. 18:1-5, Jesus addresses his disciples as they are arguing about greatness (or power). He places a child 'in the midst' to refocus their attention on the nature of the kingdom, 'I tell you the truth, unless you change and become like little children, you will never enter the kingdom of heaven'.[117]

---

[115] In my use of the 'kingdom of God' in this section see N.T Wright 'The Mission and Message of Jesus' in (Borg & Wright, 2000:31-54), also see Newbigin (1995:30-40) and Samuel & Sugden (2003:128-160).

[116] Literature on 'powers' in the NT is considerable; see Wink (1986; 1992; 1998) and Christian (1994).

[117] I return here to insights gained in interaction with the *Child Theology Movement* that takes this text and Mark 9:33-37 and Luke 9:46-48 as a point of departure from other common NT texts on care for children – Matt. 19:13-14. In Matt. 18:1-3, Jesus is

Jesus is saying that children act as a parabolic point of entry into the kingdom of God; the disciples must change to *enter* the kingdom. Children represent a paradigm of powerlessness and vulnerability that may serve as a valid starting point for transforming how power and control are understood in FBO-church partnerships. The disciples were not ready to enter the kingdom, 'becoming a child' required a change in their thinking.

This change does not mean that they will go back to being simple children, they are adults and must think and act as adults; they must change their assumptions, their priorities, and their orientation. The text in Matthew 18 is sometimes read with the idea that the disciples must be gentle, simple, humble, and naïve in order to enter the kingdom. But Jesus is speaking to them in parabolic language; they are hard of hearing. They will have to make a complete change in their orientation toward His kingdom, something that requires adult courage and maturity.

Finding their way into the kingdom would involve a special kind of learning, the kind of thinking that we cannot fully understand 'until we get inside it – and even then not fully' (Willmer, 2003:2); this is 'conversion'.

> There is an act of thinking by which sufficient wisdom is given men and women to choose the road which is for the moment the right road. There is – and this is what we mean – thinking of grace, of resurrection of forgiveness, and of eternity (Barth, 1968:437).

If children are pointers to kingdom greatness, then FBOs and churches that compete with one another for recognition, resources, or support can learn something from a child's receptivity. As when younger, vulnerable children seek an adult's protection; they gladly receive the assistance. Of course, there are children who are hostile and unwelcoming but they also give clues to the nature of living realistically in the light of the kingdom, for much work on their behalf is like 'lighting candles in the darkness', hoping and working with little certainty that interventions will be effective. This is how it is with the kingdom of God; it receives, welcomes, surprises, disturbs, and challenges human assumptions and assurances. Jesus is saying the important matter for the disciples is to 'enter', to be 'in' the kingdom, not that they strive for recognition and power. Jesus is also saying that kingdom is in front of the disciples; it is 'not yet'.

Just as the child is on the way, in transition, becoming, then disciples must be open to this way of becoming. In their argument, they assume they are 'already' part of Jesus' 'inner circle'; their horizon of expectation is 'what do we need to do *in order to be great* in this kingdom?' Jesus takes their expectations and reframes the horizon. He says the kingdom is not a matter of 'who you are', 'what you do', or 'what difference you are making'; for on

---

dealing specifically with the disciples who are engaged in a theological argument about the nature of the kingdom, 'who will be greatest'.

'these positive or negative distinctions 'much self-esteem is based and human competition thrives' (Nouwen *et al.*, 1983:19). In the kingdom of God it is sufficient to be counted as a member. Jesus offers the disciples a new way, but they must give up their fearful clinging and aspirations of greatness to enter his kingdom and 'live with Him in the fearless life of God Himself' (Nouwen *et al.*, 1983:21).

FBO-church partnerships have not 'already' arrived; they are moving together in approaching the kingdom *with* the children they are serving. The kingdom is both a present and future possibility; as the child lives with expectancy, FBOs and churches can remain hopeful in partnership. They have some signs of the 'already' of the kingdom as God invites and welcomes all who approach his way of living.

Embracing ambiguity in partnerships that point to the kingdom

Embracing tension in partnership may also remind both churches and FBOs of the reality that everything in human existence – including our love for God, one another, and children – is coloured to some degree by human ambiguity (Wolff, 1993:56). The more we love, the more our faith is vulnerable to the reality that not all is well with the world (Jeremiah 45). Leading an organization, helping a child in crisis, working with a pastor, or making decisions about partnership is rarely crystal clear. Asymmetrical leadership embraces the disjunctions and tensions described in FBO-church partnerships.[118] Human beings sometimes fear ambiguity, but ambiguity can be a gift of grace when it leads to greater discernment of the work of God and Christ. Barth is helpful on human ambiguity as we approach the living God and confront our assurances in church life. Commenting on Romans 5:1:

> The necessity of passing through the narrow gate which leads from life to death and from death to life, must remain a sheer impossibility and a sheer necessity … The comfortable and easy manner is which men advance towards this critical point [having faith in God] is the primary curse which lies upon all, or almost all dogmatic preaching, and is the lie, the poison, which is so difficult to eradicate from the pastoral ministry of the church … We only believe in what is given by God, and, moreover, our capacity reaches no further than believing that we do believe. The point where faith and unbelief part company can be defined neither psychologically nor historically. As far as we can see, our hands are empty' (Barth 1968:150).

Ambiguity serves to question untested assurances, selfish ambition, and attempts to control chaotic situations. Ambiguity can save when it leads to

---

[118]Leadership study has begun to use the term 'asymmetrical leadership' to describe action-based learning theory. Faced with rapid global change, 'asymmetrical leadership' is concerned with leading through change, momentum, and motion, in a constantly changing organizational environment..

repentance, discernment, and patience with humanity. Ambiguity means that partners will struggle as they grow in mutual surrender to God's kingdom ways. Jesus warned the disciples that his mission was not always to spread peace (Mt. 10:34-36). He described divisions in families where our most intimate personal relations are developed. Jesus also told the disciples that 'from John until now the kingdom of God has suffered violence and the violent take it by force' (Matt. 11:12).

There are times when working together in partnership requires that both church and FBO embrace this 'violence'. This is a violence of a radical turning towards the cross, the kingdom, and Christ – not a 'battlefield mentality' where partners compete for right or privilege. In embracing this sort of 'kingdom violence', FBO-church partnerships will be more discerning of the reality of God's leading. Christians who persist in this sort of faith have a chance of getting free from the 'illusionary horizons of perfection' (Willmer email, 2007). They may be more inclined to remember, 'there is no creature hidden from His sight, all things are naked and open to the eyes of Him to whom we *must give* an account (Heb. 13:4).

In their actions to take up the cause of children and identifying with their vulnerability, FBOs and churches must constantly evaluate their interventions and partnerships reflecting on Christ and His kingdom. 'Power is the freedom to let go of all that hinders the expression of sacrificial love' (Mark 10:42-45; Jn. 10:17-18; 3:1) (Kirk, 2000:196). The loss of hope and love is a major casualty in situations of poverty and oppression; children in crisis have suffered this loss. FBO-church partnerships portend to offer the child in crisis new hope, both in this world and eternity, through opportunity, restoration of human dignity, forgiveness, and a chance to assume responsibility for their futures. Children in crisis serve as reminders to FBO-church partnerships that God is their covenant partner even when their attempts to intervene may run aground or accomplish the opposite of their intended results. It is not so much the FBO-church activity that most interests God but the human beings who make the attempts.

> It remains true that God, as creator and Lord, is always free to produce even in human activity and its results, in spite of the problems involved, *parables* of his own internal good will and actions. It is more than ever true then, that with regard to these no proud abstention but only reverence, joy, and attitude are appropriate (Barth, 1960:55).

Summary

This chapter integrated the findings of the study to answer the central research question: what factors facilitated or hindered FBO-church partnership. I suggested a central category that requires 'embracing tensions in partnership', integrating the ultimate concerns of God for children, the human concerns for child, family, and community, the concerns of FBOs for intervention and programme delivery, and the concerns of the church for representing Christ in a local community. In the absence of rigorous missiological reflection, FBOs and churches worked through a number of partnership issues experientially. Partnerships that moved beyond entrenched assumptions admitted, to some degree, that neither side had all the answers; both belonged to the 'fellowship of perplexity' (Trueblood, 1970:90).

'Embracing tensions' necessitates acknowledging the potentially disjunctive factors in five domains shaping interaction: locality, sharing human resources, leadership factors, mutual accountability, and tensions between evangelism and social concern. In considering locality, I examined the church's sense of calling and long-term commitment to a specific community that at times was in tension with FBO assumptions of freedom to act in the present. Tensions in sharing human resources were observed when FBOs sought to mobilize church members and families. This required enhancing, not depleting, local church capacity. Church 'institutional memory' was noted as an important asset for incoming FBOs. Volunteers from local churches brought compassion and expressions of 'social holiness' to FBO projects, meeting the emotional needs of abandoned children.

Partnership actions in the early 1990s positively and negatively impacted levels of trust and confidence. 'Religious opportunism' reduced transparency in East-West collaboration. Learning from past mistakes enabled partnerships to move beyond 'illusions of control' to forgiveness and addressing substantive concerns for children. Romanian evangelicalism is undergoing a leadership transition, shaped by a younger generation who are now engaged in social action for children. Mutual accountability in programme management, governance, and responsibility for outcomes were instrumental to effective collaboration.

Tensions between evangelism and social action were re-examined concerning holistic outcomes. In their concern for children, some FBOs and churches have moved beyond the entrenched positions discussed earlier. Evidence was noted in overcoming social barriers and 'embracing' children from marginal and Roma ethnic backgrounds. Racial discrimination continues to be a barrier to effective gospel witness, but partnerships demonstrated that churches can be open to all (1Cor. 12:12). Care for abandoned infants in maternity hospitals and alternative residential centres for older youth were evidence that partnerships are bringing eternal and human concerns into more meaningful integration.

Theological and missiological reflection are integral to embracing tension. Categories of certitude and entitlement can be exchanged for fidelity, mutual embrace of the cross, and deeper *koinonia*. Children offer a fresh understanding of power and human competition as they rarely dominate or compete with adults. Children provide parabolic instruction in moving through life's transitions, in giving and receiving, and in setting aside our human striving and competition for 'greatness' in the kingdom. The 'child in the midst' acts as a theological pointer, serving to remind FBO-church partnerships of their mutual journey in entering the kingdom of God that is both 'already and not yet'.

Tensions in partnership were better managed when partners were less confident of stubborn assurance and willing to embrace the ambiguity of human actions. Ambiguity serves to question and dismantle arrogance and dogmatism and leads to open questions, repentance, and patience with others. Children remind us that God is committed by covenant and command to partnership with our humanity and ambiguity. I now conclude with several suggestions gleaned from this research that require further consideration in future FBO-church partnership in Romania.

Chapter 9

Conclusion

Overview of the Study and Contribution

This study provided an in-depth investigation of the relationship between selected FBOs and Romanian evangelical churches as revealed in their action for children in crisis. The analysis described operative assumptions, activities, and factors that enabled or hindered partnerships in the period 1991-2004.

In the early 1990s, FBO activity was largely reactive and disempowering towards churches. This led to a 'division of labour' – FBOs responded to human, physical, and psycho-social needs of children and churches provided what they understood as 'spiritual' care for children. This was described as a *Side A* (from above) – *Side B* (from below) approach as evidence demonstrated that FBOs and churches gave minimal attention to intentional theological integration of eternal and human concerns. FBOs and churches while working positively to care for suffering children tended to ignore the child as a 'language of God', that is, the child did not serve as a theological pointer; the child was made an object of mission and intervention.

Both FBOs and churches held confessional assurances concerning what was in the 'best interests of children'. Churches worked towards the spiritual conversion of children; conversion as transaction was contrasted with welcoming the child into the life of the believing community. The terms 'holism and transformation' were used by FBOs to describe their interventions. These terms were re-examined in light of the present pain and suffering of children. I argue that 'holistic mission' should include the life and participation of local churches and families. What began as a study to describe efficacy in partnership to assist children in crisis, led to an inquiry to understand, describe, and embrace tensions in FBO-church partnership. 'Embracing tensions' was suggested as core category to aid in the integration of eternal and human concerns and how the 'good news' might be more fully discerned in FBO-church partnership for children.

It was established that the imposition of short-sighted agendas of church on the FBO or of the FBO on the church undermined collaboration. Such actions often neglect the concerns and voices of children. These approaches also limit space for open dialogue about what God intends when he places a 'child in the midst'. Children in crisis serve to open new horizons in missiology and theology in working towards partnership that honours God.

In conclusion, I identify several positive broad-based outcomes that will continue to shape FBO-church partnership and briefly assess the current situation for Romanian children. Based on the findings in this study, I make recommendations for further theological and pedagogical reflection for future FBO-church partnership. I close with several open questions.

Identifying Positive Outcomes that continue to shape FBO-church partnership

The research described phenomena both past and present: the FBOs and churches that contributed to the research continue to work with children in crisis and new agencies are starting work.[1] Romanian evangelicalism continues to define its identity in the wider society; according to OCI Romania new churches are opened every week.[2] The following outcomes will continue to influence FBO-church partnership with wider reference in Romanian society.

Renewed interest in theology of social concern

Opportunities for broader theological education have increased since 2000; students now seek a better understanding of theology with relevance to change taking place in Romania (Mănăstireanu, 2006). Continuing education is more available to pastors; evangelical scholarship is becoming more accepted in church life.[3] Evangelicals increasingly recognize that they can make a contribution to shaping 'moral society', how they address the spiritual and physical needs of children and marginalized families should inform their evangelical ethic and mission.

> Positive change in Romanian society will take place when we come to a common ethical and moral base. The evangelical church has an opportunity as a social institution to address integrity, character, corruption, and injustice (Barbosu 2004:18).

Theological colleges still do not offer courses on 'church, child, and mission', but interest in youth work is high (Lucian, 2006). Hauerwas proposes that a believing community 'is set on its way by the language and practices of tradition, but while on its way it must often subtly reform those practices and language in accordance with its new perceptions of truth' (1981:63). The

---

[1] I continue to communicate with study participants who report that Western agencies continue to open new offices and projects.

[2] As discussed in Chapter 2, church 'planting' continues with little scholastic assessment to measure sociological, economic, or political impact resulting from 'church growth'. Romania is also now a major 'stop off point' for many international ministries that continue to promote evangelism and church growth.

[3] This represents a shift from the 1990s when 'theological education' was not as important as 'training pastors for general ministry' (Mănăstireanu, 2006). In December 2007, Corneliu Constantineanu, Silvu Rogobete, Danut Mănăstireanu, Alex Negoae, and Daniel Oprean launched a 'Romanian Institute for Evangelical Research', the first independent research venture of its kind in Romania. These and others represent a new brand of scholarship emerging in Romania.

Romanian evangelical community is in a leadership transition, which I labelled an 'emergent strategy' of FBO-church collaboration. The moral authority of scripture is highly valued; children as a language of God and pointers to the kingdom are bringing 'subtle reform' to this believing community.

Evangelicals value the gospel (as they know it); their willingness to live within its language offers opportunity to discover new horizons concerning 'God's intentions' for children and youth. The challenge is to discover and practise a contextual evangelical theology that engages Romanian society and its youngest members. The emergent Romanian church should continue to explore the possibilities of the Evangel. The child as a theological pointer is one means to encourage receptivity and openness as the evangelical church expresses its voice in Romanian society.

Dialogue with Romanian Orthodox Church concerning children

Tensions described between evangelical and Orthodox churches will continue to impact FBO-church partnerships; embracing these tensions requires theological and missiological sensitivity from both sides. Renewed evangelical efforts in theology and concern for the marginalized has contributed to greater interfaith dialogue (Rogobete, 2003; Mănăstireanu, 2004b). Evangelicals share common concerns with the Orthodox Church in ethics and moral formation of youth; both traditions seek to honour Christ and to protect children. Argyris asks, 'to what extent is Orthodoxy compatible with evangelicalism?' (2000:2).[4]

Given the outcomes of World Vision conferences where participants agreed to work together to confront child abandonment, abuse, abortion, youth and family violence, pornography, and trafficking, it is crucial that evangelical FBO-church partnerships work together with Orthodox Churches demonstrating informed missiological perceptions concerning children.[5] As a minority church in an Orthodox society, evangelicals may choose to 'explore and articulate a historical human hope that corresponds to the glory of God imagined in Christ' (Willmer, 1999:16). Evangelicals can make clear their hopes and expectations for Romanian children in light of their understanding of the kingdom of God which is a present and ultimate reality. A common concern of Orthodox and evangelicals for the eternal welfare of children invites future study in child 'spirituality', the process of salvation and conversion, and shaping faith values in Christian families.

---

[4] See Argyris (2000) 'Orthodoxy and Evangelicalism: Areas of Convergence and Divergence', a paper presented at the Conference for Eastern Orthodox Dialogue in Toronto Canada.

[5] There are hopeful signs. At a WV Romania conference held in May 2007, Romanian Orthodox and Evangelical leaders came together for two days to discuss implications for children, family, and society after the transition to the European Union in January 2007. At this meeting, new alliances were formed that could have long range consequences for Orthodox and Evangelical collaboration.

Churches and FBOs that act as 'bridges'

Several cases were labelled as 'transitional or bridge' churches. In each, there were individuals and FBOs that contributed to mobilizing the potential in the local church. Listening, learning, living with uncertainty, and acknowledging that the world and FBO-church actions in it were imperfect characterized these cases. They received children who were threatening or forgotten, offering them opportunities when others had disqualified them. In the light of God's forgiveness to the world in Christ, they embraced those who were rejected. They provided a social space for children to interact with believers. They worked within the language of faith, promise, nurture, formation, calling, restoration, and new life in Christ, while living with frustration, pain, and disappointment. They instituted new patterns of worship by receiving children from the margins into their midst.

'Receiving makes anxious disciples into powerful witnesses, makes suspicious owners into generous givers, and makes closed-minded sectarians into interested recipients of new ideas and new insights' (Nouwen, 1975:45). These 'bridge 'churches are minority faith communities. They did not fall into the trap of sectarianism; they did not 'abandon evangelism, in which the gospel is offered to all, they learned to rely on God in fresh ways rather than turning to social power or tradition' (Willmer, 1999:15). There are potentially hundreds of these 'bridges' in Romania which, as of yet, have to take an active role in caring for children in need.

Active participation by women, children, and youth

In the last 15 years, the role for women in evangelical churches has changed significantly. Where women were once given only minimal opportunity to lead in public church life, they now direct ministries to children in local churches, lead programmes started by FBOs to assist abandoned infants, and oversee foster care and placement services.[6] Increasing numbers of young women are studying psychology and social work. They provide family counselling, address the needs of children in dysfunctional homes, and care for women who suffer spousal abuse.

Teenagers, once the recipients of church-FBO interventions, are now young adults in leadership roles; they have potential to encourage child participation in programme planning. Youngsters who left the streets are leading youth ministries and shaping a new agenda for FBO-church work. These women,

---

[6] The traditional Baptist, Brethren, and Pentecostal churches still do not recognize the right of women to lead or preach in public worship. This is changing in the newer independent churches and denominations. As with other 'confessional assurances', views towards women in leadership and ministry remain largely unexamined. I credit the FBOs with helping to bring change and new initiative in this area as women have been instrumental in delivery of care to children in crisis.

children, and youth are evidence that God's freedom is not limited by church tradition or human expectations.[7] In a society where leadership is typically male dominated, hierarchical and status is ascribed, the role of women and youth is a significant marker that the 'gospel is no respecter of persons' (Acts 10:34). FBOs that plan to begin work in Romania will be well served if they invest time in listening to and learning from these individuals.

Evangelical Alliance of Romania

The Evangelical Romanian Alliance has become more unified; FBOs are more proactive in inter-denominational collaboration at local and national levels. Romanian personnel who worked with FBOs in the 1990s are being sent out from their local churches to start new ministries with children in India, Pakistan, and Turkey.[8] Romanian FBOs that were once exclusively working with children are now caring for the rural poor and elderly, developing indigenous organizational models, missiological frameworks, and a financial support base. It is critical that the evangelical alliance reflect on its theological rationale for its engagement with children inside and beyond Romanian borders.

The Present Situation for Children

Children in Romania continue to face difficulty, an indicator of continued dysfunction in the wider social system. 'Romanian's Lost Children' broadcast by CNN on July 7, 2007, described how systemic failures continue to plague Romanian's child welfare system. Despite new child welfare laws and millions of dollars from the E.U., FBO and NGO interventions, children (estimated as high as 27,000) still remain in institutions (NAPCR, 2007).[9] A UNICEF study in 2005 found that child abandonment rates (especially Roma and handicapped children) were almost as high in 2004 as during the communist era.[10] FBOs and

---

[7] Based on the evidence in this study it is reasonable to conclude that in 1991, very few pastors would have looked at a teenager living on the streets as a potential leader in the evangelical church. I identified five young men and women now in full-time ministry who were 'street children' in 1994.

[8] Since 2002, several indigenous mission societies have begun in Romania, especially by the Pentecostal and Baptist Unions. For instance, a cluster of new churches was begun in Dobrogea (Southeast Romania), several of these churches worked with Turkish gypsy children living in Romania.

[9] See http://www.cnn.com/2007/WORLD/europe/02/16/untold.stories/index.html?iref=newssearch (accessed December 2010). This archived report was a documentary on the current conditions in Romania Emma Griffiths, who interviewed a number of Romanian aid workers and child advocates in the country.

[10] See http://www.unicef.org/media/media_24892.html (accessed January 2011). UNICEF coordinated a study in 2005 with the Romanian Ministry of Health in 150 medical institutions. This study found that 4,000 newborn babies, or 1.8 per cent of all

NGOs continue to report that Romanian DCP personnel are inadequately trained to understand the causes of child abandonment. 'Children are still placed in institutions with "mental handicaps" when the problems were more likely caused by social impairment in the earliest years of their lives' (FBOL# 72, 2006).

Since joining the E.U. in January 2007, almost two million Romanians have left the country to seek employment in Western Europe. Many parents leave their children with grandparents, relatives, or to care for themselves (Griffiths, 2007). In Bucharest and Iaşi, the numbers of street children are rising as 'economic orphans' leave the villages to beg or work in the cities.[11] Drug abuse among young teens is increasing in almost all Romanian urban areas (FBOL#53, 2007). Maternity wards have become 'new orphanages'. Children who are abandoned with no identity papers or names remain 'wards of the state'. The nurses still receive inadequate training in early child development. Foreign adoptions are now illegal. An FBO director who testified to the E.U. comments:

> The Romanian adoption system had been completely corrupted by the 'baby trade' of the 1990s, by the time the reform laws were passed [2001-2002] there was no system in place to handle all these abandoned children. This means that reform has been very slow and child welfare continues to lag far behind the scale of the problem (FBOL#71, 2006).

In 2005, more than 2,500 victims of trafficking were officially registered, 366 victims were children (UNICEF, 2006).[12] INTERPOL, UNICEF, and NGOs monitor Child pornography and trafficking. Romania wants to improve the lives of its children and enhance its international image. The legacy of the earlier era contributes to a cycle that could take decades to break. I have recommended the term 'transforming' as an alternative to 'transformation' in FBO-church interventions as it is apparent that Romanian children continue to live in an unredeemed society and 'not yet' of the kingdom.

---

newborns, were abandoned in Romanian maternity hospitals immediately after delivery in 2004. Roma make up a significant percentage. This report can be compared with articles such as Traynor (2005) which dispute the claims of UNICEF.

[11] The street child phenomenon was at its worst in the late 1990s as children left the institution. The numbers of street children had significantly declined between 2003 and 2006. FBO and aid workers (2010) report a sharp rise in the number of older youth with new problems such as organized gangs and associated violence.

[12] The UNICEF representative to Romania says these official figures are low and the actual numbers of women and children who are smuggled into other European countries and sold into prostitution are much higher. For a documented summary of the current situation in Romania for children see Chronic's 'Issues Affecting Romania' available http://www.wordmadeflesh.org/romania/2010/04/the-situation-in-romania-2010/ (Accessed December 6, 2010).

Suggestions for Further Theological Reflection

Chapter 7 analysed how FBOs used the term 'holistic' mission; in Chapter 8, several indicators of integration of human and divine concerns were identified in the explication of 'tensions in evangelism and social action'. I argue that FBOs and churches should work towards more meaningful integration of '*Side A* and *Side B'*; theological and missiological reflection with a 'child in the midst' is one way forward. The Evangel embraces the individual within the social; it includes the saving of the soul for heaven and earth and the future transforming of all created things (Col. 1:20). In table 9.1, I summarize the primary categories identified in the study that were labelled as '*Side A'* and '*Side B'*.

Table 9.1 Categories identified as Side A and B in FBO-Church partnership

Side A – from Above	**Side B – from Below**
Salvation and redemption are the work of God in Christ through the Holy Spirit towards humanity. Individuals are made righteous through the work of Christ.	Samaritan theology implies caring for our neighbours as Christ works in the world through humanity reconciling society and social structures.
God's action in the transcendent realm – above all things. Concern is for the eternal world and spiritual realm; eternal life with God is taken seriously.	Human actions, obedience to God in the present world, the immanent realm. Concern is for the present, taking the physical world seriously.
God in his freedom is sometimes bracketed or left on one side. God is the 'Holy Other': illusive, and irascible in freedom, in sovereignty, and in hiddenness.	Our human activity, rationally programmemed in normal practical secularity, is held on its side that includes human ambivalence, ambiguity, creativity, and imagination.
Conversionist approach to children – they are lost in their sin and need a saviour. This can only be accomplished by the action of God.	Programmematic approach to children– a discernable order to the world, knowable through objectivity and rationality.
'Spiritual' approach to God and the Holy Spirit; pietism and holiness are strongly valued as is the miraculous or supernatural intervention of God	Pragmatic approach to social world and reliance on scientific methods as the way forward for options and solutions. God demonstrates his action in the material world.
Categories of 'faith hope and love' in Christ are used to express interventions and outcomes.	Categories of 'well-being, community or individual/social transformation as outcomes.
Churches have faith in spiritual outcomes; the final reality rests with God.	FBOs have faith in human outcomes and work to engineer social change.
An almost 'otherworldly' optimism that God can do anything; our part is to trust and obey	A 'chastened' optimism, more sceptical. A willingness to investigate illusions and ambiguity.
God wants believing people – conversion is prioritized, people are made ready for 'heaven.'	God works to shape and change the structures of our world. Justice requires working for social change.

Continuing integration of Side A and Side B

Faith-based partnerships focused on children in Romania and elsewhere offer a practical means for action and reflection on both 'from above' and 'from below'.[13] This research demonstrates that tensions can be embraced; some churches and FBOs are learning to bring these disjunctions together in their practice. A wider reading of the child's humanity and fresh openness to the Evangel will enrich and critique FBO-church delivery of spiritual interventions, child welfare, and programme management. Meaningful integration of divine and human concerns is an expression of faith in the grace of God.

It could be argued that all children are 'at risk' or vulnerable in some capacity (Samuel, 1997:27).[14] In addition to children who suffer abuse and abandonment, others are treated as invisible, idolized, or given false promises. Every social and education system falls short in representing the fullness of the kingdom. God offers an invitation to the child, the FBO, and the church to enter and receive the kingdom, to embrace Him and His way of living (Eastman, 1997:24). I have raised the question, 'what is a realistic horizon of expectation in faith-based child care'? Faith in God moves us from illusionary horizons of perfection to the reality of taking up the cross and learning of Christ crucified and risen.

> The movement from illusion to prayer is hard since it leads us from false certainties to true uncertainties, from an easy support system to a risky surrender, and from the many 'safe' gods to the God whose love for us has no limits (Nouwen, 1975:61).

As FBOs and church partnerships continue to evolve, integration of *Side A* and *Side B* will necessitate more critical thinking concerning Christological implications for childcare. Implicitly both churches and FBOs hold to the centrality of Christ; they have yet to develop an explicit theology for children. Two major themes must be accounted for: a) the image of God in children, that is, their closeness to the divine reality and b) human sin, which is to speak of their separation from God when their destiny is union with God (Loder, 1998:28).[15] This study does not develop a 'robust' theology for Romanian

---

[13] In the introduction, I said this study had applications to other contexts, especially in Eastern European countries with Orthodox majority and evangelical minorities. I am exercising caution in this conclusion, as there are limits to broad application of the specific partnership findings beyond Romania. There are applications that can be drawn from the theological and missiological recommendations in this study, especially by FBOs working in other places with evangelical partners.

[14] Samuel asks the question, 'When is a child at risk biblically? The child is 'at risk' in the mother's womb, mothers are vulnerable, not only in their own vulnerability, but because the vulnerable children they bear are specially considered' (1997:27).

[15] For discussion on sin and fallenness that can inform FBO and church dialogue see (Barth, 1956 CD. IV.1:490-505) 'The Pride and Fall of Man'. For discussion on 'God's Image in Creation' see (Moltmann, 1993b:215-43), especially 'The original designation

children but advocates effort in that direction. The use of the terms 'holistic and integral' in work with children should include biblical wholeness or 'relationality from within' (Palmer, 1993). Holism requires exploring the basic 'interconnections between theological concepts and natural scientific concepts ... if we are to do full justice to both our knowledge of God and our knowledge of the created order (Torrance, 1984:x).[16]

Theology and the humanity of children

I trace here several theological insights that informed the third phase of my study that suggest further reflection. I was assisted in analysis through a fuller comprehension of Barth's work with the Chalcedonian pattern that recognizes that in the person of Jesus Christ is an 'indissoluble differentiation', 'inseparable unity', and 'indestructible order' in the divinity and humanity of God (Barth, CD III.2:437) and reading 'The Way of the Son of God into the Far Country' (CD IV.1).[17] Loder relied on Barth's Chalcedonian method in his study of human development in theological perspective, 'as a way of working – both methodologically and materially – from below and above at the same time, allowing the objectivity of revelation to deal transformatively with the objectivity of the sciences' (1998:33). Hendry, a Reformed theologian, argues for both 'condescension' of God's grace, which the Reformers emphasized, and 'accommodation' of God's incarnation in Christ (1976:111-12). For Hendry, the humanity (of a child) to whom God accommodates is humanity endowed with a created spirit, the mark of which is human freedom. The action of God on the human spirit of the child needs further explication in Romanian evangelicalism.

The question of God's relationship to a child's humanity and created being is central to integration of *Side A* and *Side B*. God does not overrule a child's freedom but engages it in order that the 'I-Thou' of the God-child relationship

---

of human beings: Imago Dei' (:216-25). Also see the work of the Child Theology Consultation in South Africa (www.childtheology.org). This conversation in Child Theology moves beyond the two entrenched positions one usually finds in FBO-church partnership: 'Are children sinful because they are human, or is there a bias towards sinfulness in children. Does fallenness produce a state that is sinful before God because children are born that way – or do children have a propensity for evil, which when they come to exercise their wills, they act sinfully' (Eastman, 1997:24).

[16] See Torrance (1984) who advocates a dialectical dialogue between theology and modern science; he compares the transformation of conceptual frameworks brought about by quantum mechanics and relativity following Einstein to that of Barth's Chalcedonian Christology – highlighting 'indissoluble differentiation and the logical priority of theology' (1984:294).

[17] See So (2006b) for his work with this text in 'The Missionary Journey of the Son of God into the Far Country: A paradigm of the holistic gospel developed from the theology of Karl Barth'. Also see So (2006a:134-41) for discussion on Barth's treatment of Matt. 9:35-36 'he had compassion on them'.

will not be reduced to the 'I-it' order. God does not dehumanize a child in order to relate to His creation (Hendry, 1976:113). Towards the end of his career, Barth wrote, *The Humanity of God.* In this quote, I substitute the word 'child' for 'man' in the original and interpose him/her.

> The distinction due to [the child] for such through the humanity of God, however, extends also to everything with which [child as child] is endowed and equipped by God, her creator. This gift, her humanity, is not blotted out through the fall, nor is its goodness diminished. [The child] is *not* elected to intercourse with God because, by virtue of his/her humanity, he/she deserves such preference. She is elected to God's grace alone. The child is elected, however, as the being especially endowed by God. This is manifest in her special bodily nature ... and also in the fact that she is a rationally thinking, willing, and speaking being destined for responsible and spontaneous decision. Above all, however, it is shown in the fact that from the beginning [the child] is constituted, bound, and obligated as a fellow child. God concerns himself with, loves, and calls her as *this* being in his/her peculiar totality (Barth, 1960:53).

Barth provides an important clue for 'holistic' childcare in the phrase 'being in his/her particular totality' that means we cannot differentiate so easily where spirit stops and flesh begins. Human children are not divided neatly into soul, spirit, and body as some Romanian church pastors and FBOs have suggested. Children are complete human beings; they remind us that dichotomies of soul/spirit and physicality are inadequate descriptions of God's eternal love and command for children.

Reflection and Action in Partnership

In response to this challenge for more critical theological reflection and integration, I suggest a method of 'action and reflection' in FBO-church partnership. As an activist and practitioner, I could not close without at least some attempt at an action step. This is a process of learning or pedagogy, 'recognition that when people act, their action affects the way they think about that action; likewise, reflecting in a new way creates receptivity for further and more adventurous action' (Linthicum, 1991:61). Action and reflection feed on each other; action can lead to insightful reflection that results in more informed action. This is diagrammed in Figure 9.1 adopted from Linthicum.[18]

[18] Linthicum developed this model as a community organization tool. My point of departure is to focus specifically on children and include theological reflection that 'embraces' the promises of the gospel, human pain, and human fallenness.

Figure 9.1 Process of Reflection and Action in FBO-Church partnerships

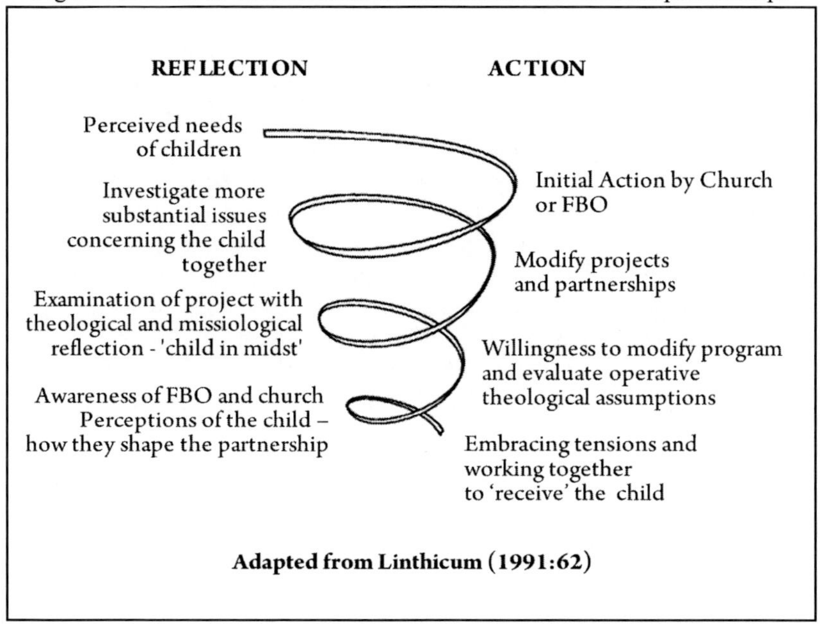

I will interpret the chart using one of the cases and offer a hopeful extrapolation. Word Made Flesh and partner churches initially responded to the perceived needs of Roma children on the streets in their community by opening a day shelter. The FBO provided services, funding, and training; the churches offered people who provided childcare. As their joint action continued, the partners met to reflect and ask questions about outcomes. Once the children's immediate needs were met, the partnership began asking more penetrating questions such as 'what are the issues for the families of the children on the streets, what are their hopes for the children?' This led to action aimed at family interventions and helping to integrate children in the formal school system. The FBO-church partnership became more involved with the Roma community.[19]

> The present [2008] long-term trend for the families in this community is emigration as older youth and parents of the children are moving to Western Europe. There they work jobs in construction or cleaning – mostly on the black market, others work in the sex trade, pimping or stealing' (Chronic email, 2008).

[19] The steps described in this paragraph are a brief description of what has taken place in this case over the last several years. The FBO and churches recognized that God offers more to the children than spending their lives on the streets; family intervention was aimed at preventing the children from going to the streets.

The following paragraphs are my 'extrapolation' applying the process of action and theological reflection.

The partnership now will seek to address causes of Roma emigration. The challenge is to build a local community that economically sustains families in which they can imagine a better future. The partnership plans to begin an income generation project. Future action requires more theological reflection: What most honours God in addressing the human and spiritual needs of these children, how does the gospel address the sense of hopelessness and 'marred identity' (Christian, 1999) in the Roma community? How does the humanity of a child in the eyes of God influence FBO-church action and prayer? The church might be asked to re-examine its understanding of evangelism as the FBO re-examines its role as both social and theological advocate for the child. Together the partners can search the scriptures with a 'child in the midst'. This will encourage dialogue about the implications of the kingdom for both social-structural change whist recognizing and embracing the exclusion, suffering, and uncertainty of the child and Roma community. 'In the church we have the basis for both spiritual and social development, this means participation for every member' (Chronic email, 2008).

As a result of theological refection, the FBO and churches can examine their common humanity in light of Christ, identify their complicity in falling short of the glory of God, and recognize and rejoice in the grace of God both for themselves and the children. They may discuss how children have been sinned against while taking reasonable action and mutual responsibility. This process, as described, unmasks the 'illusions that masquerade as reality' (Palmer, 2000)[20]; it encourages patience with humanity as partners proceed mindful of pain and hope, suffering and joy as integral to a 'holistic gospel'. Ambiguity and uncertainty are embraced as aspects of faith-based care.

The partnership may eventually confront the economic system that keeps Roma families bound in poverty, but they do so with a mutual submission to Christ, to the gospel, and to one another. As the process continues, the partnership will likely reflect on the implications of the gospel for political, economic, religious, and social systems of the community in a wider context. These fallen human systems will call the local churches forward in mission. In this model, the child acts as a catalyst and 'pointer'. Growing knowledge of Christ, the child, and the world conscientizes the FBO and church to continued action and reflection as it expresses the *Agape* of God to this community.

> So the Church is not to be understood primarily as a means to the end of transforming the society. This would be to trample over the uniqueness and infinite worth to God of the Christian community … the most amazing and

[20] A number of these illusions have been described: power and pride in partnership, perfection and certainty, programmatic responses that expect unrealistic outcomes – such as expecting the child to move 'past' human pain – impatience with the Romanian system and its labyrinth of bureaucracy leading to reactive responses.

> profound fact is the Church most transforms society when it is itself growing and being perfected in the love of Christ (Snyder, 1977:133)

Open Questions for FBOs and Churches

I close with several open questions for FBOs and churches to explore as they consider their core values and future evaluative standards and theological criteria.

In the frenetic activity of the 1990s, FBOs and churches embraced habits of work and ministry that were reactionary; few individuals were encouraged in the disciplines of reflective spirituality, critical thinking, or deeper reflection on Christ. Intentional effort is now required to move to new methods of learning and working together. Individual FBOs should allocate resources and evaluate the impact of their work over the past 17 years; this is an appropriate time for a fresh assessment of the Romanian evangelical church. FBOs will need to disconnect from patterns and methodologies that were uncritically adapted in the 1990s that are not locally sustainable. In so doing, the FBOs can reinforce the worthwhile foundations laid in the 1990s with youth and children. Research, reflection, and action, as outlined above, may encourage new initiatives in theologizing, leadership, and organizational modelling.

In their programmatic activism, FBO-church partnerships should pause and ask 'have we attended to the actual child that was set before us?' Jesus insisted that the disciples pay attention to the child He set in their midst, in her humanity and earthly reality. What future actions will lead FBO-church partnerships to recognize their failings, adjusting their thinking, values, and behaviour to serve the King? What future outcomes should FBOs and churches expect when they take seriously the child who reminds them to pray 'Thy kingdom come, thy will be done. On earth *as it is* in heaven'? (Matt. 6:10).

Future work with children entails space for scholastic attention to the Evangel in thoughtful, imaginative, and truthful ways. This will mean questioning confessional dogmatism while encouraging followers of Christ in more open dialogue with gospel, culture, and society. The emerging churches and leaders may embrace a new life of the mind where intellectual life involves 'self-awareness about alternative interpretations, which includes tentativeness in exploring the connections between evidence and conclusion' (Noll, 1994:126).[21] Such work will require awareness of God's freedom and concern for the children in their present situation. FBOs and churches are called to follow Jesus in the way of humility, service, and compassion. The biblical model of partnership goes far beyond the idea of 'forming storming, norming,

---

[21] Noll's chapter, 'The Intellectual Disaster of Fundamentalism' is especially relevant to the situation in Romania in 2008.

and performing' (Parker, 1996:114).[22] Without a Christological centre, partnership can become manipulation or 'bogus empowerment'.

Who will shape the direction of the dialogue in faith-based care for children in the next 15 years? Romanians can take a more active role in discovering and articulating the strengths in their churches and theologies that integrate God's eternal concerns and human best practice. How will the voices of the poorest families, the Roma, the marginal be included in this conversation, what will prevent their exclusion? Romanian evangelicals may chose to assume a more vocal role in shaping societal understanding of marginal children. This requires missiological clarity concerning the role of the evangelical church in the public square. How local churches, pastors, and FBOs encourage the next generation to live faithfully in the gospel is a critical question.

An estimate of evangelical churches in Romania in 2010 is approaching 6,000. There are now more than 100 FBOs working with children. The child invites both church and FBO to open their eyes to sociological realities as well as offering a theological invitation to live and practise the biblical way of forgiveness and prayer. Praying 'thy kingdom come' does not promise a just world for children; however, it calls followers of Christ to hope and responsibility as God gives foretastes and signs of that coming kingdom.

[22] This sort of language is found in leadership, partnership, and team building literature published in the West that makes efficacy and outcomes primary objectives. Biblical partnership may or may not produce tangible success. 'Every attempt to attach our hope [in Christ] to visible symptoms in our surroundings becomes a temptation when it prevents us from the realization that promises [in Christ], not concrete successes, are the basis of Christian ministry' (Nouwen, 1990:76).

Appendix A
Preliminary Survey of Child Agencies in Romania
Interview Guide – Phase One

Web pages, phone interviews, and other sources were used to gather general background data before calling or meeting agency leaders.

Interview # ____ NGO # ____ Interviewee # ____RO / INT   RO / ENG

Name: ______________ Interviewee's position: _________________
(Will be kept confidential)
Programme Name:

1) Recipients of programme helps or intervention: Who do you serve?

2) Ages? Girls? Boys?

3) Background or special needs of your clients?

4) Staff: Romanian International How many?

Partnership Issues and Questions:

5) Is your NGO/Ministry: Romanian or international in nature?

6) How would you describe your organization: examples: Working partnership, Western Funded but Romanian directed, Western Funded – Western driven, Romanian funded and Romanian directed?

7) Is your organization/NGO: faith-based or secular or government
    a. If faith-based describe closest your closest affiliation: Catholic, Protestant, Pentecostal, Orthodox, other?

8) History – how was this programme started, by whom, and what partners influenced you to start this ministry or did you start on a local initiative or with encouragement from outside sources?

9) How do you work with the church, do you partner with a local church or a denomination?

10) How important is working with the church – as you define it – to your overall strategy of working with children?

11) In the Romanian context – do you see yourself in partnership with churches or with Pastors?

Programme Goals and Evaluation:

12) Organization's purpose/goal – mission statement – do you have one?

13) Strategies/projects being implemented to reach goal. What Services are provided?

14) What services does the government provide in this community, are they accessible to you?

15) How do you monitor and evaluate the projects and the children/youth in the project – if you do not is there a reason for not doing evaluation?

16) Tell us how faith is important to your project, your staff and your children?

17) How does your programme or agency define success?

18) Do you consider the work of your NGO/ministry to be successful? Why?

Finances:

19) How many children and youth in your programme rely on your agency alone for assistance?

20) Who are your primary financial partners? What types? (Western agencies, business, local government, other NGOs, etc.)

21) What is your annual budget?

Future Issues:

22) What are the primary barriers/problems the NGO/ministry faces?

23) From your experience use the chart below and select and identify (in order 1-2-3) the top three primary causes of child welfare problems in your location and work.

Initiative of churches and others is small		Corruption at local or national level		Organizational or cultural Issues		Lack of infrastructure	
Bureaucracy		Discriminat ion		E.U. accession		Public policy	
Lack of training and general information		Governmen t attitude		Mentality of families toward children"		Children seen as not important by the society	
Financial barriers to operating our programme		Poverty of the families of children		Attitude of the community where we work		Other causes not listed here	

Appendix B
Semi-Structured Interview Guide – Case Study Locations

Main Interview Guide for Phase Two of Research
Questions used in interviewing FBO directors and church leaders:
Research on FBOs and Churches working together for at Risk Children

Interviewee Name: ___________ Interview Code #_________________
Project Name: ________________ Position of Interviewee ____________
Time with Project: ___________ Sex ( ) Age (20-30) (31-45) (45-older)

Note: Two separate questionnaires were designed for the study; they are combined here to conserve space.

Section I. Interaction between Church and FBO

1. How important is it for your FBO (or church) that the children you serve be connected to the local churches in your area?

2. What do you think a church can provide for them or the family that could not be provided elsewhere? (asked of both FBO and Church)

3. When you think of the local church and children – (local means in a specific place) what are some options you believe the FBO can offer to children at risk that maybe church cannot? (asked of FBO)

   - Do you think there are limits for a local church in caring for children?
   - What might a church offer to children at risk that a FBO cannot?

4. What are some of the specific ways your FBO works with the churches in your community? (asked only of FBOs)

4a. What has been your experience with FBOs working in your community, do they cooperate with local churches? (Asked of church leaders)

5. Do you have any public records (newspapers, letters of appreciation, invitations to conferences, workshops etc) of this interaction? (asked of both FBO and church leaders)

6. What is the perception of your organization in the community (asked of both)?

very positive ----- welcome ----- neutral ----- opposition ---- strong opposition

- In what way(s) does the local community know that your organization is a Christian organization? (asked of FBO)

7. What are the local churches able to do now that they were not doing before your FBO started working here? Do you think this is a result of the partnership with FBOs? (asked of both FBO and church leaders)

8. How would you describe your organization/church on this scale: (asked of Both)

V. conservative---somewhat conservative---progressive---v. progressive---Westernized

- Here we are using the Romanian sense of the word 'conservative' i.e. traditional church, progressive means more western or more concerned with social needs but how would you define it.

9. In your opinion, what is a sensible response from local evangelical churches to help children at risk, in other words what do you think can be done with the resources they have at their disposal? (asked of Both)

Section II. Partnership Values:

1. Show us on this scale how important collaboration or partnership is to your FBO/church?

0--------1--------2--------3--------4--------5--------6--------7
FBO completely incidental some partnership very close Church initiated

If you chose one of these words to describe your partnership – what does it mean to you?

- Independent
- Dependent
- Interdependent

2. In your experience, have you seen the most obvious benefits of working in partnership with the Churches? (Asked of FBO) and partnership with FBOs (asked of church leaders).

- What are some of the disadvantages? (asked of both)

3. What suggestions would you give to the local churches/pastors to help better cooperate with Foundations and Associations or Western partners? (Asked of FBO)

3a. What suggestions would you give to FBOs to better help them cooperate with local churches? (Asked of church leaders)

4. Can you think of any reasons churches might not want to work with outside agencies in care for children that are at risk? (Asked of both)

Section III. Organizational Dynamics

1. How does your FBO/Church understand organizational dynamics (by that we mean how does organization take place in the actual project) – are you set up like a mission, a social service agency, or other agency? (Asked of both)

   - Do you have any organizational charts, leadership, training schedules, structures, etc?

Evaluation of Impact and Change

2. Can you tell us some ways that you understand change (outcomes or impact) in the lives of children? Do you measure this in any way? (Asked of both)

   - At what level do you look for change – individual, family, other?

3. How do you describe and record the outcomes (obvious or not so obvious) you have seen in your work with children? (Asked of both)

   Explanation if needed: We are looking for ideas that reflect ways of thinking about outcomes and interventions they use. The ideas might fit these categories but ask for their own words.

   - **RESILIENCE**
   - **SOCIAL SKILLS**
   - **CHARACTER**
   - **DIGNITY**

4. Who actually does the evaluation in your projects? (Asked of both)

5. How do you measure or know if you are successful – what words describe success for you? (Make sure they explain terms like: 'fruit in their lives' – asked of both)

Section IV. Theology and children:

1. Can you tell us how you understand the spiritual or faith development of the child as it relates to your project(s)? (asked of both)

- What do you think has the most impact on children's spiritual growth (church, caregivers, family, other?) (asked of both)

2. Do you think that a focus on children as found in Mt. 18, where Jesus puts a child in the midst of the disciples can help the church understand its role in society here in Romania? Could you describe your understanding of that verse? (asked of both)

3. What do you believe God intends for the children in your programme. Please talk about this in any way that fits your biblical framework? Dignity? Worth? Purpose? (asked of both)

4. We are trying to understand how FBOs and churches understand faith in caring for children. From what you have told us so far, what do you believe are the most important aspects of a faith-based approach to the children in your programme? (asked of both)

   Possible Prompts for discussion:
   - Is it outcomes, is witness to God, building the church, or?
   - You probably expect the children to continue to face conflict and difficulty in life – how do you think faith will help them
   - What about the caregivers in your organization (family or staff) – what difference does faith make in their lives in caring for the kids?

Appendix C
Data Displays Created to Describe Partnership – Phase One

These are examples of data displays (Miles & Huberman, 1994:11) created to assist in analysis of findings. This series of data display represents some of the linkages, causality and factors involved in FBO – Church Partnerships that were induced from findings from Phase I of research.

Depiction of the overall problem:

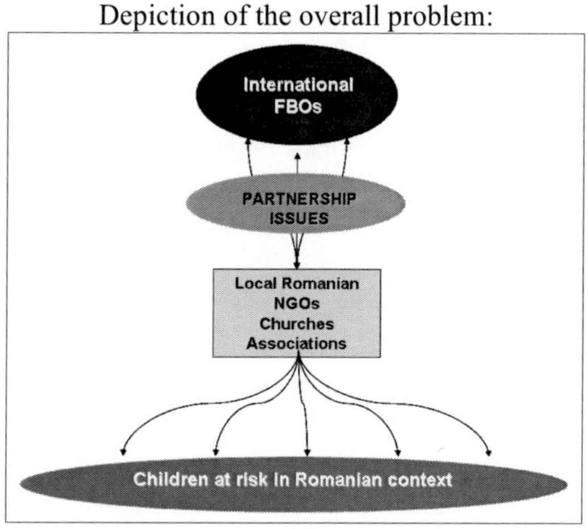

Defining FBO categories and linkages:

FBOs – categories/taxonomy

Power, control, partnership, participation, etc. understood in western ways

International FBOs

Organizational
Theological
Cultural
Sociological
} **assumptions of task/mission**

Missiologies/mandates
Ideas of church modality/sodality
Why Romania?
Theology/Sociology of child/child rights

Factors shaping partnerships with Churches:

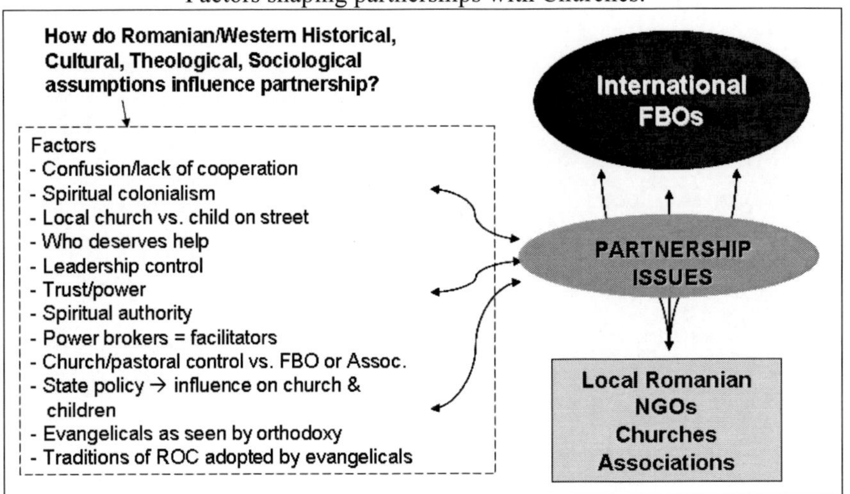

Evaluation of Outcomes in Partnership

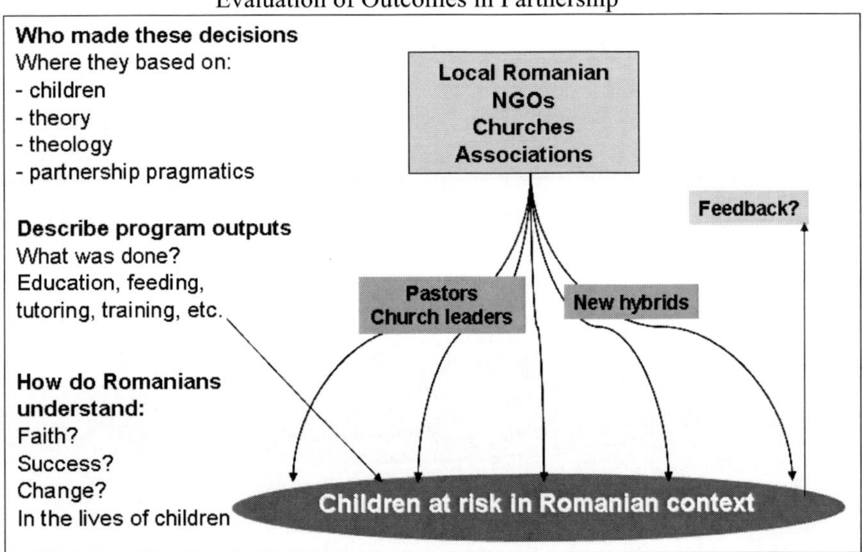

Data Display Overview of Research Problem

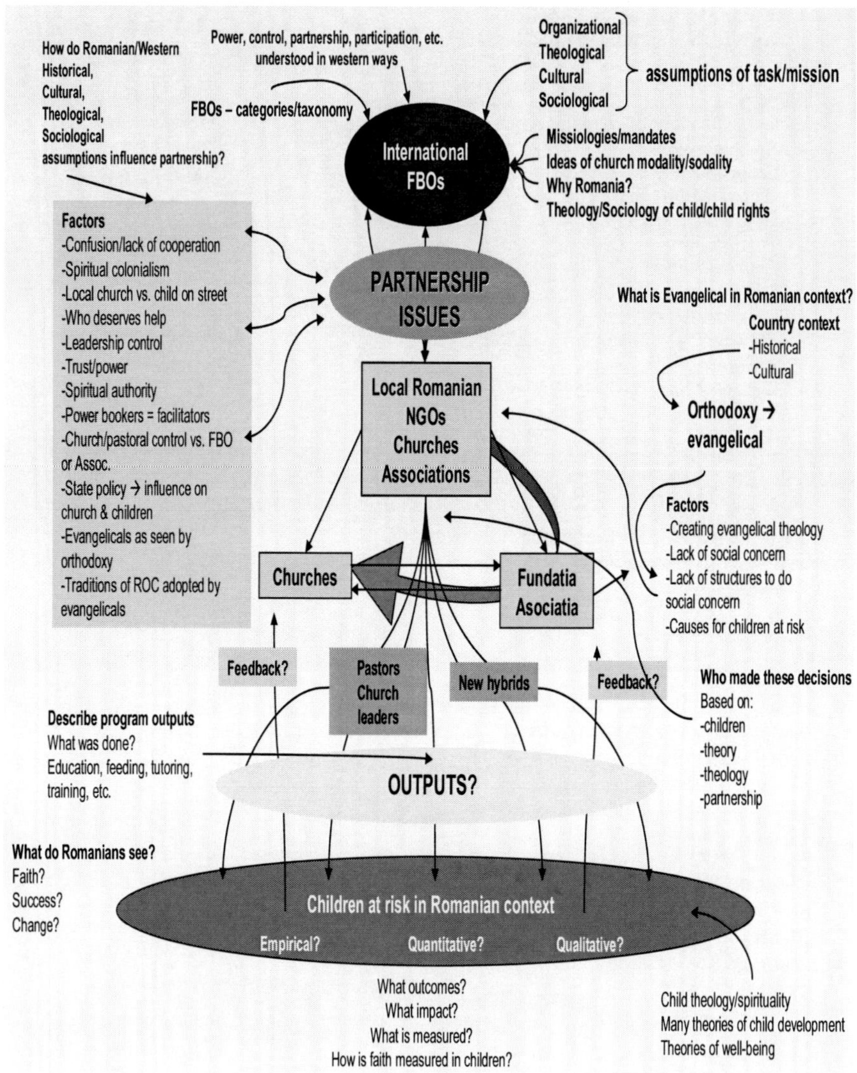

Appendix D
All Interviews by Organization and Location

This is the list of structured interviews conducted in two phases of field research. These interviewees are primary sources. The column "ID" contains the reference number that is used to indicate the source of the information. Each ID represents an identifying code to differentiate the type of interviewee. Interview transcripts were filed electronically and kept in the master database on a secure drive.[1]

I = general interview (missionaries without a specific status, students and others)
FBOL = Faith-based Organization Leader [2]
FBOS = Other Faith-based Organization people (staff, volunteers, etc.)
Pas = Pastor/Member of pastoral staff or church leader

Phase One Interviews				
#	**ID**	**Date**	**Organization**	**Location**
1	I#1	Apr 2003	Discover your Mission	Santa Ana, Cal.
2	FBOL#1	Apr 2003	OCI	Bucharest
3	FBOL#2	May 2003	WVR	Bucharest
4	I#2	Sep 2003	ITP	Bucharest
5	FBOL#3	Sep 2003	FHI-Community development	Bucharest
6	FBOL#4	Nov 2003	Nazarene Compassionate Ministries	Bucharest
7	FBOL#5	Dec 2003	Reaching Out Romania	Pitesti
8	I#3	Dec 2003	Baptist Theological Seminary	Bucharest
9	FBOL#6	Dec 2003	FDSC – Civil Society Dev.	Timisoara

[1] In Phase One, eleven of the transcripts were written by hand not transcribed as they did not contribute significant data to the study. These transcripts were kept in paper format in my home office.

[2] In Phase One, 12 of those identified with the label FBOL were also working as pastors or pastoral support roles at local churches. They were identified with the FBOL label as this was their primary role, some of these individuals answered questions about the role of the local church in guided interview.

			Foundation	
10	FBOL#7	Dec 2003	Familia/Dawn Services	Bucharest
11	Pas#1	Dec 2003	Local Pentecostal church	Bucharest
12	FBOL#8	Dec 2003	Casa Shalom	Bucharest
13	FBOL#9	Jan 2004	Viaţă şi lumină	Piteşti
14	FBOL#10	Feb 2004	Fundaţia Uşă Deschisă	Bucharest
15	FBOL#11	Feb 2004	Never Alone Foundation	Pitesti
16	FBOL#12	Mar 2004	Căminul Felix	Oradea
17	FBOL#47	Mar 2004	Children of Promise	Oradea
18	FBOL#13	Jun 2004	For God's children	Bucharest
19	FBOL#14	Jun 2004	OSCER	Bucharest
20	FBOL#15	Jun 2004	Ministry of Religion (phone interview)	Bucharest
21	FBOL#16	Jun 2004	WVR	Bucharest
22	FBOL#17	Jun 2004	Project Ruth	Bucharest
23	FBOL#18	Jun 2004	Fundaţia Mission of Mercy	Piteşti
24	FBOL#19	Jun 2004	Fundaţia Seceriş	Câmpulung Muscel
25	FBOL#20	Jul 2004	CWRWC	Bucharest
26	FBOL#21	Jul 2004	Bethany Social Services	Bucharest
27	FBOL#22	Jul 2004	Caritas	Bucharest
28	FBOL#23	Jul 2004	OCI	Bucharest
29	I#4	Jul 2004	Department Child Protection – official	Bucharest
30	Pas#2	Aug 2004	Biserica Betania	Medgidia
31	Pas#3	Aug 2004	Pentecostal Church – Babadag	Babadag
32	FBOL#48	Aug 2004	Livingstone Foundation (Holland)	Babadag
33	Pas#4	Aug 2004	Pentecostal Church – Navodari	Năvodari
34	Pas#5	Aug 2004	Pentecostal Church – Mangalia	Mangalia
35	FBOL#24	Sep 2004	Fundatia Betesda	Galati
36	FBOL#25	Sep 2004	Fundatia Child's Heart	Galati
37	FBOL#26	Sep 2004	YWAM Constanta	Constanta
38	FBOL#27	Sep 2004	Mission without borders	Sibiu
39	FBOL#28	Sep 2004	City of Hope	Bucharest
40	I#5	Sep 2004	Student at EEBC	Oradea
41	Pas#6	Sep 2004	Pastor of Pentecostal Church	Oradea area
42	FBOL#29	Sep 2004	CRY – Care and Relief for the Young	Bucharest
43	FBOL#30	Sep 2004	CRY – Care and Relief for the Young	Bucharest

44	Pas#7	Sep 2004	Asociaţia Centrul Vieţii Noi	Braşov
45	FBOL#31	Oct 2004	Mission Without Borders	Sibiu
46	FBOL#32	Oct 2004	Fundatia Familia Copiilor	Targu Mures
47	FBOL#33	Oct 2004	Asociatia "Bunul Samaritean"	Ocna Mures
48	FBOL#34	Oct 2004	GATIEF Viata si Lumina	Targu Mures (Santana de Mures)
49	FBOL#35	Oct 2004	YWAM Cluj Napoca	Cluj Napoca
50	FBOL#36	Oct 2004	Church member working with FBO	Cluj Napoca
51	FBOL#37	Oct 2004	World Vision	Bucharest
52	FBOL#38	Oct 2004	Toar	Cisnadie (near Sibiu)
53	FBOL#39	Dec 2004	Maranatha – Penilla	Iasi
54	FBOL#40	Dec 2004	Fundatia Iosif	Iasi
55	FBOL#41	Dec 2004	Calea Bucuriei	Iasi
56	FBOL#42	Dec 2004	Our little house Foundation	Iasi
57	FBOL#43	Dec 2004	Pastor of independent church	Iasi
58	FBOL#44	Dec 2004	Our little house Foundation	Iasi
59	FBOL#45	Dec 2004	Small Local FBO	Iasi
60	FBOL#46	Dec 2004	Link Romania Foundation	Iasi
			Phase Two Interviews	
#	**ID**	**Date**	**Organization**	**Location**
61	FBOL#49	Apr 2005	Asociatia Cuvantul Scris	Timisoara
62	Pas#7	Apr 2005	Pastor of Baptist church	Timisoara
63	I#6	Apr 2005	Areopagus Centre	Timisoara
64	I#7	Apr 2005	Romanian student at Elim Church	Timisoara
65	FBOL#50	Apr 2005	Touched Romania	Bucharest
66	FBOL#51	Jul 2005	Project Romanian Rescue	Constanta
67	FBOL#18	Jul 2005	Mission of Mercy	Pitesti
68	FBOL#52	Jul 2005	Mission of Mercy	Pitesti
69	I#8	Jul 2005	Mission of Mercy	Pitesti
70	FBOL#28	Oct 2005	City of Hope	Bucharest
71	FBOL#53	Oct 2005	City of Hope	Bucharest
72	I#9	Oct 2005	Student from City of Hope	Bucharest
73	FBOL#54	Dec 2005	Adoptive parent – City of Hope	Bucharest
74	FBOL#55	Dec 2005	Light & Life	Bucharest
75	FBOS#1	Dec 2005	Light & Life	Bucharest
76	FBOS#2	Dec 2005	Light & Life	Bucharest
77	FBOL#56	Oct 2005	Dorcas Ministries	Cluj (interview in U.K.)

78	I#10	Feb 2005	Pavement Project – SGM Europe	Timisoara
79	FBOL#57	Oct 2005	Pavement Project – SGM Europe	Timisoara
80	FBOL#58	Mar 2005	Mana Deschisa	Campina
81	FBOL#59	Nov 2005	Talmud Tora	Bucharest
82	I#11	Mar 2005	Teacher George Cosbuc High School	Bucharest
83	FBOS#3	Nov 2005	Heart to Heart	Bucharest
84	FBOL#60	Nov 2005	Word Made Flesh	Galati
85	Pas#8	Nov 2005	Pastor – church in Galati	Galati
86	FBOL#61	Nov 2005	Heart of a child	Galati
87	FBOL#25	Nov 2005	Heart of a child	Galati
88	I#12	Oct 2005	World Vision U.K. & Heart of a child	U.K.
89	FBOL#62	Nov 2005	Bethesda	Galati
90	FBOL#63	Nov 2005	Bethesda	Galati
91	FBOS#4	Nov 2005	Heart of a child (Together at home project)	Galati
92	FBOL#64	Apr 2005	Project Ruth	Bucharest
93	FBOS#5	Apr 2005	Project Ruth	Bucharest
94	FBOL#65	Apr 2005	Project Ruth	Bucharest
95	FBOS#6	Apr 2005	Project Ruth	Bucharest
96	Pas#9	Sep 2005	Pastor – Baptist church	Bucharest
97	Pas#10	Sep 2005	Pastor – Romanian AG church	Bucharest
98	Pas#11	Sep 2005	Pastor- PU church	Bucharest
99	Pas#12	Sep 2005	Pastor – Baptist church	Tulcea
100	Pas#13	Sep 2005	Pastor Pentecostal church	Bucharest
101	FBOL#66	Sep 2005	Bible School EEBC	Oradea
102	I#13	Sep 2005	Director of Campus Ministry	Bucharest
103	FBOL#67	Oct 2005	Veritas – open interview	Bucharest
104	FBOL#68	Jun 2006	Children to Love	Bucharest
105	Pas#14	Mar 2006	Lighthouse Pentecostal church	Constanta
106	FBOL#69	Mar 2006	Dobrogea School for Mission and Evangelism	Constanta
107	FBOS#7	Mar 2006	Turkish Gipsy ministry	Constanta
108	FBOS#8	May 2006	Asociatia Centrul Vietii Noi Brasov	Brasov
109	FBOS#9	May 2006	Asociatia Centrul Vietii Noi Brasov	Brasov
110	Pas#15	May 2006	Pastor – Brasov Christian Center	Brasov
111	FBOL#38	Jun 2006	Fundatia Toar	Sibiu

112	FBOL#70	Jun 2006	Mission without Borders	Sibiu
113	FBOS#10	Jun 2006	Mission without Borders	Sibiu
114	FBOL#71	Jun 2006	AMEC – CEF Romania	Sibiu
115	FBOL#72	Jul 2006	ROCK Ministries	Bucharest
116	FBOL#73	Dec 2007	AOG	U.S.A.

Appendix E
Key Result Areas From Survey of Churches Working with Children in Crisis

A survey was conducted in the second phase of research to evaluate key result areas (KRAs) of church-based programmes assisting children in crisis.1 This survey was conducted as a supplement to the research and to offer the churches a list of criteria that could be evaluated with little formal instruction. I visited 14 churches and the following findings were gathered through observation and limited participation.

1. Learning Environment: church classrooms for children were generally clean; if church staff had received adequate funding the class rooms were bright and well decorated. Classrooms were crowded with children who seemed interested in their activities. Children were given verbal praise for accomplishing tasks or lessons. Attendance was kept in nine of these classes.
2. Routine and Guidance: adult teachers working with children were involved and interested in the children. Most teachers followed some sort of teaching schedule; access to age appropriate education materials was a problem. The denominations in Romania have made limited investment in early child education materials; the Baptists have the most contextual curriculum. Others I examined were translated from the West and Child Evangelical Fellowship in Sibiu.
3. Boundaries for Behaviour: rules and consequences for breaking rules were understood, children were well mannered in classes or activities. The structure of Sunday school classes followed the Romanian educational model, the teacher does not facilitate discussion; instruction is rote memorization. Most classrooms for young children do not have a space for play or imaginative activities.
4. Adult-Child Interaction: conversations with teachers were open interviews. Teachers showed a high interest in the emotional and spiritual growth of children in their care. Most of the teachers are women who seemed more in tune with children than the male pastors. Ages of teachers varied from 20-60, I estimated that 1:5 had some formal training in children's ministry or education. The level of individual concern for children (especially those

[1] This assessment tool was modified from an instrument designed by Dr. Susan Greener who originally developed this tool for Compassion International (U.S.A.) and Mission of Mercy (U.S.A.).

from dysfunctional backgrounds) was high and noted as a consistent finding in this survey.

5. Parental/Caregiver Involvement: the involvement of parents was not obvious; the children were dropped at classes and picked up after services. This was noted as problematic, in the past children were taken into the adult worship services with no alternative activities, now that churches are providing programmes for children the parents did not seem involved in the activities. For the children from non-Christian families or outside programmes, if FBO staff were present (usually young adults from the church), they would take time with teachers and children to assess progress and problems.

Appendix F
Case Study Vignette:
Romanian Family Care as Extension of the Church

In the course of research, I met a number of young Romanian families like Catalin and Oltiţa Bunaciu and their four beautiful children. As I worked alongside this family, I learned that they had adopted two of their children when they worked with a small FBO in Bucharest. One of those children proved to be especially difficult. They were members of a church I attended and I asked them to describe how the church had helped them with their experience. I have shortened a series of interviews into this case vignette.

It is 1996 and winter, Bucharest can be bitterly cold in December. There are hundreds of street children and young runaways living on the streets, to escape the cold they spend their nights in the Gara de Nord (the railway station) or in the labyrinth of underground tunnels that contain the sewer and massive heating system of the city. Since the revolution in 1990, the number of homeless and street children and youth has now grown to an estimated 20,000 children. Ranging in age from infants to twenty, the majority grew up in Romania's failed child institutional system; they have learned to survive by their wits and cunning on the streets. There are very limited government social services for street children; some help is made available by NGOs and FBOs. The children and youth live in gangs, the oldest members maintaining order through violence and coercion, crime rates are high, begging, stealing, and prostitution are the surest ways to survive.

Ionuţ is three years old, his mother not yet 21 works as a prostitute, a member of a gang that specializes in both prostitution and theft. His mother abandons the boy to the gang and leaves the city; she will never see her son again. The child is sexualized and traumatized, I am certain if he had been diagnosed by a Western physician he would have been classified as undernourished and suffering from extreme attachment disorder. The boy continues to be used by the gang for begging and is passed around the gang for sexual gratification.

One day an older member of the gang takes Ionuţ with him to a drop-in shelter that offers sandwiches and a place to get out of the cold. The shelter is operated by a small FBO, *City of Hope*, at the shelter a number of young

Romanian and American volunteers spend their days providing care for street kids. Oltiţa, a young Romanian woman at the shelter notices the boy, his hair is long and full of lice, his stomach is distended and he has the look of a feral child, 'wild and crazy, not like a normal child'. She does not want to think about the boy, she has a newly born daughter at home that needs her attention but the little boy remains in her thoughts. After seeing Ionuţ at the centre a number of times, Oltiţa talks to her husband about trying to take care of the child for a few weeks, just to clean him up. This is an abridgement of our interview.

Bp: Why did you take this little boy into your home?

Oltiţa: We believed that God wanted us to try and help him; we felt we could do something but we did not know if we could help him in anything but a short term way. It did not seem right that he was so young and had been abandoned to live with this gang and be so mistreated.

Bp: What happened, why did you decide to bring him in your home?

Oltiţa: When we started, we had no idea how difficult it was going to be to try and take care of Ionuţ, he was completely out of control and he understood nothing of discipline and order. I thought we would keep him for only a few weeks, but it soon became clear that he would need more than a few weeks to help him learn to behave, I started out just wanting to teach him a few things. The next two years were the most difficult years of my life; I had to ask my mother to take care of my daughter as taking of Ionuţ took all my strength and energy. He swore, he did very vulgar things; you cannot imagine what this child was like. He had no sense of what was right and wrong, he would do things that I could not believe a young child could imagine, let alone do. Those first few months were almost impossible for me.

Bp: Did you get any professional help to learn how to take care of him; obviously he was a very troubled little boy? Did anyone from the Centre or church ask you do this?

Oltiţa: We felt this was something God was asking us to do; it was a sacrifice and it was very difficult. I wanted to give up many times, there were no social workers we could turn to; we prayed and asked God to help us. God showed us how to live through the days, it was just a matter of daily persistence and faith and we had support from our church and believing friends. I don't think anything else got me through this; people prayed for us and offered to help. I knew that God would help us and after Ionuţ had been with us for more than a few months, I could not take him back to the boy's shelter. I knew that God was helping us. We decided to adopt Ionuţ after he had been with us for about 2 years. Our faith in God helped us through this; our church is like a family… No we were not asked to do this, I would never have done this if I thought 'just a man [or organization]' was asking me to do it. The church and our faith in God were our primary resources.

Bp: How long did it take for Ionuţ to begin to behave like a more 'normal child'? Do you see signs of the trauma in his life now [he is 13 years old].

> Oltita: I think it probably took him about three or four years to recover from his experiences in the streets. He slowly learned to trust us, but it took him a long time to really believe that we were his 'parents' and family. He would go to anyone that showed him any affection but I don't think he trusted people. I believe that once he knew we were not going to leave him or abandon him, he started becoming a more 'normal child'. I think he has completely recovered now; he is very responsible boy, he takes care of his little brother and sister [her two natural children] and is making very good grades in school.

Inout was a well adjusted young Romania teenager, when I met him, I had no idea that he came from this traumatic past, he showed every sign that he will lead a 'normal life'. I used this case to illustrate how the family and church can provide a circle of care for children. The church offered emotional and spiritual support to a family that had few other resources. Their story demonstrates that faith-based care is dependent on the intervening agency of God and his church. This family continues to work with street youth in Bucharest, as directors of Teen Challenge Romania. Their focus is now children who have grown up on the streets and have become addicted to drugs and alcohol.

Bibliography

Primary Sources are listed in Appendix H and I.

Romanian Government Publications and Sources

________(1998) *Dicţionarul explicativ al limbii române [The Explanatory Dictionary of the Romanian Language]*. Bucureşti: Editura Univers Enciclopedic.

________ (2004) *Lege privind protecţia şi promovarea drepturilor copilului [Laws Concerning Protection and Promotion of Children's Rights]*, (Nr. 272/2004). Bucureşti: Official Monitor of Romania.

INSR (2004a) *Annual Statistics – 2004. Chapter 14 – Health*. Bucureşti: Institutul Naţional de Statistică – România [National Institute for Statistics – Romania].

INSR (2004b) *Population and Income, Expenditure and Consumption*. Bucureşti: Institutul Naţional de Statistică – România [National Institute for Statistics – Romania].

INSR (2005) *România în cifre [Romania in Numbers]*. Bucureşti: Institutul Naţional de Statistică – România [National Institute for Statistics – Romania], (Report).

Ministry of Health (2004) *Evolution of the HIV/AIDS Infection in Romania, between 1985-2004*. Bucureşti: National Commission on the Fight against HIV/AIDS, (Report).

Ministry of Religion (2005) *Life of the Cults – the Neoprotestant Cults*. Romanian Ministry of Religion. Available at *http://www.ministerulculturii.ro/* Accessed December 5, 2005.

NAPCR (2007) National Authority for the Protection of Child Rights Romania. Available at *http://www.copii.ro/* Accessed February 7, 2008.

Secondary Sources (Print and online)

Achim, V. (1998) *Gypsies in the History of Romania*. Bucureşti: Editura Enciclopedică.

Adeney, M. (2003) 'Culture and Planned Change' In *The Church in Response to Human Need*, Vinay, S. and Sugden, C. (eds.) (pp. 85-109). Eugene, Oregon: Wipf and Stock Publishers.

Alderson, P. (1995) *Listening to Children: Children, Ethics and Research*. Essex, U.K.: Barnardos.

Allen, R. (1962a) *Missionary Methods: St. Paul's or Ours?* Grand Rapids, MI: Eerdmans Publishing.

Allen, R. (1962b) *The Spontaneous Expansion of the Church and the Causes which Hinder It*. Grand Rapids, MI: Eerdmans Publishing.

Ames, E.W. & Carter, M. (1992) 'Development of Romanian Orphanage Children Adopted to Canada' *Canadian Psychology*, vol. 33(2):503-526.

Anderson, J. (2001) *Restoring Children of the Streets. A Guide for Mobilizing and Equipping God's People Around the World*. (3rd edn.) Manila, Philippines: Action International Ministries.

Andreiescu, V. (2001) 'A Historical and Theological Analysis of the Pentecostal Church in Romania' *The Journal of the European Pentecostal Theological Association*, vol. XXI:109-135.

Anglin, J.P. (2002) *Pain, Normality, and the Struggle for Congruence: Reinterpreting Residential Care for Children and Youth*. New York, NY: Haworth Press.

Araujo, A. (1994) 'Confidence Factors: Accountability in Christian Partnerships' In *Kingdom Partnerships for Synergy in Missions*, Taylor, W.D. (ed.) (pp. 119-130). Pasadena, CA: William Carey Library.

Araujo, A. (1996) 'Freedom and Dependency in Christian Partnerships' In *Interdev Conference* Seattle, WA: Partners International, (Unpublished Conference Paper).

Arendt, H. (1958) *The Human Condition*. Chicago, IL: University of Chicago Press.

Argyris, C. (1990) *Overcoming Organizational Defences: Facilitating Organizational Learning*. Upper Saddle River, NJ: Prentice Hall.

Argyris, C. & Schön, D.A. (1974) *Theory in Practice*. San Francisco: Jossey-Bass Publishers.

Argyris, C. & Schön, D.A. (1978) *Organizational Learning: A theory of Action Perspective*. Reading, MA: Addison Wesley.

Argyris, P. (2000) 'Orthodoxy and Evangelicalism – Areas of Convergence and Divergence' In *Conference for Eastern Orthodox Dialogue* Toronto, Can. (Unpublished Conference paper).

Ariès, P. (1962) *Centuries of Childhood: A Social History of Family Life*. New York, NY: Vintage.

Armerding, C.E. (1997) 'The Child at Risk: A Biblical View' *Transformation*, vol. 14 (2):25-26.

Ashkenas, R.; Ulrich, D.; Jick, T. & Kerr, S. (2002) *The Boundaryless Organization: Breaking the Chains of Organizational Structure*. San Francisco, CA: Jossey-Bass.

Atkinson, T. & Claxton, G., (eds.) (2003) *The Intuitive Practitioner: On the Value of Not Always Knowing What One is Doing*. Philadelphia, PA: Open University Press.

Augsburger, D. (1992) *Conflict Mediation Across Cultures*. Louisville, KY: Westminster John Knox Press.

Avarientos, E. (1996) 'Critical Factors and Standards of Children in ADPs'. Monrovia, CA: WVI Asia-Pacific Regional Office, (Internal Document).

Avery, M. (2005) *Beyond Interdependency: An Identity Based Perspective on Cooperative Inter-organizational Mission*. PhD Thesis, Fuller Theological Seminary, Faculty of the School of Intercultural Studies and Institute of Church Growth.

Bacon, W.M. (1984) 'Romania' In *Communism in Eastern Europe*, Rakowska-Harmstone, T. (ed.) (pp. 162-185). Bloomington: Indiana University Press.

Bailey, K.E. (1983) *Poet and Peasant and Through Peasant Eyes: A Literary-Cultural Approach to the Parables of Luke*. (combined edn.) Grand Rapids, MI: Eerdmans Publishing.

Balswick, J.O.; King, P.E. & Reimer, K.S. (2005) *The Reciprocating Self: Human Development in Theological Perspective*. Downers Grove, IL: InterVarsity Press.

Barbosu, C. (2004) *Legalism. Syncretism from Within*. PhD thesis (section), Deerfield, IL: Trinity Evangelical Divinity School, Intercultural Leadership.

Barnard, R. (2004) *An Examination of Dysfunctional Behaviour in Christian, Evangelical, Mission Organizations and Strategies for Managing the*

Consequences of Dysfunctional Behaviour. PhD Thesis, Open University and OCMS.

Barry, C.A. (1998) *Choosing Qualitative Data Analysis Software: Atlas.ti and Nudist Compared*. Available at *http://www.socresonline.org.uk/3/3/4.html* Accessed January 12, 2006.

Barth, K. (1936-1977) *Church Dogmatics*. Bromiley, G.W. and Torrance, T.F (eds.) Edinburgh: T. & T. Clark. (Abbreviated as CD)

Barth, K. (1960) *The Humanity of God*. Atlanta, GA: John Knox Press.

Barth, K. (1956) 'Vol. IV/1 The Doctrine of Reconciliation' In *Church Dogmatics*, Bromiley, G.W. and Torrance, T.F. (eds.) Edinburgh: T & T Clark.

Barth, K. (1963) *Evangelical Theology – An Introduction*. Grand Rapids, MI: Eerdmans Publishing.

Barth, K. (1968) *The Epistle to the Romans*. (6th edn.) Oxford: Oxford University Press.

Bass, B.M. (1990) *Bass and Stogdill's Handbook of Leadership: Theory, Research, and Managerial Applications*. (3rd edn.) New York, NY: The Free Press.

Beaver, R.P. (1970) 'The History of Mission Strategy ' *Southwestern Journal of Theology*, vol. 12 (Spring):7-28.

Bebbington, D.W. (1989) *Evangelicalism in Modern Britain: A History from the 1730s to the 1980s*. London: Unwin Hyman.

Belshaw, D. (2002) 'Towards evidence-based Strategies for Transformational Development' *Transformation*, vol. 19(April):89-82.

Ben-Arieh, A. (1999) *International Project on Indicators of Children's Well-Being*. Jerusalem: Hebrew University.

Ben-Arieh, A. (2000) 'Beyond Welfare: Measuring and Monitoring the State of Children – New Trends and Domains' *Social Indicators Research*, vol. 52(3):235-257.

Bendroth, M. (2000) 'Children of Adam, Children of God: Christian Nurture in Early Nineteenth-Century America ' *Theology Today*, vol. 56 (4):495-505.

Bendroth, M. (2001) 'Horace Bushnell's *Christian Nurture*' In *The Child in Christian Thought*, Bunge, M.J. (ed.) (pp. 350-364). Grand Rapids, MI: Eerdmans Publishing.

Berger, P. (1967) *The Sacred Canopy: Elements of a Sociological Theory of Religion*. New York, NY: Doubleday.

Bernard, R.H. (2002) *Research Methods in Anthropology: Qualitative and Quantitative Methods (*3rd edn.) Walnut Creek, CA: AltaMira Press.

Berryman, J.W. (1991) *Godly Play: An Imaginative Approach to Religious Education*. Augsburg Fortress Publishers.

Berryman, J.W. (1995) *Teaching Godly Play: The Sunday Morning Handbook*. Nashville, TN: Abingdon Press.

Berryman, J.W. (2004) 'Children and Mature Spirituality' In *Children's Spirituality*, Ratcliff, D. (ed.) (pp. 22-41). Eugene, OR: Cascade Books.

Besford, R. & Stephenson, P. (2003) 'The Churches' Ministry to Children and Their Families' In *Celebrating Children*, Miles, G. and Wright, J.J. (eds.) (pp. 143-150). Carlisle, Cumbria: Paternoster Press.

Beyerhaus,P. (1992) *God's Kingdom and the Utopian Error: Discerning the Biblical Kingdom of God from Its Political* Counterfeits. Wheaton, IL: Crossway Books

Blakeney, R.F. & Blakeney, C.D. (2005) 'Delinquency: A Quest for Moral and Spiritual Integrity?' In *The Handbook of Spiritual Development in Childhood and Adolescence*, Roehlkepartain, E.C. (eds.) (pp. 371-383). Thousand Oaks, CA: Sage Publications, Inc.

Blaxter, H.L. & Tight, M. (1984) *How to Research.* (2nd edn.) Buckingham, U.K.: Open University.

Bloesch, D.G. (1978) *Essentials of Evangelical Theology, vol. I.* San Francisco: Harper & Row Publishers.

Bogdan, R.C. & Biklen, S.K. (1992) *Qualitative Research for Education: An Introduction to Theory and Methods*. Needham, MA: Allyn and Bacon.

Bohlen, C. (1990) *Fight Against AIDS Lags in Romania.* 'New York Times International', May 9.

Boia, L. (2001) *History and Myth in Romanian Consciousness*. Budapest: Central European University Press.

Bonk, J.J. (1996) *Missions and Money: Affluence as a Western Missionary Problem.* Maryknoll, NY: Orbis Books.

Borg, M.J. & Wright, N.T. (2000) *The Meaning of Jesus: Two Visions*. San Francisco, CA: Harper Collins.

Bornstein, E. (2001) 'Child Sponsorship, Evangelism, and Belonging in the Work of World Vision Zimbabwe ' *American Ethnologist*, vol. 28 (3):595-622.

Bosch, D. (1991) *Transforming Mission: Paradigm Shifts in Theology of Mission.* Maryknoll, NY: Orbis Books.

Bosch, D. (2003) 'Toward Evangelism in Context' In *The Church in Response to Human Need*, Vinay, S. and Sugden, C. (eds.) (pp. 180-193). Eugene, Oregon: Wipf and Stock Publishers.

Bowlby, J. (1973) *Attachment and Loss: Separation, Anxiety and Anger*. New York: Basic Books.

Bowlby, J. (1998) *A Secure Base: Clinical Applications of Attachment Theory.* Paperback London: Routledge.

Bradford, J. (1995) *Caring for the Whole Child: A Holistic Approach to Spirituality.* London, U.K.: The Children's Society.

Bradshaw, B. (1993) *Bridging The Gap: Evangelism, Development and Shalom.* Monrovia, CA: MARC, World Vision Publishing.

Brant, H. (1996) 'Integrating Children's Ministry into Mission Philosophy' In *Children in Crisis: A New Commitment*, Kilbourn, P. (ed.) (pp. 103-108). Monrovia, CA: MARC Publications.

Brekus, C.A. (2001) 'Children of Wrath, Children of Grace: Jonathan Edwards and the Puritan Culture of Child Rearing' In *The Child in Christian Thought*, Bunge, M.J. (ed.) (pp. 300-328). Grand Rapids, MI: Eerdmans Publishing.

Breslau, K. (1990) 'Overplanned Parenthood: Ceauşescu's Cruel Law' *Newsweek*. Jan. 22, 1990 (pp. 33-37).

Bretherton, L. (1996) 'Chaos or Christ ' *Light and Salt*, vol. 8 (December):2-5.

Brewster, D. (1997) 'The 4/14 Window: Child Ministries and Mission Strategy' *Transformation*, vol. 14(2):18-21.

Brewster, D. (2005) *Child, Church and Mission*. Colorado Springs: Compassion International.

Briggs, C. (1986) *Learning How to Ask: A Sociolinguistic Appraisal of the Role of the Interview in Social Science Research*. Cambridge: Cambridge University Press.

Bright, J. (1995) *The Kingdom of God*. Nashville, TN: Abingdon Press.

Britton, B. (2005) *Organizational Learning in NGOs: Creating the Motive, Means, and Opportunity*. INTRAC. Available at *www.intrac.org* Accessed October 4, 2006.

Bronfenbrenner, U. (1993) 'The Ecology of Cognitive Development: Research Models and Fugitive Findings' In *Development in Context*, Wozniak, R.H. and Fischer, K.W. (eds.) (pp. 3-44). Hillsdale, NJ: Erlbaum.

Brown, C. & Brown, W. (2003) 'Progress and Challenge in Theological Education in Central and Eastern Europe' *Transformation*, vol. 20 (1):1-12.

Browning, D.S., (ed.) (1987) *Faith Development and Pastoral Care*. Philadelphia, PA: Fortress Press.

Browning, D.S.; Miller-McLemore, B.J.; Couture, P.D.; Lyon, K.B. & Franklin, R.M. (1997) *From Culture Wars to Common Ground: Religion and the American Family Debate*. Louisville, KY: John Knox Press.

Brueggemann, W. (2001) *The Prophetic Imagination*. (2nd edn.) Minneapolis: Fortress Press.

Brueggemann, W. (2004) 'Emergent Theological Converstaion with Walter Brueggemann'. All Soul's Fellowship, Decatur, GA. (Conference Proceeding) available at http://www.emergentvillage.com/weblog/walter-brueggemanns-19-theses.

Bryman, A. (1999) *Quantitative Data Analysis*. London: Routledge.

Buckland, R. (2001) *Children and the Gospel: Excellence in Ministry with Children and their Families*. Adelaide: Openbook Publishers.

Bulica, P. (2004) 'Restitutio vs. Reformatio – A Brief Comparison between the Ecclesiologies of Anabaptist and Magisterial Reformers.' In *Iosif Ton – New Horizons in Spirituality and Ministry*, Sabou, S. and Ghitea, D. (eds.), (pp.269-279) Oradea: Cartea Crestina.

Bultman, B. (1991) *Revolution by Candlelight: The Real Story behind the changes in Eastern Europe*. Portland, OR: Multnomah Publisher.

Bulzan, D. (2005) *The Status of the Evangelical Movement in Romania*. (Unpublished work).

Bunaciu, I. & Bunaciu, O. (1997) *Istoria răspândirii credinţei baptiste în România [History of the Spreading of the Baptist Faith]*. Bucureşti: Bucharest University's Publishing.

Bunaciu, O. (1997) 'Nine Baptists Beaten by Orthodox in Romania' *East-West Church Ministry Report*, vol. 5 (2):7-8.

Bunaciu, O. (2003) 'The Spiritual Life of the Believer' In *Baptists in Worship* Kiev, Ukraine, (Conference paper).

Bunge, M.J., (ed.) (2001a) *The Child in Christian Thought*. Grand Rapids: Eerdmans Publishing.

Bunge, M.J. (2001b) 'Education and the Child in Eighteenth-Century German Pietism: Perspectives from the Work of A.H. Francke' In *The Child in Christian Thought*, Bunge, M.J. (ed.) (pp. 247-278). Grand Rapids, MI: Eerdmans Publishing.

Bunge, M.J. (2004) 'Historical Perspective on Children in the Church: Resources for Spiritual Formation and a Theology of Childhood Today' In *Children's Spirituality*, Ratcliff, D. (ed.) (pp. 42-53). Eugene, OR: Cascade Books.

Bunge, M.J. (2007) 'The Vocation of Parenting: A Biblically and Theologically Informed Perspective' In *Understanding God's Heart for Children: Towards a Biblical Framework*, McConnell, D. *et al.* (eds.) (pp. 53-66). Colorado Spring, CO: Authentic.

Burch, G.W. (2005) *Community Children: A Ministry of Hope and Restoration for the Street Dwelling Child*. Miami, Florida: Latin America Mission.

Burke, M. (1995) *Child Institutionalization and Child Protection in Central and Eastern Europe*. Florence, Italy: UNICEF International Child Development Centre.

Burke, W.W. (1994) *Organizational Development: A Process of Learning and Changing.* (2nd edn.) Reading, MA: Addison-Wesley Publishing.

Bushnell, H. (1947) *Christian Nurture.* New Haven, CT: Yale University Press (orginally published 1861).

Butler, B. (1994a) 'Tensions in an International Mission' In *Kingdom Partnerships for Synergy in Missions*, Taylor, W.D. (ed.) (pp. 163-173). Pasadena, CA: William Carey Library.

Butler, P. (1994b) 'Kingdom Partnerships in the '90s: Is There a New Way Forward?' In *Kingdom Partnerships for Synergy in Missions*, Taylor, W.D. (ed.) (pp. 9-31). Pasadena, CA: William Carey Library.

Byrd, B. (1993) 'Missionary to Romania Criticizes Western Short Term Evangelism There' *East-West Church Ministry Report*, vol. 1 (4):9-10.

Byworth, J. (2003) 'World Vision's Approach to Transformational Development: Frame, Policy and Indicators ' *Transformation*, vol. 20 (2):99-111.

Campbell, D.T. & Stanley, J.C. (1963) *Experimental and Quasi-Experimental Designs for Research.* Chicago: Rand McNally.

Cantwell, N. (2005) 'Violence against Children without Parental Care' *Global Future*, Third Quarter:10-11.

Carey, W. (1981) 'An Enquiry into the Obligation of Christians to Use Means for the Conversion of the Heathens (1792, excerpts)' In *Perspectives on the World Christian Movement*, (pp. 227-236). Pasadena, CA: William Carey Library.

Carrescia, O. (2000) *Diamonds in the Dark.* Brooklyn, NY: Icarus Films. Available for order at *http://www.frif.com/new2000/diam.html* Accessed August 20, 2004.

Carson, D.A. (2005) 'Maintaining Scientific and Christian Truths in a Postmodern World' In *Can We Be Sure about Anything?* Alexander, D. (ed.) (pp. 103-125). Leicester, U.K.: Apollos.

Carter, R. (2001) *The Silent Crisis: Children in Poverty in Central and Eastern Europe and the Former Soviet Union.* Available at *http://www.samford.edu/groups/global/ ChildrenatRisk/Carter.html* Accessed June, 10 2005.

Carver, J. (1997) *Boards That Make a Difference. A New Design for Leadership in Non-profit and Public Organizations.* San Francisco: Jossey-Bass Publishers.

Cavalletti, S. (1992) *The Religious Potential of The Child: Experiencing Scripture and Literature with Young Children.* Chicago, IL: Liturgy Training Publications.

Ceauşescu, N. (1980) *Creşterea rolului femeii în viaţa economică şi social-politică a României socialiste [Increasing the Role of Women in the Economic, Social and Political Life of Socialist Romania].* Bucureşti: Editura Politică.

Cernat, P.; Manolescu, I.; Mitchievici, A. & Stanomir, I. (2004) *A Lost World. Four Personal Histories, Followed by a Dialogue with H R. Patapievici.* Iaşi: Editura Polirom.

Ceuţă, I. (2002) *Mişcarea penticostală. În evenimente şi relatări ale secolului XX [Pentecostal Movement. Events and Accounts from the 20th Century].* Bucureşti: Editura Lumina Lumii.

Chambers, R. (1997) *Whose Reality Counts? Putting the First Last.* London, U.K.: Intermediate Technology Publications.

Chapin, H.D. (1917) 'Systematized Boarding Out vs. Institutional Care for Infants and Young Children' *New York Medical Journal*, vol. 105:1009-1011.

Christian, J. (1994) *Powerless of the Poor: Toward an Alternative Kingdom of God Based Paradigm of Response.* Pasadena, CA: Fuller Theological Seminary, Ph.D. thesis.

Christian, J. (1999) *God of the Empty-Handed: Poverty, Power and the Kingdom of God*. Christian, J. Monrovia, CA: MARC.

Chronic, D. (2005) 'The Fruit of our Labour' *The Cry: The Advocacy Journal of World Made Flesh*, vol. 11 (1):14-18.

Chronic, D. (2006) *What Do We Mean by the Church*. Word Made Flesh. Available at *http://www.wordmadeflesh.com/learn/the_cry-suggestedreading.html* Accessed October 10, 2007.

Clendenin, B.D. (1995) *Eastern Orthodox Theology: A Contemporary Reader*. Grand Rapids, MI: Baker Academic.

Clinton, J.R. (1999) *Biblical Leadership Commentary: Leadership Insights from Old and New Testament*. Altadena, CA: Barnabas Publishers.

Clinton, J.R. & Clinton, R.W. (1991) *The Mentor Handbook: Detailed Guidelines and Helps for Christian Mentors and Mentorees*. Altadena, CA: Barnabas Publishers.

Cockburn, A. (1991) 'Street Children: An Overview of the Extent, Causes, Characteristics and Dynamics of the Problem' *The Child Care Worker*, vol. 9 (1):12-13.

Codreanu, M. (2002) 'The Pentecostal Phenomenon in Romania after World War I' In *New International Dictionary of Pentecostal and Charismatic Movements*, Burgess, S.M. *et al.* (eds.) (pp. 212-17). Zondervan.

Codrescu, A. (1991) *The Hole in the Flag: A Romanian Exile's Story of Return and Revolution*. New York, NY: William Morrow & Co.

Cohen, R. & Chetley, A. (1994) *Why Children Matter; Investing in Early Childhood Care and Development*. NL: Bernard Van Leer Foundation.

Coles, R. (1990) *The Spiritual Life of Children*. Boston, MA: Houghton Mifflin Company.

Coles, R. (2000) *The Moral Life of Children*. New York, NY: Atlantic Monthly Press.

Collier, J. (2004) *Report of the Cape Town Consultation on Child Theology*. Cape Town, SA: Child Theology Movement, (Consultation report).

Collins, J. (2005) *Good to Great and the Social Sectors: A Monograph to Accompany Good to Great*. New York, NY: Harper Collins Publishing.

Colson, C.W. (1992) *The Body: Being Light in the Darkness*. Dallas: Word Publishing.

Constantin, A.C. (2000) *"Decretzei": A Euphemism for a Tragic Situation (Decree 770/1966). Or: Propaganda vs. Black Humour*, (MA Thesis).

Cookingham, F. (1989) 'Value conflicts in sponsorship and development' *Together*, vol. 22 (April-June):12-15.

Cooley, R. (2005) *The Exemplary Board*. Board Seminar for Bucharest Bible University, (Board Training Seminar Paper).

Cooperrider, D.L. & Srivastva, S. (1987) 'Appreciative Inquiry in Organizational Life' *Research in Organizational Change and Development*, vol. 1:129-69.

Costas, O. (1984) *Christ Outside the Gate*. Maryknoll, NY: Orbis Books.

Costas, O. (1986) 'Proclaiming Christ in the Two-Thirds World' In *Sharing Jesus in the Two-Thirds World*, Samuel, V. and Sugden, C. (eds.) (pp. 2-16). Grand Rapids: Eerdmans Publishing.

Costin-Sima, D. & Cace, S. (eds.) (2003) *The Street Between Fascination and Slavery*. Bucureşti: UNICEF, Echosoc.

Cotrau, D. (2003) 'Linguistic Encoding of Youth Ideology by the Romanian Teen Magazines for Girls.' University of Cluj, Romania: Faculty of Letters. Available at *http://jsri.ro/old/html%20version/index/no_6/dianacotrau-articol.htm* Accessed October 2007.

Covaleskie, J.F. (1996) *Moral Reflection and Moral Education*. Philosophy of Education, University of Chicago. Available at *http://www.ed.uiuc.edu/EPS/PES-Yearbook/96_docs/covaleskie.html* Accessed June 13, 2006.

Covrig, A. (2004) 'Why Roma do not Declare their Identity – Careful Decision or Unpremeditated Refusal?' *Journal for the Study of Religions and Ideologies*, vol. 23 (8):23-36.

Cowger, C.D. (1994) 'Assessing Client Strengths: Clinical Assessment for Client Empowerment' *Social Work*, vol. 39(3):262-268.

Cox, C. (1996) 'Embracing Compassion and Fatigue' In *Compassion and Fatigue: The Washington Forum* Federal Way, WA, (WVI Published Conference Proceeding).

Craig, G. (2000) *What Works in Community Development with Children?* Ilford, U.K.: Barnardo's.

Crocker, G. (2001) *Total Quality of Charitable Service: Profiles of Excellence in Christian Relief and Development Organizations*. PhD Dissertation, Centre for Leadership Studies, Regent University, VA.

Crocker, G. (2002) 'Organizational Integrity and Ministry Success' In *Hearing God's Heart for Children VIVA International Cutting Edge 4* De Bron Netherlands, (Conference paper).

Cunningham, H. (2005) *Children and Childhood in Western Society since 1500*. (2nd edn.) New York, NY: Pearson Longman.

Currie, C. & Commins, S. (2002) *Focused Especially on the Well-Being of Children: An Integrated Paradigm for Transformation.* Monrovia, CA: World Vision International.

Curtis, P. (2004) *Under the Influence? Local NGOs and Discourse in Post-Communist Societies*. M. Sc. Thesis, London: London School of Economics and Political Science, Department of Social Policy.

Davies, R. (1991) *After Gorbachev. How Can Western Christians Help?* Eastbourne, East Sussex: Missions Advanced Research and Communication (MARC).

Dawn, M.J. (1999) 'Until Christ is Formed in You: Nurturing the Spirituality of Children' *Theology Today*, vol. 56 (1):73-85.

Dayton, R.E. & Fraser, A.D. (1980) *Planning Strategies for World Evangelization*. Grand Rapids, MI: Eerdmans Publishing.

De Pree, M. (1997) *Leading without Power: Finding Hope in Serving Community*. San Francisco, CA: Jossey-Bass Inc.

Dean, K.C. (2000) 'Proclaiming Salvation: Youth Ministry for the Twenty-First Century Church' *Theology Today*, vol. 56 (4):524-539.

Deletant, D. (1996) *Ceauşescu and the Securitate: Coercion and Dissent in Romania, 1965-1989*. Armonk, NY: M.E. Sharpe.

Deletant, D. (1999) *Romania under Communist Rule*. Oxford, U.K.: The Centre for Romanian Studies.

Dempster, M.W. (1999) 'Social concern in the context of Jesus' kingdom, mission and ministry' *Transformation*, vol. 16 (2):43-53.

Dempster, M.W.; Klaus, B.D. & Petersen, D., (eds.) (1999) *The Globalization of Pentecostalism*. Carlisle, U.K.: Regnum Books International.

Dent, S.M. (1999) *Partnering Intelligence*. Palo Alto, CA: Davies-Black Publishing.

Denzin, N.K. & Lincoln, Y.S. (eds.) (2003) *Collecting and Interpreting Qualitative Materials,* (2nd edn.) Thousand Oaks, CA: Sage Publications.

Derbyshire, M. (2001) *Voice in the Streets: A Handbook for Multi-stage Ministry to Street Children*. Oxford, U.K.: Viva Network.

DeVries, D. (2001a) '"Be Converted and Become as Little Children": Friedrich Schleiermacher on the Religious Significance of Childhood' In *The Child in Christian Thought*, Bunge, M.J. (ed.) (pp. 329-349). Grand Rapids, MI: Eerdmans Publishing.

DeVries, D. (2001b) 'Toward a Theology of Childhood ' *Interpretation*, April:161-173.

Dickens, J. (1999) 'Protecting the Rights of the Child in Romania: Children's Rights Perspectives on Romania's 1997 Childcare Reforms' *European Journal of Social Work*, vol. 2(2):139-150.

Dickens, J. & Groza, V. (2004) 'Empowerment in Difficulty' *International Social Work*, vol. 47 (4):469-487.

Dickens, J. & Watts, J. (1996) 'Developing Alternatives to Residential Care in Romania' *Adoption and Fostering*, vol. 20 (3):8-13.

Dobrincu, D. (1999) 'The Church History and the Danger of a Denominational Approach to the Research ' *Xenopoliana*, vol. VII (:3-4)

Dobrincu, D. (2001) 'We Have Come so Far by Grace. How the Church in Romania Has Grown Until the Present' In *Report on the State of the Evangelical Churches in Romania 2001*, (pp. 6-17). Bucharest: OCI International.

Dobrincu, D. (2003) 'Religious Freedom and Dispute in the Romania of Ceauşescu: the Romanian Committee for the Defence of the Religious Freedom and the Freedom of Consciousness (ALRC)' *Sighet's Annals*, vol. 10:203-227.

Dobrincu, D. (2005) 'Richard Wurmbrand's Tours to Great Britain and their International Echoes (1968-1972)' In *Romania and Britain: Relations and Perspectives from 1930 to the Present* Bucharest, (Published Conference proceeding).

Dobrisan, C. & Kachelmyer, J. (2002) *Odyssey of a Romanian Street Child*. Lake Mary, FL: Creation House Press.

Donaldson, M. (1978) *Understanding Children*. Glasgow: Fontana Press.

Downes, D. (2001) 'Planting Relevant Churches in a New Social Context' In *God's Heart for Romania*, (pp. 38-47). Bucureşti: OCI International.

Drisko, W.J. (2004) 'Case Study Research' In *The Qualitative Research Experience*, Padgett, K.D. (ed.) (pp. 100-121). Belmont, CA: Thomson Books/Cole.

Drucker, P. (1990) *Managing the Non-Profit Organization*. New York, NY: Harpers Collins.

Dyrness, W.A. (1983) *Let the Earth Rejoice: A Biblical Theology of Holistic Mission*. Westchester, U.K.: Crossway Books.

Eade, D. (1997) *Capacity-Building: An Approach to People-Centered Development (Oxfam Development Guidelines)*. Oxford, U.K.: Oxfam Publications.

Eastman, M. (1997) 'The Child and the Kingdom' *Transformation*, vol. 14 (2):24-25.

Edwards, M. (1996) 'New Approaches to Children and Development: Introduction and Overview' *Journal of International Development*, vol. 8 (6):813-27.

Edwards, M. & Hulme, D. (eds.) (1998) *Non-Governmental Organizations – Performance and Accountability: Beyond the Magic Bullet*. London, U.K.: Earthscan Publications Ltd.

Eliade, M. (1943) *The Romanians: A Concise History*. Madrid, ES: Stylos.

Eliade, M. (1991) *History of Religious Beliefs and Ideas*. Bucureşti: Editura Ştiinţifică.

Elliott, C. (1998) *Locating the Energy for Change: an Introduction to Appreciative Inquiry*. Cambridge, U.K.: International Institute for Sustainable Development.

Elliott, M. (1996) 'East European Missions, Perestroika, and Orthodox-Evangelical Tensions' *Journal of Ecumenical Studies*, vol. 33 (1):9-20.

Elmer, D.H. (1993) *Cross-Cultural Conflict: Building Relationships for Effective Ministry*. Grove, IL: InterVarsity Press.

Engel, J.F. & Dyrness, W.A. (2000) *Changing the Mind of Missions: Where Have We Gone Wrong?* Downers Grove, IL: InterVarsity Press.

Ennew, J. (1994) 'Parentless Friends: A Cross-Cultural examination of Networks among Street Children and Street Youth' In *Social Networks and Social Support in Childhood and Adolescence*, Nestman, F. and Hurrelman, K. (eds.) (pp. 409-428). New York: Aldine de Gruyter.

Ennew, J. (2000) *Street and Working Children: A Guide to Planning*. London: Save the Children.

Ennew, J. & Stephenson, P. (2004) *Questioning the Basis of our Work: Christianity, Children's Rights and Development*. London: Tearfund and Black on White Publications.

Erickson, E.H. (1963) *Childhood and Society*. (2nd edn.) New York, NY: Norton.

Escobar, S. (1991) 'Missiology in the Lausanne Movement' *Transformation*, vol. 8 (4):7-13.

Eskridge, L. & Noll, M.A. (eds.) (2000) *More Money, More Ministry: Money and Evangelicals in North American History*. Grand Rapids, MI: Eerdmans Publishing.

Evans, D. (2002) 'The Strategic Role of the Church for Children' In *Hearing God's Heart for Children VIVA International Cutting Edge 4* De Bron Netherlands, (Conference paper).

Farson, R. & Crichton, M. (1997) *Management of the Absurd: Paradoxes in Leadership*. New York, NY: Simon and Schuster.

Fiddes, P.S. (2000) *Participating in God*. Louisville, KY: Westminster John Knox Press.

Fieldler, K. (1997) *Story of Faith Mission*. Oxford, U.K.: Regnum Books.

Fischer, R.L. (2003) 'The Devil is in the Details: Implementing Outcome Measurement in Faith-Based Organizations 'In *The Role of Faith-Based Organizations in the Social Welfare System* Washington, D.C. (Published Conference Proceeding).

Flanigan, S.T. & Nicholas, B.R. (2003) 'Representing Romanian Children as Stakeholders in the Democratic Process: the Perspectives of Street Children and NGOs'. Save the Children, Romania. Bucureşti (Published Research Paper).

Fonseca, I. (1995) *Bury Me Standing: The Gypsies and Their Journey*. Toronto, Ontario: Random House of Canada Ltd.

Fowler, A. (2001) *The Virtuous Spiral: A Guide to Sustainability for NGOs in International Development*. London, U.K.: Earthscan Publications Ltd.

Fowler, J. (1981) *Stages of Faith: The Psychology of Human Development and the Quest for Meaning*. San Francisco, CA: Harper & Row Publishing.

Freire, P. (1994) *Pedagogy of Hope*. New York, NY: Continuum.

Frost, K.M. & Frost, C.J. (2000) 'Romanian and American Life Aspirations in Relation to Psychological Well-Being' *Journal of Cross-Cultural Psychology*, vol. 31 (6):726-752.

Garbarino, J. (2005) 'Violent Boys – How We Can Save Them?' *Global Future*, Third Quarter:15-16.

Geertz, C. (1973) *The Interpretation of Cultures*. New York, NY: Basic Books.

Gheorghiu, E.I. (2003) 'Religiosity and Christianity in Post-Communist Romania' *Sociologie Românească [Romanian Sociology]*, vol. 1 (3):102-121.

Ghitea, D. (2004) 'Joseph Ţon's Biography' In *Iosif Ţon – New Horizons in Spirituality and Ministry* Sabou, S. and Ghitea, D. (eds.), (pp. 9-32). Oradea: Cartea Creştină.

Gibson, D. (1993) 'Evangelical Alliances: They Make Common Cause and Common Sense' *East-West Church Ministry Report*, vol. 1 (2):3-4

Gillet, O. (2001) *Religion and Nationalism*. Bucureşti: Editura Compania.

Glaser, B.G. & Strauss, A.L. (1967) *The Discovery of Grounded Theory: Strategies for Qualitative Research*. London: Weidenfeld and Nicholson.

Glasser, A.F. (1981) 'The Apostle Paul and the Missionary Task' In *Perspectives on the World Christian Movement*, Winter, R.D. and Hawthorne, S.C. (eds.) (pp. 104-112). Pasadena, CA: William Carey Library.

Gourley, S. (2003) 'Involving Children in Programme and Policy Planning' In *Celebrating Children*, Miles, G. and Wright, J.J. (eds.) (pp. 89-93). Carlisle, Cumbria: Paternoster Press.

Grams, G.R. (2004) 'Not 'Leaders' but "Little Ones" in the Father's Kingdom: the Character of Discipleship in Mathew's Gospel' *Transformation*. vol. 21 (2):114-125.

Granqvist, P. & Dickie, J.R. (2005) 'Attachment and Spiritual Development in Childhood and Adolescence' In *Handbook of Spiritual Development in Childhood and Adolescence*, Roehlkepartain, E.C. *et al.* (eds.) (pp. 197-210). Thousand Oaks, CA: Sage Publications, Inc.

Gray, L.; Paul, R. & Whaites, A. (1996) *The Commercial Exploitation of Street Children*. Milton Keynes, U.K.: World Vision United Kingdom Policy and Research Department.

Greener, S. (2003a) 'The Effects of Failure to Meet Children's Needs' In *Celebrating Children*, Miles, G. and Wright, J.J. (eds.) (pp. 127-135). Carlisle, Cumbria: Paternoster Press.

Greener, S. (2003b) 'Factors that Optimize Development' In *Celebrating Children*, Miles, G. and Wright, J.J. (eds.) (pp. 40-47). Carlisle, Cumbria: Paternoster Press.

Greenleaf, R.K. (1977) *Servant Leadership – A Journey into the Nature of Legitimate Power and Greatness*. New York: Paulist Press.

Greenway, R. (1998) *Together Again: Kinship of Word and Deed*. Monrovia, CA: MARC.

Grenz, S.J. (2000) *Theology for the Community of God*. Grand Rapids, MI: Eerdmans Publishing.

Griffiths, E. (2007) 'Romania's Lost Children'. CNN Special Reports. Available at *http://www.cnn.com/2007/WORLD/europe/02/16/untold.stories/index.html?iref=newssearch* Accessed February 14, 2008.

Grigg, V. (1990) *Companion to the Poor*. Monrovia, CA: MARC.

Groza, V. (1999) 'U.S. Policy Promotes Institutionalization of Children in Romania'. Case Western University School of Applied Social Science. Available at *http://msass.case.edu/faculty/vgroza/international/adoption/uspolicy.htm* Accessed September 20, 2005.

Groza, V.; Ileana, D. & Irwin, I. (1999) *A Peacock or a Crow? Stories, Interviews and Commentaries on Romanian Adoptions*. Euclid, Ohio: Williams Custom Publishing.

Groza, V. & Rosenberg, K.F. (2001) *Clinical Practice Issues in Adoption: Bridging the Gap Between Adoptees Places as Infants and as Older Children*. Westport, CT: Bergin & Garvey Publishers.

Groza, V.; Ryan, S.D. & Cash, S.J. (2003) 'Institutionalization, Behaviour and International Adoption: Predictors of Behaviour Problems' *Journal of Immigrant Health*, vol. 5(1):5-17.

Gundry-Volf, J. (2000) 'To Such As These Belongs the Reign of God: Jesus and Children' *Theology Today*, vol. 56 (4):469-80.

Gundry-Volf, J. (2001) 'The Least and the Greatest: Children and in the New Testament' In *The Child in Christian Thought*, Bunge, M.J. (ed.) (pp. 29-65). Grand Rapids, MI: Eerdmans Publishing.

Guroian, V. (2001) 'The Ecclesial Family: John Chrysostom on Parenthood' In *The Child in Christian Thought*, Bunge, M.J. (ed.) (pp. 61-77). Grand Rapids, MI: Eerdmans Publishing.

Guthrie, S. (1998) 'Children at Risk: The Biggest Little Mission Field in the World? ' *Evangelical Missions Quarterly*, vol. XIV:88-94.

Hagberg, J.O. (2003) *Real Power: Stages of Power in Personal Organizations*. (3rd edn.) Salem, WI: Sheffield Publishing.

Ham, K. (1996) 'Reaching out to Russian Youth in Crisis' *East-West Church Ministry Report*, vol. 4 (2):3-4.

Hammersley, M. & Atkinson, P. (1983) *Ethnography: Principles in Practice*. New York: Tavistock.

Hammond, S.A. (1996) *The Thin Book of Appreciative Inquiry*. Bend, OR: Thin Book Publishing Co.

Harakas, S. (1977) 'The Local Church: An Eastern Orthodox Perspective'. *The Ecumenical Review*, vol. 29(2):141-153.

Harder, K. (2002) Personal Interview on International FBOs. Colorado Springs, CO

Hardiman, D., (ed.) (2006) *Healing Bodies, Saving Souls: Medical Missions in Asia and Africa*. New York, NY: Editions Rodopi BV.

Harris, H.A. (1998) *Fundamentalism and Evangelicals*. Oxford: Clarendon Press.

Harris, M.J. (2000) 'Guidelines for Contextualizing the Gospel for Russian Youth' *East-West Church Ministry Report*, vol. 8 (1):3-5.

Harrison, N.V. (2000) 'Raising Them Right: Early Christian Approaches To Child Rearing' *Theology Today*, vol. 56 (4):481-94.

Harty, H.; Van Houten, T.; Plantz, M. & Greenway, M. (1996) *Measuring Program Outcomes: A Practical Approach*. Alexandria, VA: United Way of America.

Hauerwas, S. (1981) *A Community of Character: Towards a Constructive Christian Social Ethic*. Notre Dame: University of Notre Dame Press.

Hay, D. & Nye, R. (1998) *The Spirit of the Child*. London, U.K.: Fount Harper Collins.

Hays, R.B. (1996) *The Moral Vision of the New Testament: Community, Cross, New Creation – A Contemporary Introduction to New Testament Ethics*. Edinburgh, U.K.: T&T Clark Ltd.

Heifetz, R.A. (1994) *Leadership Without Easy Answers*. Cambridge, MA: Belknap Press.

Heitmann, K. (2001) 'The Personality Cult of Nicolae Ceauşescu'. *Revista,* vol. 6 (22):10-12.

Heitzenrater, R.P. (2001) 'John Wesley and Children' In *The Child in Christian Thought*, Bunge, M.J. (ed.) (pp. 279-299). Grand Rapids, MI: Eerdmans Publishing.

Hendricks, W.L. (1980) *A Theology for Children*. Dallas, TX: Baptist Publishing Board.

Hendry, G.S. (1976) *The Holy Spirit in Christian Theology*. London: SCM Press Ltd.

Hesselgrave, D.J. (1991) *Communicating Christ Cross-Culturally*. Grand Rapids, MI: Zondervan Publishing House.

Hesselgrave, D.J. (1999) 'Refining Holism' *Evangelical Missions Quarterly*, vol. 35 (3):278-284.

Heuser, R., (ed.) (1999) *Leadership & Team Building. Transforming Congregational Ministries through Teams*. Matthews, NC: CMR Press.

Hiebert, P.G. (1978) 'Conversion, Culture and Cognitive Categories' *Gospel in Context*, vol. 1 (4):44-57.

Hiebert, P.G. (1985) *Cultural Anthropology*. (2nd edn.) Grand Rapids, MI: Baker Book House.

Hiebert, P.G. (1987) 'Critical Contextualization' *International Bulletin of Missions Research*, vol. 11 (3):34-45.

Hocken, P.D. (1991) 'The Challenge of Non-Denominational Charismatic Christianity' In *Experiences of the Spirit: Conference on Pentecostal and Charismatic Research in Europe at Utrecht University, 1989* Jongeneel, J. (ed.) (pp. 221-238). New York: Peter Lang.

Hodges, M. (1976) *The Indigenous Church*. Springfield, MO: Gospel Publishing House.

Hoekendijk, J.C. (1967) *The Church Inside Out*. London: SCM Press Ltd.

Hofstede, G. (1997) *Cultures and Organizations: Software of the Mind*. New York, NY: McGraw-Hill.

Horner, K. (1991) 'Building a New Framework for Romania's Throwaway Children ' *Together*, vol. 32:14-15.

Howard, D.A. (1981) 'Student Power in World Mission' In *Perspectives on the World Christian Movement*, Winter, R.D. and Hawthorne, S.C. (eds.) (pp. 210-222). Pasadena, CA: William Carey Library.

Huberman, M.A. & Miles, B.M. (1994) 'Data Management and Analysis Methods' In *Handbook of Qualitative Research*, Denzin, N.K. and Lincoln, Y.S. (eds.) (pp. 428-444). Thousand Oaks, CA: Sage Publications.

Hunsinger, G. (2000) 'Karl Barth's Christology: Its Basic Chalcedonian Character' In *The Cambridge Companion to Karl Barth*, Webster, J. (ed.) (pp. 127-142). Cambridge: Cambridge University Press.

Ionescu, M. & Oprea-Teodorescu, G. (1994) *History of the Brethren in Romania – the 1899-1945 period)*. (Manuscript).

Issler, K. (2004) 'Biblical Perspectives on Developmental Grace for Nurturing Children's Spirituality' In *Children's Spirituality*, Ratcliff, D. (ed.) (pp. 54-71). Eugene, OR: Cascade Books.

James, R. (2004) *Reflections on Current Thinking on Spirituality in Organisations: Contribution to a Discussion*. Sundbyberg, Sweden: Swedish Mission Council.

Jayakaran, R. (1999) 'Holistic Participatory Learning and Action: Seeing the Spiritual and Whose Reality Counts' In *Working with the Poor: New Insights and Learning from Development Practitioners*, Myers, B. (ed.) (pp. 31-38). Monrovia, CA: MARC.

Jenkins, P. (2002) *The Next Christendom*. Oxford: Oxford University Press.

Jigau, M.; Surdu, M.; Balica, M.; Fartusnic, C.; Horga, I. & Surdu, L. (2002) *The Participation and Education of Roma Children*. The Institute for Research on the Quality of Life, Bucharest: UNICEF.

Johnson, A. & Groza, V. (1993) 'The Orphaned and Institutionalised Children of Romania' *Journal of Emotional and Behavioural Problems*, vol. 2 (4):49-52.

Johnson, A.K.; Edwards, R.L. & Puwak, H.C. (1993) 'Foster Care and Adoption Policy in Romania: Suggestions for International Intervention' *Child Welfare*, vol. 72 (5):489-506.

Johnson, A.R. (2006) *Leadership in a Bangkok Slum: An Ethnography of Thai Urban Poor in the Lang Wat Pathum Wanaram Community*. PhD Thesis, University of Wales, Oxford Centre for Mission Studies.

Johnson, B.R.; Tompkins, R.B. & Webb, D. (2002) *Objective Hope: Assessing the Effectiveness of Faith-Based Organizations: A Review of the Literature.* Washington, DC: Centre for Research on Religion and Urban Civil Society.

Johnson, S. & Ludema, J.D. (1997) *Partnering to Build and Measure Organizational Capacity: Lessons from NGOs around the World.* Grand Rapids, MI: Christian Reformed World Relief Committee.

Johnson, V.; Ivan-Smith, E.; Gordon, G.; Pridmore, P.; Scott, P. & Johnson, V. (eds.) (1998) *Stepping Forward: Children and Young People's Participation in the Development Process*. London, U.K.: Intermediate Technology Publications.

Jones, E.S. (1972) *The Unchanging Person and the Unshakeable Kingdom*. New York, NY: Abingdon Press.

Jones, M.O.; Moore, M.D. & Snyder, R.C., (eds.) (1988) *Inside Organizations: Understanding the Human Dimension*. Newbury Park: Sage Publications.

Jones, P. (1991) 'Ministering to Street Children ' *Together*, vol. 32:3-5.

Jones, S.L. & Yarhouse, M.A. (2000) *Homosexuality: The Use of Scientific Research in the Church's Moral Debate*. Downers Grove, IL: InterVarsity Press.

Kail, R.V. (2000) *Children and Their Development*. Princeton, NJ: Prentice Hall College Division.

Kaplan, R.D. (1994) *Balkan Ghosts – A Journey Through History*. New York: Vintage Departure.

Kearns, K.P.; Krasman, R.J. & Meyer, W.J. (1994) 'Why Non-Profits are Ripe for the Total Quality Management' *Non-profit Management & Leadership*, vol. 4:447-460.

Kellerman, B. (2004) *Bad Leadership: What it Is, How it Happens, Why it Matters*. Boston, MA: Harvard Business School Press.

Keppeler, T. (1992) Oastea Domnului: The Army of the Lord in Romania. *Religion, State and Society*, vol. 21 (2):221-227.

Keppeler, T.J. (1996) *Beliefs and Assumptions about the Nature of the Church and its Leadership: a Romanian Case Study*. PhD Dissertation, Deerfield, Illinois: Trinity International University, International Studies.

Kilbourn, P. (ed.) (1996) *Children in Crisis: A New Commitment*. Monrovia, CA: MARC Publications.

Kilbourn, P. (ed.) (1997) *Street Children: A Guide to Effective Ministry*. Monrovia, CA: MARC Publications.

Kilbourn, P. & McDermid, M. (eds.) (1998) *Sexually Exploited Children: Working to Protect and Heal*. Monrovia, CA: MARC Publications.

Kirk, J.A. (2000) *What is Mission? Theological Explorations*. Minneapolis, MN: Fortress Press.

Klaus, B.D. (1997) 'Historical and Theological Reflection on Ministry to Children at Risk' *Transformation*, vol. 14 (2):15-18.

Kligman, G. (1998) *The Politics of Duplicity: Controlling Reproduction in Ceauşescu's Romania*. Berkley, CA: University of California Press.

Kohlberg, L. (1981) *The Philosophy of Moral Development: Moral Stages and the Idea of Justice*. New York: Harper Collins Publishing.

Korten, D.C. (1990) *Getting to the 21st Century: Voluntary Action and the Global Agenda*. West Hartford, CT: Kumarian Press, Inc.

Kotter, J.P. (1996) *Leading Change*. Boston, MA: Harvard Business School Press.

Kouzes, J.M. & Posner, B.Z. (1997) *The Leadership Challenge. How to Keep Getting Extraordinary Things Done in Organizations*. San Francisco, CA: Jossey-Bass Publishers.

Kraakevik, J.H. & Welliver, D. (eds.) (1992) *Partners in the Gospel: The Strategic Role of Partnership in World Evangelization*. Wheaton, IL: Billy Graham Centre.

Kraft, C.H. (1979) *Christianity in Culture: A Study in Dynamic Biblical Theologizing in Cross-Culture Perspective*. Maryknoll, NY: Orbis Books.

Kraft, C.H. (1990) *Christianity with Power: Your Worldview and Your Experience of the Supernatural*. Ann Arbor, MI: Servant Publications.

Kraybill, D., B. (1978) *The Upside-Down Kingdom*. Scottdale, PA: Herald Press.

Küng, H. (1976) *The Church*. Garden City, New York: Image Books.

Kusnierik, J. (1996) 'Struggling with the Past – Evangelicals in Post Communist Europe' *Light and Salt*, vol. 8 (December):4-5.

Kuzmic, P. (1991) 'Pentecostals Respond to Marxism' In *Called & Empowered: Global Mission in Pentecostal Perspective*, Dempster, M.W. *et al.* (eds.) (pp. 143-64). Peabody, MA: Hendrickson Publishers.

Kuzmic, P. (1999) 'Twelve Theses on Kingdom Servanthood for Post Communist Europe' *Transformation*, vol. 16 (1):34-40.

LaBreche, A.A. (2007) *Ethnocentrism – U.S. American Evangelical Missionaries in Romania: Qualitative Missiological Research into Representative Cross-Cultural Value Based Conflicts*. PhD Thesis, Leuven, Belgium: University of Utrecht, Theology.

Ladd, G.E. (1974) *A Theology of the New Testament*. Grand Rapids, MI: Eerdmans Publishing.

Ladd, G.E. (1996) *Jesus and the Kingdom*. London, U.K.: SPCK.

Lansdown, G. (2003) 'Disabled Children in Romania' In *Progress in Implementing the Convention on the Rights of the Child* London, (Published Conference paper).

Latourette, S.K. (1971) *A History of the Expansion of Christianity vol. 7. Advance through Storm: 1914 and After*. Exeter: Paternoster.

LeCompte, M.D. (1999) *Designing & Conducting Ethnographic Research*. Walnut Creek, CA: AltaMira Press.

Lieuwen, D. (1998) *Finding Common Ground between Orthodox and Protestants: Partial Resolution of Protestant Difficulties with Orthodox Theology*. Available at *http://www.orthodox.net/faq/protobje.htm* Accessed May 15, 2005.

Lingenfelter, S. & Mayers, M.K. (1986) *Ministering Cross-Culturally*. Grand Rapids, MI: Baker Books.

Lingenfelter, S.G. (1996) *Agents of Transformation: A Guide for Effective Cross-Cultural Ministry*. Grand Rapids, MI: Baker Books.

Linthicum, R.C. (1991) *Empowering the Poor: Community Organizing among the City's "rag, tag and bobtail."* Monrovia: MARC, World Vision.

Loder, J.E. (1998) *The Logic of the Spirit: Human Development in Theological Perspective*. San Francisco: Jossey-Bass Publishers.

Lofland, J. & Lofland, L.H. (1995) *Analyzing Social Settings: A Guide to Qualitative Observation and Analysis*. (3rd edn.) Belmont, CA: Wadsworth.

Lord, A. (2003) 'The Pentecostal-Moltmann Dialogue: Implications for Mission' *Journal of Pentecostal Theology*, vol. 11 (2):271-287.

Lucian, O. (2007) *The Development of Youth Ministries in the Romanian Pentecostal Movement: Peniel Ministry Case Study*. MA Thesis, Brussels: Continental Theological Seminary, Theology.

Maachia, F.D. (1999) 'The Struggle for Global Witness: Shifting Paradigms in Pentecostal Theology' In *The Globalization of Pentecostalism*, Dempster, M.W. *et al.* (eds.) (pp. 8-29). Carlisle, U.K.: Regnum Books International.

Maas, R. (2000) 'Christ as the Logos of Childhood: Reflections on the Meaning and Mission of the Child ' *Theology Today*, vol. 56 (1):456-468.

MacDonald, G. & Winkley, A. (1999) *What Works in Child Protection?* Ilford, U.K.: Barnardos.

Măceşaru, E. (1997) *The Christian Assemblies according to the Gospel in the History of the Romanian Christianity (1899-1943)*. Bucureşti: Romanian Bible Institute, Faculty of Pastoral-Didactical Theology.

MacLeod, H. (2000) 'Holistic Care of Children in Complex Humanitarian Emergencies: Lessons From Practitioners' In *Complex Humanitarian Emergencies*, Janz, M. and Joann Slead (eds.) (pp. 18-43). Monrovia, California: World Vision.

MacLeod, H. (2003) 'Child Protection' In *Celebrating Children*, Miles, G. and Wright, J.J. (eds.), (pp. 245-251). Carlisle, Cumbria: Paternoster Press.

Magdid, K. & McKelvey, C.A. (1987) *High Risk: Children Without a Conscious*. New York, NY: Bantam Books.

Mahar, M. (2003) 'The Potential Role of Spirituality in Conducting Field Research: Examination of a Model and a Process. *The Qualitative Report*, vol. 8(1): Available at *http://www.nova.edu/ssss/QR/QR8-1/mahar.html* Accessed June 17, 2005.

Mănăstireanu, D. (1994) *The Place of Scripture in the Orthodox Tradition*. London Bible College. Available at *http://www.ortho-logia.com/English/RomWritings/ScrpitureInBO-S.htm* Accessed February 10, 2008.

Mănăstireanu, D. (1998a) 'Evangelical Denominations in Post-communist Romania, part 1' *East-West Church Ministry Report*, vol. 6 (2):1-3.

Mănăstireanu, D. (1998b) 'Evangelical Denominations in Post-communist Romania, part 2' *East-West Church Ministry Report*, vol. 6 (3):7-10.

Mănăstireanu, D. (2004a) 'Plea for Evangelical Identity' In *Iosif Ton – New Horizons in Spirituality and Ministry*, Sabou, S. and Ghitea, D. (eds.) (pp. 327-340). Oradea: Cartea Creştină.

Mănăstireanu, D. (2004b) *What Should Non-Orthodox Christians Know about Orthodox Spirituality?* (Unpublished work).

Mănăstireanu, D. (2006) 'Western Assistance in Theological Training for Romanian Evangelicals since 1989' *East-West Church Ministry Report*, vol. 14 (3):1-4.

Mandryk, J. (2010) *Operation World:The Definitive Prayer Guide to Every Nation*. Colorado Springs, CO: Biblica Publishing

Mangalwaldi, V. (2003) 'Compassion and Social Reform: Jesus the Troublemaker' In *The Church in Response to Human Need*, Vinay, S. and Sugden, C. (eds.) (pp. 193-205). Eugene, Oregon: Wipf and Stock Publishers.

Martin, D. (1990) *Tongues of Fire: The Explosion of Pentecostalism in Latin America*. Cambridge, MA: Blackwell Inc.

Martin, S. (1996) 'The Church and the World's Children' In *Children in Crisis: A New Commitment*, Kilbourn, P. (ed.) (pp. 109-121). Monrovia, CA: MARC Publications.

Mason, J. (1996) *Qualitative Researching*. London: Sage Publications.

Maxwell, J. (1995) 'An Orthodox Response to Don Fairbairn, "Eastern Orthodoxy: Five Protestant Perspectives"' *East-West Church Ministry Report*, vol. 3 (2):5-7.

May, S.; Posterski, B.; Stonehouse, C. & Cannell, L. (2005) *Children Matter: Celebrating Their Place in the Church, Family, and Community*. Grand Rapids, MI: Eerdmans Publishing.

May, S. & Ratcliff, D. (2004) 'Children's Spiritual Experiences and the Brain' In *Children's Spirituality: Christian Perspectives, Research, and Applications*, Ratcliff, D. (ed.) (pp. 149-165). Eugene, OR: Cascade Books.

McAlpine, T. (2002) 'The Spirituality of the Child ' In *World Ministry Network WVI* Monrovia, CA (Unpublished Internal Paper).

McAlpine, T.H. (1995) *By Word, Work and Wonder: Cases in Holistic Mission*. Monrovia, CA: MARC.

McConnell, D. (2007) 'God Creates Every Unique Person as a Child with Dignity' In *Understanding God's Heart for Children: Toward a Biblical Framework*, McConnell, D. *et al.* (eds.) (pp. 13-23). Colorado Springs, CO: Authentic.

McConnell, D.; Orona, J. & Stockley, P. (eds.) (2007) *Understanding God's Heart for Children: Toward a Biblical Framework*. Colorado Springs, CO: Authentic.

McCormack, B. (2000) 'Grace and Being: The Role of God's Gracious Election in Karl Barth's Theological Ontology' In *The Cambridge Companion to Karl Barth*, Webster, J. (ed.) (pp. 92-110). Cambridge: Cambridge University Press.

McDonald, P. (2003) 'Practical and Spiritual Lessons for the Church' In *Celebrating Children*, Miles, G. and Wright, J.J. (eds.) (pp. 150-163). Carlisle, Cumbria: Paternoster Press.

McDonald, P. & Garrow, E. (2000) *Reaching Children in Need: What's Being Done, What You Can Do*. Kingsway: Eastbourne.

McGavran, D.A. (1955) *The Bridges of God*. New York, NY: Friendship Publishing.

McGavran, D.A. (1973) 'Salvation Today' In *The Evangelical Response to Bangkok*, Winter, R. (ed.) (pp. 27-32). Pasadena, CA: William Carey Library.

McGavran, D.A. (1980) *Understanding Church Growth*.(2nd edn.). Grand Rapids, MI: Eerdmans Publishing.

McIntosh, G.L. & Rima, S.D. (1997) *Overcoming the Dark Side of Leadership: The Paradox of Personal Dysfunction*. Grand Rapids, MI: Baker Books.

McKaughan, P. (1994) 'A North American Response to Patrick Sookhdeo' In *Kingdom Partnerships for Synergy in Missions*, Taylor, W.D. (ed.) (pp. 67-88). Pasadena, CA: William Carey Library.

Meeks, W.A. (2003) *The First Urban Christians: The Social World of the Apostle Paul*. (2nd edn.) New Haven: Yale University Press.

Mellis, C.J. (1983) *Committed Communities: Fresh Streams for World Missions*. Pasadena, CA: William Carey Library.

Michelson, P.E., (ed.) (1997) *Romanians and the West*. Iasi: Centre for Romanian Studies.

Miles, B.M. & Huberman, M.A. (1994) *Qualitative Data Analysis: An Expanded Sourcebook*. (2nd edn.) Thousand Oaks, CA: Sage Publications.

Miles, G. (2003) 'The Development of Children in their Families and Communities' In *Celebrating Children*, Miles, G. and Wright, J.J. (eds.) (pp. 33-39). Carlisle, U.K.: Paternoster Press.

Miles, G. & Houlihan, C. (2003) 'What the Bible Says about Why Children Suffer' In *Celebrating Children*, Miles, G. and Wright, J.J. (eds.) (pp. 200-209). Carlisle, U.K.: Paternoster Press.

Miles, G. & Wright, J.J. (eds.) (2003) *Celebrating Children: Equipping People Working with Children and Young People Living in Difficult Circumstances Around the World*. Carlisle, U.K.: Paternoster Press.

Miller, D.E. (2003) 'Emergent Patterns of Congregational Life and Leadership in the Developing World: Personal Reflections from a research odyssey' *Pulpit and Pew Research on Pastoral Leadership*, vol. No. 3 (Winter):1-37.

Miller, D.L. (1999) *Discipling Nations: The Power of Truth to Transform Cultures*. Seattle, WA: YWAM Publishing.

Miller, K.G. (2001) 'Complex Innocence, Obligatory Nurturance, and Parental Vigilance: "The Child" in the Work of Menno Simons' In *The Child in Christian Thought*, Bunge, M.J. (ed.) (pp. 194-226). Grand Rapids, MI: Eerdmans Publishing.

Mintzberg, H. (1994) *The Rise and Fall of Strategic Planning: Reconceiving Roles for Planning, Plans, Planners*. New York, NY: Free Press.

Mintzberg, H. (2006) 'Developing Leaders? Developing countries? Learning from another place' *Development in Practice*, vol. 6 (February 2006):10-21.

Mintzberg, H. & Quinn, J.B. (1995) *The Strategy Process: Concepts and Contexts*. (3rd edn.) New York, NY: Prentice Hall.

Moffitt, R. (2003) 'The Local Church and Development' In *The Church in Response to Human Need*, Vinay, S. and Sugden, C. (eds.) (pp. 234-253). Eugene, Oregon: Wipf and Stock Publishers.

Moltmann, J. (1993a) *The Church in the Power of the Spirit*. Minneapolis: Fortress Press.

Moltmann, J. (1993b) *God in Creation: A New Theology of Creation and the Spirit of God*. Minneapolis: Fortress Press.

Moltmann, J. (1994) *Jesus Christ for Today's World*. Minneapolis: Fortress Press.

Moltmann, J. (2000) 'Child and Childhood as Metaphors of Hope ' *Theology-Today*, vol. 56(4):592-603.

Monsma, T. (1996) 'Church Planting among Children: Biblical Directives' In *Children in Crisis: A New Commitment*, Kilbourn, P. (ed.) (pp. 95-102). Monrovia, CA: MARC Publications.

Morgan, G. (1997) *Images of Organization*. Thousand Oaks, CA: Sage Publications.

Morrison, L. (2004) 'Ceausescu's Legacy: Family Struggles and Institutionalization of Children in Romania' *Journal of Family History*, vol. 29 (2):168-182.

Moyle, M. (1999) 'Shadows of the Past: The Lingering Effects of the Communist Mindset in the Church and Society' *Transformation*, vol. 16 (1):17-20.

Mullinex, G. (1998) 'Church-based programs for Children – Our Approach' In *Compassion International Annual Meeting* Colorado Springs, CO, (Conference Proceeding).

Mullinex, G. (2000) 'How Does Compassion Evaluate Projects'. *Ministry Insight*. Colorado Springs, CO.

Muntean, A. & Roth, M. (2000) 'Romania' In *Child Abuse: A Global View*, Schwartz-Kenney, B.M. *et al.* (eds.) (pp. 175-195). Westport, CN: Greenwood Publishing Group.

Myers, B.L. (2001) 'What in the World Is Going on? Strategic Trends Affecting Children' In *VIVA 3rd International Cutting Edge Conference* De Bron Netherlands. Available at *http://www.viva.org/?page_id=295* Accessed September 15, 2006 (Plenary Paper).

Myers, B.L. (1992) 'State of the World's Children: A Strategic Challenge to the Christian Mission in the 1990s' In *EFMA Executive Leadership Retreat* Glen Eyrie Colorado Springs, U.S.A., (Published Conference Proceeding).

Myers, B.L. (1999a) 'Another Look at "Holistic Mission"' *Evangelical Missions Quarterly*, vol. 35 (3):285-287.

Myers, B.L. (1999b) *Walking with the Poor: Principles and Practices of Transformational Development*. Maryknoll, NY: Orbis Books.

Myers, B.L. (2000) Personal Interview concerning professionalization of World Vision. New Haven, CT. Date: March 12, 2000.

Myers, B.L. & Bradshaw, B. (1996) *Introducing the Spiritual Dimension Into Participatory Community Appraisals: Going Beyond the Physical Needs in Transformational Development.* Monrovia, CA: WWI.

Myers, R.G. (1996) 'Investing in Early Childhood Development Programs' In *The World Bank Conference on Early Childhood Development: Investing in the Future* The Carter Center, Atlanta, Georgia, (Published Conference Proceeding).

Myers, V.L. (2003) 'Planning and Evaluating Faith-Based Interventions: a Framework to Close the Theory-Practice Divide 'In *The Role of Faith-Based Organizations in the Social Welfare System* Washington, DC, (Published Conference Proceeding).

Neagoe, A. (2003) 'Mentalities and Practices of Romanian Evangelicals' In *Areopagus Romanian Culture Orientation* Timisoara, Romania. (Unpublished Conference paper).

Negruţ, P. (1999a) 'Church and Mission: An Eastern European Perspective' *Transformation*, vol. 16 (1):20-24.

Negruţ, P. (1999b) 'Sorting Out Praise and Condemnation' *East-West Church Ministry Report*, vol. 7 (1):10-11.

Negruţ, P. (2000) *The Church and the State. An Interrogation over the Byzantine Synthesis Model*. Oradea: Emanuel Biblical Institute.

Neuman, L.W. (2000) *Social Research Methods: Qualitative and Quantitative Approaches*. (4th edn.) Boston: Allyn and Bacon.

Neumann, V. (2001) 'Between Words and Reality: Studies on the Politics of Recognition and Changes of Regime in Contemporary Romania ' *Cultural Heritage and Contemporary Change, Eastern and Central Europe*, vol. 15.

Newbigin, L. (1986) *Foolishness to the Greeks, The Gospel and Western Culture*. Grand Rapids, MI: Eerdmans Publishing.

Newbigin, L. (1989) *The Gospel in a Pluralist Society*. Grand Rapids, MI: Eerdmans Publishing.

Newbigin, L. (1995) *The Open Secret: An Introduction to the Theology of Mission*. Grand Rapids, MI: Eerdmans Publishing.

Nicholls, B. & Wood, B. (eds.) (1996) *Sharing Good News with the Poor*. Carlisle, U.K.: Paternoster Press.

Niebuhr, H.R. (1956) *Christ and Culture*. New York, NY: Harper Perennial.

Noll, M.A. (1994) *The Scandal of the Evangelical Mind*. Grand Rapids, MI: Eerdmans Publishing.

Noll, M.A.; Bebbington, D.W. & Rawlyk, G.A. (eds.) (1994) *Evangelicalism. Comparative Studies of Popular Protestantism in North America, the British Isles, and Beyond, 1700-1990*. New York, NY: Oxford University Press.

Nouwen, H.J.M. (1975) *Reaching Out*. New York, NY: Doubleday & Co.

Nouwen, H.J.M. (1990) *The Wounded Healer*. New York, NY: Doubleday & Co.

Nouwen, H.J.M. (2004) *The Spirituality of Fundraising*. Richmond Hill, Ontario: Upper Room Ministries.

Nouwen, H.J.M.; McNeill, D.P. & Morrison, D.A. (1983) *Compassion: Reflections on the Christian Life*. New York, NY: Image Books.

Nucci, L. (1997) 'Synthesis of Research on Moral Development'. University of Illinois at Chicago. Available at *http://tigger.uic.edu/~lnucci/MoralEd/articles/nuccisynthesis.html* Accessed June 14, 2006.

Nye, R. (1998) *Psychological Perspectives on Children's Spirituality*. PhD Thesis, Nottingham, U.K.: University of Nottingham.

Nye, R. (2004) 'Christian Perspectives on Children's Spirituality: Social Science Contributions?' In *Children's Spirituality: Christian Perspectives, Research, and Application*, Ratcliff, D. (ed.) (pp. 72-90). Eugene, OR: Cascade Books.

O'Callaghan, R. (2003) 'What Do We Mean By Holistic Mission' *The Cry: The Advocacy Journal of World Made Flesh*, vol. 9 (Spring 1):8-10.

O'Donnell, K., (ed.) (1992) *Missionary Care: Counting the Cost for World Evangelization*. Pasadena, CA: William Carey Library.

OCI (2001) *God's Heart for Romania: Report on the state of Evangelical churches in Romania*. Bucharest: OCI International.

OCI (2001-2007) *Directory of the Network of Christian Ministries in Romania.* Bucharest: OCI International, (Annual Reports).

Oktay, S.J. (2004) 'Grounded Theory' In *The Qualitative Research Experience*, Padgett, K.D. (ed.) (pp. 23-47). Belmont, CA: Thomson Books.

Osmer, R.R. (2000) 'The Education of Children in the Protestant Tradition ' *Theology Today*, vol. 56 (4):506-523.

Overland, N. & Koenig, D. (eds.) (1998) *The Girl Child: Enhancing Life, Sustaining Hope*. Washington, DC: Washington Forum, WVI U.S.A..

Pacepa, I.M. (1990) *Red Horizons: The Story of Nicolae and Elena Ceausescu's Crimes, Lifestyles, and Corruption*. Washington, D.C.: Regency Gateway.

Padgett, K.D. (1998) *Qualitative Methods in Social Work Research*. Thousand Oaks, CA: Sage Publications.

Padgett, K.D. (2004a) 'Introduction: Finding a Middle Ground in Qualitative Research' In *The Qualitative Research Experience*, Padgett, K.D. (ed.) (pp. 1-18). Belmont, CA: Thomson Books/Cole.

Padgett, K.D., (ed.) (2004b) *The Qualitative Research Experience*. Belmont, CA: Thomson Books/Cole.

Padilla, C.R. (1983) 'The Unity of the Church and the Homogeneous Unit Principle' In *Exploring Church Growth*, Shenk, W.R. (ed.) (pp. 285-302). Grand Rapids, MI: Eerdmans Publishing.

Padilla, R.C. (1985) *Mission Between the Times: Essays on the Kingdom*. Grand Rapids, MI: Eerdmans, Publishing.

Palmer, P.J. (2000) *Let Your Life Speak: Listening for the Voice of Vocation*. San Francisco, CA: Jossey-Bass Publishers.

Palmer, P.J. (1993) *To Know as We are Known*. San Francisco, CA: Harper & Row Publishers.

Pannenberg, W. (1985) *Anthropology in Theological Perspective*. Philadelphia, PA: Westminster Press.

Parker, G.M. (1996) *Team Players and Teamwork: The New Competitive Business Strategy*. San Francisco, CA: Jossey-Bass Publishers.

Pattison, S. (1997) *The Faith of the Managers: When Management Becomes Religion*. London: Cassell.

Patton, M.Q. (1987) *How to Use Qualitative Methods in Evaluation*. Thousand Oaks, CA: Sage Publications.

Patton, M.Q. (1990) *Qualitative Evaluation and Research Methods*. (2nd edn.) Newbury Park, CA: Sage Publications.

Penner, P. (2003) 'Critical Evaluation of Recent Developments in the Commonwealth of Independent States' *Transformation*, vol. 20:13-29.

Perrow, C.B. (1970) *Organizational Analysis: A Sociological View*. London, U.K.: Tavistock Publications, Ltd.

Petersen, D. (1996) *Not By Might Nor By Power: A Pentecostal Theology of Social Concern in Latin America*. Cumbria, U.K.: Paternoster Publishing.

Piaget, J. (1932) *The Moral Judgment of the Child*. New York, NY: Free Press.

Pitkin, B. (2001) '"The Heritage of the Lord": Children in the Theology of John Calvin' In *The Child in Christian Thought*, Bunge, M.J. (ed.) (pp. 160-193). Grand Rapids, MI: Eerdmans Publishing.

Plant, S. (2003) *Freedom as Development: Christian Mission and the Definition of Human Well-being*. Henry Martyn Centre. Available at *www.martynmission.cam.ac.uk/CPlant.html* Accessed October 10, 2005.

Popa, O.D. & Horn, M.E. (1994) *Ceausescu's Romania: An Annotated Bibliography*. Greenwood Press.

Pope, E.A. (1992a) 'Protestantism in Romania.' In *Protestantism and Politics in Eastern Europe and Russia*, Ramet, S. (ed.) (pp. 157-208). Durham, NC: Duke University Press.

Pope, E.A. (1992b) 'The Significance of the Evangelical Alliance in Contemporary Romanian Society' *East European Quarterly*, vol. 25 (4):493-518.

Popescu, P. (1997) *The Return: A Family Revisits Their Eastern European Roots*. New York: Grove Press.

Popovici, A. (1989) *History of the Romanian Baptists*. Chicago: The Baptist Romanian Church Publishing House.

Putman, K.M. (2007) 'Children's Needs for Parental Love in a Systematically Broken World' In *Understanding God's Heart for Children: Toward a Biblical Framework*, McConnell, D. *et al.* (eds.) (pp. 66-76). Colorado Springs, CO: Authentic.

Putnam, R. (1994) *Making Democracy Work: Civic Traditions in Modern Italy*. Princeton, NJ: Princeton University Press.

Putnam, R. (2000) *Bowling Alone: The Collapse and Revival of American Community*. New York, NY: Simon & Schuster.

Radu, C. (2003) 'Romanian Youth Fall Prey to Heroin' *Realitatea Românească*, București.

Ram, E.R., (ed.) (1995) *Transforming Health: Christian Approaches to Healing and Wholeness*. Monrovia, CA: MARC, World Vision Publishing.

Ratcliff, D., (ed.) (1992) *Handbook of Children's Religious Education*. Religious Education Press.

Ratcliff, D. (2003) 'The Numinous Experiences of Children' In *North American Professors of Christian Education Annual Conference* Boston, MA. Available at *http://www.childspirituality.org/don/numinous.pdf* Accessed September 2007.

Ratcliff, D., (ed.) (2004) *Children's Spirituality: Christian Perspectives, Research, and Applications*. Eugene, OR: Cascade Books.

Ratcliff, D. (2007) *Ratcliff's Qualitative Research Resources*. Available at *http://www.don.ratcliffs.net/professional.htm#qual* Accessed December 15, 2007.

Rawlins, M. (2001) *An Examination of Chris Argyris' Model of Learning in Relation to its Effectiveness in Creating a Cross-Cultural, Team Learning Environment at University of the Nations Leadership Training School*. PhD Thesis, Oxford: Oxford Centre for Mission Studies.

Richmond, Y. (1995) *From Da to Yes: Understanding the East Europeans*. Yarmouth, ME: Intercultural Press.

Rickett, D. (2000) *Building Strategic Relationships: A Practical Guide to Partnering with Non-Western Missions*. Pleasant Hill, CA: Klein Graphics.
Rickett, D. (2002) *Making Your Partnership Work*. Enuimclaw, WA: Winepress Publishing.
Rickett, D. & Welliver, D. (eds.) (1997) *Supporting Indigenous Ministries: With Selected Readings*. Wheaton, IL: Billy Graham Centre.
Rinehart, S.T. (1998) *Upside Down: The Paradox of Servant Leadership*. Colorado Springs, CO: Navpress.
Robert, D. (2000) 'Shifting Southward: Global Christianity since 1945' *International Bulletin of Missionary Research*, vol. 24 (2):50-58.
Robila, M. (2002) *The Impact of Financial Strain on Adolescents' Psychological Functioning in Romania: the Role of Family Processes*. PhD, Syracuse: Syracuse University, Graduate School of Psychology.
Roehlkepartain, E.C.; King, P.E.; Wagener, L.M. & Benson, P.L. (eds.) (2005) *Handbook of Spiritual Development in Childhood and Adolescence*. Thousand Oaks, CA: Sage Publications.
Rogobete, S. (2002) 'Religion and Social Change: Some Reflections on Religion's Role in Contemporary Society' In *For a Democracy of Values: Strategies for Religious Communication in a Pluralist Society* Bucureşti, (Published Conference Proceeding).
Rogobete, S. (2003) 'Morality and Tradition in Post communist Orthodox Lands: on the Universality of Human Rights with Special Reference to Romania' In *American Political Science Association Annual Meeting* Philadelphia, U.S.A., (Published Conference paper).
Roman, D. (2003) *Fragmented Identities: Popular Culture, Sex and Everyday Life in Post- Communist Romania*. Lanham: Lexington Books.
Romocea, C.G. (2007) *Church and State: Theology and Continuity of Orthodox Religious Nationalism in Romania*. PhD Thesis, Cardiff: University of Wales, Theology.
Roseland, M.; Cureton, M.; Wornell, H. & Henderson, H. (1998) *Toward Sustainable Communities: Resources for Citizens and their Governments*. Stony Creek, CT: New Society Publishers.
Rosenfeld, R. & Wilson, D.C. (1999) *Managing Organizations*. (2nd edn.) London: McGraw-Hill Publishing.
Roth, M. (1999) 'Children's Rights in Romania: Problems and Progress' *Social Work in Europe*, vol. 6:30-37.
Roxburgh, A.J. & Romanuk, F. (2006) *The Missional Leader*. San Francisco, CA: Jossey-Bass Publishers.
Rubatos, A. (2004) *Romania Then and Now. An Inquiry into Business Culture and Transition*. Dissertation, MBA, Henley Management College, U.K..
Rubin, H.J. & Rubin, I.S. (1995) *Qualitative Interviewing: The Art of Hearing Data*. Thousand Oaks, CA: Sage Publishing.
Ryan, S.D. & Groza, V. (2004) 'Romanian Adoptees' *International Social Work*, vol. 47 (1):53-79.
Sabou, S. & Ghitea, D. (eds.) (2004) *Iosif Ton – New Horizons in Spirituality and Ministry*. Oradea: Cartea Creştină.
Salvaţi Copiii România (2002) *Report to the UN Committee on Child Rights – Geneva Concerning the Second Periodical Report by the Romanian Government on the Interval 1993-2002.* Bucureşti: Salvaţi Copiii România [Save the Children Romania], (Report).
Samuel, V. (1981) *The Meaning and Cost of Discipleship*. Bangalore: Rachna.

Samuel, V. (1996) 'A Christian Perspective on the Family' *Transformation*, vol. 13 (3):10-12.
Samuel, V. (1997) 'Theological Perspectives on Children at Risk' *Transformation*, vol. 14 (2):27-28.
Samuel, V. (2002) 'Mission as Transformation ' *Transformation*, vol. 19:243-247.
Samuel, V. & Sugden, C. (1983) 'Mission Agencies as Multinationals' *International Bulletin of Missions Research*, vol. 7 (4):152-155.
Samuel, V. & Sugden, C. (eds.) (1987) *The Church in Response to Human Need.* Oxford, U.K.: Regnum.
Samuel, V. & Sugden, C. (eds.) (1999) *Mission as Transformation: A Theology of the Whole Gospel.* Oxford: Regnum Books International.
Samuel, V. & Sugden, C. (2003) 'God's Intention for the World' In *The Church in Response to Human Need*, Vinay, S. and Sugden, C. (eds.) (pp. 128-160). Eugene, Oregon: Wipf and Stock Publishers.
Sanders, C.J. (1997) *Ministry At The Margins: The Prophetic Mission of Women, Youth and The Poor*. Downers Grove, IL: Inter Varsity Press.
Şandru, T. (1992) *Biserica penticostală în istoria creştinismului [The Pentecostal Church in the History of Christianity]*. Bucureşti: ITP.
Sanneh, L. (1989) *Translating the Message: The Missionary Impact on Culture*. Maryknoll, NY: Orbis Books.
Sanneh, L. (1993) *Encountering the West: Christianity and the Global Cultural Process*. Maryknoll, NY: Orbis Books.
Santos, H.N. (2004) 'Church Structures: The Perspective of Institutional Psychology' In *Local Church, Agent of Transformation*, Yamamori, T. and Padilla, R. (eds.) (pp. 205-224). Buenos Aires: Kairos Ediciones.
Saulean, D. & Epure, C. (1998) *Defining the Non-profit Sector: Romania.* Baltimore: The Johns Hopkins Institute for Policy Studies.
Scarfe, A. (1976) 'Romanian Baptists and the State ' *Religion in Communist Lands*, vol. 4:15-20.
Scarfe, A. (1988) 'The Romanian Orthodox Church' In *Eastern Christianity and Politics in the Twentieth Century*, Ramet, P. (ed.) (pp. 208-31). Durham, NC: Duke University Press.
Schein, E.H. (1997) *Organizational Culture and Leadership*. (2nd edn.) San Francisco: Jossey-Bass Publishers.
Schneider, S.C. & Barsou, J.L. (1997) *Managing Across Cultures*. New York, NY: Prentice-Hall.
Schön, D.A. (1995) *The Reflective Practitioner: How Professionals Think in Action*. Aldershot, England: Ashgate Publishing Limited.
Schragg, C.O. (1997) *The Self After Post-Modernity*. New Haven, CT: Yale University Press.
Schutt, R.K. (2001) *Investigating the Social World: the Process and Practice of Research*. (3rd edn.) Thousand Oaks, CA: Pine Forge Press.
Scott, D. (2007) 'Theological Dignity and Human Rights for Children' In *Understanding God's Heart for Children: Toward a Biblical Framework*, MConnell, D. *et al.* (eds.) (pp. 23-32). Colorado Springs, CO: Authentic.
Scott, D.G. & Magnuson, D. (2005) 'Integrating Spiritual Development into Youth Care Programs and Institutions' In *The Handbook of Spiritual Development in Childhood and Adolescence*, Roehlkepartain, E.C. *et al.* (eds.) (pp. 445-457). Thousand Oaks, CA: Sage Publications, Inc.
Seal, C. (1999) *The Quality of Qualitative Research*. London: Sage Publications.

Search Institute (2002) '40 Developmental Assets for Adolescents'. Search Institute. Available at *http://www.search-institute.org/downloads/#40assets* Accessed July 20, 2005.

Seel, J. (1994) 'Modernity and Evangelicals' In *Faith and Modernity*, Sampson, P. *et al.* (eds.) (pp. 287-313). Oxford, U.K.: Regnum-Lynx.

Senge, P.M.; Kleiner, A.; Roberts, C.; Ross, R.B. & Smith, B.J. (1994) *The Fifth Discipline Fieldbook: Strategies and Tools for Building a Learning Organization*. New York, NY: Doubleday.

Shawchuck, N. & Heuser, R. (1993) *Leading the Congregation: Caring for Yourself While Serving Other People*. Nashville, TN: Abingdon Press.

Shawchuck, N. & Heuser, R. (1996) *Managing the Congregation: Building Effective Systems to Serve People*. Nashville, TN: Abingdon Press.

Sherman, A.L. (2003) *Empowering Compassion: The Strategic Role of Intermediary Organizations in Building Capacity Among and Enhancing the Impact of Community Transformers*. Charlottesville, VA: Hudson Institute.

Siani-Davies, P. (2005) *The Romanian Revolution of December 1989*. Ithaca, NY: Cornell University Press.

Sider, R.J. (1999a) *Good News and Good Works: A Theology for the Whole Gospel*. Grand Rapids, MI: Baker Books.

Sider, R.J. (1999b) 'What is the Gospel?' *Transformation*, vol. 16 (1):31.

Simon, U. (1979) *A Theology of Auschwitz: The Christian Faith and the Problem of Evil*. Atlanta, GA: John Knox Press.

Sims, D. (2006) *An Evangelical Theology of Liberation for Affluent American Evangelical Children*. PhD Thesis, Durham, U.K.: University of Durham, Theology.

Sisemore, T.A. (2004) 'From Doctrine to Practice: The Influence of the Doctrine of Original Sin on Puritan Child Rearing' In *Children's Spirituality: Christian Perspectives, Research, and Application*, Ratcliff, D. (ed.) (pp. 219-232). Eugene, OR: Cascade Books.

Smith, M.K. (2001) 'Chris Argyris: Theories of action, double-loop learning and organizational learning', Available at www.infed.org/thinkers/argyris.htm. Accessed December 2007.

Snyder, H.A. (1975) *The Problem of Wineskins: Church Structure in a Technological Age*. Downers Grove, IL: Inter-Varsity Press.

Snyder, H.A. (1977) The Community of the King. Downers Grove, IL: Inter-Varsity Press.

So, D.W.K. (2006a) *Jesus' Revelation of His Father: A Narrative-Conceptual Study of the Trinity with special reference to Karl Barth*. Milton Keynes, U.K.: Paternoster.

So, D.W.K. (2006b) 'The Missionary Journey of the Son of God into the Far Country: A Paradigm of the Holistic Gospel Developed from the Theology of Karl Barth' *Transformation*, vol. 23(2):130-142.

Sookhdeo, P. (1994) 'Cultural Issues in Partnership in Mission' In *Kingdom Partnerships for Synergy in Missions*, Taylor, W.D. (ed.) (pp. 49-66). Pasadena, CA: William Carey Library.

Spradley, J.P. (1979) *The Ethnographic Interview*. New York, NY: Wadsworth Publishing.

Srinivasagam, R.T. (1994) 'Responding to Butler: Mission in Partnership' In *Kingdom Partnerships for Synergy in Missions*, Taylor, W.D. (ed.) (pp. 9-31). Pasadena, CA: William Carey Library.

Stackhouse, J.G. (2000) 'Money and Theology in American Evangelicalism' In *More Money, More Ministry: Money and Evangelicals in North American History*, Eskridge, L. and Noll, M.A. (eds.) (pp. 406-419). Grand Rapids, MI: Eerdmans Publishing.

Stackhouse, J.G. (2003) *Evangelical Ecclesiology: Reality of Illusion?* Grand Rapids, MI: Baker Book House.

Stafford, T. (2005) 'The Colossus of Care' *Christianity Today*, vol. 49 (3):50-55.

Stake, R.E. (1995) *The Art of Case Study Research*. Thousand Oaks, CA: SAGE Publications.

Stăniloae, D. (1980) *Theology and the Church*. Crestwood, NY: St. Vladimir's Seminary Press.

Stanley, B. (2003) 'Where Have our Mission Structures Come From?' *Transformation*, vol. 20 (1):39-46.

Stanley, P.D. & Clinton, R.J. (1992) *Connecting – Building Mentoring Relationships*. Colorado Springs: Navpress.

Stativă, E., (ed.) (2002) *Child Abuse in Residential Care Institutions in Romania*. Bucharest: UNICEF.

Stephenson, P. (1997) *From Sponsorship to Ownership: Building Community Capacity and Social Capital through Community-Based Child Development Programs in Latin America, East Africa and India*. MSc Thesis, Ithaca, NY: Cornell University.

Stephenson, P. (2001) 'Children's Rights: Has anyone got it right?' In *VIVA 3rd International Cutting Edge* De Bron, Netherlands, (Conference Proceeding).

Stephenson, P. (2003) 'The Rights of the Child and the Christian Response' In *Celebrating Children*, Miles, G. and Wright, J.J. (eds.) (pp. 52-61). Carlisle, U.K.: Paternoster.

Stephenson, P. & Glover, S. (1998) *Child Development Policy, Tearfund U.K.*. Middlesex, U.K.: Tearfund.

Stoica-Constantin, A.; Constantin, T.; Rogojină, D. & Baciu, S. (2000) *Drug Use Among Teenagers in Romania and The Republic of Moldavia*. Open Society Institute. Available at *http://rss.archives.ceu.hu/archive/00001135/01/143.pdf* Accessed March 10, 2005.

Stortz, M.E. (2001) 'Where or When Was Your Servant Innocent? Augustine on Childhood' In *The Child in Christian Thought*, Bunge, M.J. (ed.) (pp. 78-102). Grand Rapids, MI: Eerdmans Publishing.

Strauss, A. (1987) *Qualitative Analysis for Social Scientists*. Cambridge: Cambridge University Press.

Strauss, A. & Corbin, J. (1998) *Basic Qualitative Research: Grounded Theory Procedures and Techniques*. (2nd edn.) Newbury Park: Sage Publications.

Stricker, G. (1998) 'Stumbling Blocks between Orthodoxy and Protestant Ecumenism' *Religion, State and Society*, vol. 26:145-154.

Strohl, J.E. (2001) 'The Child in Luther's Theology: "For What Purpose Do We Older Folks Exist Other Than to Care for the Young?" In *The Child in Christian Thought*, Bunge, M.J. (ed.) (pp. 134-159). Grand Rapids, MI: Eerdmans Publishing.

Strommen, M.P. (1998) 'A Family's Faith, A Child's Faith' *Dialog*, vol. 2 (Summer):171-178.

Strommen, M.P. & Hardel, R. (2000) *Passing on Faith: A Radical New Model for Youth and Family Ministry*. Winona: St. Mary's Press.

Sugden, C. (1997a) *Gospel, Culture and Transformation*. Oxford, U.K.: Regnum.

Sugden, C. (1997b) 'Partnership' *Transformation*, vol. 14 (3):28-29.

Suico, L.U. (2000) *Sexual Exploitation of Children with Special Reference to the Role of the Evangelical Churches in the Philippines*. MA Thesis, Leeds: University of Leeds, OCMS: Theology and Development.

Swarr, D.E. (2006) *Individual Power in Organizations*. PhD Thesis, Cardiff: University of Wales, OCMS.

Swartz, C. (1994) 'Longer Term Solutions for Romanian Orphans' *East-West Church Ministry Report*, vol. 2 (2):10-11.

Swinton, J. & Mowat, H. (2006) *Practical Theology and Qualitative Research*. London: SCM Press Ltd.

Taloş, V.A. (1998) 'Religious Pluralism in the Romanian Context' *Religion in Eastern Europe*, vol. 18(August):21-34.

Taylor, W.D., (ed.) (1994) *Kingdom Partnerships for Synergy in Missions*. Pasadena, CA: William Carey Library.

Taylor, W.D., (ed.) (1997) *Too Valuable to Lose: Exploring the Causes and Cures of Missionary Attrition*. Pasadena, CA: William Carey Library.

Taylor, W.D., (ed.) (2000) *Global Missiology For The 21st Century: The Iguassu Dialogue*. Grand Rapids, MI: Baker Academic.

Tellis, W. (1997) 'Introduction to Case Study ' *The Qualitative Report*, vol. 3(2). Available at *http://www.nova.edu/ssss/QR/QR3-2/tellis1.html* Accessed May 2005.

Thatcher, A. (2006) 'Theology and Children: Towards a Theology of Children' *Transformation*, vol. 23 (4):194-199.

Thomson, M. (1996) *Family: The Forming Center: A Vision of the Role of Family in Spiritual Formation*. Nashville: Upper Room Books.

Thorup, C.L. & Kinkade, S. (2005) 'What Works in Youth Engagement in the Balkans'. Available at *http://www.iyfnet.org/uploads/WW_Youth_Engagement_2-7MB.pdf* Accessed November 11, 2006.

Tippet, A.R. (1987) *Introduction to Missiology*. Pasadena, CA: William Carey Library.

Tomkins, A. (2003) 'The Basis for the Design of Child Development Programmes' In *Celebrating Children*, Miles, G. and Wright, J.J. (eds.) (pp. 163-174). Carlisle, Cumbria: Paternoster Press.

Tomkins, A. (2002) 'HIV/AIDS and Children: How Can the Church Meet the Challenge?' In *Hearing God's Heart for Children, VIVA International Cutting Edge 4* De Bron, Netherlands, (Conference Proceeding).

Ţon, I. (1988) *The Real Faith*. Wheaton, IL: The Romanian Missionary Society.

Ţon, I. (1993) 'Towards Reformation in Romania' *East-West Church Ministry Report*, vol. 1 (2):1-3.

Ţon, I. (1996) *Suffering, Martyrdom and Rewards in Heaven*. PhD Thesis, Heverlee-Leuven, Belgium: Evanghelische Theologiesche Faculteit, Theology.

Torrance, T.F. (1984) *Transformation and Convergence in the Frame of Knowledge*. Grand Rapids, MI: Eerdmans Publishing.

Traina, C.H.L. (2001) 'A Person in the Making: Thomas Aquinas on Children and Childhood' In *The Child in Christian Thought*, Bunge, M.J. (ed.) (pp. 103-133). Grand Rapids, MI: Eerdmans Publishing.

Traynor, I. (2005) *Romania Hails Orphanage Success Story* 'The Guardian ', National Edition, London, December 3, 2005. Available at http://www.guardian.co.uk/international/ story/0,,1656707,00.html Accessed January 2006.

Treptow, K., (ed.) (1997) *Romania and Western Civilization*. Iaşi, Romania: The Centre for Romanian Studies.

Triseliotis, J. (1994) 'Setting Up Foster Care Programs in Romania: Background, Possibilities and Limitations' *Community Alternatives*, vol. 6 (1):75-92.

Trueblood, E. (1970) *The New Man for Our Time*. San Francisco, CA: Harper & Row Publishers.

Tyson, J.R., (ed.) (1999) *Invitation to Christian Spirituality: An Ecumenical Anthology*. New York, NY: Oxford University Press.

UNICEF (1993) *Early Childhood Development: The Challenge and the Opportunity*. New York, NY: UNICEF.

UNICEF (1994) *UN Convention for Child Rights: the Current Situation in Romania.* Bucureşti: Committee for the Protection of Children, (Report in English and Romanian).

UNICEF (1997) *Children at Risk in Central and Eastern Europe: Perils and Promises.* Florence: UNICEF International Child Development Centre, (Regional monitoring report), No. 4.

UNICEF (2000) 'Poverty Reduction Begins with Children'. Available at http://www.unicef.org/ *publications/files/pub_poverty_reduction_en.pdf* Accessed December 4, 2006.

UNICEF (2001) 'Violence, Abuse and Neglect'. Available at http://www.unicef.org/ *romania/ro/children_2826.html* Accessed May, 10, 2004.

UNICEF (2000-2006) *The State of the World's Children*: UNICEF, (Annual reports) Available at *http://*www.unicef.org*/sowc/* Accessed March 5, 2007.

UNICEF (2003) *Romania and the U.N. Convention on the Rights of the Child.* Bucharest: UNICEF, (Second Periodic Report).

Valdez, E. (2002) *Protecting Children. A Biblical Perspective on Child Rights.* Monrovia, CA: World Vision International, (Internal Paper).

Van Engen, C. (2000) 'Towards s Theology of Mission Partnerships'. American Society of Missiology. Chicago, IL June 16, (Conference Proceeding).

Van Gelder, C. (1985) *Mission Structures: Modality and Sodality in Tension*. Unpublished D. Miss Thesis, Pasadena, CA: Fuller School of World Mission.

Velazco, G. (2003) 'Involving Children in the Process of Assessment and Therapy' In *Celebrating Children*, Miles, G. and Wright, J.J. (eds.) (pp. 75-83). Carlisle, U.K.: Paternoster Press.

Vencer, J. (1994) 'Control in Church/Mission Relationships and Partnerships' In *Kingdom Partnerships for Synergy in Missions*, Taylor, W.D. (ed.) (pp. 101-119). Pasadena, CA: William Carey Library.

Vidal, A.C. (2001) *Faith-Based Organizations in Community Development*. U.S. Department of Housing and Community Development. Available at *www.huduser.org* Accessed February 4, 2008.

Villfane, E. (1995) *Seek the Peace of the City: Reflections on Urban Ministry*. Grand Rapids, MI: Eerdmans Publishing.

VIVA and OCMS (1997) 'Children at Risk – Statement of an International Consultation at Oxford, January 1997' *Transformation*, vol. 14 (2):1-6.

Volf, M. (1994) 'Eastern European Faces of Jesus: Theological Issues Facing Christians in Eastern Europe.' In *Consultation on Theological Education Development in Post-Communist Europe* Oradea, Romania (Published Conference Proceeding).

Volf, M. (1996a) *Exclusion and Embrace: A Theological Exploration of Identity, Otherness, and Reconciliation*. Nashville, TN: Abingdon Press.

Volf, M. (1996b) 'Fishing in the Neighbour's Pond: Mission and Proselytism in Eastern Europe' *International Bulletin of Missionary Research*, vol. 20 (1):26-37.

Volf, M. (1998) *After Our Likeness: The Church As the Image of the Trinity (Sacra Doctrina)*. Grand Rapids, MI: Eerdmans.
Voorhies, S.J. (1996) 'Community Participation and Holistic Development' In *Serving the Poor in Africa*, Tetsunao, Y. *et al.* (eds.) (pp. 123-148). Monrovia, CA: MARC.
Wagner, C.P. (1976) *Your Church Can Grow*. Glendale, CA: Regal Publishing.
Walker, J. (2008) 'Enlace: Training and Equipping Churches to Transform their Communities' *Today's Pentecostal Evangel*, 4891, Feb. 3 (pp. 7-19).
Wall, W.R. (2003) 'Social Justice and Human Liberation' In *The Church in Response to Human Need*, Vinay, S. and Sugden, C. (eds.) (pp. 108-128). Eugene, Oregon: Wipf and Stock Publishers.
Wallace, A. (2002) 'Bringing Good News to the Poor: Does church-based transformational development really work?' *Transformation*, vol. 19 (2 April):133-138.
Walls, A.F. (1996) *The Missionary Movement in Christian History: Studies in Transmission of Faith*. Maryknoll, NY: Orbis Books.
Walter, P., (ed.) (1988) *World Christianity – Eastern Europe*. Oxford, U.K.: Keston College.
Ward, P., (ed.) (1995) *The Church and Youth Ministry*. Oxford, U.K.: Lynx Communications.
Watkins, S. (1995) 'Battling the Virus in Romania ' *Together*, vol. 47:11-13.
Weller, S.C. & Romney, A.K. (1988) *Systematic Data Collection*. Newbury Park, CA: Sage Publications.
Wells, D.E. (1994) *God in the Wasteland: The Reality of Truth in a Land of Fading Dreams*. Grand Rapids, MI: Eerdmans Publishing.
Wells, D.E. & Woodbridge, J.D. (eds.) (1975) *The Evangelicals. What They Believe, Who They Are, Where They Are Changing*. Nashville, New York: Abingdon Press.
Werpehowski, W. (2001) 'Reading Karl Barth on Children' In *The Child in Christian Thought*, Bunge, M.J. (ed.) (pp. 386-405). Grand Rapids, MI: Eerdmans Publishing.
Westerhoff, J.H. (1976) *Will Our Children Have Faith?* New York: Seabury Press.
Whitall, P. (2002) 'Care for the Children' *Christianity in Action*, vol. 5 (June 2002):14-15.
White, K. (2001) 'A Little Child Shall Lead Them" – Rediscovering Children at the Heart of Mission'. VIVA International Cutting Edge 3. Available at *http://www.viva.org/?page_id=296* Accessed October 10, 2006.
White, K. (2002) 'The Ideology of Residential Care and Fostering' In *Re-framing Children's Services*, White, K. (ed.) (pp. 231-242). London, U.K.: NCVCCO.
White, K. (2003a) 'An Integrated Biblical and Theoretical Typology of Children's Needs' In *Celebrating Children*, Miles, G. and Wright, J.J. (eds.) (pp. 123-126). Carlisle, Cumbria: Paternoster Press.
White, K. (2003b) 'Key Theoretical Frameworks and Their Application' In *Celebrating Children*, Miles, G. and Wright, J.J. (eds.) (pp. 47-51). Carlisle, Cumbria: Paternoster Press.
White, K. & Willmer, H. (2006) *An Introduction to Child Theology*. London: Child Theology Movement Limited.
White, K. & Wright, J.J. (2003) 'Theoretical Frameworks Defining Risk and Resilience' In *Celebrating Children*, Miles, G. and Wright, J.J. (eds.) (pp. 117-122). Carlisle, Cumbria: Paternoster Press.

Wilkinson, J. (2000) *Children and Participation: Research, Monitoring and Evaluation with Children and Young People*. Westport, CT: Save the Children.

Willard, D. (1998) *The Divine Conspiracy: Rediscovering our Hidden Life in God*. San Francisco, CA: HarperCollins.

Willmer, H. (1995) 'Transforming Society – or Merely Making It: A Theological Discussion with the Bible in One Hand and a Very Particular Newspaper in the Other' In *Society for the Study of Theology* Leeds, U.K. (Conference Proceeding).

Willmer, H. (1999) 'Responses to Miroslav Volf ' *Transformation*, vol. 16 (1):13-17.

Willmer, H. (2001a) 'Review: Mission as Transformation ' *Transformation*, vol. 18 (3):194-196.

Willmer, H. (2001b) 'Jesus the Forgiven: Christology, Atonement, and Forgiveness' In *Forgiveness and Truth: Explorations in Contemporary Theology*, McFadyen, A. and Sarot, M. (eds.) (pp. 15-30). Edinburgh: T&T Clark.

Willmer, H. (2003) 'Child Theology' In *VIVA 3rd International Cutting Edge* DeBron, Netherlands, (Conference Proceeding).

Willmer, H. (2004) 'Child Theology is Theology ' In *Global Child Theology Consultation* Penang, Malaysia, (Conference Proceeding).

Willmer, H. (2004 – 2007) Personal correspondence by Email (PhD supervision).

Wilson, S. & Siewert, J. (eds.) (1986) *Mission Handbook: North American Protestant Ministries Overseas*. Monrovia, CA: MARC Publications.

Wink, W. (1986) *Unmasking the Powers: The Invisible Forces That Determine Human Existence*. Philadelphia, PA: Fortress Press.

Wink, W. (1992) *Engaging the Powers: Discernment and Resistance in a World of Domination*. Philadelphia, PA: Fortress Press.

Wink, W. (1998) *The Powers that Be: Theology for a New Millennium*. New York, NY: Doubleday.

Winship, C. & Reynolds, A. (2003) 'Faith, Practice and Transformation: a Theory-Based Evaluation of Faith-Based Teen Programs ' In *The Role of Faith-Based Organizations in the Social Welfare System* Washington, DC (Conference Proceeding).

Winter, R.D. (1981a) 'The Kingdom Strikes Back: The Ten Epochs of Redemptive History' In *Perspectives on the World Christian Movement*, Winter, R.D. and Hawthorne, S.C. (eds.) (pp. 137-155). Pasadena, CA: William Carey Library.

Winter, R.D. (1981b) 'The Long Look: Eras of Mission History' In *Perspectives on the World Christian Movement*, Winter, R.D. and Hawthorne, S.C. (eds.) (pp. 326-341). Pasadena, CA: William Carry Library.

Winter, R.D. (1981c) 'The Two Structures of God's Redemptive Mission' In *Perspectives on the World Christian Movement*, Winter, R.D. and Hawthorne, S.C. (eds.) (pp. 178-190). Pasadena, CA: William Carey Library.

Winter, R.D. & Hawthorne, S.C. (eds.) (1999) *Perspectives on the World Christian Movement*. Pasadena, CA: William Carey Library.

Wolff, P. (2003) *Discernment The Art of Choosing Well: Based on Ignatian Spirituality*. Liguori, Missouri: Triumph.

World Bank (1997) *Romania – Poverty and Social Policy (vol. 1&2)*: World Bank, (Sector Report).

World Bank (2003) *Romania – Poverty Assessment (vol. 1)*: World Bank, (Sector report).

World Bank (2004) *Romania at a Glance*. Available at *http://www.worldbank.org/cgi-bin/sendoff.cgi?page=/data/countrydata/aag/rom_aag.pdf* Accessed November 2006.

Wright, J.J. (2003) 'Emotional Awareness and Meeting Our Own Needs' In *Celebrating Children*, Miles, G. and Wright, J.J. (eds.) (pp. 341-347). Carlisle, U.K.: Paternoster Press.

WVI (2001) *Here We Stand: World Vision and Child Rights*. Monrovia, CA: World Vision International.

WVI (2002) *Strengthening our Bridges*. Monrovia, CA: World Vision International, (Report Submitted to the World Vision International Board from the Commission on the Church).

WV Romania (2000) 'Following Christ in Everyday Life, National Church Conference' June 15-16, 2000, Bucharest, Romania.

Yamamori, T. & Padilla, R. (eds.) (2004) *The Local Church, Agent of Transformation*. Buenos Aires: Kairos Ediciones.

Yancy, P. & Brand, P. (1999) *Pain: The Gift Nobody Wants*. New York, NY: Harper Collins Publishing.

Yin, R.K. (1984) *Case Study Research*. Beverly Hills, CA: Sage Publications.

Yin, R.K. (2003) *Case Study Research: Design and Methods*. (3rd edn.) Thousand Oaks, CA: Sage Publications.

Zamfir, C., (ed.) (1995) *Dimensions of Poverty: 1994*. Bucureşti: Editura Expert.

Zamfir, C., (ed.) (1997) *For a Child Centered Society*. Bucharest: UNICEF.

Zamfir, C.; Abraham, P. & Nicolae, A. (eds.) (1999) *Social Policies in Romania: 1990-1998*. Bucureşti: Editura Expert.

Zamfir, C.; Pop, M.A. & Zamfir, E. (1994) *Romania during the '89s-'93s: The Dynamics of Living Standards and of Social Protection*. Bucureşti: Editura Expert.

Zamfir, C.; Postill, K. & Stan, R. (eds.) (2001) *Poverty in Romania*. Bucureşti: Editura Expert.

Zamfir, C. & Zamfir, E. (1993) *Ţiganii între ignorare şi îngrijorare [The Gypsies between Ignorance and Concern]*. Bucureşti: Editura Alternative.

Zamfir, C. & Zamfir, E. (1996) *Children at Risk in Romania: Problems Old and New*. Florence, Italy: UNICEF International Child Development Centre, (Report), No. 56.

Zonabend, F. (1992) 'The Monograph of European Ethnology' *Current Sociology*, vol. 40 (1):49-60.

Zuck, R. (1996) *Precious in His Sight: Childhood and Children in the Bible*. Grand Rapids, MI: Baker Books.

FBOs in study and generic online sources

AD 2000 Movement: Available at http://www.ad2000.org/ad2kbroc.htm Accessed March, 2007.

City of Hope: Available http://www.romanianchildren.org/home.html Accessed March 2008.

Centre for New Life (ACVN Brasov): Available at http://www.cry.org.uk/page/romania, Accessed March 2008.

Cleaford Christian Trust U.K.: Available at http://www.riac.org.uk/ Accessed August 2006.

Global Action for Children: Available at http://www.globalactionforchildren.org/ Accessed March, 2007.

Global Movement for Children: Available at http://www.gmfc.org/ Accessed March 2007.

Heart of a Child Romania: Available at http://www.inimadecopil.ro/ Accessed March 2008.
Houston Chronicle series on HIV in Romania: Available at http://www.chron.com/content/interactive/special/Romania Accessed December 12, 2006.
Lausanne Movement: Available at http://www.lausanne.org Accessed March 2007.
Mental Disabilities Rights International: Available at http://www.mdri.org Accessed December 13, 2006.
Mission of Mercy: Available at http://www.missionofmercy.org/ Accessed March 2008.
Mission Without Borders: Available at http://www.mwbi.org/ Accessed March 2008.
New Horizons Foundation: Available at http://www.new-horizons.ro Accessed March 2008.
Nicolae Ceausescu – Life and Times: Available at http://www.Ceausescu.org/ceausescu_texts Accessed February 2008
OCI Romania: Available at http://www.oci.ro Accessed February 10, 2008.
Prevette Research Site: Available at http://www.prevetteresearch.net Accessed March 2008.
Project Ruth Romania: Available at http://www.projectruth.ro/index.html Accessed March 2008
Tearfund U.K.: Available at http://www.tearfund.org Accessed July 2007.
Viva Network: Available at http://www.viva.org/ Accessed March 2007.
U.S. Embassy in Romania: Available at http://www.usembassy.ro Accessed June 2003.
Word Made Flesh Romania: Available at http://www.wmfromania.com/Eng/Index.html Accessed March 2008.
World Vision International: Available at http://www.wvi.org Accessed March 2008.
World Vision Romania: Available at http://www.worldvision.ro/ Accessed March 2008.
Youth with a Mission: Available at http://www.ywam.org Accessed April 2007.

Index

REGNUM EDINBURGH CENTENARY SERIES
Series Listing

David A. Kerr, Kenneth R. Ross (Eds)

Mission Then and Now

2009 / 978-1-870345-73-6 / 343pp (paperback)

2009 / 978-1-870345-76-7 / 343pp (hardback)

No one can hope to fully understand the modern Christian missionary movement without engaging substantially with the World Missionary Conference, held at Edinburgh in 1910. This book is the first to systematically examine the eight Commissions which reported to Edinburgh 1910 and gave the conference much of its substance and enduring value. It will deepen and extend the reflection being stimulated by the upcoming centenary and will kindle the missionary imagination for 2010 and beyond.

Daryl M. Balia, Kirsteen Kim (Eds)

Witnessing to Christ Today

2010 / 978-1-870345-77-4 / 301pp

This volume, the second in the Edinburgh 2010 series, includes reports of the nine main study groups working on different themes for the celebration of the centenary of the World Missionary Conference, Edinburgh 1910. Their collaborative work brings together perspectives that are as inclusive as possible of contemporary world Christianity and helps readers to grasp what it means in different contexts to be 'witnessing to Christ today'.

Claudia Währisch-Oblau, Fidon Mwombeki (Eds)

Mission Continues

Global Impulses for the 21st Century

2010 / 978-1-870345-82-8 / 271pp

In May 2009, 35 theologians from Asia, Africa and Europe met in Wuppertal, Germany, for a consultation on mission theology organized by the United Evangelical Mission: Communion of 35 Churches in Three Continents. The aim was to participate in the 100th anniversary of the Edinburgh conference through a study process and reflect on the challenges for mission in the 21st century. This book brings together these papers written by experienced practitioners from around the world.

Brian Woolnough and Wonsuk Ma (Eds)

Holistic Mission

God's plan for God's people

2010 / 978-1-870345-85-9 / 277pp

Holistic mission, or integral mission, implies God is concerned with the whole person, the whole community, body, mind and spirit. This book discusses the meaning of the holistic gospel, how it has developed, and implications for the church. It takes a global, eclectic approach, with 19 writers, all of whom have much experience in, and commitment to, holistic mission. It addresses critically and honestly one of the most exciting, and challenging, issues facing the church today. To be part of God's plan for God's people, the church must take holistic mission to the world.

Kirsteen Kim and Andrew Anderson (Eds)
Mission Today and Tomorrow
2010 / 978-1-870345-91-0 / 450pp

There are moments in our lives when we come to realise that we are participating in the triune God's mission. If we believe the church to be as sign and symbol of the reign of God in the world, then we are called to witness to Christ today by sharing in God's mission of love through the transforming power of the Holy Spirit. We can all participate in God's transforming and reconciling mission of love to the whole creation.

Tormod Engelsviken, Erling Lundeby and Dagfinn Solheim (Eds)
The Church Going Glocal
Mission and Globalisation 2011 / 978-1-870345-93-4 / 262pp

The New Testament church is... universal and local at the same time. The universal, one and holy apostolic church appears in local manifestations. Missiologically speaking... the church can take courage as she faces the increasing impact of globalisation on local communities today. Being universal and concrete, the church is geared for the simultaneous challenges of the glocal and local.

Marina Ngurusangzeli Behera (Ed)
Interfaith Relations after One Hundred Years
Christian Mission among Other Faiths 2011 / 978-1-870345-96-5 / 334 pp

The essays of this book reflect not only the acceptance and celebration of pluralism within India but also by extension an acceptance as well as a need for unity among Indian Christians of different denominations. The essays were presented and studied at a preparatory consultation on Study Theme II: Christian Mission Among Other Faiths at the United Theological College, India July 2009.

Lalsangkima Pachuau and Knud Jørgensen (Eds)
Witnessing to Christ in a Pluralistic Age
Christian Mission among Other Faiths 2011 / 978-1-870345-95-8 / 277 pp

In a world where plurality of faiths is increasingly becoming a norm of life, insights on the theology of religious plurality are needed to strengthen our understanding of our own faith and the faith of others. Even though religious diversity is not new, we are seeing an upsurge in interest on the theologies of religion among all Christian confessional traditions. It can be claimed that no other issue in Christian mission is more important and more difficult than the theologies of religions.

Beth Snodderly and A Scott Moreau (Eds)
Evangelical Frontier Mission
Perspectives on the Global Progress of the Gospel
2011 / 978-1-870345-98-9 / 312pp

This important volume demonstrates that 100 years after the World Missionary Conference in Edinburgh, Evangelism has become truly global. Twenty-first-century Evangelism continues to focus on frontier mission, but significantly, and in the spirit of Edinburgh 1910, it also has re-engaged social action.

Rolv Olsen (Ed)
Mission and Postmodernities
2011 / 978-1-870345-97-2 / 279pp

This volume takes on meaning because its authors honestly struggle with and debate how we should relate to postmodernities. Should our response be accommodation, relativizing or counter-culture? How do we strike a balance between listening and understanding, and at the same time exploring how postmodernities influence the interpretation and application of the Bible as the normative story of God's mission in the world?

REGNUM STUDIES IN GLOBAL CHRISTIANITY

(Previously GLOBAL THEOLOGICAL VOICES series)

Series Listing

David Emmanuel Singh (Ed)

Jesus and the Cross

Reflections of Christians from Islamic Contexts

2008 / 978-1-870345-65-1 / 226pp

The Cross reminds us that the sins of the world are not borne through the exercise of power but through Jesus Christ's submission to the will of the Father. The papers in this volume are organised in three parts: scriptural, contextual and theological. The central question being addressed is: how do Christians living in contexts, where Islam is a majority or minority religion, experience, express or think of the Cross?

Sung-wook Hong

Naming God in Korea

The Case of Protestant Christianity

2008 / 978-1-870345-66-8 / 170pp

Since Christianity was introduced to Korea more than a century ago, one of the most controversial issues has been the Korean term for the Christian 'God'. This issue is not merely about naming the Christian God in Korean language, but it relates to the question of theological contextualization - the relationship between the gospel and culture - and the question of Korean Christian identity. This book demonstrates the nature of the gospel in relation to cultures, i.e., the universality of the gospel expressed in all human cultures.

Hubert van Beek (Ed)

Revisioning Christian Unity

The Global Christian Forum

2009 / 978-1-870345-74-3 / 288pp

This book contains the records of the Global Christian Forum gathering held in Limuru near Nairobi, Kenya, on 6 – 9 November 2007 as well as the papers presented at that historic event. Also included are a summary of the Global Christian Forum process from its inception until the 2007 gathering and the reports of the evaluation of the process that was carried out in 2008.

Young-hoon Lee

The Holy Spirit Movement in Korea

Its Historical and Theological Development

2009 / 978-1-870345-67-5 / 174pp

This book traces the historical and theological development of the Holy Spirit Movement in Korea through six successive periods (from 1900 to the present time). These periods are characterized by repentance and revival (1900-20), persecution and suffering under Japanese occupation (1920-40), confusion and division (1940-60), explosive revival in which the Pentecostal movement played a major role in the rapid growth of Korean churches (1960-80), the movement reaching out to all denominations (1980-2000), and the new context demanding the Holy Spirit movement to open new horizons in its mission engagement (2000-).

Paul Hang-Sik Cho
Eschatology and Ecology
Experiences of the Korean Church
2010 / 978-1-870345-75-0 / 260pp

This book raises the question of why Korean people, and Korean Protestant Christians in particular, pay so little attention to ecological issues. The author argues that there is an important connection (or elective affinity) between this lack of attention and the other-worldly eschatology that is so dominant within Korean Protestant Christianity.

Dietrich Werner, David Esterline, Namsoon Kang, Joshva Raja (Eds)
The Handbook of Theological Education in World Christianity
2010 / 978-1-870345-80-4 / 759pp

This major reference work is the first ever comprehensive study of Theological Education in Christianity of its kind. With contributions from over 90 international scholars and church leaders, it aims to be easily accessible across denominational, cultural, educational, and geographic boundaries. The Handbook will aid international dialogue and networking among theological educators, institutions, and agencies

David Emmanuel Singh & Bernard C Farr (Eds)
Christianity and Education
Shaping of Christian Context in Thinking
2010 / 978-1-870345-81-1 / 374pp

Christianity and Education is a collection of papers published in *Transformation: An International Journal of Holistic Mission Studies* over a period of 15 years. The articles represent a spectrum of Christian thinking addressing issues of institutional development for theological education, theological studies in the context of global mission, contextually aware/informed education, and academies which deliver such education, methodologies and personal reflections.

J.Andrew Kirk
Civilisations in Conflict?
Islam, the West and Christian Faith
2011 / 978-1-870345-87-3 / 205pp

Samuel Huntington's thesis, which argues that there appear to be aspects of Islam that could be on a collision course with the politics and values of Western societies, has provoked much controversy. This study is offers a particular response to Huntington's thesis by making a comparison between the origins of Islam and Christianity.

David Emmanuel Singh (Ed)
Jesus and the Incarnation
Reflections of Christians from Islamic Contexts
2011 / 978-1-870345-90-3 / 250pp

In the dialogues of Christians with Muslims nothing is more fundamental than the Cross, the Incarnation and the Resurrection of Jesus. Building on the *Jesus and the Cross*, this book contains voices of Christians living in various 'Islamic contexts' and reflecting on the Incarnation of Jesus. The aim and hope of these reflections is that the papers weaved around the notion of 'the Word' will not only promote dialogue among Christians on the roles of the Person and the Book but, also, create a positive environment for their conversations with Muslim neighbours.

REGNUM STUDIES IN MISSION
Series Listing

Kwame Bediako
Theology and Identity
The Impact of Culture upon Christian Thought in the Second Century and in Modern Africa
1992 / 978-1870345-80-2 / 508pp

The author examines the question of Christian identity in the context of the Graeco–Roman culture of the early Roman Empire. He then addresses the modern African predicament of quests for identity and integration.

Christopher Sugden
Seeking the Asian Face of Jesus
The Practice and Theology of Christian Social Witness in Indonesia and India 1974–1996
1997 / 1-870345-26-6 / 496pp

This study focuses on contemporary holistic mission with the poor in India and Indonesia combined with the call to transformation of all life in Christ with micro-credit enterprise schemes. 'The literature on contextual theology now has a new standard to rise to' – Lamin Sanneh (Yale University, USA).

Hwa Yung
Mangoes or Bananas?
The Quest for an Authentic Asian Christian Theology
1997 / 1-870345-25-5 / 274pp

Asian Christian thought remains largely captive to Greek dualism and Enlightenment rationalism because of the overwhelming dominance of Western culture. Authentic contextual Christian theologies will emerge within Asian Christianity with a dual recovery of confidence in culture and the gospel.

Keith E. Eitel
Paradigm Wars
The Southern Baptist International Mission Board Faces the Third Millennium
1999 / 1-870345-12-6 / 140pp

The International Mission Board of the Southern Baptist Convention is the largest denominational mission agency in North America. This volume chronicles the historic and contemporary forces that led to the IMB's recent extensive reorganization, providing the most comprehensive case study to date of a historic mission agency restructuring to continue its mission purpose into the twenty-first century more effectively.

Samuel Jayakumar

Dalit Consciousness and Christian Conversion

Historical Resources for a Contemporary Debate 1999 / 81-7214-497-0 / 434pp

(Published jointly with ISPCK)

The main focus of this historical study is social change and transformation among the Dalit Christian communities in India. Historiography tests the evidence in the light of the conclusions of the modern Dalit liberation theologians.

Vinay Samuel and Christopher Sugden (Eds)

Mission as Transformation

A Theology of the Whole Gospel

1999 / 978-18703455-13-2/ 522pp

This book brings together in one volume twenty five years of biblical reflection on mission practice with the poor from around the world. This volume helps anyone understand how evangelicals, struggling to unite evangelism and social action, found their way in the last twenty five years to the biblical view of mission in which God calls all human beings to love God and their neighbour; never creating a separation between the two.

Christopher Sugden

Gospel, Culture and Transformation

2000 / 1-870345-32-0 /152pp

A Reprint, with a New Introduction, of Part Two of Seeking the Asian Face of Jesus

Gospel, Culture and Transformation explores the practice of mission especially in relation to transforming cultures and communities. - 'Transformation is to enable God's vision of society to be actualised in all relationships: social, economic and spiritual, so that God's will may be reflected in human society and his love experienced by all communities, especially the poor.'

Bernhard Ott

Beyond Fragmentation: Integrating Mission and Theological Education

A Critical Assessment of some Recent Developments

in Evangelical Theological Education

2001 / 1-870345-14-2 / 382pp

Beyond Fragmentation is an enquiry into the development of Mission Studies in evangelical theological education in Germany and German-speaking Switzerland between 1960 and 1995. The author undertakes a detailed examination of the paradigm shifts which have taken place in recent years in both the theology of mission and the understanding of theological education.

Gideon Githiga

The Church as the Bulwark against Authoritarianism

Development of Church and State Relations in Kenya, with Particular Reference to the Years after Political Independence 1963-1992

2002 / 1-870345-38-x / 218pp

'All who care for love, peace and unity in Kenyan society will want to read this careful history by Bishop Githiga of how Kenyan Christians, drawing on the Bible, have sought to share the love of God, bring his peace and build up the unity of the nation, often in the face of great difficulties and opposition.' Canon Dr Chris Sugden, Oxford Centre for Mission Studies.

Myung Sung-Hoon, Hong Young-Gi (eds.)

Charis and Charisma

David Yonggi Cho and the Growth of Yoido Full Gospel Church

2003 / 978-1870345-45-3 / 218pp

This book discusses the factors responsible for the growth of the world's largest church. It expounds the role of the Holy Spirit, the leadership, prayer, preaching, cell groups and creativity in promoting church growth. It focuses on God's grace (charis) and inspiring leadership (charisma) as the two essential factors and the book's purpose is to present a model for church growth worldwide.

Samuel Jayakumar

Mission Reader

Historical Models for Wholistic Mission in the Indian Context

2003 / 1-870345-42-8 / 250pp

(Published jointly with ISPCK)

This book is written from an evangelical point of view revalidating and reaffirming the Christian commitment to wholistic mission. The roots of the 'wholistic mission' combining 'evangelism and social concerns' are to be located in the history and tradition of Christian evangelism in the past; and the civilizing purpose of evangelism is compatible with modernity as an instrument in nation building.

Bob Robinson

Christians Meeting Hindus

An Analysis and Theological Critique of the Hindu-Christian Encounter in India

2004 / 987-1870345-39-2 / 392pp

This book focuses on the Hindu-Christian encounter, especially the intentional meeting called dialogue, mainly during the last four decades of the twentieth century, and specifically in India itself.

Gene Early

Leadership Expectations

How Executive Expectations are Created and Used in a Non-Profit Setting

2005 / 1-870345-30-4 / 276pp

The author creates an Expectation Enactment Analysis to study the role of the Chancellor of the University of the Nations-Kona, Hawaii. This study is grounded in the field of managerial work, jobs, and behaviour and draws on symbolic interactionism, role theory role identity theory and enactment theory. The result is a conceptual framework for developing an understanding of managerial roles.

Tharcisse Gatwa

The Churches and Ethnic Ideology in the Rwandan Crises 1900-1994

2005 / 978-1870345-24-8 / 300pp

(Reprinted 2011)

Since the early years of the twentieth century Christianity has become a new factor in Rwandan society. This book investigates the role Christian churches played in the formulation and development of the racial ideology that culminated in the 1994 genocide.

Julie Ma

Mission Possible

Biblical Strategies for Reaching the Lost

2005 / 978-1870345-37-1 / 142pp

This is a missiology book for the church which liberates missiology from the specialists for the benefit of every believer. It also serves as a textbook that is simple and friendly, and yet solid in biblical interpretation. This book links the biblical teaching to the actual and contemporary missiological settings with examples, making the Bible come alive to the reader.

Allan Anderson, Edmond Tang (Eds)

Asian and Pentecostal

The Charismatic Face of Christianity in Asia

2005 / 1-870345-43-9 / 596pp

(Reprinted 2011)

(Published jointly with APTS Press)

This book provides a thematic discussion and pioneering case studies on the history and development of Pentecostal and Charismatic churches in the countries of South Asia, South East Asia and East Asia.

I. Mark Beaumont

Christology in Dialogue with Muslims

A Critical Analysis of Christian Presentations of Christ for Muslims from the Ninth and Twentieth Centuries

2005 / 1978-1870345-46-0 / 228pp

This book analyses Christian presentations of Christ for Muslims in the most creative periods of Christian-Muslim dialogue, the first half of the ninth century and the second half of the twentieth century. In these two periods, Christians made serious attempts to present their faith in Christ in terms that take into account Muslim perceptions of him, with a view to bridging the gap between Muslim and Christian convictions.

Thomas Czövek,

Three Seasons of Charismatic Leadership

A Literary-Critical and Theological Interpretation of the Narrative of Saul, David and Solomon

2006 / 978-1870345-48-4 / 272pp

This book investigates the charismatic leadership of Saul, David and Solomon. It suggests that charismatic leaders emerge in crisis situations in order to resolve the crisis by the charisma granted by God. Czovek argues that Saul proved himself as a charismatic leader as long as he acted resolutely and independently from his mentor Samuel. In the author's eyes, Saul's failure to establish himself as a charismatic leader is caused by his inability to step out from Samuel's shadow.

Jemima Atieno Oluoch

The Christian Political Theology of Dr. John Henry Okullu

2006 / 1-870345-51-4 / 137pp

This book reconstructs the Christian political theology of Bishop John Henry Okullu, DD, through establishing what motivated him and the biblical basis for his socio-political activities. It also attempts to reconstruct the socio-political environment that nurtured Dr Okullu's prophetic ministry.

Richard Burgess

Nigeria's Christian Revolution

The Civil War Revival and Its Pentecostal Progeny (1967-2006)

2008 / 978-1-870345-63-7 / 347pp

This book describes the revival that occurred among the Igbo people of Eastern Nigeria and the new Pentecostal churches it generated, and documents the changes that have occurred as the movement has responded to global flows and local demands. As such, it explores the nature of revivalist and Pentecostal experience, but does so against the backdrop of local socio-political and economic developments, such as decolonisation and civil war, as well as broader processes, such as modernisation and globalisation.

David Emmanuel Singh & Bernard C Farr (Eds)

Christianity and Cultures

Shaping Christian Thinking in Context

2008 / 978-1-870345-69-9 / 260pp

This volume marks an important milestone, the 25th anniversary of the Oxford Centre for Mission Studies (OCMS). The papers here have been exclusively sourced from Transformation, a quarterly journal of OCMS, and seek to provide a tripartite view of Christianity's engagement with cultures by focusing on the question: how is Christian thinking being formed or reformed through its interaction with the varied contexts it encounters? The subject matters include different strands of theological-missiological thinking, socio-political engagements and forms of family relationships in interaction with the host cultures.

Tormod Engelsviken, Ernst Harbakk, Rolv Olsen, Thor Strandenæs (Eds)

Mission to the World

Communicating the Gospel in the 21st Century: Essays in Honour of Knud Jørgensen

2008 / 978-1-870345-64-4 / 472pp

Knud Jørgensen is Director of Areopagos and Associate Professor of Missiology at MF Norwegian School of Theology. This book reflects on the main areas of Jørgensen's commitment to mission. At the same time it focuses on the main frontier of mission, the world, the content of mission, the Gospel, the fact that the Gospel has to be communicated, and the context of contemporary mission in the 21st century.

Al Tizon

Transformation after Lausanne

Radical Evangelical Mission in Global-Local Perspective

2008 / 978-1-870345-68-2 / 281pp

After Lausanne '74, a worldwide network of radical evangelical mission theologians and practitioners use the notion of "Mission as Transformation" to integrate evangelism and social concern together, thus lifting theological voices from the Two Thirds World to places of prominence. This book documents the definitive gatherings, theological tensions, and social forces within and without evangelicalism that led up to Mission as Transformation. And it does so through a global-local grid that points the way toward greater holistic mission in the 21st century.

Bambang Budijanto

Values and Participation

Development in Rural Indonesia

2009 / 978-1-870345-70-4 / 237pp

Socio-religious values and socio-economic development are inter-dependant, inter-related and are constantly changing in the context of macro political structures, economic policy, religious organizations and globalization; and micro influences such as local affinities, identity, politics, leadership and beliefs. The book argues that the comprehensive approach in understanding the socio-religious values of each of the three local Lopait communities in Central Java is essential to accurately describing their respective identity.

Alan R. Johnson

Leadership in a Slum

A Bangkok Case Study

2009 / 978-1-870345-71-2 / 238pp

This book looks at leadership in the social context of a slum in Bangkok from a different perspective than traditional studies which measure well educated Thais on leadership scales derived in the West. Using both systematic data collection and participant observation, it develops a culturally preferred model as well as a set of models based in Thai concepts that reflect on-the-ground realities. It concludes by looking at the implications of the anthropological approach for those who are involved in leadership training in Thai settings and beyond.

Titre Ande

Leadership and Authority

Bula Matari and Life - Community Ecclesiology in Congo

2010 / 978-1-870345-72-9 / 189pp

Christian theology in Africa can make significant development if a critical understanding of the socio-political context in contemporary Africa is taken seriously, particularly as Africa's post-colonial Christian leadership based its understanding and use of authority on the Bula Matari model. This has caused many problems and Titre proposes a Life-Community ecclesiology for liberating authority, here leadership is a function, not a status, and 'apostolic succession' belongs to all people of God.

Frank Kwesi Adams

Odwira and the Gospel

A Study of the Asante Odwira Festival and its Significance for Christianity in Ghana

2010 /978-1-870345-59-0 / 232pp

The study of the Odwira festival is the key to the understanding of Asante religious and political life in Ghana. The book explores the nature of the Odwira festival longitudinally - in pre-colonial, colonial and post-independence Ghana - and examines the Odwira ideology and its implications for understanding the Asante self-identity. Also discussed is how some elements of faith portrayed in the Odwira festival can provide a framework for Christianity to engage with Asante culture at a greater depth.

Bruce Carlton

Strategy Coordinator

Changing the Course of Southern Baptist Missions

2010 / 978-1-870345-78-1 / 268pp

This is an outstanding, one-of-a-kind work addressing the influence of the non-residential missionary/strategy coordinator's role in Southern Baptist missions. This scholarly text examines the twentieth century global missiological currents that influenced the leadership of the International Mission Board, resulting in a new paradigm to assist in taking the gospel to the nations.

Julie Ma & Wonsuk Ma

Mission in the Spirit:

Towards a Pentecostal/Charismatic Missiology

2010 / 978-1-870345-84-2 / 312pp

The book explores the unique contribution of Pentecostal/Charismatic mission from the beginning of the twentieth century. The first part considers the theological basis of Pentecostal/Charismatic mission thinking and practice. Special attention is paid to the Old Testament, which has been regularly overlooked by the modern Pentecostal/Charismatic movements. The second part discusses major mission topics with contributions and challenges unique to Pentecostal/Charismatic mission. The book concludes with a reflection on the future of this powerful missionary movement. As the authors served as Korean missionaries in Asia, often their missionary experiences in Asia are reflected in their discussions.

S. Hun Kim & Wonsuk Ma (eds.)

Korean Diaspora and Christian Mission

2011-978-1-870345-91-0 / 301pp

As a 'divine conspiracy' for Missio Dei, the global phenomenon of people on the move has shown itself to be invaluable. In 2004 two significant documents concerning Diaspora were introduced, one by the Filipino International Network and the other by the Lausanne Committee for World Evangelization. These have created awareness of the importance of people on the move for Christian mission. Since then, Korean Diaspora has conducted similar research among Korean missions, resulting in this book

Jin Huat Tan

Planting an Indigenous Church

The Case of the Borneo Evangelical Mission

2011 / 978-1-870345-99-6 / 343pp

Dr Jin Huat Tan has written a pioneering study of the origins and development of Malaysia's most significant indigenous church. This is an amazing story of revival, renewal and transformation of the entire region chronicling the powerful effect of it evident to date! What can we learn from this extensive and careful study of the Borneo Revival, so the global Christianity will become ever more dynamic.

GENERAL REGNUM TITLES

Vinay Samuel, Chris Sugden (eds.)
The Church in Response to Human Need
1987 / 1870345045 / xii+268pp

Philip Sampson, Vinay Samuel, Chris Sugden (eds.)
Faith and Modernity
Essays in modernity and post-modernity
1994 / 1870345177 / 352pp

Klaus Fiedler
The Story of Faith Missions
1994 / 0745926878 / 428pp

Douglas Peterson
Not by Might nor by Power
A Pentecostal Theology of Social Concern in Latin America
1996 / 1870345207 / xvi+260pp

David Gitari
In Season and Out of Season
Sermons to a Nation
1996 / 1870345118 / 155pp

David. W. Virtue
A Vision of Hope
The Story of Samuel Habib
1996 / 1870345169 / xiv+137pp

Everett A Wilson
Strategy of the Spirit
J.Philip Hogan and the Growth of the Assemblies of God Worldwide, 1960 - 1990
1997 /1870345231/214

Murray Dempster, Byron Klaus, Douglas Petersen (Eds)
The Globalization of Pentecostalism
A Religion Made to Travel
1999 / 1870345290 / xvii+406pp

Peter Johnson, Chris Sugden (eds.)
Markets, Fair Trade and the Kingdom of God
Essays to Celebrate Traidcraft's 21st Birthday
2001 / 1870345193 / xii+155pp

Robert Hillman, Coral Chamberlain, Linda Harding
Healing & Wholeness
Reflections on the Healing Ministry
2002 / 978-1- 870345-35- 4 / xvii+283pp

David Bussau, Russell Mask
Christian Microenterprise Development
An Introduction
2003 / 1870345282 / xiii+142pp

David Singh
Sainthood and Revelatory Discourse
An Examination of the Basis for the Authority of Bayan in Mahdawi Islam
2003 / 8172147285 / xxiv+485pp

For the up-to-date listing of the Regnum books see www.ocms.ac.uk/regnum

Regnum Books International

Regnum is an Imprint of The Oxford Centre for Mission Studies
St. Philip and St. James Church
Woodstock Road
Oxford, OX2 6HR
Web: www.ocms.ac.uk/regnum